Wasatch Mts., Utah, June 8, 1960   Allan D. Cruicksh

MALE LAZULI BUNTING AT NEST

Life Histories of North American Cardinals, Grosbeaks, Buntings, Towhees, Finches, Sparrows, and Allies

Order Passeriformes: Family Fringillidae

PART ONE
Genera Richmondena through Pipilo (part)

ARTHUR CLEVELAND BENT and COLLABORATORS

Compiled and Edited by
OLIVER L. AUSTIN, JR.
Florida State Museum, University of Florida
Research Associate, Smithsonian Institution

DOVER PUBLICATIONS, INC., NEW YORK

Published in Canada by General Publishing Company, Ltd.,
30 Lesmill Road, Don Mills, Toronto, Ontario.
Published in the United Kingdom by Constable and Company,
Ltd., 10 Orange Street, London WC 2.

This Dover edition, first published in 1968, is an unabridged
and unaltered republication of the work originally published in
1968 by the Smithsonian Institution Press as United States
National Museum *Bulletin 237*.

International Standard Book Number: 0-486-21977-1
Library of Congress Catalog Card Number: 68-55072

Manufactured in the United States of America

DOVER PUBLICATIONS, INC.
180 Varick Street
New York, N. Y. 10014

Publications of the United States National Museum

The scientific publications of the United States National Museum include two series, *Proceedings of the United States National Museum* and *United States National Museum Bulletin*.

In these series are published original articles and monographs dealing with the collections and work of the Museum and setting forth newly acquired facts in the fields of Anthropology, Biology, Geology, History, and Technology. Copies of each publication are distributed to libraries and scientific organizations and to specialists and others interested in the different subjects.

The *Proceedings*, begun in 1878, are intended for the publication, in separate form, of shorter papers. These are gathered in volumes, octavo in size, with the publication of each paper recorded in the table of contents of the volume.

In the *Bulletin* series, the first of which was issued in 1875, appear longer, separate publications consisting of monographs (occasionally in several parts) and volumes in which are collected works on related subjects. *Bulletins* are either octavo or quarto in size, depending on the needs of the presentation. Since 1902 papers relating to the botanical collections of the Museum have been published in the *Bulletin* series under the heading *Contributions from the United States National Herbarium*. Since 1959, in *Bulletins* titled "Contributions from the Museum of History and Technology," have been gathered shorter papers relating to the collections and research of that museum.

This work forms number 237, parts 1–3, of the *Bulletin* series.

FRANK A. TAYLOR,
Director, United States National Museum.

Contents

PART ONE

Family Fringillidae: Cardinals, grosbeaks, buntings, towhees, finches, and
    sparrows—Continued   Page

Contents

PART TWO

Family Fringillidae: Cardinals, grosbeaks, buntings, towhees, finches, and
sparrows—Continued

Contents

PART THREE

Introduction

This is part 1 of the twenty-first and last in a series of bulletins of the United States National Museum on the life histories of North American birds. Previous numbers have been issued as follows:

107. Life Histories of North American Diving Birds, August 1, 1919.
113. Life Histories of North American Gulls and Terns, August 27, 1921.
121. Life Histories of North American Petrels and Pelicans and Their Allies, October 19, 1922.
126. Life Histories of North American Wild Fowl (part), May 25, 1923.
130. Life Histories of North American Wild Fowl (part), June 27, 1925.
135. Life Histories of North American Marsh Birds, March 11, 1927.
142. Life Histories of North American Shore Birds (pt. 1), December 31, 1927.
146. Life Histories of North American Shore Birds (pt. 2), March 24, 1929.
162. Life Histories of North American Gallinaceous Birds, May 25, 1932.
167. Life Histories of North American Birds of Prey (pt. 1), May 3, 1937.
170. Life Histories of North American Birds of Prey (pt. 2), August 8, 1938.
174. Life Histories of North American Woodpeckers, May 23, 1939.
176. Life Histories of North American Cuckoos, Goatsuckers, Hummingbirds, and Their Allies, July 20, 1940.
179. Life Histories of North American Flycatchers, Larks, Swallows, and Their Allies, May 8, 1942.
191. Life Histories of North American Jays, Crows, and Titmice, January 27, 1947.
195. Life Histories of North American Nuthatches, Wrens, Thrashers, and Their Allies, July 7, 1948.
196. Life Histories of North American Thrushes, Kinglets, and Their Allies, June 28, 1949.
197. Life Histories of North American Wagtails, Shrikes, Vireos, and Their Allies, June 21, 1950.
203. Life Histories of North American Wood Warblers, June 15, 1953.
211. Life Histories of North American Blackbirds, Orioles, Tanagers, and Allies, February 27, 1958.

Arthur Cleveland Bent started work on this monumental series in 1910, more than a half a century ago. Originally conceived as a continuation of the work on the nests and eggs of North American birds left incomplete in 1896 by the late Major Charles E. Bendire, Mr. Bent expanded its scope "to cover more ground, with the different phases of the life histories arranged in a more definite and uniform sequence." The coverage and format he developed for the first volume have remained essentially unchanged. They are followed in this volume with only minor changes.

From the beginning Mr. Bent regarded the Life Histories as a cooperative venture to be shared in by everybody concerned with North American birds. He sought information for them not only

from the published literature, but from the unpublished notes of
volunteer contributors. For this purpose he maintained an enormous
correspondence with a host of amateur and professional ornithologists.
He was modest, amicable, generous, and self-effacing; his friends were
legion. In the introductions to the successive volumes he produced,
he acknowledges contributions and help from more than 800 individuals by name.

Mr. Bent entrusted the preparation of two life histories in the first
volume, those of the puffin and the great auk, to his friend Dr. Charles
Wendell Townsend. The next four volumes he wrote himself, except
for a short account of the New Mexican duck by its discoverer,
Wharton Huber, in volume 4. Starting with volume 6, which contains
five histories by Dr. Townsend and one by Thomas E. Penard, Mr.
Bent entrusted more and more accounts to others, especially when he
felt others were more familiar with the species than he. The total in
the 20 volumes is 170 histories, contributed by 28 authors, as follows:

Winsor M. Tyler	34	Josslyn Van Tyne	2
Alfred O. Gross	23	Arthur A. Allen	1
F. C. R. Jourdain	23	Mary M. Erickson	1
Charles W. Townsend	19	Wharton Huber	1
Bertram W. Tucker	13	Alden Miller	1
Alexander Sprunt, Jr	10	E. E. Murphy	1
Milton P. Skinner	9	Thomas E. Penard	1
Robert S. Woods	8	Gale Pickwell	1
Alexander Skutch	4	George M. Sutton	1
Edward S. Dingle	4	Wendell Taber	1
Jean M. Linsdale	2	G. J. Wallace	1
E. C. Stuart Baker	2	F. G. Weaver	1
Bayard Christy	2	Francis M. Weston	1
James L. Peters	2	Laidlaw Williams	1

Though a fall from a tree during a youthful egging exploit left him
with a permanent tremble in his right hand, Mr. Bent possessed a
remarkable physique and amazing vitality and drive. His mental
facilities remained sharp and clear, and he researched and wrote
almost to the day of his death on Dec. 30, 1954 at the age of 89. In
the late 1940's, realizing he probably would not live to finish the final
volumes, he asked the Nuttall Ornithological Club of Cambridge,
Mass., which he had joined while a senior at Harvard in 1888, to assume
the responsibility for their completion. The Nuttall Club, then
under the presidency of James Lee Peters, was happy to accept this
obligation. Shortly after Peters died in 1952, Mr. Bent appointed
as his literary executor my close personal friend and fellow member
of the Nuttall Club, the late Wendell Taber.

At the time of his death, Mr. Bent had finished the accounts of
the icterids for volume 20, and Taber saw it through the press in
1958. He had also completed a respectable number of fringillid

histories, 14 main species accounts plus 34 lesser ones of accompanying subspecies. These are the accounts that appear here without a "contributed by" authority listed in the heading. He had also arranged with other ornithologists, myself among them, to write on species with which he had had little or no personal experience in the field. In his files awaiting publication were a number of histories by such seasoned contributors to previous volumes as Alfred O. Gross, Alexander Sprunt, Jr., Winsor M. Tyler, and Robert S. Woods. Dr. Tyler, of whom Mr. Bent wrote, "He should have been named as one of the authors," had predeceased Mr. Bent, and his 35th and final life history, that of the eastern goldfinch, appears in this volume.

Aware of the magnitude of the task ahead of him, Taber began soon after Mr. Bent's death to recruit volunteers to help him complete the series. Within the next few years he was able to assign most of the unfinished species to ornithologists familiar with them, while he himself tackled the remaining few with his customary zeal and enthusiasm. That he was not overly well I learned only when he wrote me early in August 1960, asking me to assume his life history responsibilities in the event he was unable to complete them. Despite his failing health, he continued to work hard and faithfully at the task he had set himself until the very day of his sudden and premature death, August 31, 1960.

Ornithology is not a static science and the decade since Mr. Bent's death has seen many changes in its concepts as well as additions to our knowledge in the form of new discoveries. To reflect these changes and developments, and at the same time to keep this final volume in as close accord as possible with its predecessors in content and style as well as format, it has been necessary to establish a number of editorial policies.

Though we have followed the A.O.U. Check-List of North American Birds, 5th edition, 1957, for the scientific names of species and subspecies, for conformity with the earlier volumes we have retained the vernacular names for subspecies used in the 4th edition. A few slight changes in these vernaculars have been deemed advisable. The only other departure from the 5th edition not indicated clearly in the text has been the dropping of the melodious (Cuban) grassquit, which has no rightful place in the North American avifauna (see *Auk*, 1963, p. 73).

Unfortunately none of the histories that Mr. Bent left, or that Taber added to the files, bears a date of completion. Several accounts by other authors I know antedate Mr. Bent's demise. Two of my own contributions, those of the Japanese hawfinch and Cassin's bullfinch, date from 1949. I have found it necessary and advisable to update these older manuscripts in a few cases where significant new information has become available since their completion. These added paragraphs, each of which is signed or initialed by its contributor, I have tried to keep to a minimum.

As with the preceding volumes, the data on and descriptions of eggs have been provided by William George F. Harris, and the distribution and migrations sections have been prepared by Chandler S. Robbins through the courtesy of the Bureau of Sports Fisheries and Wildlife. The editor and the respective contributors consequently claim no credit and assume no responsibility for these sections.

Exceptional thanks are due to Aretas Andrews Saunders, who not only contributed much information directly to the *Voice* sections, but made available to the series his unpublished manuscript, "The Songs and Calls of American Birds," prepared under a grant from the American Philosophical Society and now in the Josselyn Van Tyne Memorial Library at Ann Arbor, Michigan. Richard R. Graber most generously allowed us to quote his unpublished thesis on juvenal plumages. Most of the illustrations were selected and their captions prepared by Arthur W. Argue. Oscar M. Root has been particularly helpful in checking bibliographies, reading proof, and in general "trouble-shooting."

For their whole-hearted and enthusiastic cooperation I take great pleasure in thanking the following authors who, in addition to those mentioned above, have contributed material to these final three volumes:

Anders H. Anderson
Donald Henry Baepler
James Baird
Paul H. Baldwin
Richard C. Banks
Henry E. Baumgarten
Marguerite Heydweiller Baumgartner
Andrew John Berger
Hugh M. S. Blair
Mary Sutherland Blair
Charles Henry Blake
Emmet Reid Blake
James Bond
Verdi Burtch
John B. Bushman
Henry E. Childs, Jr.
Roland Charles Clement
Howard L. Cogswell
William Maitland Congreve
John M. Conkey
James Ensign Crouch
Frederic W. Davis
John Davis
William Ryan Dawson

Barbara Blanchard DeWolfe
Robert W. Dickerman
Joshua Clifton Dickinson, Jr.
Keith Lee Dixon
Audrey C. Downer
Stephen W. Eaton
John Jackson Elliott
Mary Marilla Erickson
George M. Fairfield
J. Bruce Falls
Norman Roger French
Ira N. Gabrielson
Jean W. Graber
W. E. Griffee
Neil F. Hadley
Wilson C. Hanna
Ed. N. Harrison
Travis G. Haws
C. Lynn Hayward
Matti Helminen
Carl Helms
Norman Pierce Hill
Thomas Raymond Howell
John B. Hurley

R. Roy Johnson
David W. Johnston
Richard Fourness Johnston
Junea Wangeman Kelly
Emerson Kemsies
James Roger King
Herbert Krause
John Lane
Anne L. LeSassier
Jean Myron Linsdale
James K. Lowther
Joe T. Marshall, Jr.
Alden H. Miller
Gale Wendell Monson
L. J. Moriarty
John D. Newman
Margaret Morse Nice
Donald J. Nicholson
Val Nolan, Jr.
Robert Allen Norris
Robert Thomas Orr
Christopher M. Packard
Fred Mallery Packard
Robert Treat Paine, 3rd
Ralph Simon Palmer
David Freeland Parmalee
John R. Pemberton
Sidney B. Peyton
James Harvey Phelps, Jr.
Allan Robert Phillips
Frank A. Pitelka

William F. Rapp
Oscar Mitchell Root
John S. Rowley
Charlotte E. Smith
Robert Leo Smith
Wendell Phillips Smith
Doris Heustis Speirs
John Murray Speirs
Robert Miller Stabler
Louis A. Stimson
Gardner D. Stout
William DeMott Stull
James G. Suthard
Lewis McIver Terrill
Donald Mason Thatcher
Harrison B. Tordoff
Charles H. Trost
Robie W. Tufts
James Veghte
Lawrence Harvey Walkinshaw
Jackson Dan Webster
Francis Marion Weston
David Kenneth Wetherbee
Nathaniel Ruggles Whitney, Jr.
Frances C. Williams
Francis S. L. Williamson
Lloyd R. Wolfe
Glen Everett Woolfenden
William Youngworth
Dale A. Zimmerman

And finally, to possible critics who may lament the omission of information they think should be here, I have the honor—and pleasure—of repeating Mr. Bent's words: "If the reader fails to find mentioned in these pages some things which he knows about the birds, he can blame himself for not having sent them to:"

OLIVER L. AUSTIN, JR.

Florida State Museum
Gainesville, Florida
March 1965

List of Plates

Order PASSERIFORMES: Family FRINGILLIDAE
Genera RICHMONDENA through PIPILO (PART)

RICHMONDENA CARDINALIS CARDINALIS (Linnaeus)
Eastern Cardinal
PLATES 1 AND 2

HABITS

As we travel southward from New England's ice and snow to meet spring halfway, we are greeted by the loud *peto, peto* of the tufted titmouse, the lively, striking song of the Carolina wren, and the rich, whistling notes of the cardinal redbird, three birds we rarely see in New England. They seem to be welcoming us to the land of sunshine and flowers, and their music brings a heart-warming change from the bleak and silent woods we have left behind.

We formerly considered the cardinal a southern bird, a member of the Carolinian fauna of the Austral Zone. Our 1886 Check-List gave its range as only casual north of the valley of the Ohio River, which forms the northern boundary of Kentucky; the 1895 edition extended the range to the Great Lakes; and the 1910 edition included southern Ontario and the southern Hudson River valley.

During recent years, it has been gradually extending its range northward. It is steadily increasing in abundance and has established itself as a breeding bird in regions where it was formerly only a casual visitor.

The advance has been most rapid and most extensive in the Mississippi Valley and has occurred mainly during the last decade of the past century and the first three decades of the present century. Much of the advance seems to have come in winter, where winter feeding has encouraged it to remain. In Iowa, where it is now a permanent resident, Philip A. DuMont (1934) reports that in "1923 eight observers found thirty-six cardinals, and in 1929 seventeen observers reported one hundred and forty-nine," on a Christmas census.

For southern Ontario, where the cardinal is now well established as a breeding bird, Saunders and Dale (1933) report:

The first record for this species was one taken at London, on November 30th, 1896. * * * They remained of very rare or casual occurrence until 1910. * * * Reports were infrequent during the next two or three years, but since about 1914

1

they have come to be looked upon as permanent residents, a very delightful addition indeed to our fauna.   During the winter of 1916–1917, J. C. Middleton had eight Cardinals feeding at his home on The Ridgeway, London, as well as a variety of other birds.   Thirty-one were reported in our Christmas Census for 1929.   They often nest within the city in lilac bushes, or other shrubbery, several nests having been collected after the birds had finished with them. * * *

O. E. Dovitt (1944b) reports: "A marked incursion of Cardinals occurred throughout Southern Ontario during the fall and winter of 1938–39."

Evidently the species is still extending its range and increasing in abundance everywhere east of the Plains and even as far west as North Dakota.

In South Dakota, Herbert Krause (1956) points out, the species over a 52-year period has followed up the streams east of the Missouri River and become established as a breeding bird, wintering in "appreciable numbers."

Norman A. Wood (1951) comments on the spread and expansion of breeding status throughout Michigan beginning in 1904.

Throughout the southern portion of its range, the cardinal is universally abundant, familiar, and generally distributed in the vines and shrubbery about houses and the dense hedges of Cherokee roses, in the streamside thickets and the more open woodlands intermingled with dense bushes, and in thickets overgrown with climbing vines. It avoids the more open places and the forest treetops, but, in the cities and villages, it is omnipresent, semidomesticated, and generally beloved for its beauty and song.   In Mississippi, according to Charles R. Stockard (1905), it also nests in orchards and in "the thickest canebrakes."

Where it has become established farther north, it prefers similar haunts wherever it can find them, even coming into the towns and cities and nesting in lilac bushes near houses and in other shrubbery in parks and gardens.

Courtship.—Evidences of affection between mated pairs and courtship to secure new mates may be observed before the end of winter. The male shows more tolerance toward the female on the feeding shelf, allows her to feed with him, and often puts food into her beak. Singing by both sexes becomes more frequent and seems to play an important part in the courtship performance.

Shaver and Roberts (1933) write: "The singing of the male became more frequent in February and parts of songs could be heard at almost any hour of the day.   It was about the middle of February before the female started to sing.   From this time on to nesting time, the male and female often appeared to sing against each other, i.e., the female would sing a song and then stop while the male repeated the same song.   Then he would wait for her to sing again.   At these

PLATE 1

EASTERN CARDINAL COVERING YOUNG

Toronto, Ontario

Cowley County, Kans., July 7, 1929   W. Colv

NEST OF EASTERN CARDINAL

South Florida   A. D. Cruicksha

FLORIDA CARDINAL

times male and female usually sang the same songs. When the female changed the song, the male did too. Sometimes they would sing in unison."

They noted other types of behavior, as follows:

Two pairs of cardinals were in one tree, the males chasing the females from branch to branch. When the males alighted for a moment, their necks were stretched out and their crests raised high so that they looked exceedingly long and slender. They sang and swayed their bodies from side to side, frequently bowing also. Soon one pair flew away and the male of the remaining pair flew to the top of a high tree and sang with wings partly spread and drooping. He sang the *whoo-ett, whoo-ett, whoo-ett, tuer tuer tuer* song. The female came to the shrubbery below. The male sang low and soft. The female flew over the fence and called until he came to her. * * *

Another type of behavior is closely linked with the swaying of the exceedingly slender body with pointed erect crest. The male may fly to the same limb on which the female is perched, alighting usually higher up on the branch. Then with his crest, neck and body extended, and singing very rapidly, he may step sideways down the limb to the female. During this time he appears fairly to slide down. If this process is interrupted by the female flying to another tree, the male may pursue her flying directly towards her with outstretched crest and neck, and singing on the wing. * * *

Quite frequently the behavior just discussed ends with coition at the end of the male's slide down the limb towards the female.

They noted that the female took part in the courtship performance by stretching out her neck as far as possible, and that both sexes swayed their bodies from side to side and both sang, often in unison.

Verna R. Johnston (1944) writes: "On March 2, 1940, two male cardinals chased one female up and down and around trees for twenty minutes, the female always in the lead. The two males flew at each other several times, pecking and ruffling their feathers and uttering an angry buzzing note when in combat. Several times the males dashed headlong from the top branches of a tree toward the ground, only to swoop up again when within six feet of it. When the female stopped and perched in a tree, usually high up, the two males perched close by and took turns singing, flying at each other and diving toward the ground while the female watched them."

Much of the singing and fighting is closely connected with the establishing of the breeding territory. Mrs. Laskey (1944) says: "The groups and loose flocks, formed during fall and winter, disband gradually as males choose territory and obtain mates. * * * Cardinals do not defend territory so pugnaciously as Mockingbirds, for example, do, but there is some mild fighting in spring. A mated male will fly at an intruder of his own sex; a mated female will chase another female, but each is usually tolerant of the opposite sex, never becoming an ally of its mate against the intruder."

Nesting.—Cardinals build their nests in a variety of situations, in bushes, tangles of vines, saplings, and small trees, with no decided preference for any particular species. Very few are placed in trees; most of them are built in tangled thickets or dense shrubbery. A. Dawes Du Bois has sent me his notes on 14 Illinois nests; 2 of these were in saplings 6 feet from the ground, 1 in woods, and 1 in a ravine; 1 was in a tangle of old vines on a fallen stump in some river-bottom woods; the others were all in bushes, at heights ranging from 2½ to 6 feet above the ground; the bushes were located along the banks of creeks, at the roadside, and in woods or thickets; 2 were in blackberry bushes or tangles, 1 in a gooseberry bush, and 1 in spirea bushes close to a house; another was "in a large bush in Washington Park in Springfield, where automobiles passed only about 20 feet away."

W. E. Shore writes to me about some Toronto nests: "Five nests which I visited this year were all within the city limits. One was in High Park, within 2 or 3 feet of one of the busiest walks and, no doubt hundreds of people daily walked by within arm's reach of the nest, which was only 3 feet from the ground in an Austrian pine. Another was 12 feet from the ground in an orange-blossom bush in a back yard in the heart of the city. * * * Another nest noted was in a rose arbor 6 feet high in a city garden, and another was in a vine growing on the side wall of a back porch. The door of the porch, through which people passed all day, was only 3 or 4 feet from the nest and the kitchen window was directly over it.

"One other nest that I would like to mention was built in a small bush in a greenhouse connected with a flower shop in the center of the city. Entrance was gained through a broken pane, which the owner kindly refrained from repairing until the young had been led out."

Gertrude Fay Harvey (1903) photographed a nest in a rose vine in a conservatory.

Frederick S. Barkalow, Jr., writes to me of an Alabama nest that was 5 feet from the ground in a small *Pinus taeda*, 1 foot from the trunk.

Mrs. Amelia R. Laskey (1944), who has found a total of 103 nests near Nashville, Tenn., writes:

As nest sites, Cardinals choose young evergreens of many varieties; privet hedges; many species of vines, including rose and honeysuckle; shrubbery; and saplings of hackberry, elm, hawthorn, and locust. I have found them from 2½ to 12 feet from the ground, but 4 to 5 feet is the usual height. * * * Most nests are concealed in forks of twigs and small branches or in mats of vines stems, but one at my home was built upon a platform of twigs which I had placed in a privet shrub where the pair had tried to anchor material in unsuitable forks. Another was built on the ledge of a lattice fence between poultry wire with nothing for concealment. * * * E. Copeland (1936) describes a Cardinal nest built in a feeding shelf outside a second-story window.

Nests are composed most commonly of weed stems, small pliable twigs, strips of bark, grasses, vines, and rootlets, with leaves and paper interwoven. They are bowl-shaped, some compactly built and well-lined, others very flimsy with scarcely any lining.

She says that the nest is usually built by the female alone. Three nests that she watched from start to finish were completed in 3, 4, and 9 days, respectively; and the first egg was laid within 5 or 6 days after the nest was finished. "Four nestings in a season are not uncommon."

G. M. Sutton (MS.) specifies a wide variety of nesting habitat. The nesting site may be wholly removed from the feeding grounds in shrubbery in swamplands, in cedars in dry old fields, or in sassafras trees in the shade of tall oaks and hickories. Sutton's study of 21 nests in Oklahoma showed the highest 15 feet up, the lowest 15 inches; average height was 5.9 feet. There were 15 clutches believed complete, with 3.2 eggs per clutch. In two nests containing 4 eggs each, only 3 eggs hatched.

Nests have been recorded as high as 20 feet by Trautman (1940) and 30 feet, very rarely, by Oberholser (1927). Harold M. Holland (1930 and 1934) reports cardinals nesting for two different seasons in a woven-wire sparrow trap on a beam in an outbuilding.

William Youngworth (1955a) comments that a pair with a nest 6 feet up disregarded his Siamese cat throughout the entire nesting period. Much of the time the female was away from the nest and the male nowhere in sight. Something drove the female from the nest just before 10:00 p.m. one night; the bird returned almost an hour later. He comments on the ability of the bird to see in the dark. The female stopped night-brooding the lone nestling when it was 5 days old. On the 10th morning after hatching, the young bird, after 2 hours of calling by both parents, scrambled from the nest and flew 6 feet to a tree. Upon this, the mother bird flew away and Youngworth did not again see her near the offspring or in the neighborhood. She left the bird in the care of the male.

Oscar Hawksley and Alvah P. McCormack (1951) describe a doubly occupied nest. At one time both females were actually on the nest, facing in opposite directions.

Andrew J. Berger writes Taber that the breeding season of this species in Michigan, formerly almost unknown there, is from mid-April to mid-September. He found a female incubating four eggs on April 19, 1954. A nest held three eggs on August 26, 1955, and on September 7 the three young were still in the nest. On September 17 he collected a young bird (tail 1.5 inches long) still being fed by adults, and he saw another family group with young of about the same age in another area.

Eggs.—The cardinal lays from two to five eggs, with three or four most often forming the set. They are ovate, occasionally tending to elongated-ovate or short-ovate, and are somewhat glossy. The ground color is grayish white, buffy white, or greenish white, and is generally well speckled and spotted with such shades of brown as "pecan brown," "cinnamon brown," "mummy brown," and "Brussels brown," with underlying spots of "pale Quaker drab," "light mouse gray," or "pale violet gray." In most cases the markings are fairly evenly distributed over the entire egg, with tendency to become more concentrated toward the large end, but some eggs are so thickly speckled that the ground is almost obscured, while others may be very sparsely spotted or boldly marked with irregular spots or blotches.

The measurements of 50 eggs average 25.3 by 18.2 millimeters; the eggs showing the four extremes measure *27.9* by 18.3, 24.9 by *19.8*, *21.8* by 17.6, and 26.9 by *16.8* millimeters.

Young.—Incubation is performed normally by the female, but the male has been seen occassionally to sit on the nest for short periods.

Hervey Brackbill says in his notes: "Observations on two nests in Baltimore indicate that, although some sitting is done earlier, incubation at full intensity is not begun until the final egg has been laid. At an early May nest there was some incubation on the day the first egg was laid, but the bird did not roost on the nest until the second had been laid, and apparently did not begin steady sitting until the third was laid."

According to Mrs. Laskey (MS.), the period of incubation is 12 to 13 days. Three eggs, marked by Brackbill, hatched in 11 days 13 hours, 12 days 1 hour, and 12 days 1¼ hours.

Mrs. Laskey (MS.) says that the young remain in the nest normally for 9 or 10 days, but may leave at 7 days of age when disturbed, or may stay in the nest until 11 days old. Young cardinals are fed by both parents while they are in the nest, and for some time thereafter. Brackbill (1944) made some observations on a brood of color-banded young cardinals that "showed weak but effectual flight on the day of nest-leaving, at about 10 days of age, the birds being able to keep to cover well above the ground; strong flight by the age of about 19 days, partial independence at about 38 days, complete independence at 45 days, and severence of family ties at 56 to 59 days. * * *

"In the presence of a parent both of the juveniles that I kept under observation begged for food to the very end of their association, although during the final 12 or 14 days the begging was always futile."

Gertrude Fay Harvey (1903) watched both parents feed the young that were raised in her conservatory. "The food was grubs and insects, which the old birds swallowed and gave to the young by regurgitation during the first week. Afterwards it was given directly and it was interesting to see what large mouthfuls the little fellows could accommodate. When nine days old, one of them swallowed, without choking, a grub two inches long and as large as a lead pencil."

At a nest McAtee (1908) watched for 6½ hours, the young were fed 178 times, an average of 89 times each. The longest interval between visits was 35 minutes and the shortest was 2 minutes. G. M. Sutton (MS.) says the adults turn their heads sideways to feed the young, as the food is far back in the gullet.

Mrs. T. E. Winford writes of watching the female lead two full-grown young into a garage to feed them grubs taken out of a dislodged wasp's nest.

Apparently, three or four broods of young are often raised in a season; probably three broods are raised normally, as nesting begins early and ends late in the season. W. E. Shore writes to me that one pair, in Toronto, built five nests in one season, and another pair raised four broods successfully.

J. Van Tyne (1951) observed a male which, with its beak filled with the type of green worms it had been seen feeding the young, stopped at a feeding tray, disgorged the worms onto the shelf, cracked, ate some sunflower seeds, picked the worms up again, laid them down again, ate more seeds, then picked them up again and flew off presumably to feed the young. He repeated the procedure a second time later in the day.

Plumages.—Dwight (1900) describes the natal down of the cardinal as "mouse-gray." Of the juvenal plumage, in which the sexes are alike, he says: "Above, sepia-brown, wings darker and suffused with dull dragon's-blood and brick-red, the tail, crest and forehead largely brick-red, traces of black on lores and chin. Below wood-brown, cinnamon tinged on throat, sides and flanks."

A complete molt occurs in August, or earlier in early broods, producing in the male a scarlet plumage practically indistinguishable from that of the adult and much veiled with olive-gray edgings. The first nuptial plumage is acquired by wear, the loss of the gray edgings intensifying the bright red of the spring plumage. There is no molt. Adults have a complete postnuptial molt in late summer and the brighter male spring plumage is acquired by wear. The sequence of molts is the same in the female, but she never assumes the full red plumage, although her crest, wings, and tail are tinged with dull red.

Food.—In his excellent paper on the food of the grosbeaks, W. L. McAtee (1908) gives the results attained from the examination of nearly 500 stomachs of this species. The examination showed that "the bird's diet is about three-tenths animal and seven-tenths vegetable."

The animal food consists almost entirely of insects. He lists 51 species of beetles, including ground beetles, click beetles, wood borers, fireflies, lamellicorn beetles, long-horned beetles, snout beetles, leaf beetles, billbugs, and bark beetles. Twelve species of Hemiptera are listed, including cicadas, treehoppers, leafhoppers, plant lice, and scale insects. Four species of grasshoppers and crickets are included, as well as the larvae of eight species of Lepidoptera, ants, sawflies, dragonflies, and other flies. Other invertebrates include spiders, centipedes, snails, slugs, and small bivalves. He mentions that a male cardinal was seen eating a field mouse.

He says that the nestlings of the cardinal are highly insectivorous: "During the preparation of this report 4 have been examined, with the result that 94.75 percent of their food was found to be animal matter and 5.25 vegetable. * * * The proportions of the principal food items of the four nestlings are as follows: Cicadas, 17.25 percent; grasshoppers, 20; caterpillars, 21.25; and beetles, 23.25."

Among the vegetable food, he includes corn, rice, Kafir corn, oats, and wheat, making up only 8.73 percent of the total food, but much of this is waste grain.

He lists 33 species of wild fruits, including nearly every kind of tree, shrub, or vine that is available, and 39 species of weed seeds, as found in the stomachs of this grosbeak. But he does not mention any damage to cultivated fruits.

In his summary, he writes:

The cardinal has been accused of pilfering certain grains, notably corn, to an injurious extent, which charge the evidence from stomach examination neither proves nor disproves. But in view of the fact that only 8.73 percent of the total food is grain, and that more than half of that amount is waste, the loss is greatly overbalanced by the destruction of weed seeds alone, which compose more than half of the vegetable food. Moreover, some of the weeds consumed are especially destructive to grain crops.

In securing its insect food the cardinal injures us in 1 case and benefits us in 15. In other words, considering animal food alone, only one cardinal does harm to 15 which do good. * * *

* * * The following list of important pests the bird has been shown to prey upon is in itself sufficient proof of the cardinal's value. The list includes the Rocky Mountain locust, 17-year cicada, potato beetle, cotton worm, bollworm, cotton cutworm, cotton-boll weevil, codling moth, rose-beetle, cucumber-beetle, figeater, zebra caterpillar, plum scale, and other scale insects.

Rev. J. J. Murray writes to me: "I once noted a pair of cardinals visiting the holes made in a maple tree by sapsuckers. It was early in March, when the sap was running freely. They were drinking greedily."

Mrs. Laskey says in her notes: "March 12, 1939, I saw cardinals eating elm buds, blossoms, or seeds in the treetops.

"May 1, 1947, as winged termites emerged from the base of a large silver maple, a male cardinal ate avidly and fed a few to his mate."

At feeding stations, cardinals seem to prefer sunflower seeds, but they also eat raisins, pieces of apples, corn bread, wheat bread, scratch feed, and millet.

Behavior.—In the cardinal we have a rare combination of good qualities, brilliant plumage, a rich and pleasing voice, beneficial food habits, and devotion to its mate and family. Many of our best singers are not clothed in brilliant plumage, and many of our hand-somest birds are not gifted musicians.

Dispositions vary among individuals. Mrs. Nice (1931) writes, regarding birds that visited her feeding station: "Three were amiable birds, but the other two were quite the opposite, tyrannizing over the smaller birds, especially Harris Sparrows, and driving away their future mates; both were afraid of Mockingbirds. But from late March to September the male is a model husband and father, bestow-ing sunflower seeds upon his mate and feeding the young of the first brood almost up to the day the second brood hatches, in one case even two days afterwards! Two different years young males have been fed by their fathers for 17 days after they were fully grown, till July 10 and Sept. 30, respectively!"

Although amiable at times, the cardinal is generally mildly domi-nant at feeding stations and sometimes decidedly belligerent, as indi-cated in some of the following notes from Mrs. Laskey: "There have been occasional instances of dominance; usually one male runs at another male, one female at another female. One moves out of the way but does not leave.

"At a ground feeding spot, where sunflower seed had been placed, two male cardinals rose at least 5 feet into the air as they struck at each other.

"Some groups are made up of cardinals that are mild mannered or only mildly domineering. Again, there may be one or more indi-viduals that are pugnacious and continually driving their companions away, either by running at them or actually fighting."

Bayard H. Christy (1942) quotes Maurice Brooks of West Virginia University:

Cardinals are decidedly social, particularly in the winter. Aggregations that gather about a favorite feeding place are almost always fairly evenly divided in the matter of sex, since most of the birds seem to remain mated, at least through-out a year's time. During the early winter months a male cardinal would not tolerate the presence of a female, even his mate, on a small feeding shelf. An intruding cardinal was either driven off, or it in turn drove off the first. Other and smaller song-birds were, however, tolerated without any threatening move-ments. In late winter and early spring male birds became much tolerant of fe-males, and both sexes often fed together. During the nesting season the female, on her brief visits to the feeding shelf, was often intolerant of the presence of a male.

As further evidence of its pugnacity, the cardinal occasionally indulges in "shadow boxing," fighting its own image in a window pane or mirror, as if it were a rival. Both sexes do this.

Chapman (1912) refers to the cardinal as "rather a clumsy fellow. His body appears to be stiff, as if it were made of wood, different in every way from the pliant, lithe body of the Catbird, for example. He hops about on the ground with tail held well up out of harm's way, and comes heavily down upon his feet, as if his body were really very solid. In fact, he is not at all a graceful bird."

Thomas S. Roberts (1932) says: "It is a rather restless, uneasy bird, moving constantly about, and when disturbed, registers its annoyance by elevating the crest to the fullest extent and accompanying its rather feeble *chip* by quick jerks of the long tail."

Some observers have stated that cardinals seldom bathe, or that the male rarely does so. But there is considerable evidence that both sexes bathe, and in all sorts of weather. Mrs. W. W. Dickinson, of Bluefield, W. Va., writes to Mrs. Laskey (MS.) that she has many records of both male and female cardinals bathing. She has several records for December, January, and February. On Dec. 23, 1945, with a foot of snow on the ground, she observed five males and two females bathing that day, all separately, as she has never seen more than one cardinal bathing at a time. On Mar. 5, 1947, a male bathed with two house sparrows about noon when there was 5 feet of snow, and there was ice in the water.

Mrs. Laskey says in her notes: "January 5, 1946, about noon, with a steady rain falling, a male cardinal stood on our driveway, shaking wings and tail, going through the motions of bathing as the driving rain came from the southwest. Once he flew to a tree, but returned to the driveway to resume bathing in the rain."

Cardinals, like some other birds, are sometimes addicted to the curious habit of "anting"; this consists of picking up ants, crushing them and rubbing them through the plumage, under the wings, about the thighs, and at the base of the tail; the object of it may not be fully understood, but it is supposed to be for the purpose of anointing the plumage with formic acid to discourage vermin; after thorough "anting," the plumage appears wet, as though the juice had been squeezed out of the ants.

Referring to the gregarious character of the cardinal, Nuttall (1832) says:

But though they usually live only in families or pairs, and at all times disperse into these selective groups, yet in severe weather, at sunset, in South Carolina, I observed a flock passing to a roost in a neighboring swamp and bushy lagoon, which continued, in lengthened file, to fly over my head at a considerable height for more than 20 minutes together. The beautiful procession, illumined by the last rays of the setting sun, was incomparably splendid as the shifting shadowy light at quick intervals flashed upon their brilliant livery. They had been observed to pass in this manner to their roost for a considerable time, and, at daybreak, they were seen again to proceed and disperse for subsistence.

Harvey B. Lonell (1948) comments on the frequency with which the cardinal removes aluminum bands from its tarsus.

Stanley Logan (1951) mentions a pair of cardinals that lost nest and young in a windstorm. The adults built a new nest. The male, before the second brood hatched, undertook to feed four young robins and was almost as active in that respect as the parent robins. Ultimately the cardinal's second nesting proved successful, and the male cardinal fed both its own young and the robins'.

Voice.—Although the cardinal could hardly be rated as one of our finest singers, it has a great variety of rich, flutelike notes, which are very pleasing and are sure to command the attention of even the casual observer. It is a very persistent singer throughout most of the year, and it has been heard singing occasionally during every month in the year, but in the northern states, the main song period is from March to August, and according to J. Rowland Nowell (1899), in the vicinity of Anderson, N.C., the cardinal sings in February. Both sexes sing, and the song of the female is but little inferior to that of the male, though usually softer.

Mrs. Laskey (1944) says that cardinals "have at least 28 different songs, but male and female song are indistinguishable. Cardinal song may sometimes be heard the year round, but full song for the male usually extends from February to September, and for the female, from March until July to August. Whisper singing, antiphonal singing, and night singing are all common with cardinals."

Rev. J. J. Murray writes to me: "Once, on the last day of March, I watched a female that was moving through a thicket, followed by a male. Occasionally she stopped to whistle a low, sweet song, *peer, peer, peer, peer*, the male silent all the while. Sometimes a cardinal, disturbed at its roosting place, will react by singing, even in the middle of the night."

G. M. Sutton (MS.) points out that prior to nesting the first song for any given day may be uttered by either sex. Singing by the female subsides with nesting. During that period the male greets the day with "trial" songs, which may be three whistled *chuck-er whee* phrases, usually preceded by a few chirps similar to the alarm notes. Similar call notes are uttered in the evening for several minutes before the male flies to its perch for the night. In midsummer ebullient singing, by both sexes, may be followed by nesting, during which singing becomes practically nonexistent.

Hervey Brackbill says in his notes: "I have once seen a cardinal sing on the wing. During a flight of about 70 yards, early one March

morning, the bird gave a steady succession of the *chyou* notes that
have the quality of a taut wire sharply struck. It was still singing
when it alighted in a tree, and continued singing there for some
seconds."

Witmer Stone (1937) gives us the following account of the voice
of the cardinal: "The Cardinal has quite a repertoire but all of his
vocal efforts come under the head of whistles rather than songs.
There is the loud emphatic call—which I have recorded as *whoit,
whoit, whoit,* often followed directly by the longer drawn out *cheer,
cheer, cheer,* and sometimes a bird utters quite a different call *cheedle,
cheedle, cheedle, cheedle.* On one occasion a bird called rapidly and
continuously *whit, whit, whit, whit, whit,* etc., like the Flicker's rapid
call, while another had a very low modification of the *cheer* call—
pheu, pheu, phey."

Aretas A. Saunders writes me that "The song of the cardinal is
one of the most distinctive and pleasing of American bird songs. The
notes are delivered in a loud, somewhat reedy whistle. Certain notes,
slurs, or phrases are usually repeated rhythmically, and rather rapidly.
In many songs a particular slur or phrase is repeated throughout the
song. In other songs there are two distinct parts, the bird changing
abruptly, somewhere in the middle of the song, from one kind of slur
or phrase to another.

"The pitch of the songs varies from G'' to C'''', three and a half
tones more than an octave. The pitch of the repeated phrase may
not change or may become lower near the end of the song, very rarely
higher. This repeated phrase may be a slur, *teeyo* or *toowee*, or a
single note and slur, as *wheeteeyo* or *whitowee*. The slur may be up or
down, or both, or absent. Songs vary in length from 1.8 seconds to 4.2
seconds, usually even in time, occasionally with marked acceleration
toward the end, but never slower. The song is loud, with great carrying power. There may be a marked increase in loudness toward the
end, but never a decrease.

"Consonant sounds, both explosive and liquid, are prominent, and
include phrases such as *whitcheeah* or *toolit* or *tayo*, or *to to to to to*.
The individual bird has many songs, all the way up to seven."

In his unpublished manuscript Saunders emphasizes the variable
length and number of notes. In his 98 records the number of notes
varies from 4 to 43, with the average about 16. Songs vary in length
from 1 to 5⅖ seconds, averaging about 2¾ seconds. In this manuscript
he states that the pitch varies from D_5 to C_7.

Albert R. Brand (1938), in his studies of the vibration frequencies of
passerine bird song, found that the pitch of the cardinal's whistled
notes "averages lower than one would presume." Its average is 2800
vibrations per second, "a shade above the highest F of the keyboard";

the highest note recorded on his film was 4375, and the lowest 2200 vibrations per second.

Young cardinals begin to sing at an early age. Mrs. Laskey (1944) writes: "The first songs of immature Cardinals are very soft warblings, totally unlike adult song; these 'indefinite' warblings are called 'ancestral,' 'primitive,' or 'tribal' by various authorities (Nice, 1943). I have records for four young cardinals singing in August, two wild birds and two hand-raised, free-flying females. One of the latter began warbling at three weeks of age, the other at four weeks. One of the wild birds (probably a female) appeared to be about a month old; the other, a male, nearly two months old, used some adult phrases in his lengthy warbling performance."

Enemies.—In addition to the well-known predators, furred and feathered, that prey on all small birds, the cardinal seems to have a number of troublesome enemies among other birds. Perhaps the worst of these is the cowbird, of which Friedmann (1929) says that the cardinal is a "fairly common victim. * * * In some places this bird seems to be one of the commonest hosts, while in other localities its status is quite different. * * * The Cardinal is parasitized chiefly in the central parts of its range, as the Cowbird is a rare breeder along the Atlantic seaboard south of Virginia * * * There is a case on record of a Cardinal building a two-storied nest, the lower floor containing two eggs of the Cowbird (*M. ater obscurus*)."

Mrs. Horace P. Cook (1934) says of a pair of cardinals that nested for several years near her home: "In the summer of 1932 they first nested in the yard of a neighbor to the east of us, in a dense shrub, but cats or Blue Jays destroyed the nest and the eggs were thrown out on the ground. They then built in the yard west of ours, about eight feet up in a mulberry tree, where sprouts grew upright, making a perfect nesting site. But when the young were beginning to feather, a pair of Blue Jays tried to do away with them. The brave parents fought them off in a terrific battle, to come out victors, although the birds were barely saved."

House wrens sometimes puncture the eggs of the cardinal, and catbirds and English sparrows occasionally compete with them for nesting sites.

Harold S. Peters (1936) lists two species of lice, one fly, one mite, and three species of ticks, as external parasites of the eastern cardinal.

Dr. Rudolph Donath, of the Communicable Disease Center, Department of Health, Education, and Welfare, Atlanta, Ga., writes Oscar M. Root that the cardinal has been found to carry antibodies of the eastern equine, western equine, and St. Louis encephalitis.

D. A. Zimmerman (1954) mentions four birds found dead on highways, and Andrew J. Berger writes Taber of seeing a fox squirrel destroy the eggs in a cardinal's nest beside his house in Michigan. The adult birds flew about in neighboring bushes, giving alarm notes. Alexander W. Blain (1948) includes this species in a list of birds injured or killed by hitting "picture windows."

Mrs. Laskey (MS.) mentions a cardinal that fell to the ground with one wing bound to its body by spider webs.

As to the longevity of cardinals she (1944) says: "Of 1,135 Cardinals whose life span could have been three or more years, 30 (2.6 percent) have reached the ages of three to six years, the oldest female being 4½ years old; two males reached the ages of six years. A male and a female 10 years of age and a male 13½ years are cited from the literature."

This very old bird was banded by A. F. Ganier (1937) in February 1924 and was last seen in November 1936; he seemed very feeble when last seen, though he had mated and reared a brood that year.

Fall.—The cardinal can hardly be classed as a regularly migratory species. Many individuals are decidedly sedentary, remaining in the same locality for breeding and wintering, and seldom wandering more than a few miles from where they were hatched. On the other hand, banding records have shown that many others have wandered considerable distances from where they were banded and in various directions. A bird banded at Elberton, Ga., Apr. 4, 1944, was recovered in Dickinson County, Va., Jan. 18, 1945, 105 miles to the northeast. Another banded at Takoma Park, Md., May 10, 1939, was taken at New Kensington, Pa., July 20, 1940, nearly 200 miles to the northwest.

The records show a decided trend of movement northeastward and northward in the fall and late summer, which may account for the many northern winter records and for the eventual northward spread of the species   Where encouraged by feeding stations, some of these birds have remained and bred.

Winter.—In their winter haunts, cardinals often gather into large flocks of sometimes more than 60 or 70 birds and resort to the more sheltered localities. Milton B. Trautman (1940) says of such resorts in the vicinity of Buckeye Lake, Ohio: "In the coldest portion of the year, especially when there was much snow, the bird was largely confined to the dense cover of the larger of the brushy thickets, fallow fields in which giant ragweed (*Ambrosia trifida*) and other weeds had grown rank and tall, weedy fields of uncut corn, and the dense shrub layers and grapevine tangles of woodlands. * * * A few remained throughout winter in the dense shrubbery about farmhouses, cottages, and in villages, especially where they were fed."

There is no more pleasing, soul-warming sight than one of these bright red birds enlivening with color the somber woods or leafless shrubbery when the ground is covered with snow and the world seems lifeless. And, perhaps on a sunny winter morning, he may cheer us with a few notes of his flutelike song.

DISTRIBUTION

Range.—The eastern cardinal is resident from southeastern South Dakota (Union and Clay counties), Central Minnesota (Madison, St. Cloud), northern Wisconsin (Washburn and Lincoln counties), northern Michigan (Mackinac, Emmet, and Cheboygan counties), southern Ontario (Owen Sound, Port Hope), western New York (Rochester, Geneva), northwestern Vermont (Burlington), and eastern Massachusetts (Waltham, Arlington, Annisquam), south through central Nebraska, western Kansas, and western Arkansas to northeastern Texas, central Louisiana (Lepcompte), the Gulf coast of Mississippi and Alabama, the western panhandle of Florida, and southern Georgia (except the southeastern section).

Casual records.—Casual north to eastern Colorado (Littleton), central northern and central North Dakota (Minot, Bismarck), southern Saskatchewan (Craven), southeastern Manitoba (Winnipeg, occassionally breeding), eastern Ontario (Algonquin Park), Quebec, Maine, and Nova Scotia (Halifax). Range is extending steadily northward.

Introduced.—Hawaii.

Migration.—Essentially nonmigratory. Some wandering of immature birds in fall; some movement, mostly local in scope, in March.

Egg dates.—Georgia: 32 records, April 19 to July 8; 17 records, May 1 to May 23.

Illinois: 53 records, April 15 to July 28; 20 records, May 6 to May 30.

Maryland: 187 records, April 10 to August 19; 94 records, April 28 to June 2.

Michigan: 82 records, April 20 to August 27; 43 records, May 12 to June 15.

New Jersey: 20 records, March 2 to July 11; 10 records, April 21 to May 10.

New York: 22 records, April 16 to August 16; 11 records, May 10 to June 10.

Ontario: 20 records, April 21 to July 15; 10 records, May 7 to May 25.

South Carolina: 4 records, April 24 to July 13.

Tennessee: 2 records, April 28, May 11.

Texas: 34 records, March 24 to July 28; 17 records, April 29 to June 7.

Florida Cardinal

PLATE 2

HABITS

Ridgway (1901) describes the cardinal of peninsular Florida as similar to the eastern cardinal, "but decidedly smaller and darker; adult male with terminal margins of feathers of back, etc., distinctly olivaceous instead of gray, the red of the under parts, etc., deeper or darker; without the purity of red of western (Mississippi Valley and Texan) specimens; adult female with upper parts more distinctly olivaceous and under parts more tawny."

This cardinal is an abundant resident throughout the peninsula of Florida, as far west on the Gulf coast as Apalachicola and on many of the Keys, as well as in southeastern Georgia. In northwestern Florida it is replaced by the eastern cardinal, with which this race intergrades on the border of its range.

Arthur H. Howell (1932) says that it "is found in a number of different habitats, but seems to require thickets, or at least bushes, as an essential feature of its environment. The birds often select village gardens or dooryards for their home, and they are equally contented in the dense hammocks overgrown with cactus and lianas near Cape Sable. They follow the canals into the Everglades, and have become domiciled in the bushes growing on their banks. They are common in the deep, timbered swamps along the rivers in northwestern Florida, as well as in the custard-apple jungle on the shores of Lake Okeechobee. Even on the big prairies and in the pine woods they are usually found wherever hammock conditions, with undergrowth occur."

Phyrne S. Russell (1951) watched several of these birds snipping off blossoms of "turk's cap" or "sleeping hibiscus," *Malvaviscus arboreus* and holding them in the uptilted beak. Examination of discarded blossoms showed that the calyx was slashed just where the petiole was attached to the sepals.

Nesting.—Howell (1932) continues: "Nesting begins about the first of April and may continue to July. The nests are usually from 2 to 8 feet from the ground, placed in palmetto or oak bushes, small orange trees, or clumps of vines. The eggs usually number 3—rarely 4. A nest found in a hammock near Brooksville, May 17, 1929, was composed largely of Spanish moss, and placed 7 feet up in a small sapling; the female bird was sitting on the nest, with her wings spread widely to protect the young from falling rain."

Donald J. Nicholson made a detailed study in 1954. He writes that singing commences the second—even the first week in January. The male breaks into desultory singing at daybreak during the courtship period, continuing into the late afternoon. The female sings on the nest, but there is little singing after the eggs have hatched. In one instance, a male was at the top of a large oak 175 feet distant from the nest. In nest building, the male may accompany the female but does not actually assist in the construction. One nest was found saddled on a limb of a mango tree right against the trunk, anchored by sprouts, 5 feet above ground. The male does not incubate. Both sexes eat the fecal matter—never take it away. The female is quite tame when on the nest.

Eggs.—The measurements of 40 eggs average 24.9 by 18.3 millimeters; the eggs showing the four extremes measure *27.7* by *19.3*, *21.8* by *17.6*, and 22.8 by *17.0* millimeters.

DISTRIBUTION

Range.—The Florida cardinal is resident from the eastern part of the panhandle of northern Florida (Apalachicola) and southeastern Georgia (Okefenokee Swamp, St. Marys) south through the Florida Peninsula.

Egg dates.—Florida: 74 records, March 30 to August 8; 30 records, April 4 to April 24; 30 records, May 5 to May 25.

RICHMONDENA CARDINALIS MAGNIROSTRIS (Bangs)
Louisiana Cardinal

HABITS

Outram Bangs (1903) gave this race the above name, based on a series of 12 skins from West Baton Rouge Parish, La. The characters given are: "Bill larger and heavier than in any of the other races" of the species; and "otherwise, most like *C. cardinalis floridanus*, but wing slightly longer, tail shorter, and foot and tarsus larger. In color the male has the same olivaceous edging to the feathers of the back, but the red of the head and under parts is not so dark as in the Florida bird, though decidedly more intense than is usual in *C. cardinalis cardinalis*. The female is colored as in *C. cardinalis floridanus*, the back being olivaceous and the under parts strongly buffy; the middle of belly, however, is rather paler—more whitish.

"In both sexes the area occupied by the capistrum is greater than in the other races; and in the female the capistrum is not only more extended but decidedly darker, more sooty grayish in color, and much more conspicuous."

Its haunts and habits seem to be similar to those of the Florida cardinal. Bailey and Wright (1931), in southern Louisiana, "found several nests in the low mesquite, and one was located within fifty feet of the Gulf. The nest was made of grass and Spanish moss, and was decorated with a big piece of snake skin. * * * Another nest observed contained young, and the adults were feeding them on cicadas."

Eggs.—The measurements of 40 eggs average 24.8 by 18.5 millimeters; the eggs showing the four extremes measure *27.9* by 18.2, 23.9 by *19.8*, *21.8* by 17.9, and 24.0 by *17.5* millimeters.

DISTRIBUTION

Range.—The Louisiana cardinal is resident in southeastern Texas (Columbus, Beaumont) and southern Louisiana (Erwinville, New Orleans).

Egg dates.—Texas: 14 records, April 10 to June 1.

RICHMONDENA CARDINALIS CANICAUDUS (Chapman)

Gray-tailed Cardinal

HABITS

Dr. Chapman (1891), in naming and describing this Texas race, gives its subspecific characters as follows: "Male similar to the male of *Cardinalis cardinalis*, but with a less conspicuous black frontlet; female averaging grayer than the female of *Cardinalis cardinalis*, and with the tail feathers broadly margined with gray instead of being narrowly edged with olivaceous brown." Of the females, he says further: "In some of the Texan specimens the gray color occupies nearly all of both vanes of the median feathers, leaving only a narrow, reddish shaft streak; in most cases the gray occupies all of the tip of the feather, and when seen from below gives the appearance of an irregular terminal grayish band."

The haunts of this cardinal seem to be similar to those of the species elsewhere, such as thickets, brushy places, and the shrubbery about houses and gardens. It is an abundant and familiar bird, resident throughout its range.

George Sennett (1878) says that, about Brownville: "We found them quite common, yet very shy. A number of nests and sets of eggs were obtained. They were generally taken in dense thickets, some five feet from the ground; but we found one nest and two eggs, seven feet from the ground, in a bushy tree; and another, only two and one-half feet from the ground, in a thicket. * * * The nests vary greatly, according to location; some are bulky, and others hardly more than would answer for a Carolina Dove."

George Finlay Simmons (1925) describes the nest, as observed in the Austin region, as: "A loose, rather frail structure, composed principally of dead leaves, cedar bark strips, and dead weed stems, frequently containing Spanish moss, paper, green weed stems, grasses, and grapevine strips, and occasionally a few slender twigs, Indian tobacco, strips of dry corn shucks, straws, and pieces of rag. Lined with fiberous rootlets and fine grass stems; less commonly with fine weed stems, horsehair, grass, fine weed tips, and bits of straw."

This cardinal is sometimes imposed upon by the bronzed cowbird. Miss Mariana Roach of Dallas wrote me of a pair successfully raising a cowbird, renesting a foot from her porch screen, abandoning the nest with two eggs after she removed a newly hatched cowbird, then nesting a third time 8 feet up in a cherry laurel tree, 2 feet from her window. The parents successfully raised two young after laying four eggs. Miss Roach found the first nest early in May. The birds commenced to build the third nest on June 28; there were three eggs in this nest June 30, and four the next day. At least two young hatched July 13. One fledgling left the nest July 21, the other the following day. The family remained together into August.

Eggs.—The measurements of 40 eggs average 24.0 by 18.4 millimeters; the eggs showing the four extremes mesure *26.9* by 19.3, 24.9 by *19.8*, *21.5* by 17.9, and 22.7 by *17.5* millimeters.

DISTRIBUTION

Range.—The gray-tailed cardinal is resident from northern Texas (Randall and Armstrong counties) and western Oklahoma (Ellis County) south through central Texas and central and eastern Mexico to Michoacán and Hidalgo.

Egg dates.—Texas: 5 records, April 21 to May 7.

RICHMONDENA CARDINALIS SUPERBA (Ridgway)
Arizona Cardinal

HABITS

In his original description (1885) Ridgway describes the southern Arizona race of this species as: "Similar to *C. cardinalis igneus*, but decidedly larger, and the female more richly colored."

Later on (1901) he describes it as: "Similar to *C. c. cardinalis* but much larger, with relatively stouter bill; adult male paler red, with black of lores not meeting across forehead; adult female more deeply colored than that of *C. c. cardinalis*—almost exactly similar in coloration to the same sex of *C. c. floridanus*, but back, etc., much grayer, and size much greater."

Its haunts and habits do not seem to differ materially from those of the species elsewhere; it is essentially a bird of the thickets and shrubbery, even in the vicinity of human habitations. We found it fairly common in the canyons of the Catalina Mountains, and very common in the mesquite forest south of Tucson, where we found a nest with two eggs on May 19, and nests with young on May 19 and 20, 1922.

In this same region, Griffing Bancroft (1930) found these cardinals breeding plentifully: "Most of them selected the larger and denser trees and built well inside, so that the nest was carefully concealed. They frequented the thicker riparian undergrowths, where the tangle on the alluvial soil attained a height of twenty feet or more." For further notes on this race, see pages 30, 34.

Eggs.—The measurements of 40 eggs average 24.9 by 18.5 millimeters; the eggs showing the four extremes measure *26.9* by 18.8, 25.5 by *19.8*, *22.2* by 17.6, and 23.8 by *17.0* millimeters.

DISTRIBUTION

Range.—The Arizona cardinal is resident from southern California (Long Beach, Earp), central western and southern Arizona (Bill Williams River, Fort Verde, Salt and Gila river valleys), and southwestern New Mexico (Redrock) south to northern Sonora (Puerto Libertad, Carbo, Pilares).

Egg dates.—Arizona: 40 records, April 6 to July 31; 18 records, May 15 to June 15.

RICHMONDENA CARDINALIS SEFTONI (Huey)
Santa Gertrudis Cardinal

HABITS

Laurence M. Huey (1940) has given the above names to a local race of this species that he discovered in the vicinity of the Santa Gertrurdis Mission, which "is situated in a rocky canyon of the western slope of the main peninsula mountain chain, in the extreme northesatern section of the Viscaino Desert," in central Lower California.

He says of its characters: "Intermediate in size between the smaller *Richmondena cardinalis ignea* of the Cape region and the larger *R. c. superba* of northern Sonora and southern Arizona. *R. c. seftoni* is considerably paler and has a smaller beak than either of the above compared forms, which, geographically, are its nearest relatives. Both of these characters are at once evident when comparisons are made, and the color feature marks this Cardinal as one of the palest of the group."

He does not indicate that its habits are in any way different from those of other neighboring races of the species.

DISTRIBUTION

Range.—The Santa Gertrudis cardinal is resident in central Baja California, from lat. 28° 22′ N. (Santa Teresa Bay) south to lat. 27° 14′ N. (10 miles south of Santa Rosalía).

Egg dates.—Baja California: 30 records, March 22 to August 28; 10 records, May 20 to June 26; 10 records, August 5 to August 9.

RICHMONDENA CARDINALIS IGNEA (Baird)
San Lucas Cardinal

HABITS

The cardinal of the Cape region of Lower California is described by Ridgway (1901) as similar to the Arizona cardinal, "but smaller, with relatively shorter and thicker bill; adult male rather deeper red; adult female paler, both above and below, with capistrum obsolete, very pale grayish or grayish white, and general color of under parts light clay-buff, the chest and sides of head never (?) touched with red."

William Brewster (1902) says of its haunts: "It occurs practically everywhere from the shores of the Gulf to among the foothills of the mountains, but apparently not on the summits or upper slopes of the latter. Mr. Frazar found it most numerously at La Paz and Triunfo, least so at San José del Cabo, while he did not meet with a single specimen on the Sierra de la Laguna. Mr. Bryant saw the bird occasionally 'among thick high shrubs and trees,' on Santa Margarita island, and it was common at Comondu, while further northward he traced it nearly to latitude 29°."

He says of its nesting: "Mr. Frazar took four nests of *C. c. igneus* at San José del Rancho in July, the first on the 14th, the last on the 20th of the month. These were in bushes, the fourth in a small tree, the height above ground varying from four to ten feet. They all closely resemble nests of the eastern Cardinal. The eggs, three in number in each instance, were all fresh or but slightly incubated."

Griffing Bancroft (1930) found some half-dozen nests in the mesquites along the dry river beds, placed on the overhanging lateral branches.

Eggs.—The measurements of 40 eggs average 24.1 by 18.0 millimeters; the eggs showing the four extremes measure *27.2* by 18.0, 23.8 by *19.9*, and *20.3* by *15.8* millimeters.

DISTRIBUTION

The San Lucas cardinal is resident in the Cape district of Baja California from lat. 27° N. south to Cape San Lucas, including Santa Margarita, Carmen, and San José Islands.

Egg date.—Baja California: 1 record, June 27.

PYRRHULOXIA SINUATA SINUATA (Bonaparte)

Texas Pyrrhuloxia

Contributed by ALFRED O. GROSS

HABITS

The pyrrhuloxia was first described by Bonaparte (1837) under the name *Cardinalis sinuatus*. The type specimen was an adult male which was later acquired by the British Museum in 1855. It has a label "W. Mexico Type" and on the reverse side "*Cardinalis sinusatus* No. 3." Later the name was changed to *Pyrrhuloxia sinuata* Bonaparte (1850). Robert Ridgway (1887b) described two new races, one *Pyrrhuloxia sinuata beckhami*, the Arizona pyrrhuloxia, with a distribution of southern Arizona and New Mexico, and the form *Pyrrhuloxia sinuata peninsulae*, the San Lucas pyrrhuloxia, from a type taken at San José del Cabo, Lower California, with a habitat in the arid tropical zone of the Cape district as far north as lat. 26°40'. Ridgway (1897), after seeing the original description of *Cardinalis sinuatus* and discovering that the locality of the type was western Mexico, concluded that the name *sinuatus* in a constricted sense belongs to the form which he had described as *Pyrrhuloxia sinuata beckhami* in 1887. The eastern form known by the vernacular name of Texas cardinal was given a new name, *Pyrrhuloxia sinuata texana*, which according to Ridgway was the true *Pyrrhuloxia sinuata* with a range that includes the Lower Sonoran Zone from Nueces, Bee, Bexar, Kendall, and Tom Green Counties, Texas, south through eastern Mexico to Puebla. Thus the status of these three forms of the pyrrhuloxia stood until the whole matter was reviewed by A. J. van Rossem (1934a). Van Rossem has shown conclusively that Bonaparte's type specimen is a good example of *Pyrrhuloxia sinuata texana* Ridgway and that the name *Pyrrhuloxia sinuata sinuata* (Bonaparte) should be applied to those birds. According to van Rossem, the type of *Pyrrhuloxia sinuata beckhami* Ridgway, which was taken at El Paso, Tex., is in the same category, since modern skins from the same locality cannot be distinguished from lower Rio Grande birds. Therefore the form *Pyrrhuloxia sinuata sinuata*, the Texas pyrrhuloxia, includes all these birds in the Lower Austral Zone of southeastern New Mexico southeastward across Texas and south through Mexico to Puebla and Zacatecas. The fulvous-toned western bird that is smaller in size and with a virtual absence of black intermixture in the red of the face is given a new subspecific name, *Pyrrhuloxia sinuata fulvescens* van Rossem. This race is distributed in south-central Arizona from the vicinity of Tucson, south through the Lower Sonoran and Arid Tropical Zones of Sonora, Sinaloa, western Durango, and Nayarit of Mexico. The two races, according to van Rossem, occupy ranges that are apparently completely isolated one from the other, but distribution is practically continuous within the range of each race.

The common name of the form *sinuata*, Texas pyrrhuloxia, is very appropriate, for the stronghold of this subspecies in the United States is the State of Texas. It is especially abundant along the Rio Grande River, as well as in southwestern Texas. According to Austin P. Smith (1910) the Texas pyrrhuloxia is very abundant on the coast east of Brownsville, Tex., where as many as 50 of these birds may be observed in a morning walk along the Gulf. On Oct. 28, 1909, after a severe northern storm, the autumn migration reached a maximum, when immense flocks of pyrrhuloxias were seen. The Texas pyrrhuloxia is a shyer bird than the gray-tailed cardinal, though more communistic, going about in small flocks at least during the winter months. The males are more suspicious, and there seem to be remarkably fewer of them than of the duller-colored females. Allan Brooks (1933) reported that at Brownsville, Tex., during the winter of 1927–28 there was a very small proportion of adult males, and he estimated that there were six dull colored to every pink one. The birds are difficult to follow when disturbed because of flights of considerable distance taken at short intervals. Though often found feeding on the ground, they are much less terrestrial in habit than the cardinal. Mesquite beans form a favorite food during a portion of the winter. In Brooks County, Tex., about 125 miles northwest of Brownsville, Smith (1913) states that the pyrrhuloxia is a common resident, largely replacing the gray-tailed cardinal. With the advent of the nesting season the Texas pyrrhuloxia loses much of its shyness and resorts to the neighborhood of human habitation, where along with the western mockingbird and the curve-billed thrasher its song is a most striking feature of the advent of spring.

Nesting.—Van Tyne and Sutton (1937) found the Texas pyrrhuloxia in various parts of Brewster County, southwestern Texas, especially where mesquite thickets grew. A nest containing three eggs was found May 21, 1934, in an open thorny bush about 3 miles northeast of Burnham Ranch, and two young recently out of the nest were taken at Glenn Spring on June 4 and 5, 1935. Burleigh and Lowery (1940) found the birds on the open desert east of Guadalupe Peak of the Guadalupe Mountains at an elevation of 4,800 feet on April 29, 1939.

Herbert Brandt (1940) describes the nest and habits of the Texas pyrrhuloxias he observed in Brewster County, Tex., as follows:

> In the three-forked crotch, shoulder-high, of an ungainly, blooming catclaw was the grass-formed nest of a Texas Pyrrhuloxia containing two fresh, well marked eggs, which are noticeably smaller than those of the Cardinal—a bird we did not encounter in this region, although the Pyrrhuloxia was a common thicket dweller in the chaparral bordering watered places. The Texas Pyrrhuloxia is one of the most startling creatures that I have ever lured to my call. As he approaches, with loud round chirps, a vivid flash of crimson, a great blunt bill of rich old ivory, and a tall crest tipped with deep wine red are one's first impressions. Closer inspection shows his lower mandible to be conspicuously thicker than even the broad upper one, which is sharply decurved and gives the bird a parrot-like countenance; while the variable expressive crest creates a versatility of facial expression. His cheery whistle is neither as loud nor as pure as the Cardinal's, having a rather reedy quality, nor does he seem to be so persistent a singer. But like the latter, he responds eagerly to human imitation of bird-calls, approaching the observer with his motile crest sharply erect. In hand, each light gray feather of the breast has but the tip sprayed more or less with crimson, and the breast looks as though a paint brush had been passed hastily but once across the bird's plumage, yet this fiery pigment is so intense that in life it amazes the eye and arouses the admiration of the beholder. * * * The female lacks that lively color, and thus simulates protectively the more modest tones of her dun desert home.

In Mexico, Sutton and Burleigh (1939) found the Texas pyrrhuloxia about Monterey, Nuevo León, during the period Jan. 28 to Feb. 8, 1938. It was fairly common in the San Pedro district of Coahuila and in Victoria, Tamaulipas. On Feb. 15–17, 1938, they found it present at an elevation of 2,500 feet on the Mesa del Chipinque. Burleigh and Lowery (1942) found several pairs in a small arroyo in the open desert country west of Saltille, Coahuila, Mexico, on Apr. 22, 1941. Amadon and Phillips (1947) collected an immature Texas pyrrhuloxia at Las Delicias, Coahuila, Aug. 10, 1946. Sutton and Burleigh (1940b) found these birds in thorny thickets about Valles, San Luis Potosí. These and other records show the Texas pyrrhuloxia to be well represented throughout northeastern Mexico.

Eggs.—The number of eggs laid by the pyrrhuloxia varies from two to four, and rarely five, with three or four composing the usual set. They are usually ovate in shape and somewhat glossy. The ground is grayish white or greenish white, variously speckled, spotted, or blotched with shades of browns such as "pecan brown," "mummy brown," "sayal brown," "tawny-olive," or "Soccardo's umber," with undermarkings of "pale mouse gray," "pale Quaker drab," or "dark Quaker drab." Generally the markings are well scattered over the entire egg, which may be either heavily speckled or sparingly colored with large irregular spots or blotches. The eggs of the pyrrhuloxia cannot, with certainty, be distinguished from those of the cardinal, although they average somewhat smaller.

The measurements of 50 eggs average 24.5 by 17.8 millimeters; the eggs showing the four extremes measure *27.2* by 18.8, 24.7 by *18.9*, *21.9* by 17.0, and 22.9 by *16.0* millimeters.

DISTRIBUTION

Range.—The Texas pyrrhuloxia is resident from southern New Mexico (Mimbres, Tularosa, Lakewood) and western, central, and southeastern Texas (Kendall County, Colmesneil) south to Michoacán (San Agustín), Querétaro, and southern Tamaulipas (Juamave).

Egg dates.—Texas: 66 records, March 13 to July 29; 38 records, April 23 to May 19.

PYRRHULOXIA SINUATA FULVESCENS van Rossem

Arizona Pyrrhuloxia

PLATE 3

Contributed by ANDERS H. ANDERSON*

HABITS

As Mr. Bent points out, the above generic name is a combination of two Latin words, *pyrrhula*, a bullfinch, and *loxia*, a crossbill. This bird resembles a bullfinch in its short, thick bill, but its resemblance to a crossbill is not so apparent, although its upper mandible is somewhat decurved. The Latin *loxia* is derived from a Greek word meaning crooked. The name may be perfectly logical as a scientific name, but it seems a pity that this handsome bird could not be known by some simpler and more euphonious common name. It has been called the bullfinch cardinal, on account of its similar bill, and the name gray cardinal has been suggested, since so much of its plumage is in a soft and pleasing shade of gray. Either of these names would be appropriate and popular.

The specimens from which this species was first described by Bonaparte, under the name *sinuata*, came from the vicinity of Mexico City. Since then the species has been subdivided into three races, the Texas bird, the Arizona bird, and the San Lucas bird. A. J. van Rossem (1934a) is the authority for the above subspecific name for

---

* Incorporating material from an unfinished manuscript by Mr. Bent.

the Arizona bird. He says that this race, in comparison with *sinuata*, is slightly smaller, with "paler and more fulvous coloration, and a virtual absence of black intermixture in the red of the face and crest of the males * * *." In rearrangement of the races found within the United States, he assigns *P. s. sinuata* (Bonaparte) to the "Lower Austral Zone of southern and southeastern New Mexico, southeastward across Texas and south through Mexico to Puebla and Zacatecas." He gives the range of *P. s. fulvescens* van Rossem as: "South-central Arizona, from the vicinity of Tucson south, through the Lower Sonoran and Arid Tropical Zones of Sonora, Sinaloa, western Durango and Nayarit."

If one takes Mr. Bent's comments literally, this statement of the range of the Arizona bird is somewhat inaccurate. There are large areas of the Lower Sonoran Zone where no pyrrhuloxias are to be found. It is a bird of the mesquite edge, and this edge is usually the border of a large arroyo, or a remnant of mesquite forest on the bank of an eroded river valley, or the thorny brush at the lower, widened portion of a mountain canyon. The deeper river bottom growth of cottonwoods and willows and the fringe of *Baccharis* and *Hymenoclea* in the sands may harbor a few cardinals, but seldom pyrrhuloxias. On adjacent farmlands on the benches above the larger intermittent rivers, man has created a most favorable habitat. His fences, overgrown untidily with mesquite, hackberry, and elder, furnish shelter, nesting sites, and food; there is food, too, in the cultivated fields nearby.

The pyrrhuloxia is common to abundant along the Santa Cruz River from Tucson southward; it follows the San Pedro River from Aravaipa Creek to the Mexican border. Sutton and Phillips (1942) reported it from various points in the Papago Indian Reservation westward as far as the border of the Organ Pipe Cactus National Monument. It ranges to the live oak edge of the Upper Sonoran Zone at Oracle, at the base of the Santa Catalina Mountains, and in the Santa Rita Mountains. Bailey (1923) reported it as found "in Madera Canyon at 4,900 feet, where there was a patch of Lower Sonoran mesquite." Swarth (1929) found it at the "north end and along the western base of the Santa Ritas." Phillips (1933) found it at the Fresnal ranch at 4,000 feet in the Baboquivari Mountains. Brandt (1951) thought they were more numerous along the San Pedro River than along the Santa Cruz.

No migration has been observed, although concentrations of birds in the winter, probably near plentiful food supplies, sometimes give the impression of group wanderings. Christmas bird counts are revealing in regard to abundance. In most localities in Texas, *P. s. sinuata* is far outnumbered by the cardinal. Near Tucson *P. s. fulvescens* is

PLATE 3

son, Ariz., May 16, 1954 R. Quigley, Jr.

NEST OF ARIZONA PYRRHULOXIA

cson, Ariz. A. D. Cruickshank

ARIZONA PYRRHULOXIA FEEDING YOUNG

A. D. Du B

NEST OF ROSE-BREASTED GROSBEAK

Toronto, Ontario

H. M. Hallid

MALE ROSE-BREASTED GROSBEAK FEEDING YOUNG

likewise behind the cardinal in the Rillito drainage valley. However, along the Santa Cruz River the pyrrhuloxia leads in almost every winter census. In 1947 there were 53 pyrrhuloxias and 25 cardinals recorded. No summer counts are available.

Why the pyrrhuloxia has not established itself in the irrigated farm-lands along the Gila River westward to the Colorado River is not known. Certainly it cannot be because of the higher temperatures of the lower elevations, because the species occurs in Sonora, Mexico, at probable equally high temperatures and also at sea level.

Mr. Bent found a few pairs of the Arizona bird in the mesquite brush along the San Pedro River near Fairbanks, and found it com-mon in the mesquite forest along the Santa Cruz River, south of Tucson. In the Santa Rita Mountains, Mrs. Bailey (1923) reported it as found "in Madera Canyon at 4,900 feet, where there was a patch of Lower Sonoran mesquite" and in stony gulches "bordered by mes-quite." It might well be called the mesquite cardinal, since it seems fond of this association, but it is also seen at times in trees about houses.

Territory.—Some years before the intensive studies of territorial behavior of birds began, Willard (1918) expressed the belief that pyr-rhuloxias remain mated for life. He had found them nesting year after year in the same locations. Very probably it was the location and not necessarily the pair that was constant. We know today that good territories are usually occupied regularly. Whatever the status of the birds' bond, the pairing must begin very early in the spring, even when groups of individuals are in evidence. By the middle of February singing can be heard. Although the extent of territorial boundaries is not known, Brandt (1951) gave us a hint of the presence of territorial boundaries when he reported finding a pair of pyrrhu-loxias "about every hundred yards" near the San Pedro River.

Gould (1961) studied the behavior of cardinals and pyrrhuloxias on a 42-acre tract 10 miles south of Tucson, Ariz. He reported that their behavior is "basically very similar," and writes:

With the break-up of winter flocks in late February and March, the males of both species became highly pugnacious. This initial activity consisted pri-marily of individuals chasing each other and it occurred within groups of up to five birds. * * * Female pyrrhuloxias, but never female Cardinals, were noticed to engage in chasing activities, often with the males. These chases apparently establish a dominance order between the individuals so that the most aggressive male succeeds in taking the best territory. * * * During late April and early May definite territorial boundaries became established. As in the early stages of this process, only the male Cardinal, but both the male and female Pyrrhuloxia were involved. On one occasion a pair of Pyrrhuloxias was noticed moving about an area which eventually became their territory. At one point another pair was encountered and all four birds engaged in a vigorous fight. The intruding pair was driven out and was never noticed to encroach on that area again.* * *

Territories once established were maintained almost entirely by the males of both species. The female assisted in defense only when the nest or young were threatened directly. * * * When a Pyrrhuloxia nest and eggs were examined the female completely disappeared, but the male often stayed in the same tree and sang vigorously. If young were in the nest, the male, and sometimes the female would fly around excitedly singing or giving their chatter call.* * * Territory was maintained in three primary ways: combat, proclamation, and patrolling. Combat, which includes both fighting and chasing, was noticed in both species but it was much more vigorous in the Pyrrhuloxia. An intruding bird would be met, usually near the boundaries of the territory and either a fight or a chase, and often both, would follow. In all cases the intruder was forced to leave the area. If contact was made well within the territory, the intruder was much more prone to take flight, resulting in a chase. If contact was made near the boundary then a fight was more likely to occur. For the most part, intrusions were made only by males of adjoining territories. Unmated birds passing through the area were generally tolerated, but an established bird never was. * * *

Proclamation of territory consisted of intensive singing on the part of the males of both species. It was most frequent during the early morning, when a chorus of many birds could be heard. At this time singing would usually be from a favored site within the center of activity of the territory. Occasionally during the day competitive singing between males of the same species was heard. This was equally common in the Cardinals and Pyrrhuloxias. The males sang either in unison or alternated with each other. This type of song was most common between males of adjoining territories. Competitive singing between widely separated males was heard on only a few occasions.

Patrolling was noted in both species; however, only the Pyrrhuloxia followed a regular pattern. * * * After the initial singing in the morning the male would make his rounds, singing a few songs in one bush and then in the next, until a complete circuit had been made. He was never observed outside of the area * * *.

Once the young are out of the nest, territorial defense and maintenance were reduced, and they stopped entirely if it was late in the season. If a nest was destroyed, territorial activity increased although it never reached the peak of the initial activity. Individual pairs of both species were seen to make as many as three attempts at renesting, with a recurrence of high territorial activity, if their nests were abandoned or destroyed.

Gould says that cardinals defend their territories only against trespass by other cardinals and that pyrrhuloxias defend their areas only against other pyrrhuloxias. In the 42 acres of the study area, he reports that—

territories of six Cardinals and ten Pyrrhuloxias were established * * *. The total portion of the study area occupied by Cardinals was 54.5 per cent, wheras that occupied by the Pyrrhuloxias was 60 per cent. Both species required a suitable amount of woodland within each territory. An average of 45 per cent of the territory of each pair of Cardinals and 43 per cent of the territory of each pair of Pyrrhuloxias included mesquite woodland * * *. Cardinals appeared to require denser woodland in which to nest than did Pyrrhuloxias. An example of this was the fact that, although Cardinals were occasionally seen and heard to sing from an open mesquite patch, none established a territory there. One pair of Pyrrhuloxias, however, was able to establish a territory at this spot and raise one family. This patch consisted of small and widely spaced mesquite trees with much open, weed-covered ground between them. In other areas near Tucson,

Cardinals were found nesting in hedgerows between open fields, but these were always fairly dense and contained large trees. In these same areas the Pyrrhuloxias were often found nesting in trees with little or no vegetation around them.

Both Cardinals and Pyrrhuloxias appear to prefer an open field within the limits of their territory. * * * The fact that one territory did not include such an area shows that this is not absolutely necessary. * * * Often birds of both species were seen feeding together in groups outside of their territories. No conflicts were noticed on these occasions, indicating that these feeding areas were not part of established territories.

Gould found that the shape of the territories was roughly circular. Seven pyrrhuloxia territories averaged 2.5 acres each; they ranged from a minimum of 1.3 acres to a maximum of 3.5 acres. His trapping results showed that the pyrrhuloxias outnumbered the cardinals in the area by about 2 to 1.

Gould observed that: "The size and shape of the territories remained fairly stable during the summer. However, a few minor fluctuations were noted. These were primarily the result of the shifting of the center of activity when a new nest was built. If the new nest was built on the opposite end of the territory from the old one, then the region of the old nest was not defended as often nor as vigorously as before. This allowed a neighboring pair to gain control of the vacated area." He observed that nest sites were "placed without regard to the size or shape of the territory. Some were in the middle and others were at the edge * * *."

Nesting.—Courtship feeding, which we might call marital feeding because it also occurs during incubation, begins in February. On February 28 a female came to our feeding table in the back lot. A few moments later a male landed beside her. At once she flew into a nearby creosote bush and perched, waiting. The male fed for several minutes, then suddenly flew up to the female and fed her. He then returned to the table and resumed his meal. She waited, while he finished and left. Not until then did she venture back to the food.

Nest building apparently does not start until April. My earliest record is April 7, when a pair started a nest in a mistletoe clump in a catclaw bush near Rillito Creek. Unfortunately, they discontinued work the same day, perhaps undecided or alarmed at my discovery. By April 20 they had built another nest in similar surroundings a short distance away, which contained three eggs when we found it (Anderson and Anderson, 1946). Nesting continues at least until July, but whether more than one brood is attempted has not been determined. Late nests may indicate earlier failures. Brandt (1951) says the height of the season is the first week in June. He reports nests with eggs in late May. Sutton and Phillips (1942) found eggs just hatching on June 7 on the Papago Indian Reservation.

Additional observations are furnished by Gould (1961) from his research in the Tucson area. He writes:

Nest building is apparently carried out primarily by the females of both species. Observations on one Cardinal and one Pyrrhuloxia nest under construction showed only the females building, while the males stayed far back in the trees singing. Most nest material, with only one observed exception, was gathered within the established territory. I never saw material gathered within the territory of another pair.
* * *
Egg laying may occur any time in the months of May, June, July, and early August * * *. The most active period for both species was the first two weeks in June. Pairs found nesting in August had probably been unsuccessful in earlier nestings. Clutch size of the cardinal varied from two to four eggs and averaged three. Clutch size of the Pyrrhuloxia varied between two and three eggs, both numbers being equally common.

Nests have been observed in mesquites, catclaw, and condalia bushes at heights from 5½ to 7 feet above the ground. When placed in the dense leafless mistletoe (*Phoradendron californicum*) common to desert leguminous shrubs, there is a measure of concealment. Mrs. Bailey (1928) says that in New Mexico, the nest is placed "in mesquite and thorny bushes," is "small and compactly built of twigs, inner bark, or coarse grass, lined with a few rootlets or fine grass and fibers." Brandt (1951) gives us more detail: "Nest situated 5½ feet up in a bushy mesquite shrub of many boles; a gray affair, made of a variety of weed stems and some cobwebs, but no large leaves or pepper grass as used by Cardinal; lining of pale brown rootlets; nest neat, small, compact, with well made rim. Measurements, height, 3.50; width, 4 by 4.25; bowl depth, 2; bowl width, 2.25 by 2.50 inches. Contents, 3 eggs, incubation 4 days."

Gould (1961) found that:

Nests and nest sites of the species were very similar. Eight Cardinal and 20 Pyrrhuloxia nests ranged between 5 and 15 feet above the ground, both averaging 8 feet. In the study area both preferred to nest either in mesquite or graythorn. One nest of the pyrrhuloxia was found in an elderberry. In other areas around Tucson, Cardinals were found to use tamarisk (Tamarix) trees, and Pyrrhuloxia nests were not uncommon in palo verde (Cercidium). Both species seemed to prefer thick patches of brush or dense hedgerows; however, of the two species, the Pyrrhuloxia utilized more open situations. Cardinals were much more apt to place their nest against a major trunk of a tree than were Pyrrhuloxias, but both usually placed it in the small twigs that occur on the secondary branches. Neither species anchored the nest securely to the twigs or branch on which it was placed. * * *
The nest of the Pyrrhuloxia was almost always constructed of dead material. Of 20 nests only one contained green material, and this amounted to only a few mesquite leaves that had been added to the outside. The nature of the material often gives the nest a very decidedly grayish appearance with brownish highlights. The cup was usually well lined with rootlets, and occasionally thin strips of bark, horse hairs, or very small plant stems and fibers were used. The

nest was generally smaller and more compactly built than that of the Cardinal, but the difference was not as great as would be expected from the size difference between the two species.

Gould (1961) found the period of incubation to be 14 days from the laying of the last egg.

Incubation is probably performed entirely by the female. I have never found the male on the eggs. As we watched a nest one morning in May, the male arrived. The female uttered a few *squick* sounds, not quite sharp enough to suggest alarm. Then the male flew to the edge of the nest, slowly reached forward and gave the female a small black insect which he carried in his bill. It was a thrilling and altogether pretty sight—like two painted figures in red and gray on a background of green.

Both sexes assist in feeding their nestlings. When the fledglings are sure of their wings, they follow their parents farther afield. Sometimes they traveled 300 to 400 yards from an abandoned nest in the riverbank thicket to our back yard. They probably returned to the safety of the mesquites each evening. The latest nesting I have noted (Anderson and Anderson, 1946) was when "On September 9, 1945, a female appeared with a partly grown young bird that followed her about, begging vociferously until it was fed. This begging note, a *tseep* or *seep* sound, was heard frquently around our house during the following days and, usually when we looked outside, we found the female feeding the young bird. This dependence continued into the period of molt of the female. She appeared ragged on October 1. On October 12 she was last seen feeding her offspring which, at that time, was acquiring the male plumage. If we assume that the incubation period is approximately two weeks, and that the nestlings remain in the nest about ten days, then the eggs were probably laid about the middle of August."

Most of the adult birds seen in the latter part of October have completed their fall molt.

Eggs.—Gould (1961) reported that "The eggs of the two species are very similar and cannot always be told apart. In the Tucson area Cardinal eggs are somewhat larger and have a more bluish background color than those of the Pyrrhuloxia. The pattern of speckling is identical."

The measurements of 50 eggs average 23.9 by 17.7 millimeters; the eggs showing the four extremes measure *26.2* by 17.2, 24.9 by *19.1*, *22.2* by 17.5, and 23.0 by *16.0* millimeters.

Plumages.—Mr. Bent says the young pyrrhuloxia in juvenal plumage is much like the adult female, but the plumage is softer, more woolly, and the underparts are lighter in color, dull light grayish buff, nearly white on the abdomen; the middle and greater wing coverts are narrowly tipped with pale grayish buffy; the loral, orbital, and malar regions are tinged with red. The young male has the median underparts tinged more or less with rosy red, while there is no trace of red on these parts in the young female.

Food.—Once in late February I saw a male nibbling at the fresh catkins of a low cottonwood tree. The small but attractive bright red fruits of the Christmas cactus (*Opuntia leptocaulis*) also may be eaten. Although pyrrhuloxias sometimes perch in the spiniest of our taller, arborescent chollas, I have never seen them touch the fruit.

In the autumn, along the narrow roads of the San Xavier Indian Reservation south of Tucson, groups of birds gather in the vicinity of abundant food supplies. Here the fences are overgrown with mesquite, elder, hackberry, and graythorn. Near the end of October when the hackberries were nearly gone, I found pyrrhuloxias eating green berries in the elder bushes, crowding out a few Gambel white-crowned sparrows that had been attracted there first. Some of the nearby fields had been left fallow and were densely covered with pigweed and Johnson grass. Other fields had good stands of ripe hegari of two varieties. On all sides the ground and vegetation fairly moved with hordes of grasshoppers. They were everywhere, even in the upper branches of the mesquites, yet nowhere could I find a pyrrhuloxia actually eating a grasshopper, although I counted 42 birds on a 2-mile road, at least 20 in a strip about 200 yards long adjacent to a hegari field.

At a fence corner, where the hegari came right up to the mesquites, I found three females perching carefully on top of the 4- to 6-inch-long seed spikes. Each bird leaned over, pulled loose a large round seed, straightened up and ate it. As I watched, other pyrrhuloxias came at intervals to feed. They always clung to the top, ate off the top, and gradually worked downward by leaning forward till their bills were lower than their feet. The seeds in this area of about 10 feet square had been eaten almost entirely, while the hegari farther away from the mesquites appeared untouched. Here and there close to the fence hedge I saw many partially consumed spikes. One got the feeling that had the Indians planted their hegari farther from the mesquites, the pyrrhuloxias might not have ventured into the open so frequently. Perhaps all the blame should not be placed on the pyrrhuloxias, for they had as companions numbers of Abert's towhees, brown towhees, Gambel white-crowned sparrows, house finches, and even a few house sparrows, any of which may have helped consume the Papago Indians' hegari crop.

Near cotton fields the pyrrhuloxia must certainly be beneficial. Mrs. Bailey (1928) says: "In August and September (in which months all the stomachs examined were collected) the animal food amounting to 28.81 per cent was made up almost exclusively of harmful species, among which are the most important pests of the cotton plant, the cotton worm and the cotton boll weevil. Caterpillars, grasshoppers, and weevils are its favorite insects. Practically seven-tenths of the food consisted of weed seeds, the pernicious foxtail and burr grass amounting to 43.59 per cent of the food."

Behavior.—Elsewhere, Mrs. Bailey (1902) writes:

Though not so brilliant as the *Cardinalis* group, the pyrrhuloxias when among their native mesquites seem even more beautiful. The rose-colored vest that lights up their soft gray plumage gives an exquisite delicacy and freshness that adds charm to their individuality and sprightliness. Their expression changes astonishingly with the movement of their crest. When it is flattened the short curved bill and round head suggest a bored parrot in a cage, but when the crest is raised to its full height and thrown forward, the beautiful bird is the picture of alert interest and vivacity. * * *

A pair whose nest was stumbled on in the mesquite showed their mutual solicitude in such a charming manner, the male bursting into song to draw our attention from his mate and nest, that it seemed as if rare pleasure lay in store for the bird student with leisure to study their attractive ways.

Along the Rillito Valley, at the north edge of Tucson, Ariz., there are many homes scattered among the mesquites, still undisturbed by the expanding real estate boom. Here the pyrrhuloxias are often found around the dooryards. They hop about on the ground searching for food beneath the shrubbery, and are easily attracted to a feeding table by various kinds of kitchen scraps. The numerous house sparrows do not bother them because the pyrrhuloxia is a larger bird and the sparrows wait their turn. Occasionally a pyrrhuloxia takes a bath in a pool, and less frequently it dips its bill for a drink. Like most desert birds they probably depend upon insects to satisfy their water requirements during the spring and summer. Loss of water is reduced by keeping in the shade as much as possible.

The flight of the pyrrhuloxia is noisy and undulating like that of the cardinal—a few wing beats, then a glide, a few more wing beats, then another brief glide. Flights are usually short, but once I saw a female take off across the street, above the telephone wires, for a distance of 200 feet. When flushed suddenly from a mesquite row they flutter noisly out a bit, then turn rapidly in again, sometimes gliding beautifully into the safety of the tangle.

Various observers have described the pyrrhuloxia as a shy bird. It invariably seeks cover when disturbed on its feeding grounds, or when pressed too close while singing.

Voice.—Mr. Bent writes: "The loud whistling calls of the pyrrhuloxia are among the most delightful voices of the birds to be heard in the mesquite forest and gulches. One note is somewhat like the whistle of the cañon towhee, and others suggest some of the loud notes of the eastern cardinal." As Merrill wrote to Mrs. Bailey (1928), "in spring it is a veritable temptation to forsake the trodden paths of duty and take to the open as it [the pyrrhuloxia] perches on the top of a mesquite nearby and repeatedly calls *queet, queet, queet—queet, queet, queet—quee-u, quee-u*. During the season of rearing the young, a variety of calls are given, varying from the rattling *cheek, cheek, cheek*, when molested, to soft family notes of a liquid, purring, interrogative character."

So far as I have observed, only the male sings. He may use any elevated perch in the vicinity—electric poles and power lines furnish excellent points of vantage. There are exceptions, of course; once I saw a male singing vigorously on the ground.

Peterson (1941) interprets the song as "a clear *quink quink quink quink quink*, all on one note; also a slurred whistled *what-cheer, what-cheer*, etc., thinner and shorter than Cardinal's song."

To me this similarity to the cardinal's song is often so exasperating that one is tempted to speculate upon which bird is mimicking the other. Even the experts can be puzzled. Herbert Brandt (1951) wrote of the Arizona race: "This bird's merry whistle is, in some of its renditions, so much like some songs of the Cardinal that even Doctor Oberholser, who is an expert song student, was unable always to detect the difference. On one occasion we were sitting in the car listening to a persistent cardinal-type, whipping whistle, whereupon I asked the Doctor which bird it was, and he replied, 'A Cardinal, probably.' Putting a field glass on the distant bird, however, proved it to be a male Pyrrhuloxia in full voice." The same can be said of the commonest call-note, the explosive note of alarm that is heard every time a bird is disturbed. Once, after a morning's study in the field, I concluded that the pyrrhuloxia uttered a sharp *squick* or *stick*, while the cardinal emitted a more metallic *tik*. The extent of the alarm can be gaged by the rapidity and number of these sounds. Often three to five or more are fairly sputtered out as a bird takes flight. Some days later when I had the opportunity to try out my conclusion on an unseen bird, the pyrrhuloxia turned out to be a cardinal.

Again Gould's (1961) careful work furnishes us with interesting observations. He reports:

Singing is important in the establishment and maintenance of territory in both the Cardinal and the Pyrrhuloxia. Their songs are so similar that they are often indistinguishable. The major difference in their songs lies in the phrasing used during one singing period. Individuals of both species are capable of a wide variety of song types. In the Cardinal one type is used over and over during one singing period, but the Pyrrhuloxia alternates different types. Although the females of both species are capable of singing, the female Pyrrhuloxia is rarely heard to do so. * * *

Both species have calls that differ greatly. * * * The Pyrrhuloxia has a harsh chattering call that is used in territorial disputes and as a contact device between members of a pair.

Songs of both species were heard as early as the second week in February. It was not until the middle of March that singing in both species reached its peak. Since nesting began in May, song probably served in mating and pair formation as well as in establishment of territory. Singing subsided during the latter stages of incubation and was rarely heard after the young were hatched. Singing was renewed after the first brood became independent if a second brood was attempted. Song in September was reduced to only a few scattered half-songs by one or two individuals.

Enemies.—Dr. Friedmann (1934) mentions two nests of this bird containing cowbirds' eggs.

Field marks.—According to Mr. Bent, the adult male pyrrhuloxia is conspicuously marked; the dark gray back and pale gray under parts are offset by the crimson crest and the rose-red face and median under parts; even the wings and tail are tinged with red. The female is similar to the male, but there is much less red in the crest, under parts, wings, and tail; the under parts are buffy brown, with only a suggestion of red.

I would emphasize, however, that the bill provides the surest field mark. In the summer it is a clear yellow, while that of the cardinal is bright pink, almost a translucent agate pink. The bill of the cardinal retains this color for the entire year, but that of the pyrrhuloxia, as early as October, changes to brown or horn color. The shape of the bill, too, is distinctive. In fact, when one comes upon an immature bird, the only reliable character is the parrotlike curve and notch of the bill.

DISTRIBUTION

Range.—The Arizona pyrrhuloxia is resident from central southern and southeastern Arizona (Sacaton, Tucson, San Bernardino Ranch) south to northern Nayarit (Acaponeta River) and western Durango (Tamazula).

Casual record.—Casual in southern California (Mecca).

Egg dates.—Arizona: 20 records, April 4 to June 15; 10 records, May 11 to May 29.

PYRRHULOXIA SINUATA PENINSULAE Ridgway

San Lucas Pyrrhuloxia

HABITS

This Lower California race is similar in coloration to the mainland race of western Mexico but is decidedly smaller and has a larger bill.

William Brewster (1902) says of its distribution: "This bird appears to be strictly confined to the Cape Region, where it is nowhere very common. Mr. Belding considered it more numerous in the interior than near the coast, but Mr. Frazar found it in the greatest numbers at Triunfo and San José del Cabo, the latter place being, of course, directly on the coast. About La Paz, however, only a single specimen was seen, and but one was obtained on the Sierra de la Laguna. At Santiago four were taken, and there is a skin in the collection from San José del Rancho. The bird is doubtless resident wherever found."

Its haunts and habits are probably similar to those of adjacent races.

Eggs.—The measurements of 15 eggs average 24.3 by 18.1 millimeters; the eggs showing the four extremes measure *25.7* by *19.8*, *22.8* by 18.0, and 23.4 by *16.7* millimeters.

DISTRIBUTION

Range.—The San Lucas pyrrhuloxia is resident in Baja California from about lat. 27° N. (San Ignacio, Santa Rosalía) south to Cape San Lucas.

Egg dates.—Baja California: 6 records, April 19 to August 5; 3 records, May 3 to May 9.

PHEUCTICUS LUDOVICIANUS (Linnaeus)

Rose-breasted Grosbeak

PLATE 4

HABITS

When I was a boy we never looked for the rose-breasted grosbeak about our home grounds; if we wanted to see it, we had to hunt for it in the second-growth woodlands, far from human dwellings, on the wooded borders of swamps and streams, or wherever there was a dense growth of small trees and bushes along the edges of the woods or neglected pastures. Such places are still its favorite haunts. But, within the past 50 years it has, like that other woodland dweller, the wood thrush, learned to find sanctuary and a congenial home closer to the haunts of man in our towns, villages, and suburban grounds, where we can more easily enjoy its beauty of plumage and the richness of its song. The rear half of my grounds is well wooded with trees and shrubbery, though close to the center of the city, and here a pair of these grosbeaks have for several years built their nest and reared their young within a stone's throw of brick buildings.

Perhaps they find some protection from their natural enemies, and they certainly make delightful neighbors for bird lovers.

Spring.—Some of the early migrants vary considerably in their times of arrival, but there are two colorful summer visitors to our grounds, the Baltimore oriole and the rose-breasted grosbeak, that we look for with considerable confidence fairly early in May. Winsor M. Tyler sends me his impression of the grosbeak's coming as follows: "About midway in the May migration in New England, after many birds have long since returned to their breeding grounds, when we have listened to the robin's song for weeks, and we have almost come to look for that late comer, the wood pewee with his sweet, solemn song, there comes a new singer to the chorus. It stands out from the others—from the robin's alternating unending repetition and from the tiring reiteration of the red-eyed vireo. It adds a voice of its own to the month of May and a very welcome one. It sings a long phrase with a well-defined form like a pretty little poem, sung in the softest of tones full of delicacy and charm, a voice of syrupy sweetness like no other bird. It is the rose-breasted grosbeak, pleasing both to eye and ear.

"A characteristic habit of the male grosbeaks in spring is to take their stand on a roadway and hop about in a small company showing their black and white pattern with the blotch of rose on the breast. I have seen them year after year, always when newly arrived, on the paved streets which surround Lexington common, perhaps half a dozen in full view, silent, but very conspicuous. Later in the year they keep well hidden in the shade trees and resume their glorious song."

Courtship.—Tyler contributes the following note: "The courtship of the rose-breasted grosbeak, or its culmination, is a quiet, dignified act. There is none of the hot pursuit of the bobolink with almost a rape at the end. The two grosbeaks appear truly fond of each other. We see the female bird turn her head upward toward her mate and their beaks come together in a sort of kiss. All is harmony and peace, a picture of affection and contentment, not uncontrolled passion. They are on a branch of a tree or shrub, perhaps near where their nest will be. Their behavior resembles the love-making of the scarlet tanager under similar circumstances, quiet and staid with none of the abandon of the farmyard."

But there is nothing peaceful in the preliminaries to courtship, when the males often engage in fierce combat, more spectacular, however, than harmful, except for the loss of a few feathers. Sometimes several males may be seen hovering about one female, fighting among themselves and singing to her at the same time.

H. Roy Ivor writes Taber of the unusual courtship behavior of a male which had undertaken the feeding of its young, inasmuch as the female had started building a second nest some distance away. In one instance the feeding was long delayed. When the male finally did come and feed the young, it departed to a ravine outside its territory. Says Ivor: "His voice now was the courtship song, so different from the territorial; so entrancingly beautiful that words cannot describe it, and his courtship display an exquisite tableau. He spread and dropped his rapidly quivering wings so low that the tips of the primaries grazed the ground upon which he stood. His body was held in a crouching position with the breast almost touching the ground: his tail partly spread and slightly elevated: his head retracted so far that his nape lay against the feathers of his back. The mating song poured forth from his open beak as he moved toward the female, waving his head and body in an erratic dance. The downward and forward sweep of his wings revealed in striking contrast the blacks and whites of the separated flight feathers, the vivid rose of the under wing coverts, and the white of the rump. The song was soft, low, and continuous, with a great variety of notes." An unmated female apparently wandering through his territory had caused temporary desertion of family. She seemed to pay him no attention, and the male returned to his family.

Nesting.—The nests of the rose-breasted grosbeak are usually placed at no great height, seldom more than 15 feet or less than 6 feet above the ground, and mostly less than 10 feet, but some notable exceptions have been recorded. At the southern end of its breeding range, in the mountains of northern Georgia, Thomas D. Burleigh (1927b) reports that most nests are found in rhododendron thickets from 5 to 15 feet above the ground, but he records two exceptionally high nests; one was 25 feet from the ground "at the extreme outer end of a yellow birch sapling"; and the other "was fully fifty feet from the ground at the extreme outer end of an upper limb of a tall slender chestnut."

From the northern end of this grosbeak's breeding range Mrs. Louise de Kiriline Lawrence of Rutherglen, Ontario, writes to me: "In the spring of 1946 I was surprised to find two pairs of rose-breasted grosbeaks building their nests in white birches at a height of between 40 and 50 feet from the ground. * * * These two are the only nests I have observed at such heights. The usual heights are from 4 to 20 feet from the ground in this area. The nesting trees I have seen used, apart from white birch and white and balsam spruce, have been red maple and white pine."

In his notes sent to me, A. D. Du Bois records, among 13 nests found in Illinois and Minnesota, 2 nests in apple trees, 2 in small elms, 1 in an osage orange hedge, and 1 in a haw bush.

W. E. Shore writes me of a nest about 5 feet up in a hemlock sapling on the edge of an overgrown pasture, north of Toronto.

Nests have also been recorded in a pear tree, box elder, choke-cherry, ironwood, and willow; probably almost any small tree or shrub would be suitable for a nesting site if sufficiently sheltered.

As to the selection of the nest site, T. S. Roberts (1932) observed a male rose-breasted grosbeak behaving in an unusual manner in the fork of a small elm tree. "A moment's watching showed that he was plainly intent upon finding a suitable resting place for the nest. Settling himself into the crotch he turned slowly around and around several times, seemingly trying its fitness for the object in view. Presently he flew to a neighboring tree, whence shortly the female appeared and went through similar movements." On visiting the spot a few days later, he found a completed nest in that exact spot, with the female sitting on it.

William Brewster (1936) gives the following account of the nest-building:

About six o'clock this morning I found a pair of Rose-breasted Grosbeaks beginning their nest in the fork of a gray birch at the east end of Ball's Hill. They flitted about together, making almost incessantly a soft, low, exquisitely tender calling to one another. The female kept trying to break off dead twigs from birches. When, after many futile attempts, she got one, she flew with it to the fork. The male regularly preceded her and settling down in the fork received from her the twig and set it in place among the few others (less than half a dozen) which had been brought when my observations began. The female invariably gave up the twig when the male reached his bill towards her for it.

The above two accounts show that the male, at least sometimes, takes a leading part in the nest building, but they do not prove that he always does so. However, as he is known to incubate the eggs and feed the young, he may take a more active interest in the nest than we realize.

The nest of this grosbeak is not a work of art, nor is it very substantial. Rev. J. H. Langille (1884) has described it very well as follows: "It is composed outside of small sticks, fine twigs, or coarse strawy material, ornamented with a few skeleton-leaves, and is lined with very fine twigs of some evergreen tree (here, of the hemlock), or with fine rootlets, sometimes being finished with horse-hair, and the whole structure so loosely put together that one can see through it from beneath."

H. Roy Ivor writes Taber that, in the case of a pair nesting under observation in semicaptivity, "the male does not seem to feed the female except just after mating or when she has her nest just finished." He also states that, in semicaptivity, two nestings take place during the season. Wild birds have only one brood yearly (Forbush, 1929).

Eggs.—The eggs of the rose-breasted grosbeak vary from three to five, with four appearing to be the commonest number in a set. They are ovate, sometimes tending to rounded ovate or elongated ovate, and have little gloss. The ground is "microline green," "pale Nile blue," "pale Niagara green," or "bluish glaucous," and they are well speckled, spotted, or blotched with such shades of brown as "raw umber," "auburn," "chestnut-brown," "cinnamon brown," and "mummy brown." Generally the spots are quite evenly scattered over the entire surface with a tendency to concentrate toward the large end, and on the heavier marked types the spots may be confluent, forming a solid cap over the top of the egg.

The measurements of 50 eggs average 24.6 by 17.7 millimeters; the eggs showing the four extremes measure *26.7* by 18.6, 25.7 by *19.1*, *20.3* by 17.6, and 23.4 by *16.3* millimeters.

Young.—Incubation is shared by both sexes, the handsome and conspicuous male doing his full share, often singing as he sits on the eggs.

Burns (1915) gives 14 days as the period of incubation for the rose-breasted grosbeak; elsewhere (1921) he states that, according to other observers, the young remain in the nest for 9 to 12 days. H. R. Ivor (1944) records the incubation period as 12 to 13 days in his aviary.

The young birds are fed by both parents. Roberts (1932) writes:

Occasionally both birds were busy caring for the young at the same time, but generally they took turns at half-hour intervals. They were feeding chiefly red-elderberries from a clump nearby. Once the male and once the female, after an absence of half an hour, returned with a supply of insect food, giving the entire amount to the nestling that happened to be nearest. On these occasions not only was the old bird's bill full of insects on arrival, but there was a considerable quantity concealed in the gullet, which was regurgitated in successive small amounts. During one of the male's turns at feeding he came and went twenty-eight times in thirty minutes, always bringing elderberries from a bush only a few feet distant and feeding the same nestling fifteen times in rapid succession.

Ira N. Gabrielson (1915) made an intensive study of the nest life of a family of these grosbeaks, spending nearly 60 hours in a blind over a period of six days. He and his helpers watched carefully from a distance of 3 to 5 feet and "did not see a single feeding that was clearly regurgitative." He explains the method of feeding in great detail. His table shows that during the 60 hours the grosbeaks brooded their young for a total of 15 hours and 49 minutes, in periods ranging from 1 hour and 19 minutes to 6 hours and 54 minutes. His food table shows the amounts of the various items fed to the young, among which larvae formed the largest item, with various seeds a poor second; insects, fed in still smaller quantities, included small butterflies and moths, flies, crickets, beetles, and grasshoppers;

there were also a few spiders and a few berries. Out of 382 feedings, 283 were by the female. Observations by Francis H. Allen (1916) were somewhat different from the above.

H. Roy Ivor sent Taber detailed observations on the rearing of young birds by adults in semicaptivity. The two young were out of the shell and dry at 8 o'clock the morning of July 5, 1938. The adults divided their attentions; when one was obtaining food, the other covered the young. The male sang while brooding as he had while incubating. The adult on the nest anticipated the return of the other by giving a vocal signal and rising slightly. On July 6 a blue jay took one of the young birds and the third egg; the female abandoned the remaining chick, and the male took over. When feeding he inserted one end of a worm in the young bird's mouth and made sure the nestling's throat muscles had a grip before letting go the other end. He broke up large worms except for the skin, and sometimes withdrew the worm from the nestling's mouth several times before becoming satisfied it could swallow the food. He spent the night on the nest. During the first day the excreta from the young bird were quite stringy and not in a sac; the adult male was careful to pull them out as they were being excreted. He sometimes, but not always, ate the droppings, and on the 14th began to be less careful in housecleaning. On the 14th the peculiar notes of the fledgling replaced the nestling's chip. Fear, first observed on the 14th, became pronounced on the 16th. The following day, the 17th, the fledgling got out of the nest, but not until July 20 could it fly fairly well. Its body was not fully grown at 19 days. Droppings were still in a sac on July 25, and the adult removed them from under the branch on which the fledgling perched. On July 29 the fledgling had its first bath, and on this date, too, the female, which Ivor had many times attempted to introduce to the nestling, fed the fledged bird, her first such behavior. On July 31 the fledgling was the size of the parents. The father then started to show it how to break open sunflower seeds. Perching beside his offspring on a branch, he cracked a seed, broke the kernel into pieces, and fed it to the young bird. He then gave it a whole kernel. Next, he pretended to give the fledgling an uncracked whole seed, but held on to it and in due time cracked the seed and fed the young bird. By August 5 irritability on the part of the parent, which had been increasing, resulted in his jamming food into the mouth of the young bird, pecking its bill, and driving it away.

Ivor also writes Taber of an instance in which two males had taken over the rearing of four and three chicks, respectively, after their mates started building second nests. The clamor arising from the nest of four during a prolonged absence of the parent proved too much for the other male, 30 feet distant. He came and fed the hungry birds, one at a time, then departed hastily. He repeated this performance a number of times.

Plumages.—H. Roy Ivor writes Taber of a nestling that hatched in semicaptivity on July 5. Quills appeared on the wings on July 10. On the 12th the breast quills were just showing and the tail quills were quite perceptible. The primaries started breaking into feathers on the 13th. The inside of the mouth, red on that date, showed a peculiar iridescent shade. The egg tooth had not yet dropped off. On the 14th some down still remained. On the 17th the bird was nearly fully feathered, but the forehead was still bare. Very fine feathers appeared on the cheeks the following day. Feather growth seemed to slow up on July 23.

Dwight (1900) calls the natal down white and describes the juvenal plumage as follows:

> Above, including sides of the head, olive-brown with cinnamon and whitish edgings. Wings and tail darker, a white area at the base of the primaries, the rectrices faintly buff tipped, the coverts edged with buff forming two nearly white wing bands. Below, pure white usually a few olive-brown streaks on the sides of the chin and throat. Broad superciliary lines and central crown stripe white, buffy tinged. The edge of the wing is of a pale rose-pink; under wing coverts duller, salmon tinged.

The first winter plumage is acquired by a partial molt, beginning the middle of August and involving the contour plumage and the wing coverts, but not the rest of the wings or the tail. He describes the male as follows:

> Above, raw umber streaked with clove-brown darkest on the pileum which has a central buff stripe, the feathers white at their bases. Below, ochraceous buff, white on chin and abdomen, streaked on throat, breast and sides with clove-brown; a geranium-pink area on the jugulum veiled with ochraceous buff. Auriculars sepia bordered with clove-brown. Superciliary stripe and suborbital region white, tinged with buff, the lores grayish buff. The under wing coverts bright geranium-pink, those of the edge of the wing black spotted, the lesser coverts or "shoulders" with a carmine tinge. Two wing bands buff.

He says that the first nuptial plumage is acquired by a partial prenuptial molt late in the winter, "which involves the body plumage, the tertiaries, most of the wing coverts and the tail, leaving only the brown and worn primaries, their coverts and the secondaries." Charlotte E. Smith writes Austin that "Roberts (1955) mentions the great individual variation in this plumage. Most males become much like full adults, but in addition to the brown wings and tail there is often a trace of the white line over the eye, and the feathers of the back, crown, and rump show some brown or white. Some individuals have a bright and well-defined rose breast patch, in others it is pale pink and blurred; some have a few black wing and tail feathers in early summer."

Dwight (1900) adds the adult winter plumage is "acquired by a complete postnuptial moult early in August. Easily distinguishable from first winter dress by the jet black wings and tail. Adults are less veiled, the brown deeper and the carmine more extensive often covering the whole throat and breast and invading the abdomen and the crown. A few black spots laterally replace the streaking of the young bird. The wing edgings are whiter than those of the first winter dress."

The adult nuptial plumage is "acquired by a partial prenuptial moult which involves the body plumage but not the wings nor the tail. Distinguishable from the first nuptial by the black wings and worn tail. The retained tertiaries and secondaries become much worn and the terminal spots are gradually lost often leaving gaps in their place." Forbush (1929) notes: "It seems possible that some birds may not acquire highest plumage until the third year or even later." Charlotte E. Smith writes Austin of a male she banded in first nuptial plumage in 1961 that still had not attained full adult plumage in 1964 at the age of four years.

Hybrids with the black-headed grosbeak, *Pheucticus melanocephalus* sometimes occur where the ranges of the two species meet. H. Roy Ivor sent Taber the following notes on the plumages of two hybrid young hatched on June 4, 1943, from the pairing of a male black-headed grosbeak with a female rose-breasted grosbeak:

"First out of egg: Head fairly good black with a few buff feathers; nape the same; back black and rich buff striping; rump light cinnamon; upper tail coverts black with cinnamon tips; under tail coverts white tinged with buff at base; tail same black as head; three outer rectrices on each side pure white on ventral surface; chin black with a few buff feathers; breast very rich, almost mahogany brown caused by apricot tinging the feathers, or rather, the color is a combination of these two shades: the apricot is not mixed with the brown but a shade made up of these two—the apricot is pure on the lower breast, forming a fairly wide streak; abdomen white tinged with cinnamon; flanks cinnamon; lesser and greater wing coverts a good black with whitish spots; primaries brown and old with one fairly good black on right wing; secondaries brown with one black on each wing.

"The younger one similar except for the apricot streak on lower breast which is more vivid and the abdomen is whiter. The head and other plumage is not quite so far advanced; the chin is salmon with a few buff and one or two black feathers. Apparently the molt so far is somewhat more advanced and taking a shorter time than in the rose-breast males. The upper mandible of the older is darker than that of rose-breasts and the lower mandible the same color as the rose-breast; the upper mandible of the younger bird is darker but not quite so dark as that of the adult black-head; the lower mandible the same as that of the rose-breast. The molt of neither is complete on this date.

"I might add here that the molt of both the black-headed and rose-breasted grosbeaks begins about the middle of January and takes about 4½ months to complete."

Myron Swenk (1936) summarizes the knowledge of hybridization between rose-breasted and black-headed grosbeaks in the Missouri Valley, and David A. West (1962) made a detailed study of those hybrids where their ranges overlap in the Great Plains.

Food.—In his exhaustive report on the subject, W. L. McAtee (1908) gives the following summary:

Examinations of 176 stomachs of rose-breasted grosbeaks show that the food is composed of animal and vegetable matter in almost equal parts, the exact proportions being 52 and 48 percent, respectively. Of the portion of the diet gleaned from the plant kingdom, 5.09 percent is grain, 1.37 garden peas, and 19.3 wild fruit. * * *

Wild fruit is greatly relished, but cultivated fruit is not damaged, and although budding is practiced to a certain degree practically no harm results.

The rosebreast preys to some extent upon such beneficial insects as parasitic Hymenoptera, ground beetles, ladybirds, and fireflies. Only a tenth of the animal food is of this character, however, while among the remaining nine-tenths, which consists almost exclusively of injurious insects, is included a large number of formidable pests. Among these are the cucumber beetles, the hickory borer, plum curculio, Colorado potato beetle, Rocky Mountain locust, spring and fall cankerworms, orchard and forest tent-caterpillars, tussock moth, army worm, gipsy [sic] and brown-tailed moths, and the chinch bug. The bird is known as an active enemy of the cankerworm and the army worm during their extraordinary ingestations, and was among the birds which preyed upon the Rocky Mountain locust and the gipsy moth at the height of their destructiveness.

Then follow long lists in detail of the various items of the vegetable and animal food.

H. Lewis Batts, Jr. (1958), specifies leaf beetle larvae, *Blepharida rhois*, favored as food for the nestlings.

Mrs. Amelia R. Laskey writes to me that she has seen a rose-breasted grosbeak eating elm seeds, "often hanging head downward like a chickadee to pluck the seeds." And Robert H. Hansman tells me that these birds may be "observed opening the long seed pods of the catalpa to obtain the seeds, of which they are very fond."

B. H. Warren (1890) mentions that all these grosbeaks, taken in May and examined by him, had been feeding on the blossoms of hickory and beech trees. Dr. Charles H. Blake writes that the birds eat buds of the white ash, *Fraxinus americana*, in spring and the fruit of the European mountain ash, *Sorbus aucuparia*, in late August.

It is an open question whether blossom eating and budding is harmful to the trees or beneficial as proper pruning.

Behavior.—H. R. Ivor (1944) has studied the behavior of two pairs of rose-breasted grosbeaks in semicaptivity in his aviaries and has published the results of his observations in great detail. His paper is well worth reading. It throws considerable light on the probable behavior of the birds in a wild state, because they were free to come and go and spent some of their time outside the aviary. After the first broods had left the nests, the young birds were cared for by the males, and the females started building their second nests outside the aviary; 13 eggs were hatched in these 4 nests and all 13 young were reared to maturity.

"When allowed freedom after the first eggs were laid, the birds regularly visited the woods to feed on insects, ceasing almost entirely to use the artificial food provided in the aviary. * * * They found the entrances to the aviary without difficulty after foraging in the woods." Referring to the word "probable" in the first paragraph above, Ivor wrote Taber, Aug. 6, 1957, "Over 25 years' experimenting has shown me that such behavior was normal."

Voice.—Aretas A. Saunders has sent me some elaborate notes on the songs of this bird, from which I quote the following parts:

"The song of the rose-breasted grosbeak consists of a series of rapid notes, largely connected by liquid consonant sounds, and rarely with two successive notes on the same pitch. It is commonly described as a warble, but, as groups of notes are separated from each other by very short pauses, it is not so definitely a warble as are some other songs, such as those of the warbling vireo and the purple finch. The quality is very similar to that of the American robin, so much so that many confuse the two songs, though there is a definite difference. It differs from the song of the robin by the much shorter pauses between phrases, so short, in fact, that the song sounds continous, whereas the robin has pauses between the phrases as long as the phrases themselves. Rarely the grosbeak puts longer pauses into its song, and then it sounds much like the robin. I have only two such records, but one other in which the first three phrases were timed like those of the robin, and the other six phrases rapid, like normal grosbeak songs."

Saunders states that the length of songs depends in part on the rapidity of the singing, but more on the number of notes or phrases. Notes vary from 10 to 23 per song, averaging 16 in 37 records; phrases vary from 4 to 14, averaging $8\frac{1}{2}$. The length of the song varies from 2 to $6\frac{4}{5}$ seconds, averaging about $3\frac{3}{5}$. Pitch varies from G_5 to D_7. Pitch intervals range from $2\frac{1}{2}$ to 6 tones, averaging about 4 tones.

In the height of the mating season, the male sings a much more prolonged song in flight when pursuing a female. Often two males, both singing, pursue the same female, and on one occasion I observed three. This pursuit flight song sounds much like the regular song, except that the phrases are more rapid and the pauses between them shorter. Saunders continues:

"I have never found songs of two different individuals that were just alike. Each individual has several different songs, but each bird is inclined to begin each song in the same way, the first three or four phrases being identical, but the endings of the songs quite variable.

"The season of song lasts from the first arrival of birds in the spring to about the middle of July. Occasionally one may hear a grosbeak sing in late August or September, but whenever I have done so and seen the bird that was singing, it proved to be an immature male.

"The common call-note is a high-pitched, short, and squeaky *kink*. Young birds, shortly after they leave the nest, are quite noisy and use a variety of notes, most of which are squeaky, but one is an upwards slurred *tyoooeee*, as soft and sweet as the call of a bluebird. When a young bird is lost and becomes hungry, its call is a downward-slurred *wheeay*."

Francis H. Allen writes to me of one of these grosbeaks "who frequently introduced into his song three long, ascending whistles, reminding me of the *weet-weet-weet* of the spotted sandpiper, though they had much more of a rising inflection. He also introduced a short *chuee*, repeated rapidly about four times, and a short, low trill suggestive of the wood thrush. These unusual notes were generally at the end of the song. Once I heard him give, after the characteristic warbles of the species, first the three long whistles, then the trill, then the *chuee, chuee, chuee, chuee*, then a sweet falling whistle with diminuendo.

"On May 28, 1947, a bird preluded his regular song with a faint and short *ti-ti-sweet* and then a louder, husky trill, *wi-wi-wi-wi-wi*, after which the song continued in normal fashion."

The male often sings while on the nest and sometimes at night. The female occasionally sings a softer and shorter song than that of the male, but similar to it. H. Roy Ivor writes Taber that the female of a pair in semicaptivity sang on the nest, and "that the male uttered a courtship song in a remarkably low, sweet voice. One has to be very close to hear all the notes of this love song."

Charlotte E. Smith sent Austin the following observations: "In addition to the common metallic 'click' call-note, which is rather soft but distinct, I have heard an alarm note which, although very similar, is noticeably different because it is louder and much sharper, with the quality (to my ears) of the call of the hairy woodpecker.

I have heard both males and females give this note when blue jays or grackles attempted to share the feeder. Some individuals, both male and female, also utter a 'distress' call when held for banding—a series of loud, piercing screeches similar, but greatly magnified, to the sounds purple finches make under like circumstances. I have never heard this distress call given under natural conditions, though conceivably attack by any predator should evoke it."

Enemies.—Friedmann (1929) calls the rose-breasted grosbeak "a fairly common victim" of the cowbird and says: "Numerous published records from all parts of this bird's range * * * have come to my notice. I know of no instance where more than two Cowbirds' eggs have been found in any one nest of this species." But Jim Hodges (1946) reports a nest of this grosbeak containing "five well-incubated eggs of the Cowbird but none of the grosbeak." And the male grosbeak was incubating them.

Hamerstrom (1951) mentions finding feathers of immature rose-breasted grosbeaks beneath the plucking perch of a Cooper's hawk. H. S. Peters (1936) lists two flies as external parasites on the rose-breasted grosbeak. A. W. Blain (1948) includes this species in a list of birds injured or killed hitting "picture windows." D. A. Zimmerman (1954) mentions two birds found dead on highways.

There seems to be no published record of one of these birds living for more than 11 years in a wild state, but Henry Nehrling (1896) says: "I knew of a Rose-breasted Grosbeak that was kept in perfect health for over fifteen years. All the white of the plumage had become in time a very beautiful rosy-red." This was a captive bird. To which C. E. Smith adds: "M. M. Wernicke (1938) discusses a 15-year-old bird; A. C. Govan (1964) describes the death of a captive male at the age of 17½ years and J. H. Ross (1942) writes of a male that was kept in captivity from the spring of 1928 to the fall of 1951, when it died in its 24th year."

Fall.—When the grosbeaks leave their summer homes on their fall migration, they are not as brilliantly colored as in the spring and are less conspicuous in their behavior. Taverner and Swales (1907) say that, while passing from Canada to the United States at Point Pelee, they "were very difficult to find, keeping well up in the tops of the high trees and hiding in the leaves, and the only indication of their presence was the sharp grosbeak click that occasionally came to us from somewhere overhead."

Frederick C. Lincoln (1939) writes:

The route used by the Rose-breasted Grosbeak, which appears to belong chiefly to the Mississippi Flyway, presents an interesting variation in convergence. * * * The extreme width of the breeding range of this species, from theMaritime Provinces of Canada to central Alberta, is about 2500 miles. Nevertheless the migratory lines converge southwardly until the width of the lane narrows down to about 700 miles, where the grosbeaks leave the United States between eastern Texas and Appalachicola Bay, Florida. Instead, however, of continuing to converge, the eastern and western limits of the migratory lane remain nearly parallel, so that the birds enter the northern part of their winter range in southern Mexico through a gate of about the same width. Further south, the tapering shape of Central America results in a greater concentration, reaching its extreme in the Isthmus of Panama. Rose-breasts that travel as far as South America spread out through Colombia, Venezuela and Ecuador.

Winter.—Alexander F. Skutch contributes the following: "With rare exceptions, the rose-breasted grosbeaks do not reach Central America until the middle of October. Carriker (1910) records a young male taken at Escazu in the Costa Rican highlands at the surprisingly early date of August 13, 1902, but my own earliest date of arrival is October 16, 1942, the locality being the basin of El General in southern Costa Rica. Soon the grosbeaks spread thinly over the entire region, settling down to spend the winter from Guatemala to Panamá, and from the lowlands of both coasts up to no less than 8,500 feet in the highlands, where they brave the heavy nocturnal frosts of the winter months. Although common as winter residents in only a few localities, they are more abundant in the highlands from 3,000 feet upward than in the warm lowlands, and in Guatemala than farther to the south in Costa Rica. Likewise they are more gregarious in the highlands, where I once counted 20 in a flock, than at lower altitudes, where it is exceptional to meet more than 3 or 4 together. They frequent clearings and plantations with scattered trees and light or open woodland; but I have not met them in heavy lowland forest. They appear to avoid excessively wet districts such as the northern slopes of the Cordillera Central of Costa Rica.

"On the Hacienda 'Chichavac' at an altitude of about 8,500 feet in the mountains above Tecpán in the Department of Chimaltenango in west-central Guatemala, rose-breasted grosbeaks often visited the vegetable garden beside the house, and its vicinity. Here I first met them in November 1930, and they were present when I returned at the beginning of 1933, when about 20 were counted. By March some of the males had put on their full nuptial attire, and were resplendent in white, black, and rose. The last of the flock departed on April 6. They remained absent for 6½ months, returning on October 19, when I found three in the hedgerow at the far end of the garden, almost in the same spot where I had seen the last of the flock the preceding spring. Two were females modestly clad in buffy-brown and grayish-white; their companion was a male attired almost as plainly as they, but there was a tinge of rose on his white breast to remind me of the warm rosy shield that had covered it when he left in the spring, and his wings were conspicuously marked with black and white, in striking c   ~ast to the general dullness of his dress. Without much doubt they were individuals who had passed the preceding winter in this garden, or their descendants; but who could tell in what far northern land they had made their nests, or what route they had followed and what districts they had passed over on their long southward journey, or what adventures befell them, or how long they had been on the way?

"The three grosbeaks promptly began to eat their favorite seeds, those of the euphorbiaceous shrub *Stillingia acutifolia*. The foliage of this bush is said to be poisonous to cattle, deadly if eaten in quantity; but the grosbeaks seemed never to suffer any harm from the seeds. They crushed the thick, three-lobed pods in their heavy bills to extract the three small seeds, making a noise that I could hear at a good distance. They were also fond of the garden peas, to obtain which they perched beside one of the long fat pods, pecked a hole in its side, and removed the plump green seeds one by one. In eating these peas they were extremely fastidious, deftly biting the germ out from its tender green seed-coat and eating only the former, allowing the empty husk to fall to the ground. Sometimes they skillfully managed to extract the germ from its coat without detaching the seed, leaving the empty seed-coat in the empty pod. In favoring these peas they showed excellent judgment, for never have I tasted sweeter peas than these grown high in the mountains.

"The Indian gardener set up among the vines a scarecrow consisting of an inverted tin pail with a white rag tied around it for a head, and some old garment draped over a cross-bar for a body; but the birds were wholly indifferent to this palpable deception. With praiseworthy patience, the gardener stretched long strings completely around and diagonally across the pea patch, and tied the long, thick leaves of the yucca to them at intervals of a foot or less, so that dangling by their tips, they might sway in the wind and alarm the thieves; but this device also failed to serve its purpose. I who had heard the rose-breasted grosbeaks' joyous music in the North thought them worthy of their epicurean fare and did not begrudge them their plunder; but I found it difficult to persuade to this point of view my neighbors who had never had an opportunity to hear the birds in song. At times these grosbeaks settled in a flock in the neighboring pasture, and hunted over the ground among the scattered straw.

"In January 1934 I found rose-breasted grosbeaks fairly numerous among the open woods on the Finca 'Mocá,' a great coffee estate lying chiefly between 3,000 and 4,000 feet above sea level at the base of the Volcán Atitlán on the Pacific slope of Guatemala. Many of the males then bore considerable rose on their breasts, but I saw none in full nuptial plumage so early in the year. Each evening a number of the grosbeaks went to roost, along with a motley crowd of small birds of other species both resident and migratory, in a dense clump of tall bamboos just outside the room that I occupied, where through the window I could watch them as I sat at my work table. They darted in among the compact foliage of the bamboos so quickly that I could not count them with accuracy, but probably 10 or 12 slept there every night.

"Early in February I once saw, in the Caribbean lowlands of Honduras, a male rose-breasted grosbeak who had practically completed the prenuptial molt and was splendidly attired in black, white, and rose. By the end of February males in nuptial dress are not rare, but others have scarcely begun the molt. I have not often heard the song of the rose-breasted grosbeak in Central America, but from March 29 to April 5, 1945, a male who had not quite completed his prenuptial molt sang repeatedly in the vicinity of my house in southern Costa Rica. In the middle of the afternoon, when the Gray's thrushes were caroling blithely on all sides, he would add his sweetly varied warble to the chorus. During the first half of April the last rose-breasted grosbeaks withdraw from Central America; my latest was seen in El General, Costa Rica, on April 15, 1937.

"Unfortunately, all the rose-breasted grosbeaks that come to tropical America do not return to the land of their birth, even if they remain alive over the winter months. All too many are trapped and kept in cages for their song and attractive plumage. Scarcely any other of the migrants from further north is more popular as a cage bird. The indigo bunting, the painted bunting, and a great variety of native birds share the same unhappy fate. One has only to travel in Latin America and witness how wild birds are held in captivity, often in a cage that scarcely allows them space to turn around, and subjected to all manner of abuses, such as remaining through the night beside an unshaded electric light bulb, to appreciate fully how great an advance the United States and Canada made when they prohibited the holding of native songbirds in captivity. It is distressing to anyone with sympathetic feeling for wild creatures to see them held in thrall; but there is something particularly exasperating in the sight of these migratory birds, which are given legal protection in the country of their birth, held captive in a foreign land. They are travelers whose passports have been dishonored, and there is no consulate to which they can appeal for redress.

DISTRIBUTION

Range.—Central Canada (east of the Rocky Mountains) to Colombia and Venezuela.

Breeding range.—The rose-breasted grosbeak breeds from northeastern British Columbia (Tupper Creek), northern Alberta (Slave River near Peace River), central Saskatchewan (Flotten Lake, Cumberland House), central western and south central Manitoba (The Pas, Lake St. Martin), western and southern Ontario (Malachi, North Bay), southwestern Quebec (Blue Sea Lake, Val Jalbert), northern New Brunswick (Jardin Brook), Prince Edward Island (Harmony Junction), and Nova Scotia (Whycocomagh) south to south central Alberta (Red Deer), southern Saskatchewan (Indian Head), central northern North Dakota (Minot), eastern South Dakota (Bijou Hills), eastern Nebraska (Long Pine Canyon, Red Cloud), eastern Kansas (Manhattan), central Oklahoma (Oklahoma City), southwestern and central Missouri (Freistatt, St. Louis), southern Illinois (Mount Carmel), central Indiana (Terre Haute, Pennville), northern Ohio (Paulding and Tuscarawas counties), eastern Kentucky (Black Mountain), eastern Tennessee (Johnson City, Stratton Bald), northern Georgia (Brasstown Bald), western North Carolina (Rocky Ridge, Boone), western Virginia (throughout mountains), southeastern Pennsylvania (Chestnut Hill), southwestern and central New Jersey (Milltown), and southeastern New York (Dix Hills, Long Island). Recorded nesting once in Colorado (Longmont), and in southern Maryland (mouth of Governors Run, Calvert County).

Winter range.—Winters from Michoacán, San Luis Potosí (Xilitla), and southern Louisiana (rarely) south through southern Mexico, Central America, and northwestern South America to northern Ecuador (Sarayacú), southwestern Colombia (Villavieja), and southwestern and central northern Venezuela (Bramón, Maracay); rarely in western Cuba.

Casual records.—Casual, chiefly in migration, west to California (now almost annually), Baja California (Santo Tomás), and Arizona (southwest to Castle Dome Mountains), and east to southeastern Quebec (Moisie River, Anticosti Island), Newfoundland (Tompkins), Bermuda, Watling Island, Cuba, Hispaniola, Jamiaca, Dominica, and Curaçao.

Accidental in Greenland and in Ireland (County Antrim).

Migration.—Early dates of spring arrival are: Guatemala—Guatemala City, March 21. Bermuda—St. Georges, April 15. Florida—Juno, March 25; Pensacola, April 2. Alabama—Dauphin Island, April 3. Georgia—Savannah, April 4. South Carolina—Spartanburg, April 18. North Carolina—Weaverville, April 15. Virginia—Alexandria, April 20; Blacksburg, April 24. West Virginia—Bluefield, April 24. District of Columbia—April 17 (average of 20 years, May 4). Maryland—Baltimore County, April 8. Pennsylvania—Bethlehem, April 12; Beaver, April 24 (average of 22 years, May 1). New

Jersey—Camden, April 4; Maplewood and Long Branch, April 23. New York—Northport, April 16; Cayuga and Oneida Lake basins, April 28 (median of 10 years, May 4). Connecticut—West Hartford, April 25; Portland, May 1 (average of 32 years, May 7.) Rhode Island—Providence, April 9. Massachusetts—Martha's Vineyard, April 15 (median of 5 years, April 20). Vermont—St. Johnsbury, May 2. New Hampshire—Walpole and Monroe, May 3; New Hampton, May 4 (median of 21 years, May 8). Maine—Cumberland Mills, April 19; Springvale, April 27. Quebec—Montreal, April 28 (median of 20 years for Province of Quebec, May 10). New Brunswick—Grand Manan and St. Andrews, May 16. Nova Scotia—Port Joli, April 10; Bon Portage, April 15. Newfoundland—Tompkins, May 24. Louisiana—Shreveport, April 8; Grand Isle, April 16. Mississippi—Gulfport, April 15. Arkansas—Perryville, April 12. Tennessee—Knox County, April 3 (average, April 28); Nashville, April 15. Kentucky—Bowling Green, April 18. Missouri—St. Louis, April 12 (median of 13 years, April 26). Illinois—Murphysboro, April 12 (average, May 6); Urbana, April 22 (median of 20 years, April 30). Indiana—Bloomington, April 21. Ohio—Painesville, April 14; central Ohio, April 24 (median of 40 years, May 2); Oberlin, April 27 (average of 18 years, May 2). Michigan—Detroit, April 19 (mean of 10 years, April 22); Battle Creek, April 29 (median of 33 years, May 4). Ontario—Ottawa, May 8 (average of 20 years, May 13). Iowa—Nevada, April 21; Sioux City, April 26 (median, May 3). Wisconsin—Milwaukee, April 8; Kenosha and Wausau, April 10. Minnesota—Winona, April 25 (average of 31 years for northern Minnesota, May 4). Texas—Sinton, March 19 (median of 7 years, April 21). Oklahoma—Tulsa, April 8; Oklahoma City, April 25. Kansas—Mound City, April 18; median of 25 years for northeastern Kansas, May 2. Nebraska—Fairbury, April 17; Red Cloud, April 27 (median of 15 years, May 7). South Dakota—Yankton, April 20. North Dakota—Kenmare, May 5; Cass County, May 8 (average, May 14). Manitoba—Margaret, April 28; Aweme, May 12 (average of 14 years, May 16). Saskatchewan—McLean, April 17; Big River, May 1. New Mexico—Albuquerque, May 5. Colorado—Boulder, May 6. Wyoming—Torrington, May 11. California—Glendale, April 23. Alberta—Flagstaff, May 8. British Columbia—Tupper Creek, May 25.

Late dates of spring departure are: Colombia—Valparaiso, March 29. Costa Rica—San Isidro del General, April 15. Guatemala—Quirigua, April 7. El Salvador—Chilata, April 22. Oaxaca—Tutla, April 30. Veracruz—Jalapa, April 18. San Luis Potosí—Tamazunchale, April 29. Haiti—Poste Charbert, April 26. Bermuda—St. Georges, April 15. Florida—southern peninusla, May 23. Alabama—Auburn, May 23. Georgia—Atlanta, May 15. South Carolina—Spartanburg, May 14. North Carolina—Raleigh, May 13. Virginia—Charlottesville, May 22. West Virginia—Fairmont, May 20. District of Columbia—June 3. Maryland—Patuxent Wildlife Research Center, June 2 (median of 7 years, May 20). Louisiana—New Orleans, May 14. Mississippi—Rosedale, May 22. Arkansas—Monticello, May 23. Tennessee—Knox County, May 23 (average, May 11). Kentucky—Bowling Green, May 15. Illinois—Chicago, June 2 (average of 16 years, May 24). Ohio—Buckeye Lake, May 26 (median, May 23). Michigan—Belding, June 3. Texas—Tyler, May 30. Oklahoma—Cleveland County, May 22. New Mexico—Clayton, June 6.

Early dates of fall arrival are: South Dakota—Milbank, August 30. Kansas—Overland Park, September 1. Texas—Midland, September 28. Iowa—Sioux City, August 15. Ontario—Presquile, August 10. Michigan—Marquette, July 28. Ohio—Lakewood, August 10; Buckeye Lake, August 20 (median, September 8). Indiana—Chesterton, August 3. Illinois—Chicago, August 6 (average of 15 years, August 21). Tennessee—Knox County, August 10 (average, September 17). Massachusetts—Worcester, August 21; Essex County, August 25. New York—Oneonta, August 20. New Jersey—Cape May, August 20. Pennsylvania—State College, August 12. Maryland—White Marsh, August 20; Patuxent Wildlife Research Center, Laurel, August 28 (median of 14 years, September 9). District of Columbia—August 29 (average of 14 years, September 4). Virginia—Rockbridge County, August 25. North Carolina—North Wilkesboro, September 10. South Carolina—Clemson College, October 1. Georgia—Athens, September 15. Alabama—Gadsden, August 28. Florida—Pensacola, August 30; Tallahassee, September 6. Bermuda—Hamilton, October 2. Oaxaca—Tapanatepec, October 19. Guatemala—Guatemala City, September 29. Costa Rica—San José, October 3. Ecuador—Calacali, October 10.

Late dates of fall departure are: California—Palm Springs, September 10. Alberta—Glenevis, September 1. Saskatchewan—Regina, September 9. Manitoba—Winnipeg area, October 21; Aweme, September 19 (average of 23 years, September 5). North Dakota—Cass County, October 5 (average, August 31). South Dakota—Milbank, October 16. Nebraska—Blue Springs, October 5. Kansas—northeastern Kansas, October 1 (median of 8 years, September 13). Oklahoma—September 26. Texas—Cove, November 7. Minnesota—Minneapolis–St. Paul, November 24 (mean of 14 years for southern Minnesota, September 18); Itasca County, November 20. Wisconsin—Oconomowoc, October 26. Iowa—Liscomb, October 6; Sioux City, October 2 (median of 38 years, September 25). Ontario—

Toronto, October 14; Ottawa, October 1. Michigan—Midland, November 15; Battle Creek, September 24 (median of 18 years, October 11); Detroit area, October 14 (mean of 10 years, October 11). Ohio—Canton, November 2; central Ohio, October 21 (average of 40 years, October 2); Lucas County, October 21 (mean of 12 years, October 2). Indiana—New Castle, October 30; Wayne County, October 10 (median of 9 years, October 4). Illinois—Beach, November 12; Chicago, November 9 (average of 15 years, September 23). Missouri—St. Louis, October 18 (median of 13 years, September 28). Kentucky—Bowling Green, October 31. Tennessee—Elizabethton, December 1; Knox County, October 18 (average, October 12). Arkansas—Winslow region, October 14. Mississippi—Saucier, October 19; Rosedale, October 12 (median of 21 years, October 5). Louisiana—Baton Rouge, October 25. Nova Scotia—Shelburne, December 15; West Middle Sable, September 17. New Brunswick—Fredericton, September 23. Quebec—Philipsburg, October 22 (median of 20 years for Province of Quebec, September 14). Maine—Winthrop, October 12. New Hampshire—Dover, December 2; New Hampton, October 24 (median of 21 years, September 20). Vermont—Wells River, November 12. Massachusetts—Adams, November 8; Ipswich, November 1. Rhode Island—Block Island, October 22. Connecticut—Westport, October 8. New York—Cayuga and Oneida Lake basins, November 12 (median of 13 years, October 9); Central Park, November 5. New Jersey—Fairlawn, October 12. Pennsylvania—Rush, October 24; State College, October 19. Maryland—Allegany County, November 25; Montgomery County, November 23. District of Columbia—October 16 (average of 14 years, October 1). West Virginia—Bluefield, October 24. Virginia—Rockbridge County, November 14; Hampton, November 12. North Carolina—Weaverville, October 25. South Carolina—Clemson College, October 15. Georgia—Atlanta, October 30; Grady County, October 25. Alabama—Gadsden, November 5; Courtland, November 1. Florida—southern peninsula, November 12; northwestern Florida, November 11. Bermuda—Hamilton, October 16. Bahamas—Watlings Island, October 20. Cuba—October 13. Guatemala—Guatemala City, November 2.

Egg dates.—Illinois: 41 records, May 17 to July 10; 24 records, May 23 to June 7.

Iowa: 3 records, May 29 to June 3.

Maryland: 10 records, May 27 to June 13; 6 records, May 31 to June 10.

Massachusetts: 55 records, May 22 to July 2; 32 records, May 25 to June 7.

Michigan: 24 records, May 23 to June 30; 15 records, May 28 to June 8.

Minnesota: 22 records, May 22 to June 25; 12 records, May 27 to June 5.

New Brunswick: 4 records, June 8 to June 19.

Ontario: 34 records, May 10 to June 24; 17 records, May 30 to June 8.

Rhode Island: 29 records, May 23 to June 15; 17 records, May 29 to June 6.

PHEUCTICUS MELANOCEPHALUS MELANOCEPHALUS (Swainson)

Rocky Mountain Black-headed Grosbeak

HABITS

A. J. van Rossem (1932) has shown that the type name, as given above, applies to the Rocky Mountain subspecies and not to the California race. The Rocky Mountain bird is larger than the California form and the postocular stripe is usually absent.

Swarth (1904) says of its haunts in the Huachuca Mountains of Arizona: "It is rather singular that though in California this species is most abundant in the willow regions of the low lands, here it is preeminently a bird of the higher mountains, and, even during the migrations, of very rare occurrence in the lower valleys. During the summer it is most abundant in the higher parts of the mountains, seldom breeding below 6000 feet; but soon after the young leave the nest a downward movement is begun, and up to the middle of August these Grosbeaks fairly swarm in some of the lower canyons, young and old gathering together in enormous, though loose and straggling flocks."

Mrs. Bailey (1928) says that, in New Mexico, this grosbeak "is characteristically a bird of the Upper Sonoran oak, juniper, and nut pine region, and of the thick cottonwood groves and deciduous trees and bushes along streams."

In southwestern Saskatchewan, we found at least three pairs of black-headed grosbeaks nesting in the timber along Maple Creek; I collected one male and a set of three eggs; Dr. Bishop and Dr. Dwight, also, collected a pair of these birds and two eggs on another creek in this vicinity.

The nesting habits, eggs, food, and general behavior of the Rocky Mountain grosbeak are apparently similar to those of the more western subspecies.

In the timber along Maple Creek, southwestern Saskatchewan, on June 16, 1906, we found a nest of this grosbeak containing two eggs.

The nest was much like that of the rose-breasted grosbeak and was placed about 7 feet from the ground in a slanting fork of a thorny bush in a thick grove of small poplars and other bushes. The male was sitting on the eggs, and it was only with some difficulty that I could drive him far enough away from the nest to shoot him; he eventually fell into the nest and broke the eggs.

We had seen this grosbeak in that same region the previous year and heard its song, which to my ears was exactly like the robinlike song of the rose-breasted grosbeak. Mrs. Bailey (1928) writes:

The call of the Blackheaded is as thin and weak as his song is rich and full of personality. At its best, the song excels in finish and musical quality. * * * As a violinist, lingering to perfect a note, draws his bow again and again over the strings, so this rapt musician dwelt lovingly upon his highest notes, trolling them over till each was more exquisite and tender than the last, and the ear was charmed with his love song. In Arizona, Mr. Henshaw had the good fortune to listen to some of the delightful concerts with which the birds closed each day. In the pine woods near Camp Apache, he tells us, "just after the sun had fairly sunk below the woods, these Grosbeaks ascended to the tops of the tallest pines, and thence sent forth their sweet strains till long after dusk had settled down upon the deep forest." (1875, p. 297).

Eggs.—This species usually lays three or four eggs, but sometimes only two, and more rarely five, to a set. They are ovate with occasionally a tendency to short-ovate, and have a slight gloss. The ground may be "Etain blue," "pale Nile blue," or "pale Niagara green," and well speckled, spotted, or blotched with browns such as "raw umber," "Argus brown," "Mummy brown," or "Prout's brown," with some underlying markings of "olive gray" or "mouse gray." The markings are generally well scattered over the entire eggs and usually in the form of speckles or spots. On most eggs the spots become more concentrated toward the large end where, on occasion, they form a solid cap. The measurements of 50 eggs average 25.1 by 17.9 millimeters; the eggs showing the four extremes measure *27.9* by 17.8, 25.4 by *18.8*, *23.0* by 17.1, and 27.9 by *16.3* millimeters.

DISTRIBUTION

Range.—Southwestern Canada to Ecuador, Colombia and Venezuela.

Breeding range.—The Rocky Mountain grosbeak breeds from southeastern British Columbia (Okanagan Landing, Creston), northwestern Montana (Flathead Lake), southeastern Alberta (Walsh), southwestern Sasatchewan (Maple Creek), northeastern Montana (Glasgow), and northwestern North Dakota (Charlson) south through eastern Washington and eastern Oregon to extreme eastern California (White Mountains, Clark Mountain), central and southeastern Arizona (Prescott, Huachuca Mountains), and the Mexican Plateau to Guerrero (Amojileca) and Oaxaca (Cerro San Felipe); east to central Nebraska (Greeley) and central Kansas (east to Cloud and Harvey counties), western Oklahoma, western Texas (Midland County), and Tamaulipas (La Joya de Salas).

Winter range.—Winters from southern Sonora (Álamos), southern Chihuahua (Chihuahua), and Nuevo León (Mesa del Chipinque) south to Guerrero and Oaxaca.

Casual records.—Casual north and east to eastern North Dakota (Fort Totten), western Ontario (Kenora), eastern Missouri (St. Charles County), central Oklahoma (Fort Cobb), and central Texas (Menard, Somerset). Casual in winter in Texas, Arkansas, Louisiana, Mississippi, Alabama, Florida, South Carolina, Virginia, Maryland, Pennsylvania, New Jersey, New York, Connecticut, and Massachusetts.

Migration.—The data deal with the species as a whole. Early dates of spring arrival are: Nuevo León—March 24. Coahuila—Sierra del Carmen, April 13. Baja California—Concepcion Bay, April 2; Agua Verde Bay, April 12. Florida—southern peninsula, April 13. Alabama—Booth, May 4. Texas—Kerrville, April 30. Oklahoma—Cheyenne, May 10. Kansas—Hayes, April 26 (Kansas median for 17 years, May 5). Nebraska—Superior, April 18. South Dakota—Aberdeen, April 21. Manitoba—Treesbank, May 30. Saskatchewan—Nipawin, June 6. New Mexico—Chloride, April 28; Los Alamos, May 2 (median of 8 years, May 7). Colorado—Grand Junction, April 20. Utah—Green River, May 6. Wyoming—Torrington, May 12 (average of 11 years, May 21). Idaho—Potlatch, May 10 (median, May 19). Montana—Fort Custer, May 14. California—San Francisco Bay area, April 2. Nevada—Mercury, April 11. Oregon—Yamhill County, April 27. Washington—Pullman, May 9; Everson, May 12 (median of 6 years, May 19). British Columbia—Victoria, May 1.

Late dates of spring departure are: Veracruz—Las Vigas, April 24. Sinaloa—Cosalá, May 13. Guerrero—Chilpancingo, May 6. Baja California—La Paz, May 4.

Early dates of fall arrival are: Texas—Austin, August 26. Missouri—St. Charles County, September 6. Louisiana—Bonnet Carré Spillway, October 25. Florida—Pensacola, October 1. Baja California—La Paz, July 22. Sinaloa—October 4. Guerrero—August 26

Late dates of fall departure are: British Columbia—Okanagan Landing, September 15. Washington—Pullman, September 6; Everson, September 5 (median of 5 years, September 3). Oregon—Multnomah, September 28. Nevada—Mercury, October 4. California—Point Bonita, October 20. Montana—Gold Creek, Powell County, August 27. Idaho—Potlatch, September 13. Wyoming—

Lusk, October 6. Colorado—Grand Junction, October 2. New Mexico—Los Almos, September 29 (median of 9 years, September 13). South Dakota—White River, September 2. Nebraska—Red Cloud, September 25. Kansas—September 18 (median of 5 years, September 2). Oklahoma—Kenton, September 24. Texas—Somerset and San Antonio, September 27. Missouri—Jefferson County, September 22. Massachusetts—Martha's Vineyard, November 11. New York—Oak Island, October 20. New Jersey—Island Beach, November 2. South Carolina—October 15. Alabama—Montgomery, October 4. Florida—Miami, November 26; northern peninsula, October 26.

Egg dates.—Arizona: 16 records, May 20 to June 21; 10 records, May 27 to June 7.

Colorado: 22 records, May 21 to July 17; 13 records, June 2 to June 12.

PHEUCTICUS MELANOCEPHALUS MACULATUS (Audubon)

Black-headed Grosbeak

PLATES 5 AND 6

HABITS

From the eastern foothills of the Rocky Mountains to the Pacific coast the handsome black-headed grosbeak replaces our familiar rose-breasted grosbeak of the eastern States. It is not quite as showy as the eastern bird, but it is richly colored, the brownish orange of the under parts contrasting well with the black head and the black and white of the wings and tail. The western race, the subject of this sketch, breeds from southern British Columbia through California to northern Lower California and western Mexico.

One should look for the black-headed grosbeak in situations similar to those in which one could expect to find the eastern rose-breasted grosbeak, in thickets of bushes, small trees or willows which grow along streams, around the edges of swamps, ponds, or damp places, as well as on the edges of open woods, where the sunlight filters down through the foliage, but almost always not far from water or low ground. S. F. Rathbun says in his notes: "On more than one occasion, when in a forest where no sign of any break was seen, we perhaps would hear from far away the clear song of this grosbeak; and then we knew that in the direction whence it came would be found some more or less open spot, possibly bordered by a bit of water or a stream. And other somewhat favored spots are about the borders of the forest that have a mixture of deciduous growth."

PLATE 5

gham City, Utah   A. D. Cruickshank

MALE BLACK-HEADED GROSBEAK ON NEST

enatchee, Wash.   R. T. Congdon

FEMALE BLACK-HEADED GROSBEAK SHELTERING YOUNG

Tulare County, Calif., May 29, 1939   J. S. Row

NEST OF BLACK-HEADED GROSBEAK

Jackson County, Fla., June 1941   S. A. Grir

EASTERN BLUE GROSBEAK FEEDING YOUNG

Henry G. Weston, Jr. (1947), writes of its haunts in California:

Grosbeaks may ordinarily be found in the woodland or in riparian groves and thickets: in these two major types of plant cover, the trees and marginal or understory bushes are used for almost all routine activities. In general grosbeaks are most often found in the open woods. The extensive peripheral foliage characteristic of open woods is advantageous in foraging for food; for singing perches, grosbeaks appear to require fair visibility, and this feature is again best afforded by open woods. Nesting occurs most commonly in streamside bushes and trees and in the live oaks of open woods. Along edges or transitions between grassland and woodland or chaparral, grosbeaks are also common; but they enter chaparral and grassland only infrequently and then only in search of food.

Mrs. Irene G. Wheelock (1912) adds: "Among the alders that border small streams in the valley, in the cherry orchards at cherry time, in the potato field when bugs are rife, in the oaks and evergreens of the lower Sierra Nevada, one may hear the metallic '*eek, eek*,' of the Black-headed Grosbeak."

Spring.—According to Weston's (1947) records, the occurrence of this grosbeak in the San Francisco Bay region "is limited normally to the months between April and September, inclusive. * * * The earliest recorded date is April 4, the latest, April 21." The males arrive about six days before the females. They "arrive singly rather than in flocks and are solitary for the few days preceding arrival of females. They begin singing upon arrival, and their activities before the females appear consist largely of foraging in the live oaks and willows and uttering frequent songs from exposed perches. Males appear to be spaced, but I saw no conflicts between them until after the arrival of females."

In the vicinity of Seattle, according to Rathbun (MS.), "one may look for the arrival of this species some time during the earlier part of May. A single bird only may be seen or perhaps several in company loosely associated. By the latter part of May they are mated and the pairs well established in the localities selected for a summer home. And each pair seems to have a defined territory, for we have never found a pair nesting anywhere near another; and should the locality not be subject to much change, the birds form an attachment for it, continuing to frequent it from year to year."

Weston (1947) noticed a number of conflicts between mated pairs in defense of their respective territories, in which the females were more aggressive than the males; the females "repeatedly postured and flew at each other, and at each attack, loud songs, calls and sounds of bodily contact could be heard."

Courtship.—The same observer writes: "The only type of display seen was a nuptial flight. Loud songs were uttered from some exposed perch near a female and then the male would suddenly fly up and out, performing a song-flight in the air above her. Flying forth on a horizontal course, the male would circle out from the summit of a tree, with wings and tail spread, uttering an almost continuous song. In the air for eight to ten seconds, he would then fly back, usually to the perch just vacated. I have never seen this display before a female coming more often than four minutes apart. Song-flights are not restricted to the courtship period but also occur, although less frequently, while the female is incubating."

Nesting.—In his study of the breeding behavior of the black-headed grosbeak, Weston (1947) writes:

Nesting usually takes place in deciduous bushes and trees bordering streams. Nests are built also in bushes or trees away from stream courses in gardens, dense brushland, closed woods and parklands; but these occurrences form a small percentage of the total when compared with nestings near streams. Records of one hundred and twenty nests, from literature and specimens, show nests placed in twenty-nine different species of plants. Close to eighty per cent of the plants used were deciduous: willows were represented most frequently and constituted thirty-five per cent of the total. Second in species representation, however, is the evergreen coast live oak (*Quercus agrifolia*), with twelve per cent of the total. Nevertheless, species of next ranking frequency are all deciduous; these are, in order, alder (*Alnus rhombifolia*), big-leaf maple (*Acer macrophyllum*), blackberry (*Rubus vitifolius*), cottonwood (*Populus*), and elderberry (*Sambucus glauca*).

Nests are placed in trees and bushes, usually at a height of six to twelve feet above the ground. Among height records of 163 nests from various localities in California, I found the average to be ten feet above ground. Seventy-eight, or 66 per cent, of these nests were placed between four and twelve feet above ground. The support for the nest usually consists of a crotch or fork in a group of horizontal or vertical secondary branches. * * *

The nest is a bulky, loosely constructed affair, ordinarily composed of slender twigs, plant stems and rootlets, in the base and outer walls, and of finer stems and rootlets in the lining. * * *

Building of the nest is done by the female. Suitable nesting material is normally sought within one or two hundred feet of the nest site and occasionally as far as 350 feet. The male usually follows her while she is gathering nesting material and he may accompany her to the general vicinity of the nest; however, I have never seen a male carry nesting material nor in any way aid in the actual construction of the nest. * * *

Construction of the nest takes from three to four days. Most of the building occurs in the mornings. Visits to the nest become less frequent and more irregular, as the day progresses, and in the afternoon the nest is visited occasionally without any nesting material.

W. Leon Dawson (1923) says: "The nest of the Black-headed Grosbeak is of singularly light and open construction, evidencing, as we suppose, the habit of the tropics, where ventilation, rather than conservation of heat, is the object sought. Some nests are so thin that the eggs may be counted from below." He mentions a nest that was kept cool by evaporation: "Instead of the usual lace-work construction," the birds "heaped up a mass of green willow leaves, plucking for the purpose the terminal twigs of the youngest trees, and wedging them to a height of nine inches in a convenient crotch. In the top of this mass, *kept cool by reason of evaporating moisture*, they set the conventional root-line cup."

J. Stuart Rowley writes to me: "I have found many dozens of nests of this bird throughout southern California. Along the western slopes of the Sierra Nevadas in Tulare County, this grosbeak is an abundant nester. Most of the nests I have found have been in manzanita bushes or in willows. The nests are so thinly made on the bottoms that frequently the eggs can be seen from the ground when looking up through the bottom of the nest."

Weston (1947) says that such thinness was not observed in any of the eight nests that he studied in Strawberry Canyon.

Eggs.—The usual set of the black-headed grosbeak consists of three or four eggs. Weston (1947) records the numbers of eggs in 192 sets. There were 18 sets of two, 96 sets of three, 75 sets of four, and only 3 sets of five eggs.

The measurements of 50 eggs average 24.7 by 17.7 millimeters; the eggs showing the four extremes measure *28.2* by 17.8, 24.4 by *19.6*, *21.8* by 17.8, and 22.9 by *15.8* millimeters.

Incubation.—This is shared by both sexes alternately during the day and is done by the female alone at night, according to Weston (1947). He says that incubation starts with the laying of the next to the last egg. "On an average day the eggs are incubated about 99 percent of the time, about 40 percent of the time by the male and 60 percent by the female. The average length of each incubation period of the male is close to 20 minutes, of the female 25 to 30 minutes." Both sexes occasionally sing at irregular intervals while on the nest, and are thus helpful in locating the nests. "Although the male sings while alone at the nest, the female usually sings only while the male is in the near vicinity. * * * The eggs begin hatching on the twelfth day of incubation. In each of three nests containing three eggs each, the last egg hatched twenty-four hours after the others." In some other cases, the eggs hatched "within a few hours of one another."

S. F. Rathbun writes in his notes for June 3, 1893: "This morning I found the nest of a black-headed grosbeak. The nest was built in the fork of a willow sapling at a height of some 10 feet, and the male bird could be plainly seen on the nest. I shook the sapling lightly, expecting to see the bird fly off, but such proved not the case, and neither did it occur when it again was shaken, so I took my knife and carefully cut the sapling, lowering it to the level of my face, not more than a foot away; and only when my free hand was advanced toward the bird did he fly, but only to alight on a limb a few feet distant."

Young.—In his summary, Weston (1947) writes: "Both sexes care for the young. During the first four days after hatching, young are fed with a soft mash. On the fourth day, whole material is introduced into the diet. Early in the nestling period, fecal sacs are eaten by either parent. As the young develop, both parents spend progressively longer periods off the nest. The nestling period is twelve days. After departure from the nest the young follow the female.'

Mrs. Wheelock (1912) says: "From watching the adults gather insects for the young, I am confident that so long as they remain in the nest, they are fed upon an animal diet, and for the first few days by regurgitation. In a little less than two weeks they hop out onto the small branches, and by instinct are soon pecking at every green thing in sight. For some time they seem to keep with the adults being fed and guarded tenderly by them."

Plumages.—James Lee Peters contributes the following: "The grayish-white natal down is succeeded by the juvenal plumage in which the sexual dimorphism is already apparent; the juvenal male nearly resembles the female and differs from the adult male in spring plumage in possessing a broad median coronal stripe of buffy bordered laterally with black, a white supraorbital stripe and gray ear coverts, the dorsal plumage is streaked rather than blotched, the black areas reduced and duller in color; the nuchal band is like the crown stripe, under parts much paler becoming white on throat and abdomen, wings and tail brown instead of black, the white spots and markings reduced in size; the lemon-yellow under-wing lining is as in the adult, but the spot of that color on the abdomen is lacking. The juvenal female is not very different from the adult female, but is duller below and with more and wider streaks on breast and flanks; the yellow abdominal patch is absent.

"The juvenal plumage is immediately followed by the immature or first-winter plumage which is acquired by a complete molt of the body feathers, but the wings and tail of the juvenal plumage are retained. In this plumage the sexes are somewhat similar above; the feathers of the upper surface with wide black centers and broad brownish edgings; below buffy cinnamon somewhat paler than in the adult, posterior portion of flanks streaked in the male; flanks, and, to a lesser extent, breast streaked in the female; the lemon-yellow abdominal spot is acquired. The immature plumage is probably completely assumed by October.

"The first nuptial plumage is acquired during late winter and early spring by a partial molt of feathers of throat, sides of head, ear coverts, wing coverts, and tertials; sometimes one or more tail feathers with their corresponding coverts are renewed at this time; other changes in the bird's appearance are by wear. Males in the first nuptial plumage may be readily distinguished by their brown wings, brown or brown-and-black tails, and the fact that the top of the head retains races of coronal stripe. Adult second-winter plumage is acquired by a complete molt involving wings, tail, and the entire body plumage; it is probably complete by October. At this time the black head, wings, and tail of the male, the latter with the conspicuous white blotches on the two outer pairs, are assumed. This plumage is essentially similar to the nuptial plumage which is acquired by the wearing off of the pale feather edges of head and upper parts."

Food.—For his report on the food of the black-headed grosbeak, Prof. F. E. L. Beal (1910) examined the contents of 225 stomachs.

These stomachs contained about 57 percent of animal matter to 43 of vegetable. The animal matter is composed of insects and spiders, with a few traces of vertebrates. Insects, such as beetles, scales, and caterpillars, constituted nearly 53 of the 57 percent of animal food.

Of the animal food, beetles are the largest item. They were found in 190 of the 225 stomachs. Of these, predatory ground beetles (Carabidae) were found in 16 stomachs, and ladybird beetles (Coccinellidae) in 2. To offset the destruction of these useful insects, the 12-spotted diabrotica, which often does serious injury to fruit trees, was found in 109 stomachs. Many weevils were found, and great numbers of several species of leaf beetles (Chrysomelidae). To this family belongs the notorious Colorado potato beetle, which at one time seemed likely to ruin the potato industry of the East. * * * When the potato beetle finds its way into California, as eventually it undoubtedly will, the black-headed grosbeak is the bird most likely to become its active enemy.

Hymenoptera in the form of bees and wasps with a few ants aggregate less than 2 percent. A worker honeybee was found in one stomach. Scale insects amount to 19.83 percent, or practically one-fifth of the whole food. Most of these were the black olive scale (*Saissetia oleae*), but a few were the plum and prune scales (*Lecaneum corni* and *L. pruinosum*). So persistently are scales eaten by this bird that they were found in 142 of the 225 stomachs, or 63 percent of all. * * *

Caterpillars, pupae, and a few moths aggregate 7.7 percent. * * * Pupae or larvae of the codling moth were found in 26 stomachs, one stomach containing the remains of 29. Flies, grasshoppers, a few other insects, spiders, and miscellaneous creatures make up something more than 1 percent.

Of the vegetable food, he says:

Cultivated fruit amounts to 23 percent of the grosbeak's food for the six months that it stays in the North. * * * Cherries appear to be the favorite fruit, as they were contained in 42 stomachs. Figs were identified in 24 stomachs, blackberries or raspberries in 23, strawberries in 2, apricots in 1, and prunes in 1. * * * During cherry season these birds were almost constantly in the trees eating cherries. They do not appear to attack apricots, peaches, and prunes so extensively, but they feed freely on figs later in the season. Blackberries and raspberries are taken whenever possible, but mostly in July and August, after cherries are gone. * * * The only wild fruit identified was the

elderberry (*Sambucus*), which constitutes the bulk of this item, and was foun
in 26 stomachs.

Seeds of various weeds and some grain constitute 14.7 percent of the food
Oats were found in 9 stomachs and wheat in 7, but the amount was insignificant
The rest of the vegetable food consists of the seeds of more or less troublesom
weeds, of which the grosbeak eats a very considerable quantity.

The stomachs of 17 nestlings were included in the study. The
youngest birds had been fed almost entirely on insects, averaging
more than 90 percent, mainly caterpillars and pupae. The olde
birds had been given a larger percentage of beetles and other insects

Weston (1947) states that, in Strawberry Canyon, a "high per
centage" of the food of this grosbeak consisted of the California oal
moth, which defoliates the live oaks. He saw them eating the worm
like larvae, and found pupa cases broken open. "Innumerable
winged adults were also captured and eaten, although the wing
were dropped before the bodies were eaten." He also lists 18 specie
of plants, parts of which were eaten.

In the Yosemite region, Grinnell and Storer (1924) noted black
headed grosbeaks "feasting on the wild blackberries which were the
ripening in abundance." And "two males were seen feeding upo
the hearts of cherry blossoms. These birds were working rathe
rapidly and a blossom would drop every fifteen of twenty seconds."
And, in western Nevada, it was observed by Robert Ridgway (1877
"to feed, in May, upon the buds of the grease-wood (*Obione conferti
folia*)."

Joe T. Marshall, Jr. (1957), discussing the species without racia
identification, states that it eats numerous pine seeds evidently
taken from open cones. He says, further, "A pair fed on the gree
seeds of a prostrate milkweed. Another grosbeak ate mistletoe in
ponderosa pine. * * * In a flowering Arizona oak, one * * * fre
quently reached toward the catkins with its bill. This female was no
at first recognized as a bird, for it resembled instead a chipmunk o
small squirrel by constantly keeping its head down and body hori
zontal; it actually crawled along the horizontal twigs." He also
describes two migrant adult males which fed in *Prunus virens*, remain
ing within a few yards of each other for 45 minutes. The birds wer
searching for certain leaves rolled up half their length, each enclosing
a large green caterpillar. "Each bird would fly to a slender twig
bending it so as to cling head-down: as it rocked up and down it woul
deftly pluck the leaf and then fly a few inches to normal posture on
steady twig. With a few quick movements of the bill the grosbea
would tear open the rolled up leaf, discard it with a shake of the head
and wind up with the caterpillar in its mouth. It subdued eac
caterpillar by biting along its length, then swallowed it whole. These
dexterous operations were achieved entirely by the bill with no hel

rom the feet, nor was there any resting or pounding of the prey against the twig." Marshall also mentions a bird joining with various other species in an attack on a flight of large termites. This bird attempted its captures by comparatively clumsy leaps and short flights from the top foliage of oaks.

Economic status.—Beal (1910) writes in his summary:

> In summing up the economic status of the black-headed grosbeak, the fact that it eats a considerable quantity of orchard fruit can not be ignored. * * * To offset its fruit eating, it eats habitually and freely the black olive scale, the codling moth, and the 12-spotted diabrotica, three pests of California fruit culture. * * * Should it ever become so plentiful as to cause serious loss, no attempts should be made to destroy the bird, but attention should be directed to devices for protecting the fruit, thus leaving the bird to continue its good work in the destruction of insects. So active an enemy of insect pests as is the grosbeak can not well be spared, especially in view of the possibility of an invasion of the State by the Colorado potato beetle.

W. L. McAtee (1908) gives a very full account of the food of this grosbeak, and remarks that "for every quart of fruit eaten, more than 3 pints of black olive scales and more than a quart of flower beetles, besides a generous sprinkling of codling moth pupae and cankerworms all prey to this grosbeak."

Behavior.—That the black-headed grosbeak is a close sitter on its nest, devoted to its charges, is shown by Rathbun's experience with it as mentioned above. It is not shy around houses and in orchards and seems to have no fear of human beings. It comes readily to feeding stations, where it is very tame and where it dominates other birds and sometimes quarrels with others of its own species. Its beneficial feeding habits, in spite of its few faults, and its delightful song make this handsome bird a desirable companion about the house and garden, where it should be encouraged.

Voice.—Its song closely resembles the rich song of its eastern relative, the rose-breasted grosbeak; to a lesser extent the song resembles that of the robin and is reminiscent of that of the western tanager, but it is richer and more varied than either. Grinnell and Storer (1924) write: "The black-headed grosbeak possesses a rich voluble song that forces itself upon the attention of everyone in the neighborhood. In fact at the height of the song season this is the noisiest of all the birds. The song resembles in some respects that of a robin, and novices sometimes confuse the two. The grosbeak's song is much fuller and more varied, contains many little trills, and is given in more rapid time. Now and then it bursts forth fortissimo and after several rounds of burbling, winds up with a number of squeals,' the last one attenuated and dying out slowly."

S. F. Rathbun (MS.) describes the song as "a succession of rich and clear whistling notes given rapidly, now and then having trills injected, closing with a few rough notes. The song has a bold and joyous quality which is very noticeable." One that he listened to in early June began to sing at 3:55 a.m., 15 minutes before sunrise, and "sang from the time it began, almost without any intermission, for a period of 3 hours, each rendition of its song being followed by another with scarcely a perceptible pause between. After this first burst of more or less continuous singing, there began to be intermissions of a few seconds between the songs. As the day wore on, the bird sang less often, but it was not until 7 hours had passed that the song was heard only at times. Then it became disconnected, only the whistling notes being heard."

Weston (1947) says:

Length of individual songs varies considerably. The shortest that I have timed lasted one second, the longest eighteen; the average song is five seconds in length. The intervals between songs in series vary from one second to twenty-seven seconds. In general, songs in the early morning are longer, louder, and richer in quality than those at other times in the day. * * *

In general, the songs of female grosbeaks are infrequent and never more than four seconds in duration and are never loud. They are uttered while the female is incubating or brooding, usually as the male comes to take his place on the eggs or young. Several times during nest-building, the female uttered songs in the vicinity of the nest and always in the presence of the male. The female will occasionally sing while foraging in the peripheral foliage of trees, but only while the male is close by. * * *

The common call-note, a sharp *spic*, closely resembles that of the Rose-breasted Grosbeak. * * * It is commonly emitted while both sexes are foraging and at these times the calls are especially frequent, being repeated over and over at regular intervals.

Fall.—The same observer states: "Fall departure is apparently irregular. Late in the season all individuals are quiet. The males cease singing after mid-July and are the first to leave, generally disappearing late in July. Females and young remain several weeks longer and usually begin to leave in mid-August. In the past thirty-two years, the last-seen dates at Berkeley have ranged from August 11 to October 9. Records after early September are probably those of transients rather than local residents."

Rathbun tells me that the black-headed grosbeaks leave the vicinity of Seattle between September 5 and 20.

DISTRIBUTION

Range.—Pacific slope from southwestern British Columbia to Oaxaca.

Breeding range.—The black-headed grosbeak breeds from south-western British Columbia (Quinsam Lake, Coquitlam) south along the Pacific coast to northern Baja California (Sierra San Pedro

Martir); east in California to Owens Valley and the San Bernardino Mountains.

Winter range.—Winters from southern Baja California (La Paz), southern Sonora (Tesia), and southwestern Chihuahua south to Oaxaca (Mitla).

Egg dates.—British Columbia: 3 records, June 3 to June 5.

California: 200 records, April 23 to July 10; 102 records, May 5 to May 23.

Washington: 6 records, June 4 to July 4.

GUIRACA CAERULEA CAERULEA (Linnaeus)

Eastern Blue Grosbeak

PLATES 6 AND 7

HABITS

For a study of the characters and ranges of the races of this species, the reader is referred to a revision by Dwight and Griscom (1927). According to them, the eastern blue grosbeak is the form that "breeds in the southeastern United States west to central Kansas and western Texas, and north sparingly to New Jersey, Pennsylvania, West Virginia, Kentucky, Illinois and Nebraska * * * "

Its favorite haunts are similar to those chosen by the indigo bunting: old fields overgrown with brambles, thickets along streams, woods or roadsides, and in hedge rows; it may also be found in orchards or in shrubbery about houses and gardens; but it does not, as a rule, frequent swamps or swampy thickets, or the interior of woodlands.

Nesting.—The nest of the blue grosbeak is usually built in a bush or small tree, at no great height from the ground, usually 3 to 8 feet up.

In Virginia, according H. H. Bailey (1913), "Second growth bushes, such as oaks and locusts, are preferred, and seem to be their natural nesting sites, while around my farm they resort to the grape vines trailed on longitudinal wires, and young trees in the orchard, notably pear and cherry."

C. S. Brimley (1890) records several nests found near Raleigh, N.C. One was 5 feet up in a small pine, one 3 feet in an alder, two in sweet gums at 5 and 5½ feet, two in mulberries at 4 and 4½ feet, and one in a grapevine.

Henry Nehrling (1896) describes several nests that he found in Lee County, Tex., as follows:

* * * I discovered the first nest on a road-side only a few steps from a much frequented wagon track. It was built in a very thorny blackberry bush, about two feet above the ground, and was so well hidden in the dense foliage that it could only be seen when the twigs were bent aside. This nest was a very pretty

and compact structure, entirely different from what I had read about it. Externally it was constructed of corn-leaves mixed with long fibrous rootlets, large pieces of snake-skin and small dry leaves. The rim was made of catkins of the oak, intermingled with spider's nests and caterpillar's silk. A little cotton also entered into the composition. The cavity was lined with fine brown rootlets. * * * All other nests found subsequently were built in the same manner, and all were discovered near dwellings. Several domiciles found in gardens in rose-bushes, and one in a dense sweet myrtle (*Myrtus communis*), displayed in their construction also a few pieces of paper, parts of strings, and muslin and in the lining a few horse hairs. Snake-skins, with the Blue Grosbeak, always are a favorite and characteristic nest-building material, forming sometimes almost the entire exterior of the nest. * * *

* * * In the following year I discovered the first nest on May 13, in a peach orchard. It was built between the trunk and a sapling of a peach tree about six inches above the ground. Weeds in great luxuriance grew all around, screening the nest from observation. It was a very peculiar, though beautiful and artistic structure, built externally of broad shreds of corn-husks, a few plant-stems, and mostly of snake-skin, the latter arranged in a turbanlike way. All over it was decorated with cinnamon-brown caterpillar nests, which gave the domicile a very odd appearance. A few days later I found another peculiar nest, which was placed in a half-pendulous way in a horizontal branch of a black-jack oak, about twelve feet from the ground. Above and below it was protected by a canopy of dense foliage. * * * A third nest was also in a rather extraordinary position. It was built in an almost pendulous branch of an oak on the woodland border and far from the trunk, about twenty-five feet above the ground, and entirely out of my reach. All the other nests were built in orchard trees and ornamental shrubs.

Charles R. Stockard (1905) mentions finding an unusual nest beside a country road in Mississippi, of which he says:

This road was used in the fall and winter for hauling cotton and some of the lint remained tangled in the bushes throughout the year. The nest was placed three and one half feet from the ground in a crotch of a small gum bush, and the outer part of it was cotton giving the whole much the appearance of a ball of lint caught in the branches. This nest and set of four eggs were taken. Two weeks later, on June 1, on chancing to pass along the same road and glancing toward the former nest bush a second nest was seen. This was exceedingly like the other, its outer part being of cotton, and was placed in the identical crotch from which the first had been removed. On approaching it was found also to contain four fresh Blue Grosbeak's eggs. This was rather quick work, building a nest and laying four eggs within fourteen days.

Mrs. Nice (1931) mentions an Oklahoma nest that "had been built almost entirely of newspaper, but was lined with reddish roots."

There is in my collection, sent to me by Eugene E. Murphey, of Augusta, Ga., a nest that is almost entirely covered externally with cast-off snake skins.

Frederick V. Hebard has sent me notes on five nests of the eastern blue grosbeak, all of which were built in oaks at from 6 to 12 feet above ground, in southern Georgia.

Daniel L. McKinley has written me about a nest in south-central Missouri which includes sassafras leaves in the base. Materials also

PLATE 7

wley County, Kans.   W. Colvin

NEST OF EASTERN BLUE GROSBEAK

ennepin County, Minn., June 1929   S. A. Grimes

NEST OF INDIGO BUNTING WITH COWBIRD EGG

Toronto, Ontario

W. V. Cri

INDIGO BUNTING AT NEST

included the stems of a small mint, English plantain, and ironwood. The lining was composed of fine, long pieces of grass stems. The inside of the nest was 3 inches long, 2⅝ inches wide, and 2 inches deep.

Mangum Weeks writes me of finding a nest with two recently hatched young in a swamp maple near a brackish creek in St. Mary's County, Md., on Aug. 3, 1950. The male in attendance was in immature plumage.

Eggs.—The set of blue grosbeak eggs is commonly four, although sometimes only two or three, and more rarely five eggs are laid. They are ovate with occasional tendency toward short-ovate, or elongated-ovate, and have a slight luster. The eggs are very pale bluish-white, unmarked.

The measurements of 50 eggs average 22.0 by 16.8 millimeters; the eggs showing the four extremes measure *24.1* by 17.9, 22.4 by *19.6*, *19.8* by 16.5, and 21.0 by *15.0* millimeters.

Young.—Incubation seems to be performed entirely by the female and to last about 11 days. According to observations made by Mrs. Archie Middleton (1899), in Nebraska, the young remain in the nest for about 13 days. They are fed while in the nest by both parents, though the male is more active in this after the young have left the nest and while the female is busy in building her second nest. Apparently, two broods are commonly raised in the southern parts of the range.

Audubon (1841) writes: "When the first broods leave their parents, the young birds assemble in small flocks composed of a few families, and resort mostly to the rice fields, feeding on the grain when yet in its milky state, and until it is gathered. The parents join them with their second brood, and shortly after, or about the first days of September, they all depart southward."

On July 31, according to McKinley (*in* lit.), the nest he watched contained two newly hatched young and one egg, which hatched later. On August 8 the flight feathers had broken from their sheaths and the abundance of pinfeathers caused the birds' heads to appear rough and spiny. The nest was crowded, and one of the young sat above the level of the rim resting on the backs of the other two young. The latter had only their heads free. On August 9 the feathers of the head, back, and wing coverts had broken from their sheaths to some extent, and the wing coverts had begun to show their bars. The nest was found deserted the evening of the next day.

Plumages.—Dwight (1900) describes the juvenal plumage of the blue grosbeak as "above, bistre, grayish on the rump, russet tinged on the pileum, the feathers with wood-brown or russet edgings. Wings and tail dull clove-brown, with wood-brown edgings, two indistinct wing bands and narrow tipping of the tail buff. Below rich clay-color, pale buff on the chin, abdomen and crissum. * * *"

The first winter plumage of the male is acquired by a partial post-juvenal molt in August, involving the contour plumage and the wing coverts, but not the rest of the wings nor the tail. Dr. Dwight says that it is similar to the juvenal plumage, but "the browns everywhere darker and richer especially noticeable on the median wing coverts which become deep hazel, the crissum which becomes cinnamon or dusky-streaked and the lores which are dull sepia-brown."

He says that the first nuptial plumage is acquired by a partial pre-nuptial molt, "which involves a variable amount of the brown body plumage and wing coverts, the tail wholly or in part and apparently the outer primaries in some cases. A mixture of brown and blue results, the key to the age of a specimen being the retained brown primary coverts. The moult must occur in mid-winter judging by the worn condition of spring specimens."

The adult winter plumage is acquired by a complete postnuptial molt. "The full blue plumage is assumed, veiled with cinnamon feather tips on the head and back, a deeper band across the throat, these edgings very pale elsewhere below. The wings are black with blue edgings, those of the lesser and median coverts rich chestnut, of the greater coverts paler, of the tertials still paler; the tail darker than the wings and with deeper blue edgings, the outer pair of rec-trices narrowly tipped with white. The lores are black."

The adult nuptial plumage is acquired by wear, without molt.

Of the plumages of the female, he writes:

The plumages and moults correspond but the female never acquires much blue, remaining in a brown plumage like the male first winter. In first winter plumage the female is pale cinnamon-brown darkest on the head and palest below and on the rump; the wings and tail deep olive-brown; the wing bands pale chestnut, the one at tips of greater coverts paler. The first nuptial plumage, assumed almost wholly by wear, is paler, the brown fading. The adult winter plumage usually shows a bluish tint in the wing edgings, the wings and tail being darker than in first winter dress. More mature birds may show blue feathers on the rump, crown, sides of head, sides of throat and across the jugulum but do not often acquire a plumage as bright as that of the male in first nuptial plumage.

Food.—Based on a study of the contents of 51 stomachs of the blue grosbeak, W. L. McAtee (1908) reports that the food consisted of 67.6 percent animal matter and 32.4 percent vegetable. The stomachs of 13 young birds, still being fed by their parents, were included in the study; in these the animal matter amounted to 99.08 percent, of which grasshoppers constituted 74.1 percent. "The remains of as many as 16 short-horned locusts were obtained from one stomach, while another contained 14. Caterpillars, among them the purslane sphinx, compose 10.7 percent of the subsistence of the nestlings, and snails 10 percent. * * *

"Among the important insect pests eaten by the blue grosbeak are grasshoppers, weevils, the purslane sphinx, and the cotton cut-worm. * * *"

Earlier he says: "Injurious beetles comprise 24.4 percent of the grosbeak's food, almost half (11.25 percent) of which consists of members of the May beetle family (Scarabaeidae). Adult June bugs, and their larvae, the white grubs, were devoured by some birds to the exclusion of other food * * *" Weevils made up 7.18 percent of the seasonal food, many of which are injurious. "Leaf-beetles (Chrysomelidae), wood-borers (Buprestidae), click-beetles (Elateridae), and long-horned beetles (Cerambycidae), nearly all of which are injurious, were also devoured.

"The most important element of the animal food, however, is grasshoppers. Crickets and long and short horned grasshoppers are eagerly consumed, composing 27.2 percent of the total food. Thirty-two of the 51 blue grosbeaks ate them, several taking nothing else. * * *"

Still earlier he says: "The true bugs (Hemiptera) constitute another group of insects, mainly injurious, and all of them eaten by the grosbeak are destructive. These include members of the squash-bug family (Coreidae), stink-bug family (Pentatomidae), tree-hoppers (Membracidae), and cicadas or harvest flies (Cicadidae)."

Of the vegetable food, he says: "Vegetable substances consumed by the blue grosbeak and constituting 32.4 percent of its food may be classified as follows: Grain, 14.25 percent; weed seed, 18.05 percent; fruit, 0.06 percent; and miscellaneous, 0.04 percent." Only 11 of the 51 birds examined had eaten grain, and only 1 had eaten it exclusively. As the birds are widely scattered during most of the summer, probably little damage is done to the grain, but later, when they gather in flocks in the fields, they are said to do considerable damage. Cultivated fruits are apparently not molested, and what little fruit is eaten appears to be of wild species.

Behavior.—The blue grosbeak is a quiet, peaceful bird, living in harmony with its wild neighbors, or with other species in captivity, where it is a popular cage bird. It vigorously defends its nesting territory against intruders of its own species, but tolerates neighbors of other species. It makes itself at home about human dwellings and is not too timid there.

Nehrling (1896) says: "The flight of the Blue Grosbeak is short and low, usually leading only from one thicket to another. During migration it mounts high into the air and then its flight is rather hurried. On the ground, where most of the food is gathered, its motions are somewhat awkward. It usually searches one place thoroughly and then hops to another. In the branches of trees and shrubs its movements denote that in these it is perfectly at home. It has a predilection of perching in the tops of low bushes and trees, where it swings up and down."

Aretas A. Saunders writes me that flocks of males arrive in South Carolina and Alabama ahead of the females. The males feed on the ground in and around plowed fields; in poor light they appear black and are easily mistaken for cowbirds. Flight is undulatory.

William Youngworth (1958) first observed this species in Iowa in 1932, and collected the first specimen for that State in 1934. He now writes, "The trend with many of the prairie birds in Iowa and Minnesota is just the opposite of the apparent spread of the Blue Grosbeak. The spread of the Grosbeak is almost unique. We have a species which 30 years ago was almost unknown to the state * * * Today we can report them as not rare in western Iowa." He says that the bird seems to be a late nester, usually arriving the end of May. "In July, when Orchard Orioles are already moving to the south, Blue Grosbeaks seem to just be getting into the swing of a second nesting." His latest record was Aug. 21, 1948, with young still being fed in the nest. Birds are still in good plumage and fine song in July and August.

Voice.—Nehrling (1896) says on this subject:

The Blue Grosbeak is a very diligent singer in the early morning hours, and in order to enjoy its song we must rise early. I have rarely heard its lively strain during noontide, and not until it becomes cooler, late in the afternoon, the lovely and varied song sounds through the air in its full beauty. While singing the bird is perched in the top of a bush or small tree, on a post, or a telegraph wire. Not infrequently it pours forth its sweet strain while hidden in dense shrubs and vine-embowered trees. The lover of bird songs will scarcely tire to listen to these, although rather short, but exquisitely sweet, clear, melodious, and somewhat metallic notes. The whole performance has something very peculiarly and indescribably pleasant. Some observers claim that the song is much like that of the Indigo Bunting, and others compare it even to the Bobolink's unrivalled reverie. In my judgement it has not the slightest resemblance either with one or the other. Probably Cooper is not far amiss when he likens the song to that of the California House-finch. To my ear the song had always a great similarity to that of the Purple Finch, though not so quick and energetic. * * * In Texas I have often heard the song late in the evening, and at such times the slower and somewhat melancholie notes make a deep impression on the hearer. The bird sings from the time of its arrival late in April until the young are hatched and have left the nest.

Aretas A. Saunders writes me that one song recorded in South Carolina and three others in Oklahoma varied in form, but were mainly composed of short notes and slightly longer trills. The pitch varied from C#$_3$ to B$_3$ and the time averaged about 2½ seconds, the longest being 3.4 seconds and the shortest 1.8 seconds. He recorded *ray ree ray tōtah ray reeray tō see see tōtay* and *trŭray trŭray trĭtray trĭtray trō trō*. A single call note he recorded as *tsink* was pitched on C_4. As a flock flew by, before the time that singing began, he recorded a long series of call notes as *zit-zit-zŭ-zit-zit-zŭ zōō-zĭēēt zĭēēt zĭēēt zĭ-zi-zi-zi-zi-zi-zi-zi*. This ranged in pitch from D_3 to A_4. He summarizes the song as being a series of notes, rather irregularly alternated up and down in pitch, the quality musical but burred. He considers the song weaker than that of the rose-breasted grosbeak and less pleasing.

Field marks.—The adult male blue grosbeak can be distinguished from the male indigo bunting by its much larger size, thicker and heavier bill, and by a broad band of chestnut on the median wing coverts and a narrower band on the tips of the greater coverts; except under favorable light conditions, it does not appear to be blue, but rather an indefinite dark color; when sitting motionless in a poor light, it might be mistaken for a male cowbird.

The female somewhat resembles the female indigo bunting, but is much larger, has a heavier bill and shows two wing bars; at certain ages, there is more or less blue in her plumage, as described above.

Fall.—After the breeding season, old and young birds gather in flocks and feed in the grainfields, grasslands, and ricefields before departing in September for their winter homes in Cuba, eastern Mexico, and Central America. Dickey and van Rossem (1938) record it as a rare migrant in El Salvador, frequenting the grasslands, fields, and mimosa brush.

DISTRIBUTION

Range.—Central Great Plains and Middle Atlantic States to Guatemala and Honduras.

Breeding range.—The eastern blue grosbeak breeds from southwestern and central northern Oklahoma (Wichita Mountains; Kay County), east central Kansas (Wilsey, Lawrence), north central Missouri (Kansas City, Columbia), southern Illinois (Olney), southwestern Kentucky (Fulton County), northern Alabama (Decatur), northern Georgia (Rome, Clayton), western North Carolina (Weaverville), eastern West Virginia (Shepherdstown), southeastern Pennsylvania (Carlisle), and southwestern New Jersey (Camden) south to central and southern Texas (Brownsville, Austin, Houston), southern Louisiana (Grand Coteau), central Alabama (Greensboro, Montgomery), northwestern Florida (Jackson County, Tallahassee), and southeastern Georgia (Blackbeard Island).

Winter range.—Winters from central Veracruz (Orizaba), Yucatán (Mérida), Swan Island, Cuba (rarely), and the Bahamas (New

Providence and Eleuthera Islands) south to Guatemala and northern Honduras (Lancetilla, La Ceiba, Yaruca); rarely to Louisiana (New Orleans), Costa Rica (Coyolan) and western Panamá (Almirante); casually Connecticut (Riverside).

Casual records.—Casual north to southwestern Minnesota (Rock County), southern Wisconsin (Lake Koshkonong), southern Michigan (north to Ottawa County), southern Ontario (Chatham, Toronto, Stirling), southern Quebec (Mille Vaches), New Brunswick (Grand Manan), and Nova Scotia (Halifax), and east to Bermuda.

Migration.—The data deal with the species as a whole. Early dates of spring arrival are: Costa Rica—Angostura, March 17. Baja California—San José del Cabo, March 29. Sonora—March 9. Florida—Lower Keys, March 20. Alabama—Jackson, April 2. Georgia—Grady County, April 4. South Carolina—April 1. North Carolina—Raleigh, April 24 (average of 24 years, May 3). Virginia—Charlottesville, April 26. West Virginia—Mannington, May 17. District of Columbia—May 1. Maryland—Laurel, April 1 (median of 9 years, May 1). Delaware—Lewes, May 7. Pennsylvania—McKean County, May 15. New Jersey—Montclair, May 11. New York—Patchogue, May 1; Manhattan Island, May 15. Connecticut—New Canaan, May 2. Massachusetts—Martha's Vineyard, April 17. New Hampshire—Boscawen, May 30. Quebec—Mille Vaches, Lower St. Lawrence, May 7. Nova Scotia—Waverley, April 13. Louisiana—Grand Isle, April 1; Baton Rouge, April 6. Mississippi—Rosedale, April 22. Arkansas—Fayetteville, April 26. Tennessee—Knox County, April 23. Missouri—St. Louis, April 24 (median of 13 years, May 4). Illinois—Metropolia, April 27. Indiana—Richmond, April 14. Michigan—Ann Arbor, May 24. Ontario—Chatham, May 18. Iowa—Sioux City, May 16. Wisconsin—Cazenovia, March 26; Green Bay, May 4. Minnesota—Beaver Creek, June 6. Texas—Sinton, April 8 (median of 5 years, April 13). Oklahoma—Oklahoma City, April 18. Kansas—northeastern Kansas, April 25 (median of 23 years, May 13). Nebraska—Red Cloud, April 12 (median of 21 years, May 12). South Dakota—White River, May 17. New Mexico—State College, May 7. Colorado—Durango, May 10. Utah—Kanab, May 12. California—Santa Cruz, April 12. Nevada—Lower Muddy and Virgin Rivers, May 7.

Late dates of spring departure are: Guatemala—Finca Chamá, April 27. Guerrero—Cuapongo, April 29. Puebla—Tehuacán, May 4. Sinaloa—Yecorato, April 28. Baja California—San José del Cabo, April 30. Tamaulipas—Gómez Farías, May 1. Florida—Leon County, May 29. Alabama—Dauphin Island, May 16. Louisiana—Baton Rouge, May 14. Mississippi—Rosedale, May 13. California—White Water, May 26.

Early dates of fall arrival are: California—Yosemite Valley, August 8. Louisiana—New Orleans, August 28. New Jersey—Island Beach, August 25. Florida—Leon County, September 1. Sonora—Guirocoba, October 5. Sinaloa—Milpillas, September 9. Morelos—Atlacomulco, October 30.

Late dates of fall departure are: California—Yerma, October 1. New Mexico—Mesilla, October 12. South Dakota—Yankton, September 20. Nebraska—Chadron, October 11. Kansas—northeastern Kansas, September 2 (median of 8 years, August 27). Oklahoma—Oklahoma City, October 25. Texas—Sinton, October 16. Iowa—Sioux City, September 19. Missouri—Kansas City, October 15. Arkansas—northwestern Arkansas, September 12. Mississippi—Biloxi, October 29. Massachusetts—North Eastham, October 13. Rhode Island—Drownville, October 12. Connecticut—East Haven, October 30. New York—Riis Park, November 11; Tiana, October 22, New Jersey—Cape May, November 1. Maryland—Talbot County, October 24; Caroline County, October 17 (median of 9 years, October 6). District of Columbia—September 20. Virginia—Charlottesville, October 22. North Carolina—Raleigh, September 27 (average of 10 years, September 12). South Carolina—November 3. Georgia—Macon, October 20; Athens, October 7. Alabama—Dauphin Island, November 8; Jackson, November 1. Florida—Leon County, October 22.

Egg Dates.—Alabama: 22 records, May 10 to August 2.

Georgia: 47 records, May 10 to July 27; 25 records, May 23 to June 20.

Maryland: 12 records, May 5 to August 30; 6 records, June 2 to June 16.

GUIRACA CAERULEA INTERFUSA Dwight and Griscom
Western Blue Grosbeak

HABITS

This southwestern race of the species is described by Dwight and Griscom (1927) as "similar to *caerulea* but larger and paler, the blue of the male less purplish (dark diva, or grayish violaceous blue), the anterior wing-band a paler chestnut, the other wing-band still paler and contrasting, both broader, and the winter veiling heavier. Like *salicaria* in color but larger, especially the bill. * * * Females and young males larger and paler than *caerulea*."

The 1957 edition of the A.O.U. Check-List defines its breeding range as from southeastern California, southern Nevada, Utah, and Colorado northeastward to central South Dakota and eastern

Nebraska, and southward to northeastern Baja California, north-western Duroyo, and central Texas.

In southern Arizona, Henshaw (1875) found it to be "a very well represented species. It does not appear to visit the mountainous districts at all, but was found on the heavily brushed streams from the time they made their appearance at the base of the mountains, till, as is usually the case in this region, the waters finally disappeared in the thirsty sands of the plains below, the luxuriant vegetation which encloses the banks ceasing when the stream sinks." We found it in the willows and other vegetation along the irrigation ditches in the San Pedro valley.

In New Mexico, according to Mrs. Bailey (1928) its "cheery song can be heard from orchards, groves, bosques, mesquites, thickets, and sunflower patches."

In 1958, Robert M. Stabler sent Taber the following notes on two successive nestings by the same pair of blue grosbeaks on his ranch 3 miles north of Colorado Springs, Colo.:

"Both nestings were in a plot about 200 yards north of an arroyo containing a flowing stream and adjacent to a dusty road heavily used by gravel trucks. The vegetation was mainly composed of: Skunk-bush (*Rhus trilobata*), wolfberry (*Symphoricarpos occidentalis*), gold-weed (*Verbesina encelioides*), Kansas sunflower (*Helianthus annuus*), horseweed (*Iva xanthifolia*), and tall tansy aster (*Aster bigelovii*).

"The first of the two nests was 64 feet from the road, the second was 58 feet NNW of the first, not far from the center of the area. Other birds known to nest in the same plot are: Sage thrasher (*Oreoscoptes montanus*), lark sparrow (*Chondestes grammacus strigatus*), and Brewer's blackbird (*Euphagus cyanocephala*). A pair of Brewer's nested only 10 feet from, and concurrently with, the first nesting of the grosbeaks.

"The first nest was discovered at 6:30 p.m. on June 8. Its rim was 31.5 inches from the ground and was securely fastened to both *Rhus* and *Symphoricarpos*. With an inside diameter of 2.5 inches and a cup depth of 2.0 inches, it was quite substantially built of small twigs, rootlets, and strippings of inner bark. Several lengths of hemp string were included. Near the periphery there was some newspaper, numerous pieces of cellophane, and several large dried leaves. The cup was lined with very fine rootlets, tendrils, and both black and white horse mane or tail hairs.

"When found it contained one freshly laid egg. Daily observations between 2:00 and 2:30 p.m. revealed one pale blue, unspotted egg added on each of the three days following discovery, the clutch being completed on 11 June. The female was flushed from the nest at each of the above four checks. On June 22 the first egg hatched, another pipped, and two remained unchanged. The following day, by 10:00 a.m. a second had hatched, and two were pipped, and by 7:30 p.m. three youngsters were out. The fourth egg, though pipped, failed to hatch the chick.

"On June 22 the first egg hatched, another pipped, and two remained unchanged. The following day, by 10:00 a.m. a second had hatched, and two were pipped, and by 7:30 p.m. three youngsters were out. The fourth egg, though pipped, failed to hatch, the chick dying. Daily inspection showed the young still in the nest on June 30. At 2:00 p.m. on July 1 binocular check revealed one bird in the nest, one on a twig some 2 feet away, and the third nowhere to be seen. All were gone the following day by 8:00 a.m.

"From the above it may be seen that this female laid an egg a day for 4 days; from clutch completion to first hatching was 11 days; that at least 2 days were required to complete hatching; and that nest occupancy was about 9 days.

"When the second nest was discovered at 7:00 p.m. on July 17, it already contained four eggs similar to the first four, so laying and incubation data on this nest were not obtainable. The nest was 38.5 inches from ground to rim, in a rather sparse clump of the *R. trilobata*. The routine check at 2:00 p.m. on July 23 revealed one damp, newly emerged chick, one pipped egg, and two eggs unmarked. The following day by 10:30 a.m. two eggs had hatched and two remained unchanged, and by 4:15 p.m. one of the latter eggs showed a slight pipping. At 10:30 a.m. on July 25 three young were out, the fourth again failing to hatch. As in the first set, examination showed the last chick here to have died just prior to emergence, although this one did not pip the shell. Using the first set's incubation data and the second set's hatching times, we may assume that the female finished her second clutch on approximately July 12, just about 1 month from the time she finished laying her first set.

"Binocular check of the nest at 11:00 a.m. on August 1 showed all young therein. At 8:30 a.m. on August 3 all the young were gone and inspection of the site indicated that the nest had been vacated the day before, on August 2. No young could be seen in the vicinity of the nest. Duration of occupancy by the second brood was, therefore, some 10 days.

"A study of the second nest showed it to be somewhat less well constructed than the first, the upper wall being such that the eggs could be seen from the outside. The inside dimensions were approximately as before, and both cellophane and newspaper had again been woven among the twigs and bark strippings. Numerous small pieces of cardboard, not found in the first nest, had also been used here. Rootlets and horsehairs again lined the cup.

"Pieces of shed snakeskin are said to be a quite common feature of this grosbeak's nests. No such material appeared in the present nests, despite the fact that bull snakes (*Pituophis catenifer sayi*), garter snakes (*Thamnophis elegans vagrans* and *T. radix haydeni*), and prairie rattlesnakes (*Crotalus* v. *viridis*) frequent the area.

Nesting.—The nesting habits of the western blue grosbeak are evidently very similar to those of its eastern relative. Mrs. Bailey (1928) says that, in New Mexico, the nest is placed in "tall weeds, vines, bushes, willows, and fruit trees" and is "made of grasses and rootlets." She says further: "In twenty-three nests located during a period of five years, twenty-one had snake skin, as a foundation."

Eggs.—The three or four eggs laid by this grosbeak are indistinguishable from those of the eastern race. Measurements of 40 eggs average 21.8 by 16.3 millimeters; the eggs showing the four extremes measure *23.9* by 16.8, 21.8 by *17.8*, *20.3* by 15.8, and 20.8 by *15.5* millimeters.

The molts and plumages, food, voice, and the habits in general of the western blue grosbeak are similar to those of the eastern bird.

DISTRIBUTION

Range.—Southeastern California, southern Nevada, Colorado, and South Dakota to Costa Rica.

Breeding range.—The western blue grosbeak breeds from southeastern California (Coachella, Needles), southern Nevada (Pahranagat Valley), southern and eastern Utah (Santa Clara River, Boulder, Vernal), central and northeastern Colorado (Sedalia and Yuma County), northwestern and central South Dakota (Belle Fourche, casually, Badlands National Monument, and Pierre), and eastern Nebraska (Lincoln) south to northeastern Baja California (Cerro Prieto), northwestern Durango (Rancho Baillon), southern Coahuila (Hipólito), and west central Texas (San Antonio, Hidalgo); east to western Kansas and central Oklahoma (Minco, Woods County).

Winter range.—Winters from southern Sonora (Guirocoba, one record) and Sinaloa south along the Pacific coast of Mexico and Central America.

Casual record.—Casual in eastern Washington (Spokane).

Egg dates.—Arizona: 14 records, June 14 to August 21; 7 records, July 17 to July 27.

Texas: 20 records, May 15 to July 3; 12 records, May 29 to June 8.

GUIRACA CAERULEA SALICARIA Grinnell

California Blue Grosbeak

Contributed by WENDELL TABER

HABITS

Joseph Grinnell (1911b) described this race as "Similar to *Guiraca caerulea lazula*, of Arizona and Mexico, in coloration and general size, but bill much smaller and proportionally less tumid, that is, outlines straighter; compared with *Guiraca caerulea caerulea* of the South Atlantic States, blue color of the male paler throughout, bill smaller, and wing and tail longer."

Grinnell and Alden H. Miller (1944), consider its life-zone in California to be chiefly Lower Sonoran and state that known breeding stations range in altitude from 178 feet above sea level up to about 4,000 feet. Miller (1951c) states that the species occurs in California, mainly in riparian woodland and fresh-water marshes.

Nesting.—J. G. Tyler (1913) emphasizes water close at hand as one of the chief requirements of this species during the nesting season. But, he says, "Quite as noticeable is their complete disregard for it after cares are over, when the grosbeaks seek the dryest grain fields and roadside weed patches, where they may often be seen clinging to swaying wild oats. This plant, together with the cultivated variety, forms one of their favorite foods during the month that they remain in this vicinity after their nesting season terminates, in late June or the first week in July." He adds that the blue grosbeak is among the last birds to arrive in the spring, and probably the first to depart, early in August. He writes that on the morning of Aug. 8, 1911, "I was attracted by a subdued finch-like song hastily executed, as the singer perched just for a moment on a telephone wire * * *. Hardly had the song been finished when the bird flew away toward the south, to be followed in a very few minutes by another that went through precisely the same maneuvers, even to perching on almost the exact section of wire that the other had occupied." The migration continued for 2 more days, all birds that he could identify being males. He says, "Each one was travelling alone, but was probably keeping within calling distance of another." He notes that 7 out of 10 nests are built in patches of plant which grow along the canals and ditches and "greatly resemble in appearance and manner of growth the Chrysanthemum." The nests are fastened to two or three upright shoots, varying in height from 6 inches to 5 feet above the ground. One clump of these plants harbors only one pair of grosbeaks, and as there are not enough clumps to go around, some nests are located "in the thick bunches of small willow saplings." Nests bear a resemblance to those of the red-winged blackbird.

Tyler also states that occasionally the grosbeak will nest in a peach orchard, with the nest 8 to 12 feet above the ground. One nest was fully 20 feet up, in a willow, "at the end of a small horizontal branch the tip of which took an abrupt vertical turn and hung out over a ditch full of water." Another nest at the end of a horizontal branch of a poplar tree in a yard was about 15 feet up. The nests "are well-made, light baskets of dry grass, weed stems and rootlets, lined with black horse-hairs if such are obtainable." Always, in his experience, there was "either a piece of paper or a dry, paper-like leaf woven into the framework somewhere." He adds, "sets of three and four eggs are found in about equal numbers, the time ranging from May 18 (1906) to June 23 (1901)." In a case of late nesting, young were just out of the nest on July 15.

Eggs.—The measurements of 40 eggs average 22.0 by 16.5 millimeters; the eggs showing the four extremes measure *24.9* by 15.2, 22.3 by *17.7*, *20.0* by 16.1, and 20.1 by *14.8* millimeters.

DISTRIBUTION

Range.—Central California and west central Nevada to Baja California and Guerrero.

Breeding range.—The California blue grosbeak breeds from the Great Valley and Inyo District of central California (Red Bluff, Furance Creek) and central western Nevada (Esmeralda County) south through southwestern California (Soledad Mission, Banning, San Diego) to northwestern Baja California (San Quintín).

Winter range.—Winters from southern Baja California (San José del Cabo) and southern Sonora (lower Yaqui River) south to Guerrero (Chilpancingo).

Egg dates.—California: 38 records, April 18 to July 12; 20 records, May 22 to June 12.

PASSERINA CYANEA (Linnaeus)

Indigo Bunting

PLATES 7, 8, AND 9

Contributed by WENDELL TABER and DAVID W. JOHNSTON

HABITS

The usual breeding range of the indigo bunting includes southern Canada and the eastern United States westward to Texas, Kansas, and Manitoba. Sporadic nesting and summer occurrences have been reported from a scattering of western states (A.O.U. Check-List, 1957). It is typically a species of forest edges, weedy fields, roadsides, shrublands, and brushy ravines. As Burleigh (1958) suggests, it is a bird of

PLATE 9

H. H. Harrison

FEMALE INDIGO BUNTING AND YOUNG

Butler County, Pa., August 1945

Shasta County, Calif., June 22, 1944　　　　　　　　　　　　J. E. Patte

NEST OF LAZULI BUNTING

Cowley County, Kans.　　　　　　　　　　　　　　　　　W. Co

NEST OF EASTERN PAINTED BUNTING

he "more open country, partially overgrown fields and slashings, hedgerows, and underbrush bordering roads. * * * [There is a] noticeable tendency for this species to be more numerous along the creeks and rivers where the woods are open and there are suitable thickets in which to nest." The male requires moderately high, open perches from which he can sing conspicuously. In sharp contrast, the female searches out the concealment of dense cover close to the ground.

Bond (1957), studying ecological distribution of breeding birds in the upland forests of southern Wisconsin, noted that indigos occasionally occur *in* the forest, but are generally a species of the more open drier woods. Several factors appear to govern their breeding distribution: decreasing canopy of the forest, decreasing moisture, decreasing sapling density, and increasing shrub density. Odum (1950) found that in the mountains of southwestern North Carolina these buntings were less numerous in mesic shrublands than in xeric shrublands where there were "numerous species of shrubs and small trees which occur in dense thickets interspersed with more open places dominated by grasses and herbs." Todd (1940), like Burleigh, believed that a habitat near water is preferred, even if the water is only a small mountain stream. In western Pennsylvania, however, dry hillside thickets and even orchards are often chosen.

In Maryland, Stewart and Robbins (1958) noted indigos in "hedgerows, wood margins, and orchards; also in brushy cut-over areas of swamp forest and of rich, moist forest on the upland." In north central Arizona, H. Dearing and M. Dearing (1946) found the species in an apple orchard on one side of a road and in native trees (pines, oaks, cypress, juniper) and shrubs along the road. The shrubs included *Ceanothus*, scrub oak, sumac, and two species of manzanita. Roberts (1932) found buntings in sparsely wooded brush country, clearings grown up in second growth, and narrow strips of timber bordering lakes and streams. In Louisiana, except for the coastal areas, Lowery (1955) recorded them in clearings at the edges of woods and along highway and railroad rights of way.

As it thrives in areas where the forest has been cleared and is at least partially reverting to its original state, the indigo bunting would be expected to increase in parts of its range where such conditions develop. In north central Florida, for example, agricultural practices have radically changed the landscape over the past few decades, converting much of the once extensive pine forests, hammocks, and swamplands to pasturelands. As some of the pastures are abandoned and undergo processes of ecological succession, the stage is set for their occupancy by these buntings. Before 1964 the species was rarely seen in the environs of Gainesville, but in that year breeding birds were found at 10 widely scattered sites. Its increase in recent years has been noted elsewhere in Florida by Sprunt (1954) and in Maryland by Warbach (1958). The comments of Wells (1958) are apropos: "Perhaps originally a bird of successional vegetation within the Eastern Deciduous Forest of North America, and of the oak openings along the prairie-forest ecotone, the Indigo Bunting was undoubtedly restricted in numbers by the relatively closed canopy of the climax forest * * *. In the East the opening of the forest canopy by agriculture, logging and burning, and in the western grass lands the planting of trees, coupled with cessation of burning, converted great areas into potential Indigo Bunting habitat. This species has apparently responded to these changes with a great increase in population and extension of range * * *."

The ecological succession of forest floras in Maine during the past century has been accompanied by marked changes in the indigo bunting population at this northern limit of its breeding range. Palmer (1949) traces the species decline there, which began in the late 19th century and continued until the 1930's. As the automobile replaced the horse, large acreages of pasture were allowed to revert to forest, and the indigos started to reappear. "There has been a marked increase during the past decade, the species again being noted as a regular migrant and breeder, especially inland in southwestern Maine * * *."

The following table indicates some of the preferred breeding habitats of this species and the breeding population densities. With few exceptions these habitats are all ecologically similar—open areas with dense cover for nesting and feeding and the availability of high singing perches.

Reference	Breeding habitat	Population count or estimate
Warbach (1958)	residential area	1/acre
Beecher (1942)	thicket	5 (nests)/7.08 acres
	unmodified woodland	2/26.87 acres
Johnston (1947)	forest edge	9–18 pairs/mile
	forest interior	3–9 pairs/100 acres
Johnston and Odum (1956)	20-year-old grass-shrub field	4 pairs/100 acres
Odum (1950)	hemlock sere: mesic shrubland	7 pairs/100 acres
	oak-chestnut sere: xeric shrubland	18 pairs/100 acres
Norris (1951)	old field and fence-row	0.7 pairs/100 acres
Stoddard (MS.)	tung oil groves	1 pair/2–3 acres
Johnston (MS.)	overgrown area once cleared for building	11 pairs/77 acres
Fitch (1958)		1 pair/2.7 acres
Brewer (fide Fitch, 1958)	swamp thicket	1 pair/0.26 acre

Stewart and Robbins (1958)	apple orchard	13 pairs/25 acres
	dense second growth	4 pairs/21 acres
	shrubby field	3 pairs/19.5 acres
	field and edge habitat	9 pairs/66 acres
	dry deciduous scrub	1.5 pairs/26 acres

Nesting.—The extensive breeding range through the many habitats noted above entails a correspondingly wide choice of nest sites. William Brewster (1906) points out that the species may nest "in raspberry or blackberry bushes near farmhouses; in barberry or hazel thickets about the edges of remote fields and pastures; and in young sprout growths on the borders of woodland." Trautman (1940) specifies the brushy edges in the openings of a swamp forest. The territory he studied was a buttonbush community.

C. R. Stockard (1905) describes nests in Mississippi as being not only in low bushes and blackberry vines near the edges of fields, but also in dense cane thickets, in which the foundation of the nest was made entirely of cane leaves. The nest was only a few feet from the ground. In Alabama, L. S. Golsan and E. G. Holt (1914) described the species as a common summer resident of old fields and ditch banks in Autauga and Montgomery counties. One nest was composed of grass and leaves and lined with fine grass. It was suspended three feet from the ground in the crotch of a hackberry bush on a ditch bank in an open hayfield. Another compact nest was four feet up in a clump of sweet gum bushes on the edge of a swamp and cultivated field. It was composed of cane leaves and weed stems, and was lined with fine grass and wool.

M. G. Vaiden wrote Mr. Bent of finding 14 nests within a cotton patch of three acres in Rosedale, Miss., between May 18 and May 29, 1936. Some contained eggs; other were not completed. "Practically all the birds were successful in rearing their young. The cotton was continually worked during the last of May, June, and July, and only two nests were destroyed. The nests in each instance were within 3 to 7 inches of the top of the growing stalk. If the bird had selected the branches, all nests would have been destroyed by the plowman."

O. A. Stevens in a letter to Mr. Bent describes a nest in northeastern Kansas on a stalk of Jerusalem artichoke (*Helianthus tuberosus*) in a cornfield. The nest was placed under one of the broad leaves. A. Lang Baily (1954) observed a nest in Colorado on Aug. 5, 1943, two feet up in a thistle (*Cirsium lanceolatum*). The site was marginal weed growth of a dense roadside thicket which included a heavy stand of ragweed (*Ambrosia trifida*) and cordgrass (*Spartina* sp.).

In South Carolina, E. E. Murphey (1937) considers the species a widely diffused and abundant summer resident, but absent from sandy oakflats, pineries, and dense swamps. The bird frequented hedgerows, roadside trees, swamp clearing, the edges of small watercourses, and particularly the cottonwood trees growing so abundantly along the banks of the Savannah River. Nests were in thickets, usually adjoining open fields, and sometimes in bramble patches. Preferred to all other locations were small canebrakes where the canes were no more than one-third of an inch in diameter, and not over six feet in height. The foundation and outer layers of the nest were usually made of the dead leaves of this cane, even when the nest had been constructed at some distance from the brake.

Trautman (1940) states that in the Buckeye Lake region of Ohio the species "nested wherever there was a fair amount of brush, and all brushy thickets, fields and meadows, overgrown fence rows, edges of woodlands, openings in wooded areas, and borders of dirt roads contained nesting pairs. * * * Nesting birds avoided the wetter portions of swamps, cleared fields, heavily grazed meadows, pastures, and woodlots, and the most mature forests with little shrub layer * * *."

Maurice G. Brooks (1944), speaking of West Virginia, calls the species a "characteristic breeding bird of the oak-chestnut forest at all elevations. Much less common in the northern hardwoods, and in coniferous forests, but abundant and generally distributed in the oak-pine areas. I have not found it in the spruce forest."

R. S. Palmer (1949) says that in Maine several pairs sometimes nest in a fairly extensive area of blackberry bushes and other brush. They seem to be drawn together by habitat requirements rather than by any tendency toward colonial nesting. Richard S. Phillips (1951) mentions specifically nests in red raspberry, wild raspberry, elm seedling, elm sapling, silver maple sapling, wild rose, and ironwood sapling. Nests were situated 5 to 200 feet from the woods. T. S. Roberts (1932) states that the species occurs on prairies rather infrequently in the groves of natural timber about lakes and streams.

William Brewster (1906) describes a nest placed "in a clematis vine trained on a wire trellis which screens the main entrance to my museum. Although no one could enter or leave this building without brushing against the foliage of the vine, the birds completed their nest, but they abandoned it after laying two eggs."

Thus, nests are generally placed in crotches of shrubs or saplings only a few feet from the ground in dense cover. Phillips (1951) found the mean height above ground for 14 nests in Ohio was 31 inches. In Grady County, Ga., Herbert L. Stoddard, Sr. (MS.) has found nests at the end of a tung tree branch not over 18 inches above the ground, but the more usual location in these trees is from 5 to 15 feet up. Evidently selection of the particular nest site, as well as nest construction, is left entirely to the female (Allen, 1939). Knight (1908) gives the measurements of a nest as: outside depth, 2½ inches; inside depth, 2 inches; outside diameter, 3¼ inches; inside diameter, 2½ inches. A. O. Gross (1947) mentions a nest in August at Brunswick, Maine, "held together in part by a few spider webs." He says, "The outside measurements of the nest were 3¾ × 4½ inches and the depth 4½ inches. The nesting cavity was 1¾ × 2 inches and a depth of 2 inches." The three young were seen in the nest on Aug. 29, 1947, and out of it the next day.

Basically, the nest is a well-woven cup containing a variety of materials—dried grasses, pieces of dead leaves, strips of bark, Spanish moss, and weed stems. Lewis McIver Terrill wrote Taber that nests in the southern part of the Province of Quebec are bulky and loosely made, and their chief feature is the "invariable use of quantities of skeletonized leaves." Bailey (1954) reports finding facial tissue and cigarette papers in a nest in Colorado. Lining materials include cotton, feathers, fine grasses, wool, rootlets, and long hairs from animals such as Angus cattle and horses. J. Suthard (1927) reports having collected "during various seasons and in different localities several nests of this species composed partially of snake skin. None of these were lined with snake skin, but all had it combined in the lower portion of the nest, or woven in the sides and brim. One nest collected July 23, 1923, has the entire lower portion composed of snake skin. There are long strips of skins streaming from the bottom of the nest."

Mr. Bent's notes mention watching a female stripping cedar bark from cedar poles. He later found the nest. He also comments on the vociferous solicitude of the parents as being of assistance in locating nests, even before the young are hatched. Hazel L. Bradley's (1948) life history study mentions birch bark as nest-building material.

Trautman (1940) states:

> The nests were made chiefly of small rootlets, grasses, inner bark of vines and herbaceous plants, and bits of leaves and were lined with finer grasses, hair, or feathers. The nests were placed in shrubs, bushes, or small saplings and were 1 to 11 feet above the ground. Females were seen carrying nesting material as early as May 20, and by May 30 nest building was well under way. The earliest nest with eggs was found May 27 (1928, 3 eggs), the latest August 4 (1932, 3 eggs); the earliest nest with young was seen June 12 (1932, 4 young), the latest September 5 (1929, 4 young); the first fledgling out of the nest was noted June 21 (1925, 1 young), and the last September 12 (1929, 2 young). Most of the nests with eggs were found from June 16 to July 20, the majority of nests with young from July 10 to August 10, and most of the fledglings out of the nest from July 15 to August 20."

Doris Huestis Speirs wrote Taber about a nest she found in Ohio June 28, 1951, about 17 inches from the ground in a small hackberry sapling. The three eggs were side by side, parallel. When first observed the following day, they were still in this same position, but on a second visit at 9:50 a.m. some 65 minutes later, the eggs had "been rearranged in a more conventional design." When approaching the nest the female first clung to the bark of a little cedar tree rising above the bush, then went to the nest. The male came down once from a hackberry tree to the cedar, then dropped into the nest-site, but quickly departed. The young hatched July 6 and were still present on July 12. On the other hand, Lillian Cleveland (1903), who watched a nest finished on May 30, never saw the male near the nest.

Eggs.—Varying with the year and location, nests with eggs may be found from May to August. Some extreme egg dates are as follows: Maine, late June–July 15 (Knight, 1908); New York, May 25–first of August (Eaton, 1914); Michigan, May 26–August 16 (Barrows, 1912; Berger, 1951); Ohio, June 6–August 7 (Phillips, 1951); Maryland, May 24–August 16 (Stewart and Robbins, 1958); North Carolina, May 22–July 16 (Pearson, Brimley and Brimley, 1959); Georgia, May 17–July 23 (Burleigh, 1958); Alabama, May 12–August 12 (Imhof, 1962). The consensus of many observers is that the species is usually double-brooded. Apparently no one has studied a marked population to prove double-broodedness, but Burleigh (1958) states: "Two broods are reared in Georgia each year, the first in late May and early June, the second in July." And Pearson, Brimley and Brimley (1959) claim that in North Carolina "two broods often are reared in a season, each, of course, in a freshly built nest." According to Parmelee (1959) "Allen says it is double-brooded and that the interval between the start of the first nest (early June) and the second (late July or early August) is long." To what extent a late nest represents renesting following an unsuccessful earlier attempt at nesting is not known.

A. A. Allen (1933) says that if the first nest is started as early as the first of June, it is the last of July or first of August before the second nest is under way. He questions whether the species customarily uses the nest a second year because of the presence of mites and the changes in the locations of the leaves that afford concealment and protection. H. C. Oberholser (1938) states that occasionally the same nest is used. E. H. Forbush (1929) goes further and says that the nest is sometimes repaired and occupied year after year.

F. M. Chapman (1932) states that the usual clutch is three to four eggs, pale bluish white, but two-egg clutches are known from Alabama (Imhof, 1962), northern Florida (Johnston, MS.), and California (Bleitz, 1958). Oliver Davie (1889) describes the color as "white, with a bluish or greenish tinge, unspotted or rarely thinly dotted with brown * * *," and Barrows (1912) found in Michigan "perhaps one nest in a hundred [with] * * * one or two eggs which have small specks of brown on the larger ends." Sometimes eggs are nearly pure white. A. D. DuBois, writing Mr. Bent about a nest in Illinois which contained four eggs on June 2, 1908, says, "The yolks in these eggs showed through the shells, neutralizing the bluish tint to such an extent that the eggs appeared quite white in the nest."

The measurements of 50 eggs average 18.7 by 13.7 millimeters; the eggs showing the four extremes measure *21.3* by 14.2, 19.1 by *15.0*, *16.7* by 12.7, and 17.8 by *11.7* millimeters.

Incubation.—The incubation period is recorded by Roberts (1932), Allen (1939), and Forbush (*fide* Parmelee, 1959) as 12 days, and by Sprunt and Chamberlain (1949) as 12–13 days. Both Bradley (1948) and Allen (1939) agree that incubation is performed by the female alone, but Forbush claims that both sexes incubate and attend the nestlings.

Young.—Extreme nestling dates are available for a few regions: Maryland, June 5–August 30; Alabama, June 3–August 28. Alexander Wetmore (1909) mentions taking a young bird just out of the nest Sept. 18, 1908, and comments on such unusually late nesting. Bradley (1948) states that 8- and 9-day old birds fledge as very weak flyers and remain at or close to the ground. Burns (1921) gives 9 days for the nestling time, Forbush (1929), 10–13 days, and Allen (1939) gives 10 days. A. L. Goodrich, Jr. (1945) says that the male "joins his mate in foraging for the clamorous youngsters until they become able to fend for themselves," and G. M. Sutton (MS.) says "the male may take complete charge" while the female renests. The males, however, apparently never brood the young birds. In fact, Dr. Sutton writes: "I have never seen a male take food to, or change places with, a brooding female, and I have never flushed a male directly from the nest." Mrs. Speirs writes that in the case of nestlings she watched, the female seemed to do most, if not all, of the feeding. Spiders of one kind or another comprised the principal diet fed the young. Other foods consisted of a bee, a few mayflies, a chrysalis, a butterfly, a winged insect, a caterpillar, a daddy longlegs, and a buff-colored moth which was stuffed, wings and all, into the mouth of a fledgling. The female removed a large number of fecal sacs.

H. Dearing and M. Dearing (1946) watched young birds in Arizona, near a benchmark elevation of 4,875 feet. Commenting that the adult male bird had first been seen on July 4, the Dearings say:

The female Indigo Bunting was not seen until July 23, when the young came off the nest. The nest was not seen but the fuzzy brownish fledglings appeared that morning, and both parents were much excited about them. The male hopped excitedly about one of the fledglings on a low branch of a walnut tree near us. The female fed a second fledgling in a near-by shrub. Another was discovered low in an apple tree. We watched it sit perfectly still for more than twenty minutes, and we wondered how the parents would find it. Without a sound from parent or fledgling, the female flew straight to the latter, fed it, and flew away. The fledgling remained in its place. * * *

On July 24, we saw the parents together carrying food to three or four young in an alder tree near the road. The next day the family was still in the alders. The male, with a green caterpillar in his beak, flew from the orchard and fed a young bird. We saw the male again on August 1 and nearly every day after that until August 8.

Hazel L. Bradley's study (1948) indicates that newly hatched birds are pinkish orange in color, almost bare, but with bits of gray natal down on some of the feather tracts. There are large bulges for the eyes, which are closed and membrane-covered at first. One bird opened its eyes at the age of four days; all had the eyes opened at five days. The large wing feathers seemed to be emerging from their sheaths at five days of age, and pin feathers also appeared along other feather tracts, particularly on the back. At six days feathers were out of the sheaths and enlarging. At 11 days of age one group of young was capable of flights of 20 feet or more. The female had removed egg shells, brooded the young, fed them, and eaten or carried away fecal sacs. Nest defense was the one activity in which the male participated.

Commenting on helpers among birds, Alexander F. Skutch (1961) notes for indigo buntings that "juveniles fed still younger birds in captivity." And Val Nolan, Jr. (1961) found that "Prairie Warblers accept and feed nestling Indigo Buntings" and that the buntings will accept young prairie warblers.

Few data are available for productivity. In Michigan, Berger (1951) notes: "From eight eggs in four non-parasitized nests, six buntings were fledged. Five parasitized nests containing seven host and ten Cowbird eggs fledged two buntings and four Cowbirds." Phillips (1951) found that 18 young fledged out of 41 eggs laid.

Cowbird parasitism.—As suggested above, a serious factor in the breeding success of indigo buntings is nest parasitism by the brown-headed cowbird (*Molothrus ater*). Berger's study (1951) in Michigan revealed the fact that five out of nine bunting nests were parasitized; three contained one cowbird egg, one contained two, and one contained four eggs. In these nests four of the cowbird eggs hatched and all four young cowbirds were successfully reared. In Ohio, Phillips (1951) found that 6 out of 14 nests were parasitized and one cowbird fledged from seven eggs laid. Howard Young (1963) gave the following summary for cowbird parasitism on the indigo bunting: 12 out of 26 nests were parasitized; 6 out of 17 cowbird eggs hatched and all 6 fledged. The first recorded breeding of the indigo bunting in California was in Los Angeles County where Don Bleitz (1958) found a nest containing one cowbird and two bunting eggs. Rarely, as Friedmann (1929) reports, a cowbird will lay her egg in the nest of a bunting already containing young.

Trautman (1940) graphically presents the susceptibility of this species to visitations from the cowbird. He states that out of 16 nests examined, 5 contained three eggs or young each of the indigo bunting; 3 contained three eggs or young of this species and a cowbird egg or young each; 6 contained four eggs or young each of the indigo bunting; and 2 contained four eggs or young of this species and a cowbird egg or young each. On more than 10 occasions Trautman observed indigo buntings feeding cowbird fledglings out of the nest.

T. S. Roberts (1943), under a discussion of the cowbird, states that the indigo bunting may "bury the Cowbird egg or eggs by building a new floor in the nest." He also gives an interesting account of the female's reaction to a cowbird's egg, saying: "Attention was directed to an Indigo Bunting's nest by the constant chipping and great agitation of the female, in which the male joined to a lesser extent. The female went repeatedly to the nest, which was low down in a gooseberry bush, and, after looking in, returned each time to the lower limbs of an overhanging tree, displaying the greatest alarm and distress. Examination showed that the nest contained two eggs of the owner and a Cowbird's egg. It was suspected that the Cowbird's egg had just been deposited and was causing the disturbance. It was removed, and after the next visit and inspection by the worried little bird, the fussing and excitement subsided at once."

A. D. DuBois wrote Mr. Bent of finding a nest that contained two cowbird eggs, but no eggs of the indigo bunting. He adds, "No eggs of 'indigo' had been added when revisited 5 days later." W. T. Allen (1881) mentions a case where "The cow-bird had apparently deposited an egg in their nest before it was quite finished, whereupon the owner built a new bottom so as to leave the obtruded egg enclosed between the two and proceeded to lay its own eggs on top."

Plumages and molts.—The definitive work on this subject was published by Dwight in 1900. Chapman's brief discussion (1911) generally agrees with Dwight's descriptions. Contrary to the usual situation in male fringillids, the male indigo has at least five recognizable plumages. The brownish mouse-gray natal down is replaced through a complete postnatal molt by the juvenal plumage. This plumage is characterized by being dark brown above, and by having a pale clove-brown tail faintly edged with greenish or glaucous blue. Underparts are dull white, narrowly streaked with sepia on the breast and sides. The bill and feet are pinkish buff; with age the former becomes dusky and the latter black.

A partial post-juvenal molt, usually commencing in August, involve body feathers, wing coverts, sometimes the tail, and sometimes fiv or six outer primaries. The resulting first winter plumage resemble the juvenal plumage except that the bird is not so brown above an the streaking of the underparts is less distinct. Generally brownis in this plumage, the lesser wing coverts, upper tail coverts, rump, an rectrices are often faintly washed with a bluish tinge. Dwigh examined a few specimens taken as late as October 2 in which a post juvenal molt of remiges and rectrices was not yet completed. H ascribes the occasional post-juvenal renewal of tail and primaries t "individual precocity of southern-bred birds."

The first nuptial plumage, acquired by a partial prenuptial molt i February and March, involves some body feathers, the tail, five o six outer primaries (sometimes all of them, but usually not thei coverts), most secondary coverts, tertiaries, and a variable number o secondaries. Thus, some individuals may undergo a complete pre nuptial molt at this age. "This moult produces a variety of birds *all with brown primary coverts*, some specimens being as bright blue a are adults. * * * A mixture of blue and brown results. The mos surprising renewal is that of the distal primaries *without their primar coverts*. * * * a new black tail edged with blue is assumed unless i has already been acquired at the post-juvenal moult. * * * Th bill becomes slaty. * * * It is natural to assume that birds whic acquired new wings and tail in the autumn are the worn duller spec mens we find in May, while the brighter less worn birds are thos which have acquired these feathers at a more recent date." In thi first nuptial plumage one can usually also see varying amounts o white on the abdomen. Birds in this plumage are known to establis territories and probably breed.

The adult winter plumage is acquired by a complete postnuptia molt occurring in August or even September. It is "strikingl different from first winter dress in the depth and richness of th brown and the marked blueness of the wings and tail. * * * Th wings and tail are black, edged with blue, * * * the primary covert are black, edged with blue which is apparently pale in the less pre cocious birds and deeper in those more vigorous."

The adult nuptial plumage is usually acquired by an incomplet molt in the spring, but there is evidence from captive birds that thi molt is sometimes a complete one (Johnston, MS.). In any even most of the body feathers, some wing coverts, and tertiaries ar replaced. "The blue of the head is always deeper than elsewher and the feathers of the lores and interramal space are black." Chap man (1911) states unequivocally that the rectrices are not include n this molt. There is no evidence to support the erroneous earlier belief that the adult male indigo plumage is acquired by wear of winter feathers without molt. Adult males undergoing this prenuptial molt have been collected between December and May.

The duration of the adult's postnuptial molt, though a complete one, is incompletely understood because some individuals migrating southward from the United States have completed the molt whereas others observed in late autumn in Jamaica and Guatemala were still molting.

Dwight suggests that "the plumages and moults of the female correspond to those of the male, the prenuptial moult, especially the first, apparently limited or sometimes suppressed." In both the juvenal and first winter plumages, females closely resemble males but have little or no bluish tint on the lesser secondary coverts and tail. "In first nuptial plumage (which is in many cases apparently the result of wear) a greenish tail and few greenish edged primaries are assumed together with a few whitish feathers below." The adult winter plumage is similar to the first winter plumage but the underparts are less obviously streaked. We question Dwight's assertion that "the adult nuptial [female] plumage is attained chiefly by wear."

Alexander Skutch wrote Mr. Bent as follows: "When they arrive in Central America in the fall, the male indigo buntings display at most scattered flecks of blue on their modest brown plumage. Gradually during the winter months they acquire the indigo-colored nuptial dress. As early as January 5 I have seen a male predominantly blue, but still flecked with brown. During February many lose all the brown contour feathers and seem to be in full breeding plumage. But other individuals, probably young males, are still merely speckled with blue when the northward movement begins in the latter part of March; and some are still noticeably flecked with brown as late as the end of April."

Again referring to Guatemala birds, Ned Dearborn (1907) points out that "By the middle of March adult males had about half of the head and breast blue, the back and underparts being still in fall plumage. Males taken in January had a few scattered blue feathers both above and below. * * * Iris dark brown."

G. M. Sutton (1935), studying Michigan birds, gives evidence suggesting that the young start molting into the juvenal plumage when about 16 days old and then undergo a postjuvenal molt in midsummer.

Food.—This wide-ranging species has adapted itself to a diversified diet. W. L. McAtee (1926) says, "Professor S. A. Forbes collected 18 specimens in an Illinois orchard infested by cankerworms and found that all but one of the birds had fed on the worms, which formed

59% of the total food of the birds. He found in these stomachs, also
remains of other caterpillars, leaf chafers, weevils, click beetles, and
bugs." McAtee also lists as food one of the locust borers (*Agrilu
egenus*), grasshoppers, plant lice, and cicadas. He says, further, tha
"the bird feeds to some extent also upon grain, as oats, and upon buds
but seems rarely to do notable damage." In another report W. E
Clyde Todd (1940) states: "According to E. H. Forbush, it consume
large quantities of objectionable insects, such as grasshoppers, cater
pillars, measuring worms, and beetles; it also eats seeds, many o
which are those of weeds. Examination of stomach contents of a few
birds collected in an orchard infested with cankerworms, revealed
that 78 percent of the total food consisted of this pest." In Alabama
(Imhof, 1962) and North Carolina (Pearson, Brimley and Brimley
1959) the species consumes a variety of weed seeds, berries, other
fruits, caterpillars, grasshoppers, beetles, and bugs.

A. W. Butler (1898), commenting on the abundance of the species
and its occurrence around farms and even small fruit gardens, says
"it is desirable that they receive the fullest protection, for at any
time they may prove of untold value in assisting to hold in check
some threated outbreak of injurious insects." As other foods he also
mentions raspberries and elderberries.

T. S. Roberts (1932) lists plant lice, flies, and mosquitoes as food
and H. C. Oberholser (1938) records curculios. O. W. Knight (1908
includes vegetable matter such as seeds of the goldenrod, aster
thistle, and other composites, as well as grass and weed seeds. E. H
Forbush (1929) says, "In late summer when the corn has 'tasseled
out,' the Indigo Buntings seem to find some food about the corn tops
and often may be found in cornfields." Witmer Stone (1937) ob
served a bird eating dandelion seeds on a lawn in early May. Mabel
Osgood Wright (1907) says, "The last of May, one of these Buntings
came to a low bush, outside my window, and after resting awhile
for the night before had been stormy, dropped to the closely cut
turf to feed upon the crumbs left where the hounds had been munching
their biscuits."

E. W. Jameson, Jr. (1942) watched migrating flocks from Aug
20 until Sept. 22, 1942 along the sand dunes and rocky shores o
northeast Lake Erie where turkey bluejoint (*Andropogon furcatus*)
grows abundantly. He says, "The birds perched just below the
racemes on the two-meter culms, bending them half way to the
ground, and then ate the grains on that culm or on an adjacent
shorter one. The grains had not yet fallen at this time, and I did not
see the buntings feeding on the ground or using any other plant for
food. At 9 A.M. on September 17, seventeen buntings were feeding
in this manner within an area of about one acre; some were perched in

nearby willows in company with Song Sparrows and Chipping Sparrows. However, I did not see these sparrows feeding on bluejoint. When I left Pint Abino on September 22, buntings were present in about the same numbers as during the previous few weeks, and bluejoint still formed the major part of their diet."

Frederick V. Hebard wrote Mr. Bent that on Oct. 12, 1945, he saw at least a hundred of these birds in southern Georgia feeding in a field well studded with crotolaria, and that about a year later, Oct. 16, 1946, a vastly larger number was there.

In southwest Georgia, Herbert L. Stoddard, Sr. (MS.) noted that "the abundance of insect life in the vetches and Crimson Clover, coupled with the mixed small grains grown for the game, provides an abundance of preferred food for the breeding Indigos and their young."

Other foods are mentioned under the section entitled *Winter*.

Behavior.—Among the conspicuous behavioral traits of male indigos is their strong territorial defense. This is manifest, first of all, by their persistent singing from tall perches as noted under *Voice*. Todd (1940) states that the male "seeks some prominent perch, such as an electric wire or a high branch of a dead tree—often the topmost one * * *." Then, too, males pursue intruding males with verve as noted by Van Hoose (1955). In this instance a male, probably breeding at San Marcos, Coahuila, Mexico, was seen chasing another male on May 5, 1954; the female followed the first of these males. Furthermore, territorial male indigos have been seen defending their territories by song and pursuit against male lazuli buntings (Wells, 1958). Thus, the species is characterized by having inter- and intra-specific territorial defense.

W. E. C. Todd (1940), while driving through a woodland, "saw a pair of indigo buntings in the middle of the road a short distance ahead, the male spreading his wings and dancing about the female. They paid no attention to the car, and, as we were too close to do more than slow down, the car passed right over them. When we looked back they were still in the same place and unhurt."

Hervey Brackbill wrote Mr. Bent as follows: "Once a male behaved protectively toward a very young fledgling that I had picked up just as it was about to be fed a caterpillar. While I was holding the young bird, the parent flew about wildly within as little as 3 feet of me, uttering a variety of notes—*chip*, *tit*, and *quit* were among them—sometimes in long strings. Then, after I had put the fledgling back on the ground, the male clearly tried to draw it away from me by flying close to it and then off in one direction or another. Finally its offspring did flutter after it into some undergrowth."

Witmer Stone (1937) mentions "a brilliant male found bathing in a rain water pool in the pine grove at the Point on July 2, 1930 * * * ."

T. D. Burleigh (1941) records an interesting observation in western North Carolina. He says: "Appearing with unfailing regularity in the fir and spruce woods (6,500 feet) in early July, this species is unique in that throughout the month only adult males are seen, singing each day from the upper branches of the larger trees. At no time have females or young of the year been noted above an altitude of 5,000 feet. Extreme dates for the occurrence of these wandering males at the top of the mountain are July 5 (1931) and July 31 (1934)."

Females, on the other hand, stay secretively low in the brush and usually can be seen only by the exertion of determined effort. W. Leon Dawson (1903) says, "she is a most prosaic creature, skulking about through thickets and briar patches or fussing with the children, * * * the soul of suspicion, and her protests are so emphatic that the inquisitor believes himself 'hot' when he may be a dozen yards away." F. M. Bailey (*in* Chapman, 1932) mentions the female twitching her tail nervously from side to side. Males do this also. In contrast, Bailey describes a male which, "day after day, used to fly to the lowest limb of a high tree and sing his way up from branch to branch, bursting into jubilant song when he reached the topmost bough."

Thomas Nuttall (1832) says, "They appear to show great timidity about their nest, and often readily forsake it when touched, or when an egg is abstracted. * * * They will not forsake their young however ready they may be to relinquish their eggs; and they have been known to feed their brood very faithful through the bars of a cage in which they were confined."

W. and E. Shackleton (1947) describe "anting" by three wild indigo buntings on four consecutive days. This is of special interest in connection with the failure of the painted bunting under study to "ant" (L. M. Whitaker, 1957).

Voice.—The indigo bunting is one of those species in which, according to Borror (1961), different individuals have songs of many different patterns with little or no overlapping between birds. In fact, he suggests: "Our recordings do not contain any instance of two different birds singing songs of the same pattern * * *." Nonetheless, in the words of Winsor M. Tyler (MS.), "this song has a character shared by no other. There is a whole-souled concentration about it. The bird, when he sings, sings just as well as he can, and I believe just as loud as he can—he gives himself up entirely to singing and throws the notes out for all he is worth. * * * [The song] often suggests a goldfinch, but a point of difference is that in the song of he indigo bird nearly every note is accented, giving it a definite haracter, and the *per-chic-o-ree* phrase, so common in the goldfinch's oice, is not introduced. A bright, far-carrying song, suggesting appiness, even exuberance."

J. H. Langille (1884) calls the song "A sort of hurried warble, uite fluent, and yet seeming to stick in the throat a little. * * * Its ones are musical, being loud at first, but growing faint at the last, s if the singer were exhausting his lungs * * *." This latter point s well taken.

Ralph Hoffmann (1923) considered the song as resembling the yllables, "*swee-swee-swee, swee-swee* (slightly lower), *sweet-sweet-weet, swee-swee* (slightly lower), *swee, swee, swee.*" Arthur A. Allen 1933) affords another interpretation, "*Sweet, sweet-where, where-here, ere—see it, see it.*"

Nuttall (1832) describes a shorter song "usually uttered at the ime that the female is engaged in the cares of incubation, or as the rood already appear, and when too great a display of music might ndanger the retiring security of his family. From a young or im-erfectly moulted male, on the summit of a weeping willow, I heard he following singularly lively syllables, *tle tle tle ta lee,* repeated at hort intervals."

Aretas A. Saunders (MS.) writes as follows: "The song of the in-igo bunting consists of a short series of high-pitched notes delivered vith a sibilant, wiry, and somewhat strident quality. The notes are rouped together, both by rhythm and pitch, in pairs, with occasional ingle notes taking the place of a pair, or more rarely three or four horter notes occupying the same amount of time as a pair, or a ingle note. Each pair or group of notes is the same pitch through-ut, but nearly always a different pitch from that of the pairs immedi-tely succeeding or preceding it. An occasional slurred note, or roup of two slurs occurs."

Saunders emphasizes the high-pitched rather brassy quality, with arsh *z*-like consonant sounds. The chief character, with which we gree, is the rhythm. Notes vary from 6 to 21, averaging about 11. ongs vary in length from 1½ to 6⅘ seconds, averaging about 2⅘. itch ranges between F_6 and $D^{\#}_7$. The pitch interval varies from ½ to 5 tones, but over half his 49 records are just 2½ tones. In a etter to Mr. Bent he says, "One remarkable song that can give an dea of the rhythm, was *zay-zay zreet zay-zay zeah zay-zay seeteeteet it-zit zeah.* The remarkable thing about this is that the rhythm is xactly that of a well-known human jingle, 'Bean porridge hot, bean orridge cold. Bean porridge in the pot, nine days old.' Occasional ongs have one or two notes standing out as louder than the rest of the song, but there is nothing definite or regular about the position of these loud notes."

He comments that songs are short during May and June and possibly the first half of July. The short songs vary from 6 to 13 notes, averaging 9½. In July normal songs are 14 notes, but sometimes prolonged to 19. "The season of song lasts from the bird's arrival in spring to about the middle of August, or somewhat later than this in certain years."

The pitch, or number of vibrations per second, as studied on one bird by Albert R. Brand (1938) ranged between 8875 and 3250. The approximate mean was 5700.

Mrs. Speirs writes that at South Bass Island, Ohio, on July 11, 1951, an indigo bunting commenced singing at 4:43 a.m. and sang 15 songs a minute for four consecutive minutes, plus one incomplete song. She counted 240 songs in 34 minutes including the foregoing. The bird sang throughout the entire day to a greater or less extent until 7:38 p.m.

T. S. Roberts (1932) watched a male that sang the "livelong day" with exact regularity from the top of a flagpole. The "song was just four seconds in length with intervals of six seconds. During June and July he began singing very regularly at 4:00 A.M. and continued with surprisingly little interruption until 8:00 P.M.—about the time the Whip-poor-will began calling. Allowing four hours for rest and feeding, there remained twelve hours for singing, which, at the rate of six songs a minute, gave 4,320 songs a day, and for the two months, disregarding late May and early August, 263,520 times that he tuned his little pipe in the sixty-one days!" He describes the usual song as "sweet-toned but rather characterless * * * delivered in a lazy indolent fashion. It has more snap early in the season, but, as the summer progresses, it becomes more and more colorless and uninteresting." Again, he says, "Occasionally the male indulges in a flight song, in which the notes are more rapid and gushing."

W. E. C. Todd (1940) states that the bird "is not at its best on arrival; but the longer it stays, the longer its song grows, and the hotter the weather, the oftener it sings. From a few bars in May and June, the song develops during July and August into a lengthy refrain with many variations." He considers the song "not particularly melodious."

Numerous observers (Chapman, 1932; Todd, 1940; Fitch, 1958) make special mention of the fact that characteristically indigo buntings continue to sing into August after most other birds have stopped. Indeed, some individuals continue to sing sporadically into September. Quantitative data of Leopold and Eynon (1961) indicate that as the breeding season progresses, the daily song period becomes markedly shortened. The light intensity values in foot-candles for the first daybreak song change from 0.014 in May to 0.022 in June to 0.74 in July. Mean light intensities in foot-candles for the evening song change from 0.51 in May to 1.00 in June to 8.92 in July.

Charles Vaurie (1946) kept records of an individual for 47 consecutive days, July 20 to September 4, 1944, on the lower slopes of a 1,000-foot hill in the foothills of the Blue Mountains in Berks County, Pa. The bird was in continuous full song with only normal intervals until August 3, then sang noticeably but with fairly long pauses until August 20. The bird ceased singing during a 6-day cold spell, then continued singing on a much reduced scale. On September 4 one particular bird out of more than two dozen was singing as at the start, in continuous full song. Vaurie considers that it "is sometimes tiresome to hear this bird sing because it can go on for hours without stopping, while the song grows harsher and harsher and begins to slur and break."

Val Nolan, Jr. (1958) watched a female near Bloomington, Ind. "This female, a bird with no blue visible in her plumage, sang during two brief intervals on May 29, 1956, a cloudy day with temperatures of 66° and 76° at the times of singing. At 0501 central standard time she mounted to the top of a 15-foot Virginia pine, the highest perch within 20 yards in scrubby old-field growth. During the next 2 or 3 minutes she sang 10 loud songs, described below, then moved a few yards and sang 10 more from a spot out of my sight. Between 0911 and 0921 she sang six times from the same general location, but again I could not see her. There was no repetition of the song during the rest of the day * * *; nor did I hear the song here on four other dawn-to-dark watches and many briefer ones between May 17 and June 8.

"The songs, which were wholly unmusical, consisted of five similar windy, vibrant notes uttered in staccato fashion and seeming to my inadequate ear to rise in pitch from first to last. I was reminded of the abrupt, choppy song of the dickcissel and could not have identified the singer's species by her voice.

"A male indigo bunting was on territory in the field, and though he sang and was in view repeatedly throughout May 29, I neither saw nor heard him while the female was singing. A female was found incubating on this territory some 2 weeks later."

In spite of this detailed account it seems possible to us that Nolan's "female" was in fact a male. The individual was not taken, and it could have been a brown first-year male or an older bird that had not molted fully.

G. M. Sutton (MS.) states that the flight song may last eight seconds or more and is given principally during the morning and evening twilights, although occasionally in full daylight. It possesses

a gushing effervescent quality reminiscent of the flight song of th
goldfinch. The bird gives the song from an altitude of 75 to 100 feet
fans the air rather laboriously or stiffly, and propels the body rathe
slowly in a straight line. Donald J. Nicholson wrote Taber about *
bird he watched July 3, 1953, at an altitude of about 5,000 feet in th
Great Smoky Mountains in North Carolina. "Flying from the top o
a 140-foot-high balsam, the bird rose some 30 feet in a huge arc, the
sank slowly down to the top of another balsam perhaps 700 feet dis
tant. During the flight's 25 to 30 seconds duration the bird poure
forth in midair a most pleasing but puzzling continuous babble o
music."

Alexander Wetmore (1909) mentions hearing the flight song "o
several occasions" in September 1908 in Kansas. According t
Howell, Laskey and Tanner (1954), "In May, Mrs. Hickey heard th
full song of" an indigo bunting flying overhead at night. Willian
Youngworth (1953) considers that there are two flight songs. Th
first is similar to the song when perched; the second suggests that o
a goldfinch.

In regions where this species is a summer resident it is, perhaps
difficult to distinguish whether a singing bird is establishing a territory, or is merely migrating through. Frederick V. Hebard wrot
Mr. Bent from southeastern Georgia where the species does not bree
that the birds "do not sing either in spring or fall migration as far a
I can tell".

The alarm note is, according to E. H. Forbush (1929), "a shar
chip, resembling the sound made by striking two pebbles together
also a *chuck*." W. M. Taylor informs us that he has noted a similarit
between the call note of this bird and that of the myrtle warbler
Aretas Saunders writes the "call-note of this bird is a short *tsick* resembling call-notes of warblers. A young bird, just out of the nes
and giving the hunger call, uttered a short *psink* pitched on 'G.' "

The distinctive call note will frequently reveal the presence of a bird
in dense fields especially during migration. Call notes are often heard
at night in the fall as they migrate overhead (Lowery, 1955).

Enemies.—Richard S. Phillips (1951) says, "On July 3, 1950, I saw
a House Wren (*Troglodytes aëdon*) fly from nest No. 11. When I got
to the nest, I found the contents of the one bunting egg beginning to
seep from a bill hole in the shell."

Arthur A. Allen (1933) refers to "mites." Mrs. Harold R. Peaseley
wrote Mr. Bent of a lazuli bunting which drove away an indigo
bunting. W. E. C. Todd (1940) states that the species "is frequently
killed * * * by cars on the roads." Dale A. Zimmerman (1954)
mentions four birds found dead on highways. F. M. Bennett (1909)
describes, as elaborated on under *Migration*, the effects of a thunder-

storm off the Florida Keys. Thomas Barbour (1923) says that in Cuba, "A very considerable number are often on sale in the bird stores, and they are great favorites as cage-birds and apparently thrive."

William Brewster (1906) includes the indigo bunting among the species "whose local decrease is probably due chiefly to persecution by the House Sparrows." Some birds, he says, ceased breeding "within ten years from the first appearance of the House Sparrows. The Indigo-birds and Least Flycatchers disappeared more slowly, but in the end almost as completely." An additional factor of importance evidently unassessed by Brewster was the change in habitat and flora resulting from the industrial and residential growth of the region. In any event, with the house sparrow becoming more and more restricted at the present time to closely built-up sections, in New England at least, the importance of that species as an enemy appears to be comparatively small.

The proximity of the nest of this species to the ground suggests that it may be especially vulnerable to snakes and other wandering marauders. In fact, H. Lewis Batts, Jr. (1958), gives this vivid account: "On June 18, 1949, a cat pounced upon a nest containing three young Indigo Buntings and one pipped Cowbird egg, ate one young, and carried away the others * * *."

It is somewhat difficult to assess completely the effects of weather on this species, but Johnston (MS.) and Bill Colson found two nests in north central Florida, each containing two cold wet eggs, probably the result of recent heavy rains. Additional mortality factors are suggested by Phillips (1951): young killed by direct sunlight on the nest and nest abandonment after having been found by humans. Tall TV towers in recent years have accounted for deaths of many migrating birds. For example, at a tower in Leon County, Fla., between 1955 and 1961, Stoddard (1962) counted 345 indigo buntings killed, most of these in the autumn. TV towers, tall buildings, and airport ceilometers throughout the eastern United States caused the deaths of 450 indigo buntings between October 5–8, 1954 (Johnston and Haines, 1957).

Field marks.—The indigo bunting approximates the chipping sparrow in size, being noticeably smaller than both song and house sparrows. The adult male in breeding plumage is the only small North American finch that appears blue all over. It could be confused with the male blue grosbeak, but the latter is a much larger bird, has brown wing-bars, and a noticeably heavier bill. Under certain light conditions, indigos may appear to be black or blue-green. Males in their first nuptial plumage may not be entirely blue; they may retain varying amounts of brown body feathers among the bluish ones and have white abdomens. The adult female, in the language of R. T. Peterson (1947), is *"the only small brown Finch devoid of obvious stripings, wingbars, or other distinctive marks."* Emphasis should be placed upon the word *"obvious"* because females are frequently finely streaked. In the fall and winter adult males are somewhat brownish but show varying amounts of blue on the body, wings, or tail. Fall immatures of both sexes closely resemble adult females, except that they are more streaked below. Immatures, like adult females, may be confused with female or immature painted buntings, but under good light conditions the latter species is obviously pale yellow-green, not brownish. Especially where their ranges overlap, female indigos could be quite difficult to distinguish from female lazuli buntings, though the latter have whitish wing-bars.

Migration.—Average dates and earliest dates of spring arrival are mentioned by Cooke (1911) for 93 localties. Migrants are, apparently, frequently carried north by major storms far in advance of their normal migration dates. Thus, Taber saw one on his lawn in Ipswich, Mass., on Apr. 19, 1954. Earle R. Greene (1946) considers the species an uncommon spring migrant along the Florida Keys; he records only seven birds. F. M. Bennett (1909), however, states that during the night of Apr. 14, 1909, "the region of the Florida Keys was the scene of a violent thunderstorm of several hours' duration, with lightning, heavy rain and high winds, blowing in squalls from the southwest. The morning brought fine weather * * *." Key West was full of land birds of several species. This species was present in vast numbers. On April 20 the indigo bunting ranked second in numbers on Loggerhead Key on the Dry Tortuges. There were still hundreds of males present, but only three females. None of the birds sang. At least two dozen had lost all their tail feathers and could fly only short distances like young birds.

Speaking of the Gulf Coast region of Mississippi, T. D. Burleigh (1944) says, "Numerous small flocks are seen in the spring and in the fall both on the mainland and on the islands. * * * Although single birds are observed from time to time, these buntings are most often seen in flocks numbering from five to twelve individuals."

In southwest Georgia, Herbert L. Stoddard, Sr. (MS.) reports that "they appear in full plumage and song early in April (Sherwood, April 6, 1937, April 8, 1947, April 9, 1943, April 11, 1948, April 13, 1944, April 16, 1934, and 1936) and become abundant by the latter part of the month. Like the Blue Grosbeak, they first flock in the vicinity of ripening small grains, especially oats, which are widely grown in the region." Farther north, in Ohio, Trautman (1940) states that at the peak of the spring migration "30 to 90 birds could be seen daily, and it was obvious that there were several hundred

resent." The peak of migration generally began on May 18 and
continued until approximately May 28.

In spite of the arguments by some investigators, it now appears
that migrant birds utilize trans-Gulf and circum-Gulf routes to
and from the United States. As early as 1911 Cooke suspected
different spring migration routes by stating "that the early migrants
do not reach Louisiana by a land journey, from either the east or
the west, but by a direct flight across the Gulf of Mexico." There
is at least one record (Bullis, 1954) of indigo buntings seen migrating
over the Gulf of Mexico, Apr. 18, 1952, and the abundant spring
records from Mexico strongly indicate some northward migration
around the Gulf. Stevenson (1957), in his study, "The relative
magnitude of the trans-Gulf and circum-Gulf spring migrations,"
believes that most of the indigos use the trans-Gulf route. A trench-
ant examination of spring migration in a single season by Bagg
(1955) indicates that birds made a through flight from Yucatan to
Maine in 36 hours. He says: "When one considers all aspects of
the situation, particularly including the April 17 Florida evidence of
heavy trans-Gulf migration of Indigo Buntings, one is led toward the
conclusion that the April 17–18, 1954, buntings in the northeastern
coastal areas were trans-Gulf migrants which flew nonstop in the
strong maritime tropical airflow." As yet undiscovered is the northward route taken by birds wintering in Jamaica and other portions of
the eastern Caribbean area, but it is probably via peninsular Florida.

Fall migration commences in late August and may continue through
early November. As compared with spring migration, fall migration
entails more flocking and larger flocks. At Gainesville, Fla., in the
autumn of 1963, indigos (and a few painted buntings) were attracted
to a small but dense field of Johnson grass, indigo, sorghum, and
beggar's lice. Between October 18 and November 8, 72 indigos
were netted and banded. They all appeared to be birds of the year,
and males out-numbered females about 3 to 1. During this time
there were only four repeats, indicating a rapid turn-over of buntings
utilizing this field. For the Mobile Bay area of Alabama, Imhof
(1962) records a maximum daily spring count of 130 indigos, but a
maximum fall count of 300.

Trautman (1940) says: "The southward migration began early
for a sparrow and was in progress while some resident birds still had
young in the nest or were in family groups. Transient flocks were
observed flying overhead during early mornings of late August, and
by early September migration had become pronounced. The peak
took place between September 10 and 27, and then the species was
as numerous as it was in spring, but was less conspicuous. In late
summer the males were quiet, and both adults and young were rather

secretive. * * * In this southward movement the species was found in the same brushy cover which it inhabited in spring and summer and was likewise found wherever herbaceous plants grew tall and abundant and the weed seed crop was large."

Lynds Jones (1910), speaking of the Cedar Point region in Ohio, says, "This is one of the species which helps form the great wave of migration in spring. I have not noticed any distinct fall movement of birds from farther north." However, E. W. Jameson, Jr. (1942) says that along the northeast shore of Lake Erie flocks of from 5 to 18 or 20 adult and immature birds were seen daily from Aug. 20 until Sept. 22, 1942.

Herbert L. Stoddard, Sr., (MS.) writing about southwest Georgia states: "After the breeding season is over and the young birds are 'on their own,' the 'Indigos' linger with us in numbers throughout October. At this season they are flocking with other finches, largely in the vicinity of 'dove fields' of Shallu, or around the occasional sorghum patch in the farming sections."

R. W. William, Jr. (1906) says that during the latter part of August he found the species "very abundant in the sweet gums and oaks scattered here and there" in Leon County, Fla. The birds were extremely wary and remained in the topmost branches of the largest trees.

J. J. Audubon (1841) says that, "Towards fall, the young congregate into loose flocks or parties of eight or ten individuals, and proceed southward. * * * They are fond of basking and rolling themselves in the roads, from which they gather small particles of sand or gravel."

Eugene P. Odum (1960) and his coworkers (Odum, Connell, and Stoddard, 1961) have made interesting studies of the migrating birds killed at a TV tower in northern Florida. Between September 23 and October 9, 55 indigos were obtained; these dead birds were ground up and their body fats extracted chemically. Total fat averaged about 2 grams per bird (13.45 percent of body weight). From these and other data, these investigators estimated flight distances from 100 to 1,820 killometers. They concluded: "According to our estimates only about six individuals out of a sample of 55 birds extracted would have been able to continue across the Gulf. Most of the individuals would have had to follow the coast or stop for extensive refueling, since the average fat index for the whole group was only about 13 percent." It now appears from the unpublished work of Johnston that a significant portion of the population migrates southward through peninsular Florida.

Winter.—Indigos spend the winter rarely in the southeastern United States but more commonly in south Florida. There are occasional winter records for the District of Columbia (Stewart and

Robbins, 1958), North Carolina (Pearson, Brimley, and Brimley, 1959), Alabama (Imhof, 1962), Mississippi (Burleigh, 1944), Louisiana (Lowery, 1955), and northern Florida (Sprunt, 1954). For the West Indies, Bond (1961) mentions specifically winter records between October 10 and May 8 on the Bahama Islands, Cuba, Isle of Pines, Swan Island, Jamaica, and Puerto Rico. He suggests, however, that the species winters "chiefly in Central America." On Cuba it is regarded as "another bird of spring and autumn passage" (Barbour, 1923). On several occasions indigos have been noted in California in winter (Williams, 1961; Wilbur, 1963).

The bulk of the indigo population appears to winter "from Jalisco [Mexico], Guanajuato, San Luis Potosi to central Panama, casually to Venezuela" (Friedmann, Griscom, and Moore, 1957). The southernmost record for the species appears to be in Columbia where de Schauensee (1964) states that it is casual, being recorded in northern Chocó and Magdalena in January and February.

For the Monserrate area of Chiapas, Mexico, Edwards and Lea (1955) state: "In the mesquite-grown fields we often encountered flocks of this species near, or mixed with, small flocks of *Guiraca caerulea*, from March 26 to April 1." Loetscher (1955) describes indigos in Veracruz as being of regular but local and uncommon occurrence during the winter along the coastal plain. From sea level up to about 4,000 feet it is locally common during migration.

Accounts of the species in Guatemala are many. In that country it is common in small flocks especially in brushy meadows, open country, forest edge, and second growth. Tashian (1953) notes that indigos were "especially abundant at Bellavista where they were usually observed in large mixed flocks of which Lesser Goldfinches formed the nucleus." Baepler (1962) took specimens at 7,600 feet elevation in scrub oak and in an oak thicket at 6,900 feet. Land (1962, 1963) records them up to 6,000 feet, and states that "three specimens taken in late November were molting. Males taken up to February 15 were at least partly in winter plumage." Ned Dearborn (1907) states that Guatemalan birds were very common all winter, at least up to 4,000 feet. He says that "At Finca Chapulco, near Los Amates, these birds were daily feeding on the ground in the floor yard. Often they were found in company with *Sporophila* among the weeds that flourish along the railroad."

J. Van Tyne (1932) mentions this species as wintering at Uaxactun in 1931 "in large flocks in the open grassy clearing. Flocks of scores were constantly to be seen feeding on grass seed. They came especially to the mule corral to pick up waste grain * * *." He banded 99 birds and recorded 120 repeats in about a month. The birds were quite tame and banding operations indicated that they were "extremely sedentary," even though the "species was common all over the clearing of hundreds of acres. On the morning of April 27th the species * * * had disappeared. A circuit of the clearing revealed no Indigo Buntings. I thought they had left for the North, but on the 28th I saw again small flocks and noted bands on the legs of some birds. However, they were very restive, wandering about and not coming to the trap. On April 30th one was retaken in the trap and other banded birds were seen. The main flock probably left for the North that night, for we saw none thereafter, though two unbanded females were taken later (May 4th and 13th) in nets in the forest." He lists birds of both sexes banded in 1931 and retrapped there in 1932.

D. R. Dickey and A. J. van Rossem (1938) describe the bird in El Salvador as a "common fall and spring migrant and winter visitant to grasslands and fields throughout the Arid Lower and Arid Upper Tropical zones. The extreme dates of arrival and departure were October 26 and April 30." They say, "good-sized flocks were found in suitable territory everywhere below 3,500 feet. Although the species was less numerous in midwinter than during migrations, still it was fairly common in grasslands, fields and pastures, and at times even invaded the more open second-growth woodland. * * * a few even penetrated the coffee groves, an environment in which they seemed strangely out of place."

Alexander F. Skutch wrote Mr. Bent as follows: "The indigo bunting arrives in Central America during the latter half of October and soon spreads over the whole length of the region, as far south as western Panama. Although on October 20, 1933, I met a migrating bunting as high as 8,500 feet in the Guatemalan mountains, I found none passing the winter in districts so high and cold. The winter range extends from the lowlands of both coasts up to possibly 7,000 feet above sea level. Indigo buntings are especially numerous between about 3,000 and 5,000 feet in the drier, deforested regions of the highlands and Pacific slope of Guatemala. At the end of October 1933 I found them in large, loose flocks in the weedy fields about Panajachel beside Lake Atitlan, 5,000 feet above sea level; here at this season they were far more abundant than any other finch, resident or migratory. In December 1934 and January 1935 they were common in the coffee-producing zone of the Pacific slope between Colomba and Finca 'Moca,' at about 3,000 feet above sea level. * * *

"Although so gregarious in districts where there are extensive grassy or weedy fields, amid the heavy vegetation of the humid lowlands indigo buntings are more solitary; in clearings amid the rain forests I have generally met them singly or a few—rarely as many as half a dozen—together, in bushy pastures, old grainfields rapidly being

overgrown with tall weeds and shrubs, and about the edges of the
tangled thickets that cover lands which have enjoyed freedom from
man's disturbance for a longer period. * * *

"On my farm, in the Basin of El General in southern Costa Rica,
I seldom meet indigo buntings. But in the afternoon of April 11, 1945,
a bunting clad in brown, without much doubt a female, came repeatedly to eat bananas at the feeding shelf in a guava tree beside my
house—the only representative of the species I ever saw there. * * *
After 6 days' attendance at the feeding shelf she left, probably during
the night of April 16; and it is now nearly 3 years since I have seen
one of her kind at my feeding-station. Incidentally, she provided
my latest spring record of the occurrence of the indigo bunting in
Costa Rica. * * *

"Most of the indigo buntings leave Central America during the first
fortnight of April, and few are seen after the middle of the month."

For Costa Rica, as a whole, Slud (1964) writes:

During migration it occurs along both slopes, much more commonly the Pacific
side and the central plateau, occasionally on the Caribbean side. It is met
in largest numbers in the southwest, mostly in the upper tropical belt, and with
fair regularity in the dry-forested lowlands in the northwest. The bird prefers
"field" habitats, that is, open-country scrub, grassy and bushy pastures, abandoned agricultural lands, and low thickety edges. Usually it occurs in small
flocks, close to or on the ground, that wander about perhaps within a circum-
scribed area or probably over longer distances. On the Caribbean side during the
winter, at any rate, a small group may briefly reappear a few times in an area
with suitable habitat, even in heavily forested regions * * *. The birds are
mostly female-plumaged, usually with a blue individual or two or several with a
touch of blue.

L. Griscom (1932) says, "Mr. Anthony writes that Indigo Buntings
were especially noticeable at Sacapulas [Guatemala] in January and
February, where they shared with *P. ciris* the honor of being the most
abundant species, hundreds being flushed from the fields of dry weeds
along the Rio Negro. In common with most, if not all, of the migrants
from the United States these birds become excessively fat, just before
they depart for the north."

In British Honduras, Russell (1964) notes that the indigos first
arrive in mid-September and by late October are common. They
frequent grassy areas, low huamil, and brushy plantation edges in
flocks of 10 to 30. Many transients were seen at Half Moon Cay,
April 16–24, and most have left the country by April 25. Two
individuals banded in March at Middlesex by Nickell were recaptured
the next year at the same locality.

After many years of ornithological experience in Panama, Dr.
Alexander Wetmore writes Johnston of its occurrence there: "In its
fall migration the Indigo Bunting comes regularly to western Panama,

and a few continue through the isthmus to Darien and northwestern Colombia. As they seek the same type of cover in dense growths of weeds and grass in old fields and marshy spots that they frequent in late summer and early fall in the north, they are seen infrequently and remain little known. Males molt into the bright color of the breeding season in February and early March, and then change completely. Toward the end of March and in early April they appear in the open at the borders of thickets, and in cultivated areas in the fruit trees and shrubbery near houses. Here they often remain in the open, rather than fly to cover when startled. It is at this season that most of the rather few records of occurrence are made. Females, however, continue their skulking habits until they leave for the north."

From Montego Bay, Jamaica, Mrs. Audrey Downer writes Johnston: "Indigo Buntings wintering in Jamaica start arriving early in November. They are usually males in various stages of the blue plumage. In January the females and juvenals begin to arrive, and soon after this singing begins. Indigo Buntings have been seen in widely scattered areas throughout Jamaica, but are only known to congregate in flocks of from 50 to several hundred in two locations in the Montego Bay area at the western end of the island. The flocks build up gradually during the first three months of the year, reaching their peak from mid-March to mid-April, when the whole area pulsates with their song throughout the day. They then depart for their northern breeding grounds, and are all gone by the first week in May. During their stay in their winter quarters some birds complete their molt, while others undergo only a partial molt. The males outnumber the females four to one.

"The habitat favoured is a wooded area with low scrub ground cover. When frightened they dive for these low bushes. After a few minutes they emerge and fly into the trees to survey the situation before resuming feeding. They come readily to bird feeders baited with 'Budgerigar seed,' crushed corn, etc. They eat only the kernel, discarding the husk. They have also been observed feeding on dried logwood seeds, various weed seeds, and an occasional flying insect. Although they roost in naseberry, tamarind, and citrus trees, they do not appear to eat the fruit.

"In 1964 a banding program was started and 177 Indigo Buntings were banded in Jamaica. No recoveries have so far been reported."

Hybrids.—In the western part of its range the indigo bunting may hybridize with the lazuli bunting (*Passerina amoena*). Sibley and Short (1959) summarize their investigations by stating: "The Indigo Bunting (*Passerina cyanea*) and Lazuli Bunting (*P. amoena*) have formed a secondary contact in the plains as a result of climatic changes and men's activities, which have provided suitable habitat in a formerly unsuitable area. Over a broad area of contact and overlap specimens show that hybridization and backcrossing are occurring, and that both parental forms are present with the hybrids at some localities * * *. Measurements and weights of the specimens show that clear size differences exist between the parental forms, and that color pattern is correlated with weights and measurements in the hybrids."

On June 26, 1929, near Warren in Marshall County, Minn., W. J. Breckenridge collected a hybrid that was singing from the top branches of a dead elm. The song was identical with that of the indigo bunting. A nest in low bushes below the singing-tree was occupied by a typical female indigo bunting. William Youngworth (1932) also collected a male hybrid, on June 1, 1932, near the Niobrara River in Cherry County, Nebr. He says, "The Indigo Bunting is a fairly common bird in this region, and here also we found several Lazuli Buntings settled for the summer." The song was typical of the indigo bunting. Mrs. Harold R. Peaseley heard what she thought was the song of an indigo bunting at about noon on July 25, 1935, near Center Chapel, some 5 miles west of Indianola, Warren County, Iowa. The bird, in the top branches of a dead tree, proved to be a male lazuli bunting. She studied the bird for an hour and says, "Its behavior seemed to indicate a territory holding bird. It had three definite singing perches in the immediate vicinity of this tree and one across a small field in an Osage orange hedge. It drove a male indigo bunting out of its territory, and in so doing, the two birds came to rest for several minutes on a wire fence directly in front of us." She relocated the bird on July 27, but a thorough search failed to reveal satisfactorily the female.

Philip V. Wells (1958) watched two pairs along Leeds Creek at about 5,000 feet elevation in the Pine Valley Mountains in southwestern Utah between June 6 and Aug. 1, 1957. Vegetation was a closed stand of evergreen chaparral. Dwarf conifers formed a sparse overstory; along Leeds Creek, birch and willow were entwined with wild grape. Edge effects were provided by the stream, by a dirt road, and by some large clearings bordered by groves of deciduous oak. The two pairs of indigo buntings were spaced about half a mile apart along the road, in both cases near clearings. The favorite singing perches were the relatively tall birches along the creek, overlooking the cleared areas, but the birds also sang from junipers and foraged in all plant communities of the area.

During June one of the male indigo buntings was seen fighting with a male lazuli bunting. The two birds would take up singing perches on trees about 100 feet apart and sing back and forth until one took off in vigorous pursuit of the other. After about June 20, the lazuli buntings disappeared from the indigo bunting areas, although still sparingly present nearby.

Don Bleitz (1958), reporting on the indigo bunting breeding in Los Angeles County, Calif., found a male indigo mated with a female lazuli. The nest of this pair contained two bunting eggs and a cowbird egg. The eggs later proved to be sterile.

Why the indigo and painted buntings (*P. ciris*) do not hybridize is something of a mystery. In certain parts of their breeding ranges in the southeastern United States, as Norris (1963) points out, the two species may be found in the same general area. Parmelee (1959) sheds some light on this situation in southern Oklahoma: "The Indigo Bunting * * * was both scarce and local, and we found no situation where it and *ciris* bred side by side, although conceivably they do just that in parts of Marshall County. * * * there are significant differences in the breeding behavior of the two species."

DISTRIBUTION

Range.—Southern Canada (east of the Great Plains) to Panama, Jamaica, Cuba, and the Bahamas.

Breeding range.—The indigo bunting breeds from southwestern South Dakota (Black Hills), southern Manitoba (Portage la Prairie, Hillside Beach), northern Minnesota (Lake of the Woods and Cook counties), western and southern Ontario (Fort William, North Bay), southern Quebec (Blue Sea Lake, Montreal, Hatley), southern Maine (Avon and Washington Counties), and southern New Brunswick (St. John) south to western Kansas (Finney County), western Oklahoma (Cheyenne), south central and southeastern Texas (West Frio Canyon, Galveston), southern Louisiana (Thibodaux), southern Alabama (Fairhope), and northern Florida (Tallahassee, Gainesville); sporadically in Colorado (Morrison), southwestern Utah (Pine Valley Mountains), Arizona (Oak Creek Canyon), and California (Los Angeles County, mated with Lazuli Bunting).*

Winter range.—Winters from Jalisco (Atoyac), Guanajuato, San Luis Potosí (Xilitla), Swan Island, Cuba, the Bahamas, and Jamaica south throughout southern Mexico and Central America to central Panama; casually south to Curaçao and northern Venezuela (Sierra de Perijá); and north to northwestern California (Ferndale), Texas, Missouri, Louisiana, Mississippi, Florida, North Carolina, Virginia, District of Columbia, New Jersey, New York, and Massachusetts.

Casual records.—Casual west to Oregon (Fort Klamath), California (Yolo County, Rialto, Carmel), and Baja California (Agua Caliente) north to Alberta (Lake la Nonne), southern Saskatchewan (Estevan),

*Hybridizes extensively with the Lazuli Bunting, *Passerina amoena*, where their ranges overlap in the Great Plains area.

central Ontario (New Liskeard), central Quebec (Mille Vaches), and Newfoundland (Placentia Bay).

Accidental in Iceland.

Migration.—Early dates of spring arrival are: Bahamas—Nassau, March 9. Florida—Miami, March 12; Pensacola, March 20. Alabama—Dauphin Island, March 26; Tuscaloosa, April 4. Georgia—Grady County, March 27; Atlanta, April 5. South Carolina—March 18 (median of 10 years at Charleston, April 4). North Carolina—Tryon, April 11; Raleigh, April 19 (average of 27 years, May 2). Virginia—Lexington, April 18. West Virginia—Morgantown, April 4; Wheeling, April 6. District of Columbia—April 18. Maryland—Prince Georges County, March 13 (median of 22 years, April 30); Gibson Island, March 22. Pennsylvania—Pittsburgh, April 6; State College, April 27. New Jersey—Summit, April 4; Pequannock, April 17. New York—Orient, April 10; Manhattan (Central Park), April 18; Cayuga and Oneida Lake basins, April 28 (median of 24 years, May 10). Connecticut—Hartford, April 19. Rhode Island—Jamestown, April 16. Massachusetts—Martha's Vineyard, March 12 (median of 20 years, April 25). Vermont—Vergennes, April 26; Burlington, May 3. New Hampshire—Concord, April 10; New Hampton, May 10 (median of 21 years, May 19). Maine—Falmouth, April 21. Quebec—Quebec City, April 30; Montreal, May 11 (median of 20 years for Province of Quebec, May 21). New Brunswick—Grand Manan, April 18. Nova Scotia—Wolfville, April 11; Scotsburn and Bon Portage, April 15. Newfoundland—La Poile, April 15; Calvert, April 17. Louisiana—Bains, March 20; New Orleans, March 26. Mississippi—Gulfport, March 16; Rosedale, April 6. Arkansas—El Dorado, March 21; Texarkana, April 3. Tennessee—Knox County, April 10. Kentucky—Murray, April 12. Missouri—St. Louis, April 10. Illinois—Anna, April 12; Chicago, May 1 (average of 15 years, May 9). Indiana—Bloomington, April 13. Ohio—Youngstown, April 12; Columbus, April 24 (median of 40 years, May 2). Michigan—Imlay City, April 28; Battle Creek, May 3 (median of 30 years, May 13). Ontario—Painecourt, April 23. Iowa—Lansing, April 22; Sioux City, May 2 (median of 38 years, May 15). Wisconsin—Wausau, April 15. Minnesota—Sherburn, April 4; Redwing, April 24 (average of 22 years for southern Minnesota, May 9). Texas—Sinton, March 18. Oklahoma—Tulsa and Okmulgee, March 26; Oklahoma City, April 14. Kansas—Kansas City, April 18 (median of 20 years for northeastern Kansas, May 6). Nebraska—Valentine, April 2; Nebraska City, April 25. South Dakota—Yankton, March 23 and April 29. North Dakota—Fargo, May 15. Manitoba—Wawanesa, May 13. Saskatchewan—McLean,

March 30; Wiseton, April 1. New Mexico—Clayton, May 14. Colorado—near Denver, May 7.

Late dates of spring departure are: Panama—Lerida, May 10. El Salvador—Chilata, April 30. Haiti—Caracol, April 26. Chiapas—near Comitan, April 13. Campeche—Ichek, April 21. Guerrero—April 10. Veracruz—May15. Florida—Sarasota, May 19; Daytona Beach and Fort Pierce, May 11. Alabama—Dauphin Island, May 25. Georgia—Savannah, May 21. Mississippi—Deer Island, May 25. Illinois—Chicago, June 1 (average of 15 years, May 27). Ohio—Buckeye Lake, median, June 2. Louisiana—Shreveport, May 19. Texas—Houston, May 16. New Mexico—Clayton, May 25.

Early dates of fall arrival are: Texas—Cove, September 13. Ohio—Buckeye Lake, median, August 26. Illinois—Chicago, August 29. New Jersey—Island Beach, September 12 (median of 6 years, September 16). Maryland—Ocean City, September 8 (median of 9 years, September 18). Guanajuato—Irapuato, October 8. Guerrero—October 1. Chiapas—Socoltenango, September 3. El Salvador—Rio Goascorán, October 26.

Late dates of fall departure are: Alberta—Veteran, August 29. Montana—Three Forks, September 23. North Dakota—Cass County, September 19 (average, September 11). South Dakota—Columbia, October 9. Nebraska—western Saline County, October 23. Kansas—Lake Quivira, Johnson County, October 11. Oklahoma—Edmond, November 13. Texas—Sinton, November 25 (median of 5 years, November 24). Minnesota—Faribault, October 15; Minneapolis and Lanesboro, October 4 (average of 8 years for southern Minnesota, September 25). Wisconsin—Madison, October 15. Iowa—Sioux City, October 8. Ontario—Point Pelee, October 14; Galt, October 10. Michigan—Battle Creek, October 5 (median of 12 years, September 24). Ohio—Columbus and Cleveland, October 16 (average for central Ohio, October 1). Indiana—Richmond, October 17. Illinois—Chicago, October 24 (average of 7 years, October 8). Missouri—St. Louis, November 2. Kentucky—Bowling Green, October 16. Tennessee—Knox County, October 25. Arkansas—Winslow, October 15. Mississippi—Gulfport, December 13 and November 7. Louisiana—New Orleans, November 2. Nova Scotia—Brier Island, October 22. Quebec—St. Bruno, September 27 (median of 15 years for Province of Quebec, September 10). Maine—South Portland, October 28. New Hampshire—New Hampton, October 9 (median of 21 years, September 25). Vermont—Putney, October 3. Massachusetts—Martha's Vineyard, October 19 (median of 12 years, September 18). Rhode Island—Providence, October 4. Connecticut—Portland, October 20. New York—Astoria, December 7;

Baldwin, November 13; Cayuga and Oneida Lake basins, November 6 (median of 13 years, October 9). New Jersey—Island Beach, October 22. Pennsylvania—State College and Renova, October 19. Maryland—Frederick County, November 1, Prince Georges County, October 17 (median of 16 years, October 8). District of Columbia—October 16. West Viginia—Bluefield, October 14. Virginia—Blacksburg, October 18. North Carolina—Raleigh, October 19 (average of 8 years, October 7). South Carolina—November 10 (median of 6 years at Charleston, October 20). Georgia—Atlanta, November 3; Grady County, October 31. Alabama—Birmingham, November 11; Dauphin Island, November 8. Florida—northern Florida, November 8; southern peninsula, November 19.

Egg dates.—Illinois: 38 records, May 25 to August 10; 20 records, May 29 to June 17.

Maine: 2 records, June 10 to June 12.

Maryland: 99 records, May 24 to August 16; 50 records, June 3 to June 23.

Massachusetts: 30 records, June 1 to June 28; 15 records, June 10 to June 17.

Michigan: 9 records for southeastern Michigan, May 27 to August 19; 5 records, June 14 to June 30. Fourteen second-brood records for northern Michigan (Charlevoix County), July 2 to August 9; 7 records, July 2 to July 11.

New York: 20 records, May 28 to July 15; 10 records, June 5 to June 23.

Ontario: 25 records, May 27 to July 31; 13 records, June 11 to June 21.

Rhode Island: 9 records, May 29 to June 17.

Tennessee: 3 records, June 2 to June 22.

West Virginia: 20 records, May 12 to June 12; 10 records, May 16 to June 1.

PASSERINA AMOENA (Say)

Lazuli Bunting

FRONTISPIECE; PLATE 10

Contributed by MARY MARILLA ERICKSON

HABITS

The lazuli bunting is a jewellike species closely related to the eastern indigo bunting, which it replaces in the west and which it resembles in behavior. During the breeding season, it is widely distributed over all the region west of the prairie States from the western parts of the Dakotas to New Mexico and from southern British Columbia south to

Lower California. It is mostly a bird of the Upper Sonoran Life Zone but may range into the Lower Sonoran and Transition Zones. It has been found from near sea level on the coast and at Furnace Creek in Death Valley to elevations of 10,000 feet in the Sierras and 7,000 to 8,000 feet in the Rocky Mountains of Colorado. Tolerant of wide ranges of humidity and temperature, it breeds in the humid coast belt and the desert mountains of the Great Basin region, as well as in many intermediate localities. In the more arid regions it is commonly restricted to the brushy cover around springs or streams or to cultivated or irrigated areas. Grinnell and Miller (1944) describe its habitat as follows:

In breeding season, clumps of bushes, broken chaparral, weed thickets and other low vegetation on hillsides or in and about water courses, but not usually over water or damp ground. * * * Diversity of plant growth and discontinuity of masses of it seem important as well as the presence of a low dense tangle used normally for nesting. Foraging takes place in this cover, or in tall grass, but song posts are to varying degrees above it—even in the tips of tall trees if these are present.

In winter the lazuli bunting is found in Mexico as far south as Cape St. Lucas on the Pacific coast and the Valley of Mexico in the interior. It is absent from the Atlantic coast of Mexico. It occurs in Lower California in fair numbers as a spring and fall migrant, is present in the summer in the northwest costal district where it probably breeds, and in winter in the Cape region. Here as elsewhere it frequents the willow association along ravines in the vicinity of seepages.

In California this species occurs as a migrant in all sections of the State and breeds throughout the State except on the coastal islands and the Lower Sonoran deserts of the southeast. It breeds from sea level in the coastal regions to at least 7,500 feet in the Warner Mountains and 8,000 feet on Mount Pinos. After breeding it may be found at even higher elevations—9,000 feet at Warren Fork of Leevining Creek in Yosemite National Park, and at 10,000 feet, the highest record for the species, in Coffee Mill Meadow of Kings Canyon National Park where J. S. Dixon (1943) saw a male in a chinquapin thicket in the summer of 1941.

In Arizona it has been found at elevations ranging from 3,500 feet to 5,400 feet both as a spring and a fall migrant.

In Nevada, W. P. Taylor (1912) found it characteristically in the Upper Sonoran and the Lower Transition Zones, never far from the mountain stream association of plants where he observed it in the quaking aspens, wild rose and gooseberry thickets, willows and alders, as well as in the sagebrush of the adjacent deserts. It was most common at elevations of 5,000 to 7,000 feet.

W. H. Behle (1944) lists it as a summer resident throughout Utah, commonly found in the lowland thickets and occasionally in similar habitat in the lower portions of the mountains. A. M. Woodbury (1941) mentions it as being attracted with other species to the oaks.

In Colorado F. M. Drew (1885) and other later observers report this species as breeding from the Plains area, elevation about 5,000 feet, to as high as 7,000 feet in the mountains. C. W. Beckman (1885) reported it as common in the vicinity of Pueblo along the rivers and creeks where vegetation is comparatively luxuriant rather than in the cactus—sagebrush wasteland. M. F. Gilman (1907) reports that at Fort Lewis in southwest Colorado, elevation 7,500 feet, it is rather common and nests in the small wild cherry shrubs and in the wild roses. In the western part of the State it frequents the open scrub-oak country in well-watered localities.

The records of this species for New Mexico are scant considering its commoness in Colorado and Arizona. There are only three positive records for the State, two at elevations of 7,000 feet.

In Oklahoma Mrs. M. M. Nice (1939) reported the lazuli bunting as a rare summer resident in Cimarron County, the most western county of the State.

This species has been reported from western Nebraska and Kansas and may breed there. In the Dakotas it is listed as an uncommon summer resident partial to the willows of the Upper Austral Zone.

A. A. Saunders (1921) describes the lazuli bunting as a "common summer resident throughout the western half of Montana, becoming rather rare eastward, but evidently found throughout the state." It breeds "in the Transition Zone, in low thicket bushes, such as wild rose, currant, gooseberry and similar shrubs. All observers in the mountainous parts of the state report this species as common, not in the higher mountains, but in the foothills." In Wyoming M. Cary (1917) listed it as among the breeding birds of the Upper Sonoran Zone and J. A. Neilson (1925) as a common nesting bird in the plum thickets of the North Laramie River at 6,000 to 7,000 feet.

This species is found throughout Idaho. In the south it breeds in the undergrowth of the willow thickets along the creeks. In the north it has been observed at elevations of 2,000 feet to as high as 6,000 feet in the wooded valleys and brushy hillslopes of the Transition Zone, in the thickets and underbrush, and in areas under cultivation.

Except in the highest mountains, it is a common summer resident of all of eastern Oregon, where it frequents the willow thickets along the streams. In the John Day region of the central part of the State it was observed by Loye Miller (1904) in the tall sage. According to Gabrielson and Jewett (1940), it is an equally abundant resident of the Rogue, Umpqua, and Willamette river valleys west of the Cascades from the valley floors to an elevation of 4,000 feet. It is less abundant on the coast.

As in eastern Oregon, this species is common everywhere in eastern Washington except in the arid sagebrush region. L. R. Dice (1918a) observed it in the cottonwoods and willows along the Touchet River and in the town of Walla Walla. P. Dumas (1950) found it about equally common in the swales and draws of the prairie where a thick shrub layer of rose, snowberry, and serviceberry occur with scattered thorn trees, and in the dense chaparral brushland of ninebark, spirea, and ocean spray. In central Washington, C. H. Kennedy (1914) mentions the lazuli bunting as one of the species that is moving from the riverside thickets into irrigated land. In the northwestern part of the State, T. D. Burleigh (1929–1930) reports it as "a rather scarce summer resident in underbrush bordering open fields."

According to Baird, Brewer, and Ridgway (1874b), Lord states that the lazuli bunting visits Vancouver Island and British Columbia early in the summer, arriving at the island in May and rather later east of the Cascades. More recently (A. Brooks, 1917; A. Brooks and H. S. Swarth, 1925; J. A. Munro, 1950), it has been reported as a moderately common summer visitant to the lowlands of southern British Columbia, but as unusual on Vancouver Island. The northern-most record is that of S. N. Rhoads (1893) at Bonaparte. The species also occurs in southern Alberta and Saskatchewan.

The lazuli bunting has been affected by the occupany of its range by the white man. W. K. Fisher (1902) lists it as a species that has rapidly invaded the lumbered areas in the vicinity of Humboldt Bay on the coast of northern California. Originally he described it as restricted to the narrow river valleys open to the coast belt. In 1902 it had a much wider distribution. It has also spread into the irrigated parts of Colorado and Washington and other States where the water has changed sagebrush or other unsuitable habitats into suitable ones. Modification in distribution in the other direction has also been observed. J. Grinnell (1914a) describes their coming down Strawberry Canyon as far as Budd Hall on the Berkeley campus in 1907, but having been seen only in the upper parts of the canyon a few years later. E. C. Kinsey writes that "several pairs which always nested in our canyon on the southern slopes have moved out completely since the war period brought in a large influx of new residents. It can not seem to adapt itself to a populous human environment."

An actual extension of the range of this species is indicated by W. Youngworth (1935) who found a male lazuli bunting consorting with a female lazuli and a female indigo bunting "approximately thirty miles from the border lines of both Minnesota and North Dakota. The record is interesting in that it shows that previous reports of the lazuli bunting in Iowa and Minnesota were not accidental and that this bunting is actually extending its breeding range eastward."

Spring.—The northward migration of the species from Mexico begins the latter part of March and reaches the United States on a broad front from the San Antonio region of Texas to the Pacific coast in April. It appears first in the coastal region of southern California where it has been recorded frequently the first week of April. In Arizona it first appears about the second week of April and becomes common later in the month. In Texas it arrives a week to 10 days later. In Arizona, where it is a common migrant but a rare breeder, the migration wave is more readily observed and appears to last 5 to 6 weeks until the latter part of May. It is probably of similar duration in other areas.

R. L. Wisner (1952) observed a case of offshore migration from a boat about 15 miles out from San Diego. At approximately 10:30 a.m. "two Lazuli Buntings * * *, a male and a female, made a visit aboard. They perched on the rail only and allowed no one to approach them. When the vessel attained full speed a few minutes later the birds left and made no attempt to follow." This occurred on May 11, 1951, after a period of mild weather, so one must judge that the birds were "at sea of their own volition." Lazuli buntings have also been observed as migrants on Santa Catalina and Santa Cruz Islands in April. Farther to the north they have been recorded as migrants on the Farallones on the first of June.

In the San Francisco Bay area they usually appear the last week of April. In the Sierras and the mountains to the east they arrive later, about the middle of May. They usually reach the western part of Oregon by the very last of April, although there is one unusual record at Thurston, Oreg. for March 13. East of the Cascades their arrival is later, about the second week in May. The same dates apply to western and eastern Washington. Mid-May is the average arrival date for the Great Basin States, Nevada, Idaho, Utah, and Wyoming, but it is late May before they arrive in Montana and Colorado. The migration wave extends east to Lincoln, Nebr., where three were recorded on May 6, 10, and 19. The late May records for southeastern South Dakota are probably also of migrants.

As is to be expected on migration, the lazuli bunting is not infrequently found in habitats other than where it would breed, as in the mesquite of the Mohave Desert or the dry hillside chaparral of the central valley of California. At Twentynine Palms, Miss F. Carter (1937) found them regularly associated with chipping sparrows; they flew up in mixed flocks from the deep grass adjacent to the springs of this region.

H. S. Swarth (1904) describes its migration through the Huachucas of Arizona as follows: "During the spring migration this species appears * * * not in great numbers, but still in tolerable abundance; but its stay is an exceedingly short one, more so than any other of the migrating species. In 1903, the first noted was on April 14; for about a week they were quite plentiful, and then abruptly disappeared. In 1902, I observed a few along the San Pedro River on April 17th; a day or two later they began to appear in the mountains, and by the third week in April had all gone on." E. C. Kinsey (letter, 1955) states that "some 30 years ago during the early April migration period male lazulis could be seen, literally in successive waves numbering hundreds of individuals slowly working their way north. * * * The males migrate separately, preceding the females from 10 days to 3 weeks." Baird, Brewer, and Ridgway (1874b) also mention seeing flocks of males in the spring before the females arrived. I saw a similar group of 11 migrant males in a small brushy draw 5 miles northwest of Santa Barbara on May 11, 1951.

Territory.—The lazuli bunting appears to follow the territorial pattern typical of many migratory song birds. The males regularly arrive first, take up territories in suitable breeding areas, proclaim their presence by singing from a series of conspicuous song perches within the chosen areas, and defend them. Soon each is joined by a female who observes the boundaries of the territory and takes part in defending the area from other pairs.

The size of the territory has not been clearly established. J. Grinnell and T. I. Storer (1924) on May 23, 1915, at Pleasant Valley in Yosemite observed 24 males during a 4-hour census. These "singing males were spaced about 100 to 200 yards apart along the Merced River and tributary ravines." This spacing corresponds to that I observed for five singing males on a brush- and mustard-covered slope at Santa Barbara, and also to that observed at the Hasting's Natural History Reservation near Carmel, Calif.

Chattin's observations at the Hasting's Reservation include two records of territorial dispute, both on May 28, 1940. The first instance involved two male buntings which fought and chased one another through the bushes and live oaks a few to 10 feet above the ground. Both gave chipping notes and also some short twitters. Twice one male sang from the top of a 6-foot live oak after it had apparently chased the other bird away. In the other instance, a male and a female lazuli bunting approached a bunting nest that was under observation. As they worked their way along in fallen branches and wild rose bushes, the female, which was 6 to 10 feet ahead of the male, lit in a wild rose bush 4 feet from the nest. The female on the nest immediately left it and chased the intruding female. The male joined in the chase and all three birds flew 10 yards to the southwest giving the chipping note and a short, harsh buzzing note. The intruding pair left after about 15 seconds of "quarreling" and flew on down the canyon. The resident female returned to her nest.

On May 10, 1939, Hubbard also observed a territorial dispute. A male was sitting in a buckeye with a female nearby, when another male chasing a female flew into the clearing near them. The first male left his female to intercept the intruding male and chased him in a large circle about 30 feet in diameter for approximately 3 minutes. The pursued male once uttered the complete normal song while flying with the other male in pursuit. On two successive days May 22 and 23, 1942, Dalquist, another observer at the Reservation saw two males in a territorial dispute. One seemed to have a favorite perch in a coffeeberry bush at the foot of a valley oak tree 20 feet from a fence. The other had a perch somewhere up the canyon. If the one from the base of the oak tree alighted in the coffeeberry bushes along the fence, the other was at him like a flash and chased him through the bushes. Similarly, if the one from up the canyon came to the coffeeberry bushes by the fence, he was attacked. The one being chased often turned after 10 or 20 feet and chased the other; a moment later they reversed again and the chase went on 2 to 8 feet above the ground. The encounters lasted about half a minute, and each bird went back to its own territory. On the 23d such a chase occurred five times between 7:45 and 8:00 a.m. The bushes near the fence appeared to be a "no man's land" where neither bird fed, but would not tolerate the other. I also observed similar encounters in the Santa Barbara area.

Courtship.—At the Grand Canyon, Florence M. Bailey (1939) gives this account of the courtship: "The gay suitor, after displaying his beautiful colors with extended trembling wings, flew to the ground and went through strange courtship antics while a demure watcher sat on a twig merely turning her head from side to side." At the Hasting's Natural History Reservation, Hubbard saw a female fly to a rock on which her mate had just landed. She chirped repeatedly while she held her tail vertically. Shortly she flew away followed by the male, both going into the brush. The female continued to chirp for about a minute when both reappeared from the brush and the male resumed his singing. On May 12, 1952, I watched a male fly into the top of a mustard clump. Here his mate was perched with her tail raised, her wings spread and quivering as she gave a low call. The male flew over to her and attempted to mount, but was unsuccessful and flew back into the mustard. The female repeated her

action and the male again flew to her and mounted her as the tw
fluttered lower into the stems of mustard out of view.

Nesting.—One of the earliest descriptions of a nest of this species i
that given by Audubon (1841). He states that the "nest, which i
usually placed in the willows along the margins of the streams, is com
posed of small sticks, fine grasses and cow or buffalo hair." J. G
Cooper (1870) describes the nest as "built in a bush not more tha
three or four feet above the ground, formed of fibrous roots, strip
of bark and grass with a lining of plant down or hairs, and securel
bound to surrounding branches." J. Grinnell and T. I. Storer (1924
state that the nests "are usually ensconced in low growths alon
cañon bottoms in situations near which the adult birds spend mos
of their time." A nest found in Yosemite Valley on June 17, 1915
was described as follows:

> It was 18 inches above the ground in the crotch of a small chokecherry growin
> in a rather sparse stand of the same sort of bush. The nest was rather thic
> walled, not tightly woven, and its exterior was composed of dried and weathere
> grass and plant stems of the previous season's growth. A few leaves of th
> cherry growing on the small branches upon which the nest had been built wer
> incorporated into the surface of the structure. The inner portion of this nes
> was made of fine rounded grass stems, while the cup was lined with horsehai
> rather loosely placed. The outside dimensions were, height 3 inches, diamete
> 4 inches; the cup was about 2 inches across and nearly the same in depth. Withi
> were four pale blue eggs in which incubation had just commenced.

Other descriptions recorded in the literature give much the sam
picture. The nests were usually found from about 1½ to 4 feet from
the ground in shrubby growths. Specific locations mentioned includ
thick willow clumps, tangles of rose bushes, low thick bushes such as
wild rose, currant, and gooseberry, chaparral thickets, small pines
willows, willows and manzanita, twigs of scrub oak, poison oak, wild o
domesticated berry vines, fork of a shoot off the base of a cottonwood
brake ferns, stalks of weeds, and thistle stands. In southern Cali
fornia, W. L. Dawson (1923) reports the broadleafed sage or mugwor
(*Artemesia heterophylla*) as the favored location for nests. In 1920
in Santa Barbara, 14 of the 19 nests he found were in pure *Artemesa
heterophylla* along streams or on half-shaded hillsides where it grew
3 to 4 feet tall, 2 were in mixed stands, 2 in poison oak, and 1 in a
blackberry tangle.

The outside of the cup is regularly described as made up of coarsely
woven dried grass stems, usually the leafy portion, and the lining as
of fine grasses or long hair.

A few reports describe nests at higher elevations. J. K. Jensen
(1923) describes a nest he found in Santa Fe County, N. Mex., placed
"8 feet up in a bunch of willows on the river bank above Santa Fe."

E. C. Kinsey (letter, 1955) reports finding nests at higher elevations. "The nest is usually situated 2 to 4 feet above the ground, well concealed and strongly built and attached to a supporting foundation * * * I have found a nest situated within approximately 9 or 10 feet off the ground * * * I have also found nests in willows and in scrub oaks considerably higher than usual. One nest located in a young peach tree on a small branch was situated beyond my reach which would be almost 8 feet. Of course, this was most unusual, as was the nest situated 10 feet above the ground."

In California nesting occurs in May and June and on into July. In San Diego County C. S. Sharp (1907), on the basis of 16 years' observation, lists April 30 as the earliest date for eggs showing no (or slight) incubation and June 2 the latest record. Florence Merriam reports a nesting completed in May and another in June in the Twin Oaks area of San Diego County. In the Pasadena area George Willett (1933) likewise reports nesting as early as April 30 and in San Bernardino County, as late as July 4. Other dates for this area are O. Davie (1889) May 4 and June 13, 1883, J. Grinnell and T. I. Swarth (1913) July 7 for incubated eggs, J. Grinnell (1908) for the San Bernardino Mountain region, one begun about the end of May and another which contained three heavily incubated eggs on July 10. W. C. Hanna (1918) found fresh eggs as late as July 4 in 1918.

In the Santa Barbara area Cooper found a nest with fresh eggs as early as May 6. In the Santa Cruz area he reported finding a nest May 7, while R. C. McGregor (1901) states that they "nest from June to the middle of August."

In the San Francisco area J. Grinnell and M. W. Wythe (1927) and others state that the nesting season "extends through May and June," and others concur. J. Grinnell (1914a) notes a nest with small young as late as July 3, 1909. In the Yosemite area nesting appears to begin in late May or June. In the Mount Shasta region, Miss Merriam observed young being fed in mid-July.

In the Grand Canyon area of Arizona M. H. Lee (1920) saw adults feeding a fledgling on June 4. W. E. D. Scott (1887) took a young male on July 27, 1884, and states that "Mr. Brown has found it breeding, but not common, about Tucson * * *."

J. K. Jensen (1923) describes a nest he found in Santa Fe County, N. Mex., placed "eight feet up in a bunch of willows on the river bank above Santa Fe. It was built of the same material as the nest of the Blue Grosbeak and although it looked small I set it down as such. June 19, I happened to pass the place again and to my surprise found the female Lazuli Bunting on the nest. * * * The nest contained a set of four eggs in which incubation had just commenced." H. Lacey (1911) found nests with four eggs May 13 and

May 26 at his ranch 7 miles southwest of Kerrville and 55 mile northwest of San Antonio, Tex. In southern Ellis County, Okla. G. M. Sutton (1938) found a nest on May 26, 1937, with two egg. He found the species common along the Washita River near Cheyenne Roger Mills County, where it nested side by side with *P. cyane* and *P. ciris*.

For Nevada R. Ridgeway (1877) reports two nests with eggs, on on July 1, 1867, and another on July 4, 1868. A. J. van Rossen (1936) collected three juveniles on July 19 and 20, 1932. At Provo Utah, H. W. Henshaw (1875) found nests "the latter part of July containing either young, or eggs just ready to hatch." In Colorad. R. B. Rockwell (1908) states that they breed "late in June an. July," while W. H. Bergtold (1917) reports them as nesting i. Chessman Park in Denver the last week in June of 1916.

Breeding records for the Dakotas are scarce. Henry reports . female carrying food on August 1, though he could not find th. nest. In Montana A. A. Saunders (1921) reports nest dates for th. State that include a nest with four eggs at Flathead Lake on July 22 another one in which one egg hatched July 30, 1911, and a thir. containing two lazuli eggs and one cowbird egg on June 15, 1910.

In the Willamette Valley of Oregon G. W. Gullion (1951) ha. breeding records from June 2 to August 25. Stanley Jewett foun. nests June 17 and 20 in Multnomah County and June 8 in Umatill. County. Patterson gives the dates of May 10 to June 8 for th. southern Cascades. At Fort Klamath J. C. Merrill (1888) report. them as "breeding among the willows and manzanita bushes" begin. ning late in May after their arrival about May 20. In central Orego. A. Walker (1917) found nests on June 17, 1913, containing young.

Dawson (1909) observed a nest in Yakima County, Wash., whic. "was begun on the 19th of June and practically completed by th. afternoon of the following day,—this altho the first egg was not lai. until the 26th." J. R. King (1954) reports nesting dates for Whitma. County in Washington as June 1 to June 30 based on earliest an. latest dates for fresh completed clutches, or derived by extrapolation.

Eggs.—The set of eggs laid by the lazuli bunting is usually four, bu. occasionally only three and more rarely five. They are ovate, some. times with a tendency toward short-ovate, and slightly glossy. Th. eggs are very pale bluish-white, and unspotted.

The measurements of 50 eggs average 18.7 by 13.6 millimeters. an. the eggs showing the four extremes measure *20.8* by 14.7, 18.8 b. *15.2*, *16.8* by 14.0, and 18.8 by *12.1* millimeters.

Young.—F. L. Burns (1915) gives the incubation period of the lazul. bunting as 12 days and (1921) the length of nestling life as 10 days. This is based on W. I. Finley's record (1906) of a nest that containe.

3 eggs on June 24. These hatched on July 6 and the young left the nest on July 16. I. G. Wheelock (1912) gives the nest period as 15 days unless the young are disturbed. At one nest observed by Hjersman at the Hasting's Natural History Reservation, the eggs hatched on July 17, 1939, and the young left the nest on July 28, the 12th day.

The female is always active in caring for the young, feeding, brooding, and shading the nestlings as necessary. The role of the male is variable; in some cases he appears to take no active part, in others he gives some assistance. From a total of 124 hours of observation at four different nests at the Hasting's Reservation the following information was obtained: At the nest observed by Hjersman mentioned above, no male was found associated with it from the start of observations which began a few days before the eggs hatched. In this case all the care was given by the female. At a second nest observed by Hjersman during the first 4 days after hatching, the female fed 47 times to 12 for the male, or 80 percent of the feedings. At a third nest observed by Chattin on the third to fifth days of nestling life, the female fed 165 times to the male's 43, or 82 percent of the times. At a fourth nest watched by Gray, observations on the 2d and 3d days showed 47 feedings by the female and none by the male; on the 7th and 8th days it was 122 to 3, and on the 11th day 30 to 0, or a total of 199 times for the female to 3 for the male.

On the first day of nestling life, the average number of feedings was 2.6 times per hour at three nests. On subsequent days, the average number of feedings per hour increased as follows: 2d day, 3.6; 3d, 4.8; 4th, 5.9; 6th, 7.2; 7th, 7.6; 8th, 8.5; 9th, 9.2; 10th, 10.9; 11th, 11.0. Usually only a single young is fed at each visit. The principal food is young grasshoppers, although large larvae are used to a considerable extent and occasionally a beetle or some other type of insect. These items all appear to be relatively large and difficult for the young to swallow, or else the young are well fed and not ready to take more. Observers report that the adult commonly presents an item to a young, retrieves it if it is not swallowed and offers it again, often three or four times before it is swallowed. Fifteen or more such presentations to one or more young have been observed before the item is successfully taken. Occasionally the female, after a series of unsuccessful tries, eats the item herself. E. L. Kinsey reports the feeding of small nestlings by regurgitation, but this was not reported at the nests observed at the Hasting's Reservation. He also found grasshoppers the commonest food brought to older young.

In addition to feeding the young, the female broods them during the night and broods or shades them as necessary during the day. During 130 hours of observation at the Hasting's Reservation, the female was seeen to brood or shade the nestlings about one-third of the time and was away from the nest two-thirds of it. As was to be expected, the time spent brooding was greater for the small young and on cooler days and was negligible with older young. At one of the nests observed by Hjersman, the female left the nest, at least the greater part of the time, when the male gave a "brzeet" call, the same as the last faint part of the song. While she was off the pair were often seen foraging together on nearby grassy slopes.

Shading of the young was common when the nest was in direct sunlight. Of the total time at the nest 78 percent was spent brooding, 22 percent shading the young. The shading was done by standing up in the nest with the wings spread. Often the female opened her mouth presumably to aid her in dissipating the excess heat.

Both parents ate or carried away any fecal sac that was deposited while they were at the nest. As with other species the female, at least, seemed to wait for the young to defecate or to stimulate it by pecking at the anal region.

At the nest Gray observed at the Hasting's Natural History Reservation, he was fortunate enough to be on hand at the time the young left the nest. On this morning, the female first left the nest at 4:26 a.m. when the light was still too dim for Gray to determine what she brought to feed the young 4 minutes later. She continued to feed at 2 to 5 minute intervals until and after the young were out of the nest. Her mate was first noticed with her at 4:54. The two chirped back and forth constantly. Most of the time the male stayed in the nest area and a number of times accompanied her on her foraging trips, but he was not seen to gather food for, or to approach, the young. The female in seeking food usually clung to a vertical rose stem and watched for a grasshopper to move. When one did, she pursued it and often was successful in capturing it. At 5:04 the female was seen to feed a young, which, unobserved by Gray, had moved about 6 inches out from the nest. At first she seemed to feed this one more frequently than the young in the nest; then the pattern was reversed.

Presently the young that had been out of the nest was discovered to have returned to it. It was not for long, however, for in a few moments at 6:12 one young flew out and disappeared into the brush 4 feet from the nest. Four minutes later a second one flew to a perch 8 inches above the nest and was followed by the third. The parents watched this, but did not call or act alarmed. A few minutes later the female came to the nest with food, then departed with it rather than going to the young. Later she returned with it and fed one of the young. For the following feedings, the female returned to the nest with food and then went to the young and fed them. Within a half hour, however, she was going directly to them. The young fluttered their wings as she approached. The location note given was a *wheet*, which was uttered once or several times and was often given when they missed their grasp on a perch as they shifted their position. Mostly they tended to stay in one place. They were frequently seen to preen. At this time the body feathers were well grown. The head and wings were dark gray, the back a lighter gray, the breast reddish, the belly gray, and the bill yellow. The wings showed two bars plainly. The head and neck still had gray down and the tail was approximately 1½ inches long. About a week later young were observed following the female closely and begging for food.

E. C. Kinsey's observations (letter, 1955) differ from these to some extent. He states: "Our observations indicate that the male does not feed the young in the nest; that the feeding is all done by the female.* * *   However, the minute the young leave the nest, whether because of being disturbed or naturally, the male takes over and is the principal feeder. Almost immediately the female solicits the male's attention and a new nest is started, usually in the immediate vicinity of the old nest. The male leads the brood of fledglings off into the thicket during the day but returns to the old nesting site in the evening. The young, so far as I have been able to observe, do not return to the nest once thay have left it. The male's territorial song during the time he is feeding the fledglings continues unabated."

The same observer gives the only information available on the number of broods. "Our experience indicates that two broods are the usual order although this spring, viz 1955, * * *.   I know of one pair that reared three broods. In past years I have felt certain in other locations and with other pairs that three broods are not unusual, at least in the northern San Francisco Bay area."

Plumages.—R. Ridgway (1901) describes the adult male as: Head, neck, rump, and upper tail coverts light cerulean or turquoise blue, changing to light greenish blue (Nile blue); back, scapulars, and lesser wing-coverts darker and (especially back) duller blue; lores blackish; middle wing-coverts very broadly tipped with white, the greater coverts more narrowly tipped with the same, forming two bands; wings otherwise blackish, the greater coverts and remiges edged with bluish; tail blackish, the rectrices edged with greenish blue; chest tawny-ochraceous, this color extending farther backward laterally than medially; abdomen, under tail-coverts, etc., white; maxilla black; mandible (in life) pale grayish blue, with black streaks on gonys; iris brown; legs and feet black or dusky brown.

Ridgway describes the adult female as: Above grayish brown, passing into dull greenish blue, or much tinged with this color, on rump and upper tail-coverts, the back sometimes narrowly and indistinctly streaked with dusky, the remiges and rectrices edged with dull greenish blue, the middle and greater wing-coverts tipped with buffy or buffy whitish; anterior and lateral under parts dull buffy deepest on chest; abdomen and under tail-coverts white or buffy white.

He states that the young are: Similar to adult female but rump and upper tail-coverts light brown, without bluish or greenish tinge and usually with chest and sides narrowly and indistinctly streaked Immature males have the blue, especially on the upper parts, more or less clouded or overlaid by cinnamon brown.

E. C. Kinsey (letter, 1955) reports that "the males have a partial eclipse of their bright cerulean blue color. The young and immatures resemble the female except that the blue wash on the rump is not so pronounced. Our young aviary birds come into full male plumage the following spring although I have seen the change retarded until summer or fall of the second year. This could be the result of captivity."

H. S. Swarth (1904) reports taking an adult male August 21 that had renewed many of the feathers of the head and back, but elsewhere retained almost entirely the old worn breeding plumage. A female taken August 11 had almost entirely renewed the plumage of the upper parts and had many new feathers scattered over the throat, breast and sides.

W. Brewster (1862a) reports an unusual male specimen taken at Tucson that had "the blue almost completely obscured by rufous which forms a broad tipping on all the feathers of the upper parts The throat, however, remains nearly pure blue."

Another male seen June 8 in the chaparral belt of the Sierras above Springville, Tulare County, Calif., by myself and a number of other observers lacked the usual band of chestnut on the breast. The blue of the throat continued uninterrupted into this region and continued ventrally for the usual distance of the reddish band.

Food.—From an analysis of 36 specimens, mostly from California with 16 taken in the spring and 30 in the summer, A. C. Martin, H. S. Zim, and A. L. Nelson (1951) report that the food of the lazuli bunting consists of 64 percent animal food in the spring and 53 percent in the summer. "Grasshoppers, caterpillars, and beetles, plus a goodly number of true bugs, bees and ants are the main animal items * * * seeds of weedy plants constitute more than one-third of the spring and summer food." Of the plant foods wild oats make up 10 to 25 percent, minerslettuce 5 to 10 percent, and canarygrass 2 to 5 percent. In the spring, annual bluegrass constitutes 2 to percent, and in the summer, needlegrass, 5 to 10 percent. Small percentages of malicgrass, velvetgrass, filaree, and chickweed are also recorded.

L. L. Hargrave (1932) observed three pairs feeding on "oats in the milk" on July 18. He saw 10 birds in the same field on July 25 and 2 on August 1.

A. H. Miller (1939) gives an interesting account of the foraging habits of one individual.

On August 3, 1939, Dr. Ernst Mayr and I watched a male Lazuli Bunting (*Passerina amoena*) that had learned a handy method of feeding on grass heads. The bird was first noted as it flew along the roadside in Strawberry Canyon, Berkeley. It alighted on the barbed wire fence ahead of our car and began feeding at once. Canary grass (*Phalaris californica*) grew to a height of 20 to 26 inches and thus extended above the lowest fence wire which was 18 inches above the ground. This species of grass appears to have insufficient rigidity to support a bunting on the tips of the stems. The bunting flew laterally from the wire to a distance of about one foot, seized a grass head in its bill and returned with it to the wire, the grass stem bending over readily. The bird then lowered its bill to the wire and clasped the compact seed head against the wire with its left foot. In this position it picked out the seeds. When the head was well broken apart and the seed supply depleted, the grass stem either slipped free or was allowed to spring back to its normal position. Immediately the bird flew out for another grass head, hovered and returned, and the feeding was continued. This activity was seen at least six times in succession, the foraging taking place to either side of the wire. The bunting seemed able successfully to gauge the distance to which it could operate. Tall grasses no more than 15 inches away always were taken. At no time did it fail through attempting to bend over a head that was too short or one that was too far away.

The fence for 100 feet passed through grass of similar height and maturity. Undoubtedly the bird had lived in or about this vicinity during the current summer and had developed, to its special advantage, this method of feeding from the fence wire.

Feeding behavior was observed by a number of the students at the Hasting's Natural History Reservation. Hubbard saw a male fly from a sycamore to the ground, catching a shoot of *Avena barbata* in its bill on the way down and bending it to the ground. He held it for about 10 seconds, then released it, flew about 3 feet in the air, caught another shoot and pulled it toward the twig on which he landed. In neither case did he succeed in feeding. On another occasion, a male perched on three or four stems of *Avena* and bent them over. He continued to sing, but between songs, he reached out and picked seeds out of the flower cluster, holding them in his bill while he bit off the awn. Bartholomew observed a lazuli perched in a dead rosebush eating seeds of *Avena barbata*. The bird took seeds only from brown stems, none from green ones which he could have reached easily. Dalquist observed a male that was flying to catch insects. First he flew vertically for several inches, then turned and lit on a blue oak twig. Next he flew to a small madrone tree 6 feet away, then back to the oak, each time for the purpose of catching an insect.

He flew 12 feet up in the oak, suspending himself with his body vertical and his wings beating as he pulled something from the lower side of an oak leaf; he then dropped down and lit on a twig 2 feet below. Twice more he flew up to pluck objects from the under side of the oak leaves. He then flew out horizontally and was seen to be pacing a large moth, probably a geometrid, which he could have overtaken with ease, but he seemed to have trouble slowing down enough to keep 8 to 10 inches behind it. When the moth landed on an oak leaf the bunting turned and flew to the oak at a faster pace.

Behavior.—On their spring migration the lazuli buntings may be associated with other species. On May 2, at Twenty-nine Palms, Calif., Frances Carter (1937) observed several lazulis start up from deep grass with a flock of chipping sparrows. This association was regularly noted the rest of that year, though no chipping sparrows were seen the following year. This association with chipping sparrows was also noticed by Joseph Grinnell on the fog-swept and bald-topped hills of Humboldt County, Calif., in June. H. S. Swarth (1904) observed that in the spring migration in the Huachuca Mountains of Arizona the lazulis "were generally in mixed flocks of migrating warblers, vireos, etc. and fed with them in the tree tops rather than on or near the ground as they usually do."

E. C. Kinsey (1934) states that lazuli buntings are devoted mates and parents. He also comments that "male lazulis are very pugnacious and defend the nesting precincts vigorously. This is particularly true with the first brood; it is not always true with the second and third broods."

Dawson (1909) has this to say about the female: "*Amoena* means pleasant, but the female amenity is anything else, when her fancied rights of maternity are assailed. Her vocabulary is limited, to be sure, to a single note, but her repeated *chip* is expressive of all words in *dis* from distrust to distress and violent disapprobation."

When J. K. Jensen (1923) approached a nest, the female left it "but kept fluttering among the branches uttering sharp 'chips' and immediately the male arrived. * * *"

A possible case of polygamy and hybridization is also reported by Youngworth as follows: "During the first week of June, 1935, the writer was working on a waterfowl survey in the Waubay Lakes region in Day County, South Dakota, and it was here near Spring Lake that a male lazuli bunting was seen on several successive days. The strange thing, however, was the fact that the bird was consorting with two females. One female was an indigo bunting and the other a lazuli bunting. On every occasion when the male lazuli bunting was flushed the two females would also flush. The writer was sorry that he could not stay longer to determine whether both females started nest-building."

Voice.—The song of this species has been characterized by various authors as lively and pleasing (Audubon, 1841); vivacious, high-pitched, intricate, rapid, and varied (C. A. Keeler, 1899); a bright and musical finch-type, and like that of *Oreospiza* and *Chondestes*, having a marked burr (F. M. Bailey, 1902); a weak song (W. A. Eliot, 1923); a cheerful little song, warblerlike in character (M. H. Lee, 1920); a hurried, shrill song (Grinnell, 1912); a rapidly uttered musical jingle (Wyman, 1925), and a high and strident finch song with well-measured phrases at varying pitches (Peterson, 1941).

It was transcribed by J. Grinnell and T. I. Storer (1924) as: *see-see-see, sweert, sweert, sweert, zee, see, sweet, zeer, see-see.* They state: "These notes follow one another with rapidity; it is really with difficulty that any syllabic rendering, such as the one just given, can be made." In addition they describe it as set in character, with certain syllables added or dropped but the general theme remaining the same. C. A. Keeler (1899) transcribed it as *"tit-a-trea-trea-trea; tree, tree, trea, tree, tree; trit-a-tree, tree, tree,"* but adds "the ending of the song is frequently lost in a confused jumble of sweet tones." R. T. Peterson (1941) comments that the introductory notes are usually paired, and R. Hoffmann (1927) states that "the song is best distinguished by its marked division into short phrases which vary distinctly in pitch, generally beginning high, falling to successively lower levels and then rising again."

Its song resembles that of the indigo bunting but is distinguishable from it as appreciably weak, less warblerlike, definite, and not rambling. It has also been compared with the voices of other species. J. Grinnell and T. I. Storer (1924) describe the song as "rather high pitched, like that of the California Yellow Warbler, yet it is not nearly so shrill," while C. Barlow (1902) says that the song of the rufous-crowned sparrow has been "likened to that of the Lazuli Bunting," but sees "little resemblance save in the general trilling style. The sparrow's note is much stronger * * *."

The song is usually given from a high, open perch such as the top branches of a moderate-sized oak, sycamore, yellow pine, willow, or other tree, or from telephone wires, or if no higher perch is available, from the topmost twig of the tallest shrub in the area.

The lazuli is a persistent singer. J. Grinnell and T. I. Storer (1924) state: "It does not confine its utterances to the morning and early evening hours, but is heard if anything less often at those times than during the warmest part of the day. In our memory the song is associated with the drowsy heat of early afternoon." This persistence in song has been noted by others and was characteristic of the individuals I watched near Santa Barbara.

J. Grinnell (1912) recorded the intervals between songs during a period of about 5 minutes. The intervals ranged from 9 to 18 seconds and averaged 12.5 seconds with a majority of the intervals falling between 11 and 13.

A male that I observed on Apr. 28, 1953, when it was proclaiming territory for the first time in this area, gave a total of 95 songs during an 18-minute period from 6:56 a.m. to 7:14 a.m., or an average of 5.3 per minute. On April 29, 23 songs were recorded during a period of 9 minutes, or an average of 2.5 per minute, and on the 30th, there were 10 songs during a 2-minute interval, or an average of 5 per minute. The frequency of song probably decreases somewhat once a mate has joined the male on his territory and nesting is under way.

Singing does not decrease as much as in some species, however, for this species has been reported as a persistent singer throughout its breeding season. A male with a family out of the nest seen on June 12, 1952, was recorded as singing eight times in 1 minute and six times in another. W. A. Eliot (1923) describes it as repeating its song by the hour during the nesting season. I. G. Wheelock (1912) comments: "Long after the other birds, worn out by family cares, have ceased their music, this blythe little 'blue boy' carols his jolly roundelay from the top of a tall tree * * *." E. W. Nelson (1875) states that they are commonly heard singing during July in the vicinity of Fort Bridger, Utah; T. D. Burleigh (1923b) likewise reports them as singing in July at Clark's Fort in northern Idaho, and O. Widmann (1911) reports several males in full song at the same time he saw fully grown young on July 15 at Fork in Estes Park, Colo. A late date for song is August 16, 1920, in the Berkeley, Calif., area.

The singing males are spaced out and each has a series of song perches that are used in sequence in the fashion typical of birds holding territory and using song as a pronouncement of this fact.

The call note of this species has been variously described as a sharp *"quit"* (L. E. Wyman and E. F. Burnell, 1925), "an emphatic *quit* or sometimes *chack*" (F. M. Bailey, 1902), or sharp chips (J. K. Jenson, 1923, and S. G. Jewett, Taylor, Shaw, and Aldrich, 1953). This is given when the birds are alarmed by the intrusion of a potential enemy.

Other notes recorded by observers at the Hasting's Natural History Reservation are a harsh buzzing note and a twitter given during a territorial dispute, a *brzeet* note of the male which called the female from the nest, and the *wheet* note of the fledglings.

Field marks.—The adult male lazuli bunting is unmistakable with his azure blue head, upper parts, and throat, cinnamon band across his breast, white belly, and white wing bars. His mate is more difficult to recognize. She is dull brown, unstreaked both above and below, with a suggestion of wing bars, and gray-blue in the wings and tail. Her smaller size and bill distinguish her from the similarily colored female blue grosbeak.

Enemies.—The lazuli bunting is one of the species parasitized by the cowbird. H. Friedmann (1929, 1934) considered it an uncommon victim as indicated by the few records from Colorado, California, and Idaho. The literature contains records of 12 nests parasitized with one or two cowbird eggs. J. R. King (1954) from his observations in Whitman County, Wash., considered the relationship decidedly not uncommon, as two of three nests that he found contained cowbird eggs, and four families of fledglings included a juvenile cowbird. H. A. Edwards (1919) comments that this is a "species whose home the white-footed mouse frequently preempts. The eggs may usually be found buried in the bottom of the nest."

A loggerhead shrike, *Lanius ludovicianus*, entered a banding trap being operated by Warren M. Pulich at Boulder Beach, Lake Mead, Nev., and killed an immature lazuli bunting, the only species that the shrike was able to kill of those in the trap.

Fall.—The records point to the fact that after nesting this species may move about and congregate in areas of suitable food. It disappeared entirely from the area in which it had nested in Santa Barbara in the summer of 1952, perhaps because of the drying up of the dense wild mustard tangle in which it had nested. A. B. Fuller and B. P. Bole (1930) saw a "considerable flock of lazuli buntings * * * on July 21, 1927, in a small juniper-studded canyon at the foot of the Wind River Mountains, near Lander [Wyoming]. Others were sunning themselves along fences beside small patches of meadow on the canyon floor." L. L. Hargrave (1932) saw three pairs on July 18 in an oat field, and a group of 10 in the same field on the 25th. E. W. Nelson (1875) described them as abundant in flocks along the roadsides near Salt Lake City, Utah, between July 27 and August 8, 1872.

In this post-breeding period it is often recorded at high altitudes and in unusual localities. J. Grinnell and T. I. Storer (1924) report seeing this species at Warren Fork on Levining Creek on September 25, at an elevation of 9,000 feet, 2,000 feet higher than any of the nesting records. Similarly F. M. Packard (1945) states that this species is "common along the foothills, but visits this park [Rocky Mountain National Park] irregularly in late summer between June 27 and August 30." On Sept. 9, 1935, at Shuschartie on the northern end of Vancouver Island, Lusher took a juvenile male, one of the two records for the island. M. F. Gilman (1937) reports "a pair of lazuli buntings, August 20" in a list of "birds not regularly seen" in Death Valley. Pulich saw one male on Aug. 14, 1952, opposite Fort Mohave, Clarke County, Nev.

In general, this species decreases in numbers in the northern part of its range during August, and by the end of the month or early September all are gone. Simultaneously they become more abundant in the southern part of their range. E. C. Kinsey (letter, 1955) states that "the males leave first on the southern migration, the females and young following later. I have taken immatures of the year as late as September 15. Indeed, we have some 20 records of young lazulis trapped at Manor during the first 2 weeks of September." At Boulder Beach, Nev., W. M. Pulich (letter, 1955) reports that in 1955 this species appeared about September 4, and on September 6 first entered traps which had been in operation from August 21. They continued to enter the traps until September 17, with September 9 the peak in numbers. A total of 22 were taken, with 11 repeats so spaced as to suggest that no individual stayed in the vicinity more than 4 days.

In New Mexico along the Pecos River, H. W. Henshaw (1886) collected a single male on August 8, the only one he saw in 3½ months between July 18 and October 28. In Arizona, H. S. Swarth (1904) reports that this species reappears at a very early date in the Huachuca Mountains. "* * * one was seen on July 22, 1902, and their numbers increased rapidly throughout August. * * * In the fall the old males were the first to appear, the females and young following later." Gradually they move southward until all have left the United States by the end of September or early October. Rarely, a few may winter in southern Arizona. G. Monson and A. R. Phillips (1941) collected two males at Patagonia in southwestern Arizona on Dec. 3, 1939, the first winter record for the State.

Winter.—Practically nothing has been recorded on the habits of this species on its wintering grounds, nor have those who have seen and collected it at this season been able to give me such information. Robert T. Moore's earliest date of arrival on the wintering ground is September 3. His collection includes two taken at Guirojqui, Sonora, Mexico, on February 2 and 4, and winter-taken specimens, mostly December and January, from Sinaloa and Durango south through Jalisco and Michoacán to Guerrero, from where he took one specimen on January 27. A. J. van Rossem (1945) reports them as winter visitants in the tropical zone of southerly Sonora. R. B. Lea and E. P. Edwards (1950) saw several in the undergrowth of the pine woods of the Lake Patzcuaro region, Michoacán, on Mar. 17,

1947. The species seemingly does not occur in eastern Mexico. (Davis, letter, and others.)

DISTRIBUTION

Range.—South central Canada to Baja California, Guerrero, and Veracruz.

Breeding range.—The lazuli bunting breeds from southern British Columbia (Chilliwack, Vernon, Edgewood), northwestern and central Montana (Fortine, Belt Mountains), southern Saskatchewan (Shaunavon, Regina), central North Dakota (Fort Lincoln), and northeastern South Dakota (Fort Sisseton) south to northwestern Baja California (San Quintín), southeastern California (Clark Mountain), southern Nevada (Charleston Mountains), southwestern Utah (St. George, Zion Canyon), central Arizona (Camp Verde), northern New Mexico (Fort Wingate, Santa Fe), and western Oklahoma (Cheyenne), southwestern Kansas (Elkhart), and central eastern Nebraska (Platte Center).

Winter range.—Winters from southern Baja California (Triunfo), southern Arizona (Tucson) and southwestern New Mexico (Cliff), south to Guerrero (Iguala, Chilpancingo) and central Veracruz (Orizaba); casually Maryland (Timonium).

Casual records.—Casual in central western British Columbia (Shushartie), central Alberta (Jasper Park, Castor), western Minnesota (Warren, Lakefield), and western Missouri (St. Joseph).

Accidental in Mackenzie (Fort Providence).

Migration.—Early dates of spring arrival are: Missouri—St. Louis, May 7; Kansas City, May 13. Iowa—Sioux City, May 14 (median of 7 years, May 15). Minnesota—Elk River, May 18. Texas—Sinton and Laguna Atascosa Refuge, April 19; Midland, April 26; Tarrant County, April 30. Oklahoma—Payne County, May 5. Kansas—Wichita, April 23. Nebraska—Hastings, April 30; North Platte, May 5. South Dakota—Sioux Falls, May 13. North Dakota—Charlson, May 31. Saskatchewan—Indian Head, May 18. Colorado—Colorado Springs, April 22; Denver, May 3. Wyoming—Green River, May 5; Guernsey, May 6 (average of 8 years for southeastern Wyoming, May 16). Alberta—Castor, May 26. Idaho—Lewiston, May 6 (median of 11 years, May 13). New Mexico—Silver City, May 1; Los Alamos, May 5. Utah—Keams Canyon, May 15. Montana—Miles City, May 11. California—coastal southern California, April 4; Dublin, April 12. Nevada—Mercury, April 30.

Late dates of spring departure are: Sinaloa—April 21. Texas—Sinton, June 19. Kansas—Bendena, June 4; Stockton, May 24. Colorado—Fort Morgan, May 28. Oregon—Douglas County, April

24. Washington—Prescott, April 6; Pullman, May 14. British Columbia—Okanagan Landing, May 4.

Early dates of fall arrival are: Texas—Fort Davis, September 2. Baja California—Cape district, August 15. Chihuahua—Ramos, September 8. Sinaloa—September 3.

Late dates of fall departure are: British Columbia—Okanagan, Landing, and Shushartie, September 9. Washington—Prescott September 13. Oregon—Multnomah, September 9. Nevada—Mercury, September 29. California—Benton, September 21; Dublin, September 6. Idaho—Lewiston, September 25 (median of 11 years, September 10). Montana—Libby, August 30. Wyoming—Laramie, September 15 (average of 5 years for southeastern Wyoming, September 2). Utah—Raft River Mountains, September 12. New Mexico—Los Alamos, September 26. South Dakota—Aberdeen, September 13. Oklahoma—Kenton, September 28. Texas—Amarillo, September 12. Missouri—St. Joseph, September 13.

Egg dates.—British Columbia: 2 records, July 1 and July 14.

California: 112 records, March 25 to July 25; 56 records, May 23 to June 9.

Oregon: 15 records, June 9 to July 20.

Utah: 12 records, May 30 to July 16; 6 records, July 1 to July 7.

Wyoming: 10 records, June 5 to June 23.

PASSERINA VERSICOLOR VERSICOLOR (Bonaparte)

Varied Bunting
Contributed by LLOYD R. WOLFE

HABITS

The varied bunting is primarily a Mexican species, but three subspecies occur within the borders of the area covered by the A.O.U. Check-List. One race (*P. v. pulchra*) is resident in southern Baja California, another race (*P. v. dickeyae*) is a very rare summer resident in central and southern Arizona, and the nominate form is a summer resident in southwestern Texas, from west of the Big Bend country inland along the Rio Grande, eastward to the Gulf where it occasionally winters. Still another extralimital race (*P. v. purpurascens*) is resident in Guatemala. These races are very similar and only can be separated by a comparison of museum specimens. Their habitats, behavior, and life history, while still not well known, are probably so much alike that most details concerning one race will undoubtedly apply to the others.

This is a bird of the desert and semiarid brush country of low and medium elevations; it is never found in heavily wooded areas. James

C. Merrill (1879), referring to the Brownsville, Tex., region, says, "This beautiful species seems to be rather abundant in this vicinity, frequenting the mesquite-chaparrel." Phillips and Thornton (1949) reported it as a bird of the mesquite-salt cedar association in Presidio County, Tex. Thornton (1951) found it in the mesquite-creosote bush association, and Pulich (1963) observed birds in the Chisos Mountains in a "fairly dense stand of vegetation, together with a few cottonwoods (*Populus* sp.)" and again in the Big Bend National Park in "typical seepwillow (*Baccharis glutinosa*)-salt cedar (*Tamarix gallica*)-mesquite (*Prosopis juliflora* and *Sophora secundiflora*) habitat, along with a few cottonwoods," and "in a typical mesquite-catclaw (*Acacia greggii*) wash with scattered allthorn (*Koeberlina spinosa*) and sumac (*Rhus* sp.), bordered with creosote bush (*Larrea tridentata*)." Land (1962), writing of birds found in the arid Motagua valley of Guatemala, says, "Recorded in July and September in scrubby woodland. Males were singing on territory in July."

Many years ago the varied bunting was reported as being abundant in the Brownsville region. Griscom and Crosby (1926), reporting on the birds of that region in the early 1920's, listed it as a fairly common summer resident; however, at present it seems to be rare in that area, probably because much of the original brushy habitat association of this species has now been converted to farm land. In recent years most reports of this bunting have been from the semidesert areas of Brewster, Presidio, Terrell, and Crockett counties of western Texas.

Nesting.—Van Tyne and Sutton (1937) reported that on May 29 a nest ready for eggs was found in a dense tangle along Maravillas Creek near Marathon, Tex. Allan R. Phillips wrote Wendell Taber that he found a "nest on 1 August 1954 about 3 feet up in the dead lower twigs of a 'bachata' bush (*Condalia lycoides*) on the northwest side, near Huasabas, Sonora. The nest was constructed of coarse old grayish grass-like blades (?bark or weeds) bound with cobwebs? to two distinct but nearly vertical twigs, and, unsupported from below, was well lined with fine brownish-buffy grasses, the lining projecting above the top of the nest. The nesting tree and others of the same kind up to 10 or 12 feet in height provided good shade. There were two pin-feathered young several days old. The female came from the northeast side three times to feed the young, the male finally came with food and departed with a fecal sac. In approaching, both parents came in low through the bushes."

Baird, Brewer, and Ridgway (1905) state that among the memoranda of Mr. Xantus, made at Cape St. Lucas, they found the following in connection with this species: "nest and three eggs * * * obtained May 5 on a myrtle hanging down from very high perpendicular bluffs,* * * nest and eggs of same found on vine ten feet high." The nest is normally placed in a thick bush, low tree, or tangled vine. The records of eight sets of eggs collected in Cameron County, Tex., indicate that each nest was in a small bush; the lowest was only 16 inches from the ground and the highest was 5 feet. The nest is cup-shaped, compactly built, but somewhat untidy in appearance. The materials used in its construction consist primarily of dry grass and small stems but may include strips of vegetable fiber, plant cotton, and other similar substances. One nest included a piece of cast-off snake skin, another a strip of paper. The nest is usually lined with rootlets and fine grasses, however five of the eight available records show that some hair was used in the lining.

Eggs.—The varied bunting normally lays three or four eggs to a set. The shape varies from short-ovate to elongated-ovate. The shell is pale bluish white, unmarked, and the eggs are practically indistinguishable from those of the indigo and lazuli buntings. Measurements of 21 eggs average 17.8 by 14.3 millimeters, the eggs showing the four extremes measure *20.0* by 14.4, 19.0 by *15.0*, and *16.5* by *13.5* millimeters.

Plumage.—After the young leave the nest in juvenal plumage, the male passes through four different changes before he reaches the adult phase in the third winter, when he is over 2 years old. The female remains nearly the same after the post-juvenal molt with only slight changes from winter to summer. The juvenal plumage, both male and female, is similar to the first winter plumage of the female, but duller and more buffy brown, and the abdomen is buffy or grayish. This is described by Ridgway (1901) as follows: "above grayish brown or drab (less olivaceous than in summer female), the edges of retrices and primaries dull glaucous, or inclined to that color, middle and greater wing-coverts tipped with pale brownish buff, forming two indistinct narrow bands; under parts dull whitish medially, pale brownish laterally and across chest."

After the juvenal stage, a first winter plumage is acquired by a partial post-juvenal molt. The male in this plumage is similar to the summer female except that he is more deeply colored and browner, both above and below, with only the center of the abdomen whitish. The female is quite similar in color but the upper parts are slightly darker and more brownish. The first nuptial plumage of the male, acquired by partial prenuptial molt, is much like that of the adult female. Van Tyne and Sutton (1937) refer to a specimen taken on May 29 and state, "A male bird taken by Semple * * * is in the first nuptial plumage, scarcely distinguishable from that of the female." The first nuptial plumage of the female is much like that of the adult female but slightly more buffy. The male in second winter plumage, acquired by complete postnuptial molt, is similar to the adult male in winter, except that the wing bars are more buffy or brownish and the posterior lower parts are duller and more grayish. The second winter plumage of the female is like that of the adult female. The second nuptial plumage of the male, acquired by wear, is much like the nuptial plumage of the adult male except that the under parts are duller and more grayish or buffy brown. The third winter plumage of the male, the adult plumage, acquired by a complete postnuptial molt, is like that of the adult, however the feather tips and edgings tend to obscure the bright colors. These gradually become more apparent as the gray-brown edges wear away until they have practically disappeared by the beginning of the spring breeding season.

Food.—Very little information is available concerning the food of this bunting; presumably, it is similar to that of the indigo and lazuli buntings. Pulich (1963) states, "an adult male and juvenile were observed feeding upon weed-seeds * * *."

Voice.—James C. Merrill (1879) wrote concerning this species, "Its song has some resemblance to that of the Indigo-bird, and is constantly uttered." George N. Lawrence (1874) wrote, "This beautiful little finch is quite a common species about the vicinity of Mazatlan, where it is a constant resident * * *. It has a sweet little song, which it often warbles in the morning and evening from the top of some bush or weed in hearing of its modestly attired mate." Herbert Brandt (1940) states of the male: "this gorgeously bedecked creature, in order to spread over the countryside its crisp, warbling whistle, invariably chooses a high, prominent perch, and although very busily engaged in song, it is ever alert, and too wary to allow a person's very close approach." Allan R. Phillips writes Taber: "the usual call is very sharp and strongly reminiscent of *Oporornis tolmeiei* * * *." Roger Tory Peterson (1960) describes the song as "a thin bright finch song, more distinctly phrased and less warbled than the painted bunting's notes; notes not so distinctly paired as in song of lazuli bunting."

Field marks.—The adult male varied bunting cannot be confused with any other bird; he has a dark purplish-plum body that looks almost black at a distance, and a bright red nape, with blue crown and lighter blue rump. The most distinctive character is the red nape and dark body. Females and young males are plain grayish brown, and very similar to those of the indigo and lazuli buntings.

Behavior.—Little is known concerning the behavior of the varied bunting; usually it is a retiring species, somewhat shy and secretive, and stays away from human habitations, remaining closely to the cover of its haunts in the semidesert brush. Consequently, the female is seldom observed. However, during the nesting season, the male selects some prominent perch in the vicinity of the nest from which he announces the occupation of his territory and utters his rather sweet song. Phillips notes that both parents assist in feeding the young.

Enemies.—Apparently the varied bunting is not an infrequent host of the cowbird in some localities. Herbert Friedmann (1963) states, "R.D. Camp collected a set of 2 eggs of this bunting with 1 of the cowbird in Cameron County, Texas, on June 4, 1927 * * *." There is another set of four eggs and one of the dwarf cowbird in the collection of the Oregon State College, taken by R. D. Camp on the same date. Of the 13 available records of the varied bunting nesting in Cameron County, two—slightly over 15 percent—include cowbird eggs. Such a small number, however, may not be representative.

Other races.—The western race, *Passerina versicolor pulchra* Ridgway, is resident in southern Baja California north to Comondu; in winter, rarely to southern Sonora and Sinaloa. Ridgway (1887a) described this race as similar to the eastern race but "rather smaller, or with shorter wing and tail; adult male with red on occiput brighter, purple of throat less reddish (never decidedly red), flanks brighter plum-purple, and rump more purplish-blue or lavender * * *." William Brewster (1902) states that the females of this race differ considerably by being decidedly grayer, especially on the under parts and on the sides of the head and neck.

The intermediate race, *Passerina versicolor dickeyae* van Rossem, was described in 1934 and has been accepted by the A.O.U. Committee. This race is a rare local summer resident in southern Arizona (Baboquivarae and Santa Catalina mountains) and breeds south through central and eastern Sonora, southwestern Chihuahua south along the Pacific slopes to Colima. It winters from southern Sonora and southern Chihuahua south to Colima and Nayarit. Van Rossem (1934b) describes this race as "Similar in size to *Passerina versicolor pulchra* Ridgway, of southern Lower California. Females and young males prevailingly rufescent brown instead of grayish brown (as in *versicolor*) or brownish gray (as in *pulchra*). Adult males very similar to adult males of *pulchra*, and distinguishable only in series by the greater extent and brighter hue of the red nuchal patch."

The third race, *Passerina versicolor purpurascens* Griscom, has been described from the arid Motagua valley of Guatemala. These birds are generally similar to those of southern Texas and northeastern Mexico, but they are much smaller, and darker and duller in overall coloration.

DISTRIBUTION

Range.—Western and southern Texas to Guerrero and Oaxaca.

Breeding range.—The eastern varied bunting breeds from western and southern Texas (Marfa, Brownsville) south through central and eastern Mexico to Guerrero (Mexcala) and Oaxaca (Mitla).

Wintering range.—Winters from southern Sonora (Chinobampo), central Nuevo León (Monterrey), and southern Texas (lower Rio Grande Valley) south to Guerrero and Oaxaca.

Casual records.—Casually north in spring and summer in Texas to Edwards County and Aransas Refuge.

Migration.—Early dates of spring arrival are: Nuevo León—China, April 17. Texas—Brownsville, April 6; Chisos Mountains, April 29. New Mexico—Guadalupe Canyon, June 9. Arizona—Tucson, May 4.

Late dates of fall departure are: Arizona—Mohave Mountains, October 27. Texas—Corpus Christi, October 27; Cameron County, September 6.

Egg dates.—Baja California: 3 records, May 5 to May 12.

Texas: 14 records, April 3 to July 8; 8 records, April 26 to July 7.

PASSERINA CIRIS CIRIS (Linnaeus)

Eastern Painted Bunting

PLATES 10 AND 11

Contributed by ALEXANDER SPRUNT, JR.

HABITS

Sometimes it seems that a language other than our own succeeds in conveying an idea more convincingly. In the case of the avian gem we know as the painted bunting, Spanish seems more appropriate, because in Spanish it is "mariposa"—butterfly. This bird, in its dazzling brilliance, seems hardly a creature of feathers at all, but rather a dancing butterfly.

No other North American species is so brightly colored, or wears such a Joseph's coat of startling contrasts. There is no blending of shades whatever, the different hues are as sharply defined as if they were cut by a straight edge. No wonder many people seeing it for the first time can scarcely credit their eyes, because nothing else approaches it. Many other bright birds occur hither and yon about the country, but for flaming, jewel-like radiance, the nonpareil, as we know it in the South, literally fulfills the name; it is "without an equal."

My acquaintance with the bird dates back to early boyhood days, and my first nonpareil is still vivid in my memory, though I was only

12 at the time.   This was on Sullivan's Island, across the harbor from Charleston, S.C., where my early ornithological researches were carried on.   I was quite convinced, on seeing the brilliant singer perched on a light wire in my yard, that I had found a brand new bird, one not listed in my bird book.

Glorying in my "discovery," I enthusiastically related it to my companions and was told rather scornfully by one advanced member of the group that I had seen "nothin' but a dern nómparel!"   Nevertheless, this practical check to my supposed contribution to ornithology did not lessen my admiration for the bird.   Seeing it today is almost as great a thrill as it was then, and though it nests annually in my yard, it remains to me a source of constantly recurring pleasure and satisfaction.

Spring.—The painted bunting is a rather late migrant in spring. Widely scattered localities, together with apparently inconsistent dates, are confusing.   Illustrative is its appearance in considerable numbers at the Dry Tortugas on April 14 and its arrival at Charleston, S.C., on April 9 the same year.

The great majority of birds winter south of this country, but their return in spring is confused in Florida by the fact that some winter there.   As Howell (1932) points out: "The presence of wintering birds [in Florida] makes it difficult to determine the date when migration begins."

Migrants have been noted in the Keys late in April (Key West, April 30, Lignumvitae Key, April 29, Miami, April 16).   Yet they arrive some years as far up the east coast as Daytona on April 12. On the west coast the dates average earlier, with birds arriving at Tallahassee and Appalachicola on April 19.   The bird drops off sharply at the latter locality, and F. M. Weston has found it rare at Pensacola: "My own coastal data on the nonpareil are: Regular spring migrant, common for a day or two in some years.   Not known to nest in the Pensacola area nor anywhere in the three western counties of Florida.   Only a single fall migration record in my 46 years' residence."

A similar condition exists along the Alabama coast where Imhof (1962) gives its status on the Gulf Coast as "an uncommon to fairly common spring transient, a rare and local summer resident, and a rare fall transient.   It is known to breed only in suburban Mobile. In the remainder of the Coastal Plain, or slightly north of it, it is a rare spring transient."

In Mississippi, Burleigh (1944) gives arrival dates as from April 8 to 26.   He calls it "a rather scarce transient both in spring and fall."

H. C. Oberholser (1938), writing on its status in Louisiana, furnishes arrival dates "from March 11th", but early April appears much more

PLATE 11

val County, Fla., June 1944   S. A. Grimes

FEMALE EASTERN PAINTED BUNTING

nnington County, Minn., June 24, 1933   S. A. Grimes

NEST OF DICKCISSEL

typical. At Baton Rouge, some 90 miles north of New Orleans, it has been noted as arriving in late April, the 22nd to the 28th.

George C. Williams (MS.), in detailed notes from Texas, states that the arrival in Rockport varies from April 9–27. Dates are later at Houston, as might be expected since it is inland, and range from April 22–27. At Harlingen, in the Brownsville area, the arrival has been noted as April 24, which seems strange, although in a series of years it corresponds with more northern areas.

Returning now to the east and the South Atlantic region, Frederick V. Hebard (MS.) reports arrival in southeastern Georgia (Refuge) from April 16 at the earliest to April 24. He states that the salt water line of the Great Satilla River lies just below Refuge. Eugene E. Murphey (1937) gives arrival dates for Augusta on the Savannah River as April 25–28.

At Charleston, S.C. the nonpareil arrives about mid-April. I usually do not look for it until the 16th, and it has arrived many times on that date. Wayne's (1910) earliest was April 9, but he did not see it in some years until April 23. The males arrive first, and are followed by the females a week to 10 days later. The earliest record for South Carolina was established by E. S. Weyl and J. M. Coombs, Jr., of Philadelphia, on Mar. 21, 1939, which is considerably earlier than the earliest observation made by resident ornithologists.

The nonpareil goes on into North Carolina as far as Beaufort, confining itself, as it does everywhere in the South Atlantic area, to the coast region. Pearson and the Brimleys (1942) state that it is present there from April 15, the exact time it usually arrives in the Charleston area, some 200 miles south. No other arrival dates have been given for North Carolina.

Any critical examination of the nonpareil's spring migration cannot fail to impress the student with the peculiar hiatus between the Apalachicola and Mississippi rivers of the Gulf Coast (Florida to Louisiana). In this area the bird is rare and unrecorded in some years. East and west of it, the bird is common.

Perhaps George G. Williams' theory of spring migration *around* the Gulf of Mexico would explain, or at least help to explain, the comparative absence of the bird in that area. Williams' (1945) theory counters the long-held idea that all birds cross the Gulf, suggesting that many of them, if not most, travel around it, both east and west. To visualize this revolutionary thought, let us suppose that the spring route follows the shape of the symmetrical sweeping curve outlined by a cow's horns. Starting at the forehead (Yucatan), one horn curves around the east Mexican coast and sweeps first west, then north and east along Texas and Louisiana to, say, Pascagoula, Miss. The other turns eastward out toward and just short of Cuba, crosses the Strait of Florida, and curves up the west coast of that state t swing westward toward Pensacola. The gap between the tips o the horns basically is the area already mentioned. At the tips o both horns the nonpareil migration almost peters out, most of th birds having cut inland (northward) along the sweep of the horn' curve into Texas, Louisiana, and Mississippi on the west, and uj through Florida on the east. This leaves only stragglers to reach th area of scarcity and, as a consequence, they are few in number an considerably scattered.

If there were a strong trans-Gulf migration of these birds directl across that body of water, one could assume that large numbers o nonpareils would make landfall in the United States at the neares point in a direct line from Yucatan. This point would be the are about Mobile and Pensacola, which is the very heart of the sectio where the bird is uncommon to rare.

After the above was written much controversial comment abou Williams' theory developed among ornithologists. Most contem porary students of migration disagree with him, holding with tha foremost proponent of trans-gulf movement, George H. Lowery, Jr. of Louisiana State University. It seems established today tha Williams' theory was too sweeping in its concept, but it remain probable that some avian species are "shore-huggers" rather tha directly trans-gulf travelers. From the evidence at hand, I an strongly inclined to put the nonpareil among these.

Courtship.—This takes place as soon as the females arrive and i an animated performance, frequently characterized by lethal battle between the males, remarkable for their savagery.

In his attentions to his prospective mate, the nonpareil carrie out most of the courtship procedure on the ground, where he flatten himself out, spreads his wings and tail, and fluffs his plumage muc like a miniature turkey gobbler. The display actions are rathe jerky and stiff, with alternating periods of activity and stillness.

Nesting.—The nonpareil is a bird of low growths, hedgerows, bushes and thick grassy areas, and is consistent in placing its nest at low elevations. Usually it is in a bush or tangle of vines 3 to 6 fee from the ground and occasionally built in a banner of Spanish mos (*Tillandsia usneoides*). When this is the case, it may well be a much as 25 feet or more high. Such nests are, of course, invisible and only can be located by seeing the female fly to a particular clump

The nest itself is well made, a deep cup woven and firmly attache to the twigs or moss strands that support it. The materials are largely grass, weed stalks, and leaves, often little more than skeleta tracery in which the grassy cup is formed. The lining is either hai or fine grass.

In most of its breeding range the bird raises two broods each season, but in the Charleston area three are raised, and at times four (Wayne, 910). Wayne has found young birds "as late as September 16th." Eggs are laid by mid-May, and, indicative of the three-brood habit, Wayne has secured fresh eggs on May 18, June 16, and July 15. Audubon states that two broods are raised in Louisiana. Wilson, speaking of that State, says that two are "probable." Oberholser 1938) says "two or more." The Rev. John Bachman, quoted by Audubon and living in Charleston near where Wayne worked, notes that "I have had them to raise three broods of young in the year in confinement." At the northern limit of its Atlantic Coast range Wilmington-Beaufort, N.C.) the nonpareil apparently reduces its nesting to no more than two, and often just one, brood.

The situation in Florida is curious. Although the bird winters here with regularity, and although it occurs there in large numbers in spring, it is far from a common breeder there. South of a line across the peninsula from Vero Beach to the Gulf of Mexico, there is apparently but one nesting record (Howell, 1932). All nesting records for Florida are coastal, and it is only in the northern half of the peninsula that it breeds at all regularly. It does not breed at all in the "panhandle".

In Georgia, Burleigh (1958) states that it is "A common summer resident on the coast and along the Savannah River as far north as Augusta. Largely of accidental occurrence in the interior of the State, * * * away from the coast it is rarely observed." Eugene E. Murphey (1937) states that it used to nest abundantly at and about Augusta, Ga., but less so in recent years. Some of the diminution he lays to the charge of "those * * * who have charge of highway construction and maintenance, who relentlessly wage a war of extirpation against all roadside vegetation," thus eliminating favored nesting sites. Augusta is the only inland locality in Georgia where the species breeds, or even occurs, regularly. It is on the Savannah River at the "fall line."

A somewhat similar situation prevails along the coastal rivers of South Carolina where the nonpareil penetrates farther inland along the course of such streams than they do in areas where there are no rivers.

Burleigh (1944) states that he knew of only two localities in Mississippi where it nested, a regular one near Pass Christian and another near Biloxi, which was for one season only.

The male has little if anything to do with the domestic arrangements, as might be inferred from the brilliant plumage, calculated to draw attention. He stays in the general vicinity of the nest and sings constantly in territorial warning. The inconspicuous female is easy to overlook.

The incubation period is usually 11 days, but sometimes 12. The fledging period lasts from 12 to 14 days. The male is not recorded as taking any part in feeding the young while they are in the nest but he occasionally feeds them after they have left it.

Eggs.—The painted bunting usually lays three or four eggs; occasionally sets of five eggs are found. In shape they vary from ovate to short-ovate. They have a slight gloss and the ground is grayish white or very pale bluish-white. The markings, in the form of speckles or fine spots, are in shades of brown such as "chestnut," "chesnut brown," "Mars brown," "pecan brown," or "russet brown," with undertones of "pale mouse gray," and "pale Quaker drab." The spotting is generally concentrated toward the large end where often a ring is formed, although some eggs are fairly well covered with very fine specks. The measurements of 50 eggs average 18.9 by 14.5 millimeters; the eggs showing the four extremes measure *21.3* by *15.2*, *17.8* by 13.7 and 18.0 by 13.2 millimeters.

Plumages.—The literature contains many direct contradictions on the nonpareil's plumage development. Wilson stated that "On the fourth and fifth season, the bird has attained his complete colors." Audubon took exception to this statement and maintained that full plumage was attained at the "second season." Actually some males do not attain their full breeding plumage until their third year.

In first fall plumage the young male resembles the female. The next spring it is still much like the female, but blue feathers begin to appear on the head and by the following year practically full plumage is attained. The patchy appearance of some birds in that interim is remarkable. Wayne (1910) collected a male that had the throat, jugulum, and eye ring bright yellow instead of red.

Dwight (1900) states the juvenal plumage is acquired by a complete postnatal molt. Both sexes are then olive-brown above and the wings are dull clove-brown with sage-green edgings, brownish on the coverts. The tail is dull olive-green. Underparts are pale grayish drab washed with buff, most marked posteriorly. The orbital ring is pale buff. The bill is umber-brown with the upper mandible darker. In dried specimens the feet are dark sepia.

The first winter plumage is acquired by a post-juvenal molt which seems to be complete, one specimen from South Carolina taken October 13 being in this dress. The birds are now bright olive-green or oil-green above, and the wings and tail have become darker than in the juvenal plumage. The coverts are wholly oil-green and the remiges and rectrices are edged with a slightly paler shade. Underparts are olive-yellow, becoming maize-yellow posteriorly and dull lemon interiorly. The orbital ring is lemon-yellow. Individual variation is considerable with some birds more yellow, or more green, and some males showing occasional blue or reddish feathers.

In the first nuptial plumage, acquired by wear, young males resemble the average adult female. The more worn primary coverts are, however, usually brown, and lack the greenish edgings. Juvenal coverts may be retained.

The adult winter plumage with its brilliant colors is acquired by a complete postnuptial molt. Probably year-old birds do not acquire remiges and coverts tinged wholly claret as in adults. This would account for the green feathers mixed with the others in many specimens in which all the feathers are equally worn. The claret and greenish remiges and the body plumage are equally fresh in November birds. The claret-tinged tail is first acquired at this molt.

The adult nuptial plumage is acquired by wear. Birds with stray green remiges are probably birds of the second nuptial stage; those having all the remiges tinged claret are probably of the third nuptial. The primary coverts are usually tinged claret at both stages and unlike the brown ones of the first nuptial period. The full adult dress is certainly assumed at the second postnuptial molt and in some cases, probably at the first.

Molts and plumages of the female correspond to those of the male. In the juvenal plumage the wings and tail are duller; in the first winter dress, relative dullness prevails but the sexes scarcely differ, and the first nuptial plumage is assumed by wear. This plumage is characterized by worn brown primary coverts as in the male. At the first postnuptial molt females assume bright green-edged remiges, rectrices, and primary coverts and are even greener above and yellower below than males in first winter dress. At the second postnuptial molt or later ones, birds tend toward the plumage of the male, developing blue or dull red feathers where brighter areas occur in the male.

Many young males cannot be distinguished with certainty from females by plumage alone. The absence of mixed plumages of old and new feathers, as found in *Passerina cyanea*, belies the occurrence of any semiannual molt as in that species.

Behavior.—The nonpareil always gives the impression of being sprightly and vivacious. That this is not altogether due to its brilliant plumage is evidenced by the fact that this applies to the female also. It is often a dooryard bird, which adds to its popularity. Abundant as it is, many people living in its range are not acquainted with it, which seems to bear out the belief of some writers that the nonpareil is a shy bird. Certainly many say that it is, but the facts do not support it. It is rather retiring in the fall and often hard to find, particularly the male, but during a lifetime spent with it I have never seen any indication that the bird deserves this reputation.

It nests freely in towns and cities, many pairs doing so annually in Charleston. It is not unusual to see a male perched on a telephone wire above a street, delivering its song completely in the open and at some distance from any cover. Regarding its tendency to frequent the proximity of human habitation, I know of no spot more closely identified with this bird than the grounds of Mr. and Mrs. Carl Williams and the latter's sister, Miss Clara Bates, in Fort Pierce, Fla. Miss Bates and nonpareils are synonymous. This charming lady has maintained a feeding station for the birds for years and has come to know the species intimately.

Miss Bates (MS.) says: "These birds of the forest edge find a perfect winter habitat in the botanically interesting Florida 'high hammock' adjoining our yard. This piece of untouched native growth, approximately three acres in extent, provides both cover and food. Cabbage palms, live oaks, red bay, hickory, gumbo limbo, and mulberry rise above the lower growth of tree-like shrubs and smaller bushes, and are festooned with many species of vines. Everything in this sub-tropical 'jungle' bears fruit or seeds. At the edge of the hammock low-growing plants and grasses add their quota of food for the birds. Because of the dense shade in the hammock many of the fruits and seeds mature in mid-winter, and because of that fact there is never any scarcity of food.

"But regardless of the abundance in the hammock, the nonpareils prefer the table spread for them in our yard. They use the hammock for cover, but I never see them in the heart of it. Their favorite hide-away is the immense spread of saw palmetto, with its impenetrable tangle of prostrate trunks and sharp-edged leaves. The huge fanlike fronds give concealment from enemies, and protect the birds from storm, or a too ardent sun. I hear them flitting and rustling in the palmettos all day long, and occasionally catch a glimpse of bright eye or gay plumage.

"My feeding station is placed three feet from the edge of the hammock, near the palmettos. A tray is fastened to the side of a red bay, and a large bush of snowberry (*Chicocca alba*) surrounds the twin trunks of this tree. I spread food underneath the bush near a large flowerpot saucer that serves as the birds' bath. I feed a commercial mixture of cracked wheat and corn, and add sunflower seeds. Water is an added attraction."

Accounts of the selection of a perch when singing are greatly confused. No less eminent an authority than William Brewster (1882b) says that "The bird almost invariably sings in the depths of some thicket, and the voice ceases at the slightest noise." How Mr.

Brewster could have made this statement will always remain a mystery, but his lead has been followed by others. Frank M. Chapman (1912) quotes C. J. Maynard as follows: "[It] is always shy and retiring, seldom appearing in the open, but remaining in the dense, thorny undergrowth * * *. Whenever the birds perceive an intruder they retire into the depths of these fastnesses, and it requires considerable beating to drive them out * * *. The adult males are especially shy, and seldom show themselves. Even while singing they remained concealed, and * * * it was with the utmost difficulty that we caught sight of the authors of the harmonious strains." Chapman evidently gave full credence to this pronouncement, which must have been based on a phenomenal local condition and which is at variance with the usual facts. Frederick Hebard (MS.) states that "They never ascend to the top of a tree or the end of a branch but sing from a perch about halfway up and halfway out from the trunk."

Such positive statements are characteristic, but almost always come from northern observers, whose observations most likely are spotty and intermittent. Contrast them with statements of those who either live in the bird's range or have spent much time there. Howell (1932) says that "When singing, the males seek a perch near the top of a small tree." Eugene E. Murphey (1937) says of the bird at Augusta that it is its custom "to perch on the top of some small bush, high grass stalk or weed to sound its beautiful song." Pearson (1942) describes the singing perch as "from some exposed twig." Now these are vastly different statements from those of Brewster, Maynard, and Hebard. In a lifetime of intimate contact with the nonpareil, I can only say that they represent the actual facts in the bird's behavior. Undoubtedly the above observers must have seen something to justify their opinions, but their descriptions not only are not characteristic but are the direct opposite.

Exposed and elevated perches (from 3 to 30 feet) are the rule. As to the song ceasing "at the slightest noise" (Brewster, 1882b), this is far from the case. As already mentioned, the birds sing freely from telephone and light wires in absolutely open situations, and often along city streets. Traffic flow does not affect it at all. I have often watched nonpareils singing from a perch distant from any cover while, a few yards beneath, children played, dogs barked, and other clamor went on.

Quite a remarkable characteristic of the bird is its marked pugnacity. For a small passerine species, it is certainly a "scrapper." Unlike most avian combats which consist of little more than feints and threats, nonpareil battles are frequently bloody and often fatal. They mean business. They usually occur during mating and in territory defense, but they are not limited to these times. Multiple fights are not unusual throughout the summer. The males fly at each other and peck savagely, buffeting with their wings and mixing up in a tight tangle. The birds are so engrossed that one can sometimes pick them up in one's hands. They appear completely oblivious to everything else in the fervor of the fight. Eyes are sometimes put out, heads streaming with blood and denuded of feathers are commonplace. Occasionally one or another dies.

I have experimented with a mounted bird lure placed near a non pareil's territory. The mounted bird was soon set upon with great energy and reduced to a wreck in a few minutes. Curiously enough, this outstanding characteristic of the bird is made little of—and frequently omitted—by many writers. Wayne (1910) describes it well as follows: "As soon as the females arrive mating begins and battles take place daily between the males, which are always extremely pugnacious. In an adult male taken June 24th, 1891, nearly every feather on the top of the head was missing, undoubtedly lost in these encounters. * * * On many occasions I have seen males engaged in combat which did not cease until one was killed. I have repeatedly caught them while fighting, and a male which I examined shortly after a fight had both eyes completely closed."

The nonpareil delights in baths and is a frequent visitor to basins and fountains. At times I have had the bird disport in the spray of my garden hose, and the effect has been beautiful. The dashing movements and glowing colors amid a rainbow of spray makes them seem like detached bits of prismatic brilliance.

As might be supposed, the nonpareil is not easily intimidated by other birds, even larger ones. Miss Bates (MS.) has interesting comments along this line: "The Nonpareil is the only bird at the feeding station not afraid of the aggressive Mourning Dove. If chased from the tray by this furious 'bird of peace,' he will immediately fly back to the tray behind the dove and continue to feed. Sometimes there are three or four Nonpareils on the tray with a dove but always behind him! They feed with Cardinals, White-eyed Towhees, Catbirds and Ground Doves and are unafraid of the larger birds. On the ground * * * they eat side by side with rabbits and squirrels.'

The nonpareil is a true finch in its habitat preferences and in all its actions. It is an open country bird, although it resorts to dense cover at times. Scattered treees, field edges, grassy situations hedgerows and shrubbery along roadsides, trailing vines and the like, are favored haunts. Its actions are distinctly sparrowlike it feeds a good deal on the ground or on bending grass stalks, and prefers low cover most of the time.

Voice.—It seems to me that the literature has been cavalier in its treatment of the nonpareil's song, which is said to be weak and acking in character and which is invariably compared unfavorably to that of the indigo bunting (*Passerina cyanea*). Nuttall (1832), for instance, says that "Their song much resembles that of the Indigo Bird, but their voice is more feeble and concise."

Alexander Wilson's (1832) terminology is practically identical with Nuttall's: "Their notes very much resemble those of the Indigo Bird but want the strength and energy of the latter, being more feeble and more concise." Later on, in his account of the species, he speaks of captive specimens singing with "great sprightliness."

Audubon (1841) is somewhat more generous in his appraisal; he too calls it "sprightly," but adds that "although not so sonorous as that of the Canary, or of its nearer relative, the indigo bunting, is not far from equalling either." Later and contemporary writers also compare it with *P. cyanea* consistently.

William Brewster (1882b) writes: "The song is a low, pleasing warble very un-Finch-like in character. I should compare it to that of the Canadian Flycatcher [Canada warbler, *Wilsonia canadensis*], but the notes are less emphatic, though equally disconnected." I agree that it is a "pleasing warble," but have never thought it "low." Compared to most small passerine birds, the song of the nonpareil does not lose volume. It can be easily heard from a distance of 100 yards, and it is, at any rate, an indefatigable performance, heard from morning till night. Two or three pairs nest close to my home annually, and seldom do many minutes pass without the song resounding clearly and cheerfully.

Mrs. T. E. Winford describes the call note as *"pik-pik-pik."*

Aretas A. Saunders wrote Mr. Bent that "the song of the painted bunting is sweet and musical, high-pitched, but rather weak. It is much more musical in quality than that of the Indigo Bunting. It is made up of single-notes, two or three-note phrases, and occasional trills, usually with abrupt changes in pitch, and it is uncommon to have two or three consecutive notes on the same pitch. Phonetic examples are: *tida dayda tida day teetayta tita; witee wi witee wi witato;* and *to taytletay weeto weeto taytletay wee.*

"In 17 records obtained in Oklahoma in 1950, the number of notes per song varied from 7 to 13, averaging a little more than 10. The length of songs varied from 1 to 4 seconds, and averaged about 2. There was a pause, however, in the 4-second song, so that by leaving it out, the average would be about 1.85. The pitch varied from D# to D'. In different songs, the pitch varied from 2 to 4½ tones, averaging about 3.

"Each bird sings a number of different songs. I recorded four different songs from one bird. They prefer a conspicuous although not necessarily high, perch from which to sing, and I heard one bird sing from the ground. In general, the song shows a tendency to start on a higher pitch and end on a lower one, seven of my records ending on the lowest note of the song."

Food.—A member of the Fringillidae, the nonpareil is primarily a seed-eater. This has been shown by stomach analyses, although these have not been extensive, and by observation.

In South Carolina, I have observed the bird closely. Its frequency not to say constant presence, in weedy fields, edges of woods and salt marshes, roadside hedges, and so forth, indicate that seeds of grasses are its main dependence. And added to the habitat is the actual sight of the bird on the stems of such growth, picking away at the heads of seed. Foxtail grass (*Alopecurus*), some pines, figs and sunflowers furnish most of the preferred seeds in the Carolina Low Country.

In Florida, Howell (1932) examined 13 stomachs, in which vegetable food composed 73 percent of the total content. Among the "considerable quantities" of seeds were those of various grasses, sedges and weeds, including dock (*Rumex acetosella*), *Panicums*, *Hypericums* and *Cyperus*. One stomach contained pine seeds, another rose seeds. Wheat was found in two, and fig seeds and pulp had been taken "in several instances." Animal matter consisted of insects, amounting to 27 percent; those represented were "beetles, grasshoppers, crickets, bugs, wasps, flies and lepidopterus larvae."

W. L. McAtee (*in* Beal, McAtee, and Kalmbach, 1916) says: "Few complaints have been lodged against the painted bunting on the score of its food habits. It is said to eat rice at times, to peck into figs and grapes, and to bite off the tips of pecan shoots. In no case that has come to notice, however, has it been charged with doing serious damage. Certainly no such charge is supported by the investigations of the Biological Survey, for no product of husbandry has thus far been found in any of the stomachs examined, 80 of which have been examined, all collected in Texas in July, August and September." He goes on to say that animal matter composed 20.86 percent and vegetable matter 79.14 percent, closely paralleling the ratio in the specimens mentioned by Howell from Florida. With the eastern and western portions of the range thus indicated, it is not to be supposed that much variation takes place in the central areas of the bird's occurrence.

McAtee further observes that 2.48 percent of the animal food "was made up of weevils, mostly cotton boll weevils. All insects of this group are destructive, but none more so than the notorious cotton boll weevil, and this species had been eaten by 18 of the 80 nonpareils examined." The cotton-worm is also eaten, and composed 3.14 perent of the animal food. Other insects listed by McAtee include 'grasshoppers, crickets, click beetles, leaf beetles, caterpillars, true bugs, and small hymenopterans. A few spiders and one snail also were taken."

In the vegetable category, he found that "The vegetable food is remarkable in consisting largely of a single item—the seeds of foxtail, or pigeon grass. This is one of the worst weeds in the United States. The 80 painted buntings made over two-thirds (precisely 67.03 percent) of their total food of its seeds. The seeds of other grasses composed 5.88 percent of the food grasses alone, thus furnishing over nine-tenths of the vegetable portion." Other seeds were those of mallow, amaranth, sorrel, and nail grass.

He sums up by saying that practically all the vegetable food is weed seeds and the animal food almost exclusively injurious insects, more than a fourth being the two greatest pests of the cotton crop. Surely this is an honorable record and one which deserves better knowledge on the part of the farmer, gardener, horticulturist, and bird student. It is easy to wish that the nonpareil's range was greater than it is.

Caged.—In the days when cage birds were in vogue in this country, the nonpareil held front rank in popularity. The practice was an old one, for both Wilson and Audubon comment on it. Wilson (1832) had the following to say concerning it:

I found these birds very commonly domesticated in the houses of the French inhabitants of New Orleans; appearing to be the most common cage bird they have. The negroes often bring them to market, from the neighbouring plantations, for sale; either in cages, taken in traps, or in the nest. A wealthy French planter, who lives on the banks of the Mississippi, a few miles below Bayou Fourche, took me into his garden, which is spacious and magnificent, to show me his aviary; where, among many of our common birds, I observed several nonpareils, two of which had nests, and were then hatching. * * * Many of them have been transported to Europe; and I think I have somewhere read, that in Holland attempts have been made to breed them, and with success.

Six of these birds, which I brought with me from New Orleans by sea, soon became reconciled to the cage. In good weather, the males sang with great sprightliness, though they had been caught only a few days before my departure. They were greedily fond of flies, which accompanied us in great numbers during the whole voyage; and many of the passengers amused themselves with catching these, and giving them to the Nonpareils; till, at length, the birds became so well acquainted with this amusement, that as soon as they perceived any of the people attempting to catch flies, they assembled at the front of the cage, stretching out their heads through the wires with eager expectation, evidently much interested in the issue of their efforts.

Though the practice of caging native wild birds has now long since been prohibited, I recall an experience similar to that of Wilson's that I had in New Orleans when I was shown the aviary of a wealthy citizen there. He was neither French nor a planter, but he was interested in birds, and had a collection housed in as fine a structure as any zoological park in the country could boast. There was a caretaker whose sole responsibility was to devote himself to the avian captives. I was assured that the necessary permits were had and like Wilson, I saw several nonpareils there.

Audubon (1841) too was impressed by the cage-bird traffic:

* * * no sooner does it [the nonpareil] make its appearance [in Louisiana] that trap-cages are set, and a regular business is commenced in the market of tha city. The method employed in securing the male Painted Finch is so connected with its pugnacious habits, that I feel inclined to describe it, especially as it is so different from the common way of alluring birds * * *.

A male bird in full plumage is shot and stuffed in a defensive attitude, and perched among some grass-seed, rice, or other food, on the same platform as th trap-cage. This is taken to the fields or near the orangeries, and placed in so open a situation, that it would be difficult for a living bird of any species to fly over it without observing it. The trap is set. A male Painted Finch passes, perceives it and dives towards the stuffed bird, with all the anger which its little breast can contain. It alights on the edge of the trap for a moment, and throwing its body against the stuffed bird, brings down the trap, and is made a prisoner. In thi manner, thousands of these birds are caught every spring. So pertinacious are they in their attacks, that even when the trap has closed upon them, they continue pecking at the feathers of the supposed rival. * * *

They feed almost immediately after being caught; and if able to support the loss of liberty for a few days, may be kept for several years. I have known some instances of their being kept in confinement for upwards of ten years. Few vessels leave the port of New Orleans during the summer months, without taking some Painted Finches, and through this means they are transported probably to al parts of Europe. I have seen them offered for sale in London and Paris, with the trifling difference in value on each individual, which converted the sixpence pai for it in New Orleans to three guineas in London.

Wayne (1910) says: "This species is easily caught in trap-cages in the months of April and May. A decoy bird is placed in a cage and the latter is then placed near some hedge where Nonpareils are present. As soon as a male perceives a bird of his species in the cage, he at once makes for it and is caught. Large numbers used to be taken in this manner. They become tame almost at once, and seem to prefer hemp seed as an article of food when in captivity."

Earle R. Greene (1946) states: "This beautiful little bird has suffered to an alarming degree from trapping and caging, practiced over many years by the Cuban population of the keys. The Cubans love birds, but their admiration expresses itself in wishing to cage them to have them about their homes and dwellings and stores. The writer found that breaking up this practice was a delicate and difficult matter, and one that required considerable public education." Prior to Mr. Greene's tenure of office at Key West, the National Audubon Society's representative there, Edward M. Moore, had been working on the cage-bird situation for several years. Thanks to his experience with West Indian peoples in former years, and his diplomatic handling of the matter, cage-bird traffic was greatly reduced.

Field marks.—The male painted bunting is so absolutely distinctive that it cannot be confused with any other species. Howell's (1932) vivid, if terse, description leaves nothing to the imagination, although none is needed. This is what he says: "Head and nape azurite blue (dark violet blue); foreback yellow-green; rump dragon's-blood red; underparts scarlet." No one could fail to recognize such a bird as that, but many of course, are not aware of its existence, and when seeing it for the first time, are somewhat incredulous of the evidence of their own eyes.

The female is so utterly unlike the male that those unfamiliar with the species would never connect the two. It is easy to understand, however, that the brilliance of the latter would be a dead give-away at the nest, while the somber colors of the female blend well into the surrounding vegetation she frequents. To quote Howell (1932) again, he says of her: "Upperparts oil green or bice green; underparts pyrite yellow (yellowish green), shading to amber yellow on the belly; wings and tail hair brown (dark drab) shaded with green." Peterson (1947) notes her primary field characteristic by pointing out that "no other small Finch is green."

In closing my remarks on the bird's appearance, let me quote Miss Clara Bates (MS.) once more. In writing of the earliest fall arrival at Fort Pierce in 1937 (August 10) she says: "This little chap was down on the shore in front of our place, feeding on a three-foot stalk of heavy-headed sea grass. It was one of the most exquisite sights I ever saw—the male in full plumage, clinging to the bending grass stem and eating the seeds, chipping softly to himself all the time. The white coral sand of the shore, the river blue as the tropical sky, and the background of deep green sea-grape, made a wonderful setting * * * his plumage was as gay as that of a painted butterfly, and he poised as lightly on the grass-stem. He was so fearless that I was able to move within a few feet of him, and could observe his vivid red eyelids without using my field glasses."

Fall.—The southward movement of the nonpareil starts rather early, but covers a considerable period. From the northern limit of its South Atlantic range (Beaufort, N.C.) the last appearance dates in fall are nothing if not vague. Pearson and the Brimleys (1942) say no more than that the bird leaves in "early autumn." In the Charleston region the species becomes progressively less common in late September and more so in October, when the males are difficult to locate. Most of the birds leave during that month, and it is unusual to see one after October 20–25. The latest record is November 4.

Murphey (1937) states that it leaves the Augusta (Ga.) region in "late October."

In North Florida, Howell (1932) gives last dates for Fernandina as October 20; Daytona, October 22; New Smyrna; November 7; and Sombrero Light, November 11. At Fort Pierce, Miss Bates (MS.) says that the earliest fall appearance (south of the breeding range) is August 7, adding that "the early fall migrants pass on rapidly." From early August on, however, she has the birds more or less continually at her place through fall and winter. Florida is the only state in which it winters with regularity, and that occurs very locally and in the southern portion. Illustrative of Miss Bates's observances from August through the remainder of the year are: August 10, 15, and 29; September 26; October 10 and 19; November 19; and December 6. From January to April she has birds in varying numbers constantly.

My own experience with nonpareils in winter in Florida embraces the Lake Okeechobee area (Okeechobee City, N.E. corner of the lake, and Clewiston, S.W. corner) where I conducted the Audubon Wildlife tours for several years. In each of these towns the species was observed regularly at several feeding stations from January through the rest of the winter months.

In 1960, the Audubon tours were shifted to Naples on the southwest coast, nearer the Corkscrew Swamp Sanctuary. Nonpareils were present in Naples the entire winter. In the beautiful Caribbean Gardens of Naples, this species frequents the close vicinity of cages housing parakeets and finches to pick up seeds scattered therefrom, and, at times, as many as a half dozen can be seen any day from January through March. Several privately maintained feeding stations in the town itself harbor nonpareils the entire winter. Therefore, the species really is a common, though perhaps local, wintering bird in Florida from Lake Okeechobee southward.

In Texas, Williams (MS.) gives departure dates at Cove (near Galveston) as from September 17 to October 19. The latest Texas departure is more than 2 weeks earlier than the latest South Carolina date.

Winter.—Alexander F. Skutch contributes the following. "Painted buntings arrive in Guatemala early in October. During the winter months they are found throughout the length of Central America as far south as western Panama, but are more abundant in the north than in the south, and on the Caribbean side of Costa Rica appear to be absent. Although on Nov. 15, 1930, I met a single male at 8,500 feet in the mountains above Tecpán, Guatemala, he had probably not yet settled down for the winter; certainly while in Central America the great majority of painted buntings spend this season between sea-level and 5,000 feet. A. W. Anthony

(Griscom, 1932) found this bird abundant in January and February in the arid valley of the Río Negro at Sacapulas in northern Guatemala, but I have never anywhere known it to be common. In parts of Central America that I have visited, I have met at most scattered individuals of the painted bunting; it has always appeared to be rarer than the indigo bunting, which winters in the same localities. The seeming rareness of painted buntings may be caused in part by the dense cover they haunt, in riverside brakes of tall wild cane, high grass, pastures overgrown with bushes and weeds, and similar low, crowded vegetation. Adult males, of course, wear their variegated nuptial attire throughout the year; and as early as mid-March I have seen males and females keeping company as though mated. I have never heard the painted bunting sing in Central America. My latest spring record is of a female seen near Los Amates in the Motagua Valley of Guatemala on April 18, 1932."

DISTRIBUTION

Range.—Missouri, Tennessee, and North Carolina to Veracruz, Yucatán, and Cuba.

Breeding range.—The eastern painted bunting breeds from southern Missouri, southwestern Tennessee (Memphis), southern Alabama (Mobile), central South Carolina (Columbia), and southeastern North Carolina (Beaufort) south to southeastern Texas (Houston), southern Louisiana (Calcasieu Lake, Pass a Loutre), southern Mississippi (Biloxi), and central Florida (Punta Rasa, New Smyrna).

Winter range.—Winters from southern Louisiana (Cameron, New Orleans), central Florida (Seven Oaks, Fort Pierce), and the northern Bahamas (Grand Bahama, Berry Islands, New Providence) south to southern Veracruz (Tres Zapotes), Yucatán (Chichén Itzá), Quintana Roo (Cozumel Island), and Cuba; casually north to South Carolina (Winnsboro), North Carolina (Fayetteville), New Jersey (Haddonfield), and Massachusetts (Falmouth).

Casual records.—Casual north to the District of Columbia, Maryland, New Jersey, New York, and Massachusetts.

Migration.—Early dates of spring arrival are: Nayarit—Tres Marias Islands, April 26. Florida—northern peninsula, March 9; southern peninusla, March 21. Alabama—Dauphin Island, March 26. Georgia—Savannah, April 7 (average, April 14). South Carolina—March 21; median of 10 years at Charleston, April 15. North Carolina—Brunswick County, May 2. Maryland—Laurel, May 1. New Jersey—Cape May, May 4. New York— Easthampton, May 13. Louisiana—New Orleans, March 11; Baton Rouge, April 6. Mississippi—Gulfport, April 8; Rosedale, April 23. Arkansas—Little

Rock, May 2. Tennessee—Memphis, May 2. Minnesota—near Madison, May 2. Texas—Austin, April 4; Sinton, April 5 (median of 6 years, April 19); Cove, April 14. Oklahoma—Tulsa, April 11, Custer County, April 17. Kansas—Winfield, April 28. Nebraska— Hastings, May 19. Colorado—Denver, May 17.

Late dates of spring departure are: El Salvador—Chilata, April 27. Veracruz—southern Veracruz, Apirl 6. Campeche—Ichek, April 22. Florida—Lower Keys, June 13. Alabama—Grove Hill, May 23. Mississippi—Deer Island, May 9. Texas—Central Coast, May 30.

Early dates of fall arrival are: Arizona—Cave Creek Canyon, Chiricahua Mountains, August 11. New Hampshire—New Hampton, August 21. Maryland—Ocean City, August 31. El Salvador— Divisadero, November 12.

Late dates of fall departure are: Arizona—Fort Huachuca, September 13. New Mexico—Mesilla, September 30. Oklahoma—Fort Sill, September 6. Texas—Cove, October 19; Austin, October 14. Mississippi—Deer Island, November 1. Louisiana—Baton Rouge, October 23. New York—Manhattan, October 19. New Jersey— Island Beach, September 29. Virginia—Blacksburg, September 7. South Carolina—November 5. Georgia—Augusta, October 21. Alabama—Dauphin Island, November 1, October 17. Florida— Fowey Rocks Light, November 20; Leon County, October 31.

Egg dates.—Florida: 2 records, May 16 and May 27.

Georgia: 72 records, May 1 to July 26; 36 records, May 18 to May 31.

PASSERINA CIRIS PALLIDIOR Mearns

Western Painted Bunting

Contributed by WENDELL TABER

HABITS

Mr. Bent stated that this race is larger than its eastern relative. The red under parts of the male are paler vermilion red, and the female is more grayish green above and more buffy, less yellowish below. These color differentiations may well be associated with the somewhat different type of habitat. Charles H. Blake writes to point out that this race inhabits the drier part of the range of the species. He also quotes R. W. Storer (1951) who says that replaced tail feathers in the male may be of female type and red may occur in the plumage of first year males and also adult females. Blake comments that these phenomena have also been observed in the purple finch and can be expected to be general in species with strong sexual dimorphism.

Florence M. Bailey (1928) states the nest is located in hackberry, cat-claw, or chaparral, about six feet from the ground, made of grasses and sometimes leaves, lined with finer grasses and hairs. There may be four or five eggs. Practically all of the vegetable food is weed seeds, two-thirds of it being seeds of foxtail grass. The measurements of seven eggs, furnished by E. N. Harrison, average 19.1 by 14.9 millimeters; the eggs showing the four extremes measure *20.0* by *15.0*, 18.6 by *15.2*, *18.3* by 14.8, and 18.4 by *14.5* millimeters.

DISTRIBUTION

Range.—New Mexico, Oklahoma, and Kansas to Panama.

Breeding range.—The western painted bunting breeds from southeastern New Mexico (Mesilla, Carlsbad), central Oklahoma (Blaine County, Oklahoma City), and central eastern Kansas (Solomon, Lawrence) south through western and central Texas to southern Chihuahua (Camargo), southern Coahuila (Hipólito), and southern Texas (Edinburg, Victoria).

Winter range.—Winters from central Sinaloa (San Lorenzo), San Luis Potosí (Xilitla), and central Tamaulipas (Victoria) south through Mexico (exclusive of the Yucatán Peninsula), and Central America to western Panama (Chiriquí).

Casual records.—Casual in California (Tia Juana River Valley), Oregon (Malheur National Wildlife Refuge), Arizona (Nogales, Huachuca Mountains, Chiricahua Mountains), and Colorado (Denver).

Egg dates.—Texas: 39 records, March 28 to July 26; 22 records, May 21 to June 10.

TIARIS BICOLOR BICOLOR (Linnaeus)

Bahama Black-faced Grassquit

Contributed by JAMES BOND

HABITS

Black-faced grassquits are among the most characteristic and familiar birds of the West Indies and are also known from the extreme northern portion of South America. They are lacking, however, from any part of the mainland of Cuba. Seven subspecies are recognized, of which the nominate race is confined to the Bahama Islands and cays off the northern coast of Cuba.

The first North American record of this species was a female of the Bahaman race collected at Miami on Jan. 19, 1871, by H. W. Henshaw. It was found in bushes bordering a clearing near the old fort. Maynard (1874) gives the following vivid account of the taking of this specimen.

"Mr. Henshaw was collecting here [at Miami] with me on the 19th of January, 1871, when his quick eye detected a small bird among the thick bushes, and he instantly shot it. After making his way into the thicket and searching for a time he returned, bearing his prize but with a puzzled expression on his countenance, that instantly communicated itself to mine when I saw the little gray bird which he held in his hand, for it was a species which I had never beheld. It proved to be the Black-headed Finch, the first and, up to this date the only specimen ever taken in the United States".

A second record is based on a pair of wings from a bird that struck the lighthouse at Sombrero Key, Monroe County, Fla., Apr. 17 1888. The lightkeeper forwarded these, together with the remains of a number of other birds that had struck the lighthouse in passage, to the U.S. National Museum. There, Robert Ridgway misidentified the wings as of *Tiaris canora*, the Cuban or melodious grassquit, one of the few errors in identification he ever made. On the strength of this, the melodious grassquit remained on the American list for almost 75 years, when a re-examination of the wings revealed their true identity (cf. Austin, 1963).

In view of the abundance and widespread distribution of this grassquit in the Bahama Islands, it is strange that there are so few subsequent records of its occurrence in Florida. The only ones are recorded by Sprunt (1963) as one seen at Everglades National Park by Louis A. Stimson and C. Russell Mason, Oct. 29, 1960, and one found dead near West Palm Beach by Ralph Browning in mid December 1962.

In the Bahamas this tiny finch, which is only about 4½ inches in length, is found chiefly about the settlements, in gardens and plantations and the borders of thickets. It is common in Nassau and is one of the first birds seen by the visitor to that picturesque town. When feeding, it may be seen on lawns or in tall grass or shrubbery near the ground, and often allows a close approach when so engaged. At times small flocks are flushed by the wayside.

Nesting.—The nest is a rather roughly built but compact structure, globular in shape, with an opening at one side that varies in size. It is composed outwardly of coarse grasses and weed stalks, the interior cup lined with softer, finer grasses.

Bonhote (1903) states that the nest is situated at heights varying from 4 to 10 feet above the ground, and "generally placed on the top of a small sapling." A nest in process of construction that I found in Nassau was at least 20 feet above the ground in a dead frond of a royal palm. Another was in a flower pot that hung from the ceiling of a hotel porch in Nassau.

The breeding season, at least in the northern Bahamas, evidently begins in March and continues well into the summer. It is likely that more than one brood is raised yearly.

Dr. Virgilio Biaggi, Jr., wrote Mr. Bent that the Puerto Rican race, *Tiaris bicolor omissa*, builds its nest in the center of low bushes, and he believes the nest is used only once. A nest discovered on May 25, 1949, was constructed in about 3 days. Beginning on May 28, four eggs were laid on successive days. While the last egg was laid the morning of May 31, incubation started the previous afternoon. The female alone incubates. All four eggs hatched during the night or early in the morning of June 12. Both parents fed the young, which left the nest on June 23. The abandoned nest contained a great quantity of fecal matter.

Eggs.—The set of eggs laid by the Bahama grassquit varies from two to five, sets of three and four being most common. The eggs in the Museum of Comparative Zoology are ovate and slightly glossy. They are grayish white, speckled and spotted with "auburn," Brussels brown, argus brown, and "cinnamon brown," with underlying spots of pale drab-gray and "mouse gray." On some the specklings are scattered over the entire egg with a concentration toward the large end; others have confluent spots forming a cap over the large end with only scattered dots over the rest of the egg. The measurements of 33 eggs average 17.3 by 12.9 millimeters; the eggs showing the four extremes measure *18.3* by 13.9, 17.9 by *14.1*, *16.2* by 12.3, and 16.5 by *12.0* millimeters.

Plumages.—Ridgway (1901) describes the juvenal plumage of the Bahama black-faced grassquit as "Similar to adult female but rather paler." He adds that "Immature males are variously intermediate in plumage between adult males and females," implying that they show more or less black on the head and under parts.

Food.—The food of this grassquit consists almost entirely of seeds of grasses and weeds. Wetmore (1927) states of the subspecies inhabiting Puerto Rico (*T. b. omissa*) that seeds "are usually swallowed entire and ground up in the muscular gizzard with the sand which is eaten for that purpose, but may occasionally be hulled neatly before being swallowed." Danforth (1936), writing of the same race, notes that it occasionally eats insects.

Behavior.—The normal flight is rapid and direct, but rarely sustained for more than a few yards. In the breeding season I have frequently seen the adult male perform what may be described as a courtship flight. This is much slower than normal flight, and is accompanied by trembling wings and a puffed-up appearance with the head drawn back, while the bird sings repeatedly.

Voice.—The song is a simple, buzzing *tik-zeeëë*, or *tik-tik-zeeëë*. It is uttered a little more deliberately than that of any of the Antillean races, and with more emphasis on the introductory notes. The call-note is a weak *tst*.

DISTRIBUTION

Range.—The Bahama black-faced grassquit is resident in the Bahamas from Grand Bahama and Abaco southeast to Great Inagua and the Caicos Islands (unrecorded from Turks Islands), and on cays off northern Las Villa Province, Cuba (Cayo Tio Pepe, Cayo Punta de Piedras); vagrant to southern Florida (Sombrero Key, Everglades National Park, Miami, West Palm Beach).

Egg dates.—Puerto Rico and Vieques (*Tiaris bicolor omissa*): 28 records, 8 in February, 10 during late May, June, and July, 1 in October, 7 in November (earliest on the 18th), and 2 in December.

SPIZA AMERICANA (Gmelin)

Dickcissel

PLATE 11

Contributed by ALFRED O. GROSS

HABITS

The dickcissel is one of the commonest of the birds to be seen in the open meadows and pastures of our Middle Western States. Anyone traveling along the highways of that section of the country is certain to notice the male, who constantly and lustily announces his presence by his earnest and incessant calls from the top of a fence post or weed stalk. The clear accented notes of the monotonous song at once suggest the bird's common name. Often in the same fields one also sees the meadowlark, and because both species have yellow breasts with conspicuous black patches and other similarities, the smaller dickcissel is locally known as "the little meadowlark." The name "black-throated bunting" which appears frequently in the writings of the older ornithologists is seldom heard today. The dickcissel not only contributes its beauty and cheerful song to its environment, but also consumes scores of destructive insects as well as hundreds of seeds of noxious weeds. It thus ranks high among the economically important prairie birds.

The nesting range of the dickcissel is limited chiefly to the region of the Middle West between the Alleghenies and the Rocky Mountains and from Michigan, Wisconsin, Minnesota, and North Dakota south to Alabama, Mississippi, Louisiana, and Texas. It is abundant and, according to numerous reports, apparently is becoming more so throughout Indiana, Illinois, Missouri, Iowa, Kansas, Nebraska and South Dakota. Today it is rapidly extending its breeding range to the north and south as well as to the west of these states.

The dickcissel is very erratic in its distribution. Its numbers, even in the center of its nesting range, fluctuate greatly from year to year. A locality may have an abundance of dickcissels, only to have them practically disappear after a few years. Sometimes this fluctuation extends over so large an area of one or more States that we may speak of "high" or "low" years for the species.

A most remarkable feature of this erratic bird has been its recession from and its recent reoccupation of eastern North America. During the 19th century it nested commonly in a wide range extending from the Carolinas through Pennsylvania, New Jersey, and New York to Rhode Island and Massachusetts. Stragglers were collected as far south as Florida and as far north as New Hampshire and Nova Scotia (Gross, 1921). By the end of the century it had practically disappeared from the vast area east of the Allegheny Mountains. Many contemporary accounts tell of its diminution in numbers, and predictions were freely made that it was destined to be completely extirpated from this part of its former range. This happened during the first quarter of the 20th century. It nested in Mississippi as late as 1900 (Stockard, 1905), and the last record of its breeding in the northern section of this area was a nest found at Plainfield, N. J., on July 3, 1904, by W. De W. Miller (1904). It then disappeared, and the mystery of its disappearance has never been solved.

Just as baffling is the recent reappearance of great numbers in the region it deserted 50 years ago. After 1920 stragglers again appeared in the east, and a pair nested in Georgia in 1925, as reported by Burleigh (1927a), but the year 1928 marks the date when the dickcissel gave the greatest promise of a general return. In that year records ranged all the way from localities in Florida, the Carolinas, Pennsylvania, Maryland and New Jersey to the Bay of Fundy as follows, arranged in chronological order: April 11, Pensacola, Fla. (Howell, 1932); April 26, Tallahassee, Fla., 1 male (Williams, 1929); May 18, Columbia, S.C., 1 bird (Smyth, 1930); May 19, Raleigh, N.C., 1 pair (Snyder, 1928); May 25, Columbia, S.C., colony of 50 birds (Smyth, 1930); May 26, June 9, 18, Darling, Pa., 1 male, 1 male, 1 pair (Stone, 1928a; Smyth, 1930); June 5, S.C.–N.C. State line on Route 1, 1 bird (Smyth, 1930); June 10–11, Sharptown, N.J., 1 male (Stone, 1928b); July 15, 22, Dickerson, Md., 6 males, female feeding young (Wetmore and Lincoln, 1928); August 6, Hendersonville, N.C., 2 males singing (Pearson and the Brimleys, 1942); September 23, aboard a steamer in the Bay of Fundy, a male in winter plumage (Rand, 1929); November 5, aboard a ship 140 miles off Cape Charles, Va., 1 female (Holt, 1932). These many records in 1928 gave observers reason to believe the dickcissel was staging a substantial comeback in the east. The dickcissels have fluctuated in numbers there ever since, but with no notable increase over the numbers reported in 1928.

The detailed summary of records of numbers in "New England Bird Life" (1936–1944) and its successor, "Records of New England Birds" (1945 to the present), are helpful, at least, in hinting at the status of the dickcissel in New England from year to year. The number of birds reported each year by these two publications are as follows: 1937, 1; 1938, 3; 1939,1; 1940, 6; 1941, 1; 1942, 0; 1943, 3; 1944, 0; 1945, 4; 1946, 18; 1947, 9; 1948, 19; 1949, 50; 1950, 51; 1951, 72; 1952, 122; 1953, 288. This represents a total of 647 dickcissels in 398 separate reports in the New England States alone. It will be seen that from 1948 on the increase was extraordinary. The 647 birds were distributed by States as follows: Maine 53, New Hampshire 6, Vermont 6, Massachusetts 489, Rhode Island 44, and Connecticut 49. The extremely large number reported from Massachusetts is due in part to the larger number of active field observers in that State, but even so, it is obvious that the density of the recent invasion of dickcissels in New England is centered there.

If we arrange the 647 New England records according to months of the year we have the following: January 77, February 44, March 25, April 28, May 4, June 0, July 0, August 34, September 128, October 114, November 88, and December 105. Thus the dickcissels appear in New England during August, reach their maximum in September and October, and then drop off slowly until April. Only 4 dickcissels were reported in May for the 17 years of records; none was reported for June and July. What becomes of the birds after the end of April each year? I believe that most migrate back to their midwestern breeding grounds.

Most of the reports tabulated above are for one or two birds, rarely as many as three or five, the average being 1.6 birds to a report. Many winter records are of individuals that visit feeding stations where they often associate with house sparrows. At the feeding stations these two birds, somewhat similar in size and appearance but of different families and radically different in nesting habits, have food habits in common that bring them together. Observations at many feeding stations have greatly augmented the number of records. In fact feeding stations may be a factor in attracting them and encouraging them to remain in New England throughout the winter.

The records in the regional reports of the "Aubudon Field Notes" indicate that the recent dickcissel invasion occupies the region from the Middle Atlantic States through New England to maritime Canada.

According to Godfrey (1954) three birds were observed and a specimen collected as far north as the Moisie River on the Gulf of St. Lawrence, and another was collected 150 miles farther east on the north shore of the Gulf at Baie Johan Beetz. The northeasternmost record is of one observed and one found dead at Terra Nova in central eastern Newfoundland. There are a number of records for Nova Scotia and New Brunswick. This spread to northeastern United States and Canada suggests that the dickcissels come directly westward from the great breeding grounds of the Middle West and travel north of the barrier of the higher Appalachian mountains, probably aided by the prevailing winds at that time of the year. They continue eastward until stopped by the Atlantic Ocean, which most of them reach on the Massachusetts coast. From there they fan out northward to Maine and Canada, and possibly a few to the south. This assumption seems reasonable when we consider that the great majority of records are from coastal New England, many from such islands as Block Island, R.I., Nantucket and Martha's Vineyard, Mass., Monhegan Island, Me., and Machias Seal Island in the Bay of Fundy. Some that continue on have taken refuge on boats at sea (Fleisher, 1926; Holt, 1932; Rand, 1929; Lamm, 1956). No doubt some adventurous individuals are lost at sea.

In the spring the dickcissels wintering east of the Alleghenies probably return to their Middle West nesting area by a direct east-west migration over the route previously mentioned. This east-west and west-east migration has a parallel in several other species, for example the evening grosbeak, in which it has been a gradual but now a fixed habit. Even as the evening grosbeak is now nesting in northeastern United States and southeastern Canada, the dickcissel may again nest in New England, although it is not safe to predict the future status of so erratic a bird.

As yet I know of no recent nesting record of the dickcissel in New England and eastern Canada. All the eastern nesting records thus far have been from New York and the more southern States. John W. Aldrich's map of the breeding distribution of the dickcissel taken from U.S. Fish and Wildlife species distribution card file show the following number of localities in the States east of the Mississippi and Ohio Rivers: Mississippi 1, Alabama 6, Georgia 2, Tennessee 2, Kentucky 1, West Virginia 2, Pennsylvania 2, and New Jersey 1 (Aldrich, 1948). A considerable number of nesting records, chiefly in the Gulf and southern States, have been made since Aldrich's map was published.

I am inclined to believe that the dickcissels nesting in our southern States reach there from the south in the spring rather than coming directly from the west in the fall over the route suggested for our northern winter visitors. During the spring migration it is conceivable that some of the birds on the regular migration, on reaching the midsouthern United States, instead of following the Mississippi Valley route, are diverted to the eastern part of the United States. Many of the dates of arrival in our southern States correspond to the spring migration dates of the appearance of these birds in the Mississippi Valley.

Regardless of how the northern and southern contingents of dickcissels arrive, the sudden change of the status of this bird in the eastern part of the United States is most extraordinary.

Spring.—The dickcissel winters in Central America and in northern South America, but in much of Central America, especially in the coastal plains and lowlands, it appears only as a migrant. Peters (1931) collected specimens at Chiriquicito, Panama, as late as April 18, 1928. Dicky and van Rossem (1938) state that the dickcissel is a common spring migrant through the more open districts of the lower foothills and coastal plain of El Salvador. A male specimen was taken from a large flock at Divisadero on Apr. 12, 1926. Alexander F. Skutch states in correspondence that it is widely distributed over Central America during the winter months, but considers its status as a winter resident in the Caribbean lowlands doubtful. Near Los Amates in the lowlands of Guatemala he did not meet with it until Mar. 28, 1932, more than a month after he began work in that region. J. L. Peters (1929) also suspects that it is only a migrant in the Caribbean lowlands. He did not encounter it until March 29, when he saw two at Lancetilla perched on a wire fence running beside the railroad track where he passed six times a day, making it certain that the birds were new arrivals from the south. Several years previously Peters saw dickcissels appear at Quintana Roo for the first time on April 5. Van Tyne (1935) secured specimens at Uaxactun, Guatemala, April 13 to June 20, and at Chuntuqui April 29 to May 8. He states: "Dickcissels were frequently seen at the Uaxactum clearing in flocks of about ten to thirty. Some came regularly to the mule corral to feed on waste corn. The last were noted April 28, when several flocks were still in the clearing."

Russell (1964) writes: "The Dickcissel has been observed in British Honduras only from the end of February to May 14 with the majority of the observations occurring in the period of April 12 to 27. Migrants may stop in any open area, especially on the keys and the grassland of pine ridges at all elevations. Flocks of 15 to 30 individuals of this common transient are often seen. Some birds are extremely fat * * *. The gonads of birds taken in late April were slightly enlarged, and Peck states that in May many Dickcissels were singing." Sutton and Pettingill (1942) saw the first dickcissel near

Rancho, Tamaulipas, Apr. 15, 1938. It was noted daily from April 22 to May 1, usually in small flocks in weed-grown fields. Singing was heard from April on. A male collected on April 27 had considerably enlarged testes.

The above records indicate that the dickcissels do not leave Panama and Central America until April, and some individuals may linger into May. G. C. Williams (1945) states that dickcissels migrating from their winter quarters follow the coastal region of Mexico and Texas to reach their breeding grounds. The many spring records from that region confirm this route for a large percentage of the individuals. Lowery (1945 and 1946), however, has shown that many birds, including at least some dickcissels, make the trans-Gulf migration. Obviously certain contingents of dickcissels may take either route (Stevenson, 1957).

The first dickcissels arrive in Texas during April to breed in the prairie sections of the State. Florence Merriam Bailey (1902) writes: "When in southern Texas during the spring migration we met with flocks of dickcissels on their way to the north. In places on the open prairie two to three hundred would be sitting in rows on the wire fences like swallows on telegraph wires. * * * When not in compact flocks they were scattered through the chapparal singing on the tops of the bushes. Their song had a mouthed, furry quality, but was none the less sunny and enjoyable. When they are on their breeding grounds their song is one of the pleasantest features of the big grain fields."

At Baton Rouge and New Orleans the dickcissels arrive regularly on April 15th and are often abundant by April 20 (Lowery, 1945). The earliest record for Louisiana is of one seen at New Orleans on Apr. 6, 1894 (Oberholser, 1938).

In its continued route up the Mississippi flyway it arrives in Arkansas the latter part of April or the first week of May. Baerg (1930) has recorded the first arrivals in northwestern Arkansas for the years 1924–1928 as follows: 1924, May 3; 1925, April 26; 1926, April 30; 1927, April 27; and 1928, May 1. Meanley and Neff (1953) state that the dickcissel is now one of the most common breeding passerines in the Grand Prairie region of Arkansas. The species was not previously recorded as a winter resident in Arkansas, but the authors found single birds during the winters of 1950–51 and 1951–52 associating with English sparrows about most of the farmyards they visited. The dickcissels fed with the sparrows in the barn lots, on straw stacks, and in open sheds on dates ranging from mid-January to April.

In Missouri (Widmann, 1907) the males arrive the fourth week of April, the females not until the first week of May, and the great bulk of the birds are present during the second week of May.

In 12 years of records taken in Buchanan County, Iowa, Pierce (1930) states that during 5 years the dickcissels arrived the first week of May while in 7 of the 12 years they arrived the last half of May. Youngworth (1933) gives the earliest date for Sioux City, Iowa, as May 5, 1928.

For Minnesota Roberts (1932) gives the two earliest records for the State as being one seen May 5, 1898 at Faribault, Rice County, and one seen May 6, 1926, at Red Wing, Goodhue County. The average of 16 annual first dates, varying from May 5 to May 27, is May 18. Monson (1934) gives the earliest date for Cass County, as May 8, 1928, when they were very numerous. The average date for that county is May 29. The average arrival for 5 years at Fargo, N. Dak., is May 30 (Stevens quoted by Roberts (1932)).

Stray individuals pass on into Canada where they have been reported in most of the southern provinces: Newfoundland (Tuck, 1952; Nova Scotia and New Brunswick (Godfrey, 1954); Quebec (Lewis, 1924; Ball, 1943); Ontario (Dale, 1932; Devitt, 1935; Lloyd, 1944; Mitchell 1946); Manitoba, Criddle, 1921; Taverner, 1927; Saskatchewan, Mitchell, 1924; Potter, 1943; Houston, 1949); British Columbia (Brooks, 1923). I have been unable to find any recent published records of the dickcissel nesting in Canada, but several of the observers mentioned above have suspected the birds were breeding.

In Wisconsin the first dickcissels appear in the south-central counties early in May, but they do not reach the counties to the westward and northward to Green Lake County until the last week of May according to a spring migration map prepared by Taber (1947). According to Taber the average southern Wisconsin nesting chronology is as follows: May 25 the male arrives and sings, June 2 the female joins the male, June 7 the nest is begun, June 14 the first egg is laid, June 27 the eggs hatch, and July 6 the young leave the nest. Barger (1941) gives the earliest date for Wood County, Wis., as Apr. 27, 1941, but most of his first arrivals appear after the middle of May. The dickcissel does not breed in northern Wisconsin.

In Michigan (Wood, 1951) the spring arrivals occur principally in the last 2 or 3 weeks of May. In the Toledo-Erie marsh area the species has appeared by May 9, the first arrivals averaging May 14 and the main flight May 21. The average for 5 years in the vicinity of Battle Creek is May 28. One specimen was obtained at Kalamazoo as early as May 3, 1879. There are according to Wood only two or three dozen breeding records for Michigan, chiefly from the southern-most two tiers of counties.

The first male dickcissels make their appearance in central Illinois about the last week of April or first week of May. The males invariably sing from the time they arrive and, since they always perch in con-spicuous open places such as the top of the highest weed stalk, a fence post, or telephone pole, they are not apt to escape the field observer's notice. The arrival of the females is never heralded by song, and they are often overlooked. In general I found they arrive about 6 to 10 days after the males. Field trips made daily during the migration period at Urbana for 18 consecutive years recorded the first arrival of the males as follows: 1901, May 7; 1902, May 2; 1903, May 16; 1904, May 5; 1905, May 11; 1906, May 5; 1907, May 5; 1908, April 25; 1909, April 29; 1910, May 10; 1911, April 29; 1912, May 2; 1913, May 4; 1914, April 28; 1915, April 28; 1916, May 5; 1917, April 24; and 1918, May 2. The average of these 18 years is May 3. The average of a 7-year series of records made by T. E. Musselman at Quincy, in extreme western Illinois, is April 29, 4 days earlier than those at Urbana. The earlier dates at Quincy, which is on the Mississippi River, support the view that the vanguards of the migration waves follow the large river courses.

In addition to the States included in the preceding account of the spring migration, the dickcissel also nests in the Great Plains States as far west as eastern Colorado. Individuals have strayed farther west to the western slope of Colorado (McCrimmon, 1926); to southwestern Wyoming (McCreary and Mickey, 1935); on the shore of Lake Mead, Nev. (Pulich, 1953); Grand Canyon National Park, Ariz. (Bryant, 1952), and Santa Monica, Calif. (Stager, 1949). In fact wanderers may be expected in any part of western United States. Dickcissels also nest abundantly eastward in Indiana and Ohio, and are now nesting in increasing numbers in the eastern States, especially the more southern States of the Atlantic seaboard.

Nesting.—In central Illinois the first nests of the dickcissel may be found during the last week of May, soon after most of the individuals have arrived at their summer haunts. My earliest record is of a nest found May 22, 1899, in a meadow of clover and timothy near Atwood, Ill. The earliest nest reported by I. E. Hess at Philo, Ill., is one of five eggs found May 31, 1896. T. E. Musselman, of Quincy, Ill., found a nest of four eggs near a putting green on the Quincy golf links as early as May 21, 1918. As would be expected, first nesting dates are somewhat earlier in our southern States. For example, in Mis-sissippi Charles L. Stockard (1905) reports that the dickcissels appeared late in April 1900, in a field of luxuriant vetch. During May, 14 nests were found and at least as many more could probably have been located with careful searching. Of the 14 nests 11 contained five eggs and three contained four eggs each. All were collected from May 9 to 23, 1900. In Texas Harry P. Attwater (1887) found 20 nests in a low area along the Medina River south of Antonia on May 15, 1884. Nearly all were completed, some containing four fresh eggs.

Though nests are not uncommon in Illinois in May, the dickcissel does not reach the height of its nesting season there until late June and July. Then practically every meadow in the central part of the State has several pairs of these interesting birds. The latest nesting record reported by Hess is of a nest with four eggs found Aug. 1, 1898, near Philo. My own latest record is a nest with four eggs found in a clover field near Atwood on Aug. 12, 1918. R. M. Anderson (1907) found a nest containing two eggs and two young in Winnebago County, Iowa, on Aug. 19, 1893. These late dates probably represent a second nesting attempt for the season.

The usual and most typical location for the nest of the dickcissel in central Illinois is in a thick growth of grass or other low dense vegetation. The nest, if not placed in a natural depression in the earth, is supported but a few inches above the ground. It is usually so well hidden by the rank growth of clover, alfalfa, grass, or weeds that it is difficult to locate. Meadows provide the larger number of nesting sites, but the dickcissel is by no means confined to them. The following nest situations that came under my direct observation reveal the diversity in choice that different individuals may exhibit:

Meadows or similar situations resembling meadows:
Meadows:	
Clover	28
Timothy or other grasses	17
Alfalfa	5
Weeds and grass along fences or between cultivated fields	8
Wheat mixed with clover	2
Weeds and grass along roadsides	2
Wild roses or vines growing among grass and weeds	6
Total	68
Other situations:	
Hedge fences (osage orange)	5
Scrub apple tree	2
Thorn bush	2
Small crabapple tree	1
Total	10
Grand total	78

The largest number of nests (68) were found in meadows or in places containing vegetation approaching that present in the clover and grass fields. Only 10 of the 78 nests were in situations radically different from that ordinarily found in meadows. Of these 10 nests, all except 2 were found late in the season and probably represented second nesting attempt, after the mowers and reapers had taken their toll of nests from the meadows and grain fields. One of the nests found in a thorn bush early in the season was undoubtedly so placed because of the wet, swampy condition of the nearby fields. The nests in trees and hedges were at heights from about 2 feet to a little more than 6 feet from the ground; the highest was in a tall osage orange hedge. Albert J. Kirn (1915) found a nest with four eggs on Aug. 8, 1912, near Vinita, Okla., 14 feet up in a persimmon tree. Though nests are sometimes placed at considerable distances from the ground, these do not represent the typical or usual situation in central Illinois.

R. M. Anderson (1907) reports somewhat different nesting habits of the dickcissel in Iowa: "Many observers give the species as building its nest on the ground, but of the dozens of nests which I have examined none were directly on the ground; a few were placed in clumps of tall grass a few inches above the ground, several in Canada thistles, and the majority in small bushes and low trees, rose bushes, willows, wild crab, scrub oak, wild cherry, apple trees, etc., from a few inches to three and one-half feet above the ground. July 11–12, 1902, found four nests in a young orchard, all in small apple trees two or three feet up * * *."

The nests of the dickcissel are bulky and somewhat crude in general appearance, but are substantial structures. They vary little in size and shape; the average measurements of 10 typical nests are as follows: outside diameter 12.2 cm., inside diameter 6 cm. by 6.8 cm., outside depth 6.3 cm., inside depth 4.6 cm. The materials used seem to be those near at hand and vary according to the immediate surroundings. The exterior of the nest is usually composed of coarse weed and grass stems, or cornstalk fibers interwoven with a few leaves and grasses; the interior is lined with finer grasses, rootlets, or hair. Some nests may be made up almost entirely of one type of grass, including the lining. Though most nests are firm and well made, those built well above the ground are often so insecurely attached to their support that the least disturbance may dislodge them. Two nests under daily observation had to be tied to the vines in which they were built to prevent an untimely end of the young birds.

One nest was found in the process of construction. The female gathered all the materials and performed all the work of building and shaping the nest. All that the male contributed was his song, which perhaps served as a source of encouragement to his mate. The nest was completed in 4 days and the first egg was laid 2 days later. Unfortunately this nest was destroyed. Dr. Gordon C. Sauer (1953), who made a fine life history study of dickcissels near

St. Joseph, Mo., discovered a nest when it was 75 percent constructed. Two days later the nest contained two blue dickcissel eggs and one brown-speckled cowbird egg, and in 2 more days on June 23, 1952 four dickcissel eggs and one cowbird egg. At noon on July 5, 1952 one dickcissel young was found in the nest which had not been present 24 hours earlier. The incubation period of this bird was 12 to 13 days. The other three dickcissel eggs and the cowbird egg did not hatch. The young bird left its nest between July 12 and July 14 at the age of 7 to 9 days.

Eggs.—The eggs of the dickcissel are immaculate pale blue. The measurements of 50 eggs average 20.8 by 15.7 millimeters; the eggs showing the four extremes measure *23.4* by 17.0, 21.8 by *17.5*, *18.5* by 15.2, and 20.1 by *14.5* millimeters. The average weight of 20 eggs is 2.76 grams.

The number of eggs in a set varies from three to five, but four is the usual number. Of 29 nests containing complete sets of eggs, 5 had three eggs, 18 had four, and 6 had five eggs each; 3 of the nests containing only three eggs were under daily observation and no more eggs were added, but one or more eggs may have been destroyed before observations were begun.

The large number of sterile eggs found was surprising; of 11 nests studied during the summer of 1918, 5 contained one sterile egg and a 6th nest had two. It was thought possible that the embryos had been killed perhaps by chilling, but examination of the unhatched eggs proved that development had never started, or at least had not proceeded to an appreciable degree. Incubation is entirely by the female. Sauer (1953) determined the incubation period to be 12 to 13 days. When the fully developed embryo is ready to emerge, the egg shell and membranes break around the entire circumference midway between the blunt and pointed ends. The break seems to be made by the exertions of the struggling embryo to straighten its neck and to extend its legs in the effort to free itself. After the egg cracks, it is only a few minutes before the young frees itself entirely. A freshly-hatched chick appears almost naked, for the meager patches of natal down while wet and matted are practically invisible.

Nesting.—The study of the home life of a pair of birds that nested in the tall weeds and grass along a country roadside supplied many interesting incidents which help portray the character and behavior of the dickcissel. I made the following notes during the nesting season from blinds at close range. One nest, built about 10 inches above the ground, was composed of materials loosely interwoven among the stems of the tall grass and weeds. The tops of the grass and weeds arched over this little home, protecting the eggs and young from the direct rays of the sun and concealing them from the view of all who might pass. A barbed-wire fence that ran through the thicket also helped protect the nest from trampling by stray animals or people. The fence, as well as the nearby telephone poles and wires, provided excellent sentinel posts for the male and convenient perches for the cautious female when she went to and from her nest.

A blind was built in the tall weeds along the fence about 12 feet from the nest and completely covered with cut grasses and weeds. The day after the blind was completed the birds were conducting their home life in an apparently normal way and, so far as could be determined, they paid little attention to the blind. The female flew from the nest when I entered the blind the first time, but after a few minutes she returned to the telephone wires overhead to utter in unison with her mate the usual chirps of disapproval. The two birds continued chirping for about 25 minutes, when the female flew down to the fence close to the nest. Something seemed to arouse her suspicions, for she returned almost immediately to her mate. She now exhibited her uneasiness by flying repeatedly back and forth between the telephone wires and the fence. Suddenly, and for no apparent reason except possibly for deception, she flew far across the fields as if abandoning all desire to return to the nest. The male now ceased chirping and tuned up to his full song. In 10 minutes the female returned to the telephone wire and without hesitation flew to the fence post nearest her nest. From that point she carefully surveyed her surroundings, and especially scrutinized the blind where a human being had so recently disappeared. The male now sang louder than ever, but his mate did not utter the faintest chirp. The situation seeming favorable, she slipped into the weeds and noiselessly made her way to her nest. The birds played their parts well and without doubt their shrewdness misleads many enemies.

The birds repeated this performance on following visits to the nest, but after a few days they paid little attention to my coming and going. Nor did they seem to be disturbed by the teams and automobiles that passed along the road. Even when the driver sounded his horn directly opposite the nest the birds made no visible response. However, when an automobile or team stopped in the road near the brooding female, she invariably scooted off the nest into the grass. If the people came no nearer and their actions seemed free of suspicion, she returned to the nest; otherwise she flew to the telephone wires to chirp until they left. The female then took her usual precautions in returning to the nest, while the male seemed to sing with the purpose of attracting any attention that might otherwise be directed toward his mate.

At the time the young hatch the female's behavior undergoes a noticeable change, though the male seems unmoved and unchanged by this important event. The female becomes extremely fidgety and excitable, yet very daring. She readily hazards many dangers she would not have faced before her parental instincts were quickened by the appearance of her young. Without the least hesitancy she will return to her nestlings while an observer stands in full view only a few yards away. When this mother bird returned for the first time after the young hatched she uttered a series of low subdued notes. She then carried the egg shells away and dropped them far from the nest. This habit, held in common with many other birds, is a regular part of the dickcissel's housekeeping. All refuse and filth from the young birds is also immediately disposed of or carried away, so that the nest and its surroundings always present a neat and clean appearance.

The first food, a larva, was delivered to the young about 30 minutes after it emerged from the egg. The larva was crushed into small pieces which were thrust, at intervals of several seconds, into the nestling's gaping mouth. Meanwhile the male sat on top of his favorite telephone pole and poured forth a volume of song, seemingly oblivious to what was happening in the weeds and grass below him. The following day two more eggs hatched, but the fourth egg was sterile and remained in the nest unbroken until after the fledglings left, 9 days later.

During the first 3 days the female brooded her young very closely and left the nest only to obtain food. Even during the heat of the day when the mercury rose above 90°F. she clung closely to the nest. When the heat became excessive she panted incessantly and her partially spread wings protruded over the edge of the nest. She remained faithful to her family through the hottest weather, while the male did nothing but encourage her with his song. On the fourth and fifth days she spent less time on the nest, and from the sixth to the ninth days, when the ever-increasing appetites of her young demanded more and more food, she seldom lingered at the nest any length of time. After the sixth and seventh days the sprouting feathers and the contact of the young birds' bodies with one another easily retained the high body temperature without the aid of the parent. The temperature of nestlings 6 days old which had been left alone in the nest for an hour was 106°F., normal for birds, while the surrounding temperature was only 80°F.

The male dickcissel attends strictly to his own affairs and seldom meddles with the life of other birds nearby. When strangers intrude on his premises he not only leaves them alone, but often exhibits a marked timidity. One day a young kingbird alighted on the fence wire just above the dickcissel's nest. It was followed by its parent, which continued to feed the fledgling there for more than 20 minutes.

During this time both dickcissels seemed exceedingly disturbed, but neither offered any objection nor expended any effort in defending their territory.

Many birds, such as mourning doves, bobwhites, vesper sparrows, migrant shrikes, and others, came near the nest, but only once did I see the dickcissel muster enough courage to assert his feelings about an intrusion. One afternoon a foreign young dickcissel about 3 or 4 weeks old perched on the fence near the nest. The male stopped his singing abruptly, ruffed his feathers, and dashed fiercely at the innocent intruder, which flew for its life and escaped in the tall weeds and grass. This incident seems to signify that the dickcissel is ready to assert his authority over his own kind, but will not tackle a bird as large or larger than himself.

One usually thinks of the dickcissel as a finely colored male perched on a post or weed stalk pouring forth a volume of cheerful song. Such qualities have made the male dickcissel the favorite of many bird lovers, but more intimate acquaintance with the species' domestic life reveals the less admirable side of his character. He takes no part in nest building or incubation, nor does he help his mate feed or care for the young. In fact his attitude is one of complete indifference to them. One morning as I watched a female returning to her nest with a beakful of food for her 5-day-old young, a sharp-shinned hawk appeared out of nowhere and carried her off. Her mate seemingly paid no attention to the tragedy enacted in front of him, but continued singing from his regular post nearby. He continued to sing the rest of that day, and the next 2 days, while the young slowly starved to death.

Plumages.—The natal down of the dickcissel when dry is pure white, with no traces of the brown or gray tinges so common in the down of other passerines. It grows in 12 distinct tracts on the upper surface of the young bird as follows: 3 small areas on the dorso-posterior part of the head, 1 median and 2 lateral, collectively known as the head tract; 1 tract on each scapular region; 2 smaller tracts on the dorsal side of each wing; 1 elongated tract in the middorsal line; and 1 shorter tract on each side running parallel to the middorsal tract. The ventral aspect of the body shows no down and the entire underparts remain bare until the juvenal plumage appears.

The natal down is retained throughout the period in the nest; sometimes parts of it persist several days after they leave the nest as filaments at the apices of the feathers of the juvenal plumage. The postnatal molt is usually completed at about the 9th to 12th day after hatching, 1 to 3 days after the young leave the nest.

The first feather papillae of the juvenal plumage to appear are those of the primaries and secondaries, which protrude through the epidermis of the wing the second day after hatching. All other tracts, both dorsal and ventral, are well defined by protruding papillae at the end of the fourth day. Those of the head and caudal tracts are the last to appear.

The growth of the feather papillae is extremely rapid, and by the end of the sixth day those of the wing tract begin to unsheath at the tips. Unsheathing now progresses very rapidly; by the end of the 10th day the exposed tips of nearly all the contour feathers are out of their sheaths.

The growth of the tarsus, toes, and nails is practically complete when the young leave the nest, whereas the tail, which is more than 15 centimeters long in the adult, is less than one-half centimeter in length at this time. The time required for development is closely correlated with the time the bird acquires the use of the respective parts. The legs and toes are called upon to serve the bird the moment it leaps from the nest, but a long tail would be a nuisance in the crowded nest and is not essential as a rudder until flight is attempted.

The growth of most parts of the bird is rapid until the eighth day. Weight increases in the nest at the rate of almost 2 grams per day. One young that weighed 2.8 grams at hatching weighed 18 grams when it left the nest on the eight day. Growth slows after the young leave the nest; one young bird lost weight.

Each of 18 dickcissel nestlings of five broods was tagged for later identification. A number of them recaptured from 1 to 6 days after leaving the nest made it possible to complete a series of weights, measurements, descriptions, and photographs through their first 2 weeks of life. The young, though often at a considerable distance from the nest, were easily located by watching the feeding operations of the adult female. It became increasingly difficult to find them as they acquired the ability to fly or to run rapidly through the grass. A tagged bird 18 days old was collected a mile away from the nest where it was reared, a fact which explains the difficulty in securing later stages of the tagged young. Although the young dickcissel cannot fly when it leaves the nest, it acquires the ability within 2 or 3 days, and when about 11 days old is able to fly from 100 to 150 feet. When given the advantage of a start from an elevated perch, some flew even farther at this age.

The following description of the juvenal plumage is based on a study of the young at about the time they leave the nest. The colors were determined with the use of Ridgway's Color Standards and Nomenclature. While considerable care was exercised in comparing these colors, they are at best approximations:

Upper parts buffy brown shading to sepia on the crown; feathers of the back fuscous black edged and tipped with cinnamon buff;

unsheathed parts of the primaries and secondaries mouse gray to chaetura black narrowly margined with pallid neutral gray; wing coverts olivaceous black with broad margins of cream color; edge of wings, superciliary, and malar stripes light ochraceous buff, but in some younger fledglings these parts approach an orange-buff and even a deep chrome in color; chin and lower breast light buff shading to a lighter tint on the belly; breast and upper portion of flanks chamois, but in younger specimens in which the ventral feathers have just unsheathed and not been exposed to strong light the breast approaches buff yellow. No birds at this stage have black streaks in the breast feathers. The beak and legs are pale flesh color, but these parts darken as the bird grows older.

The dickcissel undergoes several changes by the 14th day. The natal down is entirely lost; this disappears, even earlier in birds that live a normal life in the grass fields where it frays away more quickly. The general coloration of this stage of the juvenal plumage is similar to that of a bird 8 or 9 days old, but is duller in tone, with none of the rich ochraceous-buff which is so conspicuous in recently unsheathed feathers. This change in color is apparently due to a chemical change caused by exposure either to light or to air or to both. The unsheathing of the feathers in a dickcissel 14 days old is so far advanced that from a casual glance it seems complete. Many feathers, however, such as the primaries and secondaries still retain a portion of their sheaths. Unsheathing proceeds slowly; even in a bird 18 days old the outer primaries are not completely freed of their envelopes.

The dorsal plumage of an 18-day-old dickcissel is very similar in color to that found in the 14-day bird described above. The ventral aspect of the older bird differs as follows: Bordering the sides of the throat two well-defined fuscous malar stripes extend posteriorly to the breast. The sides of the chamois-colored breast are distinctly streaked with fuscous. In the center of the breast, many of the feathers have narrow but distinct median fuscous stripes, all of which at 18 days are completely concealed from view by the overlapping tips of the feathers. A close examination of the breast region reveals other similarly marked feathers in various stages of development. These new feathers represent the first winter plumage, destined to replace those of the juvenal phase. The breast feathers in the first winter plumage differ from those of birds in the juvenal stage not only in color but in their coarser texture. The transition from the juvenal to the first winter plumage is not so sharply defined as the change from the nuptial to the adult winter plumage, which involves a complete post-nuptial molt. The post-juvenal molt is only partial and occurs so gradually that it is difficult to determine just when the juvenal plumage ends and the first winter plumage begins.

Birds in transition between the juvenal and first winter plumages were collected during the last week of June and the first week of August, representatives of the first and second broods respectively. A study of these specimens leads me to believe that the transition from the juvenal to the first winter plumage is more prolonged in first broods than in those reared later. No young birds were found in the completed first winter plumage before the last week of July. At this time, though a graded series showed all stages between the juvenal and the first winter plumages, most individuals could be placed readily in one of the two groups, those with complete first winter plumage or those still in the juvenal stage with few or no winter plumage feathers. This substantiates the rearing of two broods each nesting season.

The post-juvenal molt, which includes all but the primaries, secondaries, and rectrices, is well advanced in young birds 5 to 8 weeks old but many feathers of the first winter plumage still remain undeveloped. The following description is based on five birds ranging from 5 to about 8 weeks of age. Males and females are similar in color. Crown, back and sides of the neck and rump buffy brown or olive-brown; crown streaked with fuscous-black, back snuff brown and light clay color, the feathers with large conspicuous streaks of black. Primaries, secondaries and tail feathers as described for the juvenal plumage. Greater and lesser wing coverts and tertiaries fuscous black broadly margined with sayal brown but in some specimens edged with tawny; edge of the wing and line over the eye yellow ocher; auriculars, breast and flanks buffy brown; breast and flanks streaked with black; throat and chin cartridge buff margined by malar streaks or stripes of black; broad, short maize-yellow bands lateral to the black malar stripes; lower breast and belly light cream color; unstreaked crissum and under tail coverts light buff.

The completed first winter plumage shows the following changes: The yellow of the bend of the wing and malar and superciliary stripes is more extensive and approaches a buff-yellow or light orange-yellow. In some specimens a yellow wash extends down to the region of the belly. One female and one male bird showed a small obscured patch of chestnut brown which sharply divided the buff of the throat and the yellow of the breast. The lesser and greater wing coverts vary from cinnamon-rufous to bay. The streaks of the breast are not so conspicuous as in younger birds. In all other respects the older birds in the first winter plumage resemble those 5 to 8 weeks old.

Some of the young are partially dependent on the adults for food until they attain full winter plumage. I have often seen females at the roosts feeding young in the most advanced stages of winter plumage. In this way the family groups retain their identity even after the birds gather in large flocks before they migrate.

The first and the adult nuptial plumages are acquired by a partial prenuptial molt which involves the head, throat, and breast, but not the rest of the body nor the remiges and rectrices.

The adult male nuptial plumage has the top of the head, back and sides of the neck, the lores and auriculars pale neutral gray; crown and forehead tinged with olive ocher; an amber yellow line over the eye becomes white posteriorly; back mouse gray tinged with cinnamon-drab and streaked with black; rump and tail coverts smoke gray without streaks; lesser and middle wing coverts cinnamon rufous; edge of wing empire yellow; secondaries, primaries, and rectrices fuscous and narrowly edged with pale mouse gray; malar stripe amber yellow anteriorly, broadening posteriorly into a white area on either side of a black throat patch; chin white; breast wax yellow fading to pure white on the belly and under tail coverts; mandibles dusky slate blue; the legs and feet Prout's brown; iris dark brown. Males in nuptial plumage collected June–July show a small black patch of variable size near the middle of the yellow breast, and in all except one this spot is completely separated from the black area of the throat.

In the nuptial plumage of the adult female the upper parts are similar to those of the male, but the gray is replaced by shades of brown; crown with fine black streaks and with very little yellow; the general coloration very much duller, especially the rufous of the wings and the yellow of the breast, which are much reduced in amount as compared with the male; in three specimens the rufous of the wings is practically absent, being instead gray and fuscous, the coverts being fuscous with only a few of the feathers margined with cinnamon-rufous; chin and throat white; pronounced black lateral chin stripes bordering the maize-yellow malar stripes. In six females the black throat patch, so conspicuous in the male, is entirely lacking, but one adult female taken August 2 has a reduced patch of chaetura black on the throat which connects on either side with the lateral throat stripes. In all specimens the straw-yellow breast is finely streaked with dark brown; flanks white, washed with avellaneous and finely streaked with fuscous or brown; the primaries, secondaries, tail, bill, and legs similar to those of the male. Females collected during the late summer toward the close of the nesting season have very soiled and worn plumage; the barbs of the outer tail feathers of some August females are completely worn off, leaving nothing but the naked shafts. The plumage of the males is then only slightly worn, reflecting their small part in the rearing of the brood.

This description of the adult winter plumage of the male is base
on four specimens collected in Illinois during August 1918, thre
specimens collected during the last week of August 1908 at Mat
moros, Mexico, and one collected at Bolson, Costa Rica, De
13, 1909. Two of the Illinois birds are in transitional postnupti
molt, but the others have acquired the complete adult winter plum
age. This plumage is similar to the nuptial plumage, but the enti
coloration is very much brighter and the color bands and patch
more sharply differentiated. The gray of the pileum and neck
the nuptial plumage is replaced by a rich dark olive-brown; back snu
brown streaked with black; the rufous of the lesser and middle wir
coverts a deep chestnut color; greater wing coverts broadly edge
with mikado brown instead of gray; white edgings of the primarie
very prominent; the yellow of the breast more extensive anterior
and posteriorly, even the middle of the belly being tinged with yellow
the yellow of the breast approaching cadmium yellow; chin tinge
with cream color; superciliary and malar stripes light cadmium; th
posterior part of the superciliary stripe light yellow and not white a
in nuptial plumage; the black throat reduced in size and is more or les
obscured by pale cream tips of the feathers; no traces of black on th
lower breast; auriculars and flanks plain olive-brown; crissum c
under tail coverts warm buff instead of white as in nuptial plumage

No females in the adult winter plumage were secured. Dwigh
(1900) thus describes the female plumages: "The plumages and moult
correspond to those of the male. In juvenal plumage females ar
indistinguishable from males. The first nuptial is acquired by
limited prenuptial moult. In subsequent plumages the throat re
mains pale brown with lateral black chin streaks without the blac
patch of the male and the colors elsewhere are regularly duller.
He gives no detailed description of the adult female winter plumage

The abnormal plumages of albinism and melanism are rare in th
dickcissel. Of Townsend's bunting (*Spiza townsendi* (Audubon))
which Cockrum (1952) considered a hybrid between the dickcisse
and the blue grosbeak, the 1957 A.O.U. Check-List states: "Known
only from the type specimen, taken May 11, 1833, [in Pennsylvania
by John K. Townsend. Its peculiarities cannot be accounted fo
by hybridism or apparently by individual variation."

Food.—The following account of the food of the dickcissel is base
on the contents of the stomachs and crops of birds collected nea
Atwood, Ill., and on observations made in the field during the nestin
season of 1918. The author is indebted to E. R. Kalmbach of th
U.S. Biological Survey and to A. N. Caudell of the U.S. Bureau o
Entomology for the identification of the stomach contents of 19 o
the 33 birds collected. Results of stomach examinations presente

by Judd (1900, 1901) and observations by others are also included. The birds obtained in Illinois for stomach examinations were collected chiefly in August, when insects and seeds form the most important part of the food of the dickcissel. These stomachs contained 68 percent vegetable matter and 32 percent animal food. Examinations by the U.S. Biological Survey (Judd, 1901) show that stomachs of 152 dickcissels collected from May to August, chiefly in Kansas, some from Minnesota, Wisconsin, and Texas, contained 70 percent animal and 30 percent vegetable matter, a ratio almost the reverse of that of my birds. All but four of the Illinois stomachs were from young of the year, which may explain their higher content of vegetable matter. Young inexperienced birds are not so adept as their parents at finding and capturing insects and naturally depend on food that is more easily obtainable. Seeds, the chief and practically only vegetable matter eaten, were present everywhere in limitless quantities during August, when the birds were collected.

About 53 percent of the vegetable matter, or 36 percent of the entire contents of the stomachs, was seeds of weeds that are of no value to man, many of them a nuisance to agriculture. Of the nine species of weeds represented, two species, *Chaetochloa glauca* and *Chaetochloa viridis*, made up 33 percent of the entire stomach contents. *Syntherisma sanginuale* was represented by 1.6 percent, three species of *Polygonum* (*convolvulus, persicaria* and *aviculare*) 0.6 percent, and seeds of *Stellaria media* and sedge grasses were present in small numbers.

Unfortunately for the good reputation of the dickcissel, grain amounted to 32 percent of the entire contents, divided between wheat (6.5 percent) and oats (25.5 percent). No grain was found in the stomachs of adult birds. Judd's (1901) examinations of dickcissel stomachs collected during August showed more than a tenth of the food to be millet. He states that millet, pigeon grass, and closely related species formed almost the whole of the vegetable food.

The animal matter consists of insects with traces of spiders and phalangids. The large number of Orthoptera found in the stomachs (28 percent), and the fact that at least traces of grasshoppers were found in all stomachs except one, uphold the dickcissel's reputation as a destroyer of these noxious insects. The Orthoptera found all belong to two families: Acrididae 26 percent, and Locustidae present as 2 percent of the entire contents. Species of *Melanopus* were the commonest grasshoppers found in the stomachs. A cricket, *Nemobius fasciatus*, was taken from the beak of an adult bird.

Lepidoptera, chiefly caterpillars, amounted to 3 percent; Coleoptera, though represented by traces of eight or more species, were in amounts (0.2 percent) too small to be of importance. There were traces of two flies, two species of ants and an ichneumon fly, all in small quantities.

A. A. Forbes (1882), in a study of the relations of birds to an orchard infested with cankerworms, found that 10 out of 11 dickcissels collected had eaten cankerworms, which made up 43 percent of the food eaten by the entire group. Lepidoptera as a whole composed two-thirds of the food. Butler (1898) states that caterpillars are eaten in May in the ratio of about 20 percent, while they make up 70 percent of the food of birds collected during cankerworm infestations.

The stomach contents are clearly in the dickcissel's favor. Though 32 percent of the food of the Illinois specimens was grain, this was counterbalanced by the 36 percent weed seeds and 32 percent insects mostly destructive grasshoppers. As the stomachs were taken after the oats and wheat had been removed from the fields for threshing probably all the grain they contained was waste. The grain I have seen dickcissels eat in the fields before harvest time was chiefly from heads or panicles lying on the ground, which the binder cannot gather and therefore can be classed as waste.

The analyses of stomach contents reveal much of interest regarding the food of the dickcissel, but daily observations at the nests when the young are being fed supply even better evidence in the case of the dickcissel versus man. Not until we observe its feeding habits during the nesting season does the dickcissel receive the full credit it deserves as a destroyer of insects, especially grasshoppers. Judd (1900) found that 14 stomachs of nestlings contained chiefly grasshoppers and crickets. Regarding adults Judd (1901) states that stomachs collected in summer contained more crickets and grasshoppers than those of any other bird whose food habits the Biological Survey investigated.

The first food given the newly hatched dickcissels in Illinois were small green lepidopterous larvae and soft-bodied winged insects. Though the adult birds delivered scores of these larvae and insects their stomachs contained very few. One female made regular trips every few minutes to an elm tree for bright green caterpillars 2 or 3 centimeters long (species undetermined). These caterpillars constituted probably 90 percent of the young birds' food during their first 2 days of life. As the female averaged 10 trips an hour, she destroyed more than 100 larvae daily. On the third and fourth days she added other insects to the diet of the young: aphids, a few unidentified winged insects, and a considerable number of small grasshopper nymphs. With these additions the number of caterpillars decreased correspondingly.

From the fifth day until the young left the nest 4 days later, their food was practically all grasshopper nymphs and adults garnered from a nearby clover field they were overrunning, stripping the clover stems and leaves. During the fledgling's last days in the nest grasshoppers were delivered at the rate of one every 3 or 4 minutes

A conservative estimate shows the two adults and their four young ate about 200 grasshoppers daily.

At this rate the Illinois dickcissels, estimated to number more than 1,000,000, destroyed about 100,000,000 grasshoppers in a single day during the nesting season. As Prof. Lawrence Bruner, entomologist of the Nebraska Experiment Station, estimates each grasshopper eats about one and a half times its own weight or about 0.05 ounces of grass per day, 100,000,000 grasshoppers destroy about 156 tons. Hay during the summer of 1918 brought about $30 per ton. Hence the Illinois dickcissels saved the State about $4,680 daily during the nesting season by the destruction of grasshoppers alone. Though the bird's great value may not be fully appreciated by the average farmer, the dickcissel nevertheless is a favorite with many of them. No well-informed farmer wantonly destroys them, nor does he willingly permit anyone else to do so. This strong popular sentiment has been an important factor in their recent increase and extension of range throughout the Middle West.

In their winter habitat the dickcissels live chiefly on weed and grass seeds and grain. Alexander Skutch has sent us the following observations on their food at San Isidro del General, Costa Rica: "Along the meandering Quebrada de las Vueltas was a level of rice several acres in extent. I first saw dickcissels in some bushes early in the morning of January 26, the day when the farmer began to harvest his rice. Later in the morning I watched one of these birds eating grain at the edge of the field, as doubtless other members of the flock were doing deeper in the stand of rice where I could not see them. Despite the removal of the standing grain, the flock of dickcissels continued for the next 2 months to frequent the vicinity, possibly finding fallen grains amidst the stubble." Near Los Amates in the Caribbean lowlands of Guatemala Skutch watched dickcissels and blue grosbeaks feeding on the pollen of bamboo flowers in tall timber bamboos near the Rio Morja.

The many dickcissels now wintering in New England have food habits similar to those of the house sparrow with which they frequently associate. Both species visit feeding stations and feeding shelves for various seeds and grain. The dickcissels seem especially fond of millet.

Economic status.—In a statistical ornithological survey Forbes (1907, 1908, 1921) and Gross (1921) made in Illinois in 1906–1907 and 1909, the dickcissel ranked fifth in a list of 85 species recorded for the whole State during the summer of 1907, with an average of 32.2 birds per square mile. In 1909 it stood 11th among 117 species in abundance, with an average of 18.0 birds per square mile. As has already been stated, the dickcissel population fluctuates greatly from year to year, but during the 1909 low the state's 56,000 square miles supported more than a million dickcissels. They were about equally abundant in southern and central Illinois, but north of about latitude 42°, nearer their northern limit of summer distribution, their density dropped to about half as many per square mile.

In the summer of 1909 the dickcissels were distributed by crops in the following numbers per square mile: Meadow 81.2, waste and fallow 34.4, oats 21.4, wheat and rye 19.7, pasture 12.4, and corn 5.2. This indicates, as would be expected, that the dickcissel is preeminently a bird of open meadows, to which it is attracted not only by the many grasshoppers and other insects that supply much of its substenance, but also by the low dense vegetation that provides the kind of nesting sites it prefers. Meadows with the densest growth of clover and alfalfa, especially if they have a liberal sprinkling of weeds and dewberry vines, are preferred to those of timothy and other grasses. Though pastures present conditions similar to those of certain meadows, their much lower population densities of only about 12 to the square mile are explained by the continual disturbance created by the grazing stock. The waste and fallow areas, ranking next to the meadows in numbers of dickcissels per square mile, have vegetation favorable for the birds and are the least disturbed by man. There the plow and the devastating mower and binder never bring the birds' home life to a sudden and disastrous ending.

In the grain fields the dickcissel is present in numbers intermediate between those of meadows and of pastures. The number found per square mile in oats is practically the same as that in wheat and rye fields. Of all the areas listed, the cornfields support the lowest density, because they provide neither food nor favorable nesting sites. Furthermore corn is cultivated most heavily during the early part of the nesting season, which is certain to destroy any nests. The small number of dickcissels found in cornfields, only five to the square mile, was almost accidental. Other areas in which the dickcissel was recorded, but in numbers too small to be important, were swamps, gardens, shrubbery, orchards, and timberlands.

Voice.—The song of the dickcissel is simple, yet, like many bird notes, it is difficult to put into words. It has been written in as many ways as there have been writers to describe it, so it seems needless to contribute another to the long list of versions, a few of which are as follows: Wilson (1832) describes the song (under black-throated bunting) as consisting "of five notes, or, more properly, of two notes, the first repeated twice, and slowly, the second thrice, and rapidly, resembling *chip chip che cche ché*." Nuttall (*in* Chamberlain, 1891) states: "With us their call is '*tic 'tic—tshĕ tshĕ tshĕ tshĭp*, and '*tshĭp tshĭp, tshĕ tshĕ tshĕ tshĕ tshĭp*." Elliott Coues interprets it as "Look

Look! see me here! see!" and again he writes, "the simple ditty sounds like *chip-chip-chee, chee, chee*." To the Rev. J. Hibbert Langille (1894) it sounds like "*chic-chic-chélac-chick-chick-chick*" or "*chick-ticktshe-chick-chick-chick*." E. A. Doolittle (1920) describes the song of a male when it first arrived as "a raspy *Schreeee-schree, schree schree*. P. M. Silloway (1904) who made a special study of the song in Illinois writes: "His first song was like this: *Dick, dick, ciss ciss sell*, and this rendition proved to be his favorite production. Frequently I could hear in it: *Quick, quick, sell sell sell*, both songs being emphasized at the last syllable." Amos W. Butler (1898) writes: "comes to me characteristically as five metallic sounds— something like the noise made by dropping six silver dollars, one upon the other, into one's hand: *clenk, clenk, clenk-clenk-clenk*." Robert Ridgway (1889) writes: "[They] perch upon the summits of tall weed-stalks or fence-stakes, at short intervals crying out: '*See, see—Dick, Dick-Cissel, Cissel*.'" This latter is a much quoted interpretation of the song and one which has given popularity to the common name.

One can imagine the dickcissel singing almost any of the varied sets of words given above, yet to the reader who has never heard the song, some of these interpretations might be very misleading. If I were to select from the above descriptions the ones which seem best to depict its character, it would be a combination of those written by Nuttall and Ridgway, "*See See—Dick! Dick! tshe tshe tshe tship* (or *chisl*)." The *See See* which serves as a prelude is very faint and heard only at close range. These preliminary notes are often omitted, and I have failed to hear some males utter them at all. The *Dick!* is loud, strongly accented, and repeated slowly, usually once, some-times twice. It is followed by a rapid succession of three or four notes that sound like *tshe* or *chee*. The last note ends abruptly and is slightly different from the others, sounding more like *tship* or sometimes *chisl* or merely *isl*. When the bird is weary, and often in excessively hot weather, the song is simplified to *Dick! Dick!-isl* and sometimes merely to *Dick! Dick!* at irregular intervals.

Aretas A. Saunders writes in the unpublished accounts of the bird songs he studied and analyzed: "The song of the dickcissel is chattery and sibilant, and not of musical quality, though it is definitely rhythmic, and the notes can be definitely pitched. Each song con-sists of two parts, the first usually of two notes of the chattery type and the latter of three that are sibilant. The first two notes are short and staccato and separated by short pauses, and the latter three, though equally short, follow each other rapidly without pause. If one counts seven, evenly and rather rapidly, and then does it again in the same time, omitting the 2 and 4, so that it goes 1–3–567, he

gets the rhythm of the song. If he says the words *dick-dick sisis*
to this rhythm he has a good impression of what the song is like.

"There are many variations, however. I have 19 records collecte
in various localities, from southern Illinois, Oklahoma, and north t
South Dakota and Minnesota. In some localities the first part c
the song is higher pitched than the last. In others it is lower. I
one Minnesota record the two parts are on the same pitch.

"While two notes for the first part and three for the second are th
commonest forms, some records from Minnesota and South Dakot
have only one note for the first and four for the last; and one recor
from Illinois has three notes for each part. A number of Oklahom
records have the first notes rapidly slurred, so that they sound lik
clip or *twait* or *taweet* and in one case, slurred downward into *tleeu*
The notes of the second part vary from *sisisis* to *zayzayzay* or *tsitsitsi*
From Missouri I have one record, of three first notes only, and anothe
of four *sisses* only.

"The pitch of these songs varies considerably from F'' to B''
2½ tones more than an octave. Songs are usually about 1.4 second
in length, and vary little, but when more than the ordinary fiv
notes are used they are longer by about a fifth of a second for eac
extra note.

"A harsh call-note I recorded as *Ka-kakakakakakakaka*, all on th
same pitch, which was B''. A call of a female bird I wrote as *gzzzz*
and found it on E''."

The dickcissel begins singing as soon as it arrives in the spring
indeed, the arrival of the male newcomer is usually announced b
its loud characteristic call. During the nesting season the song ca
be heard at nearly all times of the day, but it is by no means th
first of the bird voices heard in the morning. During the earl
hours while waiting in my blind for the coming of dawn, the weir
call of the pheasants, the booming of the prairie hens, the cooing c
the mourning doves, the whistled bobwhite calls, and even the swee
notes of the song and vesper sparrows were heard long before th
dickcissel added his voice to the chorus. As the day wore on an
the heat increased the first voices were silenced one by one, but th
dickcissel kept up his singing with an undiminished earnestnes
Even at midday, when the almost unbearable waves of heat tha
rose from the fields drove most birds to cover, the song of the dick
cissel was still heard. His earnestness and persistence are traits w
are compelled to admire.

The songs of the dickcissel follow in such rapid succession an
with such regularity that records of the number of calls per minut
during different times of the day are interesting. For this purpos
a male was selected whose mate was brooding her young in a nes

few yards from my blind. His favorite perch was a gnarled stump, the highest point near the nest. For 16 minutes, from 5:05 to 5:21 a.m., he sang 114 times, an average of 7.1 times per minute. For 6 minutes from 9:55 to 10:11 a.m. he sang 122 times, or 7.6 songs per minute. For 16 minutes from 12:00 to 12:16 p.m. there were 32 songs at 8.2 per minute. In the last minute the bird uttered 5 songs an average of one every 4 seconds the highest count made the entire summer.

Thus from dawn to noon the rate of repetition does not diminish, but actually increases as the day becomes warmer. When the heat was excessive (above 100° F.) the quality of the song was greatly interfered with by the bird's rapid respiration or panting and the song often became a repetitive *tship, tship* without the prelude or the usual ending.

The average number of chirps the female uttered when disturbed, taken over similar periods of time, varied from 10 to 50 per minute, depending on her state of excitement.

Though the dickcissel is not the first to begin the morning song, he is one of the latest singers at night. Even after the glow of sunset is gone I have heard his voice sound above the hoarse calls of the toads and the varied tones of the myriads of singing insects. The only bird note I heard on those prairie fields after the last dickcissel had settled for the night was the shriek of a screech owl awakening from his day nap in the tall hedge across the field.

During the first or second week of August the clover fields that resounded with dickcissel music in June and July become quiet. By mid-August you may find a number of females still busy feeding and caring for their young, but the males have deserted the nesting haunts to join others at secluded roosts. Here they change their nuptial suit for a new and brighter plumage before their fall migration. Though the birds remain several weeks longer, the male song is now silenced, and to the casual eye the dickcissels seem to have left their prairie homes.

The dickcissel is also known to sing during the winter (see Alexander F. Skutch's account on page 186). I have never heard any of our New England winter dickcissel visitants sing, but Mrs. Lydia Gatell, Berlin, Conn., writes that a male dickcissel that remained on her premises from Nov. 22, 1950 to Apr. 6, 1951, sang frequently and with zeal, especially on stormy days.

Enemies and accidents.—Dickcissel nests on or near to the ground are subject to the usual enemies—weasels, minks, skunks, coons, opossums, and especially semiwild domestic cats. Hawks and owls take their toll. I saw a sharp-shinned hawk capture a female dickcissel as she carried food to her young at a nest near Atwood, Ill.

Stevenson and Meitzen (1946) report that a dickcissel was brought to the nest of a Sennett's white-tailed hawk.

A certain number of dickcissels are casualties of the highway Starrett (1938) found four killed by automobiles in central Illinois and Smith (1938) reports one killed in flight by a passing car a Sydney, Nova Scotia. Tuck found a dickcissel that had been run over by a railway train near Terra Nova, Newfoundland. Jame Hodges (1950) reports that a dickcissel was caught in small interlace wires of an electric line and starved to death.

A nest I found in central Illinois July 2, 1918, in a thick cluster c grapevines 5 feet above the ground had become so badly infested wit mites that the young were almost killed. I found the same mite less abundant, in a number of nests. Nathan Banks of the Museum of Comparative Zoology identified them as a new species of *Liponysu* allied to the common poultry mite.

Perhaps the greatest foe of the dickcissel, especially those that nes in clover and alfalfa fields, is the mowing machine. Cutting the firs crop destroys the early nests, and the late or second nest are ofte victims of a second harvest. In one 20-acre field near Atwood, Ill I found four nests, three with eggs and one with young that a mowin machine had destroyed. Spurrell (1921) notes frequent destructio of nests in Iowa by the cutting of clover fields. He found man eggs while loading hay. Destruction by mowers may be seriou enough to affect materially local dickcissel populations.

Fall.—The fall migration of the dickcissel has been given le attention than the more spectacular spring arrival. It is, neverthe less, quite as interesting. In August at the close of the nesting seaso the dickcissels rove about for a short time as family groups. Thes soon unite with others, which in turn may join still larger aggregatior to form roosts of several hundred individuals. In 1908 a roost tha contained considerably more than 300 birds on August 20 had ver few on September 1, and was deserted by September 10. A roost watched the summer of 1918 occupied the banks of a large drainag ditch whose sides, for a distance of nearly a mile, were covered wit giant ragweeds and horseweeds 8 to 10 feet high. Although th season was excessively hot and dry, the ditch contained refreshingl cool water. This and the admirable concealment the tall weed provided made it an ideal concentration center for many dickcissel A few could be seen feeding on the weed seeds or bathing in the ditc almost every hour of the day, but the mass of individuals came i between sunset and dark. On August 5 it sheltered only about 5 birds and on August 8 about 125. On August 10 I counted 485 adul and young, and doubtless more than twice that number were conceale by the dense growth. By August 15 a marked diminution in th

umbers at the roost was perceptible, and there was every reason to
believe the fall migration had begun. I had to leave Illinois at
his time, and so could not record the later developments at this
oost. Most dickcissels leave central Illinois by September 10 to
5, but a few stragglers may linger several days longer. My latest
ecord is of a young male collected Oct. 2, 1907.

Dates when the dickcissel was last seen in Minnesota are: Fillmore
County, Aug. 20, 1888; Minneapolis, Aug. 28, 1928; Pipestone County,
Sept. 8, 1930; and McLeod County, Sept. 12, 1893 (Roberts, 1932).

For Wisconsin, Taber (1947) gives the following dates when birds
vere last seen: Rusk County, Aug. 2, 1934; Dane County, Aug.
5, 1943; Jefferson County, Aug. 17, 1939; Jefferson County, Aug.
30, 1941; and Racine County, Sept. 30, 1939. Taber states that
he bulk of the dickcissel population leaves Wisconsin by mid-August.

In Michigan (Wood, 1951), the migration takes place mainly in
August. Specimens were taken at Jackson Sept. 8, 1941, and in
Washtenaw County Sept. 28, 1923. Birds have been noted in
he Toledo-Erie Marsh until mid-August, and sometimes as late as Sep-
ember 10. Specimens were collected there Sept. 9, 1934, and
Sept. 5, 1936.

The latest record for Buchanan County, Iowa is September 1, but
he species has usually disappeared by August 15 (Pierce, 1930).

In Ohio Trautman (1940) states: "The few transients seen during
he southward movement indicated that migration took place principally in late August. In this movement the bird was very inconspicuous, it remained chiefly where weeds grew in profusion."

Otto Widmann (1907) writes of the fall migration at St. Louis, Mo.:
"* * * we sometimes see parents feeding young after the middle of
August. When the breeding season closes, families gather into small
flocks and are seen flying south in the early hours of the day from
August 20 to September 10. To the general observer the species is
are after the middle of September, but for one who knows the roosts
he last has not gone before the first of October."

W. W. Cooke (1888) writes of the species' fall migration in the
Mississippi Valley: "In the fall of 1884 the last Black-throated
Bunting [dickcissel] left Des Moines, Iowa August 29. The bulk
eft Mount Carmel, Mo., September 6, and the last September 20.
At Unadilla, Nebr., none were seen after August 23. At San Angelo,
Tex., where it is an abundant migrant, the first appeared November 6,
and the last was seen November 23.

"* * * In the fall of 1885 none were seen at Huron, S. Dak., after
July 7; Iowa City, Iowa, August 29; Mount Carmel, Mo., September
20, and Saint Louis, Mo., September 26."

Winter.—Alexander F. Skutch has sent us an excellent account o the winter habits of the dickcissel in Costa Rica. It is presented ir its entirety, although a brief excerpt has already been given in the section on food. "Dickcissels reach Guatemala by the last week o August and Costa Rica by the beginning of September. During the winter months they are distributed widely over Central America particularly in the lowlands of the Pacific side and in the interior up to about 5,000 feet. They live in close flocks of few to many indi viduals, and are frequently abundant in regions where rice is grown I have enjoyed only transient encounters with them except in 1939 when I dwelt near San Isidro del General at about 2,200 feet above sea level. The little rustic cabin that I had rented for 6 months stood on a rise of ground in a bushy pasture facing the meandering Quebrada de las Vueltas, whose sluggish current was shaded by low trees and shrubs. Beyond the stream was a level field of rice several acres in extent. I first saw dickcissels in some bushes close to the house early in the morning of January 26, the day when the farme began to harvest his rice. Later in the morning I watched one o these birds eating grain at the edge of the field, as doubtless othe members of the flock were doing deeper in the stand of rice where could not see them. Despite the removal of the standing grain, the flock of dickcissels continued to frequent vicinity for the next months, possibly finding fallen grains amidst the stubble.

"As early as my first meeting with the dickcissels on January 26, heard them deliver brief, hurried snatches of song, punctuated by their rather harsh, 'thick' monosyllabic call note. All through February I continued to hear their calls at sunrise, and often, too shortest wisps of song. On February 27 I watched a male who perched on a dry weed stalk at the edge of the stubblefield, and sang a whisper-song so low that I might not have credited my ears, had not at the same time watched the vibrations of his throat through my fieldglasses. In March this songfulness increased. Every morning as the sun floated up above the wooded crest of the eastern ridge and sent its first cool beams through the chill gray mist which during the night had settled over the valley, the dickcissels gathered in the bushe that lined the banks of the river in front of my cabin, and on the tal weeds and shrubs in the adjoining pasture. Here the males, ofte several resting in the same bush, sang with zeal that increased as the season advanced and the date of their northward departure drew nigh. I have never met the dickcissel on his nesting-ground and know not what gifts of minstrelsy he may there display, but here his musi was of most inferior quality—a sort of animated chirping, rising and falling, and punctuated frequently by sharper, detached *chips*. Thi homely performance was continued for minutes together; and ofte several birds in various parts of the pasture, not far apart, would be chanting at once.

"By mid-March the males had practically completed the prenuptial molt. Each had a bright yellow breast and belly, and on the throat a heavy black patch that on some individuals extended well downward into the yellow of the breast, with perhaps a few detached black feathers below the termination of the solid black gular patch.

"The flight of the dickcissels is rapid, with frequent abrupt shifts in direction. In their winter home they travel in compact, quick-moving flocks of a few or many together, which wheel and turn in characteristic fashion. No other small Costa Rican bird that I know, whether resident or migratory, flies in flocks so large and compact, which rise so high and turn so quickly; parrots may travel in even larger flocks, but there is little likelihood of confusing these relatively big and noisy birds with the small and nearly silent dickcissels; nor are the straggling, slow-moving flocks of migrating kingbirds, more constant in direction, likely to be mistaken for them. I believe that I can recognize a flock of dickcissels while they are so far distant that they appear as mere motes against the sky.

"On April 3, 1939, I saw the last of these dickcissels in the vicinity of my cabin. The following year, at a point a few miles higher up the valley, I saw a lone dickcissel, singing in flight, on April 23. By the end of the month they have disappeared from Costa Rica, but the last stragglers have been recorded in Guatemala as late as May 4.

"In the Caribbean lowlands, the status of the dickcissel as a winter resident is somewhat doubtful. In the vicinity of Tela, Honduras, Peters (1929) first met dickcissels on March 29, when he saw two perching on a fence wire beside a railroad track over which for the preceding 2 months he had been accustomed to pass six times a day. They were not seen again. Near Los Amates, in the Caribbean lowlands of Guatemala, I did not meet the dickcissel until March 28, 1932, more than a month after I began fieldwork in that region. These dickcissels were in a clump of tall timber bamboos close beside the Rio Morja, in company with numerous blue grosbeaks; and both kinds of finches appeared to be eating the pollen of the bamboo flowers. Some of the male dickcissels in this flock seemed to have completed the prenuptial molt, but others were still in transitional plumage. Although I continued to study birds on this same plantation for the next 3 months, I did not again meet dickcissels, thus strengthening my belief that in this region they were only transients.

"Early dates of fall arrival in Central America are: Guatemala—*passim*, August 26 (Griscom). Costa Rica—Basin of El General, September 8, 1942, September 12, 1943, and September 24, 1945; Buenos Aires de Osa, September 4 (Carriker).

"Late dates of spring departure are: Costa Rica—El General April 3, 1939, April 23, 1940; Bebedero (Carriker), April 27. Guatemala—*passim*, May 4; Uaxactun, El Peten, April 28, 1931 (Van Tyne)."

Carriker (1910), in writing of the dickcissel in winter in Costa Rica, states: "An abundant winter visitor throughout almost the whole of Costa Rica wherever cultivated or grass-lands are to be found. They usually arrive about the first week in September and some linger on till late in April before leaving. They prefer the plateau region to the lower and hotter coastal plains, where food is also less plentiful. During their entire stay in the south they always remain in flocks of from five to six up to as many as fifty at times. The rice-fields in the region west of San Jose (from Turrúcares to San Mateo) are favorite localities for them."

As stated earlier in this account, an increasingly large number of dickcissels now spend the winter in the north, especially in northeastern United States and Canada. Here they are usually seen as lone individuals or at most three to five, and are frequently associated with house sparrows, tree sparrows, and other sparrows at feeding stations. They are usually silent except for a characteristic *cack* but at times may utter snatches of song. Dickcissels now also winter occasionally in the breeding areas of the Middle West.

DISTRIBUTION

Range.—South-central Canada to Colombia, Venezuela, and British and French Guiana.

Breeding range.—The dickcissel breeds (sporadically in eastern part of range) from eastern Montana (Miles City), northwestern North Dakota (Charlson), southern Manitoba (Oak Lake, Winnipeg), northwestern and central Minnesota (Fosston, Milaca), northern Wisconsin (Alden, Kelley Brook), central Michigan (Grand Traverse, Charlevoix, and Otsego counties), and southern Ontario (Sarnia, St. Thomas) south to central Colorado (Canyon City), western Oklahoma (Kenton), Texas (except the western Panhandle), southern Louisiana (Lake Charles, Diamond), central Mississippi, and central Alabama (Greensboro, Barachias), and locally in the piedmont of Georgia (Atlanta, Augusta), South Carolina (Columbia, York), and central Maryland (Clear Spring, Dickerson). Formerly from Massachusetts south through the Atlantic lowlands to South Carolina.

Winter range.—Winters from Michoácan (Apatzingán) south through Central America to central Colombia (Villavicencio), southern Venezuela (Caño Cataniapo), British Guiana (Abary River), and French Guiana; regularly in small numbers north to Arkansas, Mary-

and, New Jersey, New York, Connecticut, Rhode Island, and Massachusetts; casually to British Columbia, Kansas, Tennessee, Maine, and Nova Scotia.

Casual records.—Casual west to Baja California (San Jose del Cabo) and California (Santa Monica, Arcata); north to British Columbia (Victoria, Vaseaux Lake), southern Saskatchewan (Old Wives Lake), eastern Ontario (Ottawa), and Quebec (Baie Johan Beetz, Anticosti Island); and east to Newfoundland (Terra Nova), Nova Scotia (North Sidney, Sable Island), Maine, mid-North Atlantic Ocean (39° 33' N, 49° 58' W), Bermuda, Cuba, Jamaica, Aruba, Curaçao, and Trinidad.

Migration.—Early dates of spring arrival are: Costa Rica—El Hogar, March 25. Nayarit—Santa, April 22. Tamaulipas—April 15. Florida—Seven Oaks, April 8; Marathon, April 19. Alabama—Wheeler Refuge, Decatur, April 10. Georgia—Augusta, April 19. North Carolina—Raleigh, May 19. Virginia—Richmond, May 7. District of Columbia—May 10. Maryland—Cecil County, April 24. Pennsylvania—Carlisle, May 2. New Jersey—New Milford, May 6. New York—Branchport, May 5; Easthampton and Riis Park, May 18. Connecticut—Glastonbury, May 11. Massachusetts—Martha's Vineyard, May 23. Maine—Bath, May 25. Louisiana—Baton Rouge, April 12. Mississippi—Rosedale, April 21. Arkansas—Fayetteville, April 29. Tennessee—Knox County, April 29. Kentucky—Versailles, April 4; Bowling Green, April 26. Missouri—St. Louis, April 19 (median of 14 years, May 1). Illinois—Urbana, April 25 (median of 20 years, May 3). Indiana—Wayne County, May 5 (median of 14 years, May 11). Ohio—Cleveland, April 18 (average for central Ohio, May 7). Michigan—Ann Arbor, May 8; Battle Creek, May 20 (median of 7 years, May 26). Ontario—Point Pelee, May 8. Iowa—Sioux City, April 6 (median of 38 years, May 10). Wisconsin—Madison, April 9; Manitowoc County, April 18. Minnesota—Faribault, May 5 (average of 16 years for southern Minnesota, May 18). Texas—San Antonio, March 25; Bee County, April 10. Oklahoma—Oklahoma City, April 17. Kansas—northeastern Kansas, April 21 (median of 21 years, May 4). Nebraska—Brady, April 19; Red Cloud, April 27 (median of 22 years, May 12). South Dakota—Rapid City, April 12; Sioux Falls, May 14 (average of 6 years, May 26). North Dakota—Cass County, May 17 (average, May 29). Manitoba—Winnipeg, June 4. New Mexico—Santa Fe, May 7. Wyoming—Wheatland, May 20. Alberta—Nanton, April 24.

Late dates of spring departure are: Colombia—Santa Marta Region, May 1. Honduras—Tegucigalpa, April 24. El Salvador—Divisadero, April 12. Chiapas—May 13. Tobasco—Balancán, May 15. Quintana Roo—Laguna Chacanbacab, May 15. Florida—Key West, April 30. Maryland—Prince Georges County, May 22.

Illinois—Chicago, June 2. Ohio—Buckeye Lake, median departure, May 30. Texas—Central Coast, May 13; Dallas, May 29.

Early dates of fall arrival are: California—Joshua Tree National Monument, September 19, Texas—Dallas, August 21; Central Coast, August 28. Ohio—Buckeye Lake, median arrival, August 25. Mississsippi—Saucier, September 17. Nova Scotia—Bon Portage Island, August 19. New Brunswick—Machias Seal Island, August 20. Maine—Brunswick, August 13. New York—Blythewood, Long Island, August 25. New Jersey—Beach Haven, August 27; Island Beach, August 31 (median of 5 years, September 13). Maryland—Ocean City, September 1 (median of 8 years, September 16). Florida—Century, August 19. Sinaoloa—Colmoa, September 9. Veracruz—August 23. Chiapas—Ocuilapa, August 23. El Salvador—Divisadero, September 24. Colombia—Santa Marta Region, September 17.

Late dates of fall departure are: British Columbia—Victoria, November 16. California—Arcata, November 19. Wyoming—Sheridan, September 7. Colorado—Boulder, September 30. Arizona—Tucson, September 11. New Mexico—Los Alamos, November 19. North Dakota—Cass County, September 19 (average, August 25). South Dakota—Faulkton, October 1. Nebraska—Holstein, October 4. Kansas—Clearwater, October 6. Oklahoma—Cleveland County, September 29. Texas—Dallas, October 22; Sinton, October 12 (median of 6 years, September 28). Minnesota—Hutchinson, September 12. Wisconsin—Trempealeau, September 6. Ontario—Point Pelee, September 20. Michigan—Washtenaw County, September 28. Ohio—Columbus, September 27 (median of 40 years, August 25). Indiana—Wayne County, August 25. Illinois—Rantoul, September 30. Missouri—St. Louis, October 15 (median of 14 years, October 2). Kentucky—Harrison County, September 19. Arkansas—Rogers, September 6. Mississippi—Saucier, September 30. Louisiana—Baton Rouge, November 15. Nova Scotia—North Sydney, December 3. New Brunswick—off Grand Manan, September 23. Quebec—Gaspé, October 18. Maine—Bowdoinham, October 25. Massachusetts—Martha's Vineyard, November 28. Rhode Island—Middletown, October 28. Connecticut—Pomfret, December 1. New York—Water Mill, October 25; Tiana Beach, October 24 (median of 5 years, October 13). At sea in North Atlantic Ocean—39°33′ N, 49°58′ W, November 5. New Jersey—Trenton, November 25. Pennsylvania—Atglen, October 29. Maryland—Unity, November 22. Virginia—Charlottesville, October 6. Georgia—Macon, October 8. Alabama—Dauphin Island, October 20. Florida—Leon County, October 31. Sinaloa—Rosario, October 28.

Egg dates.—Illinois: 100 records, May 17 to August 5; 50 records, June 3 to June 20.

Oklahoma: 15 records, May 14 to June 20; 10 records, June 1 to June 8.

Texas: 19 records, April 28 to July 7; 10 records, May 12 to June 15.

FRINGILLA MONTIFRINGILLA Linnaeus

Brambling

PLATE 12

Contributed by WILLIAM MAITLAND CONGREVE
and
HUGH MORAY SUTHERLAND BLAIR

HABITS

The claim of the brambling to a place on the A.O.U. Check-List is based on the occurrence of a vagrant male captured in the watch house at Northeast Point, St. Paul Island, Bering Sea, Oct. 25, 1914. The specimen is defective in that it lacks the tail feathers.

This finch is one of the most characteristic and generally distributed birds of the great forests of northern Eurasia. Indeed its summer range can be said to extend from ocean to ocean, some breeding stations overlooking the Atlantic, while others lie as near to the Sea of Okhotsk. There are reports of nests being found in Britain, but all save one of these must be considered doubtful. The brambling breeds regularly, however, no farther away than western Norway—in some places, close to the coastline. Farther inland, on the forested slopes of the great highlands of Norway and Sweden, this becomes one of the commonest birds. Within the Arctic Circle it breeds freely down to sea level, the drawling song of the male being one of the bird notes most reminiscent of the woods that give so much beauty to the little ports such as Tromsö. Bramblings are equally plentiful in northern Finland, where they are to be seen down to at least the 62d parallel. It was from Finland that the first bramblings' eggs known to science were sent to England, a century ago, by that great pioneer of oology, John Wolley, then on his first visit to the North. Wolley reached his future headquarters on the Muonio too late to obtain a nest himself that season, most bramblings having hatched out their young by the time of his arrival; and for these historic specimens he was indebted to the local priest.

Everywhere within its breeding range, the brambling—like other northern finches, such as the mealy redpoll (*Carduelis flammea*) and the pine grosbeak (*Pinicola enucleator*)—is more numerous in some years than in others. Most naturalists who have lived for some time in its haunts can remember a "brambling-summer." On the other hand, the species can be disappointingly scarce even in districts where it is normally well represented. In his account of the fauna of East Finmark, Schaanning (1907) noted that in one year not a single pair of bramblings could be found nesting in a wide stretch of forest where three summers before the birds had been abundant.

Spring.—A few migrating bramblings have been seen in February as far north as the Faroes, but the spring passage does not normally become evident anywhere in western Europe until well into March, and reaches its height in April. At some time in the latter month, bramblings appear in the birch woods along the coasts of Norway—the first summer haunts to be reoccupied. Large flocks alight in arctic Finno-Scandia a week or two later, in the second half of May, when the vernal immigration into the Russian forests may be expected.

Little has been recorded of the courtship display of the brambling beyond that it does not differ much from that of the closely allied chaffinch (*Fringilla coelebs*). No sooner have the returning flocks dispersed than the females may be seen darting through the forest, each with her mate in close pursuit. When at length she alights, he settles close by, to spread his tail and flutter his drooping wings, just as would a city sparrow. It is then, as he flits by the white-trunked birches, that a male brambling appears at his best; the glossy blue-black feathers of his head and mantle offsetting the snowy-white rump and the chestnut shoulder patches.

While bramblings are generally common enough in mixed forest, their strongholds are those lovely northern woods where the graceful birch predominates above other trees. Though these finches cannot be described as colonial in the narrowest sense of the word, several pairs may often be found within a small compass. Their neighbors at times include a varying number of fieldfares (*Turdus pilaris*), and no one who has watched a party of the big thrushes hustling a crow or hawk can doubt that the association benefits the smaller birds. Frequently also a pair of merlins (*Falco columbarius*) will take up their quarters close by. As under such circumstances the little falcons hunt at some distance from their home, their presence—so far from being a menace—affords further security to the finches and thrushes around them.

Bramblings breed right up to the tree line—in some districts, well beyond the outskirts of the forests proper. It is amongst such surroundings that scattered pairs are to be found in the extreme north of Norway and Finland. Both writers recall laborious, yet ever pleasant, quests for these and other birds' nests in a wilderness of scrub around Vadsö. One particularly lovely brambling clutch was found there, but only after struggling through dense thickets of low sallows and stunted

PLATE 12

refjell, Norway, 1950   H. D. England

MALE AND FEMALE BRAMBLINGS

stport, Conn.   A. D. Cruickshank

EASTERN EVENING GROSBEAK

birches, where a tangle of interlacing, springy branches impeded every step.

Nesting.—In its choice of nesting site the brambling shows a marked preference for birch trees. Nests in conifers are by no means rare, however, and "The Old Bushman," H. W. Wheelwright (1871), regards a spruce as the normal situation in parts of Sweden. The Pearsons discovered that in Russian Lapland the earlier nesting bramblings built mostly in pines, while the later birds resorted to birches, which suggested that the latter tree was chosen only when it bore sufficient foliage to shelter and conceal a nest. Occasionally a pair of bramblings will build in an alder or, yet more rarely, an oak. In a long series of records from different sources the heights at which bramblings' nests have been found ranged between 3 and 30 feet, most of them being placed between 5 and 15 feet. The little nest can be very inconspicuous, and if well up in a birch, it can be very difficult to reach without the aid of climbing irons.

For the foundation of its nest the brambling builds a platform of small twigs and dry grass. This supports a cup of grasses interwoven with fragments of birchbark, feathers, and strands of the black, hair-like lichen (*Usnea*) that festoons the pines of the northern forests. Catkins, vegetable down, scraps of gray lichen plucked off the bark of a nearby tree, spiders' webs, and (perhaps only rarely) wasp paper are attached to the outside of the cup. The warmly felted lining consists of fine grasses, *Usnea*, hair, vole or lemming fur, and, at times, spores of one of the clubmosses. Near peasants' holdings bramblings frequently take horsehair or cowhair for their nests, while farther afield they collect the castings from the reindeers' pelts. Dresser (1905–1910) describes a striking nest built of "white marsh-cotton." A curious, abnormal example seen by Pearson (1904) in Lapland was built up to a height of a foot.

In appearance a brambling's nest closely resembles that of the better known chaffinch. As a general rule, though there are exceptions, the chaffinch's is the smaller of the two and the more neatly finished. One experienced Norwegian oologist, the late J. A. Thome, made careful notes of the many bramblings' and chaffinches' nests he came across and found that the former measured between 110 and 120 mm. in diameter, with cups between 50 and 60, while in the latter the overall measurements varied between 90 and 95 mm. with cups between 50 and 55 mm. Some bramblings' nests, though by no means all, may be further distinguished by the free use of feathers as lining material, it being exceptional to find many in a chaffinch's.

Eggs.—Six or seven eggs constitute a normal clutch with the brambling, but sets of five are not uncommon. Occasionally a nest will hold as many as eight or even nine eggs, while, on the other hand, some birds content themselves with four. Despite the difference in latitude (10°) large clutches occur as regularly toward the southern limit of the breeding range, in southern Norway, as in the extreme north. Even in a small series these eggs show considerable variation. In color they range from a clear blue to a dull olive, with markings of dark brownish purple, reddish brown, and lilac, some being heavily blotched, others thinly spotted, while in quite a number the overlying pigments are smeared to give an attractive clouded effect. Henry Seebohm (1884), one of the authorities of his day, recorded immaculate specimens. The type most frequently seen has a greenish ground with brownish-purple streaks and blotches, which often show a penumbra of paler shade. Another less common but very characteristic type of the species is a clear, pale blue relieved by scattered, almost black spots. In a third variety, on the other hand, the grayish-blue ground color is almost completely overlaid with flecks of reddish pigment, some such eggs being very handsome. The least attractive specimens are grayish buff with few and very small markings. One hundred eggs measured by Jourdain averaged 19.5 by 14.6 mm., maximum 22.2 by 15.6 mm., minimum 18.1 by 13.5 mm.

Eggs of the brambling may easily be confused with those of the chaffinch. If normal types are compared, those of the former species will appear the darker and greener, but this cannot be regarded as an entirely reliable diagnostic character. As the chaffinch breeds alongside its ally over a wide area, the greatest care must always be exercised in identifying nests.

Young.—Very little has been recorded of the incubation and fledging periods of the brambling. M. A. England, who kept two nests under close observation, found that the female alone covered the eggs throughout an incubation period of 14 days. After the eggs had hatched, the bird was seen to remove the shells, which she carried some distance away. The male, as far as could be discovered, took no interest in the nest until the young appeared, when he came to feed his mate and, later, the brood. England's notes suggest that the female did not settle down to incubate before the last egg was laid. On the other hand, the owner of a nest found by Congreve certainly started to incubate before completing her clutch, some of her six eggs containing noticeably larger embryos than others. Svein Haftorn (1952) records a family of six young examined on July 23, 1952, of which one was at least 4 days old, while another had just left the shell. In June 1938 Blair found a brambling sitting hard on three eggs in southwest Norway. None of the eggs showed any trace of incubation, however, and the sitting bird may have been only covering them against the heavy rain which was falling at the time.

The female brambling usually sits very closely, and when forced to leave her nest, she will scold the intruder from the nearest tree, the male usually joining her. Some birds become surprisingly tame. One picked Pearson's fingers while he was examining her nest although the eggs showed no sign of incubation. Among the notes contributed by the late A. Landmark to Collett's "Norges Fugle" is an account of a yet more trusting bird which finally took food from his hand as she brooded her eggs.

The fledging period of the brambling probably does not exceed the 13 to 14 days noted for some allied finches. Only one brood appears to be reared in the season.

Food.—Throughout the colder months, the brambling's food consists largely of seeds and, in the fall, small fruits. The seeds of the spruce and the red berries of the mountain ash are greatly relished, and Norwegian writers tell us that fewer bramblings may be expected to leave that country when these two fruits are plentiful than at other times. In western and central Europe bramblings consume quantities of beech-mast, woods where such fruit can be obtained being among their favorite haunts. Elder trees too are frequently despoiled of their blue-black berries. In hard weather a flock of bramblings will settle for weeks on and about a farm, to feed on the spilt grain and to do much good by keeping down such weeds as the knot grass. In the summer the birds vary their diet with insects. Collett found masses of geometer larvae in the stomachs of those he dissected at that time of the year, and he noted that young broods were entirely reared on small insects such as *Tipulidae*.

Voice.—In fall and winter, flocked bramblings keep up a rapid, low-pitched twittering, which Tucker rendered as *chuck-chuck-chuck*. A sharp *scape* is the note most commonly heard in the breeding season, the bird's voice becoming louder and harsher if any danger threatens the nest. The song of the male—if song it can be called—is a drawling *dree-e-e-e* repeated again and again and often followed by a churring note. It recalls that of the European greenfinch (*Chloris chloris*), and bears some resemblance to the trill of the clay-colored sparrow (*Spizella pallida*) of America. Although this simple performance can occasionally be heard in early spring from males still in their winter quarters, some ornithologists prefer to regard it as a kind of subsidiary song. Collett described the true song as sweet and melodious, consisting of several flutelike notes, somewhat resembling the redwing's (*Turdus musicus*) and heard only for a little while after the birds' arrival on their breeding grounds. It should be added that although many naturalists have visited the brambling's summer haunts, some of them—including one of the present writers—early in the season, Collett alone appears to have been fortunate enough to hear this "true" song.

Field marks.—The brambling can readily be distinguished from allied birds by its white rump, while at close quarters the dark head, buffish breast, and—in the male—orange lesser wing coverts are further aids to identification. In all its actions this is a typical finch, and particularly in its characteristic dipping flight. The bird moves forward with a few swift movements of the wings, and then closes them, losing height as it does so. At the end of the flight, the wings are stiffly extended as the bird glides to its perch. When in company, bramblings fly closely packed, and some writers claim that this formation alone will distinguish a distant flock.

Fall.—In some years, and especially when the spruce and mountain-ash bear heavy crops of seed and fruit, flocks of bramblings are to be encountered throughout the winter in districts well within the species' breeding range. The great majority, however, move southward during the fall. A few occasionally migrate in August, but overseas movements in any force do not normally take place until about the equinox. In western Europe they become most noticeable in October, and continue throughout the following month, and occasionally into December. When the migration is at its height, it is by no means unusual to see hundreds of bramblings in one flock, and still more imposing flights occur now and then. One flock seen in Yorkshire was described as "extending over 280 yards in length"; another, in Scotland, was "a quarter of a mile long and 15 yards broad." A tendency for the sexes to segregate has been reported by a few observers, some flocks in Yorkshire being composed entirely of adult males.

Bramblings, like many other birds, sometimes complete an overseas journey under cover of darkness. Large numbers have been identified at lighthouses on calm nights when the beams of the light become most attractive to passing migrants. Given less favorable conditions, it may happen that the birds encounter worsening weather before they make the land, growing very wing-weary and pitching into the first cover they reach after crossing the tide mark. Saxby (1874), the Shetland ornithologist, described how, one stormy October night, he thrust a lantern into a walled enclosure on a barren island, to find the ground "thickly covered—in some places, literally paved—with Bramblings and Chaffinches."

Gatke (1895), one of the first students of migration, once detected a brambling "drifting on the sea, at least three miles east of Heligoland. On the approach of the boat, the bird rose and at once ascended to a fairly considerable height, after the manner of birds which purpose continuing their journey after resting."

Winter.—Wherever bramblings winter, their numbers will be found to vary from year to year, the fluctuations being as remarkable as those observed on the birds' breeding grounds. Even in the most favored resorts, the season may pass without more than a few scattered parties putting in an appearance. On the other hand, some of the great incursions witnessed in Central Europe have become historic. A flock 100,000 strong wintered one year in the Thuringwold, according to Bechstein; and more than 1,600 dozens were killed in a succession of raids on roosting birds in Lorraine in 1765. A vast horde which settled in Luxemburg in February 1865 was computed to have included 60,000,000 individuals. This almost incredible estimate is exceeded by that reached by observers of the immigration into central Europe of 1950–51, when the number of bramblings congregating at two roosts alone was thought to be 72,000,000!

In winter, as in summer, Bramblings prefer woodland resorts, beech woods, as mentioned earlier, being especially favored. In Britain newly arrived birds often rest for a day or two about coastwise farms, and even in midwinter the species is often well represented in the big flocks of finches that haunt the open country. When going to roost, bramblings usually look for the security of a high perch, such as the upper branches of a high conifer, but sleeping birds may be flushed from low hedges, or even from among the rough grasses on a moorland. A prolonged cold spell may drive wintering bramblings farther south, such weather movements being reported in January and February.

Enemies.—Within its breeding range, the brambling's most dangerous enemies seem to be the merlin (*Falco columbarius*) and sparrowhawk (*Accipiter nisus*). In his outstanding work on the Norwegian birds of prey, Yngvar Hagen (1952) tabulates the local records of prey taken by the two raptors. Among the 678 birds noted as killed by merlins, and which could be referred to 47 species, 20 bramblings were identified. The 506 recorded victims of the sparrowhawk included the somewhat higher proportion of 25 bramblings. While it is probable that others among the Scandinavian raptors occasionally kill bramblings, Hagan could find evidence of only the goshawk (*Accipiter gentilis*) so doing, and that but once. On migration bramblings continue to be in danger from merlins. One of the writers remembers a sunny October day by the North Sea, when the fall migration was in full swing and the hedges alive with finches. Suddenly a male brambling, hard pressed by a merlin, topped the hawthorns and the falcon almost brushed the watcher's cheek as it sped by. Sparrowhawks also levy toll on wintering bramblings, and the buzzard (*B. buteo*) has been recorded as taking one. This finch figures too in British lists of prey for the tawny (*Strix aluco*) and long-eared (*Asio otus*) owls.

Bramblings' nests are often robbed of their eggs, the culprit most frequently being a hooded crow (*Corvus cornix*) or, in the north, a Siberian jay (*Perisoreus infaustus*). E. S. Steward remembered being roused early one morning by an uproar around his lodgings in Lapland. A number of bramblings had incomplete clutches close to the house, and it was their alarm notes, mingled with the louder voices of a pair of raiding Siberian jays, that had awakened him. Upon investigation, he discovered four bramblings' nests despoiled of their contents—undoubtedly by the jays.

In Finno-Scandia the brambling is one of the commoner dupes of the cuckoo (*Cuculus canorus*), and in most cases the parasitic egg closely resembles that of the host. The first authentic instance of this assimilation was detected by Prof. Alfred Newton and recorded by him in "Ootheca Wolleyana." Here, curiously enough, it was the dissimilarity between the cuckoo's egg and the brambling clutch which attracted notice, the former presenting what Newton described as "the average brambling colouration," while the latter were fine examples of the somewhat rare blue type. These interesting specimens were taken by a native collector trained by John Wolley, who had died only a few months previously. Wolley himself had earlier received several eggs which he cataloged as abnormal bramblings', but which may have been Cuckoos'.

DISTRIBUTION

Range.—Scotland, Scandinavia, and the Soviet Union to the Mediterranean, China, and Japan.

Breeding range.—The brambling breeds from tree limits in Eurasia east to the upper Anadyr Valley and south to northern Scotland (Sutherland), the Baltic, central Russia (Novgorod, Kazan, Ufa), southern Siberia (southern Omsk, Novosibirsk, Irkutsk, southern Yakutsk, Udskaya Bay), and Kamchatka.

Winter range.—Winters from Scotland and southern Scandinavia south to central Portugal, the Mediterranean, Syria, Iran, Baluchistan, northern West Pakistan, Tibet, southern China, and southern Japan.

Casual records.—Casual to Iceland, Madeira, and the Philippines (Calayan).

Accidental in fall in Alaska (St. Paul Island in the Pribilofs and Amchitka Island in the Aleutians). Recorded (possibly escaped cage birds) in New Jersey (Stanton) and Massachusetts (Hadley, Richmond).

Migration.—Early date of fall arrival is: Alaska—Amchitka Island, October 14.

Late date of fall departure is: Alaska—St. Paul Island, October 25.

COCCOTHRAUSTES COCCOTHRAUSTES JAPONICUS Temminck and Schlegel

Japanese Hawfinch

Contributed by OLIVER L. AUSTIN, JR.

HABITS

The Japanese hawfinch is admitted to the A.O.U. Check-List on the basis of a single specimen taken in the Pribilof Islands November 1, 1911. Evermann (1913), who reported its capture by a native at the village landing of St. Paul's Island, comments: "It was a new bird to the natives, none of them recognizing it as anything they had ever seen before." The species breeds to the limit of trees in Kamchatka and eastern Siberia, not too great a distance from American territory for strong wings to negotiate, and that it should have been recorded only this once within the Check-List area is the more remarkable because the species is a rather erratic migrant and winter wanderer.

Coccothraustes coccothraustes is a widespread palearctic species, a representative and characteristic bird of the northern forest belt of Europe and Asia. It is comparatively distinct and nonplastic, and its subspecies are not strongly marked, although five races are generally recognized and others have been described. The species tends to become paler from west to east across the continent, and exhibits minor size and other color variations along the southern and lateral peripheries of its breeding range. The nominate race breeds across northern Europe generally from the British Isles through Scandinavia and Russia. *C.c.japonicus*, the palest form of all, inhabits extreme eastern Asia from Manchuria to Japan and Kamchatka. A smaller, grayer race, *buvryi*, breeds in southwestern Europe and northwestern Africa; a darker bird, *nigricans*, inhabits the Caucasus region from the Black Sea to the Caspian Sea; a yellower subspecies, *humii*, is recognized in Turkestan and northern India.

Hawfinches are birds of deciduous woods and mixed forests rather than pure stands of evergreens. In settled lands they are confirmed and sometimes locally common dwellers in wooded parks, gardens, and orchards, where their depredations, particularly to such pitted fruits as cherries, do not endear them to agriculturists. However, they are nowhere overly abundant, and as they are rather shy and quiet, especially in the breeding season, they are not easily observed. In some areas they tend to be permanent residents and show very little migratory activity, but usually they move erratically southward throughout their range, sometimes coming into more open country in small groups, usually of less than a score of individuals, though flocks of 400 have been observed.

The life histories of none but the nominate race have been well studied, though more data are available on *japonicus* than on most of the rest. The several European ornithologists, Sowerby, Bergman, and Jahn, who have written of their first-hand field experiences with the Japanese hawfinch all remark the similarity of its habits to those of the European form. Hence I have drawn freely from accounts of the latter where details are lacking on the Asiatic bird.

Courtship.—The courtship of *C.c.japonicus* has never been described. The Witherby "Handbook of British Birds" (1938) portrays the court-ship of *C.c.coccothraustes* as follows:

E. M. Nicholson observed courtship from Feb. 25 in flock by two pairs: later apart from flock. Chief points are constant pursuit of female by very attentive male and the "kiss." Male observed to approach female on ground with "great bounding hops," halting face to face and tipping bill lightly against hers, once only, then hopping away again, all in silence without pause. "Kiss" also observed in trees amongst flock; initiative always taken by male. W. H. Thompson observed: (1) display in flock by single birds, which would stand very erect trailing and partially spreading wings and tail, showing the flashes of colour to advantage. No notice appeared to be taken by other birds. (2) Pursuit of female by male. (3) Mutual courtship of bowing and bill-touching by pair. (4) Coition, preceded by calling of female, but not by display of male; on one occasion male flew straight to female in response to call, from perch more than 100 yds. away. More observation needed on relation between (1) and (2). W. E. Teschemaker, with captive birds, observed side to side swaying action of both sexes and describes female soliciting by this movement, with drooping wings, low crooning note, and "kiss."

Nesting.—The hawfinch prefers to nest in deciduous trees in mixed forests. In Europe it is reported frequently to build near human dwellings, in trees in parks and in the yards of homes. In eastern Asia, however, it is essentially a shy forest bird and difficult to observe during the breeding season. It shows a preference for nesting in scrubby growth near the edges of heavy woods, or in brushy copses near the mouth of a river.

It builds a shallow, cup-shaped nest, usually from 2 to 3 meters above the ground, though occasionally in tall trees considerably higher. Kobayashi and Ishizawa (1933) observed four nests in Hokkaido "all made on branches of red-berried elders two to three meters above the ground," but add that in Korea "nests are made mostly in boughs of tall chestnut trees." Kobayashi later (1937) found four more nests in Hokkaido, all "two to three meters from the ground in ash trees." Yamashina (1933) reports it builds fre-quently in high conifers.

The nest itself is built on a crude platform, often in a tree fork. Kobayashi and Ishizawa (1933) describe two typical examples:

One nest obtained in Kitami Province, Hokkaido, is 20 x 17 cm. in outer diameter, 10 x 8 cm. in inner diameter, 6 cm. in height and 4 cm. in depth. It is a relatively crude structure, dead vines being used for the outside and rootlets and horse hair for the inside. Another nest from Kokaido [Hwang-hae Do], Corea, is 11 cm. in outer diameter, 6 x 7 in inner diameter, 7.5 cm. in height and 5 cm. deep. The principal material for the outside structure is dead grass, with which is mixed waste cloth and waste thread. For the inside part a large quantity of rootlets are used.

Eggs.—The normal clutch is five eggs, but sets of three to six are reported. Kobayashi and Ishizawa (1933) describe them as follows:

"They range from oval to broad oval or elliptical oval in shape, with medium lustre. The ground color is light greenish blue with spots and short streaks distributed all over the surface, particularly in abundance near the obtuse end. Shell markings are ashy grey while surface markings are dark brown in thick and thin shades. The average size of 50 eggs from 13 clutches is 23.68 x 17.45 mm., the maximum being 26.0 x 18.5 mm. and the minimum 19.3 x 16.5 mm. and 24.2 x 15.8 mm. (the average size being 23.0 x 17.5 mm.). Eighteen eggs weigh on the average 3.7 g."

Incubation.—Yamashina (1933) states that incubation of the one brood per year is by the female only, and requires 14 to 15 days. On the other hand Kiyosu (1943) states that the chicks hatch after 9 to 10 days incubation (which approximates European findings) and remain in the nest 10 to 11 more days. He also notes that the female is fed by the male while incubating, and that the young are fed by both parents.

Plumages.—Kiyosu (1943) describes the newly hatched chick as "flesh-colored with long white down, sparsely distributed in the pteryla above the eyes and on the hind neck, back, fore-wings, thighs, belly, etc. The inside of the mouth is purplish red at the top of the upper mandible and red at the basal part and the rest of the mouth, while the edge of the mouth is bright yellow."

The first juvenal plumage is replaced by a partial postjuvenal molt which occurs late in July and is completed by the end of August, and involves all but the flight feathers, secondary coverts, and tail feathers. In this plumage the bird is similar to the adult in winter plumage, which is acquired by a complete postnuptial molt in early autumn.

Food.—The Japanese hawfinch is essentially a seed, bud, and fruit eater, although it adds insects to its diet to increase its protein intake in the breeding season. Yamashina (1933) states, "They feed chiefly on cereals, beans, fruits, or seeds of pine and cryptomeria, and particularly on the fruits of the muku tree [*Aphananthe aspera*] in winter.

In spring they feed on fresh buds, and in summer on insects, chiefly beetles and larvae." Kiyosu (1943) is a little more specific: "It lives chiefly on vegetable food, preferring from autumn to spring the fruits and seeds of *Aphananthe aspera* (*Ulmaceae*), *Cinnamonum brevisfolium* (*Lauraceae*), *Rhus sylvestris* (*Anacardiaceae*), *Quercus aliena* (*Fagaceae*), *Rhodocarpus macrophylla* (*Coniferae*), *Staphyla, Bumalda* (*Staphyleaceae*), and *Styrax japonica* (*Styracaceae*), while in summer it eats *Prunus serrulata* or *Prunus* fruits of *Persica* of the family *Smygdalaceae*. In breeding season it feeds on insects, mainly *Curcurionidae* butterfly larvae." Y. Nakamura (1941) observed it eating the fruits of *Taxus cuspidata* and *Viscum coloratum*, and it has also been reported as feeding on the buds, fruits, or seeds of *Celtis sinensis, Deutzia sieboldiana*, and *Cryptotanenia japonica*.

The Japanese regard the hawfinch as a "bad bird" because of its occasional depredations to upland field crops. It shows a particular fondness for the red adzuki beans, a popular and widely grown staple used to make the sweet soups which are a gourmet's delight and to color the "red rice" so essential to all holiday feasting. Its appetite for this legume has earned it such local vernacular names as "bean-mouth," "bean-cracker," "bean-spinner," and "bean-shrike." T. Nibe (1918) reports from Akita prefecture in northwestern Honshu, "A few hawfinches came daily to feed on the bean plants laid on frames to dry. The birds did not seem unusually abundant, and seldom were more than 10 seen at a time, but they stayed there all day. Their damage to the beans was estimated as about 15%–20%."

Behavior.—The general behavior of the Japanese hawfinch seems from the available literature and from my own observations to be identical to that of the European form, as summed up so excellently in Tucker's account in "Handbook of British Birds" (Witherby, 1938).

"On ground hops rather heavily with erect carriage, or moves with highly peculiar almost parrot-like waddle (J. D. Wood). Likes to perch on topmost twigs of tall trees and feeds by preference in upper branches, but also often on ground, on fallen seeds under trees, etc. Flight quick, with rapid wingbeats; except over short distances markedly undulating * * *. Birds passing from wood to wood habitually rise to 200–1,000 ft. and are frequently picked up merely by hearing note (E. M. Nicholson). Roosts in woods, etc. in thick foliage of treetops or in winter sometimes in high thick hedges, etc. (Nauman)."

Voice.—The hawfinch is a fairly quiet bird on the wintering grounds and in migration, but usually betrays its presence by its short, sharp, rather metallic call note. Even during the breeding season it is not considered a good singer. Kiyosu (1943) syllabizes its notes as "*chichi, chi-chi, cho-cho*, metallic and sharp. In breeding season it whistles like a human."

Field marks.—Japanese hawfinches appear in the field as heavily built, grayish-brown birds, with white patches on the wing coverts which are conspicuous in flight. Their somewhat labored, undulating flight and their distinctive metallic call notes identify them at a distance. Their enormous, stout bills, and large, thick-set heads differentiate them at once from all other palearctic fringillids except the eastern Asaitic grosbeaks of the genus *Eophona*, from which, however, they are distinguishable at a glance by their chunkier, darker appearance and their much shorter tails.

Captivity.—Hawfinches are frequently offered for sale by the Japanese live bird dealers, but they are not overly popular as cage birds because neither their plumage nor their song is outstanding or appealing. Their chief virtue as an avicultural subject is their hardiness. To quote Yamashina (1933):

"This bird is neither very beautiful nor a good singer, so few are kept for pets. But it is very easy to feed, for its constitution is very strong, and all it needs is Japanese or Italian millet, and insects occasionally in summer. It is not advisable to give it much fat, otherwise it will grow too heavy. Constant moderate exercise and bath water are needed. This species has a habit of giving food to other birds' chicks, bill to bill, in cages, which has been observed several times. Nevertheless the raising of young removed from the wild nest is said to be very difficult."

Captive hawfinches are used commonly as decoys by the Japanese professional bird netters, who condition them to sing in the autumn by reversing their sex cycle. The birds are kept on a bland carbohydrate diet in a dark place all spring. Conditioning starts in midsummer by the gradual addition of fish meal to their food. The cages are brought out into a lighter place, and as autumn approaches, kept under electric lights in the evening so the birds will have a longer day of activity, and will eat more of the protein-rich food. By the time the southward flight of wild birds arrives in October and November, the decoys are in full song and ready for use. (Cf. Austin, 1947.)

Enemies.—The Japanese hawfinch is undoubtedly preyed upon by the faster bird-eating hawks just as is its European relative, and in the breeding season it must be equally subject to the depredations of squirrels, snakes, and other nest robbers, but no details are available.

Its chief enemy in the Orient is man. Large numbers are killed annually in Japan for food, taken in the mist nets (cf. Austin, 1947) with other small migrant birds, chiefly in October and November in the highlands, and lured to the nets by the singing of captive decoys. The following statistics on the catches of this species reported by Japanese netters to the Ministry of Agriculture and Forestry amply illustrate its irregularity of winter movement:

Year	No. birds	Year	No. birds
1924	10, 472	1934	11, 314
1925	32, 685	1935	39, 925
1926	71, 077	1936	8, 613
1927	24, 404	1937	39, 024
1928	12, 979	1938	13, 448
1929	61, 431	1939	83, 716
1930	14, 683	1940	12, 272
1931	9, 630	1941	16, 818
1932	32, 434	1942	13, 407
1933	24, 417		

Fall and winter.—The Japanese hawfinch apparently has a much more pronounced migration than any of the other races of *Cocco-thraustes coccothraustes*. The European hawfinch is generally regarded as resident wherever it occurs, though it does some wandering in the nonbreeding season. The Asiatic form also is found occasionally on its breeding grounds in winter, but its seasonal presence and absence and comings and goings in Japan leave no doubt that, although its movements are highly irregular and its abundance in any given locality very variable from year to year, the species has established there a fairly definite pattern of migration.

Sowerby (1923) writes of its movements on the continent: "It appears to be a little more than partially migratory in its habits, larger numbers, especially immature birds, leaving the Manchurian Region for East China, Korea and Japan for the winter.

"While in the forests of North Kirin, I noticed large flocks of these birds moving south in September, and all the specimens I secured were immature. On the other hand I saw fully adult specimens in the same regions after the first snows had fallen; and in North China in the middle of winter, when the ground was frozen hard, and the thermometer stood at a few degrees from zero, I have secured specimens of fully adult birds, both in forested mountainous areas and on the bleak, wind-swept plains."

In Japan the hawfinches generally appear in northern Honshu in mid-October, reach central and southern Honshu from early November to early December, and winter from central Honshu to southern Kyushu, and in the Izu, Bonin, and Ryukyu Islands. The van of the spring flight reaches Hokkaido in early April, and the wintering population has left southern Japan by mid-April, though stragglers may be observed there through May. Herman Jahn (1942) states (translation from the German):

"One finds the hawfinch wintering in central and western Japan from the end of October to the end of April. They are by no means abundant; here and there one observes small flocks up to as many as

10 individuals in suitable seed-bearing deciduous trees or bushes. Likewise it is not very plentiful in its breeding area in Hokkaido where I met it in light deciduous woods and meadow-copses, also in Sapporo and in the parks. Its behavior and voice are identical with those of the European form."

Yamashina (1933) says, "When migrating they move in small flocks of about 10 birds, but in winter they are mostly found singly. They fly in heavy, wavy lines, and are often found at the tops of high trees, emitting a cry like *titit*." Kiyosu (1943) says essentially the same thing, and adds, "It is most commonly seen on high trees, preferring the higher branches, though it sometimes perches on lower limbs and even feeds occasionally on the ground, where it hops around. The flight is markedly wavy, and it utters its call note on the wing."

Bergman (1935) gives the following account of the hawfinch's wintering habits in Kamchatka (translation from the German):

* * * I observed hawfinches in Tschapina village on 28 March 1921 on my winter journey from west Kamchatka to Petropavolowsk. Perhaps ten birds were staying in the village and its environs. They were very shy and it took me many hours to collect one. Yet they were numerous in Kirganik village. A few kilometers beyond this village, where the natives fish for salmon in summer and where there are many fish-drying racks, they appeared in great numbers. I saw more than 100 hawfinches and was able to collect a few. In the vicinity of Kirganik toward the large village of Milkowa where I stayed on 3 April, hawfinches appeared everywhere and acted in the same manner as sparrows in a European village. They flew around between the houses, perched on roofs and fences, and played about in the snow between the huts. In the next village of Werschne-Kamtschatsk there were still many hawfinches. On the road to this and the next village there were still a few more to be seen, but it was clear that they preferred to dwell in and near the villages. I also found hawfinches in several villages in the middle and upper courses of the Kamchatka River in March and April 1931. * * * During the following winter in December, January and February * * * I visited the villages where I had seen so many hawfinches the winter before. They had completely disappeared. Also on my later trips over Kamchatka I saw not another single one. It seems therefor that the coming of the hawfinch to Kamchatka was not regular * * *.

Concerning the population of hawfinches resident in the Kurils he says (1935), "I have found the hawfinch in the Kurils only on the island of Yeterop. It stays on the island the entire year, and is rare except in the spruce woods at the foot of Attosan volcano, where a colony of these birds winters near the town Kamikotan. In Europe the hawfinch is principally a bird of the deciduous forest. The Kamchatkan wintering colony was always in an almost purely spruce forest."

DISTRIBUTION

Range.—Manchuria, Korea, Japan, and China.

Breeding range.—The Japanese hawfinch breeds in Manchuria, Korea, and northern Japan south to central Honshu; possibly in northeastern China.

Winter range.—Winters in breeding range and south to southeastern China (Fukien Province).

Casual records.—Accidental in Formosa and Alaska (St. Paul Island in the Pribilofs).

HESPERIPHONA VESPERTINA VESPERTINA (Cooper)

Eastern Evening Grosbeak

PLATES 12, 13, AND 14

Contributed by DORIS HUESTIS SPEIRS

HABITS

The evening grosbeak was first described by William Cooper (1825) from a specimen sent to him by Henry R. Schoolcraft from Sault Ste. Marie, Mich. The first words written about it were those Schoolcraft (1851) penned in his journal for Apr. 7, 1823: "During severe winters in the north, some species of birds extend their migrations farther south than usual. This appears to have been the case during the past season. A small bird, yellowish and cinereous, of the grosbec species, appeared this day in the neighbourhood of one of the sugar-camps on the river below, and was shot with an arrow by an Indian boy, who brought it to me. The Chippewas call it Pashcundamo, in allusion to the stoutness of its bill, and consequent capacity for breaking surfaces."

William Cooper (1825), in his observation following the original description, quotes from the notes of Major Delafield who, as agent of the United States for boundaries, met the bird in August 1823 near the Savannah River, northwest of Lake Superior:

At twilight, the bird which I had before heard to cry in a singular strain, and only at this hour, made its appearance close by my tent, and a flock of about half a dozen perched on the bushes in my encampment. They approached so near, and were so fearless, that my canoe-men attempted to catch them, but in vain. I recognized this bird as similar to one in possession of Mr. Schoolcraft, at the Sault Ste. Marie.

Its mournful cry about the hour of my encamping, (which was at sunset) had before attracted my attention, but I could never get sight of the bird but on this occasion. There is an extensive plain and swamp through which flows the Savannah river, covered with a thick growth of sapin trees. My inference was then, and is now, that this bird dwells in such dark retreats, and leaves them at the approach of night.

PLATE 13

H. M. Halliday

EASTERN EVENING GROSBEAKS FEEDING YOUNG

Ontario

Ontario   H. M. Hall

JUVENILE EASTERN EVENING GROSBEAK

June Lake, Mono County, Calif., June 16, 1936   J. B. D

NEST OF WESTERN EVENING GROSBEAK

Major Delafield's inference is the source of the species' vernacular name—manifestly a misnomer. I do not doubt that the good major's birds cried out at sunset "in a singular strain" because he and his party disturbed them as they made camp. Ordinarily the species is not crepuscular, and in fact it might better be called "morning grosbeak," for it is most active early in the day. Yet its scientific name, *Hesperiphona vespertina*, is romantic, beautiful, and imaginative. As Edward H. Forbush (1929) points out: "Its generic name is derived from the Greek, referring to the *Hesperides*, 'Daughters of Night,' who dwelt on the western verge of the world where the sun goes down." And it inspired Elliott Coues (1879) to write: "A BIRD of the most distinguished appearance, indeed, is the Evening Grosbeak, whose very name of the 'Vesper-voiced' suggests at once the far-away land of the dipping sun, and the tuneful romance which the wild bird throws around the fading light of day. Clothed in the most striking color-contrasts of black, white, and gold, he seems to represent the allegory of diurnal transmutations; for his sable pinions close around the brightness of his vesture, just as the night encompasses the golden hues of the sunset; while the clear white space enfolded in these tints foretells the dawn of the morrow."

Before 1854, in addition to the localities mentioned in Cooper's account, this grosbeak had been reported from Lake Athabaska (Bonaparte, 1828), from Carlton House and the Saskatchewan plains, where it was known as the "sugar-bird" (W. Swainson and J. Richardson, 1831). Forbush (1929) tells of the eastward extension of range:

The first recorded extension of its range east of the Great Lakes was at Toronto in 1854. About the beginning of the last quarter of the nineteenth century there seems to have been some increase of the species in winter in the northern tier of mid-western states. The first verified occurrence of the species in Indiana, according to Dr. A. W. Butler, was in November, 1878, although it was reported there in 1876. In the winter of 1886–87 its numbers increased in Indiana, and it was noted in Ontario and also in some numbers in western Kentucky in the spring of 1887, and a few reached New York State. Up to the winter of 1889–90, however, it was almost unknown in the East, and even as far west as Ohio. In that winter a great eastward migration occurred, which in January, 1890, penetrated almost to the Atlantic coast of Massachusetts.

By February 1890 the birds had reached Revere Beach, on the Atlantic Coast of Massachusetts, and finally the migration reached as far east as the city of Quebec, and east in Maine as far as Orono.

Mr. Bent (MS.) writes of his first youthful encounter with "this fine, large and handsome grosbeak" as follows: "It was on March 8, 1890, that I saw my first evening grosbeak. I was leaving my father's house to go to work in a cotton mill in Fall River, when I saw three plump, handsome birds feeding on the buds of a sugar maple in the front yard. I promptly forgot about the mill job, and soon had two fine males and a female laid out on my skinning table. This was, believe, the first record for the species in southeastern Massachusetts Since then, at infrequent intervals, we have had them here at feeding stations, sometimes in large numbers."

In his comprehensive study of the summer distribution of the eastern evening grosbeak, James L. Baillie (1940) maps 82 summer records These form an almost continuous belt on both sides of the international boundary, from southeastern Manitoba to eastern Ontario, and con centrated mainly in the vicinity of the Great Lakes. He also gives (summer records for Alberta, 1 for Saskatchewan, 4 for Manitoba and (for New England. Many of these birds seen or collected in June July, or August, at least suggest the possibility of breeding. In severa cases parents were seen with recently fledged young apparentl hatched in the vicinity. Baillie's table gives full references for all th records, which he summarizes as follows:

> The more recent and regular occurrences of the species in eastern North Americ in winter seem to be correlated with an increase of the species in summer and i seems evident that its summer range has been extended eastward by gradual stage during comparatively recent years. * * * Facilitating their eastward extension has been the widespread planting in the east during the past few decases of the bo elder (*Acer negundo*) as a shade tree (Allen, 1919). The seeds of the box elder which hang on the trees all winter, are preferred by the evening grosbeak to any thing else, when available, and Taverner (1921) calls the situation a "baited high way" along which the grosbeaks have been able to pass.

In the 25 years since the publication of Baillie's paper, the grosbeaks have continued to extend their range eastward. They have now been reported from Newfoundland in winter and from eastern Quebec, New Brunswick, and Nova Scotia in summer. It is probably only a ques tion of time before their breeding in the easternmost Maritime Prov inces and Newfoundland is reported.

Spring.—"When the snow is heavy the birds congregate at feeding stations," writes Christopher M. Packard (MS.). "When it thaws and the ground and seeds begin to appear again, their attendance at feeders drops noticeably, doubtless because the birds can now find enough natural food. They can once again revert to the maple stands and rummage around through the soggy leaves in search of seeds fallen the autumn before. With the advent of warmer weather two new sources of food becomes available, the new tender buds and the maple sap, of which they are particularly fond."

At North Bay, Ontario, the grosbeaks arrived early one winter a the western edge of the town. Day by day they visited various box elder or Manitoba maple trees (*Acer negundo*) and in a kind of micro migration moved eastward across the town until, by the time the snows melted, they had reached its eastern limits. On a March day in 1945 we watched a small flock feeding in a Manitoba maple. The irds kept flying from the tree to a snow-covered house roof nearby o eat snow. Individual birds went to a dark patch on the roof where he snow was melting, filled their bills with the water, threw back heir heads and drank. My notes written at the time read: "The vind was blowing and waving the innumerable samaras to a tinkling nusic. The sound of the blowing seeds, of the birds' musical chatter, vas like an elfland symphony to our ears." Wings and seeds lay cattered in the snow beneath every Manitoba maple the grosbeaks ιad visited. We examined many of the the now seedless wings, itten off with neatness and precision.

Later that spring in the Haliburton District of Ontario we found he grosbeaks feeding beneath the mountain maples (*Acer spicatum*). A flock was actively searching for the fallen seeds amongst the forest itter. They were quiet when feeding, but punctuated their activity vith loud callnotes, as various members of the flock flew up into 'ellow birch or spruce and down to a little stream under alders to Irink. They drank the cold pure water of this northern stream with s much apparent relish as the North Bay grosbeaks drank the nelted snow from the city rooftops.

In Ontario, New York, and New England, small flocks move from eeding station to feeding station on the way to the breeding grounds. As evening grosbeaks are not early nesters, a few birds often remain n the vicinity of feeding stations until May. In recent years May eports have come from States south of New York and New England. 3ut gradually the flocks diminish in size until the last bird has left.

Courtship.—After watching a pair of evening grosbeaks on their reeding ground in northern Michigan, Bayard H. Christy (1930) ;ave the first published account of the colorful courtship display. Ie writes: "As the female * * * perched near, the male made a eautiful display. He crouched low, puffed out his plumage, extended is wings horizontally and set them quivering. The gorgeous contrast f the glossy black wings with the golden body suggested the appear- nce of a bird of paradise. There was no song; it was about half ast five in the afternoon, and the sun was still high."

On Apr. 4, 1937, at Hanover, N.H., I watched a pair of evening ;rosbeaks bowing to each other with great formality. They were ot more than a foot away from each other when the formalities egan. First the male bowed very low, then the female bowed. The male bowed again, and the female again. The rhythm acceler- ted until they were bowing so low that I almost expected to see them ose their balance and fall off the branch. The female punctuated er jerky movements with loud call-notes. As she bowed she called *eter!* and flicked her tail. From the male came no sound. The emale seemed the more enthusiastic, and continued to bow after the

male apparently had lost interest.   On April 21 I saw a female jerk
ing up and down in somewhat the same way a flicker does durin
courtship.   She seemed to be pursuing the male, or at least she move
toward him, but he disregarded her, dropped to a lower branch
and turned his back to her.

While observing two pairs at a salt lick by Clear Lake, Haliburto
County, Ontario, on June 1, 1945, I noted that the females were a
combative as the males, spreading their wings, jerking from side t
side, and clinching bills.   During one duel the two females ros
into the air as fighting male robins sometimes do.

On May 2, 1949, in Iron County, Mich., among a loosely scattere
flock in the crown foliage of tall sugar maples at noon I watche
(Speirs, 1949) a male in courtship display:

"The pair were about 40 feet up in a maple, the male about a foo
above the female on another branch.   Suddenly he threw back hi
head, lowered the yellow rump, raised and fanned his black tail an
commenced vibrating his black and white wings so fast that the
looked transparent as a hummingbird's.   He then glided along th
branch above her as swiftly as a geisha, but with his back in the forn
of a U.   The female did not look at all impressed, flew to a tre
eastward, followed by her swain."

Elizabeth Holt Downs (1958) has given a full account of the court
ship as she observed it on Glebe Mountain, South Londonderry, Vt.
in the spring of 1956.   She writes:

During the first part of April the grosbeaks began "chasing" each other and o
April 18th I witnessed the first courtship feeding. * * * the female initiated th
first feeding by "flirting" her tail (a quick spreading and closing of the tail)
bobbing her head and swinging her body slightly in front of the male.   Som
males do not respond at first to this invitation but in this instance the male fed th
female sugar maple buds.   Within a few days courtship feeding was a dail
occurrence.   On one occasion I watched a male grosbeak go through all th
motions of feeding a female but without any food to give her. * * *

Beginning with 1953 I have been able to observe much of the courtship behavio
of the Evening Grosbeaks every year.   Their courtship seems to follow a certai
pattern with possibly some slight variations.   It is initiated by the female askin
to be fed.   The first food she receives from the male is tree buds; later she is fe
salt-impregnated earth and still later (after pair formation has taken place) th
female is fed sunflower and tree seeds.   After pair formation has occurred, mor
often than not it is the male who takes the initiative and offers the seeds to th
female.   At this time when the female accepts the food (or asks for it) she assume
a posture similar to that of the young begging to be fed (crest raised, body crouche
slightly and wings fluttering).   Some females swing their bodies from side t
side and occasionally a female will "cry."   But sometimes the feeding i
accompanied by very little display by the female.

"Dancing" by the males usually begins shortly after the initial courtship
feeding and before pair formation has taken place.   When dancing, the mal
grosbeak faces the female.   With crest raised, bill and tail pointed upwards

breast almost touching the ground and wings drooped but spread wide and vibrating, he slowly pivots back and forth. He does not sing while dancing. If he utters any sound at all, it is too low for me to hear.

On June 1 she witnessed two matings. The second "was a very elaborate ceremony * * *. The pair, on the road in front of our house, faced each other. The male danced (but all his movements were more subdued than in the usual dance). The female quivered her wings (short, rapid movements with wings held close to her body) and held her tail high. Then still in this posture but with her breast thrust forward she hopped the few inches to the dancing male. I could not be certain that their breasts touched. She continued to dance. It looked as if they touched bills twice. He then mounted her."

Nesting.—For 75 years after the discovery of the eastern evening grosbeak, its breeding range remained virtually unknown. Of its nesting habits nothing was reported until L. Osborne Scott sent some notes to W. T. Macoun (1899) in which he announced: "I have seen the Evening Grosbeaks in flocks of ten to eighty on the Peace River. The Indians say they always build in Saskatoon willows (Amelanchier), though I think there are exceptions." Macoun also published Scott's account of nests he found near Winnipeg that year. "On the 18th of June I saw four nests of the Evening Grosbeak about one mile north of Winnipeg, near the Red River, in fact right on its bank. The nests were about twelve or fifteen feet from the ground in some grey willows; they were rather flat and slight, made of sticks and roots and lined with smaller roots. There were only two eggs in two nests and one each in the other two. The eggs were more blotched than those of the Red-breasted and not so spotted, and I fancy they are a little smaller."

Ten years later came a report from Sidney S. S. Stansell (1909) that he had located a nest 30 miles northwest of Edmonton, Alberta in June 1908 "which contained a dead full-fledged young male. The nest was 40 feet up in a white birch tree." Dr. S. C. Kendeigh, who found a pair building in a white birch in the Thunder Bay District of Ontario in 1945 writes:

"I found the evening grosbeak quite common in Algonquin Park and only a little less so north of Port Arthur. On June 22 I found a pair nest-building on one of my plots. Only the base of the nest was in position in a vertical crotch 55 feet up in a white birch that was 60 feet tall. I watched them only five minutes to avoid disturbing them, but in this time the female made 5 visits to the nest with dead twigs. These twigs she broke off a smaller white spruce about two-thirds of the way up. She broke them off with her bill, once dropping two before taking the third to the nest. At the nest she jumped into

the center and adjusted the stick into the structure on the outside
It was a hot day, in the high 80s, and the female was panting with
mouth open and wings partly spread. The male accompanied the
female on each trip to and from the nest but did not help in the build
ing. He would watch her intently at the nest while perched in a
branch a few feet below."

J. Stokley Ligon (1923) found five nests of the eastern evening
grosbeak on July 28, 1923, on Whitefish Point, Lake Superior, in
Michigan, about 20 miles from the Canadian shore; One young bird
was found on the ground, and the nest from which "it had fallen was
about 25 feet up on a horizontal limb of a white pine, well concealed
by small branches and needles." He climbed to this nest and ex
amined it, which "was practically indistinguishable from nests of
the Black-headed Grosbeak of the West, being almost, if not quite
as frail of construction.   * * * The body of the nest was composed
of hard, clean sticks and lined with black and brown hair-like rootlets
with a sprinkling of moss between the outer body and lining."

Thomas S. Roberts (1932) quotes an account published by A. G
Lawrence in the Winnipeg Free Press, June 20, 1930, of two nests
near Winnipeg found by L. E. McCall, of Selkirk, Manitoba. One
nest was "placed in a crotch 28 feet up in a Manitoba maple situated
in a garden bordering the public sidewalk, and * * * well concealed
except on one side." The other nest was 19 feet up in an elm overhanging the road, "on a fork of a long overhanging branch." Both
nests contained eggs and the two birds sat closely.

During the first three decades of the present century, while the
eastern evening grosbeak was extending its summer range eastward,
many records of probable nesting were based on females showing
brood patches and on adults seen feeding juveniles. At Woodstock,
Vt., Richard M. Marble (1926) saw four young come to a feeding
station with their parents. "The little ones were not quite as large
as the adults, their tails were very short and many downy feathers
still showed on their heads."

H. R. Ivor sent Mr. Bent an interesting account of some evening
grosbeaks he had in his aviary for several years. He told especially
of one pair that mated, built a nest, laid four eggs, and succeeded in
raising one young (see plates 12, 13, and 14). J. H. Fleming (1903)
also records the breeding of this species in captivity.

Louise de Kiriline Lawrence, my husband, and I found a nest near
a forest edge in Lauder Township, Nipissing District, Ontario, on
June 21, 1945 (Speirs and Speirs, 1947). The nest was 55 feet up in
a white pine and very well concealed. It contained at least three
young and through a 47X telescope we were able to watch the young
being fed. I spent 3 days observing this nesting. After the young

left we collected the nest, which is now in the Royal Ontario Museum of Zoology and Palaeontology. Its measurements are: Inside of cup—longest diameter, 3.7 in.; shortest diameter, 3.2 in.: Outer diameters—longest, 5.9 in.; shortest, 4.3 in.: Depth of cup—2.8 in.: Total depth—5.1 in. to supporting limb; 5.9 ins. including twigs below limb. Most of the foundation of the nest is of twigs from deciduous trees (maple, birch, viburnum, red-osier, dogwood), a piece of a vine (possibly bittersweet), twig of raspberry. Many of the twigs are opposite branching (maple, viburnum, dogwood). The smaller twigs are from coniferous trees, mostly from spruce, some from balsam fir, and one from tamarack. The edge of the nest is of rootlets interwoven with *Usnea* lichen. The innermost lining is of what appears to be black moss—the dead stage of threadlike lichens. Dr. C. H. D. Clarke assisted with the identification of the nest material.

The following summer (1946) grosbeaks were found nesting some 10 miles south of Lauder Township in Algonquin Park. Says C. E. Hope (1947):

During the last week of May, a road, about one and one-half miles in length, was bulldozed through a mixed forest of second-growth white pine, black and white spruce, balsam and birch. The action of the scraper exposed a myriad of rootlets which, after a few days, became dry and brittle. Coinciding with this period at least ten pairs of Evening Grosbeaks established themselves in what might be termed a loose colony, in woods adjacent to a section of this road. Pairs were frequently seen on the freshly graded earth. On June 10, a female, accompanied by her mate, was observed to carry off rootlets in her bill. On June 12, a similar observation was made and on this occasion we were fortunate enough to see where the material was taken and deposited. The performance was repeated several times, with only the female carrying the material but always accompanied by the male. The nest, situated 28 feet from the ground in a black spruce, was left undisturbed until June 22 when it was collected. It was found to be placed close to the trunk some six or seven feet from the top of the tree and almost entirely hidden by dense foliage. It contained four slightly incubated eggs.

On June 21 a second nest was discovered 30 feet 5 inches up in a balsam. Like the first, it was invisible from the ground and was situated close to the trunk, six or seven feet from the top. It contained three eggs on the date mentioned. This nest was left undisturbed until July 6. It was then found to contain three partially fledged young. One, taken for a specimen, proved to be a male. * * * The remaining two young left the nest on July 8. * * *

A point of interest concerning the structure of the two nests found is that from seventy-five to ninety per cent of the materials used consisted of rootlets such as were exposed in the newly made road. Oddly enough, the taking up of nesting territories adjacent to the road coincided with the exposure of unlimited nesting material.

Marjory B. Sanger reported in a letter to me the first nesting I have heard of for the Province of Quebec. Between May 26 and May 30, 1955, she watched a pair of evening grosbeaks gathering nesting material and carrying it into a 60-foot white birch that stood in a fairly open spruce and maple glade near St. Charles de Mandeville, Conté Berthier. The nest was about 30 feet up and the female seemed to be doing all the nest-building. The male, however, "observed her actions with obvious interest, * * * supervising with care and staying close at all times."

Evening grosbeak nests have three outstanding characteristics: They are loosely constructed "stick-nests"; some moss or lichen is woven into the structure; and the cup is not really round (as has been reported) but oblong or elliptical. They have been reported in seven species of coniferous trees: Balsam-fir, red spruce, black spruce, white pine, Norway (or red) pine, jack pine, and white cedar. The species has also nested in at least seven species of deciduous trees: Willow, aspen, white (or paper) birch, elm, Saskatoon (*Amelanchier*), and in hard and soft maples. One nesting was in an orchard.

Eggs.—The evening grosbeak lays from two to five eggs in a set, usually three or four. The eggs are ovate or, rarely, pointed ovate, thin shelled, and of smooth texture with little gloss. The ground color is usually deposited as a clear blue or bright blue-green, which during incubation changes to "pale blue-green" or "pale glaucous-green." They are blotched and spotted, particularly at the larger end, with "olive-brown," "lilac gray," or "light Quaker drab." Fine pencilled markings in black occur on a number of eggs. One with a "pale glaucous-green" shell was stippled all over with "olive-gray" and "pale mouse gray." The eggs resemble rather strikingly those of the red-winged blackbird. The measurements of 23 eggs average 24.5 by 17.5; those showing the four extremes measure *28.0* by 18.0, 26.8 by *19.0*, *21.0* by 16.0, and 21.0 by *16.0* millimeters.

Incubation.—One egg is laid each morning until the set (usually of three or four eggs) is complete. Incubation has been observed to start on the second day and is performed by the female alone. There is no record of incubation by the male, and but one observation of a male brooding a 3-day old nestling (H. R. Ivor Journal). At times during the incubation period the male feeds his mate both on and off the nest.

No data on the length of the incubation period in the wild are available, but we have several measurements from aviary nestings. A. G. Lawrence reported to Mr. Bent periods from 11 to 12 days in his aviary. Paul Kuntz (1939) writes from Winnipeg: "The bird sat steady for twelve days. On the thirteenth two young were hatched." J. H. Fleming (1903) observed in his aviary: "About the 16th of July three eggs of a second set were noticed in the nest; one had disappeared before my return, and on the 30th one of the two remaining eggs hatched." The incubation period in this case was at least 14 days. In the Ivor bird observatory at Erindale, Ontario, the incubation periods for three marked eggs were 12, 13, and 14 days, respectively.

One of Ivor's birds laid a second clutch; the first egg appeared when the only nestling of the first set was 11 days old and still in the same nest. Young birds recently fledged have been seen as late as mid-August in Ontario and on August 30 in Vermont, according to Elizabeth Holt Downs (MS.). B. M. Shaub (1958) reports a young male still in juvenal plumage at his Northampton, Mass., feeding station on Oct. 26, 1957. These records suggest the possibility of two broods occasionally in the wild.

Young.—When the young hatch, the eggshell may be removed by either parent. In one case the female ate all the shell.

At hatching, the nestling is much like the young of the rose-breasted grosbeak, but the skin is darker. The little bird appears very red, with damp gray feathers on its head. These neossoptiles are about a quarter-inch long and dry within 25 minutes. Paul Kuntz (1939) gives his impression of the young: "They were strong and healthy chicks, all black with a fluffy down. They looked exactly like young Bullfinches." My own notes read: "The white natal down sticks out from the top of the head. The membrane covering the eye looks purplish and very large. The bill is yellow. The egg-tooth is like the tiniest white bead on the upper mandible. The gape is white. The mouth and pharynx have an iridescent appearance—tones of violet and carmine." My notes for the second day state: "When the babies are not raising their heads, they throb with every 'peep' they utter. The natal down is perfectly placed to cover them as a blanket while in the nest. They lie bellies down. Bellies and throats are bare, but down grows on head, wings, and tract down the back."

Parents of newly hatched aviary nestlings at Erindale, Ontario, fed them a gruel of masticated earthworms and mealworms, which they first chewed for some time until a dark liquid stained their bills. We watched wild adults in the Nipissing District of Ontario feeding the young similarly on the masticated larvae of the spruce budworm (*Choristoneura fumiferana* Clem.). When the greenish bills of the adults become stained dark brown from masticating insect larvae, it is a sure sign they are feeding their young. The spruce bud-worm in all stages of development is the main item of insectivorous food for nestling evening grosbeaks wherever both the insect and the bird occur together. Moreover, the birds often appear for the first time or in unusual numbers wherever there is an outbreak of spruce budworm during the breeding season (see under *Food*, p. 224).

A number of evening grosbeak stomachs from the collection of the Royal Ontario Museum of Zoology, including those of juvenals, were analyzed by J. M. McGugan, Micro-Analyst of the Dominion Department of Agriculture in Toronto, and Ronald N. Root, of the U. S. Fish and Wildlife Service. Their analyses showed the most important vegetable food in the juvenal diet to be the pit of the pin- or bird-cherry (*Prunus pensylvanica*). Seeds of other native fruits such as the hawthorn (*Crataegus* sp.), blackberry (*Rubus* sp.), and blueberry (*Vaccinium* sp.) were taken to a lesser extent; also birch (*Betula* sp.) seeds. Weed seeds in the diet included those of sedge (*Carex* sp.), dock (*Rumex* sp.), bindweed (*Polygonum* sp.), goosefoot (*Chenopodium* sp.), crowfoot (*Ranunculus* sp.), wild geranium (*Geranium* sp.), and violet (*Viola* sp.).

Mr. Bent writes: "Mr. Lawrence has sent me some clippings from his articles in the Winnipeg Free Press, in which he describes how the grosbeaks fed their young in the box elder tree in Selkirk. Both adults helped in feeding the young by regurgitation of semidigested food while the nestlings were too young to take solid food. It was difficult for the old birds to insert their heavy bills into the mouths of the nestlings, but his sketches, based on photographs, show that the adults accomplished this by twisting their heads to one side. After the young were a week old they were fed caterpillars and small, soft green seeds. The young were fed at irregular intervals, and, when very young, were brooded by the female between feedings."

Foraging parents usually, but not invariably, leave and return to the nest together. When they arrive simultaneously both perch on the rim of the nest and the female feeds one nestling. Then she often takes food from the male's bill and feeds another. Finally the male may give any remaining food directly to the young.

I watched one nest with young 5 or 6 days old in Lauder Township, Ontario, on June 23, 1945, from 4:45 a.m. until 8:01 p.m. when it was getting too dark to see, except for a half-hour absence from 6:30 to 7:00 a.m. During this time the young were fed 34 times. Starting at 4:50 a.m. when both parents arrived with food, there were 14 feeding periods between dawn and noon. For 10 feedings the adults came together or nearly so. Once the mother came alone and remained to repair the nest lining and brood the young. Twice the father brought food when the mother was on the nest, and once unattended by his mate. Intervals between feedings in the morning varied from 7 to 54 minutes, averaging one feeding period every 21.5 minutes. Intervals between the 20 feeding periods from noon to the last one at 7:50 p.m. ranged from 1 to 97 minutes and averaged one every 24 minutes.

The father seemed to attend to the nest sanitation more assiduously than did the mother; he removed fecal sacs eight times, the mother only twice. In each case nest sanitation followed a feeding. The nestling on my side of the nest raised its uropygium, which was covered with white down, as if to help the father remove the fecal sac.

Both parents defend the nest and young.   On July 4, 1946 at the Algonquin Park nesting, I watched the pair drive off a gray jay by dashing at it, giving rough buzzing notes.   They treated a bronzed grackle and a robin in the same manner, and threatened a young hermit thrush. They tolerated the following species near or even in the balsam fir that held the nest: Golden-crowned and ruby-crowned kinglets, a myrtle warbler, Blackburnian and Canada warblers, and a purple finch. They chased no other evening grosbeaks and seemed tolerant of the few that appeared in the nesting vicinity.

The young birds grow quickly.   An aviary nestling measured 50 millimeters when 51 hours old and 57 millimeters when 78 hours old. The eyes begin to open on the fourth or fifth day and are fully open on the fifth or sixth day.   The sex of a healthy nestling can be determined by the ninth or tenth day.   Thus H. R. Ivor wrote in his journal of a 9-day old bird: "The nestling definitely seems to be a male.   The tail feathers have barely broken and show all black.   The white of the middle secondaries are very pure white."

C. E. Hope found a fledgling male about 12 days old from a nest in Algonquin Park, Ontario, on July 6, 1946 to weigh 32 grams. A second young male collected on August 9 weighed 61.5 grams.   The Shaubs have reported on weights of juveniles trapped at their feeding station at Saranac Lake, N.Y. in the summer of 1952 (Shaub and Shaub, 1953).   "Two females weighed 52.6 and 49.6 grams respectively.   A juvenal male weighed 55.2 grams and an adult male weighed 51.2 grams."

The young normally leave the nest on the 13th or 14th day.   One fledgling male, that had left the nest prematurely in Algonquin Park, Ontario, was fed exclusively by its father until independent.   A young aviary male at 36 days from hatching was being fed from time to time by its mother, although able to feed itself as well.

Juvenal males have golden heads, and when they raise the crest to to beg for food, as I have seen them do in Muskoka, they are very handsome.   My husband watched a juvenal female with a peach-colored breast following and begging from an adult in Muskoka on August 5, 1951.   The young bird looked as big or bigger than the adult and had a full-grown tail.   Elizabeth Holt Downs (MS.) recorded the dates of the arrival of the first young at her feeding station in Vermont for the years 1953–1957.   In 1953, 1954, and 1955 the first young appeared on June 26.   In 1956 the arrival date was July 6; in 1957, June 17.   Juveniles out of the nest have been reported as early as the first week in July in Ontario.   The latest date of juvenile feeding is a young male Mrs. Downs saw an adult male feeding in Vermont the third week in November.

Plumages.—The natal down is white. The neossoptiles are on the capital tract and on spinal, femoral, humeral, and alar tracts. Clifford E. Hope (MS.) describes a nestling about 12 days old, taken in Algonquin Park, Ontario, on July 6, 1946:

"Pin feathers of forehead, crown, occiput, and cervix 'clove brown' back 'olive': circle of whitish natal down above eye to nape: bare skin side of neck and center of breast dark red: feathers side of breast shading from 'broccoli brown' to 'pinkish buff': scapulars 'olive': rump covered with natal down. Wing: lesser coverts, sepia; middle coverts black, edged with pale gray, with some natal down protruding; greater coverts, black, edged with gray. Yellow and black feathers with white shafts forming pattern on inner edge of greater coverts and tertials: yellow mark on primaries and secondaries. Tail black: undertail coverts whitish. Down on tibia, over pale yellow and black feathers."

Mrs. Downs observes (MS): "the juvenals have a small yellowish patch composed of the four inner secondary coverts, which I call a birthmark because they lose it during their postjuvenal molts" The postjuvenal molt is not complete until the juvenal is nearly a month old. At 24 days a young male still had a small tuft of down above the eyes on either side of the crown.

Despite J. Dwight's (1900) statement: "The sexes are similar in juvenal plumage," I have found that the fledgling male can be distinguished by its tail feathers; these are usually black when they break from their sheaths and lack the series of white spots which characterize the female rectrices. Also, the male's primaries are black, while the female's are black and white, and the male has a prominent whitish patch on the inner flight feathers which the female lacks.

My notes contain the following description of a month old female: Crown, occiput, nape, auriculars, and side neck, olive-gray. Upper mandible, greenish gray; tip greenish. Lower mandible, pinkish, dark gray at gape. Throat, pale gray, edged with dark malar stripes. Back, olive-gray. Rump, olive-gray tinged with peach. Rectrices with series of white spots near tips. Undertail coverts, pinkish gray. Breast, light gray washed with peach. Side and flank, gray tinged with peach. Belly, gray, washed with pale peach; dark down exposed in places. Wings: first three primaries at leading edge, black, the remaining six edged with white and with yellowish patch forming square on wing. Wrist with pale yellow edge. Scapulars, olive-gray. Greater secondary coverts with patch of yellow on three feathers, the rest black. Middle coverts, black, with light edgings.

Lesser coverts, black with olivaceous edgings. Underwing coverts, lemon yellow.

I described a 2-month-old male as follows: Crown and cheek, "light olive brown." Supra-auricular region, "light olive-brown" with dusky line. Auriculars, "light brownish olive"; greenish on outer webs. Upper mandible, "drab," greenish at gape. Throat, "sulphur yellow." Malar stripes, dusky. Side neck, "cinnamon-buff." Back, "Saccardo's olive." Tail, black. Undertail coverts whitish, tinged with "cinnamon-buff." Wing, black; inner secondaries and their greater coverts, white, tinged with pale yellow and edged with pale buff. Feet, "army brown." At 3 months, the yellow frontal band of this juvenile male became conspicuous. As the patchwork of black and fawn spread over its crown, the cheeks were darkening, though not yet of the "bister" color of the adult.

Mrs. Downs, who has banded so many juvenals in Vermont, writes me that "there is considerable difference in the color of juvenal females and juvenal males—body color that is. Both are tan but the females are a gray-tan and males a yellow-tan. Even without seeing their wing markings we can tell a female from a male by the color of their bodies." (For further descriptions of the young, see Shaub and Shaub, 1953.).

The first winter plumage is acquired by a partial postjuvenal molt in the autumn. Of this E. H. Forbush (1929) writes: "the first winter plumage by partial postjuvenal molt of body feathers and wing-coverts, juvenal flight-feathers and tail retained, tertials may be shed in some cases." J. Dwight (1900) states that "Young may be distinguished usually by the dusky inner margins of the tertiaries but differ very little from adults."

Of the first nuptial plumage J. Dwight (1900) writes that it is "acquired by wear which removes much of the wing edgings. Browner more worn remiges and especially primary coverts with distinct edgings distinguish young birds." According to M. J. Magee (1928a) some and possibly all evening grosbeaks have a very slight spring molt. Of 93 grosbeaks he examined between April 15 and May 13, 24 showed signs of molt. These included both adults and young. The molt was most pronounced on the nape, and one to several new feathers were seen on crown, occiput, cervix, side of neck, and throat. We noted a male in partial prenuptial molt at North Bay, Ontario, as early as Mar. 4, 1944. In 1929, M. J. Magee (1930) continued his study of the spring molt. On the 50 grosbeaks he banded from April 13 to May 17, he noted signs of molt on 31. The molt was largely confined to the front of the head, including the chin and the neck.

In spring the bill color changes gradually from the winter "horn-color" (but sometimes "ecru-olive" with "citron yellow" at gape, or bright "wax yellow" or pale pink) to light green or pea green in late spring, and in June to light bluish green. It is possible to tell summer birds in collections by the bluish green color of the bills.

G. Hapgood Parks, who has banded more than 5,000 evening grosbeaks in Connecticut, wrote to Mr. Bent in 1947: "During the winter we made a study of the color of the birds' bills and learned that by late February (Feb. 28) the bills began to show signs of peeling from the tip and edges. An apparent loosening of the surface membranes gave the upper mandibles of some of the birds a whitish and swollen appearance across the base of the bill near the feathers. This latter condition became more apparent on more birds during the first week of March." In 1951 he added the following: "The actual color change of the bill is apparently due to pigmentation. The mottled stage, in which many bills are seen, bears evidence of this fact. Bills showing no peeling at all are not infrequently partly green with areas which retain the 'bone' color typical of the bills in winter. The peeling off of a colorless surface layer apparently helps to promote the 'new' polished appearance of the bill.

"The peeling is much more conspicuous on the upper mandible, although some peeling of the lower mandible also occurs. I find that my notes about the bills say, most frequently, 'bill green and peeling.' About as often the entry is, 'blue-green lower, peeling upper,' or, 'mottled lower, peeling upper.' I feel certain that the entire surface of the upper mandible peels, I am not at all sure that the same condition holds for the lower mandible. I would not dare to say that the bills of *all* of the birds peel, although I feel very strongly that such is the case."

The adult winter plumage is produced by a complete postnuptial molt. The earliest date for the beginning of the molt I have noted is June 28, when a female (one of a nesting pair at the Ivor Bird Observatory) molted a first primary and the male molted the first primary of both wings. On August 25 the male's new tail was half grown. L. H. Walkinshaw (1936) tells of a captive bird that started to molt on July 16 and did not finish until after November 1.

M. J. Magee (1926b) writes:

* * * After molting, the feathers in the white wing patches of both males and females are distinctly edged with yellow. All of the descriptions of the plumage that I have seen, from Audubon down, are very much as given by Professor Barrows in "Michigan Bird Life," in which for the male it is said, "most of the secondaries and their coverts snowy white;" and of the female, "primaries and secondaries black, boldly spotted with white." This limited description may be due to the fact that only specimens taken in spring were

examined. Practically all of my banding of these grosbeaks had been done in
the spring, until last fall (1925); and then from November 11 to March 1 I banded
eighty-four, forty males and forty-four females. The males had nearly all the
feathers in the white wing patch edged with yellow on the outer webs, except
the tips. This was true of the great majority of females as well * * *.

Either from wear or fading the yellow edging lightens; in the males first on the
white secondaries; in the females, on the white patches of the primaries. This
fading of the yellow edging has been particularly noticeable since the first of
March * * * .

According to Dwight (1900) the adult nuptial dress is acquired
by wear.

Food.—The most important native food for the evening grosbeak
is the fruit of maple trees and especially of the Manitoba maple or
box elder (*Acer negundo*). A. G. Lawrence of Winnipeg sent the
following note to Mr. Bent: "From fall to early spring the seeds of
the Manitoba maple (*Acer negundo*) form their chief food, but ash
seeds and chokecherries, both green and dried are also eaten. They
have also been reported as feeding on low-growing weeds, and on the
buds of the Manitoba maple. They eat snow, scooping it up and
swallowing it in large quantities after feeding on seeds. In feeding on
the maple seed keys, the bird snips off the pod at the basal end,
manipulates the winged portion between the mandibles to express the
seeds from their compartments, swallows or presents the seeds to a
young one and allows the winged pod to flutter to the ground. The
operation is performed so rapidly that the eye can hardly follow the
action."

Winsor M. Tyler (1916) describes in more detail the skill and precision with which the grosbeaks perform this operation, with their
apparently clumsy beaks. He concludes:

Upon examining the wings which the birds had clipped off, it was apparent that
the birds had bitten directly over the kernel itself at a point rather nearer the
wing than the kernel. But, although by this incision the kernel was exposed, it
was never severed and allowed to fall with the wing, as would have been the case
had the beak been closed and bite completed. The cutting process was always
arrested at the point after the casing had been divided, but before the meat had
been severed. All this, although the process involved the nicest precision, was
accomplished with great rapidity, the wing fluttering to the ground within a
second or two after the fruit was plucked from the stem.

E. L. Brereton, of Barrie, Ontario, wrote (MS.) on Apr. 11, 1937:
"I have always associated the evening grosbeak with the Manitoba
maple and always found them there, the sugar maple seeds being just
a change of diet, but this year found that they prefer the sugar maple
seeds when such can be obtained."

Fred W. Behrend (1946) tells of their feeding habits in the south.
He writes (in part) from Elizabethton, Tenn.:

The budding of the maple trees and subsequent shedding of the bud scales as winter was on the way out, provided a plentiful supply of food for the Evening Grosbeaks who seemed to be very fond of this vegetal matter. * * *

As spring advanced, the feeding habits of the Evening Grosbeaks underwent, by necessity, a change. No longer did the bud scales of maple trees cover the ground as they had been cleaned up methodically in one area after another, and therefore less frequently were the birds seen on the ground. They now fed on the fresh seed pods of the maple trees, and most of their time was spent in the in the trees. * * *

With respect to the most often referred to favorite food of the Evening Grosbeak, the seed of the box elder tree, the latter was non-existent in this community. * * * the writer observed them feeding on the seeds of mimosa and locust trees, on the hulls embedding the blossoms of the catawba tree and on the buds or bud scales of elm trees, all in addition to their most abundant food in the locality, the bud scales and seeds of the maple tree.

While south in the spring of 1952, we were surprised to come upon a little flock of evening grosbeaks at Windsor, N.C., on April 30. At first we saw the birds on green lawns eating maple seeds. Then we saw several feeding in and under a pecan tree decorated with green catkins, which they seemed to be eating. At Yorktown, Va., the next day, we found several in a huge chinaberry tree and heard the cracking sound as they lived up to their name of "berry-breaker."

B. R. Chamberlain (1952) quotes from a letter written by J. W. E. Joyner from Rocky Mount, N.C., which tells of their eating conifer seeds during the 1952 grosbeak invasion: "When the birds first came here they were never far from the pines, the seeds of which were apparently their chief food. Some seed from tulip poplars were also eaten. * * * In gleaning seeds from the pine cones they deliberately and slowly plucked the seed out, the discarded wings floating, rather than swirling, downward. For the past month they have continued to feed on pine mast but have also been seen eating elm, maple, and oak buds. They have become regular visitors to feeding trays, consuming quantities of sunflower seeds; the seeds going in one side and the hulls drooling out of the other."

O. A. Stevens, of Fargo, N. Dak., wrote Mr. Bent: "We usually find them feeding on fruits of Russian Olive (*Elaeagnus angustifolia*)." In February 1929, T. M. Shortt saw evening grosbeaks eating the seeds of the buffaloberry, (*Shepherdia argentea*), at St. James, a suburb of Winnipeg, Manitoba. The meaty fruit has a stone in the center, and Shortt told me the birds were biting the meat off the sides of the stones. Richard J. Eaton wrote Wendell Taber, that he had "seen these birds working on hybrid crabapples (*Malus* sp. ?) much after the fashion of cedar waxwings, pine grosbeaks, and robins." Frére Marie-Victorin (1935) tells us that in Quebec, the fruits of the red ash (*Fraxinus pennsylvanica*) which form in June and persist on the tree during most of the winter, are a preferred food of migrant winter birds, including the evening grosbeak. When evening grosbeaks visited St. John's, Newfoundland, from Nov. 18, 1951, to May 3, 1952, Leslie M. Tuck informs me they fed on the seeds of snowberry and beech.

Mary S. Shaub (1956) has contributed an important paper on the effect of native foods on evening grosbeak incursions:

The great adaptability of this species within its winter range to extremes of climate and topography is evidenced by its appearance in the Adirondacks, the White Mountains of New Hampshire, and all the way down the Appalachians to Rome, Georgia, as well as at many coastal points from Halifax, Nova Scotia, to Wilmington, North Carolina. It is also most adaptable in its acceptance of a vast array of native and cultivated seeds and fruits.

In the course of our study of the Evening Grosbeak since 1947, and in connection with our publishing of the *Evening Grosbeak Survey News* during five winters from 1950 to 1955, we have received a large number of reports dealing with foods eaten by this species. These are summarized in the accompanying list of seeds, fruits, and buds. * * *

The *box elder* is without doubt the most acceptable native food, and in many reports the Evening Grosbeaks are noted on these trees and not at feeders, even though sunflower seeds are available there. This pertains especially to southern Ontario. In several New York and New Jersey localities the birds were first noted on box elders and could not be enticed to feeding stations until the maple keys had been devoured.

Of the numerous fruits taken by the Evening Grosbeaks, they seem to favor the various *cherries, apples, crabapples,* and *sumac* to all others. * * * Even where the Evening Grosbeaks have settled down to a routine of daily feeder attendance, now and then for no apparent reason they will fly off to a stand of sumac for a meal, or at least a snack, even before the supply of sunflower seeds has been exhausted. * * *

This variation in diet of the Evening Grosbeak has been noted over a period of years by Mrs. Gerald Fitzgerald of Amsterdam, New York, where her fine plantings of *Washington hawthorn, crabapples, red* and *black chokecherries* and *cotoneasters* have been attractive to the Evening Grosbeak despite her generous supplying of over 1300 pounds of sunflower seeds in the winter of 1949–1950 and of over 900 pounds during 1954–1955.

Every spring evening grosbeaks may be observed "budding" in various trees. I have seen them budding in our elms, in the Rouge Hill area west of Pickering, Ontario. On Mar. 11, 1958, a female was budding in a tall elm, high up. My notes read: "She reached first for the end bud of a twig, then bit off each lateral bud. Then to the next twig, taking the end bud first then each lateral bud within reach on that twig. And so to the leading bud of the next twig." The following day I watched two females budding in our lilacs: "Each reached forward and took the nearest bud within easy reach, bit it off, ate it and reached for the next nearest bud. These were not terminal but lateral buds in each case." Mrs. Shaub (1956) lists numerous different kinds of trees and shrubs in which grosbeaks have been seen budding.

If tree buds may be considered springtime treats for the grosbeaks, nature has other delicacies in store for them as well.   Of their fondness for wild maple syrup Thornton W. Burgess (1947) writes: "Opposite the window of my room is a maple tree.   Squirrels have been eating the buds and when the sun warms things up in the morning the sap drips from the twigs where the buds have been nipped off.   The other morning the sun striking through these drops of sap filled the tree with glittering jewels.   A male Evening Grosbeak climbed about parrot fashion from jewel to jewel drinking them."   Mrs. Downs writes me: "our front sugar maple tree has been gashed in many places by some creature.   Today I saw the sap flowing from it and the EG's *drinking* the sap!   Sometimes they even had to 'tread air' to get the sap because there was no branch handy on which to perch."

As the breeding season approaches, the grosbeaks begin to seek out insect food, of which the spruce budworm is an important item.   G. H. and H. C. Parks (1963a, 1963b) describe graphically their studies of a concentration of evening grosbeaks nesting where a heavy infestation of spruce budworm was damaging the forest in the Patapedia River watershed of Quebec.   In June 1962 using only two 3-cell Potter traps they captured 747 grosbeaks in 11 days.   On the last day of their stay airplanes from the Quebec Department of Forestry sprayed the area with DDT.   Mr. and Mrs. Parks returned the following June and, using the same traps in the same manner during the corresponding 11 days caught only five grosbeaks.   During their visit to the same area in July 1964 they could not find a single evening grosbeak.   Parks and Parks (1965) conclude:

To explain the dense concentration of Evening Grosbeaks which we had originally found at 39-Mile Camp let us call attention to the fact that repeated sprayings during several years had been employed in an attempt to gain mastery over a spruce budworm outbreak which involved forests in New York, Maine, Ontario, and New Brunswick, as well as in Quebec.   Since the birds no longer found an adequate supply of the budworm for food in the sprayed areas they moved on to unsprayed tracts where the insect still persisted.

Examination of the maps on which the sprayed regions had been plotted shows that the effort to control a particularly obstinate budworm infestation near Quebec's Gaspé had approached, but had never quite reached, the Patapedia River prior to 1962.   So, as this "island" of budworm-infested forest (with 39-Mile Camp situated very close to its center) became smaller and smaller the concentration of Evening Grosbeaks which was attracted to its abundance of edible larvae became heavier and heavier.   Then 1962 witnessed the spraying of even this area and the resultant successful elimination of the pests which had been damaging the trees.   Come the spring of 1963, the almost completely eradicated budworm population was no longer adequate to attract and hold more than a very few of the Evening Grosbeaks which might be returning to, or migrating through, this area.

Maurice Broun, of Hawk Mountain Sanctuary, wrote Mr. Bent in 1952: "Last May, from the 10th to the 15th, from 20 to 40 evening grosbeaks, remnants of large flocks that visited us during the winter, were observed in voracious day-long feedings on cankerworms in the tops of large oaks in front of the Sanctuary headquarters. The grosbeaks spent more time helping to clean up cankerworms than they did at the feeders, where the sunflower seeds became a minor attraction." From analyses of stomach contents of Canadian evening grosbeaks, J. McGugan (MS.) states: "The animal matter of the bird's diet consisted of individuals of *Coleoptera, Araneida,* and perhaps others. The average amount of this material consumed was low but whole meals were enjoyed when the supply was plentiful."

Salted sand and gravel are sought both summer and winter. The birds are seen often in summer eating cinders on railroad beds tasting the salt-impregnated dirt on gravel roads that have been spread with calcium chloride to allay summer's dust, or to melt ice in the winter. Many casualties from cars result from their craving for salt.

An important summer food is the wild cherry, which is fed to the young before they leave the nest. To the cherry groves they are taken as soon as they can fly. The cherries are eaten even before they are ripe, and cherry pits are sought for on the tree and later on the ground until the supply is exhausted. Evening grosbeaks do not swallow berries whole, as do robins and cedar waxwings, but always break them, and their massive beaks accomplish this feat with ease. A flock may be traced to a wild cherry grove by the sound of the mandibles crushing the cherry stones. They always discard the fleshy part of the fruit, but swallow a certain amount of crushed shell with the kernel, which probably helps them digest their food.

Behavior.—Evening grosbeaks appear affable and harmonious when not overcrowded or short of food. When the conditions are reversed, they are not so attractive. Mr. Bent comments: "Although evening grosbeaks are ordinarily gregarious and sociable, feeding harmoniously when scattered openly on the ground, their behavior is quite different when crowded on the feeding trays. There they are often selfish, hostile, and belligerent, pushing their way in, sparring with open beaks, and threatening to attack or drive out a new arrival. They are bosses of the tray and are intolerant of other species, driving away even the starlings; only the blue jay seems able to cope with them. Even the females of their own species are not immune to attack by the males. But, so eager are they for their food, that the tray remains crowded full of birds as long as there is standing room. Towards human beings they are usually tame and fearless; we can almost walk among them when they are feeding on the ground; with good treatment they might learn to feed from our hands, or allow us to pick them up by hand from the feeding tray. When taken from traps, they should be handled with heavy gloves, for they can bite savagely with their powerful beaks."

G. Hapgood Parks (1946) writes of his Hartford station:

Why the flock returned morning after morning before sunrise, its population swelling until more than two hundred individuals simultaneously crowded every feeder and every shelf and filled every trap, is at least partly explained by the bushels of sunflower seed shucks which carpet our partly unspaded victory garden this spring. Only slightly less appealing to the birds seemed to be the large wooden bowl which we kept always filled with warm water. * * * As much as a gallon of water was drunk on mid-winter days when the Grosbeak traffic was at its height. Not one of the birds, however, was ever observed in an attempt to bathe in the bowl.

Later, Parks wrote to Mr. Bent: "We observed our first evening grosbeak in the act of bathing on January 15, 1947. It was a rainy day and 12 of the birds bathed briefly in puddles of water which had formed in depressions in the ice of our driveway. Three others bathed in the bird bath on sunny, mild January 18. A half-dozen isolated instances of bathing were observed during the following weeks."

Forbush (1929) says: "They are fond of bathing even in winter, and visit unfrozen parts of swift streams at this season to bathe and drink * * * ."

Mrs. A. O. Pendleton (B. R. Chamberlain, 1952), writing from North Carolina, tells of a remarkable invasion of evening grosbeaks on January 26, 1952, into her garden and her bird bath. She writes: "we heard a great chattering of birds * * *. There must have been 500 of them. Surely they must have just come in from a very long flight because the bird bath was full of them standing as close to each other as baby chicks, all drinking and bathing at once. Hovering above the bath like hummingbirds, there were dozens of them awaiting a vacant spot to alight in the water * * *."

Mrs. Lucie McDougall, of Port Credit, Ontario, reported to me that in late April, 1958, the grosbeaks sunbathed daily at her feeding station. She saw as many as four males sunbathing at once on her window-sill, a remarkable sight. Sunbathing grosbeaks assume most unusual postures. I watched one male sprawled on the ground looking, it seemed, right into the sun. Its 12 tail feathers were fanned out so the sun could reach each of them; its bill was open, its crown feathers erect. Another male cocked his head sideways, eyed the sun, and seemed bent on having its rays penetrate the skin beneath the gray down under its breast feathers.

The evening grosbeak has the undulating flight so characteristic of the finch family. It does not, however, dip in such deep loops as does the pine grosbeak, nor does the flight pattern follow the bouncing bends of the goldfinch. The undulations are definite but not deep.

As a flock moves in flight in the pathway of the sky, a ringing note, *p-teer, p-teer*, is heard with each dip, proclaiming to the listening ear below that a flock of evening grosbeaks is flying by. We watch the swift but wavy line of flight, punctuated by wild cries, until the flock disappears in the distance.

During migration evening grosbeaks fly high. At times their voices are heard when we are unable to discern the flock in the sky. Robert Ross Taylor writes me that at Scarborough, Ontario, he heard the call notes of grosbeaks high over his head flying west at about 11:00 p.m. on Oct. 6, 1957. During the same autumn, W. W. H. Gunn heard evening grosbeaks flying high above Toronto in the very early hours of the morning when he was on a rooftop observing Sputnik I. The birds were calling and moving westward. In both of these cases the night was clear. These are the first reports I have heard indicating that the species sometimes migrates at night.

Of their manner of flying in wooded country, S. E. White (Butler, 1892) remarked: "Their flight through the woods is very swift, reminding one, by the dexterity with which they avoid branches, of a Pigeon; when in the open, however, it is more like that of a Blackbird." He also notes that when on the ground they "move by hopping, holding themselves like Robins, and turn over the leaves with great dexterity, picking up the seeds from under them."

Very rarely is the bird ever seen by anyone in the evening. Ada Clapham Govan (1940) comments: "Where the grosbeaks spent their afternoons, no one in Massachusetts knew—or why they left all feeding stations by twelve or one each day."

In April 1940 I received a pair of live evening grosbeaks from Norwood, Manitoba. After a few days I noticed how early they roosted for the night. I then noted their times of retirement and measured the light intensity with a Weston illuminometer. In May they roosted on an average 45 minutes before sunset, in their 9-foot aviary spruce tree when the light intensity varied between 180 and 60 foot-candles, averaging 135 foot candles. They always fed heavily before retiring.

As the breeding season advanced, the birds became suddenly insectivorous. Departing from their usual habits, they looked continuously for insects. After June 1, although the female might retire fairly early, the male often kept up his vigilance until after dark. This might not have happened under natural conditions, where insects are more readily available than in an aviary.

In autumn I made daily observations. About November 1 the birds roosted on an average of 57 minutes before sunset, while various other fringillids in the garden—cardinals, white-throated sparrows, juncos, and tree sparrows—were still active and feeding, and robins, starlings, and the icterids in the district had not yet flown to their roosts. In December, January, and February the pair often retired shortly after 1 p.m. and hid in their spruce, sound asleep throughout the afternoon and evening. Rarely did they ever leave their roosting place unless badly disturbed.

Evening grosbeaks roost in a variety of places. Edward R. Ford wrote me in 1942 that in the sand-dune country of northern Indiana in February: "The temperature must have been near zero and there was some wind. * * * the bird took its station on one of the small twigs of a small pine, in the lee of the trunk which was not more than 5 or 6 inches in diameter. It assumed at once the attitude of sleep with the head turned to the rear and apparently resting between the scapulars." Marcia B. Clay (1930) tells of a male evening grosbeak that passed the night near her house at North Bristol, Ohio, "on the ground where the slope of the ravine and the projecting roots of an apple tree afforded protection from wind and snow." On Dec. 28, 1956, Louise de Kiriline Lawrence and Sheldon McLaren saw five evening grosbeaks flying to a roost in white pines at Mattawa, Nipissing District, Ontario at 3:30 p.m. At 8:30 a.m. on January 31, 1957, Mrs. Lawrence saw a flock of about 40 grosbeaks at Mattawa, mostly males, "coming off the night roost in a grove of tall pines." H. R. Dean of Highland Creek, Ontario, tells me grosbeaks roosted in white pines and cedars there throughout the winter of 1956-57.

Lucie McDougall wrote me that on March 31, 1947, she had "brought an injured bird around" into her house and released it at 5:00 p.m. It "flew up into a big elm next door and to my amazement I saw two others up there sleeping." Late in the evening she went out with a flashlight and found the birds still there. Again early in the morning the three grosbeaks were still high up in the big bare elm tree. She told me of other grosbeaks roosting at Port Credit in a row of tall spruce trees. We observed several evening grosbeaks roosting in just such a long row of spruces near Lake Ontario at Oakville on Mar. 2, 1958. We discovered the birds in the thick crowns of the trees at 3:40 p.m., when a squirrel frightened them into momentary flight.

Voice.—Aretas A. Saunders sent the following note to Mr. Bent: "In recent years, when evening grosbeaks have become more frequent in occurrence, I have recorded some of the sounds they produce, but I am not satisfied that any of these are songs. The commonest calls are shrill piping sounds, somewhat suggestive of spring Hylas. These are alternated with a lower pitched trilly sound. The sounds are like *peet peet kreek peet kreek peet peet*, etc. The *peets* in my records are pitched on A''' and the *kreeks* on F#'''. Another sound that is occasional, is like *tchew tchew tchew* and is used by birds feeding in a flock. The pitch is G'''."

Keyes (1888) describes his impressions: "As spring advanced they were usually seen, especially early in the morning, in the top of some tree, singing or chattering noisily, thus attracting the attention of nearly every passer-by. Their loud, clear, rather harsh, piping notes, uttered in concert, reminded one forcibly of the familiar chorus of a flock of Rusty Blackbirds in the spring, and have also been likened to the shrill piping arising from some frog pond on a quiet summer evening."

Francis H. Allen contributed the following to Mr. Bent: "The most characteristic call note I describe as a sort of *prrrreep*, or rolling whistle, with a clear ringing quality. This note, when heard in chorus, strongly suggests sleigh bells." Harrison F. Lewis (MS.) adds: "A note resembling that of the cedar waxwing, although somewhat louder. This is uttered when the birds are quiet and at ease."

Butler (1898) gives the male birds the credit for most of the noise: "The males have a loud call-note, a sharp, metallic cry like the note of a trumpet, which they utter frequently when excited. The females chatter like Bohemian Waxwings." My own observations force the conclusion that the female is more loquacious than the male and is often the noisier of the two. Once when I listened to a pair for half an hour, all the sounds, the shrill piping grosbeak notes, came from the female.

The call or flocking note, *pete* or *p-teer*, is the most characteristic note the species utters. It is very shrill and has considerable carrying power, which must help the various members of the flocks to keep in touch with one another. Individual birds feeding as units of a widely scattered flock call *p-teer* frequently, thus revealing their positions to their companions.

The evening grosbeak's chirp resembles the house sparrow's and many times I have been fooled by this resemblance. Sometimes there is quite a similarity between the grosbeak note and the *peet* call note of the robin.

The chorus-song is a purple finch-like *chip-chip-choo-wee*, or *chip-ip-chu-wee-er*. A surprisingly lovely harmony comes from a mixed choir, as both sexes join in the singing. On the day that I saw my first evening grosbeaks and heard their music I wrote: "Now the grosbeaks are talking together with a tender, tinkling sweetness, very musical and gentle, a liquid loveliness."

Usually in March individual males are heard singing their whisper-song, *chip-ip-chu-wee-er*. As the season advances, the phrases are heard many times in full strength and sung by both sexes. For several years we considered this the true song of the evening grosbeak. Then, one day in late April of 1941, at the University of Illinois Vivarium, our male bird, "Vesper," sang a song which we had not noticed before. After some introductory passages, he gave a high note that seemed to come from his nostrils, *whizz-whizz-tee-ee*. H seemed to like this new phrase in his musical repertoire and repeated it a number of times. The *tee-ee* is very high, yet it carries well From then on we detected this song often during his periods of singing J. Murray Speirs (1950) writes of a March flock in Ontario: "* * * I listen hard I can make out their very high pitched, rather starling like squeaky song, *Swi-swi-tsiee*."

H. R. Ivor (MS.) writes of a 3-month old male raised in his bird observatory: "Today I heard him singing—the first time I have ever heard an evening grosbeak sing. The song was very low and some of the notes seemed quite sweet, but were intermixed with some of the harsher evening grosbeak notes. I felt that there was some resemblance between his sweeter notes and those of the autumn song of the young rose-breast." The next year, Ivor heard the same bird singing a song like a catbird's also some notes similar to a blue bird's, as well as to the high-pitched notes of the mating song of the rose-breasted grosbeak.

The warning note of the species, given more often by a female, is *quoit*; the scold note is *dzee*; the male's invitation to nest, *bzzt*; the nestling's food-call, *see-see-see*; the fledgling's food call, *bee? bee, bee, bee*, etc.; and the parent's call to the fledgling that has left the nest is *chu-hee-chu, chu-hee-chu*.

Field marks.—The evening grosbeak is a heavily-built yellow, black and white finch between the size of a house sparrow and a robin with a very large, light-colored beak. The adult male has a brown head and neck, a black crown and a band of bright yellowish-green over the eyes. The body is mainly yellow and the tail is short, forked, and black. The wings of males of all ages are black, each with a conspicuous large white wing patch. Young males have a golden crown. The body of the female is gray, suffused with yellowish green about the nape; wings and tail are black with white markings

The flight is undulating, and the black and white wings are conspicuous in flight. When newly arrived in a locality, they are sometimes described as "wild canaries," "little parrots," or "oversized goldfinches." Reports of orioles seen in the north in winter usually turn out to be this species.

Enemies.—Evening grosbeaks are comparatively fearless in the presence of man and have proved to be attractive and easy targets. The first evening grosbeak known to science was the specimen an Indian boy shot near Sault Ste. Marie, Michigan Territory, in 1823 (William Cooper, 1825). When they appeared for the first time in the east during the great invasion of 1889–90, D. G. Cox (1891–92) wrote from Toronto, Ontario, "numbers of them were killed by boys with sticks and catapults, in the streets of our city." This remarkable tameness contributes greatly to their destruction. His report concludes: "The birds freely entered the residential parts of the city * * *. They were quite unsuspicious and tame, and were unmercifully and wantonly killed with clubs, catapults, revolvers, pea-rifles, and many were taken alive with a slip-noose attached to the end of a long stick * * *." The birds continue to be attractive targets for the irresponsible young.

In Ontario and elsewhere, evening grosbeaks are sometimes highway casualties, owing to their previously mentioned fondness for chlorided gravel with which many of the roads are sanded in winter.

The domestic cat also takes its toll. M.J. Magee (1932) writes: "With the number of birds around I found it practically impossible to keep the cats away. One time I found a place in a thicket not 100 feet away from my traps where a nice little 'house cat' had been devouring its kills. Quite a lot of feathers were scattered around and nine bands were found, two from Evening Grosbeak * * *"

A juvenal male evening grosbeak was found dead at the nest of a sharp-shinned hawk in Algonquin Park, according to Clifford E. Hope (in litt.). There is no doubt that Cooper's hawk is another enemy of this species. H. R. Ivor told me (letter, Nov. 1949) that a small flock of grosbeaks came into a sugar maple by his house. After feeding "they stayed in the maple until about noon when a Cooper's hawk struck at them." As far as he knows the hawk was not successful, but the grosbeaks disappeared.

Shrikes, also, are enemies of this species. Mrs. Govan (1940) writes:

"The fifth day of the evening grosbeak invasion dawned as a smiling but raw winter's day. With snow everywhere, my birds were awaiting me anxiously. Apparently the grosbeak flock had reached its peak * * *. At seven in the morning a shrike drove the terrorized flock before him in a madly dashing wave * * *. Then, one day, while thirty grosbeaks were feeding on the porch, a shrike cut across the yard. Shrieking their wild alarm, the grosbeaks hurtled upward in a blind panic. My last sight of them that day showed them being followed in close pursuit by the butcher bird."

Occasionally grosbeaks have been killed by striking the windows of houses. Often this has occurred at feeding stations when a bird has been stampeded by a hawk or a shrike.

To date there is but one report of the evening grosbeak parasitized by the cowbird. Near Saranac Lake, New York, in mid-June, 1949, a young grosbeak was reported at a feeding station. B. M. Shaub (MS.) writes in part: "It was said to be very much grayer than the previous ones. This young remained in the tree near the house and was frequently fed by the male grosbeak. It was not until July 7 that I saw this bird and at once recognized it as a young cowbird

(*Molothrus a. ater*), at least a week out of the nest * * *. On July 11 the male grosbeak and the young cowbird were seen again, but at this time the grosbeak's interest in the cowbird had greatly lessened and he was reluctant to feed it and only did so after much begging for food on the part of the cowbird."

Florence Huestis Simpson gave me an evening grosbeak killed at a window in Todmorden, Ontario, in March 1958. On it were several bird lice (Mallophaga) which were identified for me by K. C. Emerson, who wrote: "The two specimens you enclosed are *Philopterus citrinellae* (Schrank, 1776). The long, thin specimen mentioned in your letter was *Brüelia* sp. Also found on the host are species of the genera *Myrsidea, Menacanthus, Ricinus*, and *Machaerilaemus*."

Evening grosbeaks, however, seem to be remarkably free from bird lice. During the winter of 1945–46, G. Hapgood Parks (1947) banded 874 evening grosbeaks at Hartford, Conn. "The physical condition of most of the birds which we trapped was excellent," he writes. "They were very uniformly plump and vigorous * * *. Although a quick examination was made of every bird we were able to discover only one parasite * * *." Although the parasite was not identified, he states that its characteristics "were very similar to those of the common chicken-louse." A nestling my husband found under a nesting tree in Ontario in June 1945 had white eggs of a dipterous parasite in the mouth and on the dorsal feather tracts and also a deposit of eggs over the left eye.

When Gordon Lambert and Ross Baker collected a young bird not long out of the nest in the Mattawa region of Ontario, 14 hippoboscids flew out from the bird's plumage. The fledgling was one of four being fed by an adult, and the nest must have been heavily infested. J. C. Bequaert has written me that the only bird-fly taken thus far on evening grosbeaks is *Ornithomyia fringillina* Curtis, and adds: "All in all, the fly is rarely seen on this species of bird and perhaps only of accidental occurrence on it." He reports (1954) that there have been six published captures from the eastern race, one of which came from Alberta (Strickland, 1938) and the others from Ontario. Mrs. Downs has found these bird-flies on 10 juvenal grosbeaks at her banding station in Vermont. One was taken from an adult. Most of the birds she has handled have been free from bird-flies.

C. H. D. Clarke (1934) collected a male in Algonquin Park that had a tapeworm (Cestoda) in its intestines and microfilaria in its bloodstream. Of six specimens taken at Brule Lake, Algonquin Park, in the summer of 1934, he found three, including the one above, parasitized by blood protozoa, the second being infested by flagellates of the genus *Trypanosoma*, and the third by sporozoa of the genus

Leucocytozoon. Wenyon *in* Hamerton (1937) also lists *Trypanosoma* as a protozoal parasite in this species. *Plasmodium*, the malaria parasite, has been reported in a captive bird (Hamerton, 1939) wrongly attributed to *Haemoproteus* (Herman, 1944).

Despite these records, internal parasitism in the species is rare. A. M. Fallis examined blood slides from several banded Ontario grosbeaks captured in Algonquin Park, 1945–48, and the smears were negative. Mary S. Shaub of Northampton, Mass., who has banded so many of these birds, considers them "especially healthy" (letter). She has written me of another bander, Dorothy Driscoll of Brookline, Mass., who made blood smears from grosbeaks during an invasion recently and "found only one infection in 100 smears."

Age.—As yet no one has analyzed the wealth of banding data now available to determine the evening grosbeak's probable longevity or its rates of mortality and survival in the wild. M. J. Magee (1939) reported retaking three of his banded birds in their 9th year. Elizabeth Holt Downs at her home in Vermont banded a grosbeak July 11, 1956 as an adult female. This bird returned regularly and was at least 10 years old when she recaptured it June 10, 1965.

H. R. Ivor probably has the longevity record for an aviary bird of this species. Some years ago he received from Winnipeg a handsome adult female of unknown age which he named "Beauty." I knew the bird well. She lived in his bird observatory 16½ years and was therefore at least 17 years old when she died.

Fall.—In the autumn, adults and young are "on the move." Their long wings—longer in relation to body-size than those of any other finch—make them well equipped for extensive journeyings.

Until recent years, little was known about this bird's habits in the fall; but since it has moved eastward as a breeding species, it has been appearing in populated regions in some years, notably in 1957, early in the fall, and is therefore being observed more frequently. The birds show no interest in feeding stations at this time and are reported more often in box elder trees than in any other kind. K. F. Edwards reported that on Grand Manan Island, New Brunswick, October 11–16, 1957, a flock of 15 was feeding on cherry pits, another favored food. Louise de Kiriline Lawrence saw five on Oct. 19, 1944, at Rutherglen, Ontario: "They were eating cone seeds in the tops of coniferous trees." On November 14, she watched two settle in an aspen and sample the buds. On Oct. 27, 1947, she saw others budding in a poplar. Thus, on occasion, this species is a fall as well as a spring budder.

Winter.—Mr. Bent has written: "It is when the grosbeaks come to our feeding trays in winter that we become intimately acquainted with them and their traits. For a number of years I have maintained a feeding shelf at my study window, almost within an arm's reach as I sit at my desk, and have kept it supplied with sunflower seed, hemp seed, cracked nuts, peanuts, scratch feed, and other mixed bird food.

"During winters that they are here they flock to the shelf, often in such numbers that there is hardly any standing room; as long as there is room for one more to crowd in they come and gobble up the food, with a decided preference for the sunflower seeds; these they crack open very skillfully with their big beaks, swallow the kernel and let the shells fall where they may, which leaves quite a mess for me to clean up. When the grosbeaks are here in large numbers they consume an enormous amount of these seeds, involving considerable trouble and expense to keep the greedy birds satisfied, but they are worth it.

"Francis H. Orcutt, of Penn Yan, N.Y., writes to me on this point: 'Other bird students with feeding stations report that the grosbeaks are eating them out of house and home. At first, one or two birds began feeding, now I have 40. With sunflower seeds at 49 cents a pound, I cannot afford to feed them much longer.'

"During some winters these birds are seen in enormous numbers, hundreds or even thousands of them; some seasons, we see only a few, and in other years none at all. Probably the abundance or scarcity of food supply may explain this irregularity."

Mr. Bent refers the reader to: Butler (1892), Elon H. Eaton (1914), Arthur H. Norton (1918), Bagg and Eliot (1937), and Brackbill (1947) for records of invasions of this race from Wisconsin to New Brunswick, in the years since the discovery of the species. For a very complete picture of the years 1950–1955, the reader is referred to "Evening Grosbeak Survey News," edited by Dr. and Mrs. B. M. Shaub, which tells of the penetration of the grosbeaks south to Georgia.

Some winters, as in 1956–57, the grosbeaks stay north and only a comparatively few appear south of the 45th parallel. The evening grosbeak is well equipped to resist the cold, for beneath the contour plumage is a warm gray down. It wears its own "eiderdown" for the same reason that the eider duck wears his—insulation against the cold. The feet are very short, so short that they may be tucked under the feathers in cold weather. The unfeathered part of the leg is covered in the front with scales or scutellae. The underside of the feet, including the toes, are padded with tylari, corneous cushions in ridges, which give the feet grip on icy branches, leading J. Murray Speirs to comment: "The grosbeaks are equipped with their own snow tires."

One morning in North Bay, Ontario, when the temperature was 35° below zero, anxious to find out what the grosbeaks did on an extremely cold day, I went out. A flock of 12 were located, feeding on Manitoba maples. Above each bill, the breath of the bird could be seen like a little wreath. All were males. My notes read: I noted hat they looked noticeably larger than usual, as their feathers were luffed out as far from the body as possible, so that they were encased n warmth. Their feet were tucked into the warm down and could iot be seen at all. One of them reached far out for a pair of the winged seeds, and broke through the silver ice, with which the seeds were encrusted, with a loud snap. In spite of the icy frosting over the trees and seeds, apparently they were getting all the food they needed, and even piped prettily, *choo-wee, chorr-wee,* to each other.

DISTRIBUTION

Range.—Central and eastern Canada to Arkansas and Georgia.

Breeding range.—The eastern evening grosbeak breeds, and in some years is largely resident, in a narrow belt from northeastern Alberta (Athabaska Delta), central Saskatchewan (St. Walburg, Prince Albert), southern Manitoba (Gimli), western and central Ontario (Kenora, Strickland), central western Quebec (Barraute), and northern New Brunswick (Riley Brook, Tabusintac), south to central Alberta (Dunvegan), southern Manitoba (Indian Bay), northeastern Minnesota (Island Lake, Cramer), northern Michigan (Marquette, Seney, Whitefish Point), southern Ontario (Muskoka, Leeds County), southwestern Quebec (Kipawa, Charlesbourg), central and northeastern New York (Pittsford, Ithaca, Blue Ridge), southern Vermont (South Londonderry), and Massachusetts (Mt. Herman, Hadley).

Winter range.—Winters, irregularly and locally, south to southwestern South Dakota (Rapid City), Kansas, southwestern Arkansas (De Queen), southern Louisiana (Pride, Gramercy, Amite), southeastern Mississippi (Hattiesburg and Jackson County), southwestern Alabama (Grove Hill), northern Georgia, central eastern South Carolina (Charleston, McClellanville), and eastern North Carolina (Wilmington, Washington); east to Newfoundland (St. John's) and Nova Scotia (Wolfville).

Casual records.—Casual in summer in southern British Columbia (Okanagan Valley). Casual in winter in northeastern Quebec (headwaters of Nemiscau River, and Lake St. John).

Migration.—The data deal with the species as a whole. Early dates of spring arrival are: New York—Jamaica Bay, April 19; Central Park, Manhattan, April 23. Vermont—Topsham, April 21.

Late dates of spring departure are: Alabama—Bessemer and Gadsden, April 23. Georgia—Macon, April 17. South Carolina—Charleston, May 13. North Carolina—Washington, May 11; Rocky Mount, May 7. Virginia—Arlington, May 17. West Virginia—Charleston, May 15. District of Columbia—May 12. Maryland—Baltimore, June 2; Laurel, May 19 (median of 11 years, May 7).

Pennsylvania—Sheffield, May 26; State College, May 25. New Jersey—Mount Holly, May 14. New York—Cayuga and Oneida Lake basins, June 1 (median of 13 years, May 17); Amsterdam, May 22 Connecticut—Hartford, May 17. Rhode Island—Bradford, May 4 Massachusetts—Cambridge, June 9. Vermont—Montpelier, May 10 New Hampshire—New Hampton, June 1 (median of 21 years, May 14) Maine—S. Harpswell, May 8. Nova Scotia—Wolfville, April 28 Arkansas—Malvern, May 13. Tennessee—Knox County, May 1 Kentucky—Glasgow, May 8. Missouri—St. Louis, May 5 Illinois—Decatur, May 11. Indiana—South Bend, May 14. Ohio— Utica, May 21. Michigan—Detroit-Windsor area, May 14. Iowa— eastern Iowa, April 27; Ottumwa, April 24. Wisconsin—Polk County May 28. Minnesota—Anoka, May 24. Texas—Amarillo, May 18 Kansas—northeastern Kansas, May 13 (median of 7 years, April 18) Nebraska—Lincoln County, May 15. North Dakota—Grand Forks May 14. Manitoba—Winnipeg, May 12. Saskatchewan—Prince Albert, May 26. Colorado—Denver, May 28. Montana—Missoula June 5; Billings, June 4. California—Monterey, May 10; San Joaquin Valley, May 5.

Early dates of fall arrival are: Washington—Spokane, August 16 Nevada—Las Vegas, October 25. California—Sebastopol, November 26. Montana—Helena, September 20. Wyoming—Sundance, October 26. Colorado—Colorado Springs, August 12; Morrison, September 17. Arizona—Painted Desert, October 14. New Mexico—Tierra Amarilla, September 11; Lake La Java, September 17. Saskatchewan—Spirit Lake, September 30. Manitoba—Winnipeg, October 1 South Dakota—Waubay, October 29. Nebraska—Stapleton, October 30. Kansas—northeastern Kansas, November 6. Okalahoma— Tulsa, November 4. Minnesota—Walker, September 4; Isanti County, September 6. Wisconsin—Cedar Grove, October 5. Iowa— Cedar Falls, September 13. Ontario—Peterborough, August 17 Michigan—Marquette, October 3; Oakland County, October 10. Ohio—Lakewood, October 7. Indiana—Michigan City, October 20. Illinois—Chicago, November 3. Missouri—St. Louis, November 11. Kentucky—Mammoth Cave National Park, November 3. Tennessee—Smoky Mountains, October 1. Newfoundland—St. John's, December 13. Prince Edward Island—Port Borden, November 5. Nova Scotia—West Middle Sable, October 2. New Brunswick— Sackville, September 2. Quebec—Charlesbourg, August 27. Maine— Brunswick, August 17. New Hampshire—Monroe, August 14; New Hampton, August 18 (median of 21 years, October 10). Vermont— Topsham, September 20; East Barre, September 30. Massachusetts— Adams, September 16; Bourne, September 29. Rhode Island— Tiverton, September 14. Connecticut—Hartford, September 14.

New York—Elmira, August 20; Cayuga and Oneida Lake basins, September 25 (median of 13 years, October 15). New Jersey—West Milford, October 10. Pennsylvania—Holicong, August 24; New Hope, August 28. Maryland—Ocean City, October 8; Laurel, October 10 (median of 7 years, October 23). District of Columbia—October 4. West Virginia—Charleston, September 20; Meadville, October 5. Virginia—Deerfield, September 20; Shenandoah National Park, September 22. North Carolina—Wentworth, October 29. South Carolina—Charleston, November 18. Alabama—Birmingham and Monte Sano, November 21.

Egg dates.—Manitoba: 6 records, June 18 to June 20; 1 record, June 18.

Michigan: 1 record, June 24.

Ontario: 3 records, June 13 to June 20.

HESPERIPHONA VESPERTINA BROOKSI Grinnell
Western Evening Grosbeak
PLATE 14
Contributed by DORIS HUESTIS SPEIRS

HABITS

The western evening grosbeak is largely a bird of the higher altitudes whose plumage is a blending, a chiaroscuro, of the highlights and shadows of the great hills. Enid Michael (1926) writes from Yosemite:

The Evening Grosbeak * * * furnishes a splendid example of protective coloring in birds. It is brilliantly colored white, yellow, black and olive. It would seem to be one of the most conspicuous of high Sierran birds. Yet its brightest color is almost identical with the lemon color of the lichens found throughout our high Sierra. Any bird lover seeing the Evening Grosbeak for the first time is sure to be thrilled. In later summer it comes occasionally down to the floor of Yosemite valley, but it is seen more frequently in the high Sierra in that yet little known part of Yosemite National Park lying back of the valley proper.

Florence Merriam Bailey (1902) observes: "While watching the birds on Mt. Shasta one day, I was struck by the conspicuousness of one that flew across an open space. As it lit on a dead stub whose silvery branches were touched with yellow lichen, to my amazement it simply vanished. Its peculiar greenish yellow toned in perfectly with the greenish yellow of the lichen, * * * the lichen being a striking feature of the forests of the Sierra Nevada, Cascades, and northern Rockies, so that the unusual coloration of the bird may be of marked significance."

That the bird is no newcomer to the West Coast was proved when a diagnostic lower mandible was identified among the fossils from the

Rancho La Brea Pleistocene at Los Angeles. William R. Dawso
(1948) informs us that "Comparison with a specimen of the moder
Evening Grosbeak, shows it to be identical in every detail."

When Joseph Grinnell (1917) described this race from Britis
Columbia and named it in honor of Major Allan Brooks, he gave
the following diagnosis:

Bill thick as in *vespertina*, but longer and hence relatively slenderer; slightl
less slender on an average than in *californica* and *warreni**, but decidedly thick
than in *montana*. Color-tone of body of male decidedly the darkest as compare
with all the other subspecies; as a result, line of demarcation between black ca
and hind neck not sharply defined. Frontal yellow bar of male averaging muc
broader than in any other subspecies except *warreni* and *vespertina*, and bu
slightly narrower than in the latter form. Color-tone of body of female dark
than in any other subspecies; more sooty on top of head and back, and dark
brown beneath; decidedly less ashy about head and on lower surface than i
vespertina, most nearly as in *californica*.

According to the 1957 A.O.U. Check-List, it breeds and is largel
resident from north-central and southeastern British Columbia, wes
ern Montana, western Wyoming, and central Colorado, south throug
the mountains to northwestern and central eastern California, nort
eastern Nevada, central Arizona and central southern New Mexic
It winters from southern interior and southwestern British Columbi
south to southern California, southern Arizona, southern New Mexic
and western Texas; east to South Dakota and Oklahoma.

Spring.—From her cabin in the Driftwood Valley by Tetana Lak
British Columbia, Theodora Stanwell-Fletcher (1946) wrote in he
journal under the date of Apr. 17, 1938: "One day when we were cross
ing the meadow we saw an evening grosbeak on a tall spruce. Th
black and yellow velvet of its markings, the heavy pale blue bil
were unmistakable. We were wildly excited at this remarkabl
visitor * * * and J. tried, without success, to collect it." Farthe
south in their range, the birds are not so rare. Fred G. Evenden
Jr., Woodburn, Oreg., wrote to Mr. Bent:

"Every spring this species appears on the campus of Oregon Stat
College in flocks approaching several thousand in number. Th
reason for this is that the campus walks and streets are corridors o
elms that are beginning to bud out at that time. The flocks remai
approximately 2 months on these visits, building up from a smal
number to an abundance peak about the first of May, or the middl
of the 2-month period. They are year-round residents of the highe
forested hills of the Coast Range in the western part of Bento
County."

---

*The forms *californica* and *warreni* were later synonymized with *brooks
(A.O.U. Check-List, 1931).

In late May 1953, when I was on the university campus at Corvallis, Oreg., a flock of over 100 grosbeaks were feeding on the elm seeds scattered over the ground, or calling from a walnut orchard. Their voices made a continuous din which the students seemed not to notice, apparently taking their noisy visitors for granted. The birds, on their part, took the students for granted, and fed unconcernedly on the grass almost under the students' feet.

Nesting.—The evening grosbeak has a remarkable genius for keeping its nesting locations hidden from the eyes and ears of eager ornithologists, from nidologists, oologists, photographers, campers and hikers. Considering the comparative abundance of the species, nesting records are relatively scarce. In the breeding range of the western evening grosbeak, to date the States of Idaho, Oregon, Washington, and Wyoming have yet to report a single record of a nest, despite convincing evidence that the birds do breed in each of these States.

It took me 8 years to locate one nest of this elusive species (Speirs and Speirs, 1947), but during the quest a number of nests of the western race were reported to me and permission granted to use these data as desired. They include the first actual nesting records for British Columbia, Nevada, and Utah.

John Swinburne (1888) found the first reported nest of this subspecies in a thickly wooded canyon in the "intergrade region" of the White Mountains about 15 miles west of the little town of Springerville, Apache County, Ariz. He writes: "The nest was a comparatively slight structure, rather flat in shape, composed of small sticks and roots, lined with finer portions of the latter. * * * The nest was placed about fifteen feet from the ground in the extreme top of a thick willow bush. The slight cañon, with a few willow bushes in its centre bordering a small stream, lies in the midst of very dense pine timber at an altitude of about 7,000 feet, as far as I can judge." He climbed up to the nest and found that it contained three eggs.

Henry J. M. Barnett of Toronto discovered a nest of the western evening grosbeak on the ridge above Burrard Inlet, West Vancouver, British Columbia, on July 25, 1938. He writes me as follows: "I was up in some second growth timber at the top of 12th Street, on the side of Hollyburn Ridge. Most of the trees were deciduous trees (ash, etc.), but just a short distance higher up they were replaced by firs. There was a robin-sized nest about 18 feet up in one of these ash trees, about 10 feet from the top of the tree. On the edge of the nest, not exactly sitting on it, was a female evening grosbeak. It was impossible to get at the nest itself due to the position at the top of a very small tree. There was a noise in the nest as if there were three or four young there. It was almost dark and no further observations were made. My companion went back next day and said that both parents were bringing food." The "ash" species referred to was the mountain ash, *Pyrus sitchensis*. The other deciduous tree common in the nesting area was the red alder, *Alnus rubra*.

More nests of this species have been found in California than in any other State or Canadian Province. The altitudinal range has been from near sea level in the Coast Range (J. M. Davis, 1922) to 9,000 feet in the Sierra Nevada (Dixon, in litt.). The reader is referred to Dawson (1923), J. B. Dixon (1934), A. M. Ingersoll (1913), Mrs. H. J. Taylor (1926), and Mrs. I. G. Wheelock (1912).

J. Parker Norris (1887) reported the discovery of an evening grosbeak nest by E. H. Fiske, in Yolo County, Calif., on May 10, 1886. Though hailed as the "first" of the species to be discovered, this looks very much like a case of mistaken identity, for the location of the nest and the description of the eggs suggest they belonged to a pair of black-headed grosbeaks. We visited this region in the Sonoran Zone in 1939, and consider it a most unlikely place for an evening grosbeak to nest.

Probably the first authentic nest to be reported from California was found by Rollo H. Beck (1896) in El Dorado County near Lake Tahoe. The nest was 35 feet up, near the top of a black oak and in the fork of a small limb. He says: "The nest is a much more substantial structure than that of any Black-headed Grosbeak I have collected. It is composed of three materials. The foundation is of twigs broken from the tree. Upon this is placed the nest proper— of long moss-like rootlets of a very dark color and very small size. Inside this is the lining of light-colored rootlets and a couple of dry pine needles. The inside diameter is about three inches and the outside is four and one-half inches."

James B. Dixon, who sent Mr. Bent some extensive notes on the breeding of the western evening grosbeak in California, says: "This bird is a very erratic nester in the area around June Lake, Mono County, Calif. It seems to migrate through, and, if food conditions are right, it will stop and nest; usually from one to three pairs will be nesting in a small area. Some years none will stop, and other years they will be quite common at the right elevation and right tree growth. The 9,000 feet elevation seems to be about the top of their range, and down to 7,000 feet in the Mono area."

He sent the following data on eight nests: Of two nests found on June 23, 1932, one was in the "very top of a silvertopped fir tree, 12 feet from the ground, and held three eggs slightly incubated. The other nest held four eggs and was 50 feet up in a dense young fir tree only about 100 yards from the first nest. Nest outwardly made of hard, dry twigs and inwardly lined with fine grass fiber and rootlets.

Nests very similar to purple finch nests, but heavier and larger twigs. Nests well out on horizontal limbs."

One June 12, 1934, Dixon found two nests, one with four eggs and one with five eggs; this is the earliest date for eggs he recorded, and the set of five eggs was the first of this number he had seen. Both nests were in lodgepole pines, one in the top, the other 70 feet up and out at the extreme end of a drooping limb. On June 25, 1935, he found a nest 5 feet up in the very top of a lodgepole pine sapling. On July 6, 1935, he recorded a nest "70 feet up in a white pine in open forest," and another in a yellow pine 70 feet up and out on the extreme end of a limb. A nest found on July 13, 1935, was 50 feet up in a dense stand of lodgepole pines, and contained four young, estimated to be about days old.

Dudley S. DeGroot (1935) records three nests in tamaracks and one nest in a red fir in El Dorado County, Calif. The nests in the tamaracks were from 34 to 40 feet above the ground on horizontal limbs; the nest in the red fir was about 40 feet up. He gives a good account of nest building.

In 1935, Ira La Rivers discovered two nests of the evening grosbeak at Walker Mine, Plumas County, in the Sierra Nevada at an elevation of 6,500 feet. They were in dead white fir trees in a tailing-pond that had been "ravine-flooded" and lacked protective cover. One of the nests was 20 to 25 feet from the ground in the crotch next to the trunk of one of these trees. By climbing an adjacent tree, he saw it contained two eggs. He describes the structure as "compact from the center, ragged on the outside; the bowl not as deep or solid as a robin's nest, but approximately the size of a robin's nest." The second nest was some distance off, at the edge of the pond "nearer the forest proper." This nest was also in a dead white fir, 20 to 25 feet from the ground and in a crotch next to the trunk.

He writes me: "Concerning the nest at the pond's edge, I find a notation to the effect that 'but for the activity of two busy, markedly apprehensive birds, the nest would have been perfectly camouflaged by its age, for it shows a decrepitude which only long desertion can explain.' The resemblance to a tree-built *Zenaidura macroura* nest was quite noticeable, even more so when I found the ground-work of the structure so loose that the greenness of the egg, solitary as far as I could see, shown plainly through." Both pairs of birds manifested alarm at his approach, flew from the nesting tree, returned to perch on the edge of the nest, squawking. He remained only about half an hour in the vicinity as he did not wish to disturb the birds further. There was no protection for the nests from sun or rain, built as they were in dead trees. There are records of two other nestings of the species in dead tree tops.

Charles W. Michael, whom we visited at Yosemite the summer o 1939, had seen many nests, the earliest on May 10, 1925. A numbe were in yellow pines; one was high up in a Kellogg oak. Only on nest was less than 40 feet above the ground; two were 100 feet uj Edward B. Andrews collected the first evening grosbeak nest and egg in Colorado in early July 1904, within the western limits of Este Park, Larimer County (see F. M. Dille, 1904), at an elevation c 7,800 feet. Andrews wrote on July 4 of that year (MS.): "Saw thi nest in a yellow pine tree up the gulch on June 24. It was a nervou climb and 40 feet from the ground and I found the nest not completed I then thought it an old one. Today being near there, nest looke larger and I threw up a stick, a bird flew out and swooped off in th brush so quickly I did not recognize it. From the direction she wen there came back the whistle of a grosbeak, and the climb this tim did not scare me in the least. I found four eggs in the nest."

Clifford V. Davis (1953) has told of the first nest reported for th State of Montana: "On July 3, 1952, a nest with five partly grow young was found by the ornithology class from Montana Stat College while they were on a field trip. Both parent birds staye within a few feet of the nest while it was being inspected. Th nest was about 45 feet from the ground in a dense stand of Dougla fir (*Pseudotsuga taxifolia*). It was composed almost entirely c Douglas fir twigs and was lined with a few rootlets and two horsehair The nest was located about four miles north and east of Bozemar Gallatin County, at an altitude of about 4800 feet."

When I was in Nevada in late April, 1939, Thomas Trelease, o Sparks, took me up Slide Mountain to show me the western evenin grosbeak's nest he had found 6 feet up in the willow thicket at th lake's edge. The nest was so loosely constructed that the three egg could be observed from below. According to Thomas, the eggs "wer like robins' but slightly splotched." The nest also suggested robin's in size but was "real loose."

Of three nests Francis J. Birtwell (1901) found near Willis, N. Mex in the Pecos River Forest Reserve, one was in a large pine, the othe two in spruces, 41 and 46 feet from the ground, respectively. H remarked about the nest-building: "* * * certain it is that the Eve ning Grosbeak puts little work into the building of her nest. Th outside is of a few coarse sticks. Usnea is wadded together nex and fine rootlets make the lining."

J. K. Jensen (1930) found a nest in Santa Fe Canyon, N. Mex on June 29, 1930, of which he writes: "The nest was located abou 35 feet up in a Douglas fir, on a six-foot limb and about two feet fron the main tree trunk. * * * The nest—five inches across, was ver loosely made of twigs, but with a distinct depression one inch dee

nd three inches across, and thinly lined with pine needles, a few shreds
f moss, and two small pieces of fine grass stems." Of his experience
vith these birds, Jensen has written me: "The evening grosbeak is
ne of the most difficult birds to deal with as far as finding nests goes.
Saying this, I am speaking from my own experience in birdnesting in
everal foreign countries and several States. The birds are as a rule
ery common here in Santa Fe and it is not at all unusual to see as
many as 6,000 to 7,000 of the birds in the city, but it required 11
years of walking and climbing through the Sangre de Cristo Mts.
efore I saw and collected a nest. * * * Two years later I took a
ive set about 3 miles from the first located.

"The birds are very quiet during the nesting season and seem able
o keep out of sight. The incubating bird stays on the nest until
he climber gets up so far that he can reach out and touch
he nest. The last nest found was about 40 feet up in a Douglas fir
nd several feet out on a limb in rather open forest, and the nest
vas in plain view, so I could see the the incubating bird from the
ground. When I reached out toward the nest the female left, but
dropped straight down to within 2 feet of the ground; as she fell she
ave her danger call, and in a few seconds there were several males
colding me and fluttering very close, even alighting within 3 or 4
eet of me. I had looked over this particular mountain side several
imes and never seen a bird, but there must have been a dozen more
ests in the immediate vicinity. I never found another."

George I. Bone discovered the first evening grosbeak nest for Utah
near Salem on May 27, 1936. The nest contained 3 eggs. He writes
MS.): "The evening grosbeak is a common migratory bird here,
ppearing in large numbers in early spring. * * * In 1936, I noticed
hat at least one pair remained after the migration in a grove of maple
nd scrub oak near Salem, Utah. The grove of trees partially sur-
ounds a small pond or lake and the nest was found within 200 yards
f the lake. I saw the birds several times and thought they were
esting, so when Mr. Hutchings (Lehi taxidermist) said that they
vere not known to nest in Utah I decided to see if this pair had a
est. The birds were very friendly and not in the least afraid, but
he first day I looked for about an hour for the nest but did not find
t. The male kept singing about in the trees. About a week later
was again in the grove and stumbled onto the nest which was in
ery plain sight in a young scrub oak tree which was about an inch or
n inch and one-half in diameter. The nest was next to the trunk of
he tree and about 7 feet above the ground. I called Mr. Hutchings
nd the following Sunday we went to the nest. By this time the birds
vere setting. The male seemed to set on the eggs as often as the
emale. I reached up and pulled the small tree over toward the

ground with the male still setting on the eggs. It left the nest whe
about a foot from my head. The three eggs and nest were take
by Mr. Hutchings."

John Hutchings wrote me that the nest was "similar to that of th
black-headed grosbeak, loose saucer-shaped structure." Apart fro
being the first recorded nest for Utah, the account is of interest becaus
of the unusual behavior of the male in assisting with the incubation
the eggs (provided his identification of the bird was correct).

Eggs.—John Swinburne (1888) describes the eggs as "of a cle
greenish ground color, blotched with pale brown." R. H. Bec
(1896) observed: "On first glancing into the nest I though of B
colored Blackbirds' eggs, as the coloration and markings were qui
similar though the size was much less. The position of the eggs w
unusual but probably accidental. The eggs were in two rows, thr
in one row while the fourth had a row all to itself, with the small en
facing the middle egg of the other row."

William George F. Harris writes (MS.): "The eggs laid by th
species vary from two to five, with four being the commonest numbe
They are fairly glossy, and ovate to elongated-ovate in shape. Th
ground color may be 'court gray,' 'bluish glaucous,' or 'graphaliu
green,' and they are spotted, blotched, streaked, or clouded wit
'citrine drab,' 'deep olive,' and 'dark olive.' These markings a
somewhat sparsely scattered over the entire surface with a sligh
concentration toward the large end. On the majority of eggs th
spots or blotches are blurred rather than sharply defined, and th
ground often is clouded with patches of pale 'citrine drab,' with ver
fine speckles so pale that they almost fade into the ground, scattere
between the larger markings." The measurements of 50 eggs averag
23.0 by 16.4 millimeters; the eggs showing the four extrem
measure *25.0* by 17.8, 23.3 by *18.5*, and *20.0* by *14.5* millimeters.

Incubation.—The female alone incubates the eggs, with possib
rare exceptions such as the questionable Utah nesting describe
above. That she is a close sitter par excellence has been vouche
for by several collectors. No data on the length of the incubatic
period are available for this race.

Young.—Major Allan Brooks wrote me in 1939 from British C
lumbia: "The species nests regularly in the Okanagan region
recent years, in most years in the foothills behind my house. Th
nestlings are brought down as soon as they leave the nest to the tre
in my garden where they are fed each year for about a week. La
summer a female fed four young just in front of my windows for
days on the aphid contents of the galls on the cottonwoods; in form
years on the fruit of the black haw."

On a late August day in Yosemite Park, Enid Michael (1928) saw evening grosbeaks, young and old, feasting in great numbers on a cherry hedge. "Family groups were scattered from one end of the hedge to the other. These birds seemed to show a preference for the coffee berries, but, as the coffee bushes were few in the hedge, many grosbeaks had to be content with a fill of cherries."

While in Yosemite on July 30, 1939, I saw a flock of about 20 evening grosbeaks, including two or more young, in an oak grove with a pair of band-tailed pigeons. All were feeding in coffee bushes (cascara, *Rhamnus purshiana*). We saw young grosbeaks being fed and observed especially a fledgling female. First she was fed by a male which we presumed to be her father. Soon a second male approached and popped a berry into her bill. Each time she was given the whole fruit, while the older birds, when feeding, extracted the seeds, dropping the pulp. The ground beneath the coffee bush was littered with seed peelings in amongst the dried oak leaves and bracken. The young bird kept calling a soft double note and, when being fed, leaned forward with vibrating wings and raised crest.

Plumages.—Allan Brooks (1939) thus describes the plumage of juvenal evening grosbeaks:

The following description is from specimens of the Western race, *Hesperiphona vespertina brooksi*. The body plumage of the juvenal male is more richly colored than that of the juvenal female, more suffused with olive or yellow and generally darker and less gray; there is usually a more pronounced dark malar stripe. But the main difference is in the wing which follows the pattern of the adult male and not that of the female. The wing is black, without the three series of white markings that are found on the primaries and secondaries of females of all ages. But the tertials and outermost secondaries are white as in the adult male, forming a conspicuous patch; the tertials are more or less tinged with brown as in most second-plumaged males and usually have a narrow black inner border; all the feathers of this white patch are narrowly edged with primrose yellow. The tail in most individuals is solid black like the adult male's, but some show faint white tips to the inner webs of the outermost rectrices; these do not take the form of the large white spots found in females of all ages. The rump is dull buffy olive and the upper tail-coverts are black, sometimes with buff tips.

It will be seen that the wings and tail are essentially colored as in the adult male, the five innermost secondary coverts are pale yellow or white, narrowly edged with primrose yellow, forming a patch confluent with that on the tertials and secondaries just as in the adult male and very conspicuous in flight. The bill is dusky olive, abruptly pale green at the extreme base.

Food.—Observing the feeding habits of a large flock of evening grosbeaks in New Mexico, Herbert Brandt (1951) wrote:

Even in actions this is an avian object apart, as it moves about among the branches after the manner of a parrot, seeming to prefer reaching down to full extent for its seed food, with legs stretched wide apart; or grasping and crawling about with unhurried deliberation. * * *

This unpredictable bird during the winter feeds on the seeds of the boxelder and black locust; at other times it may visit the surrounding mountain slopes where it can eat its fill of juniper berries and pinyon nuts.

Alfred M. Bailey (MS.) writes of their food habits in the Denver, Colo., region: "They are partial to the seeds of the box elder, the fruits of the ornamental trees and shrubs, buds of willows and the green tips of maples, and they will visit feeding trays as long as sunflower seeds are provided."

J. A. Munro sent me specific records of the food being taken at Okanagan, British Columbia, in the various months of the year. The winter foods noted were seeds of box elder, chokecherry, white ash, and apple. In May, 10 birds were feeding on old seeds of the black locust. In June a flock fed on green box elder seeds. Several flocks in Vernon ate green elm seeds. Of August he writes: "A flock, probably comprising several families, visited tops of the tallest firs and seemed to be eating seeds from the cones." In September a small flock of young took green black-locust seeds. In October several fed on the berries of the red hawthorne.

Zella McMannama (1948) contributes an unusual observation. She says:

Comparatively little has been written about the animal food of this species hence it seems worthwhile to record the following observations.

On May 28, 1945, my attention was attracted by the unmistakable calls of a flock of these birds in the second-growth fir woods south of the Western Washington College campus at Bellingham. While attempting to locate the birds I saw one fly out and capture an insect after the manner of a cedar waxwing (Bombycilla cedrorum). In a moment another bird flew out, and as it turned the white secondaries of the male evening grosbeak were conspicuous. The entire flock engaged for some minutes in feeding upon large flies which were in great abundance above the trees. Frequently the birds missed their quarry and one made three successive stoops at the same insect, finally following it out of sight among the firs. This is the first time I had observed evening grosbeaks feeding upon insects.

Ira N. Gabrielson (1924) made a careful study of the food habits of evening grosbeaks from examination of the stomach contents of 127 specimens, a good number of which were of the western race. He writes:

No trace of animal matter was found in the 88 winter stomachs, seeds and fruit constituting the entire contents. Seeds of wild fruits formed 39.63 per cent; winged seeds (maple, ash, and box elder) 37.96 per cent; coniferous seeds, 14.5 per cent; and miscellaneous seeds, mast and rubbish, the remainder. The most important seeds of wild fruits in the food for this period were cherry pits (Prunus) found in 23 stomachs and amounting to 17.48 per cent of the total food; dogwood (Cornus), identified in 63 stomachs, 13.77 per cent; mountain-ash (Sorbus), taken from 13 stomachs, 3.82 per cent; and snowberry (Symphoricarpos) in 11 stomachs forming 1.77 per cent of the food of the 88 birds. Of the winged seeds, ash seed (Fraxinus) were found in 4; maple (Acer) in 30; and box elder (Acer negundo) in

13 stomachs. Juniper berries had been eaten by 14 birds, and seeds of other conifers by 13.

The nature of the contents of certain stomachs of this species gives a vivid idea of the shearing or crushing power of the beak. The seeds of cherries were broken easily and a whole one was rarely found. The flattened seeds of the snowberry were split longitudinally in nearly every case.

The food for the summer season, as determined by an examination of 39 stomachs, is 20.82 per cent animal and 79.18 per cent vegetable matter.

The vegetable food was of much the same character as that taken during the winter season. Seeds of wild fruits are 37.87 per cent of the food for the summer compared with 39.63 per cent during the winter. The greatest difference is in the relative quantities of winged seeds and those of conifers. The percentage of the latter rises from 14.5 per cent during the winter to 28.45 per cent in summer, while in the case of winged seeds the amount falls from 37.96 per cent in winter to 2.79 per cent in summer. * * * Weed seed and rubbish complete the vegetable food.

Beetles and caterpillars are the chief animal food, although small wasps and ants (Hymenoptera), bugs (Hemiptera), and spiders were also eaten. Among the beetles were found a few of the useful predacious ground beetles (Carabidae), which, however, amounted to less than 1 per cent of the food. Similar small quantities of weevils and click-beetles, both harmful forms, had been taken. The bulk of the beetles eaten was of the leaf-eating scarabaeid genus *Dichelonycha*, which feeds on pine, willow, hickory, and other trees and shrubs. One bird had taken 41 of these beetles and another 10. Caterpillars to the extent of 11.49 per cent of the total food had been devoured; and as caterpillars with few exceptions may be classed as harmful, this is to be counted in the bird's favor.

The only reference I have to possible salt-eating in this race is a letter from Gardner D. Stout, who writes:

"On July 16, 1965 I was driving in western Colorado near Meeker at about 9,000 feet altitude just about daybreak. The road was cut through a series of five rolling clay ridges, and the banks of each cut rose almost vertically beside the road. Clinging to the bank faces in each cut were roughly 150 Evening Grosbeaks apparently picking at the clay and eating it. Unfortunately I was unable to climb up to see whether or not these clay banks contained any salt, but there was no seepage from them."

Behavior.—H. Brandt (1951) gives a clear picture of its method of flying: "The flight is direct and rapid with pinions fully extended, and accompanied by constant rapid wing-beats. The white patch on the wings then produce [sic] a continuous variegated flash of signs that distinguishes this bird from others. Sometimes a whole flock of considerable size will take wing as though by a single impulse; or depart in single file."

In watching a large flock at Santa Fe, Brandt comments about their docility: "Never did I see a bird make a single hostile move toward another." Charles W. Michael tells a very different story. He writes from Yosemite (MS.): "One spring morning I happened to witness an interesting show with evening grosbeaks as the actors of the drama. A pair of these birds came winging over the meadow. At the edge of the meadow the birds came to perch in the branches of a great Kellogg oak. No sooner had the pair settled than the female was accosted by a second male who was already in the tree. The female was loyal to her escort and spurned the overtures of the fresh male. The escort showed fierce resentment toward his rival and the two males tangled on the spot. They clinched bill to bill and a rough and tumble fight was on.

"As they wrestled, shoved, and tugged they often lost their balance and tumbled down a few feet before gaining fresh foothold on some lower branch. They pulled no feathers nor did they scratch, but they held like fury bill to bill. In their fierce tussle they finally fell free of the lowest branch and came tumbling through the air like a spinning pin-wheel. A thump on the ground failed to loosen the grip and they rolled over and over, first one on top and then the other. This struggle on the ground lasted 2 minutes by the watch and then the birds separated and took to wing as though not in the least bit winded by the long battle. Pursued and pursuer disappeared through the treetops and it was not determined which had been the victor, the escort or the interloper. In any event the female * * * seemed quite willing to await the return of the victorious one whoever he might be."

Voice.—Herbert Brandt (1951), listening to a large flock when it was feeding, writes with appreciation of this grosbeak's voice: "All the while when feeding it keeps up an uninterrupted flock chatter of a mellow nature, a variety of notes just as though the members of the group were in conversation, which perhaps they are. In that case they are full of gossip, but of the pleasant kind, for not once was there any indication of a fighting spirit. * * * The notes have wide variety and intonation, are rather subdued, and without any harsh quality."

While listening to a pair in the Bridger Range of the Galatin National Forest, Mont., in 1953, we heard some sweet notes, but these were the quietest. Loud cheeps were given with *churr* notes following, and a number of really harsh *churr-churr* notes were heard, as well as the far-carrying call *p-teer* which rang across the valley.

Enemies.—Occasionally the evening grosbeak is a link in the predator–prey food chain. J. A. Munro (1929) reports seeing an adult goshawk carrying an evening grosbeak. "Instances of goshawks attacking the smaller bird species," he writes, "are comparatively rare in the writer's experience."

J. T. Marshall, Jr. (1942), in a list of animals eaten by the spotted owl (*Strix occidentalis*) based on stomach contents, includes one evening grosbeak. Maj. Allan Brooks wrote to me in 1942: "I once

ook one from the stomach of a horned owl in August." In the
ame letter he tells of a northern shrike attacking an evening grosbeak
ear his home in British Columbia:

> Once in very cold weather with 14 inches of snow on the ground I saw a fine
> dult n. shrike chase a ♂ ad. evening grosbeak and pounce on him as he took
> over almost at my feet. I expected to see a good fight as this grosbeak has a
> owerful bite as I well know (it can crack cherry stones). But there was no
> ght: the shrike killed him with one quick nip and carried his prey right away in
> s claws, not in its bill. I followed up as quick as I could get a gun but the snow
> 'as unmarked for 100 yards and the shrike must have carried its prey into some
> hick thorn bushes beyond that. There would be very little difference in their
> espective weights.

G. J. Spencer (1948) reports that a louse, *Philopterus subflavescens*
Geoffrey was taken from one of these birds in British Columbia.
The bird-fly, *Ornithomyia fringillina* Curtis, was taken from two
rosbeaks in the same province, one at Lytton and one at Okanagan
Landing (Bequaert, 1954). A liver fluke, *Olssoniella chivosca* n. sp.
vas reported by I. Pratt and C. Cutress (1949): "Western evening
grosbeaks collected during the spring migrations of 1947 and 1948
n Corvallis, Oregon, were found to be heavily infected with a trem-
atode inhabiting the bile passages of the liver." However, most
vening grosbeaks are remarkably free from external or internal
arasites.

Fall.—Otto McCreary (1939) tells us that the evening grosbeak has
een observed in the State of Wyoming during all seasons. They
re "most numerous at Green River (Dorothy Waltman) and at
Laramie during the months of May, June, October, and November,
ndicating migration at this season of the year." He wrote me that
he earliest fall record in the Laramie Mountains was October 8.
The species usually arrives at Laramie during the last week of October
nd departs early in November, but some years it remains throughout
he winter and into May, as in 1939.

R. L. Hand has written me about autumn concentrations of evening
grosbeaks in Idaho: "In the fall I recall days in the 1920's when they
vere present along the Lochsa River for miles, literally by the thou-
ands though never in compact flocks of more than 40 or 50 birds
ogether. At no time have I seen them in such abundance since."

On Sept. 9, 1924, Ira N. Gabrielson (1926) saw another impressive concentration while driving up Beech Creek canyon
(which enters the John Day valley at Mount Vernon, Oreg.). Blue
ays, magpies, robins, evening grosbeaks, and towhees were feeding
n wild cherries. "Robins and Evening Grosbeaks far outnum-
ered all the rest," he writes, "literally thousands of both species
eing present."

M. D. F. Udvardy observed a spectacular migration at Point Roberts, Wash., on Oct. 15, 1954. He wrote us that he saw 751 evening grosbeaks during the 4 morning hours.

Winter.—J. K. Jensen (1924) tells of a large winter invasion from the north:

> The winter of 1922–23 will go down in the annals of New Mexico as the year of many Grosbeaks * * *. Grosbeaks may be seen occasionally every year; as a rule only for a few days during spring and fall, and only few in number. During the winter mentioned above great flocks were in evidence from October 30, 1922 until May 1, 1923 * * *.
>
> At the United States Indian School, where most of my observations were made, we had flocks almost continually of from fifty to three hundred birds. In Santa Fe proper there were several flocks of from one hundred to five hundred, while smaller flocks of from four to a dozen birds could be seen at any time in almost every shade tree.

H. Brandt has written more recently (1951) of seeing a large flock in Santa Fe, N. Mex. He explains:

> The downtown public grounds and certain streets are well wooded with medium to large sized trees of the boxelder, or as is often called, ash-leafed maple. * * * This place is the usual winter resort of several thousand Rocky Mountain Evening Grosbeaks, which live in gregarious familiarity with themselves and the fortunate people of the town. So closely do they crowd together that I counted 16 birds on a single, small branch, literally enlivening it with slow-moving beauty, while 28 fed in perfect harmony in the grass near by, on an area less than 10 feet square. * * * When it leaves for its highland breeding grounds all the individuals depart together, so that Santa Fe is left without a single example of this rare bird to show its summer visitors. Then in 10 to 12 weeks it returns in force with its young, and again spends some 40 weeks or more as a feathered visitor in this ancient city of tourists.

DISTRIBUTION

Range.—British Columbia and western Montana to southern California and western Texas.

Breeding range.—The western evening grosbeak breeds, and is largely resident, from north central and southeastern British Columbia (Bear Lake, Monashee Pass, Jasper), western Montana (Bozeman), western Wyoming, and central Colorado (Elk Head Mountains, Colorado Springs) south through the mountains to northwestern and central eastern California (Eureka, Sequoia National Park), northeastern Nevada (Tahoe district, Tuxcarora), central Arizona (San Francisco and White Mountains), and central southern New Mexico (Sacramento Mountains).

Winter range.—Winters from southern interior and southwestern British Columbia (Comox, Chilliwack) south to southern California (Redlands, Cuyamaca Mountains), southern Arizona (Baboquivari Mountains, Tucson), southwestern New Mexico (Silver City), and western Texas (Guadalupe Mountains, Kerr County); east to South Dakota (Deadwood) and Oklahoma (Caddo County).

Casual record.—Casual in Virginia (Alexandria).

Egg dates.—California: 22 records, June 8 to July 30; 12 records, July 1 to July 12.

Colorado: 2 records, July 4 and July 10.

New Mexico: 2 records, June 22 and June 26.

Utah: 4 records, May 27 to June 15.

HESPERIPHONA VESPERTINA MONTANA Ridgway

Mexican Evening Grosbeak

Contributed by DORIS HUESTIS SPEIRS

HABITS

This colorful bird may be found from the Santa Catalina, Chirica-hua, and Huachuca Mountains of Pima and Cochise counties, south-eastern Arizona, southward in the mountains as far as the highlands of southern Mexico.

In describing some of the "birding" highlights of the Huachucas, Roger Tory Peterson (1948) writes:

What mountains these are! Where else can one follow a coppery-tailed trogon as it intones its deep *cowm cowm cowm cowm* among the oaks and syca-mores of a hot canyon, and an hour or two later see evening grosbeaks in the firs at a higher altitude? * * *

The grosbeak * * * is the same plump yellow bird with the big pale bill that one sees in the fir forests of Canada or on New England feeding trays in winter, a different race, perhaps—they call it the Mexican evening grosbeak—but to all appearances the same bird. There must be a point in the canyon, I suppose, where the oaks give way to the pines and where it is possible for a gros-beak to look upon a trogon.

Joe T. Marshall, Jr., writes me of the grosbeaks in Mexico: "It is always a pleasure to find them, particularly in the nearby mountains of Sonora and extreme northwestern Chihuahua." There he was surprised to find none of the Mexican species, the Abeillé (or hooded) grosbeak, *H. abeillei*, but only the evening grosbeak, "which becomes quite abundant in the higher parts of the Sierra Madre, and the Sierra Huachinera of Sonora." R. H. Palmer (1923) who saw the bird in a deep barranca in the state of Hidalgo, in commenting on the brightness of the plumage, says "the yellow was much brighter than I have seen in the birds of the North." The original description of this subspecies (Baird, Brewer, and Ridgway, 1874a) reads in part: "Yellow frontal crescent narrow, less than half as wide as the black behind it; inner webs of the tertials without any black; secondaries and inner webs of tail-feathers without white tips. * * * In size it is also a little smaller."

As its name indicates, this is a bird of the mountains, of the mountains of Mexico and ranging as far north as southern Arizona. The habitat it seeks in its American home is pine and fir forest. If any migration occurs from the Mexican populations of the Sierra Madre Occidental northward into Arizona, we have as yet no records to prove it.

Spring.—Roger Tory Peterson writes of his journey from Mexico to the Chiricahua Mountains (1955):

Before us on the horizon, as we crossed the Arizona line, rose the big blue Chiricahuas * * *. There they were, in the crystal morning light, rising like a massive blue island from the sea of the desert. And an island it was, in truth part of an archipelago composed of a dozen similar ranges. * * *

And, like islands, their climate, plants, their animals are as different from those of their surroundings as though they were isolated by the sea * * *.

A modest sign on the highway pointed the way to Portal, eight miles up on a gravel road that crossed the outwash plain. This frontier hamlet, well named, stood at the entrance of Cave Canyon, a dramatic canyon guarded by unscalable cliffs of heroic size * * *.

Portal is about 5,000 feet above sea level. It was here that H. H. Kimball found this grosbeak on the last day of March in the spring of 1926 (collection of Max Minor Peet). Allan Brooks came upon the bird at 9,000 feet, far above the little mining town of Paradise, on Apr. 25, 1913. In the same general locality but at an altitude of 5,000 feet, Austin Paul Smith found it April 26, 1917. Kimball also collected the bird in the Paradise region, although far above the town, in April 1924, in the area in which he collected adults in the summer of the same year.

In the Huachucas E. C. Jacot collected the bird in April 1922. Brandt (1951) has written of being in these mountains in early May. Among the big pines he saw a flock of Mexican crossbills and then discovered another bird identified by its showy, yellow pattern as "the Mexican Evening Grosbeak, another of those unpredictable forms from south of the border that are known to display themselves occasionally in these fruitful Arizona mountains. * * * The adult male is indeed a gorgeous creature and in collections is one of the rarest of our grosbeaks."

In the Santa Catalina Mountains Monson (1952b) found up to 15 birds on February 29 and again on March 25. In March of the same year J. A. Munro found evening grosbeaks at Bear Canyon at an altitude of 6,200 feet and took one pair whose clear dark "Nile green" bills indicated that they were coming into breeding condition.

Nesting.—In May 1904, F. C. Willard journeyed to the Santa Catalina Mountains with O. W. Howard. It had been an unusually dry winter and spring, and Willard (1910) writes:

While spending a couple of days here among the pines at the summit, we found the flocks of grosbeaks making their rendezvous at Bear Wallow Spring, the only spring in the vicinity which had not gone dry. Ruby-crowned Kinglets were also present in considerable numbers, tho more often heard than seen.

The Kinglets seemed to be nesting and while looking for them we saw a pair of Grosbeaks fighting a Long-crested Jay which they presently drove away. The female Grosbeak promptly disappeared in the top of an immense fir tree where Howard's sharp eyes soon located the nest. We collected the set of well incubated eggs the day following. The nest was eighty-six feet from the ground and twenty feet out from the trunk of the tree, near the tip of a horizontal branch.

Willard comments: "This was my first experience with one of our rarest birds * * *."

On July 1 of that same year, O. W. Howard found a nest with three eggs in an outer fork of a pine tree at 9,000 feet. In these same mountains on June 1, 1937, C. L. and P. H. Field collected a nest of twigs, lined with moss, also containing three eggs, at the end of a 12-foot limb in a pine tree about 50 feet from the ground. J. B. Hurley, whose collection contains the set, writes me: "The bird sat very tight and almost had to be pushed off the nest. The eggs had been incubated about a week."

Mr. Bent (MS.) writes: "We found the Mexican evening grosbeak fairly common in the coniferous forests of the Huachuca Mountains, Ariz., at elevations from 7,000 to 8,000 feet; they were very restless, often making long flights; we spent some time following them about, but did not succeed in finding a nest. After I had left for home, my companion, F. C. Willard, collected a set of three heavily incubated eggs on June 5, 1922." Willard (1910) published the account of another find:

On May 30 [1908] while returning from a long tramp on the west slope of the mountains, I heard the unmistakable note of a Hesperiphona and saw a pair fly into a large pine tree which stood by itself in the bed of the canyon. They soon flew down into the brush, to the ground, and then back to the pine, the male following the female. I watched them make several trips and was then compelled to leave them and hurry on toward my distant camp. They were building, the female carrying all the nesting material. I made a note to return for the set in ten days. * * *

On June 11 Willard returned, and found the nest "well concealed among the thick branches of needles at the tip of a branch fifty-five feet up. It was twenty feet out from the trunk and the female would not leave, tho I jarred the nest a good deal in roping the branch up to make the nest accessible. She did not leave until I almost touched her. The position of the nest was such that I could not photograph it. It was composed of twigs on the outside, then grass and rootlets with finer material for a lining."

Eggs.—Willard (1910) writes of the eggs of the Mexican evening grosbeak: "The eggs are strikingly similar to those of the Redwinged

Blackbird. Three or four eggs seem to constitute the normal clutch."

The measurements of 27 eggs average 23.3 by 16.8 millimeters; the eggs showing the four extremes measure *24.8* by 17.0, 23.9 by *18.0*, *21.3* by 16.0, and 21.9 by *15.8* millimeters.

Incubation.—Incubation is performed by the female and she is a very close sitter. The period is probably 12 to 14 days as in *H. v. vespertina.*

Young.—The young seem similar in every way to those of other races of this species. F. M. Chapman (1897) collected a young male but a few days from the nest, April 21. Because of the early date he concluded that the species bred there early in March.

H. H. Kimball found a number of juvenals with their parents in the Paradise region of the Chiricahua Mountains, Ariz., from about the middle of July. Young were taken from July 13 to 24, 1918, and from July 10 to 23 in 1919 (collections of M. M. Peet and the Chicago Nat. Hist. Mus.).

H. S. Swarth (1904) tells us that in the Huachucas in the vicinity of Miller Canyon "on July 30, 1902, I came upon half a dozen birds scattered through the pines at an altitude of about 9000 feet. An old male was observed feeding a fully fledged young * * *."

Food.—"When busy feeding, the birds are rather quiet," writes Willard (1910). "They walk along the branches from cone to cone and extract seeds which seem to form the major portion of their bill-of-fare."

W. E. D. Scott (1885) saw them "feeding on small cones in a spruce tree" in the Santa Catalinas. Brandt (1951) published a report of their fondness for apple seeds, and Wesley E. Lanyon (in litt.) found them in hackberry trees.

Allan R. Phillips has written me of a flock he found "at the lower edge of the ponderosa pines in the Santa Catalina Mts.—a point where one seldom sees them * * *. The crops (Feb. 29) were full of lenticular seeds, perhaps *Acer grandidentatum*, which as I now recall they were gathering under some walnuts."

Behavior.—The Mexican evening grosbeaks in the Canadian Zone of the Chiricahua Mountains of Arizona behave very much as do their eastern relatives in the highlands of Ontario. Both live largely an arboreal life, and many of their bird associates are similar. In summer both fly down from the trees to the little springs for water. When in the Chiricahuas in June, Peterson (1955) gives a clear picture of the bird in its environment. He tells us:

After we had zigzagged for miles up the rugged mountain flanks to the camp ground at Rustler Park we found ourselves at the edge of the Canadian Zone. Here on the cool north slopes pines gave way to Douglas fir and we were not too surprised when an evening grosbeak flew up from a spring where it had been drinking. Here also were crossbills, pine siskins, and red-breasted nuthatches, all birds of the northwood country, Canadian birds isolated on this sky island. We saw the first robins we had encountered in weeks and the first creepers since we left the eastern mountains."

W. E. D. Scott (1885) describes the grosbeaks as "not at all shy," while H. S. Swarth (1904) found them "very wild."

Voice.—Willard (1910) in watching a pair engaged in nest-building has this to say about their notes: "The male followed her all the time and 'talkt' to her. When percht he used the loud call note, a single very loud staccato note which I am unable to describe. When in flight the soft note was used. Reduced to syllables it sounded like 'Chéwey, chéwey, chéwey' with the accent on the first syllable."

Enemies.—H. Brandt (1951) tells us: "Old Jim Tomlinson lived alone in the last cabin up Miller Canyon in the Huachuca Mountains. He stated that he liked the Cooper Hawk very much, because it kept birds away from his fruit trees, especially the Mexican Evening Grosbeaks, which liked to pick the seeds out of apples growing in his small canyon orchard." So it is all in the point of view!

Two evening grosbeaks from the Chiricahua Mountains, Ariz., were found to be infected by the blood parasites *Typanosoma* and *Leucocytozoon* (S. F. Wood and C. M. Herman, 1943). One of the two birds harbored microfilarial worms.

Fall.—Two evening grosbeaks collected by Harter in the White Mountains, Apache County, Ariz., on July 21, 1933 (L. M. Huey, 1936a.) proved to represent two races, *H. v. brooksi* and *H. v. montana.* "When dissected neither bird was found to be in breeding condition. As both were in the midst of molting, it would indicate that their nesting period had passed and that they were migrating in search of a better food supply." The discovery of a Mexican evening grosbeak north of its breeding range suggests a postbreeding movement northward, noticeable in a number of species. On the other hand Swarth found the species in the Huachucas on July 30 (collection California Acad. Sci.) and, as mentioned above, Kimball found parents with their families in the Chiricahuas in late July. A male was found in the latter mountains on September 28 (Peet collection).

Winter.—W. E. D. Scott (1885) made "a four days' visit to the highest point of Los Sierras de Santa Catalina" from November 26 to 29, 1884. "The region is a dense pine and spruce forest, with here and there a sprinkling of poplars and sycamores, and a few evergreen oaks * * * It was real winter at this altitude—a little over 10,000 feet—with from two to six inches of snow on the ground." Here he found, besides Cassin's finch and two kinds of juncos, four evening grosbeaks feeding on the spruce cones.

The species was present at Portal in December 1925, and Kimball took a pair near Paradise on February 20 of the same year (Peet collection). Grosbeaks have been seen quite frequently in the Santa Catalinas during the Christmas bird counts. W. E. Lanyon wrote me of finding a flock of about a dozen on Jan. 22, 1956, at El Sabino Ranch. "This ranch is within the mesquite and saguaro association at the southern base of the Santa Catalina Mountains, about 3,000 feet. There were enough hackberry trees on the ranch to make it attractive to them, apparently. I had occasion to return on January 29 and the grosbeaks were still there."

DISTRIBUTION

Range.—The Mexican evening grosbeak is resident from southeastern Arizona (Santa Catalina Mountains, Chiricahua Mountains) south through Sierra Madre Occidental and the mountains of southeastern Mexico to Michoacan (Uruapan), Hidalgo (Tlanchinol), and Oaxaca (Cerro San Felipe). Recorded in spring and fall in western New Mexico (Reserve) and in winter in north central New Mexico (Caja del Rio).

Egg dates.—Southeastern Arizona: 10 records, May 16 to July 1; 5 records, June 1 to June 11.

Mexico: Chihuahua: 1 record, June 23.

PYRRHULA PYRRHULA CASSINII Baird
Cassin's Bullfinch
Contributed by OLIVER L. AUSTIN, JR.

HABITS

Cassin's bullfinch has the distinction of being the only Asiatic bird first known to science from North America. Its habitat is northeastern Siberia, but its type locality is Nulato Island, Alaska, where William Healy Dall collected the single specimen on which Professor Baird based his original description of the form (1869). According to Dall and Bannister's account (1869) of the capture of this historic specimen on Jan. 10, 1867:

"An Indian brought in a bullfinch alive, but badly wounded, which he had shot from a small tree near the fort. He had never seen anything like it before, nor had the Russians. On showing it to Captain Everett Smith, some time afterward, he said he had seen several flocks of the same species near Ulukuk. This specimen was a male, with black eyes, bill, and feet. It was the only bird of the kind that I saw during two years."

Ludwig Kumlein (1879) believed he saw a bullfinch in Cumberland Sound July 19, 1879, but he was unable to collect it for verification. Hence the occurrence of the species in North America was based solely on Dall's type specimen until October 1927, when Cyril Guy Harrold, collecting for the California Academy of Sciences, encountered four bullfinches, of which he was able to collect three, on Nunivak Island in the Bering Sea off Alaska. This discovery led Swarth (1934) to suggest: "The number of individuals observed takes the species out of the 'accidental visitant' category, and it will probably be found to be of fairly regular occurrence in Alaska at certain seasons and at favored localities." As the bird life of northwestern Alaska and the islands in the Bering Sea still has not been investigated as intensively as one might wish, Swarth's hypothesis is plausible, especially as the bird is a strong flier, and breeds fairly close by in Kamchatka and possibly in the Anadyr region. But only one more Alaskan specimen has been taken since then, an "unsexed bird, adult male by plumage," collected on St. Lawrence Island in May 1936 by an Eskimo collector, Paul Silook, who Friedmann (1937) reports "recognized it as a new bird in his experience as he wrote on the label '* * * unusual kind and killed very first time. * * * ' " Hence, although Alaska is its type locality, inasmuch as it has been taken only three times within Check-List territory, Cassin's bullfinch must still be regarded from the available evidence as a straggler in North America.

Bullfinches imported from Europe have been released frequently in North America but have never become established here. According to Phillips (1928):

"The European bullfinch has doubtless been liberated in many places and at many different times—certainly at Cincinnati early in the [eighteen] seventies and at Portland, Oregon, in 1889–1892 (at least 20 pairs), as well as in California, in 1891. There is no evidence of any attempt on the part of the birds to establish themselves."

The bullfinches are a distinct and well-marked genus of palearctic fringillids, of which the northernmost representative, *Pyrrhula pyrrhula*, breeding across northern Europe and Asia from the British Isles to Kamchatka, is the most widely distributed and the best known. The species is comparatively plastic, and seems to be in the process of rather rapid revolutionary development, especially in eastern Asia, where the status of its various recognized forms is still somewhat in doubt. In fact the identity of *P. p. cassinii* was uncertain until comparatively recently.

When it became apparent that no bullfinches occur regularly in Alaska or the contiguous islands in the Bering Sea, subsequent revisers of the group were faced with the problem of assigning Baird's prior name to one of the Asiatic races. The problem was complicated by the absence of adequate material for comparison, and by the fact that Baird's description of *cassinii*, based supposedly on a male specimen, called for a grayish bird with no red on the underparts. (The species exhibits considerable, though racially variable, sexual dimorphism, the males of most subspecies having reddish underparts which the females lack.) Stejneger (*in* Turner, 1886) was the first to realize that the type specimen was improperly sexed and was doubtless an immature female, but he assigned the name (1887) nevertheless to the grayest of the known bullfinch races, a south-central Siberian form in which the male shows no red or pink whatever, and which is now known correctly as *P. p. cineracea*.

The great English systematist, R. B. Sharpe (1888), suspected the correct identity of Baird's type, and suggested that it might be found identical with the nearest race geographically, then known as *kamtschatica*, the male of which is one of the reddest and handsomest of all the bullfinches. But Stejneger's arguments prevailed, and the name *cassinii* remained misapplied to the more distant bird until Harrold collected the Nunivak specimens. When Swarth (1928) compared these with the type of *cassinii*, and with additional Kamchatkan material and specimens from south-central Siberia, he was able to determine beyond question that Baird's name is applicable indeed to the Kamchatkan race, as Professor Sharpe had predicted 40 years earlier, and which is only logical on the basis of geographical proximity.

Probably less is known at first hand of the life history of Cassin's bullfinch than of any other form covered by this series. The available literature is singularly lacking in authoritative observations on its habits, behavior, and actions in the field. Its normal habitat has been visited by very few ornithologists, and none of these has had opportunity to do more than collect a few specimens. The few stragglers taken beyond the periphery of its usual range have added little to our knowledge of this interesting bird.

Hence we can only build an approximate picture of its life history by borrowing information on its various aspects from our knowledge of its better-known relatives. This is an unsatisfactory and unscientific procedure at best, and a particularly inexact one in so plastic, variable, and unsettled a group as the bullfinches. Closely allied subspecies vary but little in their general behavior, but minor distinctions in voice and habits have been noted between some races by keen observers. Such differences are probably heritable, and as such can be just as diagnostic of subspecies as the color and size characters by which they are distinguished. It must be realized, therefor, that observations on the habits of *P. p. pyrrhula*, *nesa*, *griseiventris*, and *rosacea*, the best-known races, while perhaps typical in a broad general sense for the species, are not necessarily authoritative for *cassinii*, and probably not exact in all details.

Courtship.—The breeding habits of Cassin's bullfinch are unknown. In fact there is very little available on the nesting of any of the Asiatic bullfinches. The display and posturing of the British subspecies, *P. p. nesa* are described by Jourdain and Tucker in Witherby's "Handbook of British Birds" (1938) as follows:

"Displaying male faces female, puffing out breast so as to display crimson feathers, while twisting and bowing tail from side to side (J. Weir). O. G. Pike describes both sexes drooping wings and spreading and vibrating tail."

Nesting.—Nothing is known of the nesting of Cassin's bullfinch. Its nest and eggs have never been collected. Jourdain (Witherby, 1938) notes that the European bullfinch, *P. p. pyrrhula* nests frequently in conifers, but that *nesa* breeds in England "in gardens, thick hedges, clumps of evergreens (especially box), also yews, and in plantations." Kiyosu (1943) states that the nests of the Japanese *griseiventris* are found "in the evergreen woods of the sub-alpine zone, in such trees as Veitch's silver fir and the Japanese hemlock, from 2000 to 2500 meters above sea level. Usually the nests are found on branches about 1 to 2.7 meters above the ground. The nest is built of dried twigs, dead runners, *Usnea* spp., and other mosses into a bowl-like shape, and lined with weed roots, hair, or feathers." The nest of the British bullfinch, according to Jourdain (*in* Witherby, 1938) is "usually about four to seven feet from ground, built of fine twigs and some moss or lichens, lined with thick layer of interlacing fine roots nearly always *black*. Sometimes extremely slightly, at others very stoutly, constructed." The same authority notes that the nest of *P. p. pyrrhula* is similar, "but slightly larger, and in Scandinavia often lined with hairy lichen (*Usnea barbata*)," which probably most nearly approximates the nest of *cassinii*.

Other bullfinch races are known to rear two broods annually, and possibly *cassinii* does likewise, for its first nesting is evidently quite early, probably starting in late April or early May. Taczanowski (1891) reports that Dybowski encountered in early July young "which had left the nest quite some days previously" and Bergman states (1935): "The Bullfinch breeds very early in Kamchatka, and as early as 14 June I collected a flying juvenal near Klutschi."

Eggs.—Considerable variation has been noted in the eggs of bullfinches. *P. p. griseiventris* (Kiyosu, 1943) lays four to six eggs, which are "roundish, 19–21 mm × 14.5–16.5 mm, averaging 20 × 16 mm in size, and 22–25 gr. in weight." The British form, says Jourdain (*in* Witherby, 1938) lays "usually 4–5, occasionally 6 or even 7; clear green-blue with few spots and a streak or two of extremely dark purple-brown, generally tending to form zone at big end. Varieties with reddish marking on white ground occur. Average of 100 British eggs, 19.54 × 14.49. Max.: 22.1 × 13.6 and 20.2 × 15.6. Min.: 17.2 × 13 mm." The European *pyrrhula* on the other hand lays "usually 5 or 6, occasionally only 4, clear greenish-blue in ground-color when fresh, with few spots and streaks of very dark purplish-brown. Average of 65 eggs (24 by Rey etc.), 20.42 × 14.69. Max.: 23.2 × 14.8 and 21 × 16. Min.: 18 × 14.4 and 19.2 × 14 mm."

Incubation.—In the Japanese bullfinch according to Kiyosu (1943) "the eggs are incubated only by the female, who is fed on the nest by the male. The eggs require 12–14 days brooding to hatch * * *." This agrees in general with accounts of other races, where the incubation period is given loosely as a fortnight or 2 weeks.

Young.—All accounts state that the nesting bullfinches of all races are fed by regurgitation by both parents and leave the nest 12 to 16 days after hatching.

Plumages.—Kiyosu (1943) states of *griseiventris*, "Immediately after hatching the chicks are bare, and very long primary dark grey down is seen above the eyes, hind head, upper arm, back, forearm, thigh, belly, and legs. The inner mouth is pink, the edges of the bill light yellow."

Food.—Again, nothing is known directly of the food habits of Cassin's bullfinch, but there is no reason they should vary materially from those of *P. p. pyrrhula*, which are given by Jourdain (*in* Witherby, 1938) as "mainly seeds of trees (alder, birch, and conifers), also kernels of berries, plant seeds and buds, but also some insect food, including larvae of larch moths, etc. (C. Loos)."

Behavior.—The only account of the behavior of Cassin's bullfinch ever written is Bergman's short description (1935) of his experiences with it in Kamchatka:

"The bullfinch is distributed sparsely over the birch, fir, and larch forests in Kamchatka. Nowhere is it abundant. In summer it lives very quietly and retiringly. Its habits do not seem to differ from those of the Swedish bullfinch, and its whistle was, so far as I could determine, identical to the Swedish. * * * In autumn and winter the bullfinch becomes more conspicuous, and I found it often on my ski and sled trips. It never occurs in large flocks, but habitually separate or a few together."

Its habits probably do not vary essentially from those of the Japanese bullfinch, which Kiyosu (1943) states "stays in pairs in summer and gathers in small flocks in fall and winter. They stay chiefly in trees, and come down to the ground seldom except for water to drink or to bathe in. They move on the ground by hopping, and their flight is undulating."

Voice.—The species has no proper "song" in the technical sense of the word, though both sexes have a "subsong" which Tucker (*in* Witherby, 1938) describes for the British race as "a low, broken, piping warble of poor and creaky quality, interspersed with rather louder notes; apparently also a more sustained and melodious piping." The familiar and distinctive "song" of the bullfinch is actually its call note, uttered in flight as well as when at rest, and throughout the year. It is a sweet, soft, flutey whistle, variously syllabized as "deu" or "phee," pleasing to the ear, and with considerable carrying power. The clear, single note is held on a steady monotone and is easily imitated. Birds in the wild will often answer a similar human whistle, and can sometimes be induced to raise or lower their pitch.

The quality of the call note varies somewhat between the races. Tucker (*in* Witherby, 1938) describes the note of the European bullfinch as "louder * * *, also decidedly harsher * * *, richer and lower * * *" than that of the smaller British subspecies. K. Wada (1933) considered the voice of a captive *cassinii* he saw in Aomori, northern Honshu, to be "fuller and nicer" than that of the Japanese bullfinch.

Field marks.—The northern bullfinches are medium-sized, grayish finches, with fairly long tails and markedly short, rounded bills. They have black crests and wings, and a white rump patch which is conspicuous in flight. The rosy breast of the male *cassinii* must be very striking in the field.

Captivity.—The bullfinch is a common cage bird both in Europe and the Orient, prized for its beauty and gentleness, but mainly for its sweet call note, for which purpose the female is as satisfactory as the male. It is an extremely popular cage bird in Japan, and in the little wooden cages that hang so commonly in front of the houses in country villages, bullfinches frequently outnumber all other species Yamashina (1933) states:

"It is one of the most common cage birds. Anyone who has ever become acquainted with its lovely features, gentle movements, and clear and variable song will wish to have it in a cage. It is an ideal cage bird from every standpoint, for it is hardy and easy to keep healthy. Seeds of Deccan grass and millet suffice as a basic diet, with greens added occasionally. It must be given water for bathing frequently, and allowed room to exercise, otherwise it is apt to get too fat. * * * It can be bred in captivity without difficulty, and it has often been hybridized with the canary and other birds."

Prince Taka-Tsukasa, one of the leading and most skillful aviculturists in Japan, adds the following comments (1928):

It is not long-lived in captivity, but it is hardy, and I have kept some individuals for several years, and bred them successfully in cages with other species * * * .

In Europe too its voice is admired, and it is kept commonly in cages, especially in Germany, where it is trained to kiss its master, and to do other tricks at his order. Some birds are taught to whistle such tunes as "God Save the King," "Yankee Doodle," or "The Star Spangled Banner," and command high prices. To teach them such songs, a very young bird is selected, separated from others so it cannot hear their notes, and the master teaches it part of the melody with a silver pipe or his own whistling. When the bird becomes proficient in this, it is taught the next part, and finally the entire song. The lesson is given in the calm and quiet of early morning, and when the bird has done well, it is rewarded with a bit of hemp seed. Then it is fed well for an hour or two, after which it is left without food until the next morning's lesson.

Enemies.—As with most other fringillids, bullfinches are captured in large numbers in Japan, especially during the autumn migration in October and November. Despite the fact they are found most commonly in the highlands, and seldom in the cultivated lowlands, they are regarded as economically undesirable to the agriculturist. Yamashina (1933) states: "Though it is valuable for eating noxious insects in summer, its beneficial attributes do not exceed the harm done in the spring to buds and sprouts of trees, especially the cherry tree. In Honshu its harmfulness is especially marked in the northern parts where the species is abundant in spring."

The Japanese netted it primarily for food, and most of those taken in the "toyabas" (cf. Austin, 1947) were killed for market and sold in strings of 10 birds each, their heads stuck through twists of rice-straw rope. The netters kept young birds to condition for decoys, and reserved a few for sale as cage birds. *P. p. rosacea* bore the brunt of the market netting in Japan on migration, but some *griseiventris* were taken, and occasionally in the north a few large, deeply red-breasted males appeared which were probably *cassinii*, highly prized by connoisseurs for their beauty.

The following Ministry of Agriculture and Forestry figures on the annual catch of bullfinches by netters in Japan do not differentiate between the races, but are of interest in showing the annual variation in the species' winter movements:

Year	No. birds	Year	No. birds	Year	No. birds
1924	39, 356	1931	30, 566	1938	56, 304
1925	9, 316	1932	53, 855	1939	58, 437
1926	70, 134	1933	49, 242	1940	67, 403
1927	50, 768	1934	15, 164	1941	41, 654
1928	32, 916	1935	112, 416	1942	74, 693
1929	51, 888	1936	41, 342		
1930	40, 635	1937	61, 576		

DISTRIBUTION

Range.—Cassin's bullfinch is resident in Kamchatka.

Casual records.—Casual in fall and winter in the Komandorskie Islands, Korea (Hamgyong Puktu), Japan (Honshu), northeastern China (northern Hopei), and Sakhalin Island.

Accidental in Alaska (St. Lawrence Island, Nunivak Island, Nulato).

CARPODACUS PURPUREUS NESOPHILUS Burleigh and Peters

Newfoundland Purple Finch

Contributed by CHARLES H. BLAKE

HABITS

In their description of this subspecies Burleigh and Peters (1948) distinguish it from the eastern race as follows: "upperparts in both sexes decidedly darker. Pileum of adult males deep maroon purple, in contrast to the deep wine purple of *purpureus*. Underparts duller and lacking the pinkish tinge of the nominate race. Females and subadult males less olive above, with the whitish streaks of the back broader and more numerous. In size, both sexes average slightly larger than *purpureus*."

Whether these distinctions are sufficient for the recognition of the subspecies is questionable. Further discussion will be found in Blake (1955). However, the Check-List Committee of the A.O.U. has recognized the race.

There is no evidence that the habits of the Newfoundland form differ in any essential way from those of the eastern purple finch. It is a fairly common summer resident from mid-May to late September. Four or five eggs compose the clutch. (Peters and Burleigh, 1951.)

This race has not been detected with certainty outside Newfoundland.

DISTRIBUTION

Range.—Newfoundland to Georgia.

Breeding range.—The Newfoundland purple finch breeds in Newfoundland (Bay of Islands and Glenwood south to Tompkins and St. John's).

Winter range.—Winter range is imperfectly known. Recorded from Maryland (Hyattsville), North Carolina (Swannanoa, Asheville), and Georgia (Amstell, Smyrna, Athens).

Casual records.—Casual in Illinois (Cook County).

CARPODACUS PURPUREUS PURPUREUS (Gmelin)

Eastern Purple Finch

PLATE 15

HABITS

The above name may be misleading to the novice, for it is no more purple, as we understand the term today, than it is blue or yellow Crimson finch would be a more appropriate name. (However, the "purple" of the Bible and of classical writers was not very different from the red of the male purple finch.) The species has also been called "linnet" and even "purple grosbeak."

Before the introduction and the subsequent increase of the house sparrow, during the last quarter of the previous century, the purple finch was a common summer resident in southern New England where we now know it almost entirely as a winter visitor. J. A. Allen (1869) wrote at that time: "Nearly all observers in Southern New England that I have met remark that this bird has greatly increased there during the last ten years; especially is it more numerous in the breeding season." It was certainly common enough when I was a boy in the 1870's. We could find plenty of nests in the spruces near our homes, and we caught the birds under sieves, or in cage traps; they made attractive pets as cage birds, for they sang well in captivity.

But, as the sparrows increased, the finches became steadily rarer until now, when only an occasional pair can be found nesting in southeastern Massachusetts. William Brewster (1906) tells a similar story for the Cambridge region: "Up to within twenty-five or thirty years the brilliant, ecstatic song of the Purple Finch might be heard through May, June and early July in almost every part of Cambridge— including even Cambridgeport. Many were the nests of this bird that I used to find in our Norway spruces and other ornamental evergreens, but since the English Sparrows became numerous the Purple Finches have abandoned one favorite urban haunt after another, and, excepting at their seasons of migration, I seldom see or hear them now in the older settled parts of Cambridge."

This is certainly true of the increasingly densely built up urban areas, but, reports C. H. Blake, some sizable populations still breed in the outer ring of suburbs. In Lexington, Mass., backyard trapping by Mr. and Mrs. Parker C. Reed has shown a fair number of breeding birds present. In some (approximately alternate) years many birds in juvenal plumage come to the traps in late summer and fall. They banded 343 such in 1954. Of course these represent the production of a considerable area; nevertheless singing summer males are not really uncommon 15 to 18 miles from Boston. At the present time

PLATE 15

nnington County, Minn., June 15, 1948   S. A. Grimes
EASTERN PURPLE FINCH FEEDING YOUNG

lare County, Calif., May 28, 1939   J. S. Rowley
NEST OF CALIFORNIA PURPLE FINCH

June Lake, Mono County, Calif., June 17, 1930

J. B. Dix

NEST OF CASSIN'S FINCH

Santa Catalina Island, Calif., Apr. 16, 1939

J. S. Row

NEST OF SAN CLEMENTE HOUSE FINCH

the controlling factor is more likely to be the availability of suitable nesting trees rather than the house sparrow.

Spring.—Wells W. Cooke (1914) makes the following interesting observation.

The great bulk of the individuals winter south of the breeding range, but a small percentage remain at this season, farther north in the southern part of the breeding range, and sometimes even to the middle part. There is therefore a broad belt, covering at least a third of the entire range of the species, in which migration dates are unsatisfactory, because the records of real spring migration are so mixed with notes on birds that have wintered. The case is made more involved by the fact that the Purple Finch is normally a late migrant, so that there are, in reality, two sets of notes, one of birds that have wintered unnoticed in the deep woods and are recorded when they spread to the open country during the first warm days of spring, and the other of migrants from the south that arrive two to six weeks later.

As Cooke implies, the spring migration is later than one might suppose. In Pennsylvania (Groskin, 1950) it is in March and April; in eastern Massachusetts, in April and May. While there is certainly a generally northward movement, it is questionable as to what extent migrating finches set even a roughly true north course. The data presented by Groskin (1950) show a northwestward course toward Michigan and a northeastward one into New England from his station in southeast Pennsylvania; northward recaptures of his banded birds were few and the distances mostly less than 100 miles. He was also able to show that an occasional bird makes a fairly long southward trip in spring.

Courtship.—Much has been written about the ecstatic and colorful courtship display of the purple finch. One of the best accounts of it is in the following note sent to me by Kenneth C. Parkes, who observed the performance at Ithaca, N.Y., at 5:30 a.m., daylight saving time, on May 19, 1940:

"When I first approached the pair, the male bird was hopping around with dangling wings and thrown-up chest, much in the fashion of the male house sparrow. The female was feeding on the grass nearby, not paying the least bit of attention to the male. His wings beat faster and faster until quite blurred. His tail was cocked up in the air like that of a wren. All this time he was chippering softly. Finally, with wings beating seemingly fully as fast as those of a hummingbird, he rose a foot or so straight up in the air.

"The female flew over at this point, and the male came down directly on top of her, although she immediately slipped out from under him. The male leaned over backward at an almost impossible angle, with his wings dangling against the ground and his bill pointed straight up in the air. The female gave a little jump and hit the male's bill with hers. Both birds immediately flew into the branches of a small birch, under which the performance had taken place. Although I was no more than 15 or 20 feet from the birds during the performance, and was right out in the open, they took absolutely no notice of me."

Gordon B. Wellman (1920) gives a similar account of the display, but adds some interesting features. When the male "was about two inches from and in front of" the female

he picked up a straw, dropped it and picked up a piece of grass which hung from each side of his bill. This seemed to be the signal for the greatest agitation on his part; with ecstatic dance, full song and vibrating wings he moved slowly on beating feet, back and forth before the female; then he rose six inches in the air, poured forth glorious song notes and dropped to the ground at one side of the female. He landed on his feet but instantly took a most dramatic pose by holding stiffly his spread tail to the ground and tilting back on that support with head held high, the raised crest and carmine ruff adding to the effect. Then like a little tragedian he rolled over on his side, apparently lifeless; the song ceased and the straw fell from his bill. Up to this time the female had remained oblivious as far as outward manifestation showed, but now she turned quickly and gave the male as he lay "dead" a vicious peck in the breast, whereat he came to and flew up in the tree, a normal bird once more, and was soon singing in the usual deliberate fashion from a high perch. The female busied herself about the spot where he had just danced and soon finding the straw and grass which he had dropped she picked them up in her bill and flew into the tree where she went searching from place to place for a spot to start a nest.

Sometimes the courtship consists largely of competition in song. Rev. J. H. Langille (1884) quotes an observation made by Eugene Ringueberg, who saw a female alight on a branch, after having been chased by two males, singing as hard as they could; the males alighted near her, and each "faced the female with neck outstretched and crest raised to its fullest dimensions, and leaned forward far enough to show conspicuously its bright rump, and to aid in this display, spread both wings and tail to the widest extent; and moving, or more properly dancing, up and down, poured forth such a volume of song as I did not think them capable of producing."

Mrs. Louise de Kiriline Lawrence, writing from Rutherglen, Ontario, says she watched a male dance before a female. The male had a piece of nesting material, a pine needle, in his bill. His crest was raised like a plume; his wings drooped and vibrated like a hummingbird's; his tail was raised. He uttered a continuous, soft warbling song with the most exquisite whistles and passages. The display continued for at least a minute and a half. The female paid no attention. The next day, June 3, a generally similar performance took place. This time the female flew up onto a rock, "tucked" softly, sank herself down, lifted her tail, and began trembling her wings. The male, in an ecstacy flew toward her. He had nothing in his bill. She sank down deeper, rippled her wings faster. The

ale lifted himself from the rock on wings fluttering so rapidly as to
e practically invisible and descended upon her for about two seconds.
fairy union on the rock in the sun. When the act was ended, both
irds sat motionless, facing each other for several seconds. Then
he female shook herself and flew off. A moment later the male
ollowed.

Nesting.—Nearly all the nests of the purple finch that I have seen
r read about have been placed in coniferous trees, mainly spruces.
n my egg-collecting days, we boys could always find one or more
ests in a row of white spruces, built along a suburban road as a
vindbreak. The nests were fairly well concealed in the thickest parts
f the trees and not far from the tops, perhaps 15 or 20 feet from the
round. But I once found one in an apple tree in an orchard. The
ests were made of fine twigs and rootlets and were lined with finer
ootlets and horsehair.

In the Cambridge region of Massachusetts, William Brewster (1906)
ound purple finches nesting "in hilly pastures sprinkled with Virginia
unipers among the dense foliage of which they love to conceal their
ests." They bred there so commonly at one time that he "found no
ess than six nests containing eggs or young within a space of half an
cre," on June 6, 1869.

E. A. Samuels (1883) says: "The nest is usually built in a pine or
edar tree, and is sometimes thirty or even forty feet from the
round—oftener about fifteen or twenty. It is constructed of fine
oots and grasses, and is lined with horsehair and hog's bristles.
)ne specimen in my collection has the cast-off skin of a snake woven
n the rest of the fabric; and I have seen nests lined with mosses."

Eggs.—The eggs laid by the purple finch vary from three to six,
vith four or five most commonly found. They are slightly glossy
nd ovate, sometimes tending to short-ovate. The ground color may
)e "pale Niagara green," or "Etain blue," and they are sparingly
peckled and spotted with shades of "olive-brown," "deep olive,"
'citrine drab," "mummy brown," and black. The usual type has
harp and clearly defined spots of black and browns scattered over
he entire egg. Less frequently the eggs are marked with clouded
pots of the lighter tones such as "citrine drab" and "deep olive," but
ll show a tendency to concentration of spots toward the large end
vhere they often form a loose wreath.

The measurements of 50 eggs average 20.2 by 14.6 millimeters; the
ggs showing the four extremes measure *22.4* by 14.2, 19.8 by *16.8*,
7.8 by 13.7, and 20.1 by *13.5* millimeters.

Young.—Ora W. Knight (1908) writes: "Both male and female
ssist in building the nest, but I have only once caught the male
ssisting in the task of incubation, and then he was perched on the

eggs half standing and literally bursting with melody.   * * * Th
male frequently feeds the female while she is incubating, and whe
not so engaged is perched on the top of some near by tree singin
his best.

"Incubation requires about thirteen days and the young leav
in fourteen more. Both parents feed them for a considerable whil
after they have left the nest."

Francis H. Allen (MS.) wrote in his notes for June 25, 1911: ",
young one in a shad bush, fed by its father, makes a constant swee
little *pee-wee* note. The old bird gathers the June-berries industri
ously for a long time, doubtless swallowing many, but apparentl
retaining some in the mouth or gullet, for the feeding process is
prolonged one. The young when being fed is very eager and voci
erous and follows its parent up when the latter starts away. Th
old bird chews the berries, sometimes if not always, and sometime
picks off only part of one at a time, perhaps when the fruit is no
ripe enough to be easily detached. The *pee-wee* note seems to b
characteristic. I hear it from others of the young. The syllable
are about evenly accented."

Plumages.—Dwight (1900) describes the juvenal plumage of th
eastern purple finch as follows: "Above, wood-brown, broadl;
streaked with olive-brown and showing whitish streaks if the feather
be disarranged so as to expose a lighter portion. Below, dull whit
streaked with paler olive-brown, least on the chin, throat and middl
of abdomen and crissum, the last two areas often unmarked. A
indistinct whitish superciliary line. Wings and tail deep olive-brown
edged with pale buff deepest and broadest on tertiaries and win;
coverts. * * *"

Minor exceptions may be taken to Dwight's description, accordin;
to C. H. Blake (1955). The throat is completely streaked but th
streaks are very narrow. In fact, all the streaking of the unde
parts in juvenal plumage is narrower than in first winter plumage
Finally, among birds handled in eastern Massachusetts, streaks occu
on the juvenal under tail coverts in nearly 90 percent of th
individuals.

The first winter plumage is acquired by a partial postjuvena
molt involving the contour plumage and the wing coverts, but no
the rest of the wings or the tail. This is not very different from th
juvenal plumage, but "the streaks are bolder, the brown usuall;
with a greenish yellow tinge merging into the buffy edgings.'
(Dwight, 1900.)

In eastern Massachusetts, according to Blake, the inception o
postjuvenal molt is quite evenly distributed over the period from
August 4 to September 8. The duration of this molt is probabl

about 8 weeks. In the Lexington, Mass., sample of 343 juvenile birds 26 percent (roughly half the males) showed some ruddy or pinkish tints in the first winter plumage. The available evidence from returns of banded birds is that all such birds are males. This ruddy coloring varies in intensity from a very faint tinting to color approaching that of the adult male. Its area may be very restricted or may extend to practically all the regions that are red or rosy in the fully colored male.

The first nuptial plumage is acquired by wear, most of the buffy tints being lost and the edgings becoming whitish. The birds breed in this plumage and the males sing.

The adult winter plumage is acquired by a complete postnuptial molt, beginning in July or early August, at which old and young birds become indistinguishable, the males assuming the pink plumage. Dwight (1900) describes the male as follows: "Above, pale geranium-red (often carmine or brick-red), hoary on the pileum and nape, the feathers of the back with dusky shaft lines and broad greenish buff edgings. Below, a hoary geranium-pink blending into white on abdomen and crissum, the flanks buffy with a few dusky streaks. Wings and tail clove-brown the edgings tinged with pale brick-red."

The adult nuptial plumage is acquired by wear, the hoary effect disappearing and the reds and pinks becoming clearer and brighter.

C. H. Blake reports that the molts of the female are the same as those of the male and that for 2 years or more she resembles closely the brown first winter plumage. Thereafter, in at least some populations, the female acquires a coloration very like that of the reddened first winter males described above. On the average such old females are a little less extensively reddened than the young males. A very few females develop a general yellowing of the plumage.

Dwight (1900) remarks: "In captivity pink adults assume golden or bronzed feathers at their first moult, never reassuming the pink dress."

Several articles have been published by bird banders who have noticed abnormal coloring in portions of the plumages of purple finches. Notable among these is the veteran bird-bander, M. J. Magee, of Sault Ste. Marie, Mich., who had banded and examined no less than 6,157 purple finches up to 1927, and as many as 1,168 in a single year. As his papers are too long to be quoted here in detail, the reader is referred to his titles in the Literature Cited under Magee (1924 and 1927).

Charles L. Whittle (1928) and Helen G. Whittle (1928) have noted such abnormal coloring in banded purple finches. The former writes: "Buffiness and bright yellow olive are common on the upper parts of many birds of this race, the latter usually appearing of greatest intensity on the rump of old females, and the former usually regularly placed on the sides of or including the breast of both young and old birds, especially noticeable on old birds in fresh post-nuptial plumage, when they can hardly be distinguishable from juvenile birds. Such buffy color is also not infrequently irregularly placed on the breast, one example being a well-marked band nearly one-half inch wide crossing it diagonally."

Helen G. Whittle (1928) refers to these as color-phases, "erythrism and xanthochroism." A female, "banded June 15, 1924, was a return-3 in 1927, at which time it was an olivaceous bird having a 'dull rosy rump with a central patch of rich olive-yellow.' As a return-4, May 9, 1928, the crown had a few crimson feathers, and the rump and upper tail-coverts were yellow with patches of rich reddish brown in the latter area."

Magee (1924) lists a number of females and young males showing some yellow or red in the plumage.

Some patches of yellowish or olive color, particularly on adult males, are evidently a result of feather replacement at a time when the bird's diet cannot provide the red pigment. (C. H. Blake.)

Food.—Ora W. Knight (1908) sums up the food of this finch very well as follows: "As to the food of the Purple Finch, the species is primarily a seed eater during the winter and spring, eating all sorts of weed and grass seeds, also to a lesser extent a few buds of apple, maple and birch as well as other tree buds. In late spring they eat some insects, such as beetles, green caterpillars and small larvae of various sorts. In summer they are fruit eaters to quite an extent, partaking of strawberries, raspberries, blackberries, cherries, both wild and cultivated and many other fruits. They seem to relish the fruit of the dogwoods, elders and viburnums very much."

Alexander F. Skutch writes to me: "In Maryland on October 27, 1929, I watched a purple finch feeding on the dry 'cones' of the tulip poplar. One by one it pulled the winged scales from the cluster, and with one deft bite cut out the seed from the thicker end of each, then allowed the empty wing to flutter slowly to the ground."

Hervey Brackbill (MS.) observed that, near Baltimore, Md., its food included berries of the Japanese honeysuckle, seeds of tulip tree, white ash, American elm, and Chinese elm, and buds of oaks and red maple.

Charles H. Blake (MS.) of Lincoln, Mass., says that it "eats buds of *Populus tremuloides*, *Prunus serotina*, and *Ulmus americana* in early spring. In winter, feeds on fruits of *Juniperus virginiana* and *Ilex verticillata*."

Mrs. Amelia R. Laskey (MS.), of Nashville, Tenn., has seen purple finches feeding on the berries of a privet hedge and perched on a twig, nibbling at hackberries.

Purple finches are very fond of the seed balls of the sycamore and the sweet gum in the south, and farther north they feed on sumac berries and the buds of the balsam fir, in addition to the items mentioned above. Their well-known habit of feeding on the buds and blossoms of fruit trees is discussed under their economic status, below.

Economic status.—When we see the purple finches flocking into our orchards in the spring and a shower of blossoms falling to the ground, we are apt to condemn them as detrimental to the interests of the orchardist. But here is what Edward H. Forbush (1913) has to say in its defense:

This Finch appears at first sight to be destructive, for it devours buds and the blossoms of apple, cherry, peach, and plum trees, feeding on the stamens and pistils. * * * They feed also upon the blossoms of the red maple, the seeds of such trees as the white ash, and the berries of the red cedar, mountain ash, and other trees. But, as with the Grosbeak, the pruning or cutting of buds, blossoms, and seeds of trees is not ordinarily excessive. On the other hand, this bird eats many of the seeds of the most destructive weeds, ragweed being a favorite. The Purple Finch also destroys many orchard and woodland caterpillars. It is particularly destructive to plant lice and cankerworms. Its quest of weed seeds is sometimes rewarded by some insects which it finds on the ground, among them ground beetles and perhaps a few cutworms.

In further exoneration of the purple finch as a bud and blossom eater, M. J. Magee (1926a) published two photographs of one of his apple trees, one showing the tree in full blossom and the other showing it so heavily laden with apples that the branches had to be supported. Eleven bushels of apples were taken from that tree, better apples than ever and "hardly a wormy one in the lot. I doubt if their budding does any harm, certainly not to apples in any event." More purple finches were in his trees that year than ever before.

Another exonerator, Horace Groskin (1938), who raises seckel pears in Pennsylvania, writes: "I have found, during the past three years, that the pruning the birds give the tree is decidedly beneficial. In the fall of each year when the birds were present in the spring, I have noted a very marked improvement in the amount of fruit on the tree, and last year, we not only had the largest number of pears on this tree we ever had before, but a great many of the pears were double the size of the normal seckel pear, and the flavor seemed to be decidedly improved. Let us be fair to the Purple Finch."

Behavior.—Purple finches are more or less gregarious at times, especially in winter; they are sociable and friendly at such times, except when feeding causes rivalry. Then they become selfish and belligerent. When several of them are eating at a feeding station they often seem quite hostile toward any new arrival, raising the feathers of the crown and rushing at him with wide-open bill. Occasional pecking may result, which seems to produce no great damage. The attacked one usually retreats somewhat and proceeds to feed only a few inches from his pursuer.

Hervey Brackbill says in his notes: "On one occasion a migrant in the female or immature plumage flew against the window at which my feeding tray is placed, in what appeared to be shadow-boxing. There were three such finches on the tray, the floor of which is above the window frame and runs within 6 inches of the pane. After all the birds had eaten for a while, the one nearest the window apparently noticed its reflection there. It stopped feeding and began moving back and forth along the very inside edge of the tray, with now one eye and now the other cocked toward the pane; sometimes it stood still for appreciable periods and stared. Once it rubbed one side of its head, and then after a bit the other, against the edge of the shelf; the impression it gave was that of rubbing its eyes, as if to see whether the bird in the glass would then still be there. Then it resumed its movement back and forth along the edge of the tray, always looking at the window. Finally, perhaps 1 to 2 minutes after it had first caught sight of its reflection, it flew up and struck the window pane once and then flew away. The other birds went on eating."

Sun-bathing, common with robins and some other birds, is sometimes indulged in by purple finches. Mrs. Herman F. Straw (1919) describes it as follows:

One day I noticed one of the birds squatting on the shelf, tail and one wing spread out to the fullest extent, one leg stretched as far as possible to one side, its neck turned so far around that the head seemed upside down, mouth open, and feathers fluffed out all over the body. Such a strange position! I felt sure this Finch was dying, and feared I had given it something that had poisoned it * * *. Consequently I was much relieved when another Finch, flying to the shelf just at this time, pecked the first bird, instantly restoring him to life and flight. Since then I have often seen seven or eight birds at the same time, in as many ungainly and ludicrous positions, "sunning" themselves in the bright, hot sunshine.

Voice.—Aretas A. Saunders contributes the following thorough study of the beautiful song of this finch: "The song of the purple finch is loud, clear, highly musical, and pleasing. There are three distinct ways of singing, more or less separated by the seasons of the year. The warbling song of early spring is probably the best known of these. This song is used while the birds are in flocks, and there are often several birds in the flock singing at once, in a chorus. The territory or nesting song comes a little later, after the birds are separated into pairs. The least common song is the 'vireo song,' which comes very early in the spring, or rarely in late fall or other seasons.

"The warbling song, according to 21 records in my collection, consists of from 6 to 23 notes. The notes are very rapid, and connected, with no two in succession on the same pitch. Liquid consonant sounds are common between the notes and connecting them. There is great variation in the song. Each song by one individual is likely to be followed, after a short pause, by another that is quite different in its notes and the arrangement of them. If a bird ever repeats one of these warbling songs again, exactly as it was, I have been unable to detect it. The pitch varies, in my records, from C''' to C''''. Songs vary in length from 1 to 3½ seconds, and average about seven notes to a second. It is heard chiefly from February to April, but I have some records, from the Adirondacks, dated in July, after the nesting was over.

"The territory song is heard commonly from late April till July, wherever there are breeding birds. It is quite different from the warble. A few groups of notes in it are warbled, but there is a series of rapid notes, all on the same pitch, near the beginning of the song, and a high-pitched, strongly accented note, usually near the end. The song does not vary in the individual, as does the warble, but is the same in all details when repeated. When it is sung the birds are not in flocks so that, ordinarily, only a single individual is heard at one time. The bird often sings the song over and over, several times in succession, without a pause, a habit that is also common to the entirely unrelated ruby-crowned kinglet. I have 18 records of this song. The pitch varies from E''' to D'''', and the length from 2⅗ to 3½ seconds. But when the song is repeated over and over, it is, of course, much longer than this. I once watched a bird singing this repeated song in flight, holding its wings up at an angle and floating in the air, somewhat after the manner of the flight song of a longspur.

"The 'vireo song' is the least common of the three, and is usually to be heard in early March, or in late October or November. This song is made up of phrases of two to five notes each, and these phrases are alternated, with short pauses between them, in much the same manner as red-eyed and yellow-throated vireos. The song is less variable than any of the vireos, however, generally consisting of three different phrases only. While usually a spring or fall song, I once heard it in July in the Adirondacks, and then the bird singing it was in the plumage of a female, though probably an immature male.

"I have one record, from such an immature male, of a song of primitive character—a mixture of warbles, trills, and series of rapidly repeated notes, lasting about 5 seconds and varying in pitch from A''' to D''''.

"The chief season of singing in this species lasts from late February or early March to July. There is occasional singing in October or early November.

"The call note of this bird is a short, sharp *tip* or *tick*. A young bird, out of the nest and calling for food, used a two-note phrase that sounded like *yo wee*, the second note two and one-half tones higher than the first."

Francis H. Allen writes to me: "I have records of several unusual purple finch songs. Perhaps the strangest of them was heard in West Roxbury, Mass., May 9, 1939. It seemed to be a medley of goldfinch song-notes with a recurrent imitation of the towhee's call, usually followed by a high-pitched trill suggesting the trill in the towhee's song but very rapid and beady in quality, and with a long, high pitched, even note that suggested the cowbird."

Field marks.—The adult male purple finch is easily recognized by its color; no other sparrowlike bird of that size is similarly colored in rosy crimson. The female is marked more like a sparrow, but its markings are more like stripes, its bill is much heavier, and its tail is sharply emarginate. The immature male resembles the female.

Enemies.—Man is, or rather was, one of the worst enemies of this fine bird; in my boyhood days, it was easy to trap all the purple finches in the neighborhood in cagetraps baited with a singing male; in those days, there was considerable traffic in trapped cagebirds, and these "linnets" made most attractive ones; but, happily, this traffic has now been stopped, in this country at least.

Evidently, the purple finch is not very often imposed upon by the cowbird. Friedmann (1929) says: "This species is occasionally imposed upon by the Cowbird, there being several cases on record. * * *

"As many as four eggs of the Cowbird have been found in a single nest of this bird together with seven of the owner."

Considerable has been published on the longevity of purple finches, based on the records of birdbanders. While the lifespan of the species apparently does not average more than 3 or 4 years, many individuals have managed to escape their enemies for 6 or 7 years, and a few have lived to be 8 or even 10 years old.

Fall.—The fall migrations of purple finches are somewhat erratic and irregular, varying in direction and extent. M. J. Magee (1924) writes from Michigan: "In the fall there is a tendency for the sexes to flock separately. Several times late in the fall flocks of from twenty to thirty, all crimson males, have dropped in for from a few hours to a day or two and then moved on. The following is from my 1922 notes: 'Have not had a crimson male at house from Aug. 23 to Oct. 4,' and my banding records show that after Aug. 7 I banded no crimson males although I trapped and banded 111 birds."

The migration route is usually from north to south, but Frederick C. Lincoln (1939) says that "banding studies have demonstrated that in addition to the normal north-and-south journeys there is also an east-and-west movement, since birds banded in Michigan have been subsequently recaptured at banding stations in New England."

Winter.—Most of us in New England have recently come to regard the purple finch as mainly a winter visitor since it has ceased to be a common summer resident here. We cannot always count on seeing it, as its visits are somewhat uncertain, being abundant some winters and scarce or entirely absent in others. When it does come, we welcome the little bands of rosy-colored males and striped females that flock to our feeding shelves, quarreling among themselves for the sunflower seeds and other food.

On rare occasions they have come in such large numbers as to be referred to as invasions. Such a visitation is described by Richard Lee Weaver (1940) as follows:

In the winter and spring of 1939, January to May, an unusual invasion of Purple Finches (*Carpodacus purpureus purpureus*) occurred throughout the northeastern United States and the Maritime Provinces. * * * Hundreds, and in many places thousands, of the birds congregated and fed on weed seeds and buds, or on grain supplied at many feeding stations. Sunflower seed was preferred to most other foods, and thousands of pounds of it were consumed. In one small town, over one thousand pounds of the seed were sold in one week during the invasion.

In the seven years prior to 1939, an average of 4,700 Purple Finches were banded throughout the country. In 1939 there were 21,592 birds banded. * * * Each of six or seven banders was responsible for banding over one thousand of the birds. Several people banded almost two thousand.

During their stay with us in New England, they are sometimes seen roving over the open country with flocks of siskins or goldfinches, feeding on weed seeds, wild fruits, buds, catkins, and such seeds as remain on the trees. But, where they are encouraged to do so, they congregate about our houses and grounds, where they can find food. They are hardy birds and can live through severe winter weather if well fed.

Forbush (1929) says: "They bathe in brooks with the temperature below freezing point and some have been known to sing in the clearing weather directly after a blizzard. Nevertheless a few are overcome by starvation and cold, as occasionally one has been picked up from the snow helpless or dead. * * * Purple Finches spend winter nights in dense evergreen trees or thickets, or even in some open buildings or under the shelter of a cupola roof."

They wander as far south in winter as Louisiana and northern Florida. Arthur T. Wayne (1910) says that, in South Carolina, they "inhabit only forests which are of a deciduous growth and feed upon the seed of the sweet gum (*Liquidamber styraciflua*), and sycamore (*Platanus occidentalis*) during November, December, and a portion of January. The birds evidently migrate to points to the southward of South Carolina during midwinter for few are to be seen until the ash (sp.?) and red maple (*Acer rubrum*) begin to flower about the middle of February, when there is a distinct migration."

DISTRIBUTION

Range.—Northern British Columbia, Manitoba, Quebec, and Prince Edward Island to south central Texas and the Gulf of Mexico.

Breeding range.—The eastern purple finch breeds from northern British Columbia (Atlin, Hazelton), northern Alberta (Peace River Landing, Fort Chipewyan), central Saskatchewan (Flotten Lake, Hudson Bay Junction), central Manitoba (The Pas, Norway House), northern Ontario (Favourable Lake, Lake Attawapiskat, Fort Albany), central Quebec, Prince Edward Island, northern Nova Scotia (Cape North) south to central British Columbia (Lac la Hache), central Alberta (Banff, Camrose), southeastern Saskatchewan, central northern North Dakota (Turtle Mountains), northwestern and central Minnesota (Fosston, northern Isanti County), central Wisconsin (Unity, Clark Lake), southeastern Michigan (Ann Arbor, Bloomfield Hills), southern Ontario (London, St. Thomas), northern Ohio (five northern counties), southeastern West Virginia (Cranberry Glades, Cheatbridge), western Maryland (Accident, Cranesville Swamp), northeastern Pennsylvania (Pocono Mountains), northern New Jersey (Ridgewood), and southeastern New York (Westchester County, East Hampton).

Winter range.—Winters from southern Manitoba (Brandon, Winnipeg), western and central Ontario (Port Arthur, North Bay, Ottawa), southern Quebec (Montreal, Quebec), Maine, New Brunswick (Fredericton, St. John), and Prince Edward Island southeast of the 100th meridian to south central and southeastern Texas (Real County, High Island), the Gulf Coast, and northwestern and central Florida (Pensacola, Oxford, New Smyrna).

Casual records.—Casual north to central southern Yukon (Whitehorse) and Labrador (Cartwright).

Accidental in eastern Franklin (off Resolution Island).

Migration.—The data apply to the species as a whole. Early dates of spring arrival are: District of Columbia—February 22. Maryland—Prince Georges County, February 29. New York—Cayuga and Oneida Lake basins, March 6 (median of 15 years, April 6). Missouri—St. Louis, February 7. Illinois—Urbana, February 16 (median of 18 years, April 1); Chicago, March 12. Indiana—Red Key, February 15. Ohio—Buckeye Lake, March 9 (median, April

7). Michigan—Battle Creek, March 21 (median of 20 years, April 7). Ontario—Ottawa, February 20 (average of 12 years, March 18). Minnesota—Duluth, April 12. Saskatchewan—Nipawin, April 8.

Late dates of spring departure are: Florida—northwestern Florida, May 20. Alabama—Leighton, May 10. Georgia—Atlanta, April 26. South Carolina—Spartanburg, April 28. North Carolina—Highlands, May 9. Virginia—Arlington, May 19. West Virginia—French Creek, May 8. District of Columbia—May 29. Maryland—Warrior Mountain, Allegany County, June 3. Pennsylvania—State College, May 18. New York—Central Park, Manhattan, May 26. Connecticut—Portland, May 30. Louisiana—New Orleans, April 25. Mississippi—Tishomingo County, April 17. Arkansas—Fayetteville, May 6. Tennessee—Knox County, May 6. Kentucky—Bowling Green, May 8. Missouri—St. Louis, May 30 (median of 13 years, May 2). Illinois—Urbana, May 31 (median of 18 years, May 8); Chicago, May 23. Indiana—Lafayette, March 13. Ohio—Buckeye Lake, May 18 (median, May 16). Michigan—Detroit area, June 1. Minnesota—Anoka, May 25.

Early dates of fall arrival are: Texas—Sinton, November 11. Minnesota—St. Paul, August 7. Ohio—central Ohio, September 18 (average, September 29). Michigan—Detroit area, August 20. Illinois—Chicago, August 25. New York—Central Park, Manhattan, August 21. New Jersey—Island Beach, August 23. Pennsylvania—State College, August 31. Maryland—Howard County, September 4. District of Columbia—August 26 (average of 18 years, October 3). Virginia—Rockbridge County, October 10. North Carolina—Chapel Hill, September 12. Georgia—Atlanta, October 21. Alabama—Birmingham, October 25. Florida—Oxford, October 13.

Late dates of fall departure are: Alberta—North Edmonton, October 9. Saskatchewan—Nipawin, October 25. Manitoba—Winnipeg, October 24. North Dakota—Cass County, November 9; Jamestown, October 23. South Dakota—Sioux Falls, October 27. Minnesota—St. Paul, November 30. Ontario—Ottawa, November 24 (average of 12 years, November 11). Ohio—Buckeye Lake, November 24 (median, October 25). New York—Cayuga and Oneida Lake basins, December 10 (median of 10 years, November 20). Maryland—Laurel, December 9.

Egg dates.—Alberta: 5 records, June 2 to June 12.

British Columbia: 5 records, May 1 to July 25.

Maine: 4 records, May 30 to June 25.

Massachusetts: 35 records, May 19 to July 2; 20 records, June 2 to June 11.

Michigan: 9 records, May 15 to June 20.

New York: 18 records, May 15 to June 23; 11 records, May 27 to June 7.

Rhode Island: 12 records, May 22 to June 14.

CARPODACUS PURPUREUS CALIFORNICUS Baird
California Purple Finch
PLATE 15

HABITS

According to Ridgway (1901) the California purple finch is similar to the eastern bird, but "wing shorter, with the ninth (outermost) primary usually shorter than sixth, tail longer, and coloration different in both sexes." The adult male is "darker, the rump much darker wine purple, and the back more decidedly reddish, thus giving to the upper surface a more uniform aspect * * *." In the female, the upper parts average "darker, more uniform, and decidedly more olivaceous or olive-greenish * * *."

This purple finch is the Pacific coast form, breeding from British Columbia to southern California. Two other western races have been described but have not yet been admitted to the A.O.U. Check-List.

Mrs. Bailey (1902) says of its haunts: "The California purple finch is a bird of higher breeding range and less domestic nature than its relative the house finch. In central California, Mr. Belding says, it is common from 3000 to 5000 feet in summer, though of course it comes lower in winter. In Los Angeles County Mr. Grinnell finds it a common winter visitant of the mesas and lowlands, haunting thickets and brushy places in small companies."

Mrs. Irene G. Wheelock (1912) writes: "The California Purple Finch is one of those species which indulge in a semi-annual vertical migration. Spending the winter among the lowlands, feeding through the valleys in small flocks, as soon as the snow begins to melt in the mountains, they work their way slowly to the higher levels."

Nesting.—Whereas the eastern purple finch seems to prefer to nest almost exclusively in coniferous trees, the western bird seems to show no such decided preference. Dawson (1923) writes: "Nests are placed, preferably, near water, in evergreen or deciduous trees, and at heights varying from six to forty feet. They usually occur on a bough at some distance from the trunk of a supporting tree, seldom or never being found in a crotch. Composed externally of twigs, they are lined copiously with green moss, horsehair, and string; and contain four or five handsome blue-green eggs, spotted and dashed with violet and black." Thomas D. Burleigh (1929–30) found a nest near Tacoma, Wash., that was "fifty feet from the ground and twenty et out at the outer end of a limb of a large Douglas fir at the edge of an open slashing. It was small but compact, and was built of twigs, rootlets and usnea moss, slightly lined with gray plant fibres and a few fine grasses." Mrs. Wheelock (1912) says: "Half-way up the mountains, at an altitude of from three thousand to five thousand feet, they find suitable breeding grounds in the yellow pines, oaks, and redwoods. The nest is built usually on a horizontal branch, and is composed of airy grass and fine rootlets woven into a shallow cup and lined with wool or horsehair." William A. Cooper (1878), of Santa Cruz, Calif., says of the nesting habits of this finch: "Favorite situations are the tops of tall willows, alders, trees covered with climbing ivy, and horizontal branches of redwoods." He gives the data for four nests, presumably found near Santa Cruz. One "was placed on a horizontal branch of an alder-tree, forty feet high, built on the top of a limb and barely fastened to it." Another was "on one of the topmost branches of an alder-tree fifty feet high." A third was "twenty feet from the ground, in a thick bunch of willow sprouts." And the fourth was "on a horizontal branch of an apple-tree," in an orchard.

Eggs.—The measurements of 40 eggs average 19.9 by 14.5 millimeters; the eggs showing the four extremes measure *22.2* by 14.2, 21.1 by *15.7*, *18.3* by 14.0, and 19.1 by *13.7* millimeters.

Young.—Dawson (1923) says: "Two broods are probably brought off in a season, the first about the 20th of May and the second a month or so later. A sitting female outdoes a Siskin in her devotion to duty, and not infrequently requires to be lifted from her eggs." The eastern purple finch apparently raises only one brood in a season. In all other respects, the habits of the California purple finch seem to be similar to those of its eastern relative. Its eggs are similar, the sequence of its molts and plumages is the same, it lives on practically the same kinds of food, sharing the enmity of the fruit growers in spite of the harmful insects that it destroys, its voice is equally charming and it does not differ from it in its general behavior.

DISTRIBUTION

Range.—Southwestern British Columbia to Baja California and Arizona.

Breeding range.—The California purple finch breeds along the Pacific coast from the Cascade Range and the west slope of the Sierra Nevada westward, and from southwestern British Columbia (Comox, Lillooet) south to southern coastal California (Alhambra) and through mountains of interior southwestern California to northern Baja California (Sierra Juarez); east in Washington to Naches Valley, and in Oregon to Friend and Klamath Falls.

Winter range.—Winters from southwestern British Columbia south to central western Baja California (San Ramon, Santo Domingo) east to southeastern California (Death Valley, Twentynine Palms) and Arizona (Grand Canyon, Huachuca and Santa Rita mountains)

Casual records.—Casual in New Mexico (Silver City).

Egg dates.—California: 50 records, April 13 to July 25; 40 records May 7 to May 28.

CARPODACUS CASSINII Baird
Cassin's Finch
PLATE 16
Contributed by ROBERT THOMAS ORR

HABITS

Cassin's finch is a bird of the high, cool, semiarid, coniferous forests of western North America. Locally, its range may overlap that of either the other two species of *Carpodacus* found in this general area, the house finch and the California purple finch. However, the house finch generally prefers situations that are lower altitudinally and warmer, while the California purple finch is largely confined to moist, shaded forests at low and middle elevations.

In Tuolumne County, Calif., on June 10, 1950, I made a point of examining an area where both Cassin's finches and California purple finches occur. During the course of a morning walk just west of Strawberry Lake the purple finch was found to outnumber Cassin's by about four to one. The elevation was approximately 5,600 feet, and the forest was composed of yellow pine, sugar pine, lodgepole pine, white fir, and incense cedar. On the afternoon of the same day along Herring Creek, 4½ miles to the northeast, at an elevation of about 7,300 feet, California purple finches were absent while Cassin's finches were numerous. Here the forest consisted largely of lodgepole pine with scatterings of aspen.

Grinnell, Dixon, and Linsdale (1930) make the following comments regarding Cassin's finch in the Lassen region of California:

This finch was found in loose companies or singly, on the ground or in tree tops, usually in rather open forest growths. Activity of one sort or another was definitely noted in types of trees exemplified by the following: white alders along streamlet, aspen, lodgepole pine, yellow pine, hemlock, small red fir. These trees were used for singing and resting perches and sometimes as foraging places, while a greater share of the foraging for food took place on the ground in clearings or at the edges of forest bordering large meadows * * *.

A review of all the field notes gathered by us leaves the impression that the center of the summer metropolis of this purple finch lies within the red fir belt, in other words, within the Canadian life-zone.

Grinnell (1908) records this species as very common in most of the higher parts of the San Bernardino Mountains of southern California, between elevations of 5,000 and 10,000 feet.

With regard to Cassin's finch in Oregon, Gabrielson and Jewett (1940) say: "It is particularly abundant in the Cascades, the Blue Mountains, and the Warner Mountains, where it is a conspicuous element in the avifauna from the yellow pine up to timber line."

In northwestern Montana, Burleigh (1921) says: "This was a plentiful bird not only toward the tops of the mountains but in the slashings and open woods in the valley."

Spring.—At this season as in fall and winter, these finches tend to stay in flocks, although single individuals are occasionally seen. In certain regions where there has been a downward population movement in the fall, the reverse trend may be noted in March and April. In 1927 James Moffitt (MS.) noted the first Cassin's finch on the western side of Lake Tahoe, Calif., on March 17. On April 3 another individual was seen and three more on April 7. On the 20th of that month these finches suddenly appeared in numbers and could be considered common a few days later.

Willett (1933) in summing up various published and unpublished records for this species in southern California mentioned Cassin's finches seen on March 23 in San Diego, up to April 26 in Los Angeles, and May 1 on San Nicholas Island. Such observations, of course, were made in years when these finches underwent unusual population movements during winter and spring in the areas concerned.

Scott (1887) records Apr. 27, 1885, as the latest seasonal date on which this species was observed in the Santa Catalina Mountains of Arizona.

Nesting.—The nesting season for this species begins in May, which is rather early for an inhabitant of high montane regions, and extends through July. It is only during these 3 months that Cassin's finches are not found in flocks. The nests are almost invariably situated in large conifers and usually near the terminal ends of limbs at a considerable height above the ground. Nests are constructed of fine twigs, weed stems, rootlets, and are frequently embellished with lichens. The lining is generally of rootlets and hair, and occasionally shredded bark.

Milton S. Ray (1918) observed a pair of Cassin's finches building a nest in a tall Jeffrey pine near Bijou at the south end of Lake Tahoe, Calif., on May 14, 1911. He comments that snow was still present on the ground in patches, and winter conditions in general still prevailed. The same author (1912a) referring to this species at Star Lake in the Tahoe region, on June 5, 1910, says: "The most important find on the meadow was a nest of the Cassin Purple Finch (*Carpodacus cassini*) with three eggs in a state of advanced incubation. The nest was placed on almost the top branch of a pine, about thirty feet up, on the edge of the meadow."

Grinnell and Storer (1924) write as follows regarding the nesting of this species in the Yosemite region:

At Mono Mills on May 17, 1916, an individual was seen finishing a nest 40 feet above ground in the outermost crotch of a pine branch. Near Peregoy Meadow on May 20, 1919, a female was seen to disappear into a dense fir bough 60 feet above the ground. At Ellery Lake, 9,500 feet altitude, on July 6, 1916, a female Cassin Purple Finch was observed feeding fully grown young, while at the same time the members of another pair were engaged in building a nest. A male bird taken in Lyell Cañon on July 23, 1915, had passed the height of the breeding season. It would seem, therefore, that the Cassin Purple Finch here as elsewhere has a long nesting season, beginning in late May and lasting at least until the end of July.

Rowley (1939) makes the following statement: "On July 7, 1930 near Virginia Lakes [Mono County, Calif.], Sheffler found a nest about fifty feet up in a lodgepole pine. The nest contained five heavily-incubated eggs (fig. 51), and I found one the next day with two fresh eggs about eight feet up in an aspen. In July 1939, several nests in lodgepole pines near camp at Virginia Lakes contained young about half-grown, except for one that was being built; no eggs were found." Regarding the nesting of this species in the San Bernardino Mountains, Grinnell (1908) says:

Three nests were found near Dry Lake, 9,000 to 9,200 feet altitude, June 23 and 26, 1906, each containing four eggs. One of the sets was fresh, and the other two were incubated to an advanced stage. As full-grown young were seen in the same locality June 18, 1907, the breeding season must cover at least two and a half months, which is a long period for the Boreal zone. All three nests were in tamarack pines, near the bushy ends of out-stretching branches. They were forty-five, fifty, and fifteen feet above the ground, respectively. The three nests are so much alike that a description of one will apply to all. Externally it consists of a foundation-work of coarse, dry, crooked weed stems and gooseberry twigs, in this respect something like a tanager's. But the internal cup is much better formed and deeper. It consists of fine yellow and brownish rootlets and grass stems, with an intermixture of finely slivered plant fibers, probably bark from small stems. The inside diameter of the cup is 2.30 inches, the depth 1.10.

Willett (1933) mentions four slightly incubated eggs collected by W. M. Pierce at Bear Valley, San Bernardino Mountains, on July 10, 1920. In the Lassen Peak region of California, Grinnell, Dixon, and Linsdale (1930) state: "Near Bogard R. S., on June 21, 1929, a female was watched building a nest fifteen meters up in the end of a branch of a large yellow pine at the edge of the meadow. The bird foraged on the ground for nest material."

Gabrielson and Jewett (1940), referring to this species in Oregon say: "Although the streaked newly fledged young are a familiar sight, the only definite breeding records for the State that have come to our attention are a set of eggs taken May 24, 1924, by Patterson (MS.) and a set of three eggs taken May 25, 1931, near Bly, Klamath County, by Braly." In northern Humboldt County, Nev., Taylor (1912) states that:

A nest was found June 26 in a *Pinus flexilis* near the head of Big Creek. The tree itself was surrounded by a grove of quaking aspens. The nest was located five feet from the trunk of the pine on the slender twigs of a branch thirty feet above the ground. Sticks and greenish yellow lichens had been used in its construction. The lining consisted of shreds of bark and sheep's wool. The structure was rather frail and loosely built. The depth of the cavity was 30 mm. (1³⁄₁₆ inches), its diameter 79 mm. (3⅛ inches). When it was first noted one parent was seen on the nest, but when a close examination of the site was made neither bird was seen. There were five young in the nest.

Johnstone (1949) comments as follows on the nesting of this species in the East Kootenay region of British Columbia: "June 20, 1937, a pair feeding young at Peckham's lake, nesting high up in a fir tree; July 17, 1946, male feeding young out of nest in Cranbrook; May 7, 1947, a pair carrying nest material into the top of a high fir tree in Cranbrook."

Eggs.—The number of eggs laid by this species ranges from three to six, with four or five comprising the usual set. They are ovate, sometimes tending to either elongated-ovate or short-ovate, and are slightly glossy. The ground color is "pale Niagara green" or "bluish glaucous," and they are speckled and spotted with "olivaceous black," "Natal brown," "bone brown," "dark olive," and less frequently with "Carob brown." On many eggs the very minute spots are so dark that they appear to be black, while others may have larger spots of the shades of brown with undermarkings of "ecru drab." In general, the spots are more numerous toward the top of the egg, and often form a loose wreath around the large end.

The measurements of 50 eggs average 20.3 by 14.7 millimeters; the eggs showing the four extremes measure *23.9* by *16.3*, *18.5* by 14.8, and 19.2 by *13.4* millimeters.

Young.—Mrs. Wheelock (1912) says that 12 days are required for incubation. It seems likely, however, that in some instances this period may extend a day or so longer. So far as known incubation is solely the responsibility of the female, although both parents participate in feeding the young. No information is available as to the length of time the young remain in the nest.

Ray (1912a) records finding a nest containing four fully fledged young on June 5, 1910, at Star Lake in the Tahoe region of California. Grinnell (1908) reports that full grown young were found about Bear Lake on July 31, 1905, in the San Bernardino Mountains and that they were common on Sugarloaf in August. Taylor (1912) referring to this species in northern Humboldt County, Nev., says: "Young birds out of the nest were noted as early as the middle of July. Upon their appearance purple finches were very much in evidence on the highest ridges in the mountains (altitudes of 9,000 feet and above). The juvenals kept up a continuous vociferous clatter. A bird would fly from one tree to another and then the other members of the family would follow. Feeding of the young was by regurgitation."

On Mount Rainier Taylor and Shaw (1927) comment that: "On August 8 a company of adults and young was observed at Glacier Basin, on the northeast side of the park. At this date the immature birds were still being fed by their parents. Young birds were also seen at Sunset Park a month later."

Judging from the egg dates it appears probable that, in some instances at least, two broods may be reared in a single season. By the end of the nesting season in the middle of summer family groups tend to move temporarily to higher elevations in the mountains.

Plumages.—No information is at hand regarding the natal plumage of the Cassin's finch. Regarding the juvenal plumage Ridgway (1901) says: "Similar to adult female, but streaks on lower parts narrower and less distinct, and wing-edgings more or less ochraceous or buffy." Two juvenals in the collection of the California Academy of Sciences have the feathers of the back and top of the head with decidedly buffy margins in contrast to the olive-gray tones so characteristic of the adult females. Furthermore, the central streaks on these feathers are black rather than dusky as in the adult female.

The first winter plumage is indistinguishable from that of the adult female plumage. It is acquired by the end of the first summer and retained for a year.

Arvey (1938) has presented some interesting information relating to color changes, seemingly induced by diet in a captive Cassin's finch. The bird was in the adult red plumage when captured in December. During the succeeding months it was fed on a seed diet until the start of the annual molt, at which time it was noted that the new flight feathers were nearly white. The bird was then given a soft-bill type of food containing animal matter in addition to the seeds, but the additional new flight feathers came in white and the red contour feathers were gradually being replaced by new yellow-colored feathers. Before the molt had been completed, red pyracantha berries were added to the diet with the result that all the flight feathers that came in after this time were normally pigmented, and the remaining old red contour feathers were replaced by new ones that were red, not yellow. A. J. van Rossem (1921) had previously reported an adult male Cassin's finch that had the red replaced by lemon yellow, taken in Sierra County, Calif.

Food.—Throughout most of the year members of this species are vegetarians, living largely on buds, berries, and seeds, particularly those of conifers. No doubt a certain amount of animal food is taken during the nesting season. The birds forage to a large extent on the ground according to Salt (1952).

Grinnell and Storer (1924) offer the following comments on the food of these finches in the Yosemite region: "The feeding habits of the Cassin Purple Finch are like those of the California. It forages either in the tops of the trees or on the ground, rarely feeding in bushes and then only on the outer foliage. Near Tamarack Flat, on May 24, 1919, a male of this species was seen feeding on the urn-like buds of the green manzanita. Young buds of one sort or another, especially needle buds of the coniferous trees, seem to be the preferred food. These and similar tender growths are likely the staple food of the Cassin Purple Finch during the long winter season when the ground is covered with snow."

In the Lassen region of California, Grinnell, Dixon, and Linsdale (1930) found the gullet of a bird shot from high in a hemlock to be "filled with the shelled kernels of two kinds of seeds, but no animal matter was detected." Swarth (1901) records these finches feeding in pepper and willow trees in Los Angeles in April. Arnold (1937) observed a male Cassin's finch feeding on cotoneaster berries on January 18, 1934, in the Coalinga area of California, and Gander (1929a) records seeing these finches in mixed flocks with California purple finches and house finches feeding on sunflower seeds on the grounds of the San Diego Zoo on Mar. 23, 1927.

Scott (1887) records members of this species feeding on the young buds of cottonwood in the Santa Catalina Mountains of Arizona in winter. Mrs. Bailey (1928) mentions the seeds of yellow pine found in the crop of one Cassin's finch obtained in the Manzano Mountains of New Mexico. She also mentions that in the Yellowstone these finches had been found eating rock salt spread on the ground for deer. Taylor (1912) records two individuals observed in northern Humboldt County, Nev., feeding in the foliage of a quaking aspen at 7,500 feet. Munro (1950) comments on a juvenal observed feeding on mulberries on August 21 in the Creston region of British Columbia.

Behavior.—Except during the nesting season, extending from May to July, members of this species are generally found in flocks. Cassin's finch, as Hoffmann (1927) states, "shares the restlessness of the family, starting for no apparent reason on long flights from one feeding place or perch to another."

In the Yosemite region Grinnell and Storer (1924) noted "a number of Cassin Purple Finches foraging in company with several Sierra Crossbills and a few California Evening Grosbeaks." They also add that, "In early summer when nesting duties were engaging their attention, single birds or pairs were seen as a rule; but later, after the broods had been reared, family parties were encountered." In the San Bernardino Mountains Grinnell (1908) says: "Small companies composed solely of male birds were often met with, feeding in open places among the pines. These bachelor parties were in evidence all through June and July at the same time that other individuals were paired off and occupied with their nests and young."

Taylor (1912) referring to this species in northern Humboldt County, Nev., observed that "Especially cold mornings seemed to drive the birds to slightly lower altitudes." He also states that "It was very easy to approach the females and juvenals, but the brightly colored males were more cautious." In commenting on this species in New Mexico Mrs. Bailey (1928) says: "During the month of October, 1904, when Mr. Gaut found the Cassins quite numerous in the Manzano Mountains, they stayed most of the time in the spruce timber, usually in company with Crossbills. During the middle of the day flocks could always be seen around the springs on the slopes of the mountains."

Voice.—Those familiar with the house finch and purple finch agree that the song of the Cassin's finch seems to combine the qualities of the songs of both these species yet differs in a manner that is difficult to describe. Grinnell and Storer (1924) write: "The song of the Cassin Purple Finch is more varied than that of either the California Purple Finch or the linnet, yet it reminds one strongly of the linnet's song. There are full rounded notes and also some 'squeals' like those in the song of the linnet. On the other hand Mrs. Wheelock (1912) describes the song of this species as "rich and melodious, of a softer quality than that of the California purple finch, but less varied. Its call-note is a clear 'cheep.'"

Referring to Cassin's finch in Colorado, Minot (1880) says: "To the northward a common summer resident up to 10,000 feet, often singing from a high perch almost identically with the Eastern bird [probably the eastern purple finch]. May 31, a large flock appeared at Boulder in the fields, feeding on the ground, springing up with a *che'-u-we'-u* as they flew, and all alighting in one tree, where, in a subdued way, they warbled, or almost twittered, in a confused chorus." Taylor (1912) records individuals of this species in full song in northern Nevada on June 24: "They continued singing until about the last of July when they became very quiet and correspondingly inconspicuous. Our observations with regard to the singing powers of the young males in the dull plumage of the first winter accord with those of Ridgway (1877), who asserts that they sing almost if not quite as vigorously and sweetly as those in the adult livery. On several occasions purple finches were heard singing while in flight."

Field marks.—The adult male Cassin's finch can be distinguished readily from the house finch by its larger size, faint rose throat and breast, and by the absence of dusky streaks on the flanks and belly. From the adult male California purple finch it differs in having a much paler rose on the throat and breast and by the fact that the top of the head is crimson and sharply defined from the back of the neck and back which are brown with but a faint rosy tinge.

The female and immature male may be distinguished from the house finch in comparable plumages by larger size and more sharply defined ventral streaking. From the California purple finch in female or immature male plumage Cassin's finch differs in having less of an olive tinge on the back and more sharply defined streaks on the ventral surface.

Enemies.—No doubt the Cassin's purple finch, like other small passerine birds that frequently forage on the ground, is subject to attack by a number of bird and mammal enemies. Clabaugh (1933) records collecting a pigmy owl with a freshly caught Cassin's finch in its claws on Aug. 18, 1930, near Hat Creek, Shasta County, Calif. Dixon and Dixon (1938), after listing a number of species of birds, including a pair of Cassin's finches, that were found nesting within 100 yards of a goshawk nest in Mono County, Calif., wondered "if these nesting birds did not gather there for the protection afforded from other predators which might be driven off by the hawks."

Late spring and summer storms are undoubtedly a serious hazard to birds of the high mountains. De Groot (1935) records finding a Cassin's finch frozen to death on her nest and three eggs one morning in the latter part of June, 1934, at Echo Lake in the Tahoe region. There had been a freak snowstorm the night before. Hanford (1913) comments as follows on the effect of heavy rain and hail in midsummer in the central Sierra Nevada at Lake of the Woods: "A mother Cassin Purple Finch continued to feed her young in a nest high up in a hemlock during a few hours of rain; at the first crashing downpour of the hail, the nestlings were silenced and the parent was seen no more."

Fall.—Throughout many parts of the range of this species, especially in the Great Basin region, there appears to be a downward migration after the flocks are formed in fall. Taylor and Shaw (1927) mention a flock of 25 to 50 seen August 21 flying over Mount Ruth (8, 700 feet) in Mount Rainier National Park, Wash. They believed that these birds were either migrating or preparing to do so. A downward movement of Cassin's finches was noted by van Rossem (1936) in the Charleston Mountains of southern Nevada in the autumn.

Henshaw (1877) comments that this species was not common in September in the Lake Tahoe region of California and that after this month none was seen. It has been the experience of others, however, that during most years a few of these finches regularly remain in this region the year around.

Winter.—Although some Cassin's finches remain in the higher mountains throughout the winter, these birds are frequently encountered in foothill and valley regions at this season. Willett (1933) referring to this species in southwestern California says: "In winter occurs occasionally in foothill country and sometimes straggles down into valleys. Has been recorded by H. Michener (Condor, *27*, 1925: 222) at Pasadena from February 9 to April 7 (1925); by H. S. Swarth (Condor, *3*, 1901:66) at Los Angeles from February 25 to April 26 (1901), and by F. F. Gander (Condor, *31*, 1929:131) at San Diego March 23, 1927, and February 25, 1929. Immature male (D. R. Dickey coll.) taken by H. H. Sheldon on San Nicolas Island May 1, 1929." Barlow (1900) recorded a Cassin's finch that was shot on Jan. 1, 1896, 5 miles south of San Jose, Calif., where it was found in company with a flock of juncos in a eucalyptus tree.

Johnson, Bryant, and Miller (1948) state: "These finches were present as winter visitants chiefly in the sagebrush–juniper area above 5,000 feet altitude in the Mid Hills section of the Providence Mountains [California]. In the vicinity of Stott's house, five miles northeast of Granite Well, they were especially abundant. Solitary individuals and small flocks foraged in piñons on rocky hillsides and in junipers on the adjacent flats. The largest flock, seen on January 2, contained 39 birds. Sometimes these finches perched quietly for long periods in the centers of junipers."

Taylor and Shaw (1927) state that "In winter the Cassin purple finch is a not infrequent visitor in the valley lands of eastern Washington." Regarding this species in Oregon, however, Gabrielson and Jewett (1940) comment as follows: "Our field notes and those of other members of the Biological Survey show it to be a regular permanent resident of all of the principal ranges of Oregon, except the Coast Ranges." In Nevada Linsdale (1936) says that Cassin's finch is "probably of regular occurrence in the valleys in winter."

A. J. van Rossem (1936) found this species principally in the piñon belt between 6,000 and 8,000 feet in the Charleston Mountains of southern Nevada in winter. Scott (1887) records a large flock of these finches at Tucson, Ariz., on Feb. 19, 1886.

DISTRIBUTION

Range.—British Columbia and Alberta to Zacatecas and San Luis Potosí.

Breeding range.—The Cassin's finch breeds from southern interior British Columbia (Stuie, Arrow Lake), southwestern Alberta (Waterton Lakes Park), northwestern, central, and southeastern Montana Fort Howe in Powder River County), and northern Wyoming (Yellowstone Park, Black Hills) south through eastern Washington and Oregon (west to Cascade Mountains) to interior northwestern California (Horse Mountain, South Yolla Bolly Mountain), interior southern California (San Jacinto Mountains), northern Baja California Sierra San Pedro Mártir), southern Nevada (Charleston Mountains), northern Arizona (Grand Canyon), and central northern New Mexico mountains near Taos).

Winter range.—Winters from southern British Columbia (Okanagan Landing), northwestern Montana (Missoula), and northwestern and central eastern Wyoming (Teton County, Converse County) south to coastal and southern California (Berkeley, San Nicolas Island, San Diego), and southeastern Arizona (Tucson), and through the highlands of Mexico to Zacatecas (Jerez) and San Luis Potosí (Charcas).

Casual records.—Casual east to southeastern Colorado (Fort Lyon), Nebraska (Crawford, Monroe Canyon), and Kansas (Hays), south to Tres Marías Islands, Valley of Mexico, and Veracruz (Orizaba, Mirador in June).

Migration.—Early dates of spring arrival are: Idaho—Moscow, March 11 (median of 11 years, April 8). Montana—Libby, February 16 (median of 6 years, April 5). Wyoming—Laramie, February 25 (average of 5 years, April 21); Casper, March 10.

Late dates of spring departure are: New Mexico—Los Alamos, May 15 (median of 7 years, April 25). Colorado—Boulder, May 21. Wyoming—Casper, May 11.

Early dates of fall arrival are: Colorado—Denver, September 8. Arizona—Tucson, October 21. New Mexico—Los Alamos and Silver City, October 5 (median of 5 years at Los Alamos, November 11).

Late dates of fall departure are: Montana—Missoula, October 18; Libby, October 6 (median of 6 years, August 27). Wyoming—Laramie, November 1 (average of 5 years, October 12). Arizona—Nogales, November 12.

Egg dates.—British Columbia: 5 records, April 18 to July 15.

California: 70 records, May 29 to July 13; 52 records, June 15 to June 29.

Colorado: 10 records, June 11 to July 10; 5 records, June 20 to June 30.

CARPODACUS MEXICANUS FRONTALIS (Say)

House Finch

PLATE 17

Contributed by ROBERT S. WOODS

HABITS

The house finch, more familiarly known as the linnet, is a species whose repute varies according to the interests and point of view of those who regard it. To the average city dweller, its domestic tastes, cheerful song, amiable manner, and the bright coloring of the male make it a pleasing adjunct to the dooryard or window sill; but a grower of the softer varieties of fruit who watches flocks of these birds descend like locusts upon his ripening crop finds difficulty in appreciating their esthetic values. Because of these destructive tendencies, the house finch has long been denied the protection of the law in California, at least, but nevertheless continues to be the most abundant species of bird throughout much of its range, which consists in general of the Upper and Lower Sonoran Zones of the Pacific and southwestern States, together with Mexico.

Most numerous about towns and cultivated lands, this species is by no means a stranger to uninhabited wastes and deserts. However, competent observers agree that the sight of a house finch is one of the surest signs that water is near; hence the linnet cannot be considered a characteristic or generally distributed bird of the desert regions. In California and New Mexico the species is reported to breed at altitudes as high as 8,000 feet, but in California, at least, the mountains are not a favored habitat, and it is not among the birds that one ordinarily expects to encounter in the higher country. In the United States its centers of greatest abundance are the valleys of the Pacific slope of central and southern California, but its natural range extends north to Washington and east into Wyoming, Colorado, and western Texas.

In recent years extensions of territory have occurred. Ralph C. Tate (1925) reported an apparently permanent incursion into the Oklahoma Panhandle, approximately 40 miles southeast of the border of the previously known breeding range. Ian McTaggart Cowan (1937) found a pair nesting at Victoria, British Columbia, in 1937, and stated that the species had been noted as a regular breeding resident in the interior of the same province for the previous 3 or 4 years. Most striking was the establishment in the early 1940's of a population of house finches on the eastern seaboard. As Austin (1961) describes it: "In 1940 cage-bird dealers in southern California shipped numbers of these birds, caught illegally in the wild, to New York dealers for sale as 'Hollywood finches.' Alert agents of the Fish and Wildlife Service spotted this violation of the International Migratory Bird Treaty Act and quickly put an end to the traffic. To avoid prosecution the New York dealers released their birds. The species was soon noted in the wild on nearby Long Island, and it has slowly been increasing its range ever since. The Mexican House Finch has now pushed northward into Connecticut and southward into New Jersey. It has also been introduced to Hawaii." On Feb. 26, 1963, a young male was collected at Zebulon, N.C., a considerable southward extension of the range.

The house finch has not only expanded the boundaries of its range in some degree, but to a much greater extent the coming of civilization has enabled it to occupy new habitats and to increase the density of its population within its original range. In reporting on a visit to the Farallone Islands near San Francisco, Milton S. Ray (1904) tells of discovering house finches, "several pairs of which, for the first time, were nesting here and challenging the Rock Wren's long-defended title of being the island's only song bird. Were it not for the grove of friendly evergreens, where these birds would have nested is a puzzle." In his comprehensive account of the species in Colorado, Dr. W. H. Bergtold (1913) says: "Previous to the advent of the English Sparrow in Denver (about 1894, according to the writer's notes) the only bird at all common about the buildings of Denver was this finch. Before the present extensive settlement of Colorado, the House Finch was, so far as one can gather from the reports of the various early exploring expeditions, to be found mainly along the tree covered 'bottoms' of the larger streams, along the foot hills, to a small extent up the streams into the foot hills, and possibly along the streams as they neared the east line of the state." He estimated the population of house finches in Denver at the time of writing to be at least four for each of the 35,000 houses or other buildings, and possibly much higher.

That the adaptation of the species to civilized environments was not, however, an instantaneous process is indicated by a statement of Charles E. H. Aiken (Aiken and Warren, 1914): "I found none nesting in those early days in Cañon City, Pueblo, Colorado Springs, or Denver, but at Trinidad, in July, 1872, I first saw them utilizing human habitations. It was many years before the northern birds took up with the advance of civilization and made their homes in towns. When I returned to Colorado, in December, 1895, after some years absence, I found them frequenting the city."

According to the fifth edition of the A.O.U. Check-List (1957), the other subspecies of *Carpodacus mexicanus* are mostly confined to Mexico, with the exception of *clementis*, an inhabitant of islands off southern California. The present widely distributed subspecies is characterized by a great amount of variation, but Ridgway (1901) pronounced these differences individual rather than geographical, and they have been generally so regarded. This decision was based on an examination of adults only. In view of the striking differences in the natal covering as described hereinafter (p. 302), it may be pertinent to note the conclusion of Aiken (1914) "that the House Finches of Colorado east of the mountains and probably of southeastern Wyoming are subspecifically distinct from those of California, Arizona and New Mexico as far east as the Rio Grande River. If further investigation proves this conclusion correct the more western and southern form becomes *Carpodacus mexicanus obscurus* McCall. Local birds are true *frontalis* since Say's type locality is the Arkansas Valley."

In a review of the house finches, Robert T. Moore (1939) goes much farther and divides that portion of the species north of the Mexican border into the subspecies (1) *frontalis* Say, centering in southern Colorado and New Mexico, (2) *smithi* Figgins, farther to the north, (3) *solitudinis* Moore, in Nevada and adjacent arid regions, (4) *grinnelli* Moore, on the Pacific coast, and (5) *clementis* Mearns, on San Clemente Island, the birds of the remaining territory being considered intergrades or undetermined.

Courtship.—In spring the male linnet may often be seen following the female, singing and fluttering his wings. Ralph Hoffmann (1927) says: "At the height of the breeding season the male hops about the indifferent female with tail up, wings drooping, head up and crest feathers raised, singing and making a sound like a sharp intake of breath. The female in the height of the mating period utters a few notes that suggest the male's song."

Various writers have referred to "courtship feeding" of the female by the male, but these incidents are usually described as occurring during incubation, and Anders H. and Anne Anderson (1944) state that at Tucson, "No 'courtship feeding' was noted during nest building or before. The nest building is done entirely by the female. The male follows, singing frequently from perches close to her work. At intervals both of the birds search for food in the vicinity." However, in the following description by Laurence M. Huey (1925) of "pre-nuptial" feeding at a feeding table in San Diego, the date mentioned is presumptive evidence that incubation had not yet commenced:

On the afternoon of March 19, 1925, a pair alighted on the edge of the table and my attention was soon attracted by a peculiar twittering call given by the female. It was rather unusual, so I watched them carefully and observed the male feed the female regurgitated food several times. His actions were much the same as those of any bird raising partly digested food from its crop; the head was bent sharply downward several times and the pellet was seen to rise up through the gullet. At the moment the female, with much twittering and flipping of wings, would open her beak to receive the tidbit.

* * * After the performance was over, they both ate freely of the damp, broken dog-biscuit that was on the table.

Bergtold (1913) "suspects that this species mates permanently: it is apt, in all seasons of the year, to come to the food and drinking dishes in pairs." This is a question which their social disposition makes more difficult to determine.

Nesting.—The greater part of the nesting activities occur in April and May, but are continued in some degree through June and July. In one of the earliest detailed studies of the species, Charles A. Keeler (1890b) says: "During the month of February the males sing more or less constantly, but it is not until a month later that love-making begins. * * * By the middle of March they are nearly all mated and by the latter part of the month nest-building is fairly under way. During the early part of April both sexes are busy in constructing a home, the male merely assisting by bringing material and finding abundant opportunity to sing while his mate is at work."

Extreme dates for fresh eggs in southwestern California as listed by George Willett (1933) are March 22 and August 1. Although Philbrick Smith (1930) reports the discovery of eggs under incubation in Contra Costa County, Calif., on November 24, it appears from available data that nesting of the house finch in California is confined rather closely to the four months first mentioned. While Bergtold (1913) also found April and May to be the most active nesting months, the following quotation indicates that early nesting may be more frequent in Colorado than in California, notwithstanding the colder winters: "Cold weather has a positive deterrent effect on egg laying, a fact clearly established by the writer's records. On the other hand, pairs of House Finches, unquestionably mated, have been observed looking for eligible nesting sites in every month of the year, not excepting the period from September to February. The earliest active nest building noted by the writer was on January 30, and the latest July 23; while pairs have been noticed gathering material as late as December 22, these attempts have been classed, however, by the writer as due to a fleeting spell of warm weather."

Nesting sites chosen by house finches are of such infinite variety that it is useless to attempt to mention all the diverse situations that have been reported. Any cavity or projection on a building which is capable of holding a nest may be utilized, provided that some concealment is afforded if near the ground; higher up, nests are often placed in plain sight on lookout timbers. About orange groves, the trees are often used as nesting sites, and in this case certain generalizations may be made. The nests are not placed in the dense outer foliage, as is the custom of the brown towhee and the lark sparrow, nor in the upper branches, as favored by the goldfinch and the phainopepla, but rather in the more open interior of the tree, often in the fork of an upright limb. The usual height of the nests is from 5 to 7 feet, but when favorable sites do not occur within these limits, they may be located at slightly less or much greater heights.

Of the house finches of Santa Fe County, N. Mex., J. K. Jensen (1923) says: "They are not at all particular about a nesting site as they build in the branches of a tree, in cavities of trees and walls, in tin cans hanging on fenceposts, and I have even seen a nest on the ground under a rabbit weed. It is one of the few birds that will use a 'cholla' cactus for nesting site." At the writer's home in the San Gabriel Valley, where there is no scarcity of nesting sites, a specimen of a "cholla" cactus, *Opuntia tunicata*, at one time contained four occupied linnet's nests, showing that they have an actual preference for these spiny plants. From his observations in San Diego County, Calif., H. W. Henshaw (1894) wrote:

> So tame and confiding have these pretty Finches become that I am persuaded that the larger proportion of their nests are built not in trees and bushes as formerly, but in all sorts of odd nooks and crannies about the house and barn; and even when they are compelled by the lack of facilities to resort to bushes and shrubbery, they choose those as close to the house as possible.

> The pertinacity with which the House Finch clings to a chosen nook about a house when their nests are destroyed is amazing, and is equalled only by the English Sparrow. I have known five nests with their contents to be destroyed one after another, and each time the same pair set to work with apparent unconcern to build anew.

Writing from San Jose, Calif., Ernest Adams (1899) summed up the matter thus: "Experience has taught me that the House Finches *may* nest anywhere. I have found them occupying nests of orioles, towhees, grosbeaks, cliff swallows, blackbirds and portions of hawks' abodes; besides tin cans, old hats and stove pipes and now I shall add hollow limbs. One bird entering the opening of a small cavity actually squeezed her way back for two and a half feet to sit on her eggs in total darkness. Another reared her brood in the deep cavity of a Californian Woodpecker in an oak while a third selected a similar hole in a telegraph pole. The latter contained six eggs." F. C. Willard (1923) discovered a nest in a woodpecker hole about 30 feet up in a large sycamore in southern Arizona, but in this case the nest was placed so that the bird could look out while incubating. In the vicinity of Salt Lake City and Ogden, Utah, states Howard Knight in an as yet unpublished manuscript, the Colorado blue spruce appears to be the house finch's favorite nesting tree, probably because its form of growth provides snug nesting sites and its numerous sharp needles discourage predators. Knight also found a nest at the unusual height of 35 feet in a Carolina poplar, where it was situated in a cup-shaped depression in the broken end of a vertical limb, surrounded by a circle of erect branches.

Old oriole nests are frequently used by the house finches, according to Willard and others, and in California nests of the black phoebe are often appropriated, a layer of new material being added in some, at least. Harold M. Holland (1923) relates one instance in which the linnets did not wait for the phoebe's nest to be vacated, but alternated with the rightful owners in the deposition of eggs until the nest contained six eggs of the phoebe and five of the house finch, after which it was deserted by both pairs. In two different years Wilson C. Hanna (1933) found a recently built phoebe's nest occupied by linnets, while the phoebe had rebuilt a few feet away, the location in both years being under a bridge. D.I. Shephardson (1915) cites instances of the invasion of newly built or occupied nests of Arizona hooded orioles, cliff swallows, and black phoebes. That the house finch may occasionally assume the role of benefactor rather than that of usurper is indicated by the observations of Alfred M. Bailey and Robert J. Niedrach (1936) in Denver:

Two instances of Western Robins (*Turdus migratorius propinquus*) and House Finches (*Carpodacus mexicanus frontalis*) using the same nests have come to our attention during the past three years. In May, 1934, we were informed that House Finches were feeding young robins in a nest on a front porch in east Denver, Colorado. On investigation we found four half-grown robins, two newly hatched finches and four finch eggs. There were two female finches apparently with the same mate, and the three finches and the two adult robins fed the young regularly. Unfortunately, however, the large robins smothered their small nest mates. We did not determine whether the four remaining eggs hatched. All three adult House Finches fed the young robins in the nest, and after the young had left the nest.

On May 15, 1936, in a similar instance, the nest was on the back porch of Bailey's home, 2540 Colorado Blvd., Denver. The young robins were nearly ready to leave the nest, and there was no evidence that the pair of House Finches had laid eggs. However, both adult finches and robins fed the young regularly. The male finch was particularly solicitous and would alight on a wire a few feet from the nest and sing whenever one of the other birds brought food. The young robins left the nest May 20, and the finches were the only ones noted feeding them from that time on, although the adult robins were about and no doubt shared the responsibility.

The building of the nest is accomplished by the female with little or no practical assistance from her mate, who, however, follows solicitously and lightens her labors with song. The materials used of course vary according to the resources of the locality, but the nests observed by the writer in southern California were composed principally of slender, dry stems, often with small leaves attached. In this particular locality the linings usually consisted of the soft, woolly branch-tips of an everlasting plant, *Stylocline gnaphalioides*. In outside dimensions the nest is about 5 inches in diameter by 3 inches in depth; inside, the diameter is about 2½ inches, the depth perhaps 2 inches. When new, the nest is neat and attractive in appearance, but it soon becomes fouled around the edges after the hatching of the brood.

Other nesting materials mentioned by Mrs. Florence Merriam Bailey (1928) as used in New Mexico are grass stems, plant fibers, leaves, rootlets, twigs, hairs, string, and wool. Ray (1904) describes a nest discovered in the Farallone Islands as "closely made of island grass, with an occasional feather intermixed, and lined with bits of string, cotton and mule hair." In the Point Lobos Reserve, on the coast of central California, where the trees are hung with lichens, this material was used in the construction of nests mentioned by Grinnell and Lins-dale (1936), who state that these nests are unusually well concealed when built into masses of the same vegetation. As proof of the ability of the house finch to resort to "new and ingenious expedients," H. W. Henshaw (1894) tells of a nest built "in the corner of the piazza of a country store" in San Diego County:

Viewed from below, the nest was seen to be balanced rather than firmly placed upon a narrow joist, and I was at a loss to comprehend how it was maintained there even in calm weather, to say nothing of the high winds that prevail in this locality. By means of a step-ladder I was soon able to solve the problem. Having about one-half finished the structure, the birds evidently recognized the insecurity of its position, and the location being in every other respect eligible they hit upon the following remedy. Procuring a long piece of white string they carried one end well into the body of the nest and twined it around several sticks. Thence it was car-ried out like a guy rope to a nail that chanced to have been only half driven home, about six inches beyond the outer rim. Two turns were taken about the nail and the string then passed back to the nest and firmly interlaced with the twigs. The nest was then completed.

The string thus attached protected the nest from pitching forward—though the wind rocked it continually—while the wall protected it behind.

The work was not so deftly done as not to betray the novice in the weaving art, and a yearling Oriole might have smiled at the crude effort to steal its trade by its thick-billed relative. However, the evident purpose of *Carpodacus* was to tie down its nest so that it would stay, and appearances were but a secondary consideration. That the nest was securely anchored was evidenced by the fact that it contained five eggs upon which the female was peacefully setting quite regardless of the fact that it was within three feet of the head of every passer by.

The observation in the preceding sentence regarding the nesting bird's obliviousness to the near approach of persons is confirmed by Dr. Bergtold's (1913) statement: "The birds grow very tame if the nest be closely associated with man and his doings: they seem to be bothered in no way by slamming of doors or by passers in and out of a door close to a nest." Nevertheless it must be placed on record that those that have nested for years about the present writer's home in southern California do not show that philosophical disposition. Though they have never been persecuted, and they seem to prefer to build around the house, and often near doors which are in frequent use, if anyone passes through the doorway or approaches the nest, they invariably leave precipitately, with every indication of great alarm.

That the social tendencies of the linnet may be retained in some degree even during the breeding season could be inferred from the following instance cited by Grinnell and Storer (1924): A rather unusual case was that of partnership nesting, noted at Dudley, 6 miles east of Coulterville, on July 14, 1920, where two nests had been built on one beam inside a barn. The nests were placed so close to one another that the constituent materials were interwoven on the adjacent sides. The centers of the two nests were but 4½ inches apart. Each nest contained 4 fresh eggs, and so far as could be seen the householders were deporting themselves with model comity.

F. G. Evenden (1957) found nest construction in the region of Sacramento, Calif., took as long as 2 to 3 weeks in March or April, the chief cause for delay appearing to be weather conditions and competition with the house sparrow. In July, a nest was completed in 2 days. Between completion of the nest and the beginning of egg laying, 1 to 4 days' time elapsed, with the greatest time lapses coming early in the nesting season. In all recorded observations, eggs were laid in the early morning hours. Disturbance, as by a cat or house sparrow, might result in the skipping of a day.

The eggs are usually deposited daily until the full complement of four, or sometimes five, is reached. Incubation may begin at least a day or two before completion of the set, so that all the eggs are not hatched on the same day. To atone for his dereliction in the matter of nest building, the male undertakes the support of his mate while she alone incubates the eggs and broods the young. He feeds her by regurgitation, in the manner described under *Courtship* (p. 292). The feeding usually takes place while the female incubates, but she sometimes receives food away from the nest, after fluttering her wings and begging in the manner of the fledglings. While the female ordinarily attends to her duties quite faithfully, Bergtold (1913) says: "The eggs sometimes undergo a surprising amount of cooling without being spoiled. One set, when partly incubated, was successfully hatched after being uncovered all of a cold rainy night, the female having been frightened from the nest at about 11 p.m., not returning until daylight."

F. G. Evenden (1957) points out that early during the egg-laying period the female was found at the nest only early and late in the day, with the length of her visits increasing as the clutch was laid. Very little of the male was seen until the young hatched. Although he stayed in the area during the day, there was evidence that he joined other males in flights to a night roost. In one instance the roost was a mile and a half distant.

The house finch shows a marked tendency to return to the same nest, not only for the second brood, but in subsequent years. In this connection, Willard (1923) writes: "On the San Pedro River are some large ranches where much hay is raised. At one of these a large stack is always built in a certain deserted ranch yard and a pair of House Finches have had their nest in it every time I have visited the spot. This season, after a lapse of six years, I visited the place again, in company with Mr. A. C. Bent, and remarked as we came to the stack that I always used to find a finch's nest in it 'just about here', and, as I touched the hay, out flew Madame Finch from her nest, which held five eggs. In passing, may I remark that this was one of the few places where I could count on getting a set of five eggs. Most of the finches in that region lay four." Nests are quickly prepared for reoccupancy by adding a layer of nesting material to the top and interior to cover the filth left by the preceding brood. The second brood often follows the first with very little delay, and instances in which the broods actually overlapped were cited by Aiken (1914):

When the young in this nest were half grown the parents built a second nest under my neighbor's porch and while the male was attending the first brood the female raised another. In 1898 the breeding impluse was even stronger. The male was first noticed December 27 of the previous year to come and inspect the old nest. At intervals of ten days he came after that for several weeks before he brought his mate. In March the pair cleaned and relined the old nest and the female began incubating. Soon after the young were hatched a second nest was built adjoining the first and attached to it in which a second complement of eggs was laid and the female sat on these while the young were growing in the first nest beside her. When the second brood were hatched a third clutch of eggs was laid in the nest now vacated by the first brood and a third brood sucessfully reared.

While two broods seem to be normal in the house finch, the number may be greater, or at times less. Aiken (1914) suggests an explanation for this variation, based on his observation of one pair through a period of 10 years: "I assume and am convinced that the birds were in their first reproductive year when they built the first nest. They reached the height of reproductivity in the third year when they raised three broods. In succeeding years they dropped to two broods and then to one. This may be accepted as a law or rule applicable to other species whose habit is recorded of producing two or more broods in a season. We may conclude that the more vigorous pairs produce two or more broods some seasons but other pairs may produce but one."

Supplementing the instance of polygamy cited by Bailey and Niedrach is the following case witnessed by Harold Michener (1925a) in southern California: "On April 22, 1912, one male and two females began building a nest on top of one of the beams supporting the roof of the front porch. This position was sheltered by a wisteria vine. All three birds worked together in building the nest. Two eggs were in the nest on April 28. Ten eggs were laid, one being crowded out of the nest. After the first part of the incubation period, during which there were frequent contests between the females for the privilege of sitting on the eggs, one of the females apparently disappeared and was seen no more. The eggs had begun to hatch on May 12, but only six of them hatched."

Eggs.—The eggs of the house finch number from two to six, with four or five comprising the usual set. They are ovate, sometimes tending toward the elongated-ovate or short-ovate. The ground of the egg is bluish white and they are delicately spotted, speckled, and streaked, with comparatively few well-defined markings of "dark olive," "mummy brown," or black. In most cases the spots are confined to the top half of the egg, and often they form a very fine loose ring around the large end. Occasionally an egg may be unmarked.

The measurements of 50 eggs average 18.8 by 13.8 millimeters; the eggs showing the four extremes measure *22.4* by *15.2*, *16.7* by 13.7, and 17.5 by *11.5* millimeters.

Young.—The incubation period as determined by Dr. Bergtold (1913) in Denver averaged 14 days, but Chas. A. Keeler (1890b) reported it as 13 days (presumably in northern California), while in southern California the three sets most accurately timed by the present writer agreed at 12 days. It thus appears possible that the incubation period is shortened by a warmer climate.

Evenden (1957) says the incubation period, timed from the laying of the last egg to the hatching of the last egg, was 12 days each for two nests in June, 13 days each for six nests, 14 days for two nests, and 16 days for one nest in late April, early May. Hatching varied from one or two birds per day for 3 days, to five young hatched in 1 day. Hatching dates were between May 1, 1954, and July 29, 1951. Circumstantial evidence indicates that the first egg laid hatched first. Hatching took place both during the night and in the daytime. Significant differences in size of the young in the nests were observed infrequently. The female carried eggshells at least 20 feet away almost immediately—in fact, in one instance carried away one part of an eggshell while the young bird was still in the other part.

The development of the young is not quite as rapid as in some other small passerine birds. Not until they are about 10 days old do the young habitually hold their eyes open with an expression of alertness.

The female broods them rather closely for the first few days, after which both parents bring food, which is imparted by regurgitation. The intervals between feedings, though irregular, average longer than in those species which carry food in the bill. Emerson A. Stoner (1934), in front of whose bedroom window at Benecia, Calif., a pair of linnets accommodatingly raised their brood, makes these comments on their family life:

* * * Aided by a flashlight, the beams directed out through the window, I found that the female invariably slept with her head under one wing. Although this is what might be expected, I had never before had the opportunity of looking into a bird's nest so conveniently situated to allow night investigation without fear of disturbing the sitting bird. The female had become so accustomed to motion and noise in the room that considerable rather vigorous tapping on window failed to arouse her.

The mother did not brood her young on the final nine nights the young were in the nest. During this period it was interesting to note that the fledglings, on the last six nights prior to their departure, also tucked their heads under their wings.

Bergtold (1913) says: "The young remain about fourteen days in the nest, which is kept perfectly clean by the old birds for four or five days after the eggs are hatched." In southern California I have found the period spent by the young in the nest to range from 14 to 16 days, with the latter figure predominant. Evenden (1957) says 11 to 19 days. Howard Knight (MS.) thus describes the behavior of a brood of house finches found in a nest built in the top of a 15-foot blue spruce at Salt Lake City:

"On the first day of observation the birds were not active nor did they have much muscular control. Most of the movement was of the feet and legs which were being flexed and stretched almost constantly. The toes were curled and then extended fully almost without cessation, and the writer believes this exercise serves to develop adequate strength in the feet and legs for perching while still quite young. These birds leave their nests and perch on limbs for a few days before they fly.

"As with the young of many birds when handled, they almost always voided feces when first taken from the nest. The distended appearance of the abdomen suggests that this is a reaction to pressure on the abdomen while being lifted from the nest. During the first 3 days of observation there was no fecal soiling of the nest, so it is concluded that during this time the adults dropped the fecal sacs out of the nest, though this was not seen. On the fourth day of observation, there was considerable soiling of the edge of the nest and voiding over the edge. Very little goes over the edge, however, so in a few days the rim of the nest is a filthy mess. The purpose of this behavior is well served as the interior of the nest stays quite clean.

"Warmth is essential to these nearly naked nestlings, and they constantly seek it. When being handled they lie close to the hand holding them, and if the fingers are closed over them they are content to remain motionless until disturbed. When lying on an open hand they lie with their bare abdomen pressed to the warmth of the hand, but if the fingers are slightly curved over them, the birds struggle to get their entire bodies under the fingers. When put back into the nest there is quite a commotion and jockeying for position as each one burrows in among the others in an effort to find suitable contact positions and a comfortable temperature.

"Until the third day of observation the eyes were closed, with only a very narrow slit showing where the lids separated on the fourth day. On the third day the birds could open their eyes a tiny bit, but seemed to prefer to keep them closed. By the fourth day the eyes were open more of the time than they were closed. Bergtold reports that the eyes of the birds he observed opened on the third day.

"Most of the observations made by the present writer were made between the hours of 5 p.m. and 7 p.m. At this time the crops of the birds were greatly distended, and the contents could be seen to be largely dandelion seeds, which suggests the importance of this bird in control of this weed. The skin of the neck is very thin, loosely folded, and almost transparent. A full crop makes a large bulge on the right side of the neck. In the morning this bulge is scarcely noticeable.

"By the fourth day the birds could hold their bodies off the ground for short periods. In doing so, the wings were used as anterior props to assist the legs. They became progressively more active with each passing day. On the fifth day they developed a technique for resisting being taken from the nest. When touched they immediately cowered among their siblings and locked their toes around some of the nesting materials or the handiest part of the nearest nestling. This gripping became more tenacious on succeeding days, and it frequently took a minute or two to disengage the feet and lift the birds free of the nest." This brood had left the nest by the 11th day of Knight's observations, which would indicate that the time spent in the nest might be less than that recorded in Colorado or California.

Evenden (1957) states young never returned to the nest after the initial flight, which ranged from 12 to 125 feet in distance and up to 9 feet in height.

He (1957) also describes at length an instance of one female, in 1951, presumably with the same male, maintaining two nests, 16 feet apart, at the same time. Timing was such that the second clutch hatched the day before four of the five young in the first nest departed. A year later, "double nesting" was observed again. Other instances are suspected.

Plumages.—As it lies in the nest with head and wings retracted
the newly hatched house finch, as observed in California, appear
rather uniformly covered with fairly long grayish-white filaments
which stand erect and distinct.   The concealed portions of the body
including the neck, are nearly or quite bare.   Keeler (1890b), who
studied these filoplumes with considerable care, described them as
consisting of a straight, slender, solid stem 8 or 10 mm. in length, with
very fine alternate branches or barbs placed at considerable interval
apart.   From the third day on, he found, the growth of the feather
is continuous.   At that time the wing quills first make their appear
ance, and by the sixth day nearly all the feathers have sprouted, the
ear coverts being last.

The filoplumes persist until all the feathers are fully grown
and the filaments standing erect among the feathers of the crow.
furnish the last identification mark by which the more recently fledge
individuals can be distinguished.   After losing these vestiges of
natal down, the young linnets differ in appearance from the adult
females principally in the streaking, which is rather narrower and
appears to stand out more conspicuously, perhaps because of th
cleaner plumage.   Also, the wing coverts of the young are tipped
with buffy.

Surprisingly, in the cooler climate of Denver the natal covering
seems to be much less developed than in southern California.   Dr
Bergtold (1913), by setting up removable nest boxes outside his
windows, was able to study closely the development of the young
nestlings there, which he describes as follows:

* * * the young up to the fourth day seem naked, but are really partly covered
by a minute down which appears in streaks, there being four lines on the head, *i.e.*
one along the skull in the long axis of the body, one over each eye, and one over the
occiput, transverse to the long axis of the head.   There is also one along the
dorsum of each wing, one over each scapula parallel with the vertebral column, an
inter-acetabular dorsal patch, a streak down the outside of each thigh, and
sternal streak which bifurcates, one fork going under each wing, and on the second
day an interscapular vertebral streak appears.   All these areas grow rapidly and
soon appear to coalesce; and by the fourth day the body seems to be covered all
over with down except the belly, and, by this time, the wing quills are just budding

Since available literature furnished little information concerning the
finches of the Great Basin region lying between these east and west
extremes of the range, an inquiry was addressed to A. M. Woodbury
This resulted in studies by Howard Knight of the University of Utah
who kindly supplied the following description of a brood of recently
hatched house finches at Salt Lake City: "These nestlings did not have
their eyes open, but did have several streaks of down on them.   One
streak was slightly crescent shaped across the occiput with the point
of the crescent running forward.   The top of the head or crown was

bare. Between the center line of the head and either eye there were two streaks of down running from the base of the beak backward to a point just behind the eye. These last four mentioned tracts measured 6 mm. in length, and the down tufts themselves measured from 3 to 8 mm. in length.

"The cervical region and the anterior part of the back were bare. At a point between the wings the dorsal down tract began and extended posteriorly to terminate abruptly above the oil gland. The humeral down streaks were 4 mm. wide, and the tufts measured 3 to 5 mm. in length. A short femoral tract measured 10 mm. in length, while the downy tufts varied from 5 to 10 mm. in length. The wings at their widest point were 8 mm. across, and bare except for a tract of down 3 mm. long on the posterior edge. There was a little down on the shank of the legs, and it was scattered about without pattern or design. Downy tufts at the tarsus measured 3 to 4 mm. in length, and were confined to the outside of the leg.

"The abdominal region of these birds was very bare except for two lateral streaks of down appearing in narrow tracts between the legs. The tracts were 10 mm. long, and the tufts measured 3 to 5 mm. in length. There were two rows of pin holes in the skin of the latero-ventral region where the feather tracts later developed."

Assuming that there had been no significant change between hatching and the discovery of the brood, this seems to represent an intermediate condition, in that the natal covering was much more conspicuously developed than in the Colorado nestlings, while on the other hand, the down of the head, though disposed in a different pattern from that described by Dr. Bergtold, still occurred in linear tufts, unlike the California birds.

The great variations which occur in the normally red portions of the male house finch's plumage have been the subject of much comment and study. It is well known that in captive birds the red color eventually changes to yellow, and this is also true of those which were introduced into the Hawaiian Islands. On the other hand, F. C. Lincoln (1917), in writing of the birds of Rock Canyon, Ariz., says: "The males of this region are remarkably brilliant; much more vermilion than any in my series of Colorado specimens. This may be the result of the intense sunlight." Even in a single locality and under natural conditions, moreover, bright red may in certain individuals be replaced by tawny orange, deep yellow, or pinkish, while the extent of the reddish area is also variable. In the course of studies carried on in connection with their banding operations, Harold Michener and Josephine R. Michener (1931) discovered that the paler hues were usually replaced by red in subsequent years, and that in some individuals the red areas increased in extent with age, while the reverse changes were of much

less frequent occurrence. Their conclusion was that the paler or dull[e]
coloration normally represents the first adult plumage of a substanti[a]
percentage of individuals. In a discussion of the linnet of the Hawa[i]
ian Islands, Joseph Grinnell (1911a) makes the following gener[a]
observations on the plumage of the house finch:

At its post-juvenal molt the male acquires a first annual plumage not percep[
tibly different in matter of intensity or extent of color from that assumed at an[
later or more "adult" period of life. A corollary of the fact last stated is the[
during the winter and spring—from September until the time of appearance [of
full-fledged young the following season—there are no male linnets without colo[
This is very different from the case in *Carpodacus purpureus* and *C. cassini*, whe[n
the post-juvenal molt of the male leads into an uncolored first annual plumag[e
practically identical with the plumage of the normal adult female. The abov[
facts are abundantly indicated by the extensive series of specimens in the Cal[i
fornia Museum of Vertebrate Zoology.

* * *

In the large series of males of the California linnet, leaving out the rare exam[
ples which are distinctly yellow or orange, striking variation is shown in the tir[
of the red. But arrangement of the component examples by date, from Septem[
ber to July, shows this variation to parallel the lapse of time beyond the fa[ll
molt, and to be altogether due to the effects of wear. There is no spring mol[t
and the notion that an influx of new pigment into the feather towards sprin[g
serves to produce the bright colors of the nuptial dress is, of course, withou[t
foundation. In the fresh fall plumage the red is of a conspicuous pinkish ca[st
(burnt carmine of Ridgway's *Nomenclature of Colors*, 1886 edition); there [
thereafter a gradual change through crimson, until by summer a brilliant popp[y
red is displayed.

* * *

Microscopical examination of various appropriate feathers shows the followin[g
conditions. In the newly-acquired, unworn feather, the red pigment is restricte[d
to the barbs of the contour portion of each feather, except for their termin[al
portions to a distance of one millimeter from their tips. These barb-ends, whic[h
together thus constitute a grayish band terminating each feather, and all th[e
barbules, are white. In the extremely old abraded (summer) feather these un[
colored end-portions of the barbs in the overlapping feathers, and all of the ba[r
bules, have simply been broken off and lost, thus removing the grayish obscuratio[n
from the bright red in the barbs.

The Micheners (1932) also conducted experiments on male linnet[s
which were frequent visitors to the traps, by plucking the feathers o[
the rump at intervals during the year and comparing the colors of th[
successive replacements. They found that red was replaced by mor[
yellowish or brownish tones, thence through brown shades to grayis[h
olive. However, with the renewal of the entire plumage at the tim[
of the molt, the rump again became red. Though red coloring i[
very rare in the plumage of the female house finch, H. S. Swart[h
(1914) obtained two females which showed scattered red feathers i[
some of the areas where that color occurs in the male.

Weights.—J. L. Partin (1933) made more than 1,000 weighings of 800 individuals to determine the possible influence on weight of season, time of day, sex, and age, with the following results:

1. There is a seasonal variation in the weight of the House Finch; the minimum average for adults occurs during November, and is about 93.7% of the maximum, which occurs in February, while there is a tendency for a low average weight all along from May to November.

2. Immatures average lightest in June, being about 92.8% of the adult average for that month, and reach 98% of the adult weight in September.

3. There is a daily variation in the weight of the House Finch, with a decidedly uniform increase for adult birds during the morning, breaking away from a smooth curve in the afternoon, but reaching a maximum during the latter period. The average daily fluctuation for the adults amounts to about 3.5%.

4. Immatures are more erratic in weight in the forenoon but tend toward a smooth curve in the afternoon, reaching a maximum near the close of the day, with a differential of about 5% between a.m. and p.m. weights.

5. The females average heavier during the breeding season than the males, while the males are heavier during the prenuptial season, November to March.

6. There is a strong indication that territorial variations occur, possibly because of variations in food supply, or in hereditary influences, or in both.

Food.—In relation to the house finch, food is a most important, not to say controversial subject, and it is by all means unwise to arrive at any generalized conclusion. Each locality or each set of circumstances should be considered on its merits. Bergtold (1913) sums up as follows his observations on the food of house finches in Denver and its environs:

The House Finch will eat almost anything vegetable, though it prefers seeds, and experiments with different seeds show that hemp is selected to the exclusion of all others. Nevertheless it feeds in our streets and alleys, gathering bread crumbs, eating from pieces of bread, apples, oranges, and, in fact, from almost any piece of table refuse. It will consume large quantities of fat, more especially suet. In winter when the ground is unusually deeply covered by snow, these birds wander far and wide over the prairie and vacant city lots, eating weed seeds, particularly those of the so-called Russian Thistle (*Salsola tragus*). It was, to the writer, a most satisfying discovery to find that the nestlings were, whenever possible, fed as soon as hatched and hereafter, on dandelion seeds. * * *

If not fed on dandelion seeds, the nestlings are given such food as the old ones usually consume but the writer has never detected any animal food in the crops or stomachs of House Finch nestlings. This Finch has never been seen feeding from the horse manure of the streets.

The House Finch exhibits, in common with many other birds, a fondness for maple sap, sipping it as it oozes from the cut branches of a spring pruned tree. The only objection my friends hereabout have against the House Finch is that it eats in the spring, leaf and blossom buds from bushes and trees—for example, lilac bushes and apple trees.

Insofar as the food of the adults is concerned, it is probable that the foregoing statements would apply almost equally well to the city of Los Angeles. However, in an agricultural environment in the same county, where for many years a feeding table has been maintained and sporadically supplied with such table scraps as crumbs and cheese parings, we have never known any of the numerous house finches present to show the slightest interest in these offerings, which are watched for and eagerly eaten by towhees, song sparrows, and some other birds. Apparently the diet of the house finches in this part of the San Gabriel Valley has consisted entirely of three items: soft fruits, seeds, and buds. The first of these items is seasonal, as the birds are unable to penetrate the skins of the year-round fruits, namely, oranges and avocados, and they show no taste for the berries of the pyracantha and other shrubs, highly favored by mockingbirds and waxwings. On buds their attacks are not systematic and persistent, like those of the purple finches during their occasional visits. It is plain, therefore, that seeds constitute their staple food.

The fruits that suffer most severely from the linnets are peaches, apricots, nectarines, plums, sweet cherries, pears, summer apples, and loquats. Persimmons would probably be equally acceptable, but they ripen at a time when these birds are not numerous in the orchards. In the San Gabriel Valley they have shown no great interest in the berry fruits such as grapes and mulberries. The variety of seeds used is undoubtedly great. Among naturalized plants, the seeds of the sweet alyssum and the tree tobacco (*Nicotiana glauca*) are especially popular.

The most thorough study of the house finch's diet was that made by F. E. L. Beal (1907), who examined the contents of 1206 stomachs and found them to consist in the aggregate of weed seed 86.2 percent, fruit 10.5 percent, animal matter 2.4 percent, miscellaneous 0.9 percent. Excerpts from Beal's report follow:

Observations in orchards show that in the fruit season the linnet is not backward in taking what it considers its share of the crop, and as it spends much of the time there, field observations alone would lead to the conclusion that fruit was its principal article of diet. Examination of the stomach contents, however, proves that such is not the case, and when we find how small is the relative percentage of fruit eaten, it seems strange that its fruit-eating proclivities should have attracted so much attention. But it must be borne in mind that the bird is wonderfully abundant, which is one of the primary conditions necessary for any species to become injurious.

* * * Seeds of plants, mostly those of noxious weeds, constitute about seven-eighths of its food for the year, and in some months amount to much more. In view of this fact it seems strange that the house finch has acquired such a reputation for fruit eating, and it can be explained only upon the principle already laid down that in the fruit districts the bird is too numerous for the best economic interests. While each house finch eats but a small modicum of fruit, the aggregate of all that is eaten or destroyed by the species is something tremendous. * * *

Examination of linnet stomachs does not reveal any very considerable number of blossom buds, and it is probable that but little of the alleged mischief to fruit blossoms is done by this bird. Moreover, it may be stated that in most cases budding by birds does little, if any, damage. It is only in very rare instances that birds take the buds from a tree, or even enough to cause considerable loss. * * *

Before the settlement of the Pacific coast region it is evident that the linnet must have subsisted almost entirely upon the seeds of plants growing wild in the valleys and canyons. With the advent of civilization two new articles of food were presented—grain and fruit. It would seem natural for the linnet, especially equipped as the bird is to extract the kernel of seeds, to have chosen the former, as did the blackbirds, doves, and some other species; but for some reason best known to itself it selected fruit. How much the character of the food had to do with the bird's choice it is impossible to say, but it is probable that attendant conditions greatly influenced the result. Grain is grown on large, open areas, with few or no trees to afford nesting sites, while orchards offer every inducement to linnets as a permanent residence. Moreover, much of the fruit-growing section of the State is divided into small holdings, each with a dwelling with accompanying barns, sheds, and other buildings that afford ideal homes for these birds. * * *

Although the great bulk of fringilline birds normally subsist principally upon seeds, at certain times, notably in the breeding season, they eat a considerable quantity of animal food, mostly insects. Moreover, their young while still in the nest are usually fed largely, and in some cases entirely, upon insects. Quite the contrary is true of the linnet. The adults eat only a small percentage of animal food, even in the breeding period, and feed their nestlings no more, perhaps less, than they eat themselves. In this respect the linnet is probably unique in its family. Such animal food as the bird does eat, however, is much to its credit. Plant-lice (Aphidae), especially the woolly species, constitute a large portion of this part of the linnet's food; caterpillars and a few beetles make up most of the remainder.

M. P. Skinner (1930) writes: "The house finches * * * of the San Joaquin Valley are certainly developing a great fondness for watermelon. On July 7 and 8, 1930, I watched them at a feeding station thirty miles north of Bakersfield. During the morning hours, and still more during the afternoon hours, there was a steady stream of these birds to some watermelon rinds for the ripe watermelon pulp still present. Most of these feasting birds were young of the year, but there was also a fair number of both adult males and adult females. At first I thought the birds were attracted because of thirstiness; but soon after that, I noted that pulp that was almost dry was taken as well." Esther Reeks (1920) noticed these birds eating regularly from a block of pressed salt and sulphur, apparently being the only birds attracted to it. Various observers have commented on the important part cactus fruit plays in the linnet's diet where other food is scarce. Some individuals, at least, show a marked liking for sugar syrup.

From available evidence, it would seem that the economic status of the house finch might be summarized somewhat as follows: In the case of fairly large commercial orchards, their depredations should not be overly serious, and in years when there is overproduction they might be actually beneficial to the grower, since the attacks of the birds, unlike many insect infestations, in no way impair the vitality and future productive capacity of the trees. It is in small home orchards that they become most annoying and destructive, especially since, as Beal points out, their concentration is greatest in such an environment. On the other hand, their consumption of weed seeds is undoubtedly of great benefit, though this cannot be expressed in terms of actual monetary value.

Behavior.—The house finch is eminently social in disposition, and outside the breeding season is usually seen with others of its kind, in numbers ranging from small groups to immense flocks. Among themselves, as well as with other birds, they are comparatively peaceable and not especially given to aggression. Bergtold (1913), whose intimate study of the birds enabled him to know many of them as individuals, stressed the high degree of variation found among them, not only in physical characteristics such as color and markings, but in such attributes as tameness, quarrelsomeness, and gentleness. The notable differences in the timidity of nesting birds, as mentioned previously, may perhaps be taken as examples of these marked individual or clan variations. Clearly it is useless to attempt to define too closely the behavior pattern of such a species.

The linnet's flight is bounding and free, usually clearing the tops of trees and buildings rather than passing between them. Descent to the ground is ordinarily only for the purpose of feeding on weed seed, and they prefer to eat fruit still hanging on the tree rather than that which has fallen to the ground. When idle, they choose comparatively high perches, and great numbers may often be seen lined up on transmission wires. Grinnell and Storer (1924) comment on the behavior of this species in the foothills of the Sierra Nevada:

Linnets, like purple finches, when frightened usually seek safety in flight rather than in dodging into the protection of trees or brush as many sparrows are wont to do. If a flock of linnets is come upon suddenly, while feeding in a weed patch or on the ground, they get up quickly with an audible whirring of wings and make rapidly off in ascending course. The flock is usually dense when it first rises. Then it opens out and the individuality of the members is expressed as each pursues its own undulating course. Linnets, more perhaps than any other of the finches, are accustomed to strike out into the open, mounting high into the sky and circling for a time, before descending again.

The song of the male linnet is heard off and on through the greater part of the year. After the annual molt begins, in late summer, singing is indulged in sparingly and the birds usually remain relatively quiet until some protracted warm spell during the late winter, or until the first days of actual spring. From then on, their voices resound, in favorable places, from early dawn until late dusk. During the courting season they are as apt to pour forth their melodies while in flight high overhead as when perched.

After the couples have become established, the male and female of each pair stay close together, both when perched or when in flight, and when alone or with other pairs. In flight, the male usually keeps a little behind and to one side of the female, and when foraging he is quick to follow any changes in her location. After she begins the work of incubation he is wont to post himself on a perch close to the nest, where he is seen and heard much of the time.

In the cool coastal climate of the Point Lobos Reserve, Grinnell and Linsdale (1936) made the following observation: "Ordinarily linnets exhibited a marked preference for open places, exposed to the sunshine. Flocks were observed in winter in the dead tops of pines at the margin of the woods, on wires of telephone and power lines, in live oaks, in the dead and leafless cypresses and also in the live ones, on the ground where the cover of vegetation was sparse, in the tops of brush piles, and in extensive patches of mustard and radish. Some of these places were occupied as forage sites, but others serve only as safety refuges or as perches where, seemingly sunshine could be absorbed."

George A. Bartholomew and Tom J. Cade (1956) showed that water consumption increased directly with increasing ambient temperatures. Mean consumption at 39° C. was over 40 percent of body weight per day. A bird might drink over 100 percent of its body weight in 24 hours. Birds were hyperactive at this temperature, and some individuals panted almost continuously. At 20° down to 6° the birds were under no apparent stress. Succulent food proved important for birds in the deserts and enabled them to maintain body weights during a 7-day test period without water.

Voice.—The linnet household furnishes an outstanding example of a "musical family." The male is an indefatigable songster, the female also sings on occasions, and the fledglings, lined up on a wire, literally "sing for their supper." To human ears, the keynote of all house finch utterances is cheerfulness. The song suggests happiness, and even the notes that express anxiety over peril to the nest have a cheerfully rising inflection. Entirely absent from their vocabulary are the strident bickering cries and harsh scolding notes that are so freely used by many other species. In the words of Myron H. and Jane Bishop Swenk (1928), "The House Finch is a joyous bird, and it expresses its joy in its rollicking, warbling song. The song itself is not long, but it is rapidly repeated many times, producing a long-continued flow of singing. The song has many variations; in fact, but rarely do you hear two songs that are exactly alike. Different individuals will sing slightly differently, and the same bird will vary his song from time to time, but the song always has the same basic structure, is rather consistently given in 6/8 time, and all of the songs share the same general quality."

To the casual observer the notes of the house finch are not impressive in their variety, but Bergtold's (1913) account indicates that this apparent limitation of expression may be attributable rather to a lack of acuteness or attention on the part of the listener:

* * * During the cold months the birds are comparatively silent but they frequently break into song on bright sunny winter days. * * * From the middle of January onward, the singing increases with the lengthening days * * * .

* * * There is a distinct and recognizable difference in the alarm note over the sight of a dog or a cat if it be near the drinking place, and the alarm when one examines the nest. The writer has learned to know when the young are ready to leave the nest by the peculiar coaxing notes of the old birds. During nest building, the male often feeds his busy mate, as he would a young bird, and at such times the notes uttered by the female are peculiar to this part of the nesting habits. During August and September the song is at ebb, but starts afresh, on a subdued scale, in October.

Aretas A. Saunders says of the species as it sings in the Eastern United States: "The following notes were obtained from a single individual that appeared in Canaan, Conn., in June 1954:

"The song is bright, rapid, extremely musical, consisting of series of rapid notes, with slurred notes before or between the series. An example might be written phonetically as *tāyō tātātātā tāyō titititi tēēēyōtitit*. The number of short notes in the series varied from 2 to 10, but was most frequently 4. The pitch varied from D_6 to A_6, the slurred notes mainly downward from 1½ to 2½ tones.

"A call note recorded I wrote as *queet*. It was pitched on A_6."

Field marks.—In the valleys of California very few species of birds have red in the plumage; there the male linnet is usually recognized at a glance. In none of its range, in fact, is it likely to be confused with any birds other than the purple finches of the same genus. From them it differs in its normally brighter and less purplish shade of red, the red areas being rather more restricted and more sharply defined, with no suffusion of red over the remaining plumage. Ralph Hoffmann (1927) says: The darker gray of the female Purple Finch and the dark patch on the cheek bordered above by a light line distinguish her from the female House Finch. The absence of marked streaking on the flanks and the deeply notched tail distinguish the male Purple Finch from the male Linnet." This species is also noticeably more slender than the purple finches. From most of the streaked, brownish sparrows the female can be distinguished by the heavy, convex bill and the rather broad and comparatively uniform streaking of the under parts; also by the less terrestrial habits.

Oakleigh Thorne (1956) states that persons encountering difficulty in identifying finches for banding purposes, with the bird in the hand, have a number of distinguishing marks to guide them. Particularly, the bill of the house finch is very stubby as compared with that of the Cassin's finch, or other races, including the eastern purple finch. The house finch is slightly smaller than the Cassin's and has a more "round" head. Cassin's usually shows a slight crest. The house finch tends to have a square-ended tail, whereas the tail of the purple finch is rather forked. The Cassin's tends to sit rather still while feeding at a banding station and flies away silently after banding. The house finch is more noisy and nervous, and inevitably utters a chirp upon being released. The house finch has rather long, slender tarsi: those of the Cassin's are rather short and stocky

The foregoing statements apply to both sexes and all ages. Female or young house finches have brown streakings on a buff background on the breast, Cassin's has darker brown streaking, or elongated dots, on a white background, and thus appears to be the more distinctly streaked bird. The house finch shows a uniform tone over the whole head; the Cassin's shows distinct areas of light and dark. Ear, or cheek patches, and malar stripes are darker.

The adult male Cassin's has a rose-red or "old rose" colored head. The bright red is restricted to the crown, with a wash, rather than dense color, on the face and breast. In the house finch this bright red includes most of the head and breast. Cassin's has an unmarked belly, whereas the house finch has brown streakings on the belly and breast.

Enemies.—The abundance of the house finch is evidence that it has no enemies serious enough to hold it in check where food, water, and shelter are available. Its habit of nesting around buildings protects it from many wild predators, though domestic cats take their toll of any nestlings that leave the nest before they are in full command of their wings. For some unexplained reason there are very few records of parasitism by cowbirds, despite the fact that the nests are not very well concealed.

In some parts of California poisoning campaigns have been carried on by orchardists, but the effects, if any, have been local. Bergtold (1913) expressed the fear that the house finch would ultimately be supplanted by the house sparrow in the cities, because of the latter's aggressive disposition, superior strength, and longer breeding period. However, the waning of the house sparrow's ascendency in more recent years would seem to lessen that danger, and there is no need to fear for the future of the house finch.

As to the parasitic insects and mites, Bergtold (1913) says: "The young and nests of the House Finch are always infected by a minute parasite, some of which were collected and sent to an entomologist, who determined that they were not true bird lice (Mallophaga) but mites, probably belonging to the family Gamasidae * * *." At a later date, Bergtold (1927) reported capturing a young finch "which seemed unusually docile. An examination of the bird disclosed a good sized swelling in the cellular tissue just below the right eye, a swelling that proved to be an abscess containing three small living larvae which were removed by expression. Thereupon the bird was liberated, was seen about my premises all that day and was much more lively than before." The flies raised from these larvae were identified as *Protocalliphora splendida*.

An unusual form of hazard to which these birds are subject was revealed by Clinton G. Abbott (1931), who reported the discovery on Point Loma by J. W. Sefton, Jr., of an adult female linnet fluttering helplessly on the ground. "He picked it up and saw that the flight feathers of the left wing were securely attached by spider's webbing to the left foot. In his estimation the bird could never have disentangled itself, but with his aid it was able to proceed on its way." Abbott suggests that this "probably represents the maximum size of bird that could be so ensnared in this country."

Rudolph Donath of the Communicable Disease Center, Department of Health, Education, and Welfare, Atlanta, Ga., writes on Oct. 17, 1958, that the house finch has been found to carry antibodies of western equine and St. Louis encephalitis.

Fall.—With the close of the nesting season in late summer, house finches of all ages begin to gather in flocks and search out the larger tracts of maturing weeds, whence they flush and circle in clouds before the passer-by. Referring to the vicinity of Denver, Bergtold (1913) says: "During August and September of each year there is a noticeable diminution of Finches about the city. This is the time when the burdens of nesting and raising of young are practically over, permitting young and old to flock on the prairies to feed on weed seeds * * *."

Winter.—Even in the mildest regions of coastal California, the numbers of the house finch are distinctly less in winter, though some remain throughout the year in almost all localities. Since H. W. Henshaw (1875) spoke of them as "very abundant at Camp Apache the first of December, frequenting the ravines and hill sides covered with piñons and cedars, as well also as the stubble fields and weeds," it seems not improbable that there is a partial migration to the desert regions where the winter sun shines warmer. That the birds are able to withstand winters of considerable severity, however, is shown by the following observations of Bergtold (1913):

Winter in Denver seems to have no terrors for this species. It appears to the writer that the cold season does not trouble the House Finch much as long as the bird is well fed, though many, doubtless, suffer frosting of feet during extremely cold spells, resulting in mutilations referred to later on. The birds roost at night, whenever possible, close to buildings, in vines next to a wall, in a nook or on a moulding under an overhanging eave, and in the folds of awnings, for which places the birds have many fights until all are located for the winter, each going to its accustomed place a considerable time before sunset. The young birds sleep in trees after leaving the nest. They have never been observed to sleep two or more together, but appear, on the contrary, to desire separate places, each by itself. It has seemed odd to find that the birds never use the nesting boxes to sleep in, after the nesting season is over. In December they go to roost early, 4:15 p.m. and sleep with the head under the wing, puffed up like little feather balls.

DISTRIBUTION

Range.—British Columbia, Idaho, and Wyoming to Baja California, Sonora, Chihuahua, and Texas. Also (introduced) Connecticut to North Carolina; Hawaii.

Breeding range.—The common house finch breeds, and is largely resident, from southwestern and south central British Columbia (Victoria, Williams Lake, Okanagan Landing), central, western, and southern Idaho (Moscow, Boise, Pocatello), central, northern, and and southeastern Wyoming (Big Horn Valley, Torrington), and western Nebraska (Kimball County, Haigler) south through California, including the northern Channel Islands, to central Baja California (Todos Santos Islands, Cedros Island, Santana), central Sonora (Tiburón Island, San Pedro Mártir Island, Oposura), northwestern Chihuahua (Chihuahua), and western and south central Texas (Boquillas, Somerset, Austin). Introduced in Hawaii, and on Long Island, N.Y., from where it has spread as a breeding species north to southwestern Connecticut (Greenwich Township, Fairfield County) and south to New Jersey, eastern Pennsylvania, and northern Maryland (Towson).

Winter range.—In winter to the Gulf coast of southern Texas. Descendents of the birds released in New York migrate south regularly to Maryland and have been recorded south to the District of Columbia, Virginia, and central North Carolina (Zebulon), and north to Massachusetts.

Casual records.—Casual north to Alberta (Topaz Lake) and Montana (Santon Lake), east to central Kansas (Cloud County), and northeastern Texas (Fort Worth), and south to southern Sonora (Chinobampo).

Migration.—Early dates of spring arrival are: New Jersey—Oakhurst, February 19. Texas—northwestern Atascosa County, February 2; Haskell County, March 28. New Mexico—Clayton, February 26. Montana—Stanton Lake, February 11. Nevada—Carson City, March 9. Washington—Pullman, March 16. British Columbia—Okanagan Landing, March 21.

Late dates of spring departure are: Texas—Haskell County, May 8; Rockport, April 26. Nebraska—Red Cloud, February 26. New Mexico—Clayton, May 3. Colorado—Platteville, March 17.

Early dates of fall arrival are: Washington—Camas, September 11. Nevada—Clark County, October 5. Texas—El Paso, August 7.

Late dates of fall departure are: British Columbia—Okanagan Landing, October 24. Nevada—Clark County, December 5. Wyoming—Laramie, November 25. Utah—Pine Valley, December 31. Colorado—Platteville, December 27. Arizona—Tombstone, December 20. New Mexico—Clayton, December 13. Kansas—Morton and Hamilton counties, November 19.

Egg dates.—Arizona: 37 records, March 16 to June 30; 20 records, May 10 to May 26.

British Columbia: 50 records, April 13 to July 18; 25 records, April 22 to May 23.

California: 268 records, February 28 to August 7; 104 records, May 1 to May 17; 72 records, April 6 to April 26.

Colorado: 16 records, April 24 to July 22; 9 records, May 13 to May 26.

New Mexico: 12 records, April 12 to June 26.

Oregon: 31 records, April 7 to July 25; 16 records, May 6 to May 22.

Texas: 9 records, April 5 to July 12.

Utah: 37 records, April 16 to July 4; 19 records, April 20 to June 1.

Washington: 23 records, April 15 to June 30; 13 records, April 25 to June 13.

CARPODACUS MEXICANUS POTOSINUS Griscom

San Luis House Finch

HABITS

Ludlow Griscom (1928) gave the above name to this subspecies and selected an adult male from San Luis Potosí, Mexico, as the type. He gave it the following subspecific characters: "Similar to *Carpodacus mexicanus rhodocolpus* Cabanis, but adult male in breeding plumage a darker bird throughout, the red areas more crimson or carmine, less scarlet; brown of upperparts darker, and brown streaking below heavier, darker and more distinct; adult male in winter plumage with the red areas a rose purple shade as in *rhodocolpus*, but more heavily and darkly streaked below, and underparts with pronounced gray edgings, giving almost a hoary effect, particularly noticeable on the hind-neck and auricular region; females darker above and more heavily streaked below."

For a further discussion of this subspecies, the reader is referred to a review of the house finches by Robert T. Moore (1939).

DISTRIBUTION

Range.—The San Luis house finch is resident from south central and eastern Chihuahua (Chupadero) and the middle Rio Grande Valley of Texas (50 miles northwest of Comstock, Fort Clark), south to Zacatecas (Sombrerete, Lulu), San Luis Potosí (San Luis Potosí), and Nuevo León (Linares).

CARPODACUS MEXICANUS RUBERRIMUS Ridgway

San Lucas House Finch

HABITS

Ridgway (1887a) proposed the above name for the house finch of the southern half of Lower California. He says in a footnote: "A considerable percentage of the specimens which I have been able to examine are so peculiar that nothing approaching them can be found in the very large series from other localities. These peculiarities consist, (1) in the smaller general size, (2) rather more swollen bill, and (3) greater extension of the red. This last peculiarity is carried to such an extreme that in all of the 'Cape St. Lucas' specimens the under tail-coverts are deeply tinged with pink, while in some even the wing-bands are pinkish; in several the pure deep madder-pink of the breast is continued backward over the belly and flanks, where the usual dusky streaks are entirely obliterated."

William Brewster (1902) writes:

This is one of the most abundant birds of the Cape Region, throughout which it is very generally distributed, save on the higher mountains, where it was not seen by either Mr. Belding or Mr. Frazar. The latter found it building at Triunfo the last week in April. Young of the first brood were on the wing and their parents laying a second time by the last week in June. One pair had taken possession of an old nest of the Arizona Hooded Oriole, which was attached to the under side of a palm leaf.

Mr. Bryant says that most of the nests of the St. Lucas House Finch which he found at Comondu "were in palm trees and well nigh inaccessible"; but one was on the "under side of a veranda awning of an *adobe* house" among the branches of a vine.

In central Lower California, Griffing Bancroft (1930) found this finch to be a "common and conspicuous bird about houses and gardens, but rare in natural surroundings. * * * " The nesting sites "most frequently chosen are on the outsides of occupied houses. Where the walls are of tule stems the linnets work their way between the upright stalks. The beams under the eaves and even the thatched roofs of adobes are also favored spots. We found many nests in olive trees and in various odd locations. On the desert, mistletoe in mesquites or flicker holes in cardon are most frequently used."

The eggs are practically indistinguishable from those of the species elsewhere. The measurements of 40 eggs average 18.9 by 13.9 millimeters; the eggs showing the four extremes measure *20.9* by 14. 9, 19.5 by *15.0*, *17.5* by 13.0, and 19.4 by *12.9* millimeters.

The plumage changes, food, voice, and other habits probably do not differ from those of other races of the species.

Distribution

Range.—The San Lucas house finch is resident in the southern half of Baja California (33 miles west of Calmallí, Cabo San Lucas, offshore islands), southern coastal and central interior Sonora (Guaymas, Río Sonora north to lat. 30° N., San Esteban Island), northern Sinaloa (Río Fuerte), and southwestern Chihuahua (Barranca de Cobre).

Egg dates.—Baja California: 4 records, April 26 to May 18.

CARPODACUS MEXICANUS CLEMENTIS Mearns
San Clemente House Finch
PLATE 16

Habits

Edgar A. Mearns (1898) described and named this finch, based on a specimen taken on San Clemente Island, Calif. He gave it the following diagnosis: "Similar to *Carpodacus mexicanus frontalis* (Say), but with larger legs and feet and heavier coloration. The striping of the under surface is much broader than in typical specimens of *frontalis* from the eastern base of the Rocky Mountains. The wings are shorter, the tail perhaps a trifle longer, and the bill much larger and more convex above. It is, in fact, intermediate between the form of *frontalis* inhabiting the neighboring mainland of California and *Carpodacus mcgregori* Anthony, from San Benito Island, about twenty miles west of Cerros (or Cedros) Island, Lower California, which latter (*C. mcgregori*) is but another step towards *Carpodacus amplus* Ridgway of Guadalupe Island."

In commenting on the status of this subspecies, A. J. van Rossem (1925) remarks: "For some years past, the standing of *Carpodacus mexicanus clementis* Mearns has suffered assault by various writers," and then goes on to say: "The extent of red or yellow on the males, the proportion of red to yellow males, and the measurements of wing and tail in either sex are all items to which no diagnostic value can be attached. The tarsi and feet of *clementis* are slightly heavier in appearance but are not longer than in *frontalis*, and, considering the variation displayed, this tendency will not bear stressing. The characters which appear to provide the most secure basis for differentiating the island race are the decidedly heavier bill, the intensity or brilliancy of coloration in the males and the heavier streaking of the females."

There is very little to be said about the habits of this island form, which do not seem to differ much from those of its mainland relative.

A. Braziar Howell (1917) says of it: "The breeding season is a long one, and at least three broods must be raised each year. * * * Nesting sites originally were in cactus plants or in niches of cliffs, but the birds are now taking advantage of the chance to occupy more sheltered situations in buildings and sheds, where such occur. * * * Linnets are fond of congregating about the opuntia patches, on the ripe fruit of which they feed extensively."

Earlier he says: "Two phases of coloration occur in this form, the usual red phase and another in which the red is replaced by yellow. Every intergradation between these two is encountered. I have seen specimens in which the yellow was of very limited extent, a male marked like a female except for a faint red tinge on the chest, a female showing a trace of red, and another with a tinge of yellow."

The measurements of 40 eggs average 19.6 by 14.3 millimeters; the eggs showing the four extremes measure *22.5* by 14.9, 19.4 by *15.3*, *17.9* by 14.9, and 19.3 by *13.5* millimeters.

DISTRIBUTION

Range.—The San Clemente house finch is resident on Santa Barbara, San Nicolas, Santa Catalina, and San Clemente Islands off southern California and Los Coronodos Islands off northwestern Baja California.

Egg dates.—Santa Catalina Islands: 12 records, March 15 to July 13; 6 records, April 8 to April 23.

San Clemente Island: 21 records, February 7 to May 30; 15 records, March 23 to March 30.

CARPODACUS McGREGORI Anthony

McGregor's House Finch

HABITS

This large-billed house finch is characterized by its describer, A. W. Anthony (1897) as "nearest *C. amplus* but slightly smaller, with more compressed and laterally flattened mandible, longer tail and different coloration; larger than *C. mexicanus frontalis*, bill much larger, its lateral outlines viewed from above, parallel for nearly half the length. Red colors replaced by orange tints."

He describes the coloration of the adult male as follows: "Above dark olive gray heavily streaked with blackish slate; rump pinkish orange; forehead, superciliary stripe, and malar region orange vermilion; chin, throat and breast lighter, approaching orange chrome; rest of lower parts whitish, heavily streaked with slaty; wings and tail dusky brown; primaries and tail feathers edged with whitish; wing-coverts edged and tipped with buffy white."

Of its habitat on the San Benito Islands off the west coast of Lower California, Anthony says: "McGregor's Finch seems to be rather rare but well distributed over the island that we explored, the largest of the group of three. There is very little vegetation on this island, which is little more than a reef less than two (?) miles in extent, and it is rather surprising that a species of this genus should be found there at all."

Richard C. McGregor (1898), for whom this species was named, writes:

We found examples of *C. mcgregori* distributed over the two large Benitos, but on account of their extreme shyness they were difficult to obtain. We were at the islands too late to collect eggs, but I secured three young birds about ready to leave the nest. The parents had constructed their nest about two feet above the ground in a century plant (*Agave*). It was made after the fashion of *C. frontalis*, of a miscellaneous lot of bark, twigs, and fibre. The three young are of different sizes, of which the smallest is here described.

* * * The young plumage differs in coloration but little from that of the adult female. Upper parts heavily marked with clove brown, edges and tips of the feathers cinnamon; lower parts streaked with clove and cinnamon; tertials and rectrices broadly edged and tipped with wood brown.

One set of four eggs reported by E. N. Harrison from Lower California April 1, measures 20.0 by 15.0, 20.0 by 15.1, 20.1 by 15.5, and 19.5 by 15.5 millimeters.

DISTRIBUTION

Range.—McGregor's house finch is resident on the San Benito Islands and, rarely, on Cedros Island off central western Baja California.

CARPODACUS AMPLUS Ridgway
Guadalupe House Finch

HABITS

A larger house finch, with an even larger bill, lives on Guadalupe Island, off the west coast of Lower California.

Ridgway (1901) describes it as "similar to *C. mexicanus mexicanus*, but much larger, the bill especially; coloration darker and browner above, more broadly streaked with dusky beneath; the adult male with red (or yellow) of throat, etc., extended over breast."

It seems worthwhile to consider the environment in which the Guadalupe house finch still continues its somewhat precarious existence on an island where at least two endemic forms have already become extinct and others seem to be threatened with a similar fate. The following extracts are from a paper by John E. Thayer and Outram Bangs (1908):

Guadaloupe Island, the northern end of which lies about 160 miles southwest from San Antonio point, Lower California, is about 20 miles long and from 3 to 7 miles wide. It is of volcanic origin, and is traversed throughout its entire length by a chain of mountains, the highest of which is some 4500 feet above sea level. The western and northern sides of this range slope rapidly toward the ocean, ending in many places in high perpendicular cliffs. Toward the south the slope is more gradual and ends less abruptly. The southern part of the island, which is lowest, is rocky and barren, and during May and June, 1906, was a sun-burned waste with hardly a leaf of living verdure.

At the northern end of the island extending along a narrow ridge, and in some places down its perpendicular face is a fast decaying pine wood. No young trees appear anywhere and the old ones are gradually falling, the ground being strewn with decaying trunks. * * * Most of the higher parts of the island are open, rocky table land, but near the very highest part, north of Mt. Augusta, is a large cypress wood, occupying an area of nearly three square miles. The eastern edge of this large cypress grove ends abruptly at a ridge below which is another much lower table land. Upon this is a second but very much smaller grove of cypress with several springs and pools of water, more or less alkaline, near by. Here Brown and Marsden made their camp. Among the cypresses of both groves there are numerous dried stumps of some shrub now extinct in Guadaloupe. No young trees could be found in or about the groves, and most of the old trees show the marks of the teeth of goats, and many are dying. Far down the northwestern slope there is a large grove of cabbage palms, and another smaller one near Steamer Point on the west shore. Among the palms are a few fine oaks, from 30 to 65 feet in height, and under a cliff east of the cabins several stunted ones that branch very low down like shrubs * * * .

The domestic goat and cat turned loose upon the island many years ago, are of course responsible for the destruction of its flora and ornis. Brown and Marsden estimated the numbers of the goat to be between six and eight thousand. It eats up every growing thing. All shrubs have long been exterminated and not a young tree, palm, oak, pine or cypress can be found in the island. The cat is also very numerous and undoubtedly has caused the extinction of two of the island's native birds—the towhee and the Guadaloupe wren—while the rock wren, junco, flicker and petrel, suffer much from its depredations.

In spite of its environment and enemies, the house finch seems to be flourishing, for the same authors say in the same paper:

The house finch is by far the commonest bird of the island. Mr. Brown has sent us the following account of it: "On our arrival—May 1—well grown young were about with the old birds, and at that time the house finches were scattered about in large numbers all over the island. On the cliffs and about the rocks near the landing there were several hundred of them. Late in June they gathered in flocks and all left the lower altitudes, even those, some thirty or forty, that had been living about our cabins. Empty nests were found in a variety of situations, in the pines and cypresses, in cactus plants, and in crevices in the rocks. Their food seemed to consist chiefly of grass seeds and insects, but the birds that lived near our cabins were very partial to goat meat and made our meat-shed their headquarters."

Nesting.—Walter E. Bryant (1887) gives the following account of the nesting habits of the Guadalupe house finch:

Two nests were found in cypress trees nearly completed by February 22. A nest and set of five fresh eggs (No. 792, author's oological collection), which in consequence of a heavy storm had been deserted, was taken on the 1st of March. From this date began the nesting season of this species.

The last nest, taken April 7th, contained five eggs, with small embryos in them. In nearly every instance, the birds selected for a nesting place the upper side of a cypress branch in the angle formed by its intersection with the trunk, thus avoiding the storm-shaken foliage. They seemed to show a preference for the leeward side of a tree, where the nest would be protected from prevailing winds. One prudent couple had built in a clump of mistletoe, at a height of twenty feet.

Several pairs built in the tops of palms. The nests were ordinarily not more than ten or fifteen feet from the ground.

The birds make but slight demonstrations while their nest is being removed, uttering only a few notes of protest, or silently witnessing a wrong hitherto unknown to them.

The material used for the outer structure of the nests consisted of the dark, dead stems of weeds, only the finer ones being selected. One nest found in a pine tree, had the foundation and sides made of pine needles, with the invariable lining of goat's hair, black and white being used indiscriminately. The external diameter of the nest is about 130 mm., with a central cavity about 65 mm.

Eggs.—He says of these: "The eggs, sometimes four in number, but oftener five during the early part of the season, are colored precisely like the average specimens of *C. frontalis rhodocolpus*, the spots being either sparingly applied or entirely wanting. They also resemble them in general shape, but the size seems to distinguish them. The five eggs of set No. 792, measure respectively 22 × 15; 22 × 15.5; 22.5 × 15.5; 23 × 15.5; 23 × 16.5 mm. The length measurement varies from 19.5–24 mm., and the width 15–16.5 mm. The average of thirty-two specimens is 21.3 × 15.5 mm."

The measurements of 50 eggs average 21.5 by 15.6 millimeters; he eggs showing the four extremes measure *24.1* by 15.7, 23.0 by *16.5*, and *19.0* by *14.9* millimeters.

Plumage.—According to C. H. Blake, the adult male has both the rown and the red darker than in the Mexican house finch (*C. m. nexicanus*), with the red extending in lighter shades down onto the streaked area of the breast. The distribution of color resembles the nuch paler San Clemente house finch. The red of the forehead and crown is less extensive than in the common house finch. The females and immature males are darker than those of the Mexican house inch, and the ventral streaks are broader, resembling in this respect he San Clemente house finch.

Food.—Bryant (1887) says: "The dissection of specimens showed he food to consist chiefly of seeds from the cypress tree, mingled with green seeds of 'chick-weed.' Some of those taken near camp had heir crops well filled with bits of tallow picked from the body of a goat which had been dressed and hung under a tree."

Behavior.—Bryant (1887) noticed nothing in either their habits or song that differed from those of the mainland forms, and adds: "Soon after settling on the top of the island in December, 1885, the 'Gorrions' began to collect about the camp, making the mornings joyous with heir song.

"By our refraining from discharging fire-arms in the immediate vicinity of the camp, they soon became quite tame, hopping about camp during the day, and roosting at night in the thickest cypress, or, during a storm, under the eaves of the palm-thatched huts."

Enemies.—Bryant (1887) says: "They are easily entrapped under a box, and it was in this way that the Mexican women at the settlement succeeded in catching, during my stay, as many as two or three dozen, which they ate."

But their chief enemy is the introduced cat, and it is largely due to their nesting in the spiny chollas, or other inaccessible places, that hey have survived the predation of this animal. However, A. W. Anthony (1925) makes the following statement: "Formerly one of the most abundant land birds on the island but now reduced to about 10% of its abundance 25 years ago, the destruction being due to the thousand of cats that infest all parts of the island. The species nests largely in the cactus found over most parts of the island, which fact saves the nestlings until able to flutter to the ground, where they fall an easy prey."

DISTRIBUTION

Range.—The Guadalupe house finch is resident on Guadalupe Island off central western Baja California.

Egg dates.—Guadalupe Islands: 14 records, March 21 to May 25; 7 records, March 24 to March 26.

SPOROPHILA TORQUEOLA SHARPEI Lawrence

Sharpe's Seedeater

HABITS

Some confusion has existed in the nomenclature of the seedeaters, but I understand that the above name is now established for the race of these tiny finches (the white-collared seedeater of the 1957 A.O.U. Check-List) that is to be found in the lower Rio Grande Valley of southern Texas and in adjacent regions in northern Mexico. Other races of the species occur elsewhere in Mexico and Central America.

As I had but a fleeting glimpse of this little midget near Brownsville, Tex., and as very little has been published about its habits, we must be content with what our contributors have sent to us regarding this and closely allied forms of the species.

I wrote to L. Irby Davis, who lives within the breeding range of this subspecies at Harlingen, Tex., for information about it. He has sent me some interesting notes from which I quote: "The males had regular territory areas selected by early April and spent considerable time each day in singing from several favorite perches within the area. They usually moved from one perch to another in about 5 minutes time, but sometimes even less. The females were seldom seen, as they were feeding in the grass most of the time before nesting. They are not extremely vigorous in defense of territory; however, a male will often chase an intruder quite some distance when the latter approaches a singing post that is occupied at the moment. When the male is at the far side of his territory, a visiting male may perch in a favorite bush or feed beneath it without being disturbed."

Alexander F. Skutch has sent me a copy of his chapter on this species for his proposed work on life histories of Central American birds. He says that the seedeaters "live in open, grassy places, including pastures, roadsides, weedy fields, and even marshlands covered with tall coarse grasses."

George B. Sennett (1879) says "its habit of frequenting low bushes and weeds preclude its frequent observation where there is so much undergrowth. One specimen was shot in a small tree, and about nine feet from the ground, which was the only one observed at such height. It is tame and quite fearless."

Nesting.—Davis writes to me of a nest that he had been watching. "The nest was 3 feet up from the ground in the crotch (where a

ngle stem of about one-half inch diameter branched out into a
rcle of about 12 flowering branches) of an upright weed. The
lant was about 5 feet high and was growing in a community of
milar plants in an abandoned field at the side of an irrigation canal.
he nest was about 2 inches in diameter and 1½ inches deep. As
usual with this species, other pairs occupied adjoining territories
1 both sides of the canal. Most nests are placed in weeds as far
s I have been able to observe; however, I did find one nest in a pile
f vines. The giant ragweed (*Ambrosia aptera*) is a favorite nesting
lant here.

"It would seem, however, that any tall upright weed which grows
1 rather dense stands would be just as acceptable. Most of the
ests which I have found have been about 4 to 5 feet up. As far as
can recall, the limits have been about 3 feet to 5½ feet. The nest
ported on was constructed almost, if not quite, entirely from a
ngle type of slender fiber. One of these was examined with a hand
nse and found to be the denuded rachis of a spike of Rhodes grass
Chloris gayana)."

Edward R. Ford has sent me the following data for a nest and
aree eggs of Sharpe's seedeater that was collected on Apr. 26, 1937,
ear Santa Maria, Hidalgo County, Tex. The nest site was on the
lge of a thicket by a roadside and near a resaca. The nest was
egun on April 15; there was one egg in it on the 22nd and three on
1e 26th. "The nest was placed 3 feet up in a slender, thorn-bearing
1rub (not a desert species) supported by two upright twigs. It
·as composed almost entirely of fine rootlets, light brown in color,
ith one or two small, straight plant stems, giving the whole a degree
f rigidity, and a strand or two of long black hair, together with a
it of vegetable down. The floor of the nest was partly afforded
y the branchlets which supported it. It measured 2¼ inches in
utside diameter and 1¾ inside. Outside depth was 1⅜ inches."

Alexander F. Skutch (MS.) gives the following account of nest-
uilding by a closely related subspecies in Central America: "The
est is built by the female alone. Her first operation is to cover
1e supporting twigs with cobweb.

"Standing in what is to be the nest cavity, she wraps strands of
obweb about the surrounding branchlets, and soon has the entire
est outlined, or better, sketched in with cobwebs, while there are
ill only a few wisps of firmer material. It is remarkable that a
ird with so short and thick a bill, apparently little suited for work
ith stuff so light and delicate as cobweb, should handle it so well.
[ext the seedeater gathers fine rootlets, fibers, or delicate branches
·om the inflorescences of grasses, for the body of the nest. These
re sparingly used and form a thin, open fabric through which much

light passes.   The lining may be of horsehairs when these are available

"Five or six days of leisurely work suffice to complete the sligh structure."

James C. Merrill (1879) reports two nests of Sharpe's seedeater at Fort Brown, Tex., both in bushes, supported by twigs, and place 3 and 4 feet from the ground.   Of one of these he says: "It is delicate little nest, supported at the rim and beneath by twigs, an built of a very fine, dried grass, with which a few horse-hairs, a lea or two, and a small rag are interwoven: it is 1.70 wide by 1.50 i depth.   Both these nests are open and transparent."

Eggs.—Skutch (MS.) describes the eggs of this species as follows

"The eggs vary from pale blue to bluish white or pearl gray i ground color and are finely mottled with light brown or chocolate the markings usually heaviest in a wreath about the thick end, bu by no means absent from the remaining surface.   Some eggs bea a few heavy blotches of black or deep brown in addition to the fine and lighter flecking.   The measurements of 13 eggs average 16.3 b 12.7 millimeters.   Those showing the four extremes measure *17.5* b 12.3, 15.9 by *13.5* and *15.5* by *12.3* millimeters."

The two sets of eggs in the Harvard Museum of Comparativ Zoology are ovate in shape.   The ground is pale bluish white, an they are profusely spotted and blotched with shades of "clov brown," "seal brown," "light seal brown," "Rood's brown," an "mummy brown," with undermarkings of "light mouse gray." Some eggs are so heavily marked that the spots almost obscure th ground, and are confluent toward the top of the egg forming a soli cap.

The measurements of 50 eggs average 16.1 by 12.3 millimeters the eggs showing the four extremes measure *17.5* by 12.2, 15.7 b *13.5*, *15.0* by 12.6, and 15.9 by *11.5* millimeters.

Young.—Skutch (MS.) writes: "Incubation is performed by th female alone.   In one instance, the eggs hatched in 13 days.   Th nestlings are attended by both parents and remain in the nest 10 o 11 days."

Davis writes to me of a nest that he found on June 10: "Fou seedeater eggs were being incubated along with two cowbird eggs Two of the seedeater eggs were pushed far down into the nest materia by the cowbird eggs, and the latter were removed.   The two youn hatched on June 12 and left the nest on June 20.   Both parent attended the young in the nest."

Plumages.—Ridgway (1901) describes the young of *morelleti* (th name then in use for this race) as follows: "Similar to the adult female but wing bars deep buffy and plumage of a much looser texture."   Thi doubtless refers to the juvenal, or first, plumage.   He goes on to say

Immature males are variously intermediate in coloration between
the fully adult male, as described above, and the adult female, two or
three years being probably required for attainment of the full plumage.
Some freshly molted adult males, especially those showing traces of
immaturity, have the under parts posterior to the black jugular band
more or less buffy, sometimes quite strongly so. These occur in same
localities as specimens with the same parts pure white."

Lawrence (1889) adds the following: "The most mature males of *S.
sharpei* are grayish above, with the crown and sides of the head black,
and the back blotched with black; the under parts are pale fulvous
white with an indistinct collar of black, though the latter character is
seen in but few specimens."

Voice.—Davis gives, in his notes, the following impressions of the
song of Sharpe's seedeater: "The song most often heard here (or should
I say noticed?) is a loud, clear *sweet sweet sweet cheer cheer cheer*.
There are a number of variations, but they are usually weaker and
hence not noticed as often. Variations are: *Sweet sweet cheer cheer
cheer chee swee swee r r r r r r r*, the end being a low, dry roll; *sweet
sweet chip pip swee; sweet sweet sweet chip; chip chip chip suwee suwee;
se swee churrrrrrr.*

"The call is a soft, plaintive *che*, given at intervals of 5 to 12 seconds,
when disturbed."

In Mexico, he heard songs that were quite different from those he
heard in Texas.

Field marks.—Davis tells me: "Our birds do not show white collars
cross the back of the neck nor black bands across the breast. These
so called typical marks of the adult male bird do not become conspicuously noticeable in the field until one gets down to central Vera Cruz,
as far as I have been able to observe. That, I presume, means that
such marks are seen mainly in the nominate form."

In this connection, it is interesting to note that, apparently, neither
Lawrence (1889) nor Ridgway (1901) had seen any fully adult males
showing the above characters fully developed, from the region of the
lower Rio Grande.

Lawrence said, when he gave it the subspecific name, *sharpei*, "none
of the numerous specimens received from Texas had the black band on
the throat, which exists in the full-plumaged male of *S. morelleti*."
And Ridgway, some years later, when he treated *sharpei* as a synonym
under his description of *S. morelleti*, wrote: "It is true specimens representing the fully adult male plumage described above are wanting in
the series from the State of Tamaulipas and the adjacent parts of Texas;
but males from that district agree exactly in plumage with immature
males from more southern localities, and I believe that fully adult
males have simply not yet been taken in the region designated."

Winter.—Davis writes to me: "I have not been able to detect a∎ evidence of migration among the seedeaters here. We seem to ha∎ just as many in winter as in summer. There is some local shifti∎ about of population, and sometimes we see loose flocks of 100 or mo∎ in winter. Such flocks are likely to be found in tall grasses alo∎ resacas."

DISTRIBUTION

Range.—Sharpe's seedeater is resident from central Nuevo Le∎ (Monterrey) and southern Texas (Rio Grande City, Port Isabe∎ south to eastern San Luis Potosí (Valles) and northern Veracr∎ (Laguna Tamiahua).

Egg dates.—Texas: 37 records, March 12 to September 3; ∎ records, April 26 to May 25.

PINICOLA ENUCLEATOR LEUCURA (Muller)

Canadian Pine Grosbeak

PLATE 18

HABITS

One winter morning many years ago, during my boyhood days, ∎ looked out of one of our windows and was surprised to see a numb∎ of strange birds in one of our maple trees; they were sitting quiet∎ or moving about slowly, apparently feeding on the leaf buds; th∎ looked very plump and seemed to be dark gray in color. Eve∎ after one was shot, I could not identify it until I had consulted t∎ bird books in the public library and decided that it was a pine gro∎ beak. We saw much of them that winter, and we boys amused ou∎ selves by catching them under a sieve, propped up by a stick with ∎ string attached to it. They were so tame that we could walk up ∎ them and almost catch them in our hands. We kept one rosy ma∎ in a large cage, where he proved to be a docile pet and a good singe∎ but we released him in the spring.

This grosbeak makes its summer home in the coniferous forests ∎ Canada, northern New England, and possibly in some of the extrem∎ northern parts of some of the more western States. It breeds ∎ far north as the limit of trees in northern Canada, from the Anders∎ River region to northern Ungava and Labrador. South of the Cana∎ dian border it is rare or extremely local.

Courtship.—Dr. and Mrs. J. Murray Speirs observed courtshi∎ feeding near North Bay, Ontario, on Mar. 30, 1944. Mrs. Spei∎ writes that, while snow was falling with a southwest wind, a ma∎ that had been feeding on willow buds flew suddenly toward a fema∎

PLATE 17

E. Porter

Arizona, Apr. 17, 1941

FEMALE HOUSE FINCH AT NEST IN CHOLLA CACTUS

Toronto, Ontario

H. M. Hall

CANADIAN PINE GROSBEAK

lso present. From the eminence of a raspberry cane 6 inches above
ιe female the male reached down toward her and offered something
rge and white which she accepted. The male then glanced upward,
ιd both birds flitted their tails. The female then ate a few shriveled
ιspberry seeds that were still clinging to the cane and twice during
ιe process reached up and pecked her mate under the tail. Both
ιrds then flew off with bouncing flight.

Nesting.—MacFarlane (1891) reported a nest in northern Mac-
ensie, of which he says: "In the spring of 1861 an Indian discovered
nest of this species on a pine tree some 60 miles south of Fort
nderson, but unfortunately while descending therewith he fell and
estroyed both nest and eggs; and although we frequently observed
)me birds at the post and elsewhere, we never succeeded in finding
nother nest." In another publication (1908) he refers to this same
est as being "in a spruce tree," which seems more likely.

James Bond writes to me of a nest found by Edward Finkel near
Iount Lewis on the Gaspé Peninsula on July 17, 1946. He says
ιat "it was in the crotch of a low shrub, about 2 feet above the
round and that the trunk was about 2 inches in diameter." It
)ntained two small young. Harry B. Goldstein, a member of the
arty, writes to me that the nest "was compactly built; its founda-
on was composed of small twigs and roots; the interior was made
p of very fine rootlets, fine bits of grasses and lichens."

Harold F. Tufts (1910) gives an interesting account of the finding
f a nest of the pine grosbeak near Shelburne, Nova Scotia, on June
0, 1910: "The wood road which I was following led through a large
rea of wet bog or mossy swamp, rather thickly overgrown with
tunted spruce and hackmatack and scattered bunches of swamp maple
nd laurel bushes." By following up a singing male he found the
ιate and followed her:

Following the course taken by the female as nearly as I could, I searched care-
ιlly among the densely branched spruces for a nest. After nearly an hour of
ιunging through the bog, knee deep in water and slime, till darkness was setting
ι and failure seemed certain, finally I noted a dark mass some fifteen feet up in
slender young spruce, close to its top. Giving the tree a slight tap with my
ιnd the bird flew off and I was delighted to recognize the female Pine Grosbeak
ι she fluttered about close at hand.

The nest, a rather bulky sprawling affair of twigs and grasses, resembled some-
hat in both situation and general make-up that of the Blue Jay. The three
ιggs were rather advanced in incubation, containing young well formed—but
·ith the use of caustic potash the shells were properly emptied.

Positive evidence of nesting in Maine was furnished by Miss
ιarie Kaizer Maddox, who wrote to Ora W. Knight (1908) as follows:
Four years ago in the month of May I found a Pine Grosbeak's nest
bout seven miles north of Jackman, near a sporting camp at Hale

Pond. The nest was not in thick woods but in open pasture near tł
Canada Road. It was woven of twigs and moss, lined with rabbit
hair and contained four pale-green eggs, flecked with purple ar
hardly to be distinguished from the moss itself. This nest was in
fir tree about four feet from the ground. It was neatly woven b
much less substantial than most nests of that size. Probably tł
fact that the region is three thousand feet above sea level accoun
for a nest in that latitude."

Henry Nehrling (1896) writes: "I am in the happy situation
report of the Pine Grosbeak's breeding in northern Wisconsin. M
A. J. Schoenebeck found a nest of this bird May 5, 1890, near Boyd
Creek, six miles west of Chaguamegon Bay, Bayfield County, Wi
It was built in a hemlock about nine feet above the ground and seve
feet from the trunk. The ground was dry and the forest consiste
of deciduous and coniferous trees. The structure was composed
hemlock and other twigs, and the interior of grasses and rootlet
lined with finer grasses and a little moss."

Eggs.—The pine grosbeak lays from two to five eggs with for
being the most frequent number. They are ovate to elongate
ovate, and have a slight luster. The ground is "deep bluish gla
cous," "bluish glaucous," "court gray," or "Etain blue"; speckle
spotted, and blotched with shades of "dark grayish olive," "dar
olive," "bone brown," "mummy brown," and black, with unde
markings which may be in the form either of small spots or blotch
of "light mouse gray" or "light neutral gray." Some eggs are un
formly marked over the entire surface; others have a decided concer
tration toward the large end where often a wreath is formed.

The measurements of 40 eggs average 26.0 by 18.3 millimeter:
the eggs showing the four extremes measure *28.8* by 18.2, 25.9 b
19.3, and *22.4* by *17.0* millimeters.

Young.—Miss Maddox wrote further to Knight (1908): "I fin
that the incubation was completed on May 27, being the thirteent
day after the fourth and last egg of the clutch appeared in the nes
The female bird as far as I could learn did all the sitting. Severa
times I surprised the male bringing her food and saw her leave tł
nest and receive it from him, near but never on the nest. Bot
parent birds fed the fledglings after they left the nest, which occurre
the twentieth day after they were hatched."

Plumages.—Dwight (1900) describes the juvenal plumage of tł
pine grosbeak as follows: "Above, bistre, tinged on crown and rum
with dull ochre-yellow. Wings and tail clove-brown with pale bu
edgings sometimes whitish especially on tertiaries and tail. Win
bands indistinct, pale buff. Below, hair-brown or drab, washed

pecially on breast and sides, with ochraceous, the feather edgings
ood-brown." The sexes are alike.

The first winter plumage is acquired by a partial postjuvenal molt,
ginning early in September and involving the contour plumage
d the wing coverts, but not the rest of the wings nor the tail. He
scribes this plumage in the young male as follows: "Above, chiefly
le olive-brown, sometimes with reddish or yellowish tinge veiled
th smoke-gray edgings; the crown, auriculars, rump and upper
il coverts ochre to gallstone-yellow, often orange, the feathers
rk centrally, usually a sprinkling of brick-red feathers and some-
nes the yellows completely replaced by red, occasionally carmine.
low, smoke-gray, the breast and throat usually with some red
d yellow not very pronounced.

"Wing coverts tipped with white forming two distinct bands the
sser coverts plumbeous and ochre tinged."

The first nuptial is "acquired by wear, brightening [the] colors
d assuming a golden sheen, this optical effect being due to loss of
rbules * * *."

A complete postnuptial molt occurs in late summer or early fall,
oducing the well-known pinkish plumage of the adult winter male.
ear again produces the brighter colors seen in the spring.

Of the plumages of the female, Dwight says: "In juvenal plumage
e sexes are practically indistinguishable. In first winter plumage
ller than the corresponding dress of the male; above, olive brown
th smoke-gray edgings, the crown and rump ochre or dull olive-
llow, entirely smoke-gray below. * * * The adult winter plum-
;e is similar to male first winter, but duller with only a tinge of
d at most on crown, rump or breast."

Food.—Knight (1908) says that, in Maine, the pine grosbeaks "eat
ds of the maple, elm, birch, apple, mountain ash, elder, pear,
plar, willow and other native trees, and the seeds of birch, hackma-
ck, pines, fir, spruce and in general almost any of the grass and
ed seeds at a pinch. Their prime choice in the free state is seem-
gly crab-apples, mountain ash fruit, pine seeds and maple buds.
y captive birds eagerly ate flies, beetles, angle worms, caterpillars
d insects of other kinds."

Forbush (1929) adds: "Among the fruits eaten are those of the
sh or mountain cranberry, barberry, mountain ash or rowan tree,
rginia juniper or red cedar, crabapple, apple, black alder, privet,
wthorn, buckthorn, sumac, Japanese barberry and waxwork
elastrus scandens). * * * It takes also seeds of roses. It is very
nd of sunflower seeds and eats those of hemp, burdock, ragweed,
mb's quarters and other weeds."

Ira N. Gabrielson (1924) reported on 394 stomachs of which 3(were taken during the winter months, October to March, inclusiv Distribution was from Alaska, 5 Provinces of Canada, and 13 State He says the pine grosbeak "feeds in flocks which usually settle down one tree or more and feed for some time, making a full meal on or variety of fruit or seed if not disturbed. Local conditions, such relative abundance and availability, probably govern the selection food. For example, a series of stomachs from New Hampshire co tained little except seeds of blackberries (*Rubus*) and the stamina flower buds of pine. When both gizzard and gullet were examined was usual to find the gizzard filled with one of these foods and the gull with the other. * * * Stomachs of a series from British Columb were filled with seeds of snowberry (*Symphoricarpos*)."

Continuing, Gabrielson says winter food was 99.1 percent vegetab) *Rubus* seeds occurred in 207 stomachs and amounted to 14.37 perce) of the winter food. Coniferous buds were found in 166 stomachs an made 24.22 percent. "Both had been taken from many differe) regions by birds which were collected in every winter month." Oth(items show high percentages because they constitute the entire conte) of a few stomachs from one locality, as snowberry, which amounted (17.3 percent, having been eaten almost exclusively by 69 birds in or place. Weed seeds formed 7.67 percent of the diet, juniper berri(and other coniferous seeds 4.15 percent. He lists a great variety (wild fruit, which totaled 14.34 percent. Mast, probably compose largely of beechnuts or acorns, was 5.66 percent. The various forn of animal food listed were nearly all found in coniferous buds and ma well have been devoured accidentally with them.

Gabrielson says the few summer stomachs contained 83.83 percen vegetable food and 16.17 percent animal. The percentage of wil fruit was higher; maple and ash seeds were absent. Grasshopper ants, spiders, and caterpillars accounted for 15.08 percent of the tot(food. There were a few small flies and beetles.

In Nova Scotia in July Harrison F. Lewis observed a bird eatir ripe fruit of *Amelanchier*, or shad bush. The bird would pick or fruit at a time, manipulate it in its beak, extract and swallow the see(The outer skin and attached pulp fell to the ground. A day later h wife watched a male which seemed to be eating scales of rust off fence-wire. Another bird, in female plumage, was noted the followir day picking repeatedly at the ground on bare, gravelly soil. The(could have been wind-blown seeds present. Another summering bir ate the seeds of mountain holly, *Nemopanthys mucronata*, in fashio similar to that employed on the shad bush.

William Youngworth (1955b) mentions seeing a bird splitting th green seed pods and extracting the seeds of a Persian lilac.

Maurice Brooks (1956) in referring to an invasion into West Virginia uring the winter of 1954–55 states that the birds "fed on frozen fruits particularly apples), seeds of maple and white ash, and on some ortion of the twigs of conifers, especially pitch pine (*Pinus rigida*). n addition they made extensive use of other plant foods, some of hich would not be available northward. These included seeds of ulip poplar, wild grapes (*Vitis* sp.), black haw and wild raisin (*Viurnum prunifolium* and *V. cassinoides*), flowering dogwood (*Cornus orida*), and greenbrier (*Smilax* sp.)." The birds were also noted eeding on fruits of staghorn sumach (*Rhus hirta*).

R. E. Mumford wrote Mr. Bent of observing birds on Dec. , 1951, eating the red berries of nightshade, *Solanum dulcamara*, uring an invasion into Indiana. One bird fed on the jack pine cones *Pinus banksiana*). Birds also ate the seeds of a planted variety f privet and of a cultivated honeysuckle.

Albert E. Allin writes Taber that the fruit of the "Rowan tree," ctually the showy mountain ash, *Pyrus decora*, is by far the most avored food for the great numbers of pine grosbeaks wintering in the egion of Fort William, Ontario. Initially, the birds feed in the trees. Melting snow in the spring reveals a further food supply on the ground. Next in favor come lilacs, probably *Syringa villosa*. Ornamental pples (crabs) are, perhaps, equally popular once the rowan crop has een depleted. Stragglers remaining after the main flocks of birds ave moved on southerly or in other directions feed at times off the amaras of the black ash, *Fraxinus nigra*, and, at times, partake of igh-bush cranberries, *Viburnum trilobum*. Occasionally birds feed off he box elder, *Acer negundo*, and white birch, *Betula papyrifera*.

Behavior.—In Newfoundland, the pine grosbeak is called "the nope," a most appropriate name for a bird that spends so much ime sitting still or moving about very slowly. When with us in vinter it is surprisingly tame or unafraid, allowing closer approach han does any of our other common birds.

It seems stupidly tame; one has no difficulty in catching it in the implest trap, with a slip noose, or in a hand net; I have tried picking t up by hand, but have never quite succeeded. It adapts itself eadily to captivity and makes an attractive pet. Knight (1908) ays that "one never knows the real loveliness of their character until he has studied them close at hand for a protracted period as vas my privilege for about seven years. In captivity the male sings lmost continuously during the morning hours and more or less luring the whole day in the spring months, and though not quite as ull of music at other seasons, there is hardly a day in the year but hat my captive birds sang more or less."

Edgar A. Mearns (1880) writes: "They appear to be utterly devoi of fear of man. If their ranks are thinned by the gunner, the surv vors will rarely be driven away, but come close up to the hunter and h from branch to branch in his vicinity, scrutinizing him closely ar uttering a reproachful note like that of the Fox Sparrow (*Passerel iliaca*); they often fly down to inspect the dead bodies of their cor panions lying upon the ground."

The flight of the pine grosbeak is slightly undulating, but not much so as with the woodpeckers or the goldfinch.

Forbush (1929) says: "During the winter these birds bathe in tl soft snow, standing in it, either on the ground or on the thick folia; of coniferous trees, fluttering their wings and throwing the snov spray over their plumage in the same manner in which many bir bathe in water."

Voice.—Mearns (1880) pays the following tribute to the song this bird:

The Pine Grosbeak's song is one of the finest, but I have only been privileg to listen to it on a single occasion—in March, 1875. * * * It was one fros morning, as I was following the course of a stream that flowed at the bottom of deep ravine, that I heard, most unexpectedly, a new song. It proceeded fro far up the glen. The notes were loud, rich and sweet. I listened to them wi a thrill of delight and wonder, and then pressed forward to identify the new v calist. Soon I discovered perched upon the top of a tall hemlock, a beautif red Pine Grosbeak—the author of one of the most delicious songs that I ev heard. Its carmine or rose-colored plumage, and its mellow notes, were a fea alike to the eye and ear; and, though I may never hear the Pine Grosbeak si again, I shall ever cherish towards it feelings of admiration and gratitude for tl revelation of beauty and melody which I so keenly appreciated on that occasio

Wendell Taber writes that the flight song may be classified somewhat of the type of the purple finch. The song of the latte bird, however, is rather slurred, with one note running into the nex No confusion between the two songs is possible. The song of th pine grosbeak is a sweet melodious carol, loud and distinct, and carrie quite a distance. Each note is clear-whistled rapidly and is sej arated by an infinitesimal break from the next succeeding not The various commonly heard call notes are scattered at interval through the song and are easily recognizable individually. Th song covers a much wider range of pitch, especially in the uppe range, than does that of the purple finch.

Harrison F. Lewis writes of a bird singing near his home in She burne County, Nova Scotia, in the early afternoon of Mar. 23 1953, a sunny day with maximum temperature of about 60° F. H has recorded two types of song. The ordinary song is a short, cor tinuous musical warble, not loud, but weak and altogether lackin in vigor and emphasis, in marked contrast to the vigorous, arden

ong of the purple finch, which it otherwise somewhat resembles.
The song gives the impression of flowing forth without the exercise
f any effort on the part of the bird either to utter it or to terminate
t. The singer does not seem interested in its song. Sung from a
erch in a tree, each song continues for 2 seconds or a little more.
Ie considers the flight song as being much less vigorous than that
f the purple finch.

Knight (1908) says: "Though it is a pleasure to watch a flock of
hese warmly clothed, plump, robust birds feeding cheerfully on a
old winter morning, the real pleasure of knowing them has not been
eached until the song of the male has been heard. Soft, tender,
ventriloquial and caressing at times, at others rising clear and loud
out always full of trills and warbles, the song of the Pine Grosbeak
easily places it on equal footing with any of our song birds."

He also mentions "a peculiar querulous whistled *caree* or *c-r-r-r-u*
or *ca-r-a-r*," which is evidently a note of warning, "for when one of
a flock of feeding birds utters it all cease feeding and stand trans-
ixed, looking cautiously about for danger or suddenly taking flight."
Another call, often uttered when a bird has just alighted, "sounds
ike a warbled *pee-ah-pree-pu*" and is "designed to call others to the
spot. When feeding they keep up a low whistled conversation
among themselves."

Francis H. Allen has sent me the following notes: "On June 28,
1888, Bradford Torrey and I found two or three singing males on
Mount Lafayette in New Hampshire. The song most resembled
that of the purple finch but was sweeter, wilder, and more interesting.
It was really a beautiful song.

"Besides the familiar flight call, suggestive of that of the greater
yellowlegs, the pine grosbeak has when feeding a soft, short whistle,
sometimes with a little roll in it, but usually unmodulated."

Wendell Taber had the experience of having four birds fly in and
alight beside him, uttering the while an amplified version of the
common flight call of the goldfinch. The imitation was so perfect
that Oscar M. Root, some 30 yards distant, turned to look
for goldfinches.

Field marks.—The pine grosbeak can generally be recognized by
its shape; it is a plump, stocky bird, about the size of a robin, but
much more robust, with a short, stubby black bill, two white wing
bars, and a slightly forked tail. Except in the rosy-colored males,
the colors are not conspicuous, the females showing only dull yellowish
ochre on the crowns and rumps. They are stolid birds and very
deliberate in their movements.

Winter.—Pine grosbeaks are not strictly migratory. They do not
make regular latitudinal movements in spring and fall. Those indi-

viduals that spend the summer in the mountains of northern Ne
England move down into the lowlands for the winter, while tho
that breed farther north at lower elevations either remain on or ne
their breeding grounds throughout the year or move southward whe
their food supply becomes scarce and they are forced to look for
elsewhere. These movements are irregular and erratic, sometim
insignificant in numbers, but at other times so impressive in volume
to be called invasions. J. Murray Speirs (1939) has publishe
some data showing that, in the vicinity of Toronto, periods of greates
abundance have occurred at intervals of 5 or 6 years, usually
The records for Massachusetts show intervals of only 2 years in on
case, 5 years in two, and 6 years in one case, with some longer inte
vals between invasions. Ludlow Griscom (1923), referring to th
New York City region, says: "There have been ten marked fligh
in the past ninety-six years, the last in the winter of 1903-04. Th
last eighteen years is the longest interval between flights of which
have any record." Some of the greatest invasions into Massachuset
occurred in the winters of 1869–70, 1874–75, 1892–93, and 1903–0
William Brewster (1895) has published a full account of the remarkab
flight that occurred during the winter of 1892–93, to which th
reader is referred.

That these great southward flights are not caused by severe winter
is shown by their absence during some of our hardest winters an
their presence in large numbers during some of our mildest and mos
open winters. The movements seem to be governed entirely by th
food supply. Referring to the causes of these flights, Forbush (1929
suggests:

When there is a heavy crop of beechnuts in northern Maine and the souther
Canadian forests, the Pine Grosbeaks sometimes swarm in those regions an
few come to Massachusetts, but a lack of wild fruit, cones and seeds in norther
forests might compel these birds to seek food to the southward.

* * * A dry spring and summer in the north, resulting in a scarcity of wil
fruit and seeds, may be the chief cause of the great southward flights, especiall
if the dearth of food comes the next season after a year of plenty with its con
sequent increase in the numbers of the birds. A fire sweeping through a grea
forested region or a great eruption of spruce-destroying insects, such as sometime
occurs, might have a similar effect.

The favorite haunts of the grosbeaks during their winter visit
with us are the more open coniferous forests or the hillsides covere
with an open growth of red cedars, which furnish shelter as wel
as food; we can almost always find them in such places when the
are with us. But they also resort to deciduous trees and shrub
about our homes, to orchards and to shade trees along the streets
of towns and cities, feeding on such fruits and seeds as are available

or on the leaf buds. William Brewster (1895) draws the following attractive picture of a flock of pine grosbeaks:

When I first saw them they were assembling in a large white ash which over-hangs the street. This tree was loaded with fruit, and with snow clinging to the fruit-clusters and to every twig. In a few minutes it also supported more than a hundred Grosbeaks who distributed themselves quite evenly over every part from the drooping lower, to the upright upper, branches and began shelling out and swallowing the seeds, the rejected wings of which, floating down in showers, soon gave the surface of the snow beneath the tree a light brownish tinge. The snow clinging to the twigs and branches was also quickly dislodged by the movements of the active, heavy birds and for the first few minutes it was inces-santly flashing out in puffs like steam from a dozen different points at once. The finer particles, sifting slowly down, filled the still air and enveloped the entire tree in a veillike mist of incredible delicacy and beauty, tinted, where the sunbeams pierced it, with rose, salmon, and orange, elsewhere of a soft dead white,—truly a fitting drapery for this winter picture,—the hardy Grosbeaks at their morning meal.

Albert E. Allin writes Taber that in the Fort William region of Ontario, where this species winters in great numbers, the relative winter abundance is associated directly with the relative abundance of fruit of the rowan tree, *Pyrus aucuparia*, which border the streets in quantity. Birds commence to arrive in October or early No-vember, appearing first on the outskirts of the cities, then pene-trating within. The pine grosbeak population builds up to a peak around Christmas or early in January, then decreases as the rowan fruit is consumed. A minor upsurge takes place again in late Feb-ruary or early March, but the high count of 200 birds as late as March 2, 1941, was unusual.

DISTRIBUTION

Range.—Mackenzie and Labrador to northern United States.

Breeding range.—Breeds from central Mackenzie (Great Bear Lake, Fort Reliance), northern Manitoba (Churchill), northern Ontario (Fort Severn, Fort Albany), northern Quebec (Richmond Gulf, Fort Chimo, George River), and northern Labrador (Okak) south to northern Alberta, central Saskatchewan, central Manitoba, central Ontario (Temagami, occasionally to Sundridge), and central Labrador (upper Hamilton River, Stag Bay).

Winter range.—Winters in southern parts of the breeding range, south casually to central Alberta (Edmonton), Nebraska (Neligh), Kentucky (Hickman), Maryland (Assateague Island), Massachusetts (Cambridge), southern Maine (Buckfield, Brewer), and Newfoundland (Pasadena, Bay Bulls).

Casual records.—Casual in Kansas (Hays).

Accidental in northern Keewatin (Repulse Bay).

Migration.—The data deal with the species as a whole. Late dates of spring departure are: North Carolina—Mt. Olive, April 10. West Virginia—Ona, April 25. Maryland—Garrett County, March 1. Pennsylvania—State College, May 1. New York—Tompkins County, May 5 (median of 5 years for Cayuga and Oneida Lake basins, April 9). Connecticut—Bloomfield, April 8. Rhode Island—Providence, April 28. Massachusetts—Falmouth, April 17. Vermont—Topsham, April 22. New Hampshire—Dublin, April 21; New Hampton, April 14 (median of 13 years, March 27). Maine—Presque Isle, April 23. New Brusnwick—Fredericton, March 21. Kentucky—Hickman, March 19. Illinois—St. Joseph, April 7; Lake Forest, March 14. Michigan—Detroit, March 2. Ontario—Toronto, April 23. Iowa—Iowa City, April 28. Wisconsin—Baraboo, April 23. Minnesota—Minneapolis, April 12. Kansas—Harper, March 31. North Dakota—Wilton, April 17. Manitoba—Treesbank, March 30. Saskatchewan—Skull Creek, May 15. Alberta—Glenevis, March 30.

Early dates of fall arrival are: Alberta—Clagary, November 26. Saskatchewan—Regina, October 9. South Dakota—Sioux Falls, October 29. Colorado—Denver, November 6. Michigan—Detroit, November 10. Ontario—Gooderham, October 21. Minnesota—Squaw Lake, October 18; Ely, October 27. Illinois—Lake Forest, November 17. Quebec—Quebec City, October 8. New Hampshire—New Hampton, September 30 (median of 13 years, October 14). Connecticut—New Haven, October 31. New Jersey—Morristown, November 7. New York—Cayuga and Oneida Lake basins, October 16 (median of 8 years, November 9). Pennsylvania—Allentown, October 26. Maryland—Monument Knob, Washington County, November 6. Virginia—Greene County, November 16.

Egg dates.—Labrador: 5 records, June 11 to June 24.

PINICOLA ENUCLEATOR ESCHATOSUS Oberholser

Newfoundland Pine Grosbeak

Contributed by CHARLES HENRY BLAKE

HABITS

This is still another of the relatively recently recognized races (described in 1914) from the northeastern corner of the continent. As is true of most other such forms, there are almost no indications that it differs in any essentials of its habits and life history from the subspecies adjoining it to the west and south.

The Newfoundland pine grosbeak is smaller than the Canadian, and the color is a darker gray with the males more scarlet, less rosy. Van Tyne (1934) reported the form from Michigan and Ohio and gives the weight of *eschatosus* as 52 to 61 grams compared with 70 to 83 grams for *leucura*.

Peters and Burleigh (1915) tell us that this bird is known locally in Newfoundland as "mope" because of its inactivity and tameness. It occurs in flocks of 5 to 10, or occasionally 20 to 30, most commonly in partly barren areas with clumps of dwarf spruces and larches, or Labrador tea. It is especially fond of the berries of the mountain ash. The nests are placed rather low in conifers and are built of twigs and moss. The clutch consists of three or four eggs.

DISTRIBUTION

Range.—Breeds from central Quebec (Mistassini Post, Anticosti Island) and Newfoundland south to northern New Hampshire (Connecticut Lakes), central Maine (Somerset County; King and Bartlett lakes), southern New Brunswick (Milltown, Saint John), and Nova Scotia (Neil Harbour, Barrington, Sable River); once in Connecticut (Wilton).

Winter range.—Winters south to Wisconsin (Madison), northern Ohio (Fulton County, Painesville), Pennsylvania (Tionesta, Warren, State College), and Virginia (Shenandoah National Park).

Casual record.—Accidental in northern Keewatin (Repulse Bay).

Egg dates.—New Brunswick: 2 records, June 15 to June 24.

Newfoundland: 3 records, May 26 to June 28.

PINICOLA ENUCLEATOR KAMTSCHATKENSIS (Dybowski)
Kamchatka Pine Grosbeak

HABITS

This race of the widely distributed species breeds in Kamchatka, and has been taken only once in North American territory. J. H. Riley (1917) reported that a specimen in the United States National Museum, transferred there by the Bureau of Fisheries, was "taken on the tundra of St. George Island, Pribilofs, Alaska, Oct., 1915."

The best condensed description of the subspecies seems to be that of Hartert (1910), which James L. Peters has kindly translated for me as follows:

"The Eastern Siberian Pine Grosbeak differs from the European West Siberian form through noticeably thicker, higher, and shorter bill; also, as a rule, the color is somewhat paler, the red of the male lighter and the underparts perhaps paler gray. The feet appear to be somewhat stronger. Bill 15 mm."

We seem to have no information on its habits, which probably do not differ materially from those of adjacent races.

DISTRIBUTION

Range.—The Kamchatka pine grosbeak is resident in Kamchatka. Also recorded in the Komandorskie Islands.

Casual records.—Casual in winter south to Japan and the Kurile Islands.

Accidental in Alaska (St. George Island in the Pribilof Islands).

PINICOLA ENUCLEATOR ALASCENSIS Ridgway
Alaska Pine Grosbeak

HABITS

Ridgway (1898) described this northern race as similar to the Canadian pine grosbeak "but decidedly larger, with smaller or shorter bill and paler coloration; both sexes with the gray parts distinctly lighter, more ashy."

The 1957 Check-List gives it the following range: Breeds, and partly resident, in central Alaska (Cape Prince of Wales, Fairbanks), Yukon (Russell Creek, Carcross), western Mackenzie (Aklavik, Fort Simpson), and northeastern British Columbia (Lower Laird Crossing). Winters south to southeastern Alaska (Chitina, Wrangell), central Oregon (Sisters, Camp Harney, Ironside), and northern North Dakota (Turtle Mountains, Devils Lake).

Nelson (1887) writes of its distribution and habits in northern Alaska: "It is limited by the range of spruce, pine, and cotton-wood forests. Dall found the crops of these Grosbeaks filled with cotton-wood buds at Nulato, on the Yukon. During winter, while traveling along the frozen surfaces of the water-courses of the interior, it is common to note a party of these birds busy among the cotton-wood tops uttering their cheerful lisping notes as they move from tree to tree. * * * They rarely paid any attention to us, but kept on their way, and were, ere long, lost to sight in the midst of the bending tree-tops. * * * These birds withstand the severest cold in these forests, even within the Arctic Circle, and appear to be about equally distributed throughout the wooded region."

Joseph Grinnell (1900a) found this grosbeak "to be a common resident throughout the year in wooded tracts from the delta eastward through the Kowak Valley. * * * In September and October Pine Grosbeaks were quite numerous, being often met with in companies of six to a dozen, immatures and adults together. They were usually among the scattering birch and spruce which line the low ridges. * * * In the severest winter weather they were not often seen in the spruces, but had then retreated into the willow-beds."

Nesting.—Grinnell (1900a) says on this subject: "Not until May 25th did I discover a nest. This was barely commenced, but on June 3rd, when I visited the locality again, the nest was completed and contained four fresh eggs. The female was incubating, and remained on the nest until nearly touched. The nest was eight feet above the ground on the lower horizontal branches of a small spruce growing on the side of a wooded ridge. The nest was a shallow affair, very much like a Tanager's. It consisted of a loosely-laid platform of slender spruce twigs, on which rested a symmetrically-moulded saucer of fine, dry, round-stemmed grasses. Its depth was about one inch and internal diameter 3.25."

He found two other similar nests, on June 11 and 12, about 6 feet up in dwarf spruces.

Eggs.—Grinnell (1900a) continues: "The eggs are pale Nile blue with a possible greenish tinge, dotted and spotted with pale lavender, drab and sepia. The markings are very unevenly distributed, the small ends of the eggs being nearly immaculate, while there is a conspicuous wreath about the large ends. The markings are not abruptly defined, but the margins of the spots are indistinct, fading out into the surrounding ground-color. One of the eggs is more thickly and evenly sprinkled with various tints of bistre. The eggs are rather ovate in shape, but the small ends are blunt. They measure 1.05 × .71, 1.05 × .72, 1.04 × .74, 1.03 × .75."

The measurements of 17 eggs average 26.3 by 18.4 millimeters; the eggs showing the four extremes measure *26.8* by 18.3, 26.3 by *19.0*, *22.9* by 16.8, and 26.8 by *17.8* millimeters.

Food.—Grinnell noted that "until the snow covered the ground, they fed on blueberries, rose-apples and cranberries. During the winter their food was much the same as that of the redpolls—seeds and buds of birch, alder and willow, and sometimes tender spruce needles."

DISTRIBUTION

Range.—Alaska to western Canadian border states.

Breeding range.—Breeds and is partly resident in central Alaska (Cape Prince of Wales, Fairbanks), Yukon (Russell Creek, Carcross), western Mackenzie (Aklavik, Fort Simpson), and northeastern British Columbia (Lower Liard Crossing).

Winter range.—Winters south to southeastern Alaska (Chitina, Wrangell), central Oregon (Sisters, Camp Harney, Ironside), and northern North Dakota (Turtle Mountains, Devils Lake).

Egg dates.—Alaska: 5 records, May 26 to June 29.

PINICOLA ENUCLEATOR FLAMMULA Homeyer

Kodiak Pine Grosbeak

HABITS

Ridgway (1901) describes the pine grosbeak of Kodiak Island as follows: "Similar to *P. e. canadensis* in length of wing, tail, and tarsus, but with much larger, relatively longer, and more strongly hooked bill; in shape and size of bill is in coloration more like *P. e. enucleator*, but decidedly larger (except bill), the adult male with the red rather brighter, especially on upper parts, the adult female and immature male usually with much less of yellowish olive on breast and with more of the same color on rump and upper tail coverts."

Ralph B. Williams, of Juneau, writes to me of its status in southeastern Alaska as follows: "Winter migrant, scarce resident, occasionally nesting in the Hudsonian Zone of the mainland north of Juneau and away from the beaches and inlets. These birds are most often encountered, however, during December and February. The first seen on January 12, 1947, was a small flight of 14 individuals, equally divided as to sex. They were feeding on the fruit of the European mountain ash. This tree was introduced into this section a number of years ago and now has become established as a 'native', being found from sea level to above timberline. Its adaption and spread has been made possible by robins, waxwings, and grosbeaks feeding on the fruit throughout the town then repairing to spruce and hemlock stands in the forest surrounding the town to roost. Many seedlings of the European mountain ash can be found near these roosts. High and low bush cranberries also provide food for the grosbeaks while on migration through this area of southeastern Alaska."

He also comments that the flight is undulatory, wings closed on the dip, and at a distance the birds cannot be distinguished from Bohemian waxwings, which they resemble in flight to a remarkable degree. Perched amid scarlet clusters of ash berries, the birds converse in soft notes. Now and then they utter a loud, mellow two- or three-syllable whistle, which is most frequently heard in flight and appears to prevent the separation of the flock. Occasionally one or two birds will sit on lower branches, a few feet from one's head, and feed in unconcerned fashion.

In 1948 the birds arrived on November 27. The first flocks were mainly females or immatures. A few days before Christmas the flocks became more conspicuous as the number of males in brilliant plumage increased, with many young males just beginning to show traces of rose-red coloration about their heads and rumps. As time passed and the ash berries were consumed, the grosbeaks turned their attention to devil's club buds and berries, *Echinopanax horridus*, high-bush cranberries, and the buds of the willows and alders. The flocks departed about Mar. 20, 1949, but on June 11 he observed two brilliant rose-red males and three females feeding on dandelion seeds, among a flock of some 20 to 30 pine siskins.

Joseph C. Howell wrote Williams about a nest he found June 9, 1944, at Middle Bay, 25 miles southeast of Kodiak. The nest was 4 feet up in a small spruce 6½ feet high. The nest was loosely built of twigs and lined with light brown rootlets (much like the nest of a mockingbird), and was 6 inches across, 4 inches in depth. The three eggs were a dull greenish blue, lightly splotched with light brown. There were three or four old nests, considered to belong to this species, within 150 feet. The female flushed at 2 feet. Her scold was a not very musical peep, much like the call of a spring peeper. She remained in a willow about 12 feet away. Soon two immatures (or females) appeared and spent much time chasing each other. One of these latter birds was most often in a willow 18 feet away.

Joseph Grinnell (1909) records that Dixon reported "A scattered company * * * in a patch of windfalls at about 1800 feet altitude" on Chichagof Island near Hooniah, Alaska, on June 25, 1907. Dixon continued, "The snow was just melting and many small plants were coming up in the open spaces that were exposed to the sun. The birds in pairs were feeding on these sprouting plants. The song had a clear, snappy, flycatcher-like accent to it." Dixon found the Kodiak pine grosbeak fairly common at Coppermine Cove, Glacier Bay, in July, and added: "The males would perch on the very tip of some spruce and indulge in a jerky but clear-cut song. Sometimes they were found feeding in the alders, where we saw them tearing the young alder buds apart, and supposed at first they were eating them; but upon examination we found their crops full of small green worms and it was evidently these the birds were after and not the buds themselves."

Elsewhere Grinnell (1910) writes: "The crop of a grosbeak taken by Dixon July 19 at La Touche Island contained sprouting weed seeds. The bird was flushed from the ground. A family of adults and young met with near the same place August 5 were also feeding on the ground where they were gathering soft weed seeds. This shows that the species probably resorts regularly to other sources of food than the leaf-buds of trees."

DISTRIBUTION

Range.—Coastal southern Alaska to Washington and Idaho.

Breeding range.—Breeds in southern Alaska (Kodiak Island, Kenai,

Sitka, Dall Island) and northwestern British Columbia (Telegraph Creek, Tetana Lake).

Winter range.—Winters from southern Alaska (Juneau, Wrangell) south to Washington (Port Angeles, Dayton), central eastern Oregon, and northwestern Idaho (Cedar Mountains).

PINICOLA ENUCLEATOR CARLOTTAE Brooks
Queen Charlotte Pine Grosbeak

HABITS

Allan Brooks (1922), in naming this race, based on a small series of specimens from the Queen Charlotte Islands, gives it the following subspecific characters: "Smallest and darkest of all the American subspecies; tail much shorter than in the other American races. Red of male deeper and more scarlet (less of carmine); yellow of females and old males darker and suffusing the entire plumage more or less, except the center of belly, lower tail coverts, and under wings and tail."

This race seems to be confined during the breeding season to the islands for which it is named.

There seems to be no information available on the nesting, food, or other habits of this grosbeak, which probably do not differ materially from those of the other forms of the species.

DISTRIBUTION

Range.—The Queen Charlotte pine grosbeak is resident on the islands and along the coast of western British Columbia (Queen Charlotte Islands, Porcher Island, Rivers Inlet, Vancouver Island).

Casual records.—Casual inland in southern British Columbia (Lillooet).

PINICOLA ENUCLEATOR MONTANA Ridgway
Rocky Mountain Pine Grosbeak
Contributed by WENDELL TABER

HABITS

Robert Ridgway (1898) described this race as being similar to *P. e. californica* but decidedly larger and slightly darker, the adult male with the red of a darker, more carmine, hue. The 1957 A.O.U. Check-List gives its breeding range as central interior British Columbia and southwestern Alberta south through the northern Cascade Range and Rocky Mountains to central and southeastern Washington, northeastern Oregon, south-central Utah, central eastern Arizona, and central northern New Mexico.   The race winters from southern British Columbia and southern Alberta south to southeastern Oregon, southwestern New Mexico, northwestern Texas, and western Nebraska.

Except for slight variations arising out of a habitat involving a more western type of flora, the life history of this race differs doubtfully from that of the other races.   I. N. Gabrielson and S. G. Jewett (1940) state that the habits and behavior of this race are quite similar to those of *P. e. alascensis* and that it is impossible to separate the two in the field.   W. L. Dawson (1909) says that the pine grosbeaks breeding on the higher mountain ranges in British Columbia occupy a zone from timber line downward about 2,000 feet, and that the birds favor hemlock and balsam timber.   He found the race (which he treated as *alascensis*) in the Cascade Mountains due north of Mount Baker on both sides of the 49th parallel, breeding close to timber line.   Young were being fed on July 17.   He failed to note any red males, although many gray males were singing in the early norning from the topmost spray of balsams.   Alden H. Miller (1940) noted a young bird that had nearly finished its post juvenal molt on September 7, 1939.

Habits.—Norman R. French (1954) studied this race at an elevation of 10,000 feet in the Uinta Mountains in northeast Utah between June 10 and July 30, 1953.   The Engelmann spruce, *Picea engelmanni*, and the alpine fir, *Abies lasiocarpa*, were the two dominant trees.   *Carex* prevailed in a wet meadow.   The snow had a uniform depth of at least 3 feet, with drifts of many times that depth, on June 10.   On June 11 French observed an adult pair of these birds feeding amid debris from the spruces scattered on the snow, in company with at least a dozen red crossbills, two pine siskins, a gray-headed junco, and a male black rosy finch.   The adult pine grosbeaks ate principally seeds of the spruces.   One bird had its esophagus filled with tender new growth from the tips of spruce boughs.   Other food included seeds of *Silene acaulis*, the ovaries of glacier lilies, *Erythronium grandiflorum*, and insects.   One female fed steadily in flycatcher fashion, taking insects on the wing.   The male acted similarly once.

Nesting.—A nest he located July 4 was near the end of a sloping Engelmann spruce limb and contained two young birds.   These were last seen in the nest on July 14.   The nesting territory had a diameter of about 1,200 feet.   The adults tolerated strange pine grosbeaks on two occasions, but this happened late in the nesting period.   Gray-headed juncos nested at the base of the same tree.   The parent pine grosbeaks united to drive off Canada jays; the male grosbeak drove off a red squirrel.

In feeding the young, both parent birds approached the nest at the same time with their throats noticeably distended by the filled gular sacs. Whichever sex arrived first at the nest, the other perched opposite. Either sex might choose either side. Generally, but not always, the first parent to arrive fed the young first. At times it removed a fecal sac from the nest and then usually waited at the nest or on a perch nearby for its mate. Except for three occasions when the female remained to brood, the parents departed together. Frequently, this departure involved a chasing ceremony with one bird diving at its perched mate, forcing it to fly, and chasing it across the meadow. Either sex might be the chaser.

The measurements of 12 eggs average 24.9 by 17.5 millimeters; the eggs showing the four extremes measure *26.3* by *17.9*, *23.3* by 17.3, and 25.4 by *16.9* millimeters.

DISTRIBUTION

Range.—Boreal summits of Rocky Mountains from Alberta to New Mexico.

Breeding range.—Breeds from interior British Columbia (Puntchesakut Lake, Mount Revelstoke) and southwestern Alberta (Jasper House, Banff) south through the northern Cascade Range and Rocky Mountains to central and southeastern Washington (Mount Rainier), northeastern Oregon (Wallowa Mountains), south central Utah (Cedar Breaks), central eastern Arizona (White Mountains), and central northern New Mexico (Truchas Peak).

Winter range.—Winters from southern British Columbia (Point-nopoint, Alta Lake, Okanagan Landing), and southern Alberta (Red Deer) south to southeastern Oregon (Crane), southwestern New Mexico (Kingston), northwestern Texas (Pampa), and western Nebraska.

PINICOLA ENUCLEATOR CALIFORNICA Price

California Pine Grosbeak

HABITS

This high Sierran form was described by William W. Price (1897) as follows: "It differs from *P. e. canadensis* in the much larger, more hooked and less turgid bill, and in the almost entire absence of dark centers to the feathers on the back and scapulars."

He says of its haunts: "This apparently very distinct *Pinicola* is an inhabitant of the higher Sierra Nevada Mountains of Central California. It is strictly an alpine species; I have never seen it below 7000 feet and I have taken it near timber-line. It is peculiar to the belt of tamarack pine (*Pinus murrayana*) and the beautiful red alpine fir (*Abies magnifica*), and most of the specimens taken were from the latter tree. According to my observations this bird is uncommon, for, during several vacations spent in the high Sierra, I have met with it only on rare occasions."

Milton S. Ray (1912) has published an interesting paper, describing the summer haunts of this grosbeak and the difficulties encountered by him and his party in their search for its nest, in which they were finally successful. The paper is well illustrated with 16 photographs, showing the ruggedness of the snow-covered heights. The story is far too long to be repeated here, but it is well worth reading, as illustrating the scarcity of the bird and its erratic habits.

Nesting.—After much hard work, extending over several seasons in the same general region, Ray and his companions at last succeeded in finding two nests and collecting two sets of eggs of the elusive California pine grosbeak. Of the first nest, he says: "Measurement showed the nest to be sixteen feet above the ground, four feet from the trunk and twenty-one inches from the tip of the branch. The red fir in which it was placed was on a sloping mountain side where the rather scattered timber rose among huge boulders, fallen trees and fast melting banks of snow. * * *

"The nest was simply a rough platform of twigs, principally fir, and was thickly lined with very fine light-colored grasses. So thick is this grass lining that eggs in the nest were not visible from below. The twig platform measures 6 × 8 inches, the grass nest cavity, 5 by 4½ by 1¼ inches deep."

He describes the finding of the second nest as follows: "The female was seen to fly to a nearby tree where she began hopping from branch to branch until a height of about 25 feet had been attained whereupon she flew to, and disappeared in, the thick foliage of a hemlock bough. Advancing nearer, Littlejohn could just discern the tail of the bird projecting over what might be a nest and which on my climbing the tree proved so to be. Being situated eight feet out near the end of the limb, and in a thick patch of foliage, it could not be seen from above except by spreading the branches apart. On doing this and after the sitting bird had been urged off with a long stick the nest was seen to contain three eggs." The nest was similar to the first one.

Both of these nests were found in the vicinity of Pyramid Peak, Eldorado County, Calif., at elevations between 6,500 and 8,000 feet, and were under observation for several days between June 15 and 19, 1912.

Richard Hunt (1921) found a nest of this grosbeak in Plumas County, Calif., on July 12, 1921, containing three young almost ready to fly. It was 20 feet up in a lodgepole pine and was much like those described above.

"The nest was placed on a horizontal forked branch about 3 inches from the main trunk (at this height 1⅜ inches in diameter), and supported laterally by branches growing level with the rim. It was not attached to its support, but was fairly well *crammed* between the supporting branches and was reasonably firm. The eggs could be seen through the bottom."

Eggs.—Ray (1912) illustrates his two sets of eggs of the California pine grosbeak and describes them as follows, using the color names in Ridgway's Nomenclature of Colors, 1886: "The ground color of the eggs approaches closely to Nile Blue (no. 17, Plate IX), but is slightly deeper and more rich in shade. The surface markings are spots and blotches, chiefly around the larger end, and in the form of a rough wreath, of black and of a rich deep brown called Vandyke (no. 5, Plate III). There are underlying scattered spots of Wood Brown (no. 19, Plate III), and splashy shell markings of Olive Gray (no. 14, Plate II). The eggs are ovate in shape and measure as they lie in the picture 1.02 × .69, 1.02 × .67, and .98 × .71." The eggs in the second set measure in inches 1.02 by .68, 1.00 by .68, and 1.06 by .68.

The measurements of 40 eggs average 26.1 by 17.7 millimeters; the eggs showing the four extremes measure *28.8* by 17.4, 25.1 by *18.6, 24.4* by 17.5, and 24.7 by *16.8* millimeters.

Voice.—Ray (1912) writes:

The song of the California Pine Grosbeak does not, I think, bear so much resemblance to that of *Carpodacus cassini* (which Price has compared it with) as it does to that of the Black-headed Grosbeak. However, as it is so much more varied, melodious and rich than that of the Black-headed Grosbeak, the comparison merely serves to give a general idea of its style. The song consists of a series of trills, warblings and mellow, flute-like notes that must be heard to be appreciated. The bird as a songster ranks easily with the best of the Sierra vocalists like the Ruby-crowned Kinglet, Water Ouzel and Sierra Hermit Thrush. Unlike the Western Robin which, perched on some tree top, will sing through almost the entire day, the Pine Grosbeak is not a persistent singer and only on rare occasions have I been given the opportunity of hearing its song.

Winter.—Not until the winter storms come and swirling clouds of snow cover much of their favorite feeding grounds are these hardy birds forced to move downward to the lower levels in the mountains in search of food. There they find shelter in the dense thickets of mountain alders and abundant food in the berries of the western mountain ash.

DISTRIBUTION

Range.—The California pine grosbeak is resident in the Sierra Nevada of central eastern California (10 miles south of Blairsden, Dinkey Lake in Fresno County). Recorded in summer in western Nevada (Carson Range).

Egg dates.—California: 11 records, June 4 to June 30.

LEUCOSTICTE TEPHROCOTIS UMBRINA Murie
Pribilof Rosy Finch

HABITS

Olaus J. Murie (1944) has given the above name to the rosy finches that breed on the Pribilof Islands and St. Matthew and Otter islands in the Bering Sea, which formerly bore the same name as the birds breeding on the Aleutian Islands. He describes this new form as follows:

Similar to *L. t. griseonucha* in general coloration, but breast Prout's brown, mixed with indistinct black streaks and suffusions that give it a darker appearance, graduating to black on the throat. Back almost the same basic color, though appearing paler due to more restricted black streaking and some paler feather edges. The breast color, because of admixture of black, has a more luminous, richer color effect than the mere naming of these tints would indicate. Flanks, belly, rump, and wing coverts suffused or spotted with old rose, more like geraneum pink in some lights. Back of neck and cheeks gray, as in other forms of *tephrocotis*. Crown and lores black. Bill black (in breeding season). Feet black.

Spring.—Preble and McAtee (1923) write: "Although a few may be present [on the Pribilof Islands] in winter the bulk of the summer residents arrive in early spring. Hahn recorded them as numerous on St. Paul April 4, 1911, when they were heard singing for the first time, and as evidently pairing on April 5. Hanna, making observations on St. George in 1914, noted the birds as very common, singing and apparently mating, on March 28 and April 8, and estimated the number seen on the latter date as 500. On April 22 he considered them much more abundant than in the winter, and on May 6 estimated a total of 2,000 birds seen."

Nesting.—The same authors (1923) say: "During the summer of 1914 the writer found the bird common on St. Paul Island. On June 22 a nearly completed nest was found on a narrow shelf beneath an arched rock about 15 feet from the ground. On July 4 this nest contained its complement of 5 eggs. Another nest found the same day in a small cavity on the face of a cliff contained 5 eggs which were obviously on the point of hatching. The first young out of the nest were seen on July 2. * * * The nests are quite bulky and are built of grasses and the dry stalks of various herbaceous plants, with a lining of fine grass and feathers. Hanna found a nest on St. George in 1914 which had a lining of reindeer hair."

G. Dallas Hanna (1922) writes: "While nests have been found in old buildings, the favorite site for nest building is in some crack or crevice of the precipitous cliffs on the shores of the Pribilofs." The nests are usually less than 25 feet from the base of a cliff, and on rare occasions may be reached by hand, "but the birds are seldom so injudicious as to run such risks. * * *

"The length of time a female remains off her nest depends, of course, upon the state of incubation of the eggs; when she returns to it, the male settles on some favorite nearby rock and pours forth his beautiful song, repeating it time and time again. The serenity of the scene is interrupted only by some wandering finch which must be chased away most vigorously."

Eggs and young.—Hanna (1922) says: "The normal set consists of five eggs, but four and six are not infrequent. While the color is usually pure, immaculate white, in some cases there are faint reddish or yellowish brown spots or, more often, specks, many of which are almost microscopic in size.

"Two broods of young are raised each year under normal conditions, and hence this species increases rapidly in numbers if free from enemies. The period of incubation is not definitely known, but the second sets are laid by August 1 in the majority of cases. It is believed that the same nest is used for both sets, or at least the same location. Sometimes it appears that a portion of the old nest is torn out and then reconstructed."

Food.—Preble and McAtee (1923) report on the contents of 22 stomachs from the Pribilof Islands as follows:

The food in these stomachs was found to be vegetable, 75.5 percent; and animal, 24.5 percent. The plant diet was chiefly seeds, but in a few cases bits of leaves and fruiting capsules were eaten. Seeds of crowberry (*Empetrum nigrum*) were found more frequently than any other (i.e., in 6 gizzards) and from 20 to 40 seeds were present in certain of these stomachs. The largest numbers of seeds eaten by any of these rosy finches were 250 and 450, in two instances, of those of brook saxifrage (*Chrysoplenium beringianum*). In one case also 160 seeds of sea parsley (*Ligusticum scoticum*) were contained in a single stomach. Other seeds eaten included those of grass, rush (*Juncus* sp.), sedge (*Carex* sp.), chickweed (*Alsine borealis*), buttercup (*Ranunculus* sp.), water chickweed (*Montia fontana*), cinquefoil (*Potentilla* sp.), and bluebell (*Campanula* sp.).

Of the animal food, approximately 21 percent of a total of 24.5 percent consisted of two-winged flies, 2 percent of beetles, and 1 percent of springtails. The flies consumed were chiefly crane flies (*Tipulidae*), and the beetles included ground beetles (*Pterostichus* sp. and others), leaf beetles (*Chrysomela subsulcata*), beach beetles (*Aegialites californicus*), and weevils. Caterpillars occurred in 2 stomachs and springtails (*Aptera: Collembola*) in 1. The latter insects were identified as *Isotoma violacea* var. *mucronata*, and the record is the first of the occurrence of this species on American territory.

Mr. Hahn noted the rosy finch feeding on seeds of poochka, or wild parsnip (*Coelopleurum gmelini*), and of rye grass, and Mr. Hanna observed that in winter they appeared to feed almost exclusively on the seeds of poochka.

Behavior.—Hanna (1922) writes: "The males spend the greater part of the summer fighting each other. * * * Often a female may be seen pursued by a half a dozen suitors. When the female is off her nest, her mate (or, at least, some mate) is constantly close beside her, and, if rosy finches are abundant, many is the battle he has to fight. Or, as she feeds along some narrow ledge, two contestants for her favors may now and then come tumbling down to the beach line, flapping and pecking at each other, their places as attendants being soon taken by a third party."

Like its relative on the Aleutian Islands, this finch spends much of its time on the wing in long, swinging curves, or darting from one perch to another, seeming to enjoy its restless agility.

Voice.—Hanna (1922) writes: "The beautiful song of the male was new to me then, and it seemed the most attractive feature of the desolate place. It is excelled by the song of no other species on these islands, and is rivalled there only by that of the Alaska Longspur and of the Pribilof Snow Bunting."

Enemies.—Hanna (1922) says:

These birds continued to be abundant from 1913 up to the winter of 1916–17, when a terrible catastrophe befell them. The Pribilofs that winter were visited by a number of gyrfalcons, and these wreaked havoc among the resident land birds. * * * The first gyrfalcons killed were examined, and in their stomachs was found unmistakable evidence of slaughter—the rosy feathers of their victims. Their prey was so easily captured on the barren Pribilofs that the falcons became extraordinarily fat. So oily were they that the preparation of specimens was exceedingly difficult. The offering to the natives of a bounty of one dollar for each capture was instrumental in securing thirteen of them, a greater number than the total which had been seen on the Pribilofs since observations commenced. * * * When the summer of 1917 came, scarcely a finch could be found. Only one pair nested on St. Paul, and one pair on Otter Island. A few more were left on St. George, but the species would have been classed as exceedingly rare even there. * * *

Through succeeding years the rosy finches were watched with great anxiety, and it was gratifying to see their numbers gradually increasing. By 1920 there were, perhaps, a dozen pairs on St. Paul Island and a hundred on St. George, but even the latter was still underpopulated.

Winter.—Although a few rosy finches are to be found on the Pribilofs all winter, there is a great falling off in their numbers during late fall and winter, as most of them gradually drift away to spend midwinter on the Aleutian Islands, or as far east, perhaps, as the islands south of the Alaska Peninsula. According to the data published by Preble and McAtee (1923), their numbers did not decrease very rapidly until December, but the birds were almost absent during January and February; and they did not return in any numbers until March.

DISTRIBUTION

Range.—The Pribilof rosy finch is resident on the Pribilof Islands and on St. Matthew and Otter islands in the Bering Sea.

Egg dates.—Pribilof Islands: 3 records, June 26 to June 28.

LEUCOSTICTE TEPHROCOTIS GRISEONUCHA (Brandt)

Aleutian Rosy Finch

HABITS

From the tip of the Alaska Peninsula westward, we found these large and handsome rosy finches generally distributed on all the islands we visited, as far west as Attu Island. They were breeding mainly in the crevices in the almost inaccessible rocky cliffs or among the loose rocks on the summits, but resorting to the shores and snow banks for feeding. Other rosy finches that breed inland and farther south make their summer homes in the alpine zones above timberline in the mountains. But there is no timberline in the treeless Aleutians, and these rosy finches find congenial summer homes from sea level up to the summits.

The Aleutian rosy finch breeds from the Commander Islands eastward to the western part of the Alaska Peninsula and in the Shumagin Islands; it wanders in winter eastward to Kodiak Island. A new name has been given to the rosy finches that breed on the Pribilof Islands and St. Matthew Island, farther north in the Bering Sea.

Stejneger (1885) says of the haunts of this finch in the Commander Islands:

Copper Island, being one mass of rugged and cracked rocks and cliffs, with steep, often quite perpendicular, walls jutting up straight out of the ocean, is the favorite haunt of these stone-loving birds, which may be said to be fairly common on that island, occurring in pairs around the whole isle during the breeding season. * * *

The "Aleutian Rosy Finch" delights especially in steep and high rocks, especially close to the sea and inaccessible to any other beings than those provided with wings. In fact, I do not think that a single pair breeds in interior of the islands, but after the young are out, the whole family will often move inland, following the rivulets up to the backbone of the mountains in the search for insects.

Nesting.—We did not succeed in finding a nest with eggs, but Wetmore found a nest on Kiska Island on June 18, containing two fully fledged young; it was in a crevice in the rocks in an almost inaccessible place on the face of a cliff. Though the birds evidently had nests among the rocks on the summits, they were too well hidden for us to find them.

Dall (1873) reports: "On the 24th of May we found a nest, situated in a crevice of a rocky bank on the shore of Captain's Harbor, Unalashka. It was of grass, very neatly sewed together, and lined with fine grass and a few feathers. It contained five white eggs in fresh condition, and was about twelve feet above the beach."

Eggs.—This species lays from three to six ovate eggs, with five being the number most frequently found. They are slightly glossy; white or light creamy white, and unspotted.

The measurements of 50 eggs average 24.5 by 17.3 millimeters; the eggs showing the four extremes measure *28.3* by 17.0, 23.4 by *18.8*, *21.3* by 16.3, and 22.9 by *15.8* millimeters.

Plumages.—Ridgway (1901) describes the juvenal plumage of this finch as follows: "Uniform grayish brown, more or less washed with a more umber tint; wings and tail dusky slate, the feathers margined with paler; edges of greater wing-coverts and tertials dull buffy; no trace of pink on tail-coverts, etc., nor of gray or black on head."

The sexes are alike in the juvenal plumage and nearly alike in all plumage, though the females may average a very little duller than the males. The seasonal changes in plumage are not conspicuous. In winter birds the pink are of a softer hue and the feathers of the breast are narrowly margined with paler. Material is not available for a study of the molts.

Food.—Stejneger (1885) examined the gullets of several specimens, of one of which he says: "Gullet crammed with an enormous mass of food, consisting of (1) several dozens of a Coleopterous insect, and (2) a similar number of larvae, etc., (3) besides leaves and buds of *Cochlearia*, and (4) some seeds."

We frequently saw these finches feeding on the snow banks, picking up seeds and insects which had been blown there by the high winds.

Behavior.—These rosy finches are restless, roving birds, often seen sweeping over the mountains in long swinging curves; while feeding on the snow banks they were usually too shy to be approached, but about the rocky summits, where their nests are well concealed, they are very tame; they will sit on some nearby rock, chirping loudly in protest, or fly about from point to point in swinging billowy flight, twittering constantly.

Voice.—Nelson (1887) says: "This bird has no song, but utters a low, mellow chirp.   * * * Dall adds that it has no song at any season, but a clear chirp-like *weet-a-weet-a-weet-weet*."

DISTRIBUTION

Range.—The Aleutian rosy finch is resident in the Aleutian Islands (Near Islands to Akutan Islands), Nunivak Island, western part of the Alaska Peninsula, Unga Island, and Semidi Islands. One breeding specimen was taken on Kodiak Island. Winters also on Kodiak Island.

LEUCOSTICTE TEPHROCOTIS LITTORALIS Baird
Hepburn's Rosy Finch

HABITS

This form has been called the gray-headed rosy finch, as its cheeks and, in typical specimens, the entire head is gray, except the black frontal patch.

As its subspecific name implies, it is a bird of the coastal mountain districts of northwestern North America, from the Alaska Peninsula eastward and southward, breeding above timberline. J. Grinnell (1909) reports that one specimen collected of a number of *leucosticte* seen at Hooniah on Chicagof Island, Alaska, June 21 to 27, 1907 was *L. t. littoralis.* According to the observer, Dixon, the birds were "around the lower end of the melting snow slides, and the rock slides near the summit of the mountain, 2,500 feet altitude." Alfred M. Bailey (1927) observed these finches at several places in southeastern Alaska, Glacier Bay, Juneau, and other places; they were evidently nesting in the precipitous cliffs at elevations of about 4,000 feet. In the Stikine River region of northern British Columbia and southeastern Alaska, Harry S. Swarth (1922) found them "after we emerged from the upper edge of the forest (about 3500 feet) and they evidently inhabited all of the open country from there on upward."

Dawson (1909) writes: "This bird is the vestal virgin of the snows, the attendant minister of Nature's loftiest altar, the guardian of the glacial sanctuaries. * * * He alone of all creatures is at home on the heights, and he is not even dependent upon the scanty vegetation which follows the retreating snows, since he is able to wrest a living from the very glaciers. Abysses do not appall him, nor do the flower-strewn meadows of the lesser heights alienate his snow-centered affections."

Taylor and Shaw (1927) say of this hardy bird: "Apparently scorning more comfortable surroundings, the rosy finch selects for his home and feeding ground bleak and wind-swept ridges of rock, dizzy crags and precipices. This is one of the hardy quartet of birds (rosy finch, pipit, ptarmigan, horned lark) which is characteristic of the Arctic-Alpine, the highest and coldest life zone on Mount Rainier."

Nesting.—To William T. Shaw (1936) we are indebted for much that we know of the nesting and other habits of Hepburn's rosy finch, and much of what follows has been taken from his two articles on the winter habits and nesting studies of this finch. His observations were made mainly on Mount Baker and Mount Rainier, Wash., where he found several old nests, as well as nests with eggs and nests with young. Of one nesting site, he says:

"Here were domes of reddish, clinker-like, porous rock, overlain with flat stratified slabs of a very hard structure. Both formations were later referred by Dr. Wm. M. Tucker of the Fresno State College, to rhyolite, differently metamorphosed in cooling. Water dripped over about half of this area. The drier parts showed irregular gas-formed crypts here and there and in two of these appeared from the distance, that which looked like nesting material. One, at least, had what was distinctly shown as loose weathered ends of grass, though very old."

Of one nest location, he says: "It was placed in a rather open space in the rock, roughly speaking about 8 inches high. It was not a secure enclosure, but was penetrated by light from two or three small openings from the side and back where the rocks did not fit tightly together besides being widely open from the front. In it the nest was set back about ten inches from the opening. * * *"

He describes another nest, located in the slab formation, as follows:

This was a bulky affair a little smaller than that of a Robin. It was constructed on the outside with considerable black, dead *Usnea* or tree moss (a lichen) and what seemed to be rootlets of what might be partridge-foot (*Lutkea pectinata*) which was found to be projecting down from the undercut sod of the moraine's knife edge. Quantities of rootlets, possibly of a sedge (*Carex*), rushes (*Juncus*) or a bent grass (*Agrostis*) were found although these fragments were difficult to determine. A few bits of old dead moss stems were also present in the outer wall. The lining was of grass culms which had the appearance of having been shredded to a considerable fineness in the bottom of the nest. Several Ptarmigan feathers were present in the lining.

Charles S. Moody (1910) discovered two nests of this finch while fishing along swift, rocky, mountain streams in northern Idaho. One was "situated upon a slight shelf of the rock near where the cliff takes a sharp angle. It was composed of dried grass stems, pine needles and moss. The structure was poorly made, and I am at loss to understand why the wind did not sweep it away. The eggs, which were about .94 × .50 inches were a bluish white, though I am inclined to believe this was due to the incubation, as they appeared about ready to hatch. I think that the eggs when first deposited are milk-white, from the fact that those in another nest discovered by me the next season were of that color."

Of another nest, he says: "While picking our way around a cliff upon which tussocks of grass were growing, a Rosy Finch started from beneath my feet. She alighted on a rock not far distant, and complained about our intrusion. The nest was situated beneath one of these tussocks, and was very similar to the one just described."

Eggs.—The eggs of Hepburn's rosy finch, usually four or five in number, are pure white and unmarked, like the eggs of other races of the species.

Young.—Shaw (1936) inferred from his studies that the incubatio period is about 14 days. Of four helpless young rosy finches he says "Tender skin was noticed, irregularly tufted with fluffy gray down which moved in the breeze. Large, dark, closed eyes,—yellow rimmed mouths, thin, wobbly necks through which pulsed spurts o warm blood from strong heart to brain, all showing most vividl when the birds were brought from their hidden retreat to open day light. No sound was uttered. Every effort was made by the fledg lings to hide the eyes from the light."

When 6 days old the young "weighed 56 grams for the four o them, or 14 grams apiece. They still retained the gray downy plum age of hatching; but now had in addition, blackish pterylae of pin feathers and stubby wing and tail quills. The eyes of one or two o them were just faintly opening and they had tiny far-away voices rarely used, at long intervals."

At 9 days of age, "they had advanced markedly and weighed 8 grams, or an average of 21 grams apiece. They were now showin distinct signs of intelligent, awakening interest. Hunger seemed t be a rather constant stimulus. Baby down was now giving way t rather coarser resistant feathers. Eyes were all open, as also wer gaping yellow-rimmed mouths on slightest provocation."

At 14 days of age, the young were beginning to leave the nest One of the remaining two weighed 26 grams. "The following day no birds, young or old remained. The Rosy Finches had abandonec their glacier nesting places for the more congenial and fruitful for aging sites beside the moist edges of the retreating snow banks o the flower-clothed moraines."

Plumages.—The molts and plumages are apparently similar in al the rosy finches. The plumages are well described under the brown capped rosy finch, but there is too little material available for a study of the molts.

Food.—Rosy finches are mainly ground feeders, picking up the seeds of weeds and wild plants. The Leffingwells (1931) made a study of the winter habits of Hepburn's rosy finch at Clarkston, Wash., and "found that 99 percent of the food consists of the seeds of weeds found abundantly on the steep slopes of the cañon walls or in the wheat fields on the tops of the bluffs, while but one percent was insect material. The seeds most commonly taken are Russian thistle, *Salsola kali*; wild grass, *Sporobolus cryptandrus*; Jim Hill mustard, *Sisymbrium altissimum*; and sunflower, *Helianthus annuus*." They list six other species of plants of which the seeds are eaten.

They also mention that the summer food of both adults and young consists more largely of insect food; in 16 birds, collected by Swarth

1922) in the Stikine River region, insect "material was found to be 9 percent and vegetable matter 41 percent of the total."

Swarth also says: "The old birds were assiduously feeding the young, and in pursuit of this duty we several times saw them fly into the air to capture flying insects, which were then carried to the waiting offspring."

Moody (1910) writes: "Like Crossbills, they are very fond of salt, and will greedily eat anything of a saline character. There is also a small black midge, or gnat, that covers the snow on certain warm days, and these the birds devour. I have also seen them industriously picking about the tops of fir trees and on the branches of white cedars."

G. W. Gullion (1957) recorded a bird feeding among cheatgrass, *Bromus tectorum*, at 6,500 feet in Nevada, Mar. 10, 1956. S. G. Jewett, W. T. Taylor, et al. (1953) mention flowers of the white heather, seeds of Russian thistle, and leaves of the saxifrage (*Saxifraga tolmiei*).

Behavior.—The Leffingwells (1931) write:

The leucostictes are decidedly gregarious; all wait till some venturesome spirit shows the way to food or starts the flight, then others follow quickly. They fly in dense masses in an undulating manner. The individual apparently keeps to no set position in the flock, which constantly whirls about, much like a group of dry leaves carried on a stiff breeze or as caught suddenly by a whirlwind and thus twisted onto another course, or set down as suddenly as it was started in flight. Upon arrival at the [roosting] rock, the birds swirl in, close to the face of the upper portion, perching abruptly. They often circle several times about the rock; then alighting they dart from jagged point to jagged point, working down, amid much chatter, to the base, stopping at intervals to pick about the lichens, and finally go to the thistle and grass to feed a few moments before roosting.

On several occasions, Prairie Falcons and Pigeon Hawks appeared at the rock. Their presence did not greatly alarm the finches which often ignored the intruder entirely or gave chase in flocks of fifteen or twenty individuals. Never did they seem very enthusiastic about mobbing the enemy.

Rosy Finches are perpetually in action, never perching longer than a few seconds at a time. It was of interest to note that, while feeding upon Russian thistle or Jim Hill mustard, which protruded through several inches of snow, they walked with a staggering motion rather than hopping as is characteristic of most sparrows. After feeding here for a few moments they swirled off to a ledge of rimrock to perch and chatter and then came back to the food area.

The birds begin preparation for the night long before sunset, the flock usually appearing at the roosting site between two and three o'clock. A bird enters a swallow's nest and usually turns at once, and thrusts its head from the opening, uttering a loud cry as though challenging all others. It may remain here a few seconds or it may come out at once and repeat the same performance in another nest. Often a single bird will inspect as many as a dozen nests before finally settling in one. Usually by four o'clock the entire flock is at roost and no sound can be heard, nor can the birds be frightened from the nests.

The roosting rock, referred to above, was an outcrop of basaltic rimrock, with a perpendicular face about 200 feet high, against which were clustered hundreds of abandoned nests of cliff swallows, in which the finches roosted.

S. G. Jewett, W. T. Taylor et al. (1953) comment on a flock o about 1,000 birds which arrived at Republic, Wash., the morning o November 12, 1920. Nervous and uncertain at first, the birds finally settled about a small, open spring, and then were tame and unsus picious of an observer not more than 30 feet distant. On the ground the birds maintained a constant musical twitter, but the notes ceased when the birds took flight, rising to a great height. Again, on Jan uary 10, 1918, a flock of about 50 birds took shelter from the raw wintry wind in the mud nests of a deserted colony of cliff swallows some birds turning around to peer out curiously.

Voice.—The Leffingwells (1931) say on this subject:

While the birds are in flight there is a constant chattering, and on a dull day when they are flying at a distance their presence can be detected first by the thin clear notes uttered in rapid succession. The flock note is similar to that of the Evening Grosbeak though not so forceful and we have interpreted it variously as *terrip* or *terrp*; also as half whisper as *peeap*, *peeap* and *cheep*, *cheep*. The alarm note is a short, guttural, monosyllabic *cheep*, *peep*, *peep*. At other times it is very curt, being *cha cha*.

Few attempts at song were noted until the first of February and then the first song was somewhat sketchy. A notation on February 4, 1928, states that the birds were trying to sing, for some were giving softly a few connected notes. Most dominant at this time was soft *cheek-ah*, a soft song like that of the Purple Finch. Again on February 12, one Hepburn sat on a tree and sang a buzzy Purple Finch song. This may be the song of the birds. After this date attempts at song are common, and on February 25 a note states definitely that the males were singing. The song, a long warble, was much like that of the Goldfinch.

Field marks.—Hepburn's rosy finch can be distinguished from the gray-crowned rosy finch, with which it is often associated in winter, by its head markings, which are distinctly visible in the field, even at a considerable distance. Hepburn's has been rightly called the gray-headed rosy finch, for almost its entire head is gray, down to the sides of the head and throat, with only the forehead black, while in the gray-crowned rosy finch only the posterior half of the crown is gray, the frontal half being black. The brown body plumage, with its rosy tints, is common to all the rosy finches, which look much like large brown sparrows.

Fall and winter.—As cold weather approaches, the rosy finches desert the alpine heights, retreat to the lower slopes, and spread out over the lowland plateaus. They become tame and confiding during the winter, adapting themselves to civilization and coming readily to feeding stations and window sills in their search for food.

Gabrielson and Jewett (1940) write: "The most abundant wintering Rosy Finch in the State is Hepburn's Rosy Finch. It gathers into huge flocks that swirl along the rocky hillsides of eastern Oregon like eaves in a storm. These winter flocks are restless, except when actually feeding. They whirl up in spiral flights, then alight for a few seconds, only to start off again with little apparent reason. Usually they alight on the ground, sometimes on buildings, once in a great while in trees or bushes, and we have seen the telephone and fence wires decorated with them for a considerable space."

Hepburn's rosy finch has been known to stray far from its western breeding range. A male was collected near Minneapolis, Minn., Jan. 3, 1889; another specimen was trapped and banded at Gorham, Maine, Dec. 15, 1936 (Gross, 1937).

The Leffingwells (1931) say:

> With the exception of active competition for roosting places, there is little quarreling among the birds early in the winter. After the latter part of January, however, the birds become more quarrelsome. This continues with increasing vigor until shortly before the departure of the flock, when the birds seem to be paired. On March 3, 1928, we observed that at the spring there was constant fighting which consisted largely of the aggressor opening his bill as though to intimidate, and making a hissing noise. He then rushed toward the opponent, caught at its bill and the two fell, fluttering and whirling, to the ground in a circular motion.

They add that the flock breaks up somewhat toward the end of the winter, shortly before the migration begins. A bird they banded in February 1928 returned and was retaken in November 1929.

DISTRIBUTION

Range.—Pacific slope of Alaska to California and New Mexico.

Breeding range.—Breeds from south central Alaska (Kenai Peninsula, McKinley Park), southwestern Yukon (Tepee Lake), and northwestern British Columbia (near Doch-da-on Creek) south through high mountains of southeastern Alaska and western British Columbia to Cascade Mountains of Washington, Oregon (Crater Lake), and central northern California (Mount Shasta).

Winter records.—Winters from southern Alaska (Kodiak Island, Kenai Peninsula, Juneau), central British Columbia (Quesnel), and central Montana (Fort Shaw, Fort Keogh) south to northern California (Chats), western Nevada (Washoe and Storey counties), northern Utah (Bacchus), and central northern New Mexico (Vermejo Park).

Casual records.—Accidental in Minnesota (Minneapolis) and Maine (Gorham).

LEUCOSTICTE TEPHROCOTIS TEPHROCOTIS (Swainson)

Gray-crowned Rosy Finch

PLATE 19

HABITS

The gray-crowned rosy finch, the type race of the species and the first of the rosy finches to be discovered, was described and figured by Swainson and Richardson (1831). They obtained only a single specimen, which was "killed on the Saskatchewan, May, 1827," near Carlton House, Saskatchewan. This race breeds in the northern Rocky Mountains, migrating east to Manitoba, south to Utah, Colorado, and western Nebraska, west to the Cascade Range, and north to Great Slave Lake. Like the other rosy finches this bird finds a congenial summer home among the mountain snowbanks and glaciers well above timberline, often up to 10,000 or 12,000 feet.

The gray-crowned rosy finch seems to migrate well inland, along the mountain ranges or in their vicinity, largely avoiding the coastal areas. Ralph B. Williams writes to me from Juneau, Alaska: "During banding operations from March 22 through April 3, 1948, the writer trapped and banded a total of 300 *Leucosticte tephrocotis littoralis* and 6 *Leucosticte tephrocotis tephrocotis.* * * * The resultant research into the available literature on the occurence of the subspecies *tephrocotis* in the Alexander Archipelago failed to bring to light any data, but I have been able to discover several records with reference to *littoralis.*"

Nesting.—Strangely enough, I cannot find in the literature any account of the nesting of the gray-crowned rosy finch in what is now known to be the breeding range of this typical race of the species. There are plenty of references in the literature under the name of the gray-crowned, but these all prove to be referable to the Sierra Nevada rosy finch, which had not been separated from the former at the time that the articles were published.

Mrs. Florence Merriam Bailey (1918) found these finches with young in Glacier National Park, which is probably near the southern end of its breeding range, but she does not say that a nest was actually found. However, as its summer haunts are similar to those of the other races, it seems fair to assume that its nesting habits are also similar.

Eggs.—The four eggs in the collection at the Harvard Museum of Comparative Zoology measure 21.5 by 16.7, 21.9 by 16.1, 22.0 by 16.3, and 22.1 by 16.1 millimeters.

Plumages.—In a general way, the plumages of the rosy finches are very much alike in both sexes, though the females are always

PLATE 19

…eau, Alaska R. B. Williams

GRAY-CROWNED ROSY FINCH

…no County, Calif., July 1935 J. B. Dixon

NEST OF SIERRA NEVADA ROSY FINCH

Mammoth Crest, Mono County, Calif.   J. B. Di

SIERRA NEVADA ROSY FINCH COUNTRY

Brooks Mountains, Wyo., June 1951   J. B. Fre

BLACK ROSY FINCH NESTING COUNTRY

aler and less rosy. It has been contended that the sexes cannot
e distinguished in life. J. C. Merrill (1880) has made a study of
ne winter plumages of the two forms of the species at Fort Shaw,
Iont., pointing out certain details by which the sexes can be dis-
nguished. The reader is referred to his paper.

In its feeding and other habits, this rosy finch does not differ
naterially from the other races of the species. Laurence B. Potter,
f Eastend, Saskatchewan, has sent me the following notes sub-
nitted by Charles F. Holmes, of Dollard, Saskatchewan: "On De-
ember 15, 1940, I noticed a dozen rosy finches, with one Hepburn's
mong them, feeding upon weed seeds on the south side of my grain-
ries; they were not at all alarmed at my presence, and remained
bout the yard for several days, going in and out of the various
uildings and even roosting at night among the rafters. About
December 20, the flock of 12 was increased to perhaps 200; they
ettled in the tall poplars, not unlike the habit of snow buntings
nd looking just as odd. They swarmed over the roof of the house,
heir feet sounding like hail as they landed, and in a few minutes
vere literally covering my feeding board, cracking and husking the
eed and squabbling for place. At one time I counted 50 feeding
n the board including two Hepburn's whilst the overflow of some
undred fed upon the ground. As far as I could judge, the Hepburn's
eemed to be in ratio of 1 to 70, though sometimes 1 to 50.

"In front of the house was a car; they perched upon the radiator,
ew in at the windows and sat upon the steering wheel; and when
went out to place more feed upon the board, they sat upon my head
nd walked over my shoes.

"As long as so many fed upon the board at one time, they were
airly peaceable, but when two or three remained, one in particular
ecame very hostile, refusing place to all and sundry and fairly romp-
ng up and down from one end of the board to the other in his efforts
o police it. He would hump his back, fluff out his feathers and, with
is topnot erect, dash at any intruder."

P. M. Silloway (1903) writes of the behavior of these finches in
'ergus County, Mont.:

A regular winter resident at Lewiston, where it is known as "brown snowbird."
t generally appears about the first of November, though in pleasanter weather
t may not be observed before the 8th or 10th. * * *

The leucostictes are our English sparrows in social manners. They feed at
he door-steps, or in the yards. On a warm winter morning I have seen from forty
o fifty of these birds sitting on a wood-pile in the door-yard, sunning themselves
nd gleaning from refuse. In the late afternoons the individuals of a flock scatter
ut to accustomed nooks for the night. A particular male, and sometimes a
emale, have regular sleeping nooks in the porch of the writer's home, and long
efore nightfall the birds seek their quarters. I have seen one enter a tubular

eavestrough, there to spend the night. Frequently they flutter under projectin eaves, and cling to some projecting support for the night.

* * *

The leucostictes feed on the seeds of the dwarf sage, or glean from th snow about the bases of such plants. They are fond of gleaning along the hil sides at the margin of the snowy areas. In the spring, when a thaw is takin place, a flock will congregate on a spot eight or ten feet across, all pecking indus trially from the bare ground. They also frequent the margins of dry ditche and a walk or fence on sloping ground, where exposed areas can be found, ar favored feeding-places. * * *

Very early the leucostictes give evidence of the approach of the nuptial seasor After the middle of January, one male will frequently chase another coquettishl\ like meadowlarks in amorous sport. Occasionally at this season a male wil sit for a few moments, uttering a pretty little trill, like *tree-ree-ree-ree-ree-ree-ree* enunciating the syllables with great rapidity. As the season approaches, and th warm sunshine of late February announces the further advance of the verna period, the leucostictes increase in their musical numbers. Sitting on the ridge c house or barn, generally at the end of the ridge, alone or in small troops, they utte their wheezy chants, sometimes with no more force than that used by the grass hopper sparrow, sometimes with greater force and more varied expression.

The males sing also while sitting on the ground, appearing to be picking uj morsels of food, and singing as a frequent variation. In such instances the son has a ventriloquial effect, appearing to issue from a point much farther awaj A male singing on the ground will sidle toward a female, and if she coyly take wing a reckless amorous pursuit will follow. * * *

In early March the wing-bars of their plumage become more prominent, the purple of the sides to show more noticeably, and the colors generally to assum their vernal or nuptial hues. By the middle of April the last of the leucosticte has disappeared.

In his notes from Salida County, central Colorado, Edward R Warren (1910b) says:

Rosy Finches were unusually abundant about Salida the winter of 1908-9 which, as stated above was very severe, and especially so in the higher mountain where the birds usually stay. Frey says in his notes: "Thousands of these bird were here at all times during the winter. Every snow that came would driv them down to the valleys; when the south hills became bare they would split uj in small bunches and scatter and climb up as the snow receded. I have taker all four varieties from a single bunch, and might say at a single shot. They seemec to be all varieties together, and the Gray-crowns were most plentiful, with Brown caps a close second, and about one in four or five would be Hepburn's, and a verj few black ones. These birds fed almost entirely on the tumbleweed (Russiar thistle) seeds, and their throats and crops were literally crammed with them."

DISTRIBUTION

Range.—Alaska and Yukon to California, New Mexico, and Nebraska.

Breeding range.—Breeds in the mountains from northern Alaska (Brooks Range), central Yukon, and western Alberta south to south eastern British Columbia (Indianpoint Mountain, Moose Pass) and orthwestern Montana (Glacier Park). Recorded in summer in entral northern Washington (Hart's Pass) and in western Mackenzie Fort Resolution).

Winter range.—Winters from southern British Columbia (Chilliwack, Clinton, Cranbrook), central Alberta (Jasper Park), southern Saskatchewan (Skull Creek, Indian Head), and southwestern Manitoba Birtle) south to northeastern California (Chats), central Nevada Reno), central Utah (Provo), northern New Mexico (Cimarron), orthwestern Nebraska (Sioux County), and southwestern South Dakota (Rapid City).

Casual record.—Casual in Iowa (Sioux City).

Migration.—The data deal with the species as a whole. Early lates of spring arrival are: Wyoming—Yellowstone National Park, February 28. Montana—Anaconda, March 12. Alberta—Banff National Park, February 26. British Columbia—Lytton, April 6.

Late dates of spring departure are: Arizona—Grand Canyon Village, March 23. Colorado—Colorado Springs, April 18; Walden, April 17 (median of 10 years, April 6). Utah—Provo, April 20. Wyoming—Jackson Hole, April 26; Laramie, April 13 (average of 7 years, March 25). Idaho—Moscow Mountain, May 11. Montana—Anaconda, May 8. Alberta—Veteran, May 9; Athabaska Landing, May 3. California—Big Creek, May 6. Oregon—Camp Harney, March 22. Washington—Pullman, March 31 (median of 5 years, March 15). British Columbia—Lac la Hache, April 26.

Early dates of fall arrival are: British Columbia—Lac la Hache, October 25. Washington—Pullman, October 17 (median of 7 years, November 1). Oregon—near Enterprise, October 30. Nevada—Ramsey, November 15. Alberta—Banff, October 4; Glenevis, October 8. Montana—Big Sandy, October 1. Idaho—Moscow, October 21. Wyoming—Wyoming Peak, October 5; Laramie, October 25 (average of 7 years, November 17). Colorado—Walden, October 31 (median of 8 years, November 13). New Mexico—near Cimarron, November 11. Utah—Zion National Park, November 4. Saskatchewan—Eastend, October 27. South Dakota—Black Hills National Forest, October 29. Nebraska—Blue Springs, November 2.

Late dates of fall departure are: Alberta—Banff, November 3. Wyoming—Yellowstone National Park, December 7 (average of 7 years, November 17).

Egg dates.—Alaska: 104 records, May 14 to August 11; 65 records, June 9 to June 30.

California: 25 records, June 15 to July 17; 17 records, June 30 to July 10.

LEUCOSTICTE TEPHROCOTIS WALLOWA Miller

Wallowa Rosy Finch

HABITS

Alden H. Miller (1939a) gave the above name to the rosy finc
that is known to breed only on the Wallowa Mountains of Oregor
its winter range being undetermined. He gives it the followin
subspecific characters:

Similar to L. t. tephrocotis, but cinnamon brown of ventral surface duller an
more sooty, the feathers bearing either dusky areas or dusky shaft streaks imme
diately distal to the downy gray basal parts. Black throat area grades les
abruptly into breast. Streaks of back somewhat darker and broader and feathe
margins distinctly more neutral brown, with less yellow and red-brown pigmen

* * *

Wallowa differs from L. t. dawsoni of the Sierra Nevada of California in slightl
sootier under parts, and in much darker, less tawny dorsal surface. Some in
dividuals of wallowa are almost indistinguishable from dawsoni ventrally but th
dark, broad dorsal stripes of wallowa are in no instance closely approximated i
dawsoni. Wallowa differs from dawsoni, as does L. t. tephrocotis, in greate
average depth of bill and in more pointed wing tip.

DISTRIBUTION

Range.—Oregon and Nevada.

Breeding range.—Breeds in Wallowa Mountains of northeaster
Oregon.

Winter range.—Winters south to central western Nevada (Ramsey
Reno).

LEUCOSTICTE TEPHROCOTIS DAWSONI Grinnell

Sierra Nevada Rosy Finch

PLATES 19 AND 20

HABITS

Joseph Grinnell (1913) gave the above name to the rosy finch o
the Sierra Nevada, "in recognition of the services to Ornithology o
William Leon Dawson." He gives it the following diagnostic charac
ters: "As compared with its nearest relative, Leucosticte tephrocoti
tephrocotis Swainson, of the northern Rocky Mountain region, in Britis
America and western Alaska: general coloration in all plumage
grayer toned, less intensely brown, size slightly less, the bill bein
distinctly less in bulk, and wing averaging more rounded; juvena
plumage much grayer especially anteriorly both above and below
breeding females less different; breeding males least different, but
still perceptibly less vivid in the chestnut about the head."

Its breeding range seems to be confined to the Sierra Nevada,
om Eldorado County on the north to Tulare County on the south,
California. Dawson (1923) gives its range as follows: "At least
e higher portions of the central and southern Sierras from Nevada
ounty south to Olancha Peak; also sparingly about the higher peaks
the White Mountains; retires in winter to lower levels, chiefly
sterly."

All the rosy finches seem to prefer to make their summer homes
d rear their young in what we humans would consider most un-
tractive, even forbidding, surroundings, and this southern member
the tribe is no exception to the rule. In the bleak and lofty heights
the Sierras, from 10,000 to 13,000 feet above sea level, among
wering cliffs and rocky slopes, where snowfields remain all summer,
ese hardy birds find congenial summer homes.

Grinnell and Storer (1924) call this "the most typically alpine of
l Californian birds. The mountaineer does not meet with it until
reaches the main Sierran crest or at least the loftiest of the out-
anding spurs."

esting.—Dawson (1923) writes:

* * * The cliff-nesters find their favorite sites available in June, and they,
cordingly, fall to early in the month. The moraine or rock-slide nesters expect
eir home sites to be buried in snow until late in June; and, subject to the varia-
on of the seasons, nest complements may be expected in such situations at any
me from the 1st to the 20th of July. The noisy scenes of courtship, therefore,
ay extend from the middle of May to the middle of July; but the actual nesting
conducted so quietly, so decorously, that the inexperienced student is likely to
utterly deceived.

* * *

The nests of the Leucos are always fully sheltered. They are set back in
ches or placed under boulders, sometimes in chambers of generous proportions,
d always beyond the reach of rain or snow. * * *
Some of the nests are drab-looking affairs, especially where weathered grasses
e the only materials available. Some, however, are wonderfully compacted
mosses, and are lined with feathers or other soft substances. * * * The nests
e, naturally, of the sturdiest construction, with walls from one to three inches
thickness, with hollows deeply cupped. * * *

A long and interesting account, fully illustrated, telling of the
iscovery of the first nest of this bird, was published by Milton S. Ray
1910), to which the reader is referred.

James B. Dixon (1936) gives the following measurements of what
e considered to be a typical nest: "Outside diameter, 4½ inches;
side diameter, 2½ inches; outside depth, 2¾ inches; inside depth,
½ inches."

Eggs.—This rosy finch lays from three to five eggs, more rarely the
tter. They are like the eggs of the other subspecies, pure white

and unspotted. Dawson (1923) gives the average measurements o
10 eggs as 22.5 by 15.6 millimeters.

The measurements of 40 eggs average 21.6 by 15.7 millimeters; th
eggs showing the four extremes measure *24.1* by 17.0, 23.1 by *17.5*
19.7 by 15.6, and 21.6 by *14.8* millimeters.

Young.—Dawson (1923) writes:

The pace of the Leuco day quickens when these white ovals part and nake
babies, to the number of four or five, are born into this world of snow-glare an
hunger. The parents, however, have capacious throats, or crops, and to obviat
the handicap of a long haul, comparatively infrequent visits are made to th
nest. I have seen parents making trips every five minutes, but ten- or fifteen
minutes are more usual, with half an hour, or such a matter, for older birds. Foo
material rarely protrudes from the parental beak, but the nature of the visi
whether parental or conjugal, may be surely determined by the presence or absenc
of the foecal sac, the laden diaper, without which no self-respecting parent wi
quit the presence of his (or her) offspring. * * *

Alden H. Miller (1941) has made the interesting discovery tha
rosy finches are provided with "buccal food-carrying pouches,"
which facilitate carrying considerable quantities of food from distan
feeding grounds to nests. These are fully described and illustrate
in his article, to which the reader is referred.

Dixon's (1936) observations indicate that the female does all th
incubating and will not tolerate the male near the nest until after th
young have hatched; from then on the male seemed to do more thar
half the feeding; the young remained in the nest about 14 days an
were fed after leaving it.

Food.—Grinnell and Storer (1924) write:

Our findings in the Yosemite Park and elsewhere along the Sierras tend to shov
that the food of the Leucosticte even in summer consists predominantly of seeds
with possibly buds, of the dwarfed plants which grow at and above timber line
This is contrary to the testimony of several observers, who, upon seeing the bird
hopping about the edges of snow banks where numbers of benumbed insects ar
often seen stranded on the snow, conclude that the birds are engaged solely i
gathering these "cold-storage bugs." * * *

The present contention as to the prevalently vegetable character of the food o
the Sierra Nevada Rosy Finch is upheld by the contents of the crops of several o
the birds taken for specimens in August, 1911, in the Mount Whitney region
These crops, ten in number, were subjected to careful examination and their con
tents found to consist 91 per cent of small seeds, and 9 percent only of insects

Dawson (1923) writes:

As the season advances and the area of the snowfields is reduced, the Leucos re
sort to the south slopes of the peaks, where yellow-winged locusts and deer-flie
and the hardy butterflies, notably *Vanessa californica*, hold forth. These the
pursue on the ground, or else seize in midair by dextrous leaps from below. The
feed also at the lower levels over the heather beds and in the vicinity of the cirqu
lakes. Once I saw a company of these Leucos feasting on caddis-flies. So eage
had they become that they alighted upon the stones which protruded above th

water of a shallow lake, where they could seize the becoming caddis-flies as they crawled out of their chrysalis cases.* * *

Behavior.—Except during the nesting season rosy finches are not particularly shy and may often be approached. Behavior about the nest is thus described by Dixon (1936):

> During nest building the female exercised no caution in approaching the nest and paid little attention, if any, to anything except building her nest as quickly as possible in the place she had selected. After egg laying, and particularly after incubation had begun, this condition changed. After incubation had begun, the female upon leaving the nest would drop vertically to the lower part of the cliff and then change her course to suit the direction of her destination. In returning to the nest extreme caution always was exercised. Usually the approach was made from level with the nest or slightly higher; and alighting first some distance from the nest the bird would carefully look the situation over and would then fly about half way to the nest and repeat the performance. If satisfied that the coast was clear she would then fly directly to the nest and enter with hardly a wing flutter to indicate where she had disappeared. In no instance did we see the male feed the female either on the nest or near it.

Ray (1910) writes: "The Rosy Finch * * * is ever active either on foot or wing, among the rocks, along the cliffs or while feeding on stranded insects upon the snow. Endowed by nature to combat the fierce gales which prevail almost continually in these high altitudes, this bird possesses great power in its broad stretch of wing. The flight is rapid, in long, graceful, sweeping curves, and the birds mount hundreds of feet even against the strong head winds without much apparent effort."

DISTRIBUTION

Range.—The Sierra Nevada rosy finch is resident in the Sierra Nevada (Mount Tallac, Olancha Peak) and White Mountains of central eastern California; probably also in the Inyo Mountains. Recorded in winter in central western Nevada (Reno).

Egg dates.—California: 1 record, July 14.

LEUCOSTICTE ATRATA Ridgway
Black Rosy Finch

PLATE 20
Contributed by NORMAN R. FRENCH

HABITS

The first black rosy finch was found in 1870 somewhere in the Uinta Mountains of northeastern Utah by the naturalist accompanying the Hayden Expedition of the U.S. Geological Survey. When Robert Ridgway of the Smithsonian Institution received this bird, a single specimen apparently in the first winter plumage, he described it as the young of the gray-crowned rosy finch. He right-fully expressed doubt about this identification, however, as the latter is cinnamon brown in body color and the new specimen was dark gray or black. Nearly 4 years later five similar specimens of wintering birds from Colorado were sent him by Charles Aiken. These he described and named the black rosy finch, calling attention to the earlier error.

This species, like other members of the genus, breeds in the high rocky regions above tree line in our western mountains. Groups may be found rapidly working across a snowfield, each bird alternately hopping and walking, gleaning insects which lie numbed on the cold surface where they were carried by the wind from lower elevations. The species is as characteristic of the mountaintops as the rocks and the perpetual snow, as the tundra with its dwarfed but brilliant flowers, or as the pipit and the pika.

In winter the birds may be found in flocks with other rosy finches, gray-crowned, Hepburn's, and, in central and southern Colorado, the brown-capped rosy finch as well. The large flocks are closely formed, the birds descending on a spot of bare ground to feed and suddenly all abandoning the spot for another farther away

Recently the taxonomic status of this bird has again come into question. Mewaldt (1950) reported a specimen from the Bitterroot Mountains on the Montana–Idaho border which was believed to have characteristics of both black and gray-crowned rosy finches More recently a thorough investigation of that mountain range has disclosed a zone at least 50 miles in length where complete and thorough mixing of the two groups occurs. To the west, in the Seven Devils Mountains near the Idaho–Oregon border, a similarly mixed population was found in 1957 (French, MS.). These were only 50 miles from a previously described dark race of the gray-crowned rosy finch, found in the Wallowa Mountains of Oregon. Thus a broad zone of hybridization or intergradation exists between the two supposed species.

Nesting.—By early April the rosy finches have disappeared from their winter haunts and begun to appear on the breeding grounds Bleak winter conditions still prevail at these high elevations when the birds return. On such a day in the Wasatch Mountains of Utah the birds were observed at 11,000 feet elevation. The snow lay deep, and the only access to the area was on skis. The only bare areas were the high rocky slopes blown clear of snow by the unceasing wind. On these the rosy finches seemed to find seeds from the previous growing season lodged between the rocks and among the small clumps of dried and abraded vegetation. A male black rosy finch attempting to display before a female was almost blown off his feet in the process.

The territory of these birds is unusual in that it centers around the female bird. It moves wherever she moves, even if it means leaving nest and eggs unguarded. Whether the female is feeding, selecting a nest site, or building a nest, her mate stays with her and continually has to drive away the one to several males constantly trying to attract her attention. This situation apparently results from the dearth of females. All observations in both winter and summer indicate that males outnumber females approximately six to one. The actual causes of this unbalanced sex ratio, which can hardly be advantageous to the birds, remain obscure.

Another consequence is that the entire work of selecting a nest site and building the nest falls to the female, the male being quite occupied by others of his kind. One female examined potential nest sites on a cliff for 8 days before finally deciding upon one and beginning nest construction on the ninth day. The nest is usually completed in 3 days. Nest building has been observed as early as June 11 and as as late as July 14.

The nest is placed in a crevice or hole at some almost inaccessible location on a vertical cliff. It is thus well protected from above and on all sides but one, which remains as an entrance. In a single unusual case the female had built her nest among the rocks of a talus slope where it was practically as well protected. The nest itself is a cupped structure, completely supported from below except when the sides happen to rest against the walls of the nest cavity. The base is generally of mosses, which may be growing in the cavity, and the upper portion is made primarily of grass, with some feathers, hair, and moss mixed in. The lining is of finer grass and hair.

Eggs.—Of the eight sets of eggs that have been observed, including three sets reported by F. W. Miller (1925), three nests contained five eggs, four nests contained four eggs, and one contained three eggs. The last of these was a replacement after the first set was destroyed, which may account for the small number. The egg is pure white and ovate pyriform in shape, giving the impression of being rather long and unusually pointed at one end.

The measurements of 16 eggs average 22.1 by 16.0 millimeters; the eggs showing the four extremes measure *23.4* by 15.7, 21.0 by *16.3*, *21.0* by 16.3, and 23.3 by *15.3* millimeters.

Young.—After 12 to 14 days of incubation the eggs hatch, producing helpless young covered on the dorsal surfaces with sparse long whitish down. At the approach of the parent bird, the gaping of the young bird exposes the bright red lining of the mouth contrasting sharply with the yellow edge of the bill. As in incubation, the task of brooding and feeding the young falls to the female. After the first week the male helps feed his offspring and both parents then continue this function until the young are independent.

On the 4th day of nest life the eyes of the young birds are opening and the nestlings begin chirping, especially at feeding time. On the 7th day the feathers begin breaking from their sheaths and, by the 11th day, the nesting bird appears completely covered by feathers. The young leave the nest at approximately 20 days of age. After this they remain among the rocks where their gray color makes them very difficult to locate, even when they call frequently. The young birds are probably fed by the parents for as long as 2 weeks after leaving the nest. During this time the young beg energetically from the parent whenever it is near and follow it as it retreats. The adults use this trait to lead their young in flight to a safe place among the tumbled rocks, where they leave them by flying off too rapidly for the young to follow. In such places several families become consolidated in a single flock. After they are thus assembled parental care of the young wanes and ceases.

Plumages.—The general coloration of a bird in juvenal plumage is lilac-gray, darker dorsally. The contour feathers have somewhat brownish edges, providing a faint buffy color, especially ventrally. The flight feathers are darker. The secondaries show broad buffy margins and the central rectrices a narrow margin of the same color. The remaining rectrices and especially the primaries show distinct but very narrow whitish margins. The primaries and their coverts have narrow margins of pink, wider proximally on the remiges. The nasal tufts are whitish, as in the adults.

In late August or September the first winter plumage is acquired by a partial postjuvenal molt. The rectrices, remiges, wing coverts and perhaps some of the tail coverts remain unchanged. With the exception of slight differences in these feathers, the first winter plumage is similar to the adult winter plumage.

There is no prenuptial molt, the adult breeding dress being acquired by wearing off of the dusky, grayish, brownish, or pinkish edgings of the feathers. Unlike the other members of the genus *Leucosticte* in North America, the black rosy finch shows rather strong sexual dimorphism. The body and head of the male are sooty black, with a light gray crescent extending from eye to eye over the back of the crown, and a pink wash on the belly, flanks, and tail coverts. The flight feathers are nearly as dark centrally as the contour feathers but are lighter below, the ventral aspect of the extended wing appearing almost pearl-gray. The primaries of a fully adult bird have even more extensive white and pinkish edgings than those of the juvenile. The pink color is most pronounced along the bend of the folded wing where the overlapping primaries, secondaries, and their coverts make an almost solid area of pink. However, the intensity of this color may vary considerably in any single population. The female is generally duller than the male, with less extensive pink and a gray crown patch that may be barely detectable.

The postnuptial molt takes place during approximately the same time of year as the postjuvenal molt and is complete. During this time also the solid black pigmentation of the bill begins to fade until the winter condition is attained, when the bill is yellow except for the very tip, which remains black. It starts to darken again during March just prior to spring migration.

Food.—The rosy finches subsist primarily on a diet of seeds but supplement this with insects when they are available. During the first few days of nest life the young are given only insects the female collects in the vicinity of the nest. When the young birds begin receiving more seeds, both parents are kept busy making long trips to the tundra where they show a preference for foraging along the edges of melting snowbanks. In winter large flocks settle on any spot of bare ground to search for seeds, or they thoroughly examine plants, such as Russian thistle, protruding from the snow.

During the breeding season rosy finches of both sexes develop a pair of gular sacs capable of considerable distension and opening from the floor of the mouth. This accessory food-carrying structure is definitely advantageous to a species whose nest may be some distance from the feeding grounds. Besides the North American species of rosy finches, gular sacs are known only from one other fringillid, the pine grosbeak, *Pinicola enucleator* (see French, 1954).

Analysis of the contents of crops and gular sacs of 70 summer specimens of black rosy finch has shown that the food of these birds consisted of 97.2 percent seeds and 2.8 percent animals, including mites, nematodes, and various insects. The seeds were those of the small tundra plants abundant in the habitat where the birds are found, the following genera being the most abundant: *Siversia, Arabis, Smelowskia, Silene, Lewisia, Sibbaldia, Claytonia.*

Behavior.—Rosy finches are very social birds. It is unusual to see an individual alone. During most of the year they may be found in large flocks, feeding together and flying off together. Only at the approach of breeding do negative social forces develop strongly enough to cause antagonism and breaking up of the groups. The groups re-form in late summer, even while the young are still being fed by the parents, as the positive social forces recrudesce.

The flocks are closely knit and, when one bird chirps and flies, the entire group literally explodes in an effort to follow. With two young birds raised in captivity, the one irresistible stimulus was flight. If one bird flew over the other's head, the second bird immediately forgot what it had been doing and flew in pursuit.

The flight of the black rosy finch is distinctive. Quick strokes of the wings followed by a glide, seemingly with almost folded wings, result in an undulating path of flight. Viewed from beneath, the luster of the undersurfaces of the wings shows plainly when they are in motion.

Voice.—The black rosy finches use only three primary notes, which, plus variations, serve all purposes. These birds, therefore, cannot be considered as having a true song. The three call notes are: A descending rather harsh *chew* or *tsew* note somewhat similar to the chirping of an English sparrow, a low, throaty sharp *pert*, and a high piercing *peent*.

Flocks in flight utter a call which resembles *pert-pert-chew*. It is heard most frequently in winter flocks and probably serves to hold the group together. When the birds go to roost on a high cliff, their roosting or territorial calls may be heard clearly from below even when the birds cannot be seen. This call consists of a series of *chew* notes, each one on a different pitch, uttered rapidly and continuously. During the breeding season it seems to function in spacing the birds. The high *peent* seems to serve as an alarm note, generally being given when a bird is startled, and resulting in the nearby birds either crouching or taking sudden flight.

Field marks.—The distinctive coloring of this species has been described under plumages and the characteristic undulating flight in the section on behavior. The long pointed wings give the rosy finch an appearance in flight somewhat similar to that of the mountain bluebird, *Sialia currucoides*. The latter, however, does not exhibit the undulating path of flight, nor does the pipit, *Anthus spinoletta*. These two birds are the ones most likely to be mistaken for rosy finches in summer. On the ground pipits walk rather than hop, as the rosy finches do frequently, but the typical bobbing or rocking of the pipit serves to distinguish this species. The same characteristics serve to distinguish the birds in winter, with the additional feature that rosy finches then occur in large flocks, frequently numbering into the hundreds of individuals.

Enemies.—The main enemy of the black rosy finch is the Clark's nutcracker, *Nucifraga columbiana*. These birds have been observed destroying nests, eggs, and young of the rosy finch and have been suspected of other nefarious activities (French, 1955). A long-tailed weasel, *Mustela frenata*, was once seen carrying off a young black rosy finch, with the adult bird chirping noisily over its head. On another occasion two weasels were searching among the rocks of a talus slope, again with rosy finches protesting nearby. This time their search was unsuccessful. In most cases the young birds are susceptible to the predations of these or other mammals for only a brief period, just after leaving the nest.

In a nest in the Absaroka Range of Wyoming the nestling black rosy finches were infested with blood-sucking larvae of a fly, later identified as belonging to the genus *Protocalliphora*. The harm resulting to the young birds could not be determined. They at least survived to the time of leaving the nest.

Fall.—The rosy finches start to flock in the high mountains by the time the young birds become independent of the parents. These flocks coalesce until they may be composed of several hundred individuals. These hardy birds remain at high elevations until well after freezing weather sets in, where they have been seen regularly throughout October and as late as November 2 in the Uinta Mountains and the Wasatch Mountains of Utah. At about this time the birds begin to appear in the valleys and deserts at lower elevations and start using their winter roosts in these areas. The exact paths and distances involved in the migration are not yet known, but a comparison of the summer and winter ranges indicates that the birds probably move about 300 miles and several thousand feet in altitude in the process.

Winter.—The winter range of the black rosy finch includes Utah, the southern half of Wyoming, and the western half of Colorado. The species has been reported in adjacent parts of Arizona, in Nevada, and even in extreme eastern California. These and the other rosy finches have communal winter roosts which they use year after year. Where the winter ranges of two or more kinds of rosy finches overlap, these birds will occur in mixed flocks that will use the same roosts. At a cave in Bingham County in southeastern Idaho, gray-crowned rosy finches, *L. t. tephrocotis*, and Hepburn's rosy finches, *L. t. littoralis*, regularly may be found roosting together in winter. In southwestern Wyoming and throughout Utah the black rosy finch occurs with these two, and in central and southern Colorado a fourth, the brown-capped rosy finch, *L. australis*, joins the winter flocks.

The winter roosts provide overhead shelter and escape from the wind. Known roosts are few, but those that have been observed include cave entrances, mine shafts, abandoned cliff swallow nests, and such man-made structures as piers, out-buildings, and barns. The birds leave the roosts at daybreak to forage in surrounding areas and return by midafternoon. Although feeding flocks met with during the day are large, the birds seem to return to the roost in small groups. The birds settle on their individual perches within the dimly lighted cave or structure well before sundown.

Banding carried on at two roosts approximately 8 miles apart west of Salt Lake City, indicated the birds returned night after night to the same roost. Only rarely did birds banded at one roost appear at the other, even when released more than 15 miles away and an equal distance from either roost.

DISTRIBUTION

Range.—Central Rocky Mountains.

Breeding range.—The black rosy finch breeds in the high mountains of north to southwestern Montana (Bitterroot Range south of Lolo Pass, Anaconda Range, Madison Range, and Crazy Mountains). *East* to western and northcentral Wyoming (Big Horn Mountains, Absaroka Range, Teton Mountains, Gros Ventre Range and Wind River Range). *South* to northern Utah (Uinta Mountains and southern Wasatch Mountains) and northeastern Nevada (Jabridge Peak and Ruby Mountains). *West* to central and western Idaho (Lost River Range, Sawtooth Mountains, and Seven Devils Mountains).

The above range includes the areas (Seven Devils Mountains and Bitterroot Range) where intergradation or hybridization with the gray-crowned rosy finch occurs freely.

Winter range.—In winter the black rosy finch is found in the valleys and lower elevations *north* at least as far as northwestern Wyoming (Mammoth, Dubois, Jackson, LaBarge and Pinedale). *East* to central Colorado (Boulder, Evergreen, and Cañon City). *South* to northern New Mexico (northwest of Vermejo Park), southern Utah (Kanab and St. George), and northern Arizona (Grand Canyon). *West* into Nevada (Pioche, Tonopah, and Reno) and as far as eastern California (Bodie and Chats).

Casual records.—Casual in eastern Oregon (Wallowa Mountains) and eastern Montana (Terry).

Migration.—Late dates of spring departure are: Colorado—Cañon City, April 20; Walden, April 18. Utah—Provo, April 20. Wyoming—Yellowstone National Park, April 5. Montana—Anaconda, May 27.

Early dates of fall arrival are: Wyoming—Yellowstone National Park, October 9; Sheep Mountain, November 24. Utah—Provo, October 10; Saltair, October 31. Colorado—Golden, November 13. New Mexico—Vermejo Park, Colfac County, November 29.

LEUCOSTICTE AUSTRALIS Ridgeway

Brown-capped Rosy Finch

PLATE 21

Contributed by FRED MALLERY PACKARD

HABITS

The high rugged mountains of Colorado are the home of the brown-capped rosy finch, a species with close affinities for the arctic environment of that region. Its range is almost entirely restricted to the western half of Colorado, although it has been found in northern New Mexico near the Colorado boundary. Nesting on peaks, usually above 12,000 feet, it migrates altitudinally to the lower hills for the winter. It rarely descends below 6,000 feet, and it has not been recorded below 5,000 feet.

Within its limited range the brown-capped rosy finch is a common bird, especially numerous on the lofty meadows of the Front Range and Arapahoe Peaks that form the eastern chain of the Rocky Mountains. An ascent of almost any suitable peak in Colorado in summer should result in the discovery of one or more groups of these finches flying up from the tundra, feeding on the lingering snowbanks, or perched on a nearby outcrop. They, with the white-tailed ptarmigan, are truly birds of the summits; of the species that nest above timberline the ptarmigan remains closer to its summer home throughout the year.

Courtship.—Although brown-capped rosy finches are plentiful and locally abundant throughout their range, few trained observers have recorded their behavior prior to the nesting season. Because much of their high alpine habitat is nearly or completely inaccessible to man until very late spring, little information about their territorial and courtship habits is available.

Lack (1940) writes that they arrive on the arctic tundra in sizable flocks, already paired. F. W. Miller (MS.) notes that "as mating takes place, the flocking is still adhered to, even with eggs or young in the nest, they always appear in company. But the flocks are less unified, and the pairs and individuals act independently." Robert J. Niedrach, Assistant Director of the Denver Museum of Natural History, who has studied the bird life of Colorado for more than 50 years, told me that during the mating period, from the last 2 weeks of June to early July, the male performs a conspicuous song flight. Undulating in a large circle that covers 10 to 20 acres, he sings on the wing steadily for 5 or 10 minutes before finally descending to the ground to feed. The male sings actively during the early part of nesting, but less so when incubation begins. Thereafter, only an occasional song in flight is heard, and the characteristic call that birds of both sexes give on the wing as they fly directly between the feeding and nesting grounds. He found flocks of 10 to 15 individuals together just before the nesting season, but during the nesting period the birds were observed singly or in pairs. Where several nests are in fairly close proximity, as on a single side of a peak, a number of individuals may be seen at one time in a limited area. At Rocky Mountain National Park I noticed that rosy finches did not occur in flocks during the nesting season.

Nesting.—The brown-capped rosy finch nests at elevations above 12,000 feet throughout the western half of Colorado and extreme northern New Mexico wherever alpine tundra, precipitous cliffs, talus slides, and slow-melting snowbanks combine to form the requisite ecological conditions. The species probably nests also along the Colorado border in Utah and Wyoming where a similar habitat exists, but evidence of this is lacking.

Despite the species' abundance in many parts of its range, very few nests have been studied or collected. F. C. Lincoln (1916), reporting the discovery of the first known nest by H. R. Durand, A. H. Burns, and himself, writes:

The nest was discovered July 11, 1915, on the southwest exposure of the south peak of Mt. Bross, Park County, Colo., at an elevation of 13,500 feet, or within 600 feet of the summit, the elevation of Mt. Bross being 14,000 feet. This altitude of the nest site here marks the limit of plant growth, the remaining 600 feet being bare rock, either slides or in the form of outcropping or small cliffs.

It was in one of these latter that the nest was found * * *. The face of this cliff had suffered considerably from erosion, resulting in "chimneys" and cavities from a few inches to several feet in diameter, and in one of the smaller of these the nest was placed. The hole, forming the upper terminus of a vertical crack, ran back twelve or fourteen inches and was about forty inches [sic] from the base of the cliff.

A number of nests from Mt. Bross were studied and added to the collection of W. C. Bradbury. About these nests, F. W. Miller in 1921 writes: "On Mount Bross, the rosy finch is abundant everywhere above timberline, though it nests exclusively on the southwestern or Buckskin side at an altitude of 12,000 feet up. This locality is ideal, the entire side of the mountain being one huge rock slide, varied and broken with cliffs and outcrops * * *. All the nests were found in cliffs; one was placed on a shelf of rock in a prospect tunnel. The usual site is in a hole or crevice in the face of a sheer rock cliff. Where the rock is in lime formation, the nest is occasionally placed several feet back in a narrow fissure. No nests or signs of nests were found in the rock slides."

PLATE 21

Colorado   Colorado Museum Natural History

NEST OF BROWN-CAPPED ROSY FINCH

ong Island, N.Y., July 5, 1942   R. T. Peterson

EUROPEAN GOLDFINCH

The nest may be placed in a blowhole or shallow crevice only a few inches within the cliff face, or it may be far back in a larger crack beyond arm's reach. Less frequently it is built behind or under a large rock amid finer detritus. One nest was discovered in a depression on the surface of a cliff protected by a large overhang of the escarpment. The nests always appear to be from 6 to 40 feet above the top of the talus slide at the base of the cliff. These sites provide shelter from the frequent blustery winds, rain squalls, lightning storms, and occasional snows that strike the alpine meadows during summer.

All the nests so far discovered appear to have been hidden in perpetual shadow, entirely out of reach of the sun's rays. Niedrach photographed parent birds feeding young in a nest on a shelf of rock 15 feet back in a cavelike opening that was so dark he could not cast light on the nest itself even with the aid of mirrors. Such sites must be very cold, especially at night. One nest on Mount Bross was frozen tightly to ice formed by the congealing of water trickling down during the frigid hours of darkness.

The nest consists of a cup of fine material tightly woven into an outer matrix of alpine moss (*Sphagnum*). Lincoln (1916) describes it thus: "The bulk of the nest was of dry grass and flower stems neatly and compactly woven together with a considerable quantity of fine moss, and lined with a fine yellow grass and a few feathers from the bird's body, with one White-tailed Ptarmigan feather. It rested well into the silt which covered the bottom of the hole, and the cup was placed to one side, thus giving walls of unequal thickness on two sides. This inequality did not, however, change the general exterior shape, which is practically round * * *."

A nest collected by A. T. Wheeler, now in the University of Colorado Museum, is practically circular, both exteriorly and interiorly, but the sides of the cup flare outward below the rim so that the cavity is wider inside than at the top. Lincoln's nest was 4.75 inches in diameter, with an overall depth of 3.00 inches; the cup was 2.50 inches in diameter and 1.60 inches deep. A nest in the University of Colorado Museum measures 5.69 inches in diameter and 2.81 inches in overall depth; the rim of the cup is 2.37 inches in diameter; the widest interior diameter is 2.75 inches; and the depth is 1.62 inches. A third nest, in the Chicago Natural History Museum, of which only the cup has been preserved, has the following dimensions: inner diameter of rim, 2.60 inches; greatest inside diameter, 2.75 inches; inside depth, 1.5 inches; overall depth, 2.50 inches.

The outside of the nest appears always to be solely of alpine moss. The cup is firmly woven into this matrix, the bowl composed of very fine grasses, flower stems, and rootlets, the rim of slightly coarser grass stems, and the underside of the cup, hidden by the moss, of still coarser bits of stem an inch or less in length, all closely woven together. The cup sometimes includes traces of a variety of other materials: ptarmigan and rosy finch feathers, rabbit and cony fur, elk and burro hair, pieces of cloth, ravelings of burlap, and, in one nest, a section of blasting fuse. One egg was found with cotton adhering to the shell. Occasionally small sharp pebbles fall into the nest and dent the fragile egg shells.

Nest building begins about June 20 or later, and the actual construction of the nest does not take long. F. W. Miller (MS.) watched a site that was vacant on July 12; on July 14 the nest was complete except for the lining; by July 16 it had been finished and two eggs laid. Three days later the set of five was complete and the female was incubating. Niedrach told me that in his experience the female builds the nest alone; he never saw a male bring material to it.

Eggs.—The number of eggs in complete sets varies from three to five. Several nests Niedrach studied in the Arapahoe Range contained the smaller number, while of 13 nests F. W. Miller and others watched on Mount Bross, 1 contained two eggs; 2, three eggs; 5, four eggs; and 5, five eggs.

F. C. Lincoln (1916) describes the eggs as "pure white, slightly glossy, unmarked; ovate pyriform in shape; measurements in inches:— .91 × .60; .95 × 63; .97 × 62." Other sets examined by the writer agree with this description, with slight variations in the measurements.

The measurements of 50 eggs average 22.7 by 15.6 millimeters; the eggs showing the four extremes measure *25.8* by 16.0; 25.1 by *16.5*; *20.5* by 16.0; and 23.2 by *14.8* millimeters.

In his notes, F. W. Miller mentions indications of pigmentation on one set of eggs he collected; but when they were blown for preservation, no trace of pigment could be seen. The shells are very thin and fragile, and of the few sets that have been collected, a number have been broken in the blowing or otherwise destroyed.

According to the limited data available, eggs are laid at the rate of one a day until the clutch is complete. The earliest date eggs have been found is June 30, when a set of four was discovered on Mount Bross. Fresh eggs have been found as late as July 19, which were the second set of five laid in a nest from which the first set had been collected on July 8. A nest completed on Arapahoe Peak, Grand County, on July 28, contained three eggs on August 7, the date the eggs were taken.

Young.—According to Niedrach, incubation probably lasts from 12 to 14 days. The earliest hatching date noted is July 8; full clutches of eggs still under incubation have been found several times as late as July 27. Incubation of second sets, when laid, probably continues into early August. No exact temperatures of the air around the nesting sites have been taken, but the sunless crevices and caves are extremely chilly, even though protected from direct winds. Trickles of water running down the surface of the rocks near the nests frequently freeze at night. The young remain in the nest about 18 days and are fed by both parents, often at the same time. The parent not on the nest at night roosts in a crevice nearby. The adults show little fear of man at this time. They frequently flew within 6 feet of Niedrach while he was taking motion pictures of them feeding their young. When the nestlings are half grown, they emit a continuous loud chirping which carries a long distance and helps locate the nest sites. The fledged young are fed on the ground until they are able to forage for themselves, and remain with the parents during August and at the least, into September, forming family groups on the alpine tundra.

Plumages.—The brown-capped rosy finch differs from all other leucostictes in lacking distinct or clear gray markings on the head. Ridgway (1901) writes: "* * * there is a quite well defined area covering exactly the same parts of the pileum as in *L. tephrocotis tephrocotis* and *L. atrata*, that is differently colored from the contiguous parts, but instead of this area being clear and perfectly uniform light ash gray the feathers are dusky brownish gray centrally, margined with light brownish gray, producing a more or less squamate or scale-like appearance; furthermore, the brown color which borders this somewhat grayish area is decidedly lighter and duller, or less rufescent than in *L. tephrocotis.*"

Of the several leucostictes, only *L. atrata* and *L. australis* show striking sexual color variation, and in *L. australis* there are also marked differences between the summer and winter plumages of each sex. Ridgway (1901) describes the adult male in summer as follows:

Pileum dusky grayish brown, becoming nearly or quite black on forehead; nasal tufts whitish; rest of head, together with neck, chest, and breast, deep cinnamon-brown or dull russet, deepest on throat, where often, as on chest and breast also, tinged or flecked with bright red; hindneck, back and scapulars similar, but duller * * *, with narrow, more or less indistinct, shaft-streaks of dusky; feathers of rump and upper tail-coverts broadly and abruptly tipped with peach-blossom pink; the remaining portion of the feathers grayish brown * * *; sides, flanks, and abdomen mostly carmine-pink * * *; under tail-coverts deep grayish brown or dusky centrally, broadly and abruptly margined with pink and white; wings dusky, with lesser and middle coverts broadly tipped with peach-blossom pink, the greater and primary coverts and remiges edged with the same—the color very bright, almost scarlet, on the wing-coverts in some midsummer specimens; tail dusky, edged with pale brownish gray and pinkish; bill and feet black.

In his monograph on the genus *Leucosticte* (1875), he adds: "In the male, the red of the lower parts extends much farther forward than in the other forms, always covering pretty uniformly the entire abdomen and sides, while it sometimes invades the breast, or even sometimes the throat and cheeks." In the adult female in summer, he says, the prevailing color is "pale grayish-brown-umber, the pileum hardly appreciably different, and the forehead scarcely inclining to black; red markings almost obsolete, and distinctly indicated only on the lesser wing coverts and rump; greater coverts, remiges, and rectrices skirted with whitish; abdomen scarcely tinged with red * * *.

"In midsummer [June and July], the pale margins of the crown and grayish brown of the plumage wear off, so it becomes more uniform, while the red of the male is heightened into an intense crimson, or harsh carmine tint."

A. W. Anthony (1887) describes the adult male in winter (January) thus:

Pileum grayish black, darkest anteriorly, slightly paling to grayish on occiput; lores dull blackish; nasal plumes white. General color above and below light umber-brown, tending to chocolate on the chin and throat. Feathers of the back with darker shaft-lines and paler edges; those of the breast but slightly tipped with whitish. Hinder parts of the body, above and below, rich carmine-red; primaries, outer four secondaries, second, third, fourth and fifth rectrices edged, and lesser wing-coverts broadly tipped with same color. Wings and tail blackish, all of the primaries and secondaries broadly, and median pair of rectrices slightly, edged with dull white. Lining of wings white, edged with rosy.

The female in winter is similar to the male in general color, but paler, and varies considerably. The rosy hues are usually very faint and may be almost entirely absent.

The immature male closely resembles the adult, the principal difference being that the greater wing coverts are edged with whitish in summer and with buffy in winter.

The juvenal plumage is generally grayish-brown, the crown being dull grayish-black with gray edges on the feathers, the sides of the head and neck grayish-brown darkening on the chin and throat. The lower parts are light brown anteriorly, each feather edged with whitish, the abdominal feathers light dusky, with pinkish and whitish edges. The back is dull brown, the upper tail coverts and lesser wing coverts with rosy markings, the wings and tail blackish.

In winter the bill is yellow, tipped with black. In early March the yellow becomes clouded with dusky horn color, and it darkens progressively through April and May until by June it is intense black. The feet are black at all times.

Field marks.—Rosy finches are rather chunky, sparrowlike ground birds that look darker than the other ground finches of the region. The brown-capped rosy finch lacks the distinct gray area on the crown common to the other leucostictes, and the general coloration is lighter brown and duller. The rosy feathers of the adult male are bright, especially in midsummer, and often extend forward to the breast or throat. Females are duller and paler than males, are less rosy, and sometimes show no pink at all. Their blended colors, lacking in contrast, help identify them. Young birds lack rosy feathers and are nondescript.

A. W. Anthony (1887) writes: "In comparing the full plumaged *australis* with *L. tephrocotis*, both in winter dress, I find the latter much the darker bird, the umber-brown on the breast and back of the female *tephrocotis* being of about the same shade as that found on the male *australis*. In *tephrocotis* the rosy hue is less extended, decidedly duller, and more broken by the ground colors of the body. In *tephrocotis* I often find the rump marked with crescent-shaped rosy spots on a chocolate ground, while in *australis*, although the rosy patch is seldom, if ever, continuous, it is usually less broken and extends farther forward."

Food.—The brown-capped rosy finch feeds principally or entirely on insects, seeds, and small plant fruits that occur on or near the ground. So far as has been recorded, it seldom, if ever, feeds in the air. In high altitudes grasses and flowering plants grow only a few inches tall and their growing season is brief. They come rapidly into seed and are quickly replaced by a new succession of plants. Thus a constantly renewed abundance of seeds and fruits is available to the rosy finches.

E. R. Warren (1916) collected two females that were foraging for their young at 11,500 feet in Elk Basin, Gunnison County, on June 28. Analysis of their stomach contents showed that in one, 80 percent was seeds of *Alsine* (*media*?) or chickweed, with shelled seeds of *Bidens*, seeds of *Eragrostis*, *Polygonum*, *Corizus hyalinus*, *Corizus indentatus*, and *Balclutha impicta*, one *Trypeta*, and traces of beetles and spiders. The other contained 50 percent *Bidens* seeds, 35 percent *Alsine*, 10 percent *Eragrostis*, and some *Corizus*, a fly, and traces of beetle. On Specimen Mountain in Rocky Mountain National Park I once watched a rosy finch fluttering over a growth of arctic willow (*Salix* sp.) but could not determine whether the bird was feeding on buds or on insects.

Rosy finches are frequently seen hopping about on the patches of snow that linger on the alpine meadows until late summer, sometimes until new snow falls in autumn. It is often assumed that the birds do so to eat the snow as a source of water, but at least for the brown-capped rosy finch, there is no valid evidence that they do so. Niedrach, who has carefully watched the activities of these birds on snowbanks, informed me that he has never seen any rosy finches actually eating snow, and that the birds are apparently seeking seeds that have blown there sometime previously. These seeds form strata or lenses in the snow that are readily visible to the eye, and become impregnated with snow water until they are very soft. As the snow melts, they appear on the surface of the patch, where the rosy finches gorge themselves on them. F. W. Miller (MS.) notes that these snowbanks are the favorite feeding grounds of the rosy finches as long as the patches remain. He observed that the birds feed extensively on dead and torpid insects that have been chilled and dropped to the ground. He says that "As the season advances and the snow disappears, the birds resort to the cliffs and rock slides, where they find a variety of insect food, including a large number of moths. After a storm, they are always out to gather up the insects that have taken refuge in the grass and litter."

The winter diet is almost completely herbaceous, except for such animal substances as may be present in refuse heaps visited by the birds. Roadside grass and weed seeds supply a large proportion of their nourishment at this season, especially the Russian thistle or tumbleweed (*Salsola* sp.), which they eat until their crops are overfull (Warren, 1910). Aiken (Ridgway, 1875) reports them to be very fond of hemp and canary seed, from which they remove the shells almost instantly.

Behavior.—Leucostictes are more at home on the ground than above it, but they do alight occasionally on bushes, trees, fences, or buildings. E. R. Warren (1915) watched a flock of brown-capped rosy finches at timberline on Mount Bross in late September and writes: "Several of them worked down a little and perched in some dead trees, in the topmost branches, something I do not recall having seen these birds do before, though when at lower elevations in winter I have seen them in low bushes or trees." During the winter when mixed flocks of rosy finches forage along the roadsides of the mountain "parks," passing vehicles often flush them from the weeds. Usually they alight on the ground a hundred yards or so away, but not infrequently some will perch briefly upon a fence wire or tall weed, seldom staying there more than a few seconds.

On their alpine meadows in summer, the rosy finches are shy and quick to fly at the approach of an intruder. By sitting quietly, however, one may watch them at fairly close range, especially if one settles near a favored snowbank where the birds come to feed. The parents of a nest of young Niedrach (MS.) was photographing showed no fear at his presence. In winter they become tame and confiding. Robert Ridgway (1875) quotes C. E. Aiken, who studied these birds at Colorado Springs during that season: "Every morning they came, usually only one or two at a time, to pick up crumbs in the door-yard, and fearlessly ventured on the porch for seeds that fell from a canary cage hung there; indeed, so tame were they that they would pick seeds at my very feet as I dropped them from my and. During two days that I remained in town I caught five alive under a common flour-sieve * * *." In Rocky Mountain National Park I have often walked to within 10 feet of winter flocks of leucostictes, and once a band settled to the ground all around me.

Their habit of carrying their bodies close to the ground gives a flock of feeding rosy finches some resemblance to longspurs, but they do not creep as longspurs do. Aiken writes (Ridgway, 1875): "They move on the ground with quick, short hops, their feet so closely drawn up into their ruffled feathers as to be almost invisible."

Enemies.—Probably rosy finches fall prey occasionally to the several species of hawks and other predators present on both their summer and winter ranges, but the only reported attack on brown-capped rosy finches appears to be that of Niedrach (MS.), who watched a merlin (*Falco columbarius richardsoni*) chase some of them unsuccessfully at a roost at Morrison.

Voice.—The note most frequently heard from the brown-capped rosy finch is a rather harsh, goldfinchlike *peyt-a-weet* the birds utter as they rise from the ground and repeat on the wing. The incessant prenuptial singing of the male has been described above, as has the continual chirping of the nestlings and the characteristic call the parents use when flying between the nest and feeding ground. After the young fledge, the adults are rather silent, occasionally emitting a thick-toned chirp, but the young birds keep up an incessant clamor, "like young chimney swifts," as F. M. Drew (1881) describes it. "The wind was very high at the time [August 17], and often while standing in a lode drift, the noise would go rushing by sounding like the distant jingle of sleigh bells."

In winter the foraging flocks are conversational, twittering together quite noisily, and the birds are very quarrelsome and noisy about their roosts. Aiken (Ridgway, 1875) describes a winter song: "I have several times heard one of them sing, a pretty, warbling song, somewhat like that of the canary, but so low as hardly to be heard at a distance of more than two or three rods." I have heard what were probably fragments of this song among the winter flocks at Rocky Mountain National Park.

Winter.—The foothills of the Front Range and of the Arapahoe Range rise abruptly from the Great Plains about 20 miles west of Denver. The first isolated ridge, known as the Hogback with an average elevation of 5,500 feet, marks the normal eastern limit of the winter range of the brown-capped rosy finch. Westward the species is found in winter in most of the basins and mountain "parks" that lie between the ranges, particularly in North Park, Middle Park, and South Park, southwestward to Mesa Verde National Park, and at a number of other places in the western half of the State. Some of these leucostictes occur in winter in immediately adjacent parts of New Mexico, casually in Wyoming, and possibly in Utah.

The descent to the lower ranges begins in late September and becomes pronounced when the first severe autumn snows strike the peaks. Through October and November, as the storms increase in severity and frequency, flocks of from 50 to more than 100 rosy finches begin to appear in the foothills. At Rocky Mountain National Park small bands composed entirely of *australis* arrived in the Transition Zone at 8,500 feet in mid-October; usually they do not remain then, but move higher again after the snow that prompted their first descent has melted. The November storms, however, produce permanent snows on the alpine meadows, and thereafter many of the birds either stay in the Transition Zone "parks," or descend into the foothills. Even at that season small flocks may be found above timberline, and a number return to the summits in winter whenever the weather clears after storms.

Niedrach found the species common during the entire winter of 1918 at 13,000 feet on Quartz Creek, at the edge of Taylor Peak, Pitkin County. The birds appeared in bands of three or four to a dozen, searched the newly turned soil of excavations for food, and ate refuse the cook threw out. Horace G. Smith, of Denver, told me that these finches were often present in large flocks in winter near mines high in the mountains, where they frequented the places where the cooks disposed of dishwater containing crumbs and other food.

In late October three other species of leucosticte arrive in Colorado from their summer ranges and join the brown-capped rosy finches to form mixed flocks which may number a thousand birds, though groups of one or two hundred are more usual. The gray-crowned rosy finch (*L. t. tephrocotis*) soon becomes the most common form, almost equaled by *australis*. Hepburn's rosy finch (*L. t. littoralis*) is fairly numerous, often making up a quarter of the total, while the black rosy finch (*L. atrata*) is always rather rare, seldom represented by more than one or two individuals. These flocks consist entirely of leucostictes; no other birds mingle with them in the meadows. Sometimes a small flock is comprised entirely of *australis*, but this is not always the rule.

Every mountain storm drives the birds to lower elevations. Severe blizzards bring thousands to the foothills, where they remain as long as the inclement weather lasts. When the weather clears, many follow the receding snowline back into the higher country; others remain for some weeks in the valleys, while still others make a daily trek in clement periods to elevations 2,000 to 3,000 feet above their roosting sites. If the fair weather is prolonged, a number return to the alpine tundra until the next storm drives them down again. Aiken writes (Ridgway, 1875): "A storm gathers them into a dense lock, when their habits are much like those of the Shore-Larks [*Otocoris*]; but, on the return of pleasant weather, the flocks are dispersed, and the birds are found singly or in small companies."

At night during the winter the rosy finches congregate in roosts, all our species together, sometimes numbering a thousand or more. Niedrach (MS.) has studied such a roost at Red Rocks Park, at Morrison, Colo., a 6,000 feet elevation. The birds begin to arrive here from the hills above about 3:00 p.m. and do considerable foraging before seeking their sleeping crannies. They quarrel vociferously among themselves over the roosting spots, flying in and out of the cliffs until it is totally dark. In this roost each bird occupies a little blowhole, which is usually soiled with a great mass of droppings. In another roost, along the Hogback west of Denver, the birds sleep in cliff swallow casings in association with juncos, house sparrows, and pine siskins.

These foothill roosts are occupied nightly until about April 10, and are then abandoned, the birds presumably moving up a few thousand feet with the retreating snows. Through April and early May many birds remain at elevations of 7,000 to 9,000 feet, the migrant species disappearing from the region gradually. A late spring storm may force the remaining birds down into the foothills briefly, but as these snows melt quickly, they soon return. As the alpine tundra blows clear of snow and the brown-capped rosy finches ascend to their nesting ranges, the wintering flocks gradually diminish.

Horace G. Smith of Denver reports that he has seen brown-capped rosy finches on two occasions in that city, both times in winter. One flew into an open window of a residence, and a band of the birds once entered a cowshed to roost for the night.

DISTRIBUTION

Range.—Wyoming, Colorado, and New Mexico.

Breeding range.—Breeds in the mountains of southeastern Wyoming (Medicine Bow Range), Colorado (near Walden, Pikes Peak) and central northern New Mexico (Wheeler Peak).

Winter range.—Winters at lower altitudes within the breeding range.

Migration.—Late dates of spring departure are: Colorado—Colorado Springs, May 28; Walden, May 21 (median of 8 years, April 10).

Early dates of fall arrival are: Colorado—Walden, November 4 (median of 7 years, November 13).

Egg dates.—Colorado: 11 records, June 28 to July 27.

CARDUELIS CARDUELIS
European Goldfinch
PLATE 21
Contributed by JOHN JACKSON ELLIOTT

HABITS

In addition to the small colony that managed to perpetuate itse
during the past half century on southwestern Long Island, N.Y., th
European goldfinch is admitted to the American list on the basis of i
successful establishment in Bermuda. The 1957 A.O.U. Check-Lis
refers all these birds to the British race *Carduelis carduelis brittannic*
but as Austin (1963) has recently pointed out, the subspecific status c
the former Long Island population is conjectural, and the Bermud
population today is unquestionably *C. c. parva*, the race of Madeir
the Azores, and the Canary Islands. Bermuda was first colonized b
goldfinches that escaped from a British ship in the harbor in 1893, bu
the stock there now has apparently descended from birds brought sub
sequently from their home islands by the large element of Azorian
resident in Bermuda. The stock released in the New York City are
in the latter half of the 19th century also came from the British Isle
but since then it doubtless received admixtures of the nominate race c
central Europe, to which most cage bird stock imported into thi
country in the 20th century is assignable.

The number of times and places this well known Old World bird ha
been introduced into North America is uncertain. Long a popula
cage bird in Europe and the British Isles, captive goldfinches may wel
have been brought here by homesick Europeans as early as the 18t
century, though we have no certain records of importations before th
mid-19th century. Since then the commercial trade has been fairl
steady. The species is still kept and raised by cage bird fanciers bot
here and abroad, and can be bought today in many pet shops through
out this country.

The earliest mention of this species in America (cf. Robert Cushma
Murphy, 1945) is in a rare volume entitled "Green-Wood Cemetery
a History of the Institution from 1838 to 1864" by Nehemiah Cleave
land, published in New York in 1866. Green-Wood Cemetery, i
Brooklyn on the extreme western end of Long Island, is famous as th
site of the first successful introduction of the house sparrow to thi
country in the winter and spring of 1852–53. Evidence on pages 7
and 134 of this rare history shows that as well as the house sparrows
some 48 European goldfinches and a number of other British bird
were released in the cemetery late in 1852. According to Cleavelan
the experiment was a failure, because all the birds except the hous
sparrows disappeared. If any of these goldfinches did survive, ther

s no record of their presence in the New York area up to the time of he Hoboken introduction in 1878.

Serious attempts were made to naturalize the European goldfinch n St. Louis in 1870, in Cincinnati around 1872, at Hoboken, N.J., n 1878, in eastern Massachusetts around 1880, and in Cuba in 1886. Though a female with her nest and five eggs was collected in eastern Massachusetts in 1890, the only consistently successful breeding records in this country have stemmed from the Hoboken introduction of 1878.

The following year some of these birds appeared in Central Park, New York City, where they bred fairly regularly for the next several decades. E. T. Adney (1886) briefly describes their nesting during his period. Elon H. Eaton (1914) writes that "In the spring of 1900 I noticed several pairs that were endeavoring to build their nests in Central Park, and in the country about Kings Bridge and Spuyten Duyvil, in New York City." In his list of permanent residents of Central Park, Charles H. Rogers (1903) reports as many as 15 individuals during the winter of 1901–02. Though Clinton G. Abbott (1902) reported to the Linnaean Society the presence in January of that year of fully 50 European goldfinches on the grounds of Columbia University at 116th Street, New York City, the birds disappeared from Central Park shortly after the turn of the century, and 20 years later Griscom (1923) reports the species had "virtually disappeared" from New York City.

Birds from the Central Park nucleus started early to radiate out into the nearby suburbs. Eaton (1914) writes of three individuals seen at Long Island City in the winter of 1889, and of "many" that A. K. Fisher observed at Dobbs Ferry, N.Y., the winter of 1891, including several found dead there in the snow. John T. Nichols (1936) reports from his journal the following records for the Englewood, N.J., region: "A flock of about eight on January 28, 1912; about six at Leonia on February 16, 1913; one on February 21, 1915; seven, one in full song, in a heavy wet snowstorm on March 6; a flock of about five at Coytesville on March 13 with the remark 'They seem to be unusually common in the Englewood region this year', and the species singing on March 23, 1915." Nichols moved to Garden City, Long Island, in 1916 where he also found the European goldfinches present and later observed several nestings.

Since the early 1900's a number of scattered sight records have been reported from the New York area and a few, as detailed later, elsewhere in North America, most if not all of these apparently based on escaped captive birds. The only population to maintain itself consistently, however, was the colony that found suitable surroundings on the south shore of Long Island, within a large triangle extending roughly from Baldwin to Babylon on the south and northward to an apex at Westbury. Here at Massapequa my parents first observed occasional small flocks visiting their composite flower beds around 1916 and called my attention to them as a reminder of their childhood days in Britain. During the next few years I saw the goldfinches often enough to regard them no longer as a novelty, and I continued to see birds intermittently through the 1920's and early 1930's. During the war years the species seemed to be increasing slowly but steadily around Massapequa. By the middle 1950's, however, the postwar building boom destroyed much of its favorite habitat in this area. The species then became progressively rarer and has now virtually disappeared.

Courtship.—On Long Island singing males appeared on the nesting grounds in mid-April, usually accompained by nonsinging birds, presumably the females. On several occasions at this time I watched a pair mount high into the air and fly about for a brief interval, during which the male burst into a very attractive flight song, which ended as both descended together on a long slant and flew into the nesting area.

The female appears much the duller of the pair when the male displays before her, posturing to make the most of his bright yellow wing patches. As Witherby (1938) describes it, the "courting male sways body from side to side and quickly turns slightly expanded wings first to one side and then to the other, with a golden flashing effect." I watched one singing male advance toward the female, swaying characteristically from side to side with his wings partly spread and flashing his bright yellow wing patches. His mate also swayed slightly and crouched, whereupon he hopped momentarily on her back. Before he actually came to rest, she slipped from under, uttered several harsh notes, and hopped unhurriedly among the near-by branches. Then she flew into a neighboring tree, and from there into another, and passed out of sight, the male following closely. At no time did I see copulation actually take place.

Nesting.—British writers list the goldfinch as nesting in gardens and orchards, in oaks, chestnuts, or plane trees (sycamores), and occasionally in shrubs, evergreens, and hedges. W. E. Glegg (1943) writes that at Minchinhampton (Gloucestershire) on Apr. 26, 1943, H. C. Playne "inspected a nest of the goldfinch (*Carduelis c. britannica*) which was built on the top of the thick stalk of a plant of brussels sprouts about 4 feet above the ground and surrounded by the flowering shoots. The female was sitting on five eggs."

In America the European goldfinch has nested principally in trees. Allan D. Cruickshank (1942) describes the nest as "placed in a conifer or deciduous tree from five to thirty feet from the ground." Among

ıe early nests found in Central Park, New York City, E. T. Adney
(886) describes one built in the long needles of a pine tree on a slender
ıorizontal branch about 12 feet from the ground. Most April and
ırly May nests here were built in conifers; deciduous trees were
ccupied later when their leaves developed more fully. Among the
eciduous trees the Norway maple appeared to be the favorite. Of
ıe 15 nests I found in Massapequa and Seaford, 12 were in Norway
ıaples, 1 in a swamp maple, 1 in a pitch pine, and 1 in an arborvitae.
'he inaccessibility of most conifers in this area within the boundaries
f private grounds perhaps accounts for the small percentage of nests
found in evergreens.

John T. Nichols (1936) writes of a female accompanied by a singing
ıale carrying nesting material into a large, thick-foliaged pine at
ıarden City Apr. 21, 1933, but the birds apparently deserted the site
 days later. On May 12, 1935, he observed "two birds flying back
ıd forth in company and saw one of them visit and thus disclose their
ssentially completed nest," which was about 14 feet up in a small
ıaple. The only nest reported in this country outside the New York
rea was found July 11, 1890, within 7 feet of the ground in an apple
:ee at Northville, near Worcester, Mass. (Churchill, 1891). This
est, with its clutch of five eggs and the female, was collected for the
fatural History Society of Worcester.

All the nest-building I witnessed was done early in the morning,
ever later than 11 a.m. The male often accompanied the female as
ıe traveled back and forth, and alighted nearby while she picked up
esting material. Following her back into the nest area, he sang as
ıe worked, but I never saw a male come very close to the nest at
ıis period. As I never found a nest just as it was started, I could
ot determine the exact period of nest building.

Nest heights at Massapequa ranged from 5 feet 9 inches in the
rborvitae to 26 feet 6 inches in the pitch pine. The trunk diameter
f the arborvitae was 1⅝ inches, its height 7½ feet. The smallest
ccupied maple stood 12 feet 6 inches tall, and its nest was 9 feet
 inches above the ground, fastened to an offset on the trunk supported
y upright sprigs. Three nests were found in fairly large maples, one
ı the upper, one in the middle, and one in the lower branches. All
ere about two-thirds the way out from the trunk, well hidden among
ıe foliage, and usually just beneath other branches that concealed
ıem from above. Supported below by the main branch, they were
ften further secured by the side walls interwoven around two or three
ııall upright twigs. The arborvitae nest was well concealed in the
ınter of the tree; the most exposed nest was the one in the pitch pine.

British nests, according to Witherby (1938) are "neatly built of
ıots, bents, moss, and lichens, interwoven with wool, lined vegetable-

down, wool; hair sometimes added." Nests in the Massapequa are showed the birds preferred to use certain plants in their construction influenced to some extent by the materials available at the season One June nest was made almost entirely of whitlow grass (*Drabe verna*, a mustard) with the small bell-like flowers still on the drying stalks. Five other June nests were built mainly of mouse-ear chick weed (*Cerastium vulgatum*), also very decorative. A late nest, buil about July 10, had walls of fibrous stems without flowers. Lining in the early nest contained such fluffy materials as could be foun nearby, in one case soft pink thread, bits of wool, absorbent cotton and plant down. A late June nest was lined almost entirely with thistle down.

Three Massapequa nest cups measured $2\frac{1}{16}$ inches across and $1\frac{1}{2}$ inches deep; their bottoms and side walls were $\frac{1}{2}$ inch thick. Although firmly supported, the nests had such weak rims that young in the later stages often broke them down, especially after heavy rain softened the excreta-covered side walls, and converted the cup into an irregular platform, which in one case measured $5\frac{1}{4}$ inches by $2\frac{1}{2}$ inches. In another nest I released a young bird whose rear end had wedged into the crack of a separated rim. At Baldwin, Long Island, an adult caught similarly in a broken rim was found dead hanging by its neck after the nesting season.

Eggs.—To quote Witherby (1938) again: "Usually 5–6, 3, 4, and 7 also on record, bluish-white ground-color with few spots and streaks of red-brown, sometimes very dark, and ashy shell-marks * * *. Average of 100 British eggs, 17×12.8 mm. Max.: 19×13.5 and 16.3×13.6 mm. Min.: 15.5×12.2 mm." In practically all American nests on record, including those I studied at Massapequa, the clutch is five eggs. I measured no eggs in the nests for fear of disturbing the birds, but some varied noticeably in size and shape. The second egg laid in one late June nest I estimated to be one-eighth inch longer than its predecessor. Before I could study this interesting egg further, and shortly after the fourth egg was laid, the nest was robbed and its plant-down lining found at the foot of the nest tree.

Incubation.—Witherby (1938) states that incubation is "by hen alone, fed by cock; begins before clutch is complete. Period 12–13 days." He adds that in Britain the breeding season starts "exceptionally in April; most eggs laid from mid-May onward * * * normally two broods: three at times, as young found in September."

From the records available at the time, Allan D. Cruickshank (1942) stated that in the New York region "There is but one brood, local egg dates ranging from April 26 to June 4." Soon after this, on July 5, 1942, Roger Tory Peterson and I found a European goldfinch's nest with five eggs that were still unhatched July 11. The

ımmer of 1944 I found a bird just starting to build her nest on July
ł. Though I was unable to continue observations of this nest,
hich was on private grounds, a successful brood could not have left
until about August 20. Thus apparently the species is double-
rooded here as it is abroad.

In four nests studied at Massapequa, one in May and three in July,
ıe five eggs were laid at the rate of one a day, either during the
ıght or very early in the morning, for the new egg was always present
y 7 a.m. The female incubated very closely and remained on the
est almost continuously after the first egg was laid. I found one
emale off her nest only twice before the first-hatched young was
days old, and both times she returned within 5 minutes after I
rrived. Voluntary absences usually lasted from 3 to 4 minutes, and
minutes was the longest time I noted an incubating female off her
est. At two nests the incubating female seldom flushed before I
ctually touched the nesting branch. When driven off the nest, the
emale was usually back on her eggs as quickly as conditions permitted,
ometimes within 30 seconds. At the nest Roger Peterson photo-
raphed with me in early July 1942, the female came back on the
est almost before preparations could be made for taking the picture,
ith the branches tied back to reveal the nest, the camera on its
latform next to it, and Peterson standing not 25 feet away operating
by remote control.

The male starts feeding the female on the nest apparently as soon
s she starts incubating. At a Massapequa nest I began watching
hen the second egg was laid, the male was already bringing food to
is mate. Feeding was always well in progress by 7:00 a.m., and the
atest I observed was at 8:03 p.m. Intervals between feedings were
hortest in the early morning, usually 15 to 20 minutes, and longest
uring the middle of the day, from 40 to 53 (the longest) minutes in
lay–June nestings. Intervals were noticeably longer in July–
.ugust nestings.

When the male brought food to his mate, he usually gave five or six
ownward thrusts of his bill as she assumed a begging pose, and then
egurgitated into her open gape. She then worked her mandibles
igorously as she swallowed the food. Before he flew away the male
isibly swallowed whatever remained in his bill. At no time did I
ee a female fed off the nest, nor did I see one voluntarily leave the nest
fter 7:45 p.m. One incubating female occasionally left with her
ıate after he fed her on the nest and sat with him a short time on
earby electric wires. She usually excreted, preened a little, and spent
few minutes wiping her bill on the wire while the male sang inter-
ıittently before she returned to her duties.

At the arborvitae nest the male usually approached it indirectly flying first to the top of the tree, then to an opening in the foliage, and finally on in with food. The female also returned furtively, often climbing several feet through the thick needles to the nest. Birds nesting in maples usually approached their nests by flying first to a nearby tree, then to the nest branch, and finally to the nest.

As incubation starts before the clutch is complete, the eggs do not hatch simultaneously. A first clutch laid May 9–13 at Massapequa hatched as follows: May 24, 7:00 a.m., first young out; May 25, 7:00 a.m., three young; May 25, 7:00 p.m., four young; May 26, 7:00 a.m., five young. In a late clutch laid July 15–19 the hatching progress was: July 30, 9:00 a.m., three young, 7:30 p.m., three young, one egg pipping; July 31, 7:00 a.m., four young; July 31, 7:00 a.m., all five hatched. Thus the last egg laid had a nest occupancy of around 12 days, and it seems unlikely that any first egg took more than 15 days to hatch.

Fledging.—Witherby (1938) gives the period of young in the nest as 13–14 days and states that both parents feed the fledglings in turn by regurgitation. At Massapequa the first young to hatch lay with their heads hanging limply over the remaining eggs. Typically the female broods the nestlings fairly closely for the first six days. Then, though she covers them continuously at night and during stormy weather, daytime brooding becomes more and more intermittent, but does not cease entirely until the young are well fledged, some three days before they leave the nest. While incubating and while brooding newly hatched young, the female is usually very tame, flushing close and seldom moving far from the nest. As the young develop, she becomes warier and more easily alarmed, leaving the nest when one approaches within 15 or 20 feet. In the final stages of fledging both adults are reticent about coming near the nest until the intruder departs. John T. Nichols noted similar behavior in a Garden City nesting in 1935.

The male continues to feed the female while she broods. While she is on the nest, he gives the food to her and she in turn feeds the young. Feeding of the brooding female was last seen in a first nesting when the oldest young was 11 days old, and in a second nesting at 8 days. In both cases the female arrived with the male, took her place on the nest, and accepted food in place of the well-grown young. Both adults immediately left the vicinity and shortly returned with more food. When both adults were feeding the young, intervals between feedings were shorter than when the male was the sole provider. Once the parents fed the young only a few minutes apart, but usually the intervals between feedings were longer, the longest in a second nesting being one hour and forty minutes.

The male was never seen to pay any particular attention to the nest. He usually left immediately after feeding the female or young, and he disappeared entirely from the vicinity at sunset. The four of five males in the Massapequa colony in 1943 seemed to maintain contact with each other and, after singing on the wires at sunset, usually flew together into a grove of large trees, apparently for the night.

As with most carduelines, the European goldfinch pays little attention to nest sanitation. During incubation, however, the female never fouled the nest with her own excrement, and she apparently removed the egg shells after hatching, because I never found a trace of them in the nest. The rim of one nest showed but a single deposit of excreta 6 days after the first young hatched, but by the eighth day it was fairly well encrusted, and heavily so by the time the young flew. In the arborvitae nest thick excrement coated the foliage several feet below the nest by the time it was deserted.

The largest number of young known to leave the nest successfully at Massapequa was four. In two nestings two of the five young disappeared from the gray ball of fluff that filled the nest cup about 10 days after hatching. The remaining three, of fairly equal size, soon filled the nest and showed no desire to leave it 17 days after the first young hatched. At this time the parents apparently tried to induce them to fly by backing away to coax them out. Though they leaned far forward from the precariously tilted, rain-weakened platform, which had lost most of its semblance to a nest, the three fledglings did not follow. That night during a heavy rain storm one fell out, and I found it dead on the ground below the next morning. The other two left the next day, 18 days after the first young hatched, or 16 days after the last one. Another time my plucking a conspicuous excreta-stained shoot from the foot of the nest tree shook it slightly and sent the three young flying off in different directions. One I retrieved and replaced in the nest was gone again within 24 hours.

Adults may continue to feed the young for an indefinite period after they leave the nest. I saw three young being fed out of the nest by one of their parents as late as August 26. The three juveniles, well grown and apparently out of the nest for some time, sat in the top of a maple in a small grove as twilight was falling. The parent regurgitated into the open gapes of the begging young, and then roosted on a branch above them. As darkness fell they all tucked their heads behind their wings and settled down for the night.

Plumages.—At hatching the almost naked young are yellowish-tan and are soon tufted with grayish down. By the time the first-hatched young are 6 days old, the nest cup appears about half filled with gray fluff out of which, when approached, the yellow-rimmed gapes are thrust. Witherby (1938) describes the nestling as: "Down darkish grey, medium length * * *. Tongue and floor of mouth crimson, posterior angles of tongue paler but not forming definite spots, roof of mouth dark lilac; externally flanges cream-colour." J. T. Nichols described the Massapequa nestling found dead (now in the American Museum of Natural History) in the flesh as follows: "Weight 913 grams; length 83 mm.; wing 44 mm.; tarsus 12 mm.; tail 14 mm.; bill 7½ mm. Upper mandible wood gray, lower mandible paler, tip dark, yellow along fissure; legs pale pinkish gray; bird scantily feathered, wings about half developed, wing patches yellowish, a brighter yellow line through the center of each."

On leaving the nest the juveniles (Whitherby, 1938) are entirely grayish-buff with indistinct dark brown spots and streaks, except for the dull white belly and the wings and tail, which resemble those of the adult but have buffier tips. The juveniles molt their body feathers in early autumn and in their first winter plumage assume the distinctive white-rimmed crimson face and black crown of the adult dress. There is no spring molt, and the adult plumage is replaced annually by a complete molt in August and September.

Food.—Witherby (1938) gives the food of the British goldfinch as "Seeds and insects, but chiefly former. Of seeds, thistles are great favourites, but many other weed seeds are eaten and also small seeds from cones, birches and alder-catkins. Of insects, small Coleoptera, larvae of Lepidoptera, Diptera, Hymenoptera, and aphides."

The species' food preferences in this country are much the same, and vary little from those of the American goldfinch. John T. Nichols sent me the following analysis of the stomach contents of the dead Massapequa nestling: "Stomach crammed full with small seeds of two or three kinds. There were also a green caterpillar, the pupa of a moth, a few red spiders, and bits of green leaf." He also observed several small flocks feeding on the seeds of sweet gum (liquidambar) at Garden City, Long Island, in the fall.

My own records show them seen feeding in spring in patches of various early-seeding grasses. Later they resorted to beds of thistle marigold, zinnia, cornflower, and other composites. I watched one bird in juvenile plumage in late August 1944 feeding almost exclusively on zinnias; it perched on the flower heads, pulled out the more or less unripe seeds, and then mashed them between its mandible before swallowing them.

In winter the small flocks about Massapequa in the early 1940' frequented patches of crab grass and barnyard weeds on an old farm at Fort Neck and, as described in Europe, were partial to old waste lands and the weedy borders of grainfields. They were practically if not entirely, independent of feeding stations, many of which were well maintained in the neighborhood. During the winter of 1943–44, six or seven foraged industriously in a large patch of burdock (*Arctium*) behind an old barn. They eagerly sought the dark seeds within the burrs, cracking them open with a slight movement of the bill and swallowing the kernel. It took them about 3 seconds to husk and swallow each seed. Five birds feeding close together on one large burdock head made a beautiful sight. They also show a preference for this plant in Britain.

Behavior.—The European goldfinch flies with the undulations typical of the American goldfinch, the redpolls, and other closely related cardueline finches, but, as Witherby (1938) notes "with noticeably light, flitting and 'dancing' action." Edmund Selous (1910) writes that "They flew in a wild, fluttering, winter-butterfly way, over the barren fields, on which they would suddenly descend before they had gone very far * * *."

Birds nesting close to a tar-surfaced road perched constantly on the electric wires bordering it to sing, preen, and wipe their bills. Their frequent and characteristic bill-wiping seems peculiar both to the species and to the breeding season, and appears possibly to have some sort of display function.

The species is strongly territorial and defends its nesting area vigorously. Pairs nesting in fairly large maples usually appropriated about one-fourth of the tree and kept it clear of smaller birds. I watched one incubating female leave her eggs to dash at a robin that flew by within 4 feet of the nest. She followed it about 20 feet before returning. To disturb the nesting birds as little as possible, I usually did not examine their nests until just before I left at each visit. Twice my suspicions of tragedy at a nest I was watching were aroused by the presence of small birds passing freely through the braches near it. In each case the nest was rifled and the contents gone.

At the arborvitae nest the male took up his perch about 40 feet away on the wire nearest the nest. Although he tolerated other species on the nearby wires, he charged all European goldfinches that came near and kept them from between him and the nest. I once watched him ward off three other goldfinches in succession with short threatening flights, then fly across to the arborvitae and enter it from the opposite side to feed his incubating mate. When I approached this nest too closely, the female flushed and joined her mate on the wire, where both pivoted back and forth, apprehensively uttering canarylike *swees*. Their swaying and *sweeing* is apparently a sign of alarm or excitement, for they so acted twice when cats appeared nearby. Both times one of the pair flew low over the cat and chased it, uttering the same notes, until it ran swiftly around a nearby house and out of sight.

In Britain (Witherby, 1938) the goldfinch is "Usually gregarious. Roosts in trees * * * hedges or bushes in parties unmixed (as a rule) with other species." On Long Island the birds seemed similarly sufficient unto themselves. The small flocks of 6 to a maximum of 17 individuals were never observed to contain other species, nor did they ever mix with the larger flocks of 60 to 70 American goldfinches wintering nearby. The latter resorted to the more open fields, while the European goldfinches remained in the tangles of burdock and composites in backyard gardens closer to dwellings.

Elsewhere in America scattered individuals have been reported consorting most often with American goldfinches, occasionally with pine siskins and juncos. Nichols (1936) reports a European and an American goldfinch feeding together in the sweetgums in Garden City. One was reported in company with American goldfinches near Flushing on the north shore of Long Island in December 1946. Doris Heustis Mills (1937) watched a lone bird at Hanover, N.H., May 13, 1937, feeding with American goldfinches on larch catkins and joining them and siskins on the ground to search for weed seeds.

Voice.—The common call note is a rapid *tswit-i-wit*, occasionally abbreviated. Like the *per-chic-o-ree* of the American goldfinch, it is given both when perched and in flight and, when learned, similarly identifies the unseen bird. Another common note is a soft, inflected, musical, canarylike *swee*, which Witherby (1938) transcribes as *mahi* and apparently expresses concern or worry. He describes the aggressive note as a grating " 'geez' * * * shorter and much coarser" than the *tswee* note of the greenfinch. Massapequa birds apprehensive of the safety of the nest uttered all these notes, and occasionally a deflected *cheeeu*, usually swaying from side to side at the same time. When startled the bird shows its alarm with a sharp *zit*.

One incubating female showed her awareness of the alarm notes of nearby robins by becoming briskly alert and moving her head toward the direction of the calls. Several times when a male, presumably her mate, flew above the nest maple uttering the *tswit-i-wit* call, she answered with a soft, inflected, musical note. The young in the nest are usually silent until a day or two before they leave, when they start to chipper softly while fluttering on the nest rim at feeding time.

The male's superb and sprightly song during the breeding season starts usually with the *tswit-i-wit* call note, continues with a couple of twittering phrases of three or four notes each, then develops richly with intermingled inflective calls, musical pipings, and trills. In late July near sunset one male uttered 27 identical phrases of 3 to 4 seconds each at about 5-second intervals, which he followed with a longer 28th phrase and then stopped. I heard another bird give two similar series of 14 and 15 phrases each within a half hour. The song may be performed in flight, but is usually given from a commanding perch in a treetop or on a wire, the singer swaying slightly back and forth in his ecstasy. Song often starts before sunrise, but stops quite regularly on clear evenings at least 5 minutes before sunset.

Witherby (1938) charts the British goldfinch's singing period as follows: exceptional or subdued song in late January and the first half of February; irregular but fairly frequent song from then into the first half of March; then steady singing into late July, after which the birds sing irregularly to late August; an interval of silence follows; then irregular song into early December.

The Long Island birds followed this pattern rather closely during the first 8 months of the year. Winter singing often constituted a subdued but continuous musical twittering indulged in by the flock, but occasionally individuals sang well. During February and March birds often sang in the rain and sleet and during mild snowstorms, usually from the shelter of conifers. Almost all this early singing was done in trees, but during the nesting season wires became the favorite singing perch. The irregular autumn singing in Britain is duplicated by only two records here. Albert R. Shadle (1930) writes of a bird that attracted his attention by singing from 200 feet away at Buffalo, N.Y., on Oct. 17, 1929. One of five birds I watched feeding in a weedy field at Massapequa, Nov. 10, 1947, sang a subdued song of 4 to 5 seconds duration. The only sound recording of the species in this country, made by Charles Brand for the Cornell collection, was of a male, probably an escapee from captivity, that remained for a week in late May around Cornell Heights, Ithaca, N.Y. (Montagna, 1940).

Enemies.—The European goldfinch has been exposed to the same predators that attack all small birds in this country. Though no cases have been reported, some doubtless fell victim to small hawks, shrikes, and housecats. Nest predation at Massapequa was often heavy. Three nests with a total of 15 eggs in 1944 fledged only two young; one nest was robbed when the clutch was just completed, the other two days after the last young hatched. Though none was caught in the act, the main predators presumably were grackles and perhaps blue jays to a lesser extent. Grackles were common in the nesting area, and one of the robbed nests was in a pitch pine directly beneath one of their favorite flight routes. Though cowbirds were plentiful in the vicinity, their attentions were apparently frustrated by the goldfinch's habit of incubating closely after the first egg is laid, for no case of cowbird parasitism was ever noted.

The greatest limiting factor to the species' success in this country unquestionably has been man. Trapping for cage bird purposes is believed to have reduced the Central Park population around the turn of the century. The recent development of the old waste farmlands on western Long Island for suburban homes has of course been the final blow. The Long Island colony was never large and was apparently barely able to maintain its numbers. The birds that wintered so regularly on the old Fort Neck farm in Massapequa before it was bulldozed into building lots numbered exactly 17 individuals in 1942, 1945, and 1946. Fewer than a dozen reports of the species were made on Long Island in 1954, none listing more than three birds, and less than half as many in 1955. The only recent report is a lone bird seen near Orient, Long Island, May 30, 1961.

Winter.—After the breeding season the Long Island European goldfinches usually appeared first in the suburban flower beds, then, turning to seed, in southern Nassau and parts of Queens and Suffolk counties. As the food in these areas became exhausted, the birds repaired for the winter to deserted farmlands where weed seeds were plentiful, just as they do abroad. Witherby (1938) describes their favored wintering grounds in Britian as "rough, neglected pastures, roadsides, and waste land, with thistle and other weeds." This certainly fits their former wintering territory at Massapequa.

As the birds shunned the more wooded and marshy areas and the shore sections, they went unreported by the bird watchers who largely concentrated on these more productive regions. This doubtless accounts for Cruikshank (1942) writing: "Immediately after the nesting season the birds seem to vanish, and records until the following spring are few and far between."

Their favored haunt at Massapequa on the old Fort Neck farm was a vacated barnyard surrounded by neglected fields full of thistle, burdock, and other weeds, and bordered by a grove of fairly large red cedars which provided them shelter during severe weather. The small wintering parties were usually restless and nervous when feeding on the ground, and flew frequently into the nearby trees. Food was usually plentiful throughout the mild Long Island winters, and the birds always seemed in good condition to withstand the winter season there. The effect of occasional spells of more severe weather with snow or sleet was to scatter them into wider territory, and it seems strange that practically none were ever reported from the many feeding stations in the area.

Its attractive appearance, interesting habits, and sweet song that began in late winter when few other birds were singing, made this little European finch a welcome addition to our avifauna. It is regrettable that it was so limited in distribution and unable to maintain itself over a wider range. During its heyday in the 1940's, bird lovers came annually from far and wide to see it in this, its last stronghold in continental North America. We probably shall never have the pleasure of its company regularly again.

DISTRIBUTION

Range.—The British European goldfinch is resident in the British Isles.

Casual records.—The British European goldfinch is casual in the Hebrides, Shetlands, and Orkneys. It was introduced in Oregon (Portland, 1890), Missouri (St. Louis, 1870), Ohio (Cincinnati, 1870), New Jersey (Hoboken, 1878), Massachusetts (probably near Boston, 1889), and New Zealand. Not well established anywhere on the North American continent. Escapes are reported from time to time in western, central, and eastern United States and Ontario. The Madeira European Goldfinch is resident in the Madeira, Azore, and Canary Islands. It was introduced in Bermuda before 1860 and is now well established there.

ACANTHIS HORNEMANNI HORNEMANNI (Holboell)

Hornemann's Redpoll

Contributed by OLIVER L. AUSTIN, JR.

HABITS

In the few notes he left in his files on this redpoll, with which he was not familiar in the field, Mr. Bent characterizes it as "the largest and whitest of the redpolls, a lovely bird when in full plumage, with a delicately rosy breast and a pure white rump." It is also one of the rarest in continental North America of the five forms of this puzzling genus currently recognized by the A.O.U. Check-List. According to the 5th edition of the Check-List, it breeds "on Ellesmere Island (Slidre Fiord), Baffin Island (Clyde Inlet), and in the northern half of Greenland (Inglefield Land to Orpik on the west coast, Germania Land to Scoresby Sound on the east coast). Has been taken in summer months in Spitsbergen and Jan Mayen Island." It winters mainly in the southern half of Greenland, but sometimes wanders irregularly southward to Manitoba, Michigan, Ontario, Quebec, Labrador, Sweden, Scotland, England, and France.

One of the few ornithologists familiar with this form on its Greenland breeding grounds, Finn Salomonsen (1950), considers its "general life-habits are very similar to those of the Greenland [greater] Redpoll. * * * In the breeding-time Hornemann's Redpoll is restricted to the interior country, where it frequents hill-slopes and mountain-sides at some altitude. The temperature is higher there than at sea level

* * *, the vegetation richer and taller. * * * The presence of willow or other shrub of some size is indispensable to it. In the valleys and in the coastal areas, which have a more rough climate, all plants trail along the ground and do not form actual bushes."

Of its status on Southampton Island, George M. Sutton (1932) reports: "Hornemann's Redpoll does not, so far as I have been able to determine, nest anywhere on Southampton. It is irregularly common as a migrant, being about equally numerous in autumn and spring. * * * During migration it associates with all the other species of redpolls which are to be found in this region, so that it is sometimes difficult to identify the birds, as they fly about together. It lingers later in the fall than the other redpolls, however, and apparently returns a little in advance of them in the spring. It is rarely seen even in mid-winter when it feeds on such seeds as have not been buried under the snow."

J. Dewey Soper (1946) observes: "As in other parts of Baffin Island, Hornemann's Redpoll does not appear to inhabit Foxe Peninsula during the summer months. In the autumn, however, these birds begin to make their appearance in varying numbers, usually in small flocks, but groups of upwards of one hundred individuals have been noted. * * * It occurs, apparently, only as an irregular migrant on Baffin Island."

Nesting.—Salomonsen (1950) briefly outlines its nesting habits as follows: "The nest is placed on hill-slopes in low shrub of willow or dwarf-birch * * * , or in crevices in the rock covered by trailing twigs of willow. * * * The nest is built of dry grass, rootlets and willow down * * * . Egg-laying takes place from the end of May to the end of June, as a rule about 1 June. Eggs, 'probably of this race' measure on an average 18.2×13 mm (14 eggs; Jourdain). Clutch-size: Up to 7 eggs recorded. Incubation lasts 11 days, fledging 11–12 days * * * . The earliest fledgings have been observed 16 June * * * . After the breeding-period the adult birds with their young wander about for some time before they start the migration."

Food.—The only report on the food of Hornemann's redpoll is that of Manniche (1910), who identified seeds of *Luzula* and various Cyperaceae in the stomach contents of birds he examined in northeast Greenland.

Voice.—Again according to Salomonsen (1950), its "song and other notes are exactly similar to those of the Greenland [greater] Redpoll."

Fall and winter.—To quote Salomonsen (1950) once more: "Hornemann's Redpoll is resident in Greenland and only rarely leaves the country. The northernmost parts of its breeding-area are vacated in the autumn, but it is known to winter as far north as Thule District on the West-coast and the Mackenzie Bay region on the East-coast. It spends the winter in the interior country, frequenting wind-swept plateaus, hilly plains and mountain-slopes where it feeds on bushes and herbs protruding above the snow. The inner, desolate parts of the country are only exceptionally visited in winter by man, and very little is known about the life-habits of Hornemann's Redpoll there. When mountain-winds blow with high temperatures, bringing a thaw, Hornemann's Redpoll appears in flocks at the settlements on the coast * * *. Hornemann's Redpoll, in contrast to the Greenland [greater] Redpoll, has never been recorded from Davis Strait in the migration time, a fact which indicates that it leaves Greenland only exceptionally. This holds good also of the East-coast population."

DISTRIBUTION

Range.—Eastern Canadian Arctic and Greenland to south central and southeastern Canada.

Breeding range.—Breeds on Axel Heiberg Island, Ellesmere Island (Slidre Fiord), Baffin Island (Clyde Inlet), and in the northern half of Greenland (Inglefield Land to Orpik on the west coast, Germania Land to Scoresby Sound on the east coast). Has been taken in summer months in Spitsbergen and Jan Mayen Island.

Winter range.—Winters in southern half of Greenland (in migration casually north to Peary Land); casually south to northern Manitoba (Churchill), Keewatin (Southampton Island), northern Michigan (McMillan, Sault Ste. Marie), southern Ontario (Galt), northern Quebec (Fort Chimo), Labrador (Kamarsuk), Scotland (Unst, Fair Isle), and England (Whitburn, Spurn).

Casual records.—Accidental in Sweden (Gallivare, Lule Lapfmark) and in France (Abbeville).

Migration.—Data apply to the species as a whole. Late dates of spring departure are: New Jersey—West Englewood, April 1. New York—Tuckahoe, March 24. Massachusetts—eastern Massachusetts, March 20. Michigan—Blaney Park, March 17. Wisconsin—Duran County, March 26. Minnesota—Kittson County, April 11. Alberta—Glenevis, April 10. British Columbia—Cranbrook, April 20.

Early dates of fall arrival are: British Columbia—Atlin, September 30. Montana—Moiese, November 27. Minnesota—St. Vincent, October 26. Wisconsin—New London, November 7. Quebec—Montreal, November 23. Maine—Skowhegan, November 25. Massachusetts—Swampscott, November 16.

ACANTHIS HORNEMANNI EXILIPES (Coues)

Hoary Redpoll

PLATE 22

Contributed by PAUL HERBERT BALDWIN

HABITS

The hoary redpoll is a circumpolar inhabitant of arctic regions. Its range extends wholly across northern Eurasia and the North American continent from Ungava to northwestern Alaska. It breeds in the far north and winters in northern and temperate latitudes southward to the northern United States. It is noteworthy for its sporadic appearances and for its sudden fluctuations in number from year to year in the wintering range. It is rarely seen in settled districts.

This bird is similar in appearance to the common redpoll (*Acanthis flammea flammea*), but it is whiter and often lacks the streaking on the under tail coverts. Apparently the darker individuals of this race are difficult to distinguish in the field from the common redpoll, with which it is very often found in company.

The southern parts of its breeding range extensively overlap the northern part of that of the common redpoll, where its habits are said to be indistinguishable from those of the latter species (Nelson, 1887).

In northern Alaska the hoary redpoll may be found breeding generally in the tundra biome where scattered low shrubs occur. It seeks the willows and alders of the drainage channels or hillsides and tends to avoid the flat tundra. However, in midsummer, cottongrass (*Eriophorum*) seeds mature and provide a food resource attracting the redpoll to open places it may not have visited earlier in the summer. In late summer it wanders around joining other species and races of redpolls to travel in mixed flocks throughout the winter.

Territory.—The hoary redpoll is not a territorial bird. Its nests may be grouped closely together, often with several nests in one small clump of bushes. The adult birds freely leave the vicinity of the nest. Gregarious behavior continues through the nesting season with the birds flitting about in loose flocks or all stopping to feed together in some spot that attracts them.

In 1953 P. H. Baldwin and E. B. Reed (Baldwin, MS.) found that at Umiat, Alaska, territorial behavior was either lacking or at a low ebb during the middle and late parts of the breeding period. They recorded no singing as taking place on perches near nests. On one occasion, however, a male was seen to chase another male from the nest. Gregarious behavior continued through the nesting period, as

PLATE 22

Yukon Delta, June 21, 1914

NEST OF HOARY REDPOLL

Churchill, Manitoba, June 14, 1940　　　　　　　　　　　　　　R. S. Palmer

FEMALE COMMON REDPOLL AT NEST

PLATE 23

Bethel, Alaska, June 13, 1946 — L. H. Walkinshaw

COMMON REDPOLL AT NEST

Virginia Lakes, Mono County, Calif., June 21, 1940 — J. S. Rowley

NEST OF PINE SISKIN

the birds frequently gathered in small groups to feed and move about. On June 12, a flock of 8 to 10 mixed males and females flitted from willow to willow constantly chirping in flight. These birds bounded up and down, ascending to heights of 50 to 75 feet, whence they dropped with folded wings. In late June, while nests were still being completed, male redpolls flew around a good deal and often gathered into small, noisy aggregations.

Nesting.—Walkinshaw (1948) notes that the hoary redpoll nests closer to water, often over shallow water, whereas the common redpoll nests in the willows on the higher tundra. He found that five nests of the hoary redpoll averaged 71 cm. above ground (30.5 to 99), 48.8 mm. in inside diameter, and 37.0 mm. in depth, while the outside measurements were approximately 104 mm. in diameter and 78 mm. in depth.

A. C. Bent (MS.) found eight probable hoary redpoll nests in little willow patches near Nome, five of the nests in one small patch. Both species of redpolls were represented in nearly equal numbers, as far as he could tell. They were very tame, and he identified them by their colors as they sat on their nests or perched nearby. The nests were all placed in crotches of the willows, from 18 to 36 inches above the ground; they were generally in plain sight, but some were partly concealed in the foliage. They were all much alike in construction, made externally of either scraggly twigs or coarse weed stems, internally of finer grasses, and lined with feathers and white willow down.

A nest in the Bent collection taken by F. Seymour Hersey on the Yukon Delta, June 24, 1914, was placed 3 feet up in a dwarf alder; it was made of coarse weed stems and grass and lined with dark feathers in the bottom of the nest and with white ptarmigan feathers about the rim.

L. H. Walkinshaw (1948) writes: "Brandt * * * states that the Common Redpoll builds the greater portion of the exterior of its nest with small twigs whereas the Hoary Redpoll uses bronze-tinted grasses interwoven with silvery plant down and threads of bark. This was true in the nests we found [near Bethel, Alaska]." Bent (MS.) found both types of nests near Nome; those with the twig foundations probably he thought belonged to the common redpolls and the others to the hoary redpolls, although this was not positively determined.

In 1952 T. J. Cade and G. B. Shaller (*in* Kessel, Cade, and Shaller, 1953) found a redpoll nest at Etivluk in the Brooks Range on June 12, 12 inches off the ground and with one egg. They found 11 more occupied nests between this date and July 15 at various localities along the Colville River. All 12 nests were believed to be those of

Acanthis hornemanni exilipes.   All were lined with ptarmigan feathers and some with caribou hair as well.

In 1953 Baldwin and Reed examined 25 nests of the hoary redpoll near Umiat on the Colville River about 75 miles south of the Arctic Ocean.   Of these nests, 16 were in or under willow, 6 were in alder, 1 in an unidentified shrub, and 2 were on artificial substrates at camp. The height at which these nests were placed varied from ground level to 84 inches.

The female redpoll constructed the nest but was accompanied during her work by the male.   The whole nest apparently was built in 3 days, and the lining of fine materials and ptarmigan feathers added in less than 24 hours.   The main nesting materials were the coarse grasses *Arctigrostis latifolia* and *Calamagrostis* sp., and also cotton from cottongrass and willow.   Lesser amounts of alder and willow twigs, heath shrub roots, caribou hair, and vole (*Microtus*) fur were used in some nests.   All nests seen were lined with ptarmigan feathers.

Eggs.—The number of eggs varies from three to six, with four or five most frequently comprising the set.   They are ovate or short-ovate, and slightly glossy.   The ground may be either "bluish glaucous" or "pale Niagara green," delicately spotted and speckled, with shades of reddish browns such as "warm sepia," "snuff brown," "Mars brown," and a few specks of black, with undermarkings of "light drab," "light cinnamon drab," or "pale brownish drab." Some eggs may be marked only with the light undertone spots of "light cinnamon drab," while in others the shades of brown such as "snuff brown" or "Mars brown" predominate.   There is, in general, a tendency for the markings to become heavier toward the large end where sometimes a fine, loose wreath may be formed; or again there may be very fine indistinct specklings scattered over the entire egg.

The measurements of 40 eggs average 16.7 by 12.5 millimeters; the eggs showing the four extremes measure *18.5* by 12.7, 17.8 by *13.5*, *14.0* by 11.9, and 17.3 by *10.9* millimeters.

Cade and Shaller (Kessel, MS.) in 1952 found nests with from one to six eggs between June 12 and July 15.   One nest contained one egg, one had two eggs, one had three eggs, four had five eggs, and one had six eggs.   Between June 25 and July 4, they found four additional redpoll nests containing five eggs and young mixed, or just five young.

Baldwin and Reed in 1953 found the average clutch size to be five eggs in 13 clutches under observation at the time the first egg hatched.   However, when seven nests discovered after at least one egg had hatched were considered, the average came down to 4.7 eggs per clutch.   The range was three to six (1 nest with three eggs, 5 nests with four eggs, 13 nests with five eggs, 1 nest with six eggs).

Incubation.—Walkinshaw (1948) notes that incubation is apparently by the female alone. Baldwin and Reed (1955) found the incubation time, defined as the interval between the laying and the hatching of the last fertile egg, to be 11 days. Incubation began following the laying of the second or third egg, the incubative behavior lasting an average of 14.4 days (four nests). Variations in the period were due to differences in promptness of starting incubation and in the number of eggs in the nests. The female did all the incubation and was fed on the nest by the male.

They also observed that during the period of incubative behavior, the male engaged in courtship feeding of the female, and the female begged food from the male. The incubating female usually became excited and restless a few seconds before the male became visible to the observer. How she became aware of his approach beyond the willow thickets is not known. At one nest, on July 3 (3:15 p.m.), the female on the nest became excited; the male came and fed her several insects; she rose to the edge of the nest to be fed, and as soon as the male finished feeding her and left, she settled down on the eggs again. This response by the female was not evoked by a wandering juvenal redpoll passing close to the nest.

Young.—Walkinshaw (1948) says: "At a nest found on June 9, three young hatched on June 10 and the fourth on June 11. On June 19, two of these young left the nest when 9 days old; the others remained at least until June 20." His notes seem to indicate that the female did all the brooding of the young and all the feeding and nest cleaning; once the male fed his mate, however. His table shows that the young increased in weight from 1.3 grams at hatching to 6.5 grams at 7 days; during the same period, the wing increased in length from 5.3 to 20.3 millimeters; the first primaries were in evidence at the end of the first week.

Baldwin and Reed (1955) found the hatchings at all redpoll nests to occur between June 6 and July 8 in 1953. Hatching occurred at any hour of the day or night. Brooding was by the female only, and the amount of time she spent settled on the nest declined progressively as the days went by. Starting with 85 percent the first day of brooding, the time on the nest decreased to 30 percent on the fourth day, to 27.5 percent on the seventh day, and to 1 percent on the tenth. By this time the nestlings were large, well-fledged, and crowding the nest, and the female ceased brooding. Both parents fed the nestlings throughout the time they stayed in the nest. The female fed the young intensively at first and somewhat less frequently after a few days had elapsed. The male, on the other hand, fed the young just half as often as did the female the fourth day, but gradually increased his feeding until it equaled the female's on the tenth day.

The dates of departure from the nests extended from June 20 to July 21, with the young in 15 nests leaving between June 20 and June 30. The departure of a brood was either sudden and complete or a gradual occurrence over a day or more. Nest departure occurred from 12 to 14 days after hatching, with 14 days representing the typical period of nest life.

Plumages.—E. W. Nelson (1887) gives the following description of young hoary redpolls in juvenal plumage in July: "The feathers on the top of head, back, and rump, sides of neck, breast, and body each with a shaft-streak of dull blackish-brown, and feathers of crown and rump edged with more or less ashy or grayish, and in some cases the gray extends down the middle of the back. Ear-coverts, edges of dorsal, and scapular-feathers buff, or dull fulvous-brownish. The two wing-bars and tertiaries are edged with a lighter shade of buff; edges of primaries and rectrices grayish, washed more or less heavily with a fulvous shade; the abdomen ashy-white; chin occupied by a concealed patch of sooty-brown feathers with a dull white wash * * *."

The red crown is acquired at the post-juvenal molt, when a first winter plumage is assumed which is very similar to the spring plumage but is more or less tinged with buff and shows broader white edgings on the wings and tail. The annual molt of adults at Umiat occurs between mid-June and mid-September.

Food.—The hoary redpoll feeds predominantly on plant materials, especially seeds but also buds. Insects are eaten to a limited extent.

In northern Alaska, according to Joseph Grinnell (1900a), "redpolls when feeding seldom utter a note, but if alarmed the flock takes flight from the brush in scattering succession with a chorus of calls. The seeds and buds of the alder, birch and willow constitute their sole food supply. When feeding, the redpolls assume all manner of postures, most often clinging beneath the twigs, back downward and picking to pieces the pods."

I. N. Gabrielson (1924) reported on the contents of the stomachs of 11 hoary redpolls. Six of these were collected by E. A. Preble in the Athabasca–Mackenzie region and contained seeds of birch and alder. The remaining five were from Michigan and Maine and contained seeds of knotweed (*Polygonum*), stink grass (*Eragrostis*), sedge (*Carex*), pigweed (*Amaranthus*), and an unidentified seed.

Baldwin and Reed (1955) made observations on the foods and feeding of hoary redpolls at Umiat in northern Alaska from June to August, 1953. From June 12 to 16, redpolls were occasionally seen feeding in situations suggestive of hunting for insects, as when a pink-breasted male fed from tall willow branches carefully and quickly searching stems and crotches. Leaves were not yet out on the willows. Frequently the birds sought seeds. Another male was seen foraging on the ground at the edge of slow-moving water under the willows, and a parent from one nest foraged on the leaf-covered ground under the willows. Willow catkins attracted the redpolls, and they often probed the cottony willow pods.

The adults fed the young a white mash of seed kernels which between July 20 and 29 was determined to be composed almost entirely of kernels of the seeds of cottongrass. The mash taken from one adult collected had insect parts mixed in it. One juvenal not long out of the nest was seen feeding at cottongrass, and the bird had cotton on its bill.

The parents ate the egg shells after the young hatched and often ate the nestlings' fecal sacs. One adult female was seen to feed its young several insect larvae. Another adult redpoll was watched 15 minutes while it industriously foraged at brown willow pods which were opening.

As the cottongrass seed heads began to mature in late July, the redpolls spent much more time on the open tundra away from the willow brush, though the willow catkins also attracted them. By August 11 the birds became much scarcer on the tundra, and examination of the cottongrass heads revealed few seeds left in them; some only had empty husks.

Field marks.—The smaller hoary redpoll is distinguished from the larger Hornemann's (Greeland) redpoll (*Acanthis h. hornemanni*) by its size and somewhat darker color. The hoary redpoll often associates with the common redpoll (*Acanthis f. flammea*) in winter flocks and is distinguished from the latter at such times by its frosty appearance. P. A. Taverner (1934) says of *Acanthis h. exilipes:* "Characteristic adults [have] feather edgings light so that a typical bird looks like a Common Redpoll * * * seen through a white veil * * *." However, the colors are frequently so similar that many hoary redpolls "are inseparable from the Common Redpoll except by other characters."

Enemies.—G. M. Sutton (1932) says that jaegers and the duck hawk are the principal enemies of the redpolls. Baldwin and Reed recovered feathers of a hoary redpoll and a fox sparrow that had been fed to two young duck hawks near their nest on a cliff at Umiat Mountain.

Winter.—Grinnell (1900a) says that in the Kotzebue Sound region in northern Alaska these redpolls—

were present in unvarying numbers throughout the year. They were obviously less noticeable up to the middle of September, or until the summer birds had all left; but during the long winter, from September 15 to May 15, they were by far the most numerous species. The days of extremest cold were invariably calm and clear, and on such days one could walk scarcely a half-hour in any direction from camp without meeting with flocks of from ten to fifty redpolls. In the morning especially, they kept constantly on the go, flying about from place to place with a continuous medley of chit-chat notes. Later, in the short winter day, they would be less noticeable, and were to be looked for in the thickets of alder and willow, where their presence would be first betrayed by the rustle of pods and dead leaves. * * * On windy days, which were very numerous in the fore part of the winter, one had to look for the redpolls in the most sheltered situations, and sometimes he would fail to find them at all. But the next calm day would bring them out again in full force.

Taverner (1934) says the hoary redpoll is the only subspecies of *Acanthis hornemanni* so far reported for southern Canada. During occasional winters this race occurs in varying numbers with large flocks of the common redpoll, but there is no regularity in its visits. Ludlow Griscom (1949) finds the hoary redpoll a rare winter visitor in the region of Concord, Mass., occurring in marked flight occasional years only.

Maurice Broun observed hoary redpolls at Hawk Mountain, Pa., in 1956 and writes (in litt.): "During the mid-afternoon of 18 March of this year, at the height of the blizzard which struck the Northeast, my wife and I, and my assistant, Alex Nagy, studied four extremely light-colored redpolls that moved restlessly in the lilacs and among the lower limbs of a black birch by Sanctuary headquarters. * * * Three were females. We concluded that these birds could be nothing else than hoarys, for the birds were white as the snow. The next afternoon they returned and again we studied them. * * * Meanwhile we had a flock of 30 or more common redpolls. But the hoarys did not associate with the other redpolls * * * these birds were a distinct homogeneous unit."

L. E. Hicks (1934) says of a specimen he collected in Ohio on Mar. 16, 1931: "The bird was engaged in feeding in several weedy patches along the margin of an extensive marsh area, a half mile south of the Lake Erie shore. This individual was exceedingly active, darting rapidly back and forth between weedy patches and several fence posts or mounting to some telephone wires or tree tops to emit repeatedly from three to five rapid indescribable notes which recalled at the same time those of both the Purple Finch and the Goldfinch."

DISTRIBUTION

Range.—Alaska, Canadian Arctic, Norway, and U.S.S.R. to northern United States, England, former East Prussia, and Kamchatka.

Breeding range.—Breeds in northern Sweden, northern Russia, and northern Siberia east to the Chukotski Peninsula, south in eastern Siberia to south central Khabarovskj and in western and northern Alaska (Hooper Bay, Bethel), northern Yukon (La Pierre House), northern Mackenzie (Fort McPherson, Anderson River, Caribou Rapids of Hanbury River), northeastern Manitoba (Churchill), northern Quebec (Fort Chimo), and northern Labrador (Nachvak).

Winter range.—Winters irregularly south to England, former East Prussia, Kamchatka, the Komandorskie Islands, southern Alaska (Kodiak Island, Chitina), southern British Columbia (Okanagan), eastern Montana (Miles City), southwestern South Dakota (Black Hills), Minnesota (Faribault), northern Illinois (Mount Carroll, near Chicago), northwestern Indiana (Mineral Springs), northern Ohio (Lucas County), New Jersey (Bergen Co.), southeastern New York (Bronx), Connecticut (East Haven), Massachusetts (Nantasket Beach), and New Brunswick (Petitcodiac).

Casual records.—Casual in Hungary, Maryland (Berlin), Saint Lawrence Island, Sakhalin Islands, and northern Japan.

Egg dates.—Alaska: 12 records, June 1 to June 29.

ACANTHIS FLAMMEA FLAMMEA (Linneaus)

Common Redpoll

PLATES 22 AND 23

Contributed by ROLAND C. CLEMENT

HABITS

When the cold air masses of winter extend their fronts into our northern tier of states, a period of welcome surcease from the storminess of the seasonal transitions descends upon regions within their influence. During this month or more of calm the days scintillate and begin to lengthen, and the dwellers of the northland, human as well as wild, come out of hiding to enjoy the sun and the cold, dry air. These are among the most beautiful days in the northland; the temperature hovers between —10° and —20° F., there is no wind, and a great silence lies upon the winter barrens. From the distant spruces that dot the valley slopes like stubble come the faint tinklings of white-winged crossbills and the occasional rattle of redpolls, sounds so faint that you must hear them repeated to feel sure that the sound is not coming from your own lungs.

Not many redpolls winter near the edge of timber, but some do, and only a year in the semibarrens, that broad, indefinite ecotone between the treeless tundra and the spruce–fir–larch forests of the taiga, can give one a sense of thorough familiarity with these small finches. To those who have not visited the northland, the redpolls remain erratic winter visitors; they rarely go south of the 40th parallel. They are rare in many years, but are sometimes abundant, often occurring then in large flocks, the members of which may be alternately wild and delightfully tame. Here is how they impressed Henry David Thoreau (1910), who wrote from Concord on Dec. 11, 1855:

Standing there I am reminded of the incredible phenomenon of small birds in winter,—that ere long amid the cold powdery snow, as it were a fruit of the season, will come twittering a flock of delicate crimson-tinged birds, lesser redpolls, to sport and feed on the seeds and buds now just ripe for them on the sunny side of a wood, shaking down the powdery snow there in their cheerful social feeding, as if it were high midsummer to them. These crimson aerial creatures have wings which would bear them quickly to the regions of summer, but here is all the summer they want. What a rich contrast! tropical colors, crimson breasts, on cold white snow! Such etherealness, such delicacy in their forms, such ripeness in their colors, in this stern and barren season!

The edge of the tundra marks their northern limits, which they penetrate only where coastal driftwood provides substitute nesting sites, as Brandt (1943) reports from the Bering Sea Coast of Alaska. "Back from the driftwood of the coast these birds were not met with," he writes, "until the rolling upland tundra was reached, where occasional patches of stunted gnarled willows grow." Ecologically, then, the common redpoll belongs in the "subalpine" or tundra–coniferous forest ecotone, as Pleske (1928) also makes clear.

Spring.—In the transition zone the redpoll arrives late and departs early. Except for stray individuals, mid-March sees them leave the more southern regions, and soon thereafter, in years of abundance, the birds often stream northward in large numbers, as emphasized by Farley's (1930) remarkable observation of "tens of thousands" of redpolls moving north across the prairie near Chamberlain, S. Dak., on Mar. 23, 1929, and Richard L. Weaver's (*in* litt.) experience with "three to four thousand birds" moving up the Connecticut Valley near West Lebanon, N.H., on Mar. 25, 1941, "a continuous stream of birds made up of small flocks of about twenty-five individuals, many of them pausing to bathe in icy pools."

At Indian House Lake, Quebec, at 56°12′ north latitude, in the heart of the semibarrens which is their home and which I shared with them during a year of military duty, the winter resident populations thins out near the end of March. Though there are signs of movement throughout April and May, there is no marked influx. Spring migrants apparently spread out so widely that their arrival is almost imperceptible near the northern limits of the range. At Point Dall, Alaska, however, between 61° and 62° north latitude, Brandt (1943) reports that mixed flocks of common and hoary redpolls arrived on May 16.

H. Bradford Washburn, Jr., reports by letter finding dead redpolls at 17,700 feet and 18,200 feet near the summit of Mount McKinley in Alaska, on May 31, 1947, and July 10, 1951, respectively. He believed the birds had been swept up to the higher parts of the mountain by the strong southwest storms which hit the peak at that time of year.

Courtship.—At Indian House Lake during 1945 the common redpoll began to sing on March 5, about a week after its more northern relative, the hoary redpoll (*C. h. exilipes*), which wintered there with it but did not summer. From March 12 to the end of the month the birds were very noisy and excited. By the last week of March many appeared paired and sneaked through the alder thickets near our camp, calling plaintively and behaving shyly. By mid-April scattered pairs had apparently selected nesting sites, but they were so extremely secretive I found it impossible to fix the status of the few pairs that wandered about near us. Some days the thickets along the lake seemed deserted, when suddenly a passing northern shrike would draw up a swirling group of 10 or so redpolls, seemingly from nowhere. Once the threat passed these sprites melted back into thickets so unobtrusively that their momentary clatter seemed to have been an error of observation.

Not until the morning of May 25, 1945, did I first observe mating. Although coitus did not actually take place, the female crouched, dropped her wings, and twittered excitedly. The male stood before her stiffly and bowed a few times. That afternoon, and again on May 30, birds were seen picking up ptarmigan feathers from our camp hillside, evidently for nest material.

No truly territorial behavior has been reported by the few naturalists who have witnessed this redpoll's prenuptial activities. Song is most active before the flocks break up, and no fighting over nesting territories appears to take place. The irregular spacing of nests, sometimes close together, seems to confirm this view.

William Dilger's studies of captive redpolls offer new enlightenment on this score (Dilger, 1957). He found that a rigid social hierarchy exists within the flock, the males being clearly dominant over females during the nonreproductive season. This dominance is linear, from high to low male, and from low male to high female to low female. The low male usually directs his attacks toward a female after losing an encounter with a male. Most significant, however, is the fact that females become aggressive and dominant over the males as the breeding season approaches. European studies suggest that this reversal of dominance is characteristic of cardueline finches in general. "Each female," Dilger states, "clearly singles out a certain male to which she behaves in a particularly aggressive manner. These are the couples between which pair bonds are ultimately formed." Once the pair bond is fully formed, the males are in almost constant song and keep as far as possible from one another. There is, thus, little overt aggression among them.

Nesting.—This absence of territorial behavior, coupled with the shyness of nesting birds, makes nest hunting difficult. The discovery of fully fledged young redpolls in the streamside alders of Indian House Lake on June 8 was a complete surprise to me. Six occupied nests were found on June 9, 14, and 25. These nests were built on a careless foundation of small twigs laid across adjacent branches out from the trunk of a small spruce, or in the crotch of an alder or willow, and from 3 to 6 feet off the ground, usually about 5 feet. On this platform is woven a loose cup of fine twigs, rootlets, and grasses or, if in the forest, black tree moss (*Usnea barbatus*). The nest is then completed by a thick layer of ptarmigan body feathers (mostly white), making a small warm cup into which the female can sink almost out of sight as she sits on her small eggs. All these nests appeared to be loosely built, and they disintegrated quickly once abandoned, their feather lining blowing away. Walkinshaw (1948), on the other hand, considered the Alaska nests very well built, and found many of the past year's nests in the low leafless willows.

L. I. Grinnell and Ralph S. Palmer (Grinnell, 1943) had similar difficulty locating nests around Churchill, Manitoba. Of nine nests found, "the bulk material was chiefly dried grasses, though in one nest, small twigs had also been used." Ptarmigan feathers were used in the lining of eight nests, plant-down in five, hair in one, and lemming fur in another. According to Brandt (1943), the use of small twigs as a nest foundation is characteristic of this species and helps to distinguish it from the nest of the hoary redpoll where the two nest together in Alaska.

The dimensions of 11 nests given by L. I. Grinnell (1943) and Brandt (1943) were as follows: Outside diameter, 7.6 to 10.0 cm., averaging 8.7; inside diameter, 4.5 to 6.0 cm., averaging 5.6; outside depth, 5.0 to 8.8 cm., averaging 6.8; and inside depth, 3.0 to 5.1 cm., averaging 4.0.

The nest site naturally varies with the type of cover available. In the semibarrens, the principal habitat of this species, it nests usually in dwarfed or poorly formed spruces, or in willow and alder thickets. Where the common redpoll ranges onto the tundra, it must perforce use any cover available, whether driftwood stranded by high tides, tufts of grass, or human artifacts. Concealment likewise varies considerably; nests in spruce are usually the best concealed, those in deciduous shrubs sometimes poorly so because they may be built before the foliage has developed enough to provide concealment. Although some nests survive the sweep of winter

winds, no one has yet reported that the common redpoll uses the same
nest from one year to the next, as Wynne-Edwards (1952) reports
is true of the arctic races on Baffin Island, and of the lesser redpoll
(*A. f. cabaret*) in Scotland.

Lee R. Dice (1918b) considers nest building the work of the female
alone, but I have seen both birds at the nest during the last phases of
construction.

Eggs.—Four to five (rarely up to seven) eggs comprise the clutch.
Brandt (1943) writes:

> The egg ranges from ovate to elongate ovate in shape, is almost without gloss,
> and somewhat delicate in structure. The ground color is prominent, and ranges
> from greenish white to pale glaucous blue and pale turquoise green. The markings
> are never conspicuous because they lack boldness, yet often the broad end of the
> egg is thickly sprinkled. These spots, while concentrated at the large end, are
> never found to be wreathed as in the case of the Hoary Redpoll. In color they
> range from pale rose purple to purplish lilac.
>
> An occasional additional kind of marking, in the form of hairline pencillings
> or small dots is to be found usually at the broad end of the egg. The latter vary
> from dull dusky purple to dull violet black.

Walkinshaw (1948) likens them to eggs of the field sparrow (*Spizella
pusilla*).

The measurements of 50 eggs average 16.9 by 12.2 millimeters;
the eggs showing the four extremes measure *20.3* by 12.9, 17.0 by
13.7, and *14.2* by *11.2* millimeters.

Preble (1908) reports a nest with one egg as early as April 24 on
the Upper Mackenzie River and Perrett (*in* Austin, 1932) records
four fresh eggs on April 28, at Nain, Newfoundland, Labrador.
These are early dates which contrast with L. I. Grinnell's (1947) late
date of July 22 for young just leaving the nest at Churchill, and
admit the possibility of a second brood in this species, something
Brandt (1943) seems confident of in Alaska. A. C. Bent (in litt.)
thought so, too, writing me: "When I was in Nome in 1911, we found
both species about equally common and both nesting * * * they
were well started on their second broods about the middle of July;
young birds of the first broods were fully grown and on the wing."
June, however, seems to be the peak month for nesting activity.
Females do all the incubating.

Although Grinnell (1943) found incubating females to be close
sitters, I found that they almost always left the nest quietly as
soon as I approached; they dropped below the level of the nest and
flew off through the alders without giving alarm. Only once did
adult birds betray their nest by showing alarm. On the other hand,
Walkinshaw (1948) says: "I soon found that when redpolls scolded
me in the region of these groups of willows, they had a nest there."

Both Walkinshaw and I have been intrigued by females that brooded an empty nest while we measured their eggs nearby.

Young.—Information on the early development of redpolls is scarce. I established one 11-day incubation period at Indian House Lake, and Lawrence I. Grinnell (in litt., 1955) agrees that his "10 or 11 days" (Grinnell, 1943) should read "probably 11 days," even though European students (Witherby, 1938) report 10 or 11 days for this species. Walkinshaw (1948), writing of Alaska observations, said, "We found that, usually, three young hatched the first day, and the fourth the following day. With five-egg sets, four usually hatched the first day."

The following information on development is drawn from Grinnell's (1943, 1947) studies: Except for faint wisps of grayish natal down on the principal feather tracts, the newly hatched young are naked and they weigh less than 1.5 grams. Motor control is limited to the ability to right themselves when turned over on their backs, and to spreading and closing the toes. So translucent are they that food can be seen in the gullet, and blood vessels give the skin an orange-red hue. The fourth day sees the eyes begin to slit, and they are quite open the next day. The sixth day sees the young vigorous and active, although the first *cheep* notes are not uttered until the tenth day, when they show the first fear reactions. Perching is first accomplished successfully on the eleventh day, and the nestlings can fly enough to leave the nest the next day. Growth in weight is rapid and steady until the ninth day, when it tapers off abruptly after attaining 12 grams. Adults weigh 13 to 14 grams.

The long days of the subarctic summer provide about 20 hours of daylight, including the colorful crepuscular hours, and the redpoll's nesting day is consequently much longer than that of related fringillids from more southern regions. Adult females are sometimes active from 3:00 a.m. to 10:30 p.m., at Churchill (Grinnell, 1943). Somewhat farther north in Alaska, Walkinshaw (1948) found activity continued around the clock. Although females average approximately equal periods off and on the nest, the colder June period at Churchill, with a 31° to 63° F. temperature range, saw an interval of attentiveness only 40 percent that of July, when the temperature ranged between 42° and 77° (Grinnell, 1947), meaning shorter periods of exposure and more frequent feedings. The same adjustment to temperature is evident in the diurnal activity cycle (Grinnell, 1943), the feeding interval being only 8 minutes between 3:00 a.m. and 6:00 a.m., but about 24 minutes for the rest of the day. The average interval between feedings diminishes with advancing age, being 38 minutes for the first 4 days, 23 minutes for the 5–7-day period, and 19 minutes for days 8 through 10.

The nestlings are usually fed directly by the female, though she sometimes feeds them by regurgitation. Although Dice (1918b) found no males helping to rear the young, both Walkinshaw (1948) and Grinnell (1943) observed males feeding them occasionally, and found that they also fed the female at the nest. The latter writes, "The female, before accepting the food from the male, opened and shut her bill rapidly several times, and while taking the food, she vibrated her wings continuously. * * * After accepting the food, the female regurgitated and fed the young. In the case of a rosy-breasted male and its mate, one parent would come alone to the nest, feed the brood of five, then fly off; the other parent would come almost immediately afterward and also feed the brood."

Writing to Mr. Bent from Mountain Village, Alaska, about nest sanitation in this species, Henry C. Kyllingstad says: "I have seen no evidence of any effort to keep the next clean. Never once have I observed the adult birds carrying off or otherwise disposing of the feces of the young. By the time the young are ready to leave the nest, it and its surroundings are extremely dirty, all twigs below the nest being white with the excreta. It is very easy to locate nests by this means if one wishes to band fledglings—simply look for a white blotch! I have seen hundreds of nests of these birds and they are all alike." I was not impressed by any lack of sanitation in the Indian House Lake nests I found, and Grinnell (1943) definitely states that the nests "were frequently cleaned by the parent birds, usually immediately after feeding the young; the parent sometimes swallowed the excreta, sometimes carried them away." Walkinshaw (1948), too, saw females swallow excreta at the nest. Absence of nest sanitation, however, is characteristic of most cardueline finches. The feces are not voided in a sac, and usually dry up and disintegrate quickly.

After leaving the nest on the 12th day, the dark, heavily streaked young I found at Indian House Lake associated in small family groups and remained in the protection of the extensive streamside alder–willow thickets for a while. By mid-July, when all the young were off the nest, their preferred habitat appeared to be the dwarf birch scrub along the upper edge of timber on the valley slopes.

Plumages.—Dwight (1900), basing his description of the juvenal plumage on a single August specimen from Labrador, called it "streaked with sepia and clove-brown above with white edgings; rump paler but also streaked." Wings and tail were clove brown with whitish or buffy edgings, and the coverts, wing bands, and tertiaries edged with pale cinnamon. The first winter plumage, he writes, is acquired by a partial post-juvenal molt late in August, involving only body plumage and wing coverts; the crown is then dull crimson, and the chin spot is dull brownish-black. A few young birds, even females, may acquire rosy breast feathers, but these are characteristic of adult males.

Continuing, Dwight adds that the first nuptial plumage is "acquired by wear, through which much of the buff is lost, the birds becoming darker and whiter with the crown spot a trifle brighter to the eye, due to loss of grayish barbules of the red barbs." A complete postnuptial molt brings the adult winter plumage. The adult nuptial plumage, like the first nuptial plumage, is acquired by wear, the rosy feathers of the male deepening in color by loss of the grayish barbules and reduction of the whitish edgings. Female plumages and molts correspond to those of the male, but the crown spot remains duller and smaller.

Food.—Availability is a powerful governing factor in the food preferences of so wide-ranging a species. In winter the redpolls that stay northward are largely dependent on the seeds of the amentiferous birches, alders, and willows. Southward they partake of a wider variety of seeds from forbs and grasses in addition to their usual staples, the lesser conifers. Grinnell (1947) has analyzed the available data from the literature and found that the redpoll is known to eat the seeds or parts of 41 genera of plants, and insects of 6 orders. A series of 10 stomachs he collected at Churchill between June 7 and 17 provide a clear index to availability of foods because they contained vegetable matter amounting to 41.2 percent (mostly seeds of *Ranunculus*, *Eriophorum*, and *Draba*), gravel (58.8 percent) and no animal matter. Insects were not plentiful that year before June 20.

Like most seed-eating fringillids, the redpoll takes insects when they are abundant, especially when feeding the young. In the sparsely settled expanses of its northland breeding ground, the redpoll seldom comes into direct contact with man's agricultural activities. When it does visit settled areas in winter, its weed-seed-eating habits recommend it even to those who are not alive to its many other charms.

Tom J. Cade (1953) has suggested that this species "has a sufficiently adventuresome disposition to utilize sub-nival situations" in food-getting during winter, and that it is thus in possession of a trait adapted to ensure survival under difficult winter conditions. Although suggestive, his single observation of redpolls feeding in tunnels formed by weeds otherwise buried in snow, provides no evidence that the birds actually excavated these openings to get at food. To me, one of the most impressive effects of snow storms at Indian House Lake during the depth of winter was that as one alder–willow thicket along shore was drifted over and made inaccessible to birds (chiefly ptarmigan), another thicket was exhumed by the same winds. This made for frequent shifts in the accessibility of food supplies but never completely eliminated them. It seems likely that each topographic region will provide strikingly different conditions in this respect.

Behavior.—The common redpoll shares much of its behavior, temperament, and voice characteristics with the other small cardueline finches, not merely the other redpolls, but with the siskin and the goldfinch as well. Close observation may disclose specific traits, some of them diagnostic for each member of the group, but these are difficult to describe and impossible to delimit.

Restlessness is certainly one of the chief characteristics of the redpoll in the open. Writing of its incessant activity, John V. Dennis (*in* litt.), who banded and carefully observed redpolls in Sharon, Mass., during the winter of 1949, says: "Even while feeding, the individual bird would never remain for long in one spot. After clinging to a weed stalk a few seconds, generally feeding with the body held horizontal to the bending stem and sometimes head downward, the bird would move on to another stalk, often just in advance of the main flock. Then, as though impelled by an innate rhythm, the flock would take wing again and the whole performance would be repeated. This was always the method of feeding in the open. Instead of relying upon a sentinel or the alarm call of an observant member of the flock, the redpolls take no chance, as it were, but fly up with pulselike precision.

"But when feeding in a sheltered region, such as a feeding tray near dense shrubbery, this instinct disappears. The flock loses its cohesion. Individuals stay at the feeders as long as they please; they come and go individually, unless an alarm sends them all away. They are much less likely to take fright at the appearance of humans than of birds of other species feeding with them."

This disregard of humans, especially by birds in sizeable flocks, is commonly mentioned in the literature and forms treasured memories of those who have known the redpolls any length of time. Mrs. Kenneth B. Wetherbee (1937) records this as part of her banding experience near Worcester, Mass., during the winter of 1935–36 and adds: "They were alarmed only by a sudden movement. By moving cautiously one could approach to within a few inches of them as they fed, and they were but mildly concerned when a hand moved slowly about among them * * *. As a rule they fed peacefully, packed as closely as they could stand on the shelf, though occasionally one would open its bill in an unfriendly attitude toward a newcomer attempting to alight * * *." She actually captured redpolls by hand and describes it thus: "The window was slowly raised, and a hand, reached cautiously out, was carefully cupped about the desired individual which was brought slowly inside without unduly disturbing its companions * * *. If an individual displayed some nervousness, instead of attempting to capture it by hand, I gently shoved it toward a trap entrance."

John V. Dennis also wrote about the remarkable tameness of these birds: "Even as I was collecting birds in a gathering cage, birds still free sought to enter the traps. Some of the outsiders would peck through the mesh of the gathering cage at the birds imprisoned within. Often, individuals would calmly feed within the trap while every effort was being made to scare them into leaving through the exit.

"While awaiting their turn to be banded, the birds in the burlap-covered gathering cage were noisy and persisted in pecking one another. But if the burlap was suddenly removed the occupants would freeze in position and remain absolutely silent for close to a minute."

W. C. Dilger (1957) found that no long period of habituation was necessary in his captive flock. Three days sufficed to work out the rigid social hierarchy which he considers typical of this species. The birds were so highly social that their various activities tended to be performed in concert. During the breeding season, however, males would not tolerate one another at less than 10 centimeters, whereas females permitted the approach of other females to about 4 centimeters before asserting their rank. Contacts between the sexes were somewhat intermediate.

An observation on feeding behavior made by William Brewster (1936) suggests the redpoll's versatility. The birds involved were feeding on the ground, pouncing with both feet, kicking and tossing leaves to get at fallen birch seed, very much as fox sparrows do. Charles H. Blake (*in* litt.) writes that, when feeding on seeds in catkins of gray birch, the birds normally perch on the twig bearing the catkin, steadying the catkin by grasping the twig and the catkin base in one foot.

The winter of 1947 brought some 300 redpolls to Hawk Mountain Sanctuary in Pennsylvania, where they are usually rare. Maurice Broun, writing to Mr. Bent about this visitation, reported that, "One Sunday in January, about 50 of the little birds were bathing and wading in the icy water of the tiny brook by our house; the temperature was 38° F., and there was much snow and ice on the ground. After a thorough bath the bathers flew up to an apple tree where they shook and flashed their feathers, chattering contentedly in low tones. These are the only birds that I have ever seen bathing—really soaking—in mid-winter." Palmer (1949) gives an interesting account of redpolls bathing in wet snow on a roof, as reported by Mrs. E. A. Anthony of Mount Desert Island, Maine:

The birds would take a series of vigorous hops to gain momentum, then plunge and burrow head first until almost out of sight. They fluttered their wings like birds taking a water bath. They would then remain quiet for several minutes, and emerge, flutter their wings, throw snow over themselves with their bills, and hop to another place to repeat the bathing. When a bird came out of a hole, another would dash into it, the first going into another hole or making a new one. About 50 birds kept this up for an hour and left the snow on the roof only after they had honeycombed it with holes.

Voice.—The difficulty of describing the dry trills and other notes of the redpoll is evident when one looks over the varied syllabifications used by authors to interpret this small finch voice. In a letter to Mr. Bent, Francis H. Allen wrote, "Besides the rattling *tshu, tshu, tshu,* as Ralph Hoffmann renders the flight-note, this species has a call-note *sweet* or *swee-e-et* of a coarser quality than the similar note of the American Goldfinch, louder but not so clear and sweet, while not so husky as that of the Pine Siskin."

Grinnell (1947) recognized three categories of notes: (1) a repeated *chit* used in flight and while feeding, (2) a trill which is a flight call, and (3) "a sweeter note, usually a perching call." He adds, "None of the above-mentioned calls seemed to fulfill the function of a song." The *chit-chit-chit* call, not loud, was most often, but not always, uttered in threes lasting just under a second. During flight these notes are often uttered while nearing the tops of their goldfinchlike undulations.

The variously written, interrogatory *tree-uh-eee?* call betokens annoyance or concern, and, according to Grinnell (1947), "is often uttered by the male when perching preparatory to feeding a nesting female. It is often reiterated at least a dozen times at intervals of about five seconds by both parents when they are anxious." Olive P. Wetherbee (1937) thought that this "call seemed to serve two purposes, those of a danger signal and a call to food. It was uttered with peculiar emphasis when there was a cat about, but was most frequently heard early in the morning while the flock was congregating * * * before starting to feed, at which time it was voiced by many members of the flock in a more rollicking manner."

Though this species has no territorial song, it seemed to me that the excited March flocks at Indian House Lake joined in a veritable songfest. I made note of a juncolike lay and wrote that the "junco song is very variable, always sweeter than its model, and sometimes elaborated into a near warble: *dre-he-he-he-teu-teu-teu,* the first part a junco-trill, the last rolling and melodious. My journal describes the voice of fledglings as raspy "catbird-like" cries. Austin (1932) describes the notes of fully fledged young as "something like the *chee-chee-chee* of the old birds' song, but delivered with a sore throat, and not unlike in quality the *mew* of the Catbird."

Enemies.—The redpoll is preyed upon by the usual enemies of small birds, the raptores in particular, but specific information is meager. Grinnell's (1947) extensive survey of the literature revealed occasional predation by falcons, harriers, and jaegers. The animosity the redpolls bore the northern shrike and the hawk owl at Indian House Lake indicates that these, too, prey upon them even though no actual chase was witnessed. Near human habitations the redpoll's tameness sometimes makes it easy prey for cats (Wetherbee, 1937).

Losses incurred during the reproductive period are more important, though at a level normal for small birds. Grinnell's (1943) study of a total of 33 eggs showed successful hatching of only 72 percent, and nestling losses reduced the survival of chicks at nest-leaving age to 39 percent. Despite these losses, the redpoll is a common bird in its own territory.

Field marks.—The recent generic lumping by some authors of the redpolls with the goldfinch and siskin and, in Europe, with the twite, serin, and linnet emphasizes their similarities in form and behavior. In America, except for the darker, yellow-flashing siskin, a small, streaked, grayish-brown, fork-tailed finch is a redpoll; the red forehead and black chin make identification specific. Some, but not all, males have a rosy breast. The species *flammea* may be told by its brownish tone, since most feathers have a buff edging, and by the streaked rump; the congeneric *hornemanni* group have frosty-white feather edgings, and an unstreaked rump for the most part. Even so, excellent observation conditions are required to separate the two species, and field identification of subspecies is unsafe. Indeed, the redpolls await a thorough monographic revision.

Fall and winter.—August sees the redpolls wandering about the brushy semibarrens in small family groups, slowly aggregating into loose flocks, so that by September the first migrants begin winging southward or to more sheltered localities. At Indian House Lake throughout October there was a distinct southward flight up the valley of small flocks of 5 to 60 birds. These birds flew directly and purposefully, 30 to 50 feet overhead, and showed a preference for the narrow, semiwooded intervale that extends for miles along the lake. They called continuously as they flew southward upstream, their high note being heard long before the birds came into sight against the usual autumn background of low, ragged clouds. By whistling almost any long-drawn note it was usually possible to make them veer from their course and pass overhead. They seldom alighted though, and when they did, it was at some distance, and they took off again immediately if I approached them. This flight was a conspicuous feature of the fall migration in the valley of the George River. Harrison F. Lewis (1939) has reported a similar movement near Moosonie, Ontario.

The southward incursions of redpolls in some years are almost certainly related to conditions—whether deep snows, ice storms, or actual failure of the catkin crop—that reduce the availability of food in their breeding grounds, but our knowledge of conditions in the subarctic is still too scanty to permit correlations.

Redpolls winter throughout the subarctic from Alaska to Labrador. Periods of bad weather cause them to disappear from their usual haunts, in alder and willow thickets which remain uncovered by drifting snows, perhaps to concentrate in sheltered woodlands. But once the storms are past, they disperse again and enliven the northern scene with their incessant chatter and trim, often colorful, forms.

DISTRIBUTION

Range.—Alaska, Mackenzie, Quebec, and Arctic Eurasia to central United States, the Mediterranean, China, and Japan.

Breeding range.—The common redpoll breeds from northern Scandinavia, northern Russia, north central Siberia, western and central Alaska (Kobuk River Valley, Nulato, Circle), central Yukon (Ogilvie Range), northern Mackenzie (Mackenzie Delta, Franklin Bay, mouth of Kogaryuak), northern Keewatin, northern Manitoba (Churchill), northern Ontario (Fort Severn), northern Quebec (Richmond Gulf, Sugluk, Fort Chimo), northern Labrador (Nachvak), and Newfoundland south to the Baltic, former East Prussia, Poland, central Russia, Altai, Sakhalin Island, Kamchatka, the Komandorskie Islands, southern Alaska (Dutch Harbor, Kodiak Island), northern British Columbia (Atlin), northern Alberta (probably Chipewyan), southern Saskatchewan (casually, Mortlach), northern Manitoba (Cochrane River, York Factory), northern Ontario (Lake Attawapiskat), central and southeastern Quebec, the Magdalen Islands (Grosse Ile), and Newfoundland. Has been taken in summer in southeastern Alaska (Thomas Bay) and central British Columbia (Fort George).

Winter range.—Winters from the British Isles, southern Scandinavia, central Russia, central Siberia, central Alaska (Nulato, Fairbanks), southwestern Mackenzie (Fort Simpson), northern Alberta (Wood Buffalo Park), northern Manitoba (Theitaga-Tua Lake), northern Michigan (Isle Royale, Sault Ste. Marie), central Ontario (Eganville), southern Quebec (Cap Rouge, Gaspé), central Labrador (Nain), and central Newfoundland south to France, Italy, Yugoslavia, Turkey, Caucasus, China (Kiangsi), Korea, and Japan (northern Kyushu); and to western Oregon (Eugene), northeastern California (Eagle Lake), northern Nevada (Ruby Lake), northeastern Utah (Uinta

Mountains), central Colorado (Colorado Springs), Kansas (Lakin, Lawrence), Iowa (Keokuk), southern Indiana (Miller), southern Ohio (Cincinnati), southeastern Virginia (Back Bay), eastern North Carolina (Hatteras), and central and southern South Carolina (Aiken, Kingstree, Bull's Island, and Beaufort County).

Casual records.—Casual on the island of Malta and at Repulse Bay, Southampton.

Accidental in Bermuda and the Bonin Islands.

Migration.—Late dates of spring departure are: South Carolina—Aiken, March 4. North Carolina—Washington, March 25. Virginia—Charlottesville, February 23. District of Columbia—March 12. Maryland—Dorchester County, March 11. Pennsylvania—State College, April 15. New Jersey—Cape May, March 26. New York—Cayuga and Oneida Lake basins, May 5 (median of 13 years, April 8); New York City, May 4. Connecticut—Southport, March 25. Rhode Island—Pawtucket, April 21. Massachusetts—Danvers, April 14. New Hampshire—New Hampton, April 28 (median of 21 years, April 8). Maine—Portland region, May 19. New Brunswick—Miscou Island, May 26. Nova Scotia—Antigonish, May 2. Prince Edward Island—Charlottetown, April 13. Newfoundland—St. Anthony, April 23. Missouri—Montgomery City, April 12. Illinois—Rantoul, March 20. Indiana—Waterloo, April 3. Ohio—Toledo, March 18. Michigan—Battle Creek, March 25. Iowa—Winneshiek County, April 5. Wisconsin—Green Bay, May 21. Minnesota—Minneapolis-St. Paul, April 17. Kansas—Clearwater, March 21. Nebraska—Gibbon, March 19. Manitoba—Margaret, March 20. Wyoming—Yellowstone Park, April 3. Idaho—Meadow Creek, April 4. Montana—Bozeman, May 16. Alberta—Cranbrook, April 20.

Early dates of fall arrival are: British Columbia—Arrow Lake, November 22. Alberta—Glenevis, October 12. Montana—Fortine, October 30. Idaho—Priest River, October 23. Wyoming—Albany County, November 8. Colorado—Weldona, October 25. Saskatchewan—Eastend, October 20. Manitoba—Treesbank, October 20. North Dakota—Fargo, October 4. Kansas—Clearwater, October 15. Minnesota—Kittson County, October 4; Minneapolis, October 19. Wisconsin—Eau Claire, September 23; New London, October 15. Iowa—Sioux City, November 10. Michigan—McMillan, October 15. Ohio—Ashtabula, October 20. Indiana—Carroll County, November 5. Illinois—Glen Ellyn, November 6. Missouri—Mt. Carmel, November 4. Prince Edward Island—North River, October 4. Nova Scotia—Pictou, October 13. New Brunswick—Scotch Lake, October 14. Quebec—Gaspé, October 20. Maine—Phillips, October 5. New Hampshire—New Hampton, October 12 (median of 13 years,

)ctober 28). Massachusetts—Waltham, October 16. Connecticut—
Iartford, October 2. New York—Cayuga and Oneida Lake basins,
)ctober 17 (median of 6 years, November 3). New Jersey—Elizabeth,
)ctober 18. Maryland—Allegany County, December 6. Virginia—
Jack Bay, December 5. North Carolina—Arden, October 29.

Egg dates.—Alaska: 124 records, April 4 to August 17; 62 records,
'une 2 to June 19.

British Columbia: 1 record, May 26.

Labrador: 13 records, June 9 to July 27.

Manitoba: 4 records, June 19 to June 29.

Newfoundland: 4 records, June 1 to June 19.

ACANTHIS FLAMMEA ROSTRATA (Coues)

Greater Redpoll*

HABITS

This is the other large and dark colored redpoll, previously men-
.ioned as being difficult to recognize in the field.

It breeds on Baffin Island, Iceland, and in Greenland, where
Iagerup (1891) called it the "most numerous of the smaller birds
ound in the vicinity of Ivigtut." He says further that: "In 1886 it
vas first observed on May 6, and was common on May 17. On
Jeptember 24 the majority had migrated southward, though a few
vere met with now and then during October. * * *

"In 1887, the first were seen on April 24, and on April 30 a few
single individuals, besides three together flying toward west-north-
vest, about one hundred feet high. On the 6th of May several ap-
Jeared in the valley, and by the 10th of the same month, they were
common."

Of its status on Ungava, Lucien M. Turner says in his unpublished
Lotes: "Rather common in winter. None to be seen from May 15 to
September 1 of each year."

The greater redpoll ranges southward more or less irregularly in
winter to southern Canada and the northern United States, as far
west as Manitoba and Montana and as far south as southern New
England, Colorado, and northern Illinois.

Ridgway (1901) describes the greater redpoll as similar to *holboelli*,
"but much larger and with a relatively thicker and more obtuse bill;
coloration rather darker and browner, with the dusky stripes on sides
and flanks usually heavier and broader; adult male with the pink
or red of chest, etc., apparently less extensive as well as less intense."

---

*For further details on the life history of the greater redpoll, see Salomonsen
(1950)—Editor.

Hagerup (1891) gives us the following information on its nesting and other habits:

These birds usually build wherever a bunch of bushes may be found, but rarely over five hundred or six hundred feet up the hillside, although I have met examples on the higher lands during the mating-season. I discovered eight nests with eggs and young. Three of the nests had the full number of eggs in May, the others in June. The earliest newly-laid eggs were found on May 20, the latest on June 26. One clutch consisted of four eggs, another of six, and the remainder of five eggs or young.

These nests were in willow bushes, generally in the lowest branches, close to the ground, and never higher than three and one half feet. An exception was a nest built upon one of the seats in an old boat which lay beside a thoroughfare within the town of Ivigtut. * * *

* * *

The nests which I found were made chiefly of dried grass and roots, the inside being lined with white plant-wool, and often with a few Ptarmigan feathers, so that it looked altogether white.

At the end of June, when the willows are in leaf, the young forsake their nests. During July and August and the first half of September, both old and young used to come about the houses, gathering in flocks on the refuse heaps outside the brewery, and, if then a cage with a decoy bird was placed near them, they were easily caught in a net. * * *

* * * During the summer they live to a great extent on insects, and one which I shot on the 2d of July had its oesophagus full of small flies.

Their song, which they deliver both when flying and perching, is but ordinary and consists mostly of trills, reminding one of the song of *Fringilla chloris.*

Winter.—In the large flocks of redpolls that occasionally visit Massachusetts in winter, greater redpolls are sometimes well represented. William Brewster (1906) mentions that "at Nantasket Beach, two young collectors, by a few random shots into an exceptionally large flock of Redpolls, secured forty specimens, of which six proved to be *linaria,* and thirty-four *rostrata!*"

Referring to the large, mixed flocks, he says that the subspecies and species "do not differ appreciably in notes, habits or general appearance. It is true that *rostrata* and *holboellii* may be occasionally recognized by their superior size, and *exilipes* by its bleached coloring, but Redpolls, as a rule, are so nervous and restless, and when in large flocks are so constantly in motion and so likely to take their departure at any moment, that a prompt use of the gun is usually indispensable to the positive identification of any particular bird * * *."

DISTRIBUTION

Range.—Baffin Island, Greenland, and Iceland to Iowa, Ohio, New Jersey, and Scotland.

Breeding range.—Breeds on Baffin Island (Clyde Inlet, Nettilling Fiord), Greenland (north to Melville Bay on the west coast, and to

avnsjord on the east coast), and Iceland. Has been taken in summer
1 Southampton Island.

Winter range.—Winters from the southern parts of breeding range
uth casually to Colorado (Magnolia), Minnesota (Kittson County,
Iinneapolis), Iowa (Iowa City), northern Illinois (Chicago area),
uthern Michigan (Kalamazoo), northwestern Ohio (Lucas County),
rthwestern Pennsylvania (Presque Isle), New Jersey (Princeton),
utheastern New York (Ossining, Shelter Island), New Brunswick
Grand Manan), Newfoundland (Locke's Cove), Ireland, and Scotland.

Casual record.—Casual at Helgoland.

ACANTHIS FLAMMEA HOLBOELLII (Brehm)
Holboell's Redpoll

HABITS

This subspecies breeds from northern Scandinavia across northern
urasia to northern and western Alaska, and migrates south in winter
) Germany, southeastern Siberia, and Japan. It wanders occa-
ionally on migration or in winter to southern Canada and the northern
Inited States, eastward to Massachusetts, Maine, and the Maritime
rovinces.

Ridgway (1901) describes it as exactly like the common redpoll "in
oloration, but averaging decidedly larger, especially the bill, the
atter usually relatively longer."

In the roving flocks of redpolls that are seen occasionally in New
England in winter we sometimes see a few that seem larger and darker
han the common redpolls with which they are associated. Unfortu-
ately for the field observer, there are two subspecies of redpolls that are
oth larger and darker than the common redpoll, either one of which
nay occur there at that season. These two forms are so difficult to
listinguish that it would seem unwise to attempt to identify them by
ight in the field. But, as Holboell's redpoll breeds as far away as
Ierschel Island and as the greater redpoll breeds in Greenland, it
vould seem that the latter might be the form more likely to occur
nywhere in eastern North America.

I have been unable to find any information on the nesting habits,
ood, or other habits of this subspecies, which probably do not differ
very much from those of the other northern races.

The measurements of 21 eggs average 16.9 by 12.0 millimeters; the
ggs showing the four extremes measure *18.9* by *13.0*, 16.0 by 12.5,
nd 17.3 by 11.9 millimeters.

DISTRIBUTION

Range.—Scandinavia, U.S.S.R., and Alaska to Manchuria an
Japan.

Breeding range.—Breeds from northern Scandinavia and norther
Russia across northern Siberia, western and northern Alaska (S
Lawrence Island, Barrow, Collinson Point), and northern Yuko
(Herschel Island) south in eastern Siberia to Kamchatka; in genera
farther north than *A. f. flammea*, though in unfavorable season
supposed to colonize within the northern limits of that form.

Winter range.—Winters from the southern parts of its range casuall
south to central Europe and central Asia; recorded in Manchuri
Japan (Hokkaido, Honshiu) central Alaska (Tanana), and th
Pribilofs.

Casual records.—Casual in southwestern Alaska (Kodiak Islan
in summer), Montana (Miles City), Minnesota (Ottertail County
Iowa (Iowa City), Wisconsin (Lake Koshkonong), Keewatin (Sout
ampton Island), Ontario (Moose Factory, Toronto), Quebec (Quebe
City), Massachusetts, Maine (North Brighton, Gorham), New Bruns
wick (Grand Manan), Newfoundland (Locke's Cove), and Grea
Britain.

SPINUS PINUS (Wilson)

Pine Siskin*

PLATE 23

Contributed by RALPH S. PALMER

HABITS

The pine siskin is a social bird the year round. Breeding indi
viduals join in social flocks away from the nesting territory, and the
sometimes feed in the tree where the nest is situated. These socia
groups are small, up to a half dozen birds, not the large flocks com
monly seen outside the breeding season. From late summer to lat
winter the pine siskin associates, roughly in descending order o
frequency, with the redpolls, the goldfinches, the two crossbills, th
purple finch, the cedar waxwing, and very occasionally, the juncos
Except for the first two mentioned, the association usually is brie
and may break off whenever a mixed flock takes flight. A commo
situation is to find the few siskins in the flocks of the other species
especially when goldfinches or redpolls are plentiful and the siskin
few.

The siskin is a relatively high and swift flier, often crossing from
ridge to ridge or peak to peak in direct flight far above the trees i

*The following subspecies are discussed in this section: *Spinus pinus pinu*
(Wilson) and *S. p. macropterus* (Bonaparte).

the intervening area. The flocks are compact, and all members execute long undulating sweeps in unison. Usually the birds fly silently, but now and again one or many may utter a sharp lisping call-note that carries well.

The decision to alight seems to come abruptly, and the flock drops down into the trees to rest or feed. It is common for the birds to be more vocal on alighting, and again as they depart. Often when feeding, there are no birds in flight; at other times part of the flock may take wing and pass over those still feeding to other food trees. As the birds thus go "leapfrogging," the entire mass of the flock of busy, lisping birds appears to flow through the forest. Then all of a sudden the lisping ceases and the flock is silent; it takes flight with a very audible whirring of wings and flies rapidly away.

By observing alders in Strawberry Canyon at Berkeley, Calif., in February, T. L. Rodgers (1937) provides a description of siskin habits that applies generally:

It began to appear as if the regular procedure of the birds was to alight in the top of a tree, forage down to the lower limbs, never spreading over an area more than 12 or 15 feet across, and then by means of a circular flight move to the top of another tree and forage down *it*. Although this was the commonest method, they were also seen to forage in a nearly horizontal line through a group of trees without foraging through any of them completely; they foraged up through a tree, and then moved by a direct route, at times even "flowing" from one tree to the next after the manner of a flock of Bush-tits. The direct flights of the flocks were either to trees far away or to those ten or fifteen feet off. This seems to bear out the idea that "circle flights" are survey flights.

The siskin's gait seems much better adapted to climbing about tree tops than to ground feeding. On the ground it walks with very short steps interspersed with occasional little hops, and its body almost seems to cling to the ground.

Many authors have commented on the siskin's tameness and boldness in its relations with human beings. Brooding females usually can be approached within inches before they leave the nest. Exceptional, however, was the experience of F. H. Allen (1888) at Newton, Mass., in late April. He observed two siskins near a heap of hops by the roadside. One flew away on his approach; the other, though able-bodied and in good condition, allowed itself to be approached closely, stroked, and caught in the hand. Allen queried: "Was this bird affected by the hops * * *?" E. R. Davis (1926) reported siskins at Leominster, Mass., to be remarkably tame in late fall. He says:

In a short time the birds came to regard me as their friend, and in the days that followed grew to be exceedingly sociable and to lose every vestige of fear. Whenever I would appear at the window, or step outside the door, down they would come and, settling upon my head, shoulders, and arms, would peer anxiously about for the food that they had learned to know I held concealed from them in a box, dish, or other receptacle. The moment I removed the cover or exposed the food, they would make a dash for it and the usual scrapping program would be on. Nor was it at all necessary for me to go outside the door * * *. In a short time the siskins discovered this opening [in a window pane], and it was only necessary for me to draw the slide when one after another would come right into my kitchen, and soon one or more of them would be perched on my head or shoulder, or hopping around on the desk where I was writing, looking for the handful of seeds that they all knew was forthcoming. * * * Now and then some members of the flock would elect to spend the night in the warm room, sleeping on the clothes-line, stretched across the room a little below the ceiling. On such occasions they seemed to be without fear and totally oblivious to people moving about the room, often within a few inches of them, turning on or snapping off electric lights.

The interested reader may want to read all of the above-quoted article by E. R. Davis. He carried out a series of conditioned reflex experiments. Only a paragraph about one of these (p. 386) is quoted here; it concerns a button rigged to release a small batch of seeds when pushed:

For quite a while the thing remained a puzzle to them. Finally, one of them happened to notice that push-button, which was a different colored wood from the rest of the contraption. He sidled up to it, looked it over for a moment, then gave it a "biff." This released the catch on the other side and down at his feet came a little handful of seeds. This frightened him, of course, and he flew away, only to return a minute later, eat the seeds that had fallen down the chute, and then tried to "press the button" arrangement again. It was not long before several of the flock had learned the secret, but it was quite a while before they became used to the seeds falling down at their feet, so that they were not afraid, and would proceed to eat them without first flying away a few inches.

A siskin's life is not always easy. During severe weather in March and April, 1939, many siskins died on Mount Desert Island, Maine (R. S. Palmer, 1949). Winter deaths, presumably from eating a poisonous chloride, are discussed under food. Various authors have reported destruction of nests, eggs, or young by wind, sleet, and rain. Heavy rains have killed young after they departed from the nest. Several observers, on finding nests empty and sometimes damaged, have suspected predation by the red squirrel and the blue jay. The domestic cat is a known predator. The cowbird, too, is a hazard, since its egg or chick in a siskin nest is detrimental to the siskin's nesting success. Both parent siskins treat the young cowbird as one of their own. At Wenatchee, Wash., R. T. Congdon (MS.) found a young siskin that had died after a foot became entangled in the nest lining.

E. R. Davis (1926) described siskin actions at the sight of a northern shrike at Leominster, Mass., in winter:

It was wonderful how quickly they would detect one of these birds in the vicinity, or even at a great distance. Instantly, if one of them appeared in the sky or on a distant tree, all activity ceased among the Siskins, and each bird, intently watching the enemy, would literally "freeze" to the spot where he was sitting, hardly moving a feather until the enemy had disappeared. On more than one occasion I have had them "freeze" on my hand, where they had been sitting when the danger threatened.

Aggressiveness is a marked siskin trait at feeding stations. Davis (1926) placed food on a shelf 3 feet square and found that "the bird that first reached the place seemed to consider himself the sole owner of the entire stand, and woe to the individual that dared dispute his claim." When feeding with purple finches the siskins are bold and usually hold their own. Generally they feed together peaceably, but now and again a siskin takes the offensive and darts at a purple finch, scaring it away. Perhaps the siskin's sharp bill gives it authority. In feeding with evening grosbeaks, the siskins keep their distance and show pugnaciousness only among themselves.

Territory.—Siskins go in flocks containing a few to well over a thousand individuals. Flocks of 50 to 200 are common.

At the close of the breeding season—usually early summer—the birds generally leave the breeding localities, although the extent and often direction of this movement is unknown. Then the birds may occur in or pass through the nesting area again in autumn. Large-scale incursions in the postbreeding period have not been noted as frequently as autumn and winter invasions. However, in Alberta beginning in mid-June and lasting into August, 1921, large numbers of siskins moved into the park country of the prairie where no evergreens occur except for small patches along river bottoms. F. L. Farley (1921) reports that at almost any hour of day one could see large flocks, "whirling here and there" in redpoll fashion. They would feed, then take flight suddenly.

In parts of the siskin's range near and along the Pacific coast, the species occurs in many localities all year, but a goodly share of the population moves altitudinally to the lowlands in autumn and to higher elevations to breed in spring. The highest altitudinal record is for a siskin that Taylor and Shaw (1927) found dead at approximately 11,000 feet on Mount Ranier, Wash.

The siskin's center of abundance is from the Rocky Mountains westward. Part of the population in the interior of the continent shows a more or less northwest–southeast movement in autumn and the reverse in spring. Thus it seems likely that the species may have spread eastward, as the evening grosbeak did at a later period, but before the event could be chronicled. M. H. Swenk (1929) wrote:

Judging from the fact that in various falls that they have occurred in Nebraska the Pine Siskins usually have been seen first in the more westerly and northerly parts of the state, and later in the more southeastern localities, and also from the further fact that they may reach western or central Nebraska commonly in seasons when they are uncommon or absent in extreme southeastern Nebraska, it is probable our Pine Siskin winter visitors are birds that summer in the Black Hills and those parts of the Rocky Mountains at a corresponding latitude, or northward.

The fall and winter wanderings, especially in the East, are so irregular in occurrence and so variable in extent that it is difficult to define the species' usual range as compared to its total range. At any rate there is usually some movement—vertical migration in mountains, horizontal elsewhere, both unpredictable regarding the amount or direction. In some years these movements become southward incursions of vast extent. Dorothy Mierow (1946) summarized as follows:

Some years are marked by exceptional flights of these birds southward. In 1896, enormous flocks were found in Louisiana, South Carolina, Missouri, and Illinois. Again in the year 1907, notable for its cold spring, flocks were observed in Florida, Tennessee, Ohio, Michigan and Missouri. This year they nested in Nebraska. The season of 1922–23 was characterized by an abundant crop of beech nuts and wild fruits, and again the siskins appeared in large numbers in Alabama, Virginia, Ohio, Wisconsin, North Dakota, and Nebraska. They were conspicuous by their absence from Yosemite National Park, California, in the fall of 1923. In 1925, they were seen in Kentucky and Michigan, and they nested in North Dakota and also at Ithaca, New York. There were abundant spruce, fir, and hemlock seeds in the Great Smokies of Tennessee in 1937. Siskins, usually rare in Tennessee, appeared in thousands during November. In other years, too, there were great flights at one place or another, but in these particular years the movement was most marked.

During an incursion into the southeast in the winter of 1946–47, R. L. Weaver (1948) saw five birds in Orange Park, Clay County, Fla., probably the southeasternmost record.

The pine siskin is commonly stated to wander continually throughout the nonbreeding season, especially during fall and winter. But when food is plentiful, many observers have noted that siskins will remain in one particular area over a long span of time. At Northampton, Mass., B. M. Shaub (1951a) analyzed his banding data for early 1947 as follows:

An examination of this record will show at once that the birds with which we were working were not, in all probability, wandering winter visitors or transients as they generally have been described. On the other hand they had more-or-less settled down in Northampton and vicinity for the winter and spring * * *. [Seven banded individuals] were with us rather regularly over a period of 2½ months, although it is possible that they could have made visits to other localities nearby and as often returned.

Courtship.—The pine siskin probably begins breeding when a year old, but data from banded birds to prove this are scant.

Richard Harlow (1951) states that there is abundant evidence that the crossbills and siskin have no definite breeding ranges. He writes: "* * * I do not know of any locality in our northeastern and northern forests where one can say, 'We will find the pine siskin here this year.' "

M. H. Swenk (1929), in his study of this species in Nebraska, correlated breeding records with temperatures of the months March, April, and May. If the mean temperatures for April were subnormal, the siskins might remain and breed; the same might happen if supernormal April temperatures were followed by subnormal May temperatures. Nebraska is, of course, outside the area where the siskin ordinarily may be expected to breed.

Usually the birds are numerous—often abundant—in areas where food is plentiful. The flocks contain both sexes. Scattered flocks tend to join, forming larger ones. By late January of most years, in localities all across the continent, the thin lispy calls of the siskin are augmented by a warbled song. At this time the flocks break up into smaller ones, then into groups of three to five birds, then into pairs.

There is considerable fighting and chasing when the flocks start to disintegrate. At Rutherglen, Ontario, Mrs. Lawrence notes: "In the midst of all this sweet singing, two birds swing into the air in an extensive 'cloud chase', their movements tightly synchronized as they alternate in the roles of pursuer and pursued."

Perhaps anticipatory to courtship- and nest-feeding is a performance observed in late April in Everett, Wash., by M. R. Thayer (1911): "Our attention was called to three birds on a [trellis] cross-bar about seven feet from where we stood. Two were close together and the third a little apart, and all three were opening and closing their bills, stretching them wide as if yawning and closing them with a snap. Before we had time to consider what it might mean, the two turned toward each other and touched their bills in a most lover-like manner. They were quiet a moment, then one opened his bill wide again and they both flew away followed by the third * * *."

Courtship feeding begins while the birds are still in flocks or small groups. On Feb. 5, 1948, at Rutherglen, Ontario, Mrs. Lawrence (MS.) noted: "The female sat on a twig. Presently the male alighted on the same twig, hopped up to her and offered her a small particle, of what I could not see. She crouched and, with trembling wings, accepted the offering."

The birds are still in flocks or groups when courtship flight with song reaches its fullest development. Two paragraphs from Mrs. Lawrence's notes describe it well: "With a beam of sun-shine illuminating his golden flashes, the male rose into the air with tail spread wide and wings in a blur of rapid motion. To the accompaniment of a flight song which seemed to express far more musical adoration than could be contained in so small a body, he described circle after circle around his chosen mate. That the female reflected none of her partner's emotion in no way seemed to dampen his ardor and, after he dropped on to a twig from pure exhaustion to catch his breath, a few moments later he rose again in a repeat performance no less ecstatic than the first.

"None of the flight song performances I saw ended in copulation. When that took place in my presence, it was an anticlimax to what I had previously seen. Two birds came to the salt lick and one of them perched in a bush. That very instant the male alighted directly upon the first bird by the pouncing technique without any sort of preliminaries. Copulation took place with both birds trembling violently. When it was over, the female begged and the male, with nothing in the bill, performed a token feeding. The female shook herself and both birds hopped down on the ground where the male strutted a little with raised head feathers."

Formation of the pair bond involves symbolic feeding, sexual flight, and song, and it occurs while the birds are in social groups. Single brood monogamy is certain, but how much longer the pair bond lasts is not known.

Nesting.—At times Siskins nest as isolated pairs. More usually, nesting is somewhat a colonial affair, with the nests rods apart. Adults join in social flocks away from the nests.

Typically, the nest is at middle height in a conifer, well out, and concealed on a densely foliaged horizontal limb. The most frequent departure from this pattern is for the nest to be located lower down, but when this happens it is still usually above 8 feet from the ground. Commonest choices for nesting are hemlock, pines, spruces, firs, cedars, redwood, cypress, and wild lilac. Introduced conifers, also transplantings of native trees, are occupied in addition to natural stands. Deciduous trees are used for nesting occasionally. For example, the siskin has nested in box elder in New Mexico (F. M. Bailey, 1928) and North Dakota (R. Reid, 1929), in maples and oaks in Oregon (C. Keller, 1891), in maple in Washington (R. T. Congdon, MS.), in the very top of a 50-foot eucalyptus in California (Carriger and Pemberton, 1907), among cottonwoods in Montana (A. A. Saunders, 1912, 1921), and two nests in lilacs in Colorado (F. M. Dille, 1900). The highest nests are at about 45 to 50 feet. In manuscript notes, S. F. Rathbun recorded a nest in Washington only 4½ feet above ground in a stunted cedar. The lowest record at hand is of a nest in Iowa, recorded by Dales and Bennett (1929) as only 3 feet up in a 4½-foot cedar on a lawn. During resting periods the birds go to tree tops.

The female chooses the nest site and is accompanied by the male as she brings nesting material. At times the birds return to social life in flocks; also, other siskins occasionally accompany the nesters on flights to the nest tree. As C. W. Bowles (1903) puts it, several pairs may be "superintending" when one is building. The small nesting territory is used for copulating—although this occurs elsewhere, too—and nesting; in addition, the male feeds his mate there during incubation and the period until the young attain flight. The defense of territory is developed slowly, being weak until after the nest is built. Weaver and West (1943) write:

> During nest building the male had been quite attentive to the female and never left the nesting area for very long periods, and he did not seem to be very closely associated with any of the other siskins or flocks which fed near the nest tree. After the eggs were laid, he would leave the area for short periods, which became longer as incubation progressed. He frequently returned in company with one of several other siskins. The female would chase these birds, as would the male, if they came too close to the nest. On several occasions, he flew off with these birds after feeding her on the nest. Other birds would enter the general nesting area and feed with one or both of the mated birds, unmolested.

As is common with a number of early nesters, the structure that the siskin builds is rather large in proportion to the size of the builder and usually well concealed in foliage. It is fairly well put together, generally somewhat flat, and often not very securely fastened to the branch. The foundation and sides consist of such materials as twigs, rootlets, and grass; the lining consists of fine rootlets, hair, fur, feathers, and other fine-textured material. The finer material, at least, is often gathered on the ground. Dales and Bennett (1929) saw a siskin dismantling an old goldfinch nest and using the materials in new construction.

Numerous photographs and descriptions of nests have been published. A good example of the latter is C. H. Morrell's (1899) of one found in March in Nova Scotia:

> It was saddled on the limb and radiating twigs but not attached to them. Considering the size of the bird, it is quite large, rather flat, and bears no resemblance to * * * [Goldfinch nests], measuring as follows: height, 1.63 inches; depth, .75; outside top diameter, 4 inches; inside top diameter, 2 inches. It is constructed mainly of dark pendulous tree-moss, with some fulvous bark from weed-stalks, plant-down, usnea, and other mosses. About the bottom of the nest is [sic] woven a few spruce twigs. The lining is entirely the pendulous moss.

From Eureka, Calif., R. R. Talmadge (MS.) writes of two nests that he considered distinct from all others he had found. The first was composed of fine grayish rootlets with a minimum of plant fiber and lined with black horsehair. The other was similar, but was lined with red hair from cattle that were in the immediate area.

Most of the nests discovered were similar in composition, but the lining was mixed, not distinct as in these two.

According to Weaver and West (1943), at Hanover, N.H.:

Three days were required to complete the outer layers and bottom of the nest. On the fourth day, lining materials were added. Several attempts to break off small twigs from the nest branch were observed. After the fifth day, materials were added to the nest sporadically until the eggs were laid. On the seventh day the female began making trips to the nest without materials and sitting on it for short periods. This procedure continued with the trips to the nest becoming more frequent and the time spent on the nest increasing to as much as fifty minutes before the tenth day, April 18, when the first of the two eggs was laid. The second egg was laid on the following day.

Eggs.—The data summarized from Mierow (1946) plus other available published and unpublished information through 1954, indicate that three-egg clutches predominate, about two-thirds as many have four eggs, a third as many have two, that clutches of five are rare but occur more often than those presumed complete with a single egg. C. W. Bowles (1903), for example, mentions sets of one (complete?), three, and four in Washington, and stated that three seemed most common. Carriger and Pemberton (1907), writing of San Mateo and San Francisco Counties, Calif., states that the "average set seems to be three eggs, but four is also a common number. Several sets of two eggs were taken in advanced stages of incubation, and also two sets of five, but these are rare." There seems to be no geographic variation in clutch size, but it is difficult to assess the data since most sets observed were from Pacific coastal states.

Carriger and Pemberton (1907) write: "The eggs are a pale greenish blue several shades lighter than the eggs of *Astragalinus* [goldfinches], and are marked with chocolate spots and irregular blotches, with a number of pale lavender blotches which appear to be beneath the surface of the shell. Eggs vary from very nearly unmarked, to well marked about the larger end and sparingly over the whole surface. The average size of all eggs at hand is .63 × .48 inches."

In a manuscript note, Robert R. Talmadge of Eureka, Calif., states: "Several sets which I have found had one or two unmarked eggs. The markings vary from small blackish spots to semi-elaborate scrolling of dark sepia and lavender."

All egg data at hand indicate that complete sets of fresh eggs usually are to be found in the United States and Canada from early April to early May. Eggs in March, or indications of their probable occurrence then, are as follows: young nearly ready to leave the nest March 19 at Woodstock, Vt. (E. H. Forbush, 1929); nest nearly completed March 15 (had three eggs on the 31st) and another started March 18, at Lincoln, Nebr. (M. H. Swenk, 1929); Siskin gathering nesting material March 16 in San Francisco County, Calif. (M. S. Ray, 1916); nest completed March 11 had three eggs on March 18, also nest with two nearly fledged young on April 13, in Lewis County, N.Y. (C. H. Merriam, 1878); nest with two eggs and two newly hatched young March 28 or 29, at Tacoma, Wash. (J. H. Bowles, 1924); clutch of four on March 29 in Nova Scotia (C. H. Morrell, 1899); nest with two eggs taken on unstated March day in Ontario (Baillie and Harrington, 1937); and unstated number of eggs the last of the month in Vermont (Tracy *in* Mierow, 1946). Fresh eggs in May and early June are common but why many fresh clutches have been found in California in early June is a matter for speculation.

The set of eggs of the pine siskin varies from three to six; sets of four and five are most frequent. They are ovate with some tendency toward short-ovate and have very little lustre. The ground color is greenish-white or bluish-white, delicately speckled and spotted with "light cinnamon drab," "cinnamon drab," "warm sepia," or "Verona brown," with a few thin scrawls of black. In general, the markings are concentrated somewhat toward the large end where they often form a loose wreath; rarely an egg is found that is almost immaculate.

The measurements of 50 eggs average 16.6 by 12.4 millimeters; the eggs showing the four extremes measure *18.0* by *13.1*, and *14.3* by *11.3* millimeters.

Eggs are laid on successive days. Weaver and West (1943) say that at Hanover, N.H., both eggs of a two-egg clutch "were laid before nine o'clock in the morning. Incubation began upon the laying of the first egg and the young hatched thirteen days later, one day apart. * * * The danger from freezing of the eggs would appear to be lessened with incubation beginning upon the laying of the eggs."

Only the female has an incubation patch and she alone incubates. Weaver and West (1943) write: "During incubation, the female stayed very close to the nest. The longest observed period that the female was off the nest for the entire period of incubation was eight minutes. She was fed by the male during incubation, and this permitted long uninterrupted periods on the nest; in fact, he began feeding her on the nest the day before the first egg was laid and in one instance was observed to feed her while she was off the nest before the eggs were laid.

Hatching is described by the same authors (1943) as follows: "Just prior to hatching, the female stood up on the edge of the nest and looked at the eggs a great many times. Hatching occurred early in the morning, before 7:30 a.m., or possibly during the night. There was no sign of the egg shell in the nest, but later a small piece was found under the tree.

Young.—In the above-mentioned nest, "feeding of the young began very soon after hatching, possibly within the hour." Weaver and West reported that, during the first few days after hatching, the female fed the young about every 10 to 15 minutes, but near the end of the nestling period feedings were about an hour apart. For the first 7 or 8 days the male fed the female on the nest and she fed the young; he increased his trips with food to twice an hour, and made even three or four trips per hour toward evening. On the 7th or 8th day he began to feed the young directly. After the 10th day, the male was not seen to feed the female and she began to forage for herself and the young.

The usual method of male feeding female when the young are small has been reported from Berkeley, Calif., by T. L. Rodgers. The bird on the nest hears *ti-er, ti-er* from the mate in another tree, and replies *ti-er*. They call back and forth three or four to a dozen times, and the food bearer flies to a position a few feet from the nest and utters one or more plaintive *pseee* notes. Then, while both are silent, it hops quietly toward the brooding bird. She flutters her wings and begs and the feeder regurgitates. Rodgers (1937) states: "The feeding process continued by the clasping of the bills of the two birds, the upper and lower mandibles of one just closing the complete gape of the other. Three or four such contacts were made, and, between each, the bird doing the feeding gulped as if bringing more food into its mouth. The bird then flew away, and the brooding bird sat quietly for eight or ten seconds before proceeding to feed the young."

This regurgitative feeding of the brooding female by the male was observed at close range at Sioux City, Iowa, by Dales and Bennett (1929), who pointed out that the process is a comparatively long one. Their description of a feeding ends thus: "Toward the end of the feeding as the male withdrew his beak from the female's mouth a string of saliva-like substance stretched between the two bills; this was immediately sucked in by the female. There must have been considerable of it, for there seemed to be a flow of it for nearly fifteen seconds. Then the male flew away."

The food-bearing male sometimes is accompanied by other siskins who do not trespass in the small defended area around the nest. They perch in the nest tree, or in nearby trees; they also accompany the male when he departs, as several observers have noted. The female also joins social groups.

Weaver and West state that the young never were left unprotected more than 11 minutes, that during the first week the female's usual duration of absence was 3 minutes. She kept the nest clean by eating all excreta for the first 7 or 8 days; later it became fouled because neither parent removed the droppings. T. L. Rodgers (1937) observed the eating of the droppings. He states that the nest was kept clean during the first 8 days and, from the 9th day on, no droppings were taken from the nest and they accumulated there.

Data on the growth and development of young siskins have not been published in detail. In New Hampshire, Weaver and West (1943) report that the brood of two young they studied showed their first fear reactions about in their 6th day. The young became very active during the last 4 days of nest life and the female then spent little time brooding them. They took turns exercising and stretching their wings, also walking on the nest rim. In their haste to be fed, they sometimes fell over the side and grasped the outer structure and pulled themselves back again. They say that "The adults seemed to approach the nest rather deliberately during the last 2 days, seemingly coaxing the young to such daring feats."

Both young left the nest 15 days after the first hatched; thus one was a nestling 14 days (it probably departed prematurely) and the other 15, which may be the usual initial flight age.

One young was seen being fed in the nest tree an hour or so after both had left the nest. Other observers have indicated that the young are with the parents and fed several days, or longer, but the span of time from nest-leaving to independence remains unknown.

Whether our bird, like the Old World siskin, *Spinus spinus*, is double-brooded is still a moot point. There is a strong probability that it is—at least in some years—and that the birds may change localities between nestings. E. H. Forbush (1929), without direct support, says: "One brood yearly, probably two in many cases." Suggestive is a single sentence by William Brewster (1938) relative to the siskin on Aug. 9, 1873, at Lake Umbagog on the Maine–New Hampshire boundary: "A male shot this morning was unmistakably breeding and yet full-grown young are about in considerable numbers." As already shown, the siskin is an early nester; also, fresh eggs are fairly common as late as early June in some localities and seasons, especially Pacific coastal states, and eggs or nestlings in July have been recorded for a number of localities widely spaced geographically. Here are some late breeding records: set of five eggs July 22 in Ontario (Baillie and Harrington, 1937); pair of siskins seen copulating July 30 on Forrester Island, Alaska (Willett, *in* Mierow, 1946); nest with young August 4 in Faith Valley, Calif. (Bassett, *in* Mierow, 1946); birds in breeding condition carrying nesting material, July 15–August 14, in the Porcupine Mountains, Mich. (W. B. Barrows, 1912); four young left the nest August 19 at Bozeman, Mont. (A. A. Saunders, 1921); clutch of three fresh eggs August 14 at Tacoma, Wash. (C. W. Bowles, 1903); and nests "containing young in early September," also at Tacoma (J. H. Bowles, 1924). Omitted are various late dates for adults reported as seen "feeding young"; it is assumed they are for young that have been flying, and for an unknown length of time.

It seems that the very long span of breeding dates can hardly be explained in terms of replacement layings after a loss of an earlier clutch or brood. More likely, either some birds breed twice in some years or different parts of the population breed at different times.

Plumages.—There is little sexual dimorphism although, after the juvenal stage, and presumably among birds of equal age and state of plumage wear, males are usually more brilliantly colored. This applies especially to the yellow portions of wing and tail.

Breeding adults are grayish brown above, heavily streaked with dusky; the paler rump is often tinged with yellow. Wings and tail are mainly dusky. The basal portions of the flight feathers are yellow, and are conspicuous in flight but almost entirely concealed when the birds are at rest. There are two narrow whitish wing bars. Underparts are whitish, heavily streaked with dusky except from the abdomen posteriorly when it is often plain. The bill is brownish or dusky at the tip, becoming paler (flesh colored or bluish) toward the base, especially the lower mandible. The iris is brown. Legs and feet vary greatly in color, but usually are medium light to a darker shade of brown. This breeding condition is a result of wear and fading of the plumage acquired months beforehand by a partial post-juvenal molt in the case of young birds and a complete postnuptial molt in the case of adults.

At Rutherglen, Ontario, in 1948, siskins were plentiful and nested. Mrs. Louise de Kiriline Lawrence (MS.) saw the first flying young on May 10. On May 22 females with incubation patches were noted going into molt and, in general, acquiring fat—first on the abdomen, then on the axilla, and last on the fulcrum. The birds then left the area, the last seen on June 3.

After the postnuptial molt—details of it have been described by T. and E. McCabe (1928)—the new fresh plumage has these characteristics: orange-buff wing bars; strong dusky markings and yellowish edges on back feathers; buffy or yellowish tint on abdomen (which may be either heavily or lightly streaked or plain); and buffy chest and flanks.

Although the natal down has been observed quite often, apparently no description of it has been published. The photographs in the article by T. L. Rodgers (1937) indicate that a well developed nestling down exists.

The development of the juvenal plumage has not been described; it is developed to the point that initial flight occurs at 15 days of age. This plumage is more buffy and warmer in general tone than the worn breeding plumage of the adults it associates with, so the two age groups then can be distinguished afield. After wear and fading, it is very similar in general aspect to that of worn adult plumage.

The juvenal plumage is worn a long time, probably two months according to Dwight (1900), but the exact time is hard to determine because of the irregular breeding season. Rockwell and Wetmore (1914) state that immature birds were still in molt in Colorado the first week in October. They mention young out of the nest July 18, but since the duration of molt is not known, one cannot estimate the time lapse before it began. Winter flocks of incursion visitants usually are preponderantly birds of the year, but this is hardly a clue in interpreting A. T. Wayne's (1906) comment for the period Dec. 12, 1896, to the following mid-March in South Carolina: "Between these dates many of the birds taken seemed to be in a state of perpetual molt."

According to Dwight (1900), there is a partial post-juvenal molt in August in eastern Canada involving body plumage but not wings and tail. The first nuptial stage, therefore, is this combination in worn condition.

Food.—The pine siskin is a tree- and ground-foraging finch. Like the crossbill, it often hangs upside down when feeding in vegetation, but it is a more generalized feeder, not tied closely to cone feeding and hence independent of the varying extent of the cone crop.

The results of food habits analyses were summarized by W. L. McAtee (1926): "The food of the siskin is principally the seeds of coniferous trees, alder, birch, ragweed, and other weeds. About one-sixth of the total food is animal, consisting chiefly of caterpillars, plant lice, scale insects, and grasshoppers. No doubt the siskin pays, in the destruction of these pests, for the forest seeds it consumes."

Two decades later Dorothy Mierow (1946), having more published information to summarize, wrote:

They feed their young mainly on aphids and seem quite content with alder, birch, and willow seeds. As they wander farther south and over the plains, their main items of diet may become weed seeds. Farther east, seeds of sweet gum, maple, and elm, as well as buds and insects, form part of their diet. In California, where they seem to be most numerous, they often feed almost entirely on the seeds of eucalyptus, extracting them from the pods either on the trees or on the ground. They also seek after the sweet liquid in the eucalyptus flowers.

The following information elaborates on the taking of some of the items already mentioned. Also, in some measure, it indicates seasonal and geographical variation in food habits, plus mentioning some items taken that might not be readily identified in analysis of contents of digestive tracts.

In early April in Ohio, examination of a siskin revealed it had been feeding on flower buds of the slippery elm (Kemsies, 1948). In June in West Virginia, Maurice Brooks (1943) saw siskins avidly eating the coated carpels of young spruces. Mr. R. E. Mumford writes of seeing birds feeding on Jack Pine cones (*Pinus banksiana*) during an invasion of Indiana during the winter of 1952–1953.

After Oct. 4, 1889, at Lake Umbagog, Maine, they were feeding exclusively on the seeds of birches (Brewster, 1938).

John F. Ferry (1907) writes that, in winter in northeastern Illinois, "they were observed to feed industriously on coneless branches of pines and spruces. The object sought was probably the dry resinous aments of these conifers. They frequent patches of thistle and seed-bearing weeds and work very actively and in perfect silence."

In South Carolina in the winter of 1896–97, a time of siskin abundance there, Arthur Wayne (1906) observed them "feeding on the seeds of sweet gum (*Liquidamber styraciflua*), and shortleaf pine (*Pinus mitis*)."

During a winter and spring when siskins were common at San Diego, Calif., F. F. Gander (1929b) noted that their food was almost entirely seeds of various species of eucalyptus, which they obtained from pods on the trees and also among fallen leaves.

In Flathead County, Mont., on Aug. 7, 1915, A. D. DuBois (MS.) recorded pine siskins eating thistle seeds along the railway. "I watched one for some time. He would fly to a thistle head and, clinging to it, sometimes nearly upside down, would pull out the cottony tufts one or two at a time, very dexterously and rather rapidly, working his bill along to the seed which he removed and then threw the fluff to the breeze, immediately working out another tuft. He pulled them part way out, a bunch at a time, afterward slipping them along until they came out one at a time or sometimes two."

In North Dakota, O. A. Stevens (MS.) wondered how the siskins got dandelion seeds. On investigation he found that they did not wait for the heads to open, but pulled off some of the bracts and took the seeds before they were fully ripe.

In two areas, on opposite sides of the continent, the siskin has reportedly done extensive damage to vegetable and flower gardens. From Independence Lake, British Columbia, T. and E. McCabe (1929) write regarding areas recently opened to farming:

None of us who have vegetable gardens has been spared by the siskins. Our own case is the most extreme, as we have attracted the species by means of amazingly effective salt and clay baits for banding purposes. It is now impossible to raise most vegetables except under wire. In rather long experience of gardens and their pests we have seen nothing to rival the instantaneous devastation which an unobtrusive flock of siskins can inflict, often before their presence in a garden has been noticed. Not once, but season after season, and time after time within the same season, we have seen long rows of seedling beets, chard, lettuce, radishes, and onions, cut neatly to the ground. * * * Peas and cole crops, as far as we know, are not taken, but we hear of the destruction of turnips. * * *

The farmers nearer the Fraser [River] suffer as much as we do, and in spite of being further from the mountains, more than most of our nearer neighbors. We know of one ranch where for years a barn door has been used as a deadfall, and the birds fed to hogs by bucketfuls. In another case great numbers are shot, and as many as thirty-five have been picked up as the result of enfilading a row of vegetables with a single charge of shot. As the typical associations of the Canadian Zone are left behind, and the greater drouth and summer heat of the river flats approached, the nuisance decreases. From the immediate vicinity of Quesnel we hear a few scattered complaints of moderate losses, but a short distance southward, within touch of the long arm of Transition Zone conditions, which stretches so far up the valley, all knowledge of the trouble seems to disappear, though we do not know where it may recur.

In Maine, siskins occurred in thousands in the spring and summer of 1925. Forbush (1929) states that they "invaded gardens, stripped beets, beans and other plants of their leaves, and ate the blossoms of many flowering plants." A correspondent in Patten, Maine, wrote Forbush that he had seen "as many as a thousand birds on a half acre."

Both the insect foods and ways of obtaining these are varied. In Ohio during a "most unseasonable and heavy snow in early October, these little birds surrounded our houses and literally skimmed the outer walls of all insect life. From foundation to eaves they hunted in every nook and corner, capturing spiders, flies, cocoons, * * *." (J. L. Parsons, 1906.)

In February at Alameda, Calif., an oak (*Quercus agrifolia*) was swarming with siskins. F. N. Bassett (1923) noted that the birds were procuring their food from the lower surfaces of the leaves. Many leaves were afflicted with the gall of a saw-fly, *Callirhytis bicornis*. Bassett reports: "The galls were attached to the midrib or a lateral vein on the lower surfaces of the leaves. They were composed of leaf material, light green in color (lighter than the leaf), from two to four millimeters long and shaped somewhat like a miniature saddle, being depressed in the middle and rising to an apex at both ends. Each contained a minute milky-white grub and many close views revealed the birds 'shelling' the galls and devouring the contents exactly as a domestic canary shells its seeds."

In February at Berkeley, Calif., T. L. Rodgers (1937) writes about siskins feeding in Monterey cypress:

I was unable at first to determine, by observation, exactly what the birds were eating, so I collected one hundred cypress tips, averaging three inches long and representative of places all over the side of a tree on which I watched many siskins foraging. Examination of the cypress tips showed many psocid-like insects, many scale insects, a few small green caterpillars, and many yellow larvae that were inside thin-walled cavities in enlarged green vegetative tips. There were few indications of broken-off vegetative tips, but some were damaged, which probably indicated that some of the yellow larvae had been torn from their chambers. The indication was quite definite that the siskins were taking only insect food.

Rodgers also saw a siskin picking aphids which it fed to a young bird just out of the nest. In April at Seattle, Wash., S. F. Rathbun

(MS.) recorded this observation: "I noticed that, when alighting on any older limb, the siskins would examine it closely until its extremity was reached, and this was particularly the case when any had the appearance of being dead. Then the bird would clip or break off the twig's end. I examined one of the twigs that fell and, in breaking it, I found deeply embedded within a fat grayish-green grub, evidently the larva of a twig-boring insect. This explained the siskins' actions."

The McCabes (1929) mention the attraction that salt and clay have for siskins. In an earlier article (1928) they state: "The attraction has always been some mineral food, relish, or medicament, natural or artificial. Ashes, deep blue clay from a cellar hole, salt, and newly-set Portland cement have all had their periods of favor." The habit has been noted in different seasons and at widely separated points. Mierow (1946) made the general statement that a "necessary item in the siskin's diet, as well as in that of other boreal finches, is some kind of mineral salt." D. S. Farner (1952) reported this habit in Crater Lake National Park as follows: "Although to a much lesser extent, siskins display 'salt-feeding habits' similar to those of the Red Crossbills. Especially during the summer of 1951 it was possible to observe siskins pecking at the powdery crusts on the andesite rocks."

In the first half of March 1941, between Saranac Lake and Tupper Lake, N.Y., the road had been treated with a mixture of sand and calcium chloride—the latter apparently added as a binder for the former. G. M. Meade (1942) quotes an observer as follows:

For several days great numbers of White-winged Crossbills and small numbers of Red Crossbills and Pine Siskins settled on the road to eat the salt. The roadbed was covered with them and it was almost impossible to scare them away even by using the horn. They appeared to be too sick to rise and even though motorists drove slowly they were killed in great numbers. The surface of the snow-covered road was actually reddened by the blood and feathers of the birds. My estimate is that there were at least a thousand birds killed.

From Rutherglen, Ontario, it is clear from the following observations for the winter of 1947–48 by Louise de Kiriline Lawrence (MS.) that salt in some form is a real desideratum of siskins. She writes: "At this time, the birds were encountered chiefly on the highway where they assembled in dense flocks, eating gravel mixed with chloride. Soon after sun-up they began to appear in these places with their numbers reaching a peak around midday, followed by a slow decline until, just before sunset, the last flock flew away to roost. Many of these birds apparently travelled considerable distances to these cherished feeding-places; I saw birds winging their way to and from the highway from the woods at least a mile away. When disturbed, the birds swung off the road as of one accord, amid exicted twitter, to alight in the trees alongside and there continue their feeding on the seeds of the evergreens, or on the buds of the white birches and aspen trees, with the siskins showing particular liking for the seeds of the alder-bushes. The siskins were a gregarious lot, associating freely with all the other finches, especially with the Gold-finches and the Red Crossbills.

"The pine siskins were first attracted to my feeding place under the pines, a little off the highway, by the coal ash pile. One day they dropped down from the surrounding trees by the dozens. I counted 92 before I got too mixed up by their numbers, all clustered into a little space 10 inches by 10 inches in front of my window. They ate the ash-dusted snow mixed with slopwater. On an old cedar stump I kept a block of salt. From rain and snow and the humidity of the air, the salt had saturated the stump and this saltlick became here-after the number one attraction. The birds crawled over the stump and picked the salt crystals from the block itself as well as from the top and the underparts of the stump, where the deposition of crystals was richest, and from the gravel around it, where the snow had been melted away by the salt. I put baited traps near the saltlick, hoping for some good banding, but not until I changed the bait to dried cedar seeds did my banding luck turn. These seeds proved irresistible to the siskins and when my supply ran out I put small dishes of water in the traps with the same excellent result. Thus, from January 7 to May 29, I banded 337 pine siskins."

Siskins can be attracted to feeding stations by millet seed and by chaff, and Forbush (1929) states that they are "extremely fond of cracked butternuts." They eat many of the vegetable foods com-monly used at feeding or banding stations, and eat suet occasionally. In winter at Leominster, Mass., E. R. Davis (1926) notes that whenever "an Evening Grosbeak came to the feeding-shelf and began cracking the seeds, he would be surrounded by several of the siskins. As he cracked the seeds, some particles of the kernel would scatter from his beak, and immediately the siskins would rush in and gobble them up. This act was not much relished by the Grosbeaks and they would often show their displeasure by a vicious peck at the intruder * * *."

Dishes of water, for drinking and bathing, have been used to bait siskins into traps for banding. At Sioux City, Iowa, a basin of water was placed under a nesting tree and both parent siskins came to drink and bathe (Hayward and Stephens, 1914). In March at Berkeley, Calif., T. L. Rodgers (1937) observed:

Several times, I saw siskins approach [eucalyptus] blossoms from above, lean over and reach into them. I had supposed that they were after insects attracted by the flowers, but twice I noticed that after reaching into the blossoms, they raised their heads after the manner of a chicken drinking. I gathered a large bunch of the blossoms and in every one examined found several drops of clear sweet liquid, with only a slight eucalyptus flavor. Later, I saw more siskins drinking from flowers, also a junco.

At Macon, Ga., in late December, a siskin was observed at borings made by a yellow-bellied sapsucker in the trunk of a sweet gum. The sapsucker chased it away (H. L. Batts, 1953).

Field marks.—It is somewhat difficult to distinguish at a distance between the pine siskin, the goldfinches, and the redpolls. Not only do these various birds mingle in flocks, but their size, manner of flight, call notes, and general habits, are all quite similar. The siskin, however, is characterized in all seasons by its dusky-streaked plumage (on grayish brown base above, more or less whitish or buffy below) two light wing bars, and, usually, considerable yellow on the basal portions of its wing and tail flight feathers. It has no red on its crown or black on its throat as the redpolls do. Siskins in juvenal plumage have the adult pattern but, for some time after they first fly, they are readily distinguished from their elders at close range by the worn plumage of the latter, the young being much buffier, their underparts often tinged with pale yellow, and their overall appearance lighter. Our siskin at any age is fairly similar in color and pattern to the female and juvenal of *Spinus spinus*, the siskin of the Old World—a species in which the adult male is redpoll-like in having a crown patch (which is black in the siskin) and a blackish chin.

Voice.—Various utterances frequently are compared with those of the goldfinch, redpolls, and canary. Call notes are given in chorus, especially when the birds alight or rest. Descriptive words commonly used by describers of siskin call notes are: weak, thin, lispy, buzzy, wheezy, and churring. In general their calls are more husky than those of the American goldfinch.

Ralph Hoffmann (1904) describes the common call note as "*chee-ee* given in a husky tone; when flying it utters a note like the syllables *tit-i-tit*. Another very sweet call, often given by a single bird to call back the flock, is identical with a note of the American Goldfinch." In winter at Anniston, Ala., R. H. Dean (1923) observes that, when siskins took flight, their utterances were *tit-i-te, tit-i-te,* several times in succession; sometimes notes were a smoother *see-a-wee.* On March 22 a new note was recorded, *z-z-z-z-z* (a prolonged *z*), weak, as are all the notes, but rather harsh. The *z* notes seem to be part of the song, "a weak prolonged chittering performance interspersed with the louder *z-z-z-z* notes." A. A. Saunders (1935) points out that the siskin has an "undulatory flight, calling *tit-a-tit* with each undulation." He also mentions a "husky but sweet *swi-sieee,* slurring upward at the end, much like the Goldfinch's similar note, except for the huskiness." He says that the siskin's song is uttered in choruses and that mixed choruses are heard when goldfinches and siskins flock together. The latter's song much resembles the former's, being a "long-continued series of notes, groups of two-note phrases, or single notes and long trills." The quality is "husky, and the trills fricative and like a loud long whisper."

From Rutherglen, Ontario, Louise de Kiriline Lawrence sends this observation: "From this day [January 29], the Pine Siskin's singing became common all over the woods. It was particularly intensive during the morning and early forenoon. The birds sang from perches, sometimes from the top of a bush along the road, at other times from the highest twig of the tallest tree. Their song included some of their common notes which seemed to serve as punctuations between the more elaborate sentences and a 'vireo' song, very like that of the Purple Finch, only with the performance in keeping with the Siskin's smaller size. A 'churry' (not 'burry') note also was interpolated often in the singing, so like that of the Evening Grosbeak that I several times mistakenly thought the Grosbeaks were present unseen amongst the trees. The weather had no effect whatever on the Siskins' vocal ardor, be the day dull and mild, or cold and clear with the temperature far below zero."

From Camrose, Alberta, F. L. Farley writes me as follows of a siskin found injured on November 29 and kept in a cage: "It is now more than two months since we have had him and we are all surprised with his musical ability. Between daylight and noon every day he sings just as continuously as most of the tame canaries, and the most interesting thing we have learned is that he combines the well known notes of Goldfinch and Redpoll and the rich ones of the tame Canary. Then, in between these songs come the nasal *squeez* or *issch* so diagnostic of the Siskin in its wild state. As I write now, he is singing quite steadily, and in between the songs he gives the Canary *e-r-e*. His songs are on a low scale and cannot be heard more than a third of the distance that a tame Canary's voice carries."

Enemies.—Friedmann (1963) writes: "Generally, the pine siskin is ecologically allopatric with the brown-headed cowbird, a fact which effectively protects it from the attentions of the parasite. However, there are places where the two species overlap and here the siskin is occasionally imposed upon. Eleven such instances have come to my notice, distributed among the following states: Iowa, Kansas, Nebraska, South Dakota; and in Canada: Ontario and British Columbia." To these may be added N. J. Ilnicky's (1963) observations of a pair of siskins feeding a newly fledged cowbird in Marquette, Michigan, on July 11, 1962.

Spinus pinus pinus is the wide-ranging subspecies occurring in North America north of Mexico. J. Grinnell (1928a) described it and its intergradation with the Mexican subspecies thus:

The birds from the northeastern United States and Canada are, in massed series, dark colored, that is, with sharpest and blackest streaking; also they include individuals showing least length of wing. The birds from Arizona, and most of those from California, are of relatively pale coloration, and some of them have longer wing than in any northeastern birds I have examined. Furthermore, there are many individuals, chiefly from southern California, which I cannot distinguish in any respect from Mexican and Lower [= Baja] Californian specimens. * * * * * * In other words, the range of variation in southwestern siskins is so great, and the possible average is so elusive, that, despite the *macopterus*-like individuals among them, I have come to the conclusion * * * [that] all north of Mexico * * * [should be called] *Spinus pinus pinus* * * *.

Spinus pinus macopterus (Du Bus) is the Mexican subspecies, about which relatively little is known. Grinnell (1928a) wrote that, compared to the northern one, it "is stated to possess longer wings and tail, and paler, less sharply streaked style of coloration."

Sutton and Burleigh (1940a) found it common and noisy in pine woods at 8,000–10,000 feet, in early April, at Las Vigas, Veracruz. They took specimens in breeding condition. For the period July 26–28, 1942, at 10,500 feet at Cofre de Perote in the same state, W. B. Davis (1945) reported that siskins "were just entering the breeding season in late July; females contained ova as large as 5 mm. in diameter and the testes of males were considerably enlarged."

DISTRIBUTION

Northern Pine Siskin (*S. p. pinus*)

Range.—Alaska, Mackenzie, Ontario, and Labrador to northern Mexico and Gulf Coast states.

Breeding range.—The northern pine siskin breeds from central southern Alaska (Iliamna, Chitina Moraine), central western and southern Yukon (Fortymile River, Carcross), central southern Mackenzie (Moose Island), central Saskatchewan (Flotten Lake, Emma Lake), southern Manitoba (Lake St. Martin), northern Ontario (Favourable Lake), central western and southeastern Quebec (Mistassini Post, Anticosti Island), southern Labrador (Hamilton Inlet), and Newfoundland south to southern California (San Jacinto Mountains), southeastern Arizona (Mount Wrightson, Graham Mountains), southern New Mexico (Cloudcroft), southwestern Texas, western Oklahoma (Cimarron County), central southern and northeastern Kansas (casual Wichita, Onaga), northwestern Iowa (Sioux City), central Minnesota (Walker, Pine County), northern Wisconsin (Mercer), central Michigan (Kalkaska County), southern Ontario (Guelph), northern Pennsylvania (Hartstown, Monroe County), New York (Tompkins County, Ossining), Connecticut (Hadlyme), and Massachusetts (Needham). Recorded in summer from northeastern Sonora (Oposura), eastern Tennessee (Cosby), and western North Carolina (Black Mountains).

Winter range.—Winters at lower elevations, probably throughout the breeding range, north at least to southeastern Alaska (Gastineau Channel), central and western British Columbia (Lac la Hache), Montana (Missoula), southern Manitoba (Brandon, Hillside Beach), western and central Ontario (Fort William, New Liskeard), southwestern Quebec (Aylmer, Montreal), central New Brunswick (Fredericton), Prince Edward Island, and central Newfoundland, south to northern Baja California (Nachogüero Valley, Río Álamo), Sonora (Nacozari), Durango (Ciénaga de las Vacas), Coahuila (Sierra de Guadalupe), Neuvo León (Mesa del Chipinque), Tamaulipas (Galindo), southeastern Texas (San Antonio, Houston), southern Louisiana (Cameron, Mandeville), Mississippi (Rosedale), and Florida (rarely south to Miami).

Casual records.—Casual in the Pribilof Islands (St. Paul Island), southern Baja California (La Paz), Labrador (Cape Mugford), and Bermuda.

Migration.—Early dates of spring arrival are: Maryland—Laurel, March 5 (median of 5 years, April 11). Quebec—Seven Islands, May 24. Tennessee—Knox County, March 20. Ohio—Buckeye Lake, March 3 (median, April 20). Minnesota—Minneapolis, March 3 (average of 8 years for southern Minnesota, March 25); Duluth, March 14. North Dakota—Jamestown, March 26. Manitoba—Treesbank, May 2 (average of 15 years, May 16). New Mexico—Glenrio, April 4; Los Alamos (median of 7 years, April 13). Wyoming—Casper, March 8. Montana—Libby (median of 10 years, March 22). Washington—Pullman, March 10.

Late dates of spring departure are: Florida—Anna Maria, May 1. Alabama—Dauphin Island, April 26. Georgia—Statesboro, May 23. South Carolina—Charleston, April 21. North Carolina—Cullowhee, June 3; Roan Mountain, June 1. Virginia—Arlington, May 11. West Virginia—Cheat Mountains, May 31. District of Columbia—May 22. Maryland—Garrett County, May 29. Pennsylvania—State College, June 6. New Jersey—Bernardsville, May 22. New York—Cayuga and Oneida Lake basins, May 29 (median of 18 years, May 19); Central Park, Manhattan, May 24. Connecticut—New Hartford, May 29. Rhode Island—South Auburn, May 25. Massachusetts—Northampton, May 29. New Hampshire—Concord, May 19. Mississippi—Rosedale, May 18 (median of 16 years, May 5). Arkansas—Little Rock, April 30. Tennessee—Knox County, May 10. Ohio—Buckeye Lake, May 22 (median, May 14). Michigan—Detroit area, May 29. Iowa—Keokuk, May 15. Minnesota—Red Wing, June 1 (average of 7 years for southern Minnesota, May

24). Texas—San Antonio, May 21. Kansas—northeastern Kansas, May 29. New Mexico—Glenrio, June 6; Hachita Grande Mountains, May 22. Wyoming—Casper, May 17.

Early dates of fall arrival are: North Dakota—Jamestown, September 5. Kansas—northeastern Kansas, October 19 (median of 7 years, November 7). Minnesota—Fillmore County, September 14 (average of 6 years for southern Minnesota, September 29). Iowa—Sioux City, September 26. Michigan—Detroit, September 5. Ohio—Buckeye Lake, October 15. Indiana—Wayne County, October 8. Missouri—St. Louis, October 5 (median of 12 years, October 30). Tennessee—Great Smoky Mountains National Park, October 15. New Hampshire—New Hampton, August 25 (median of 19 years, October 19). Massachusetts—Martha's Vineyard, September 1 (median of 5 years, October 22). Connecticut—New Haven, October 8. New York—Fire Island, Long Island, September 5; Cayuga and Oneida Lake basins, September 7 (median of 16 years, October 14). New Jersey—Cape May, October 7. Pennsylvania—State College, October 1. Maryland—Laurel, October 3. District of Columbia—October 15. Virginia—Arlington, October 24. North Carolina—Rocky Mount, October 31. South Carolina—Charleston, October 31. Georgia—Athens, October 20. Alabama—Sand Mountain, October 26. Florida—Tallahassee, November 8.

Late dates of fall departure are: Washington—Starbuck, November 15. Manitoba—Trees Bank, November 10 (average of 14 years, October 26). Minnesota—Minneapolis, November 27 (average of 7 years for southern Minnesota, November 2). Ohio—Buckeye Lake, November 29. Mississippi—Saucier, November 27. New Hampshire—New Hampton, November 30 (median of 19 years, November 18). New York—Cayuga and Oneida Lake basins, December 8 (median of 8 years, November 24). Maryland—Laurel, December 23. South Carolina—Charleston, December 12.

Egg dates.—British Columbia: 5 records, May 1 to June 20.

California: 48 records, April 9 to July 12; 24 records, May 21 to June 25.

Colorado: 12 records, May 2 to July 5; 8 records, May 9 to May 14.

New Brunswick: 2 records, June 27 and July 16.

New Hampshire: 2 records, April 17 and April 18.

New York: 5 records, April 4 to May 25.

Ontario: 2 records, April 7 and April 14.

Washington: 11 records, April 4 to May 22; 6 records, April 25 to May 10.

Mexican Pine Siskin (*S. p. macropterus*)

Range.—The Mexican pine siskin is resident in northern Baja California (Sierra Juárez, Sierra San Pedro Mártir) and in highlands of western and southern Mexico from western Chihuahua (Pacheco) south to Michoacán (Cerro de Tancítaro, Cerro Moluca), Mexico (Mount Popocatepetl), and central western Veracruz (Las Vigas). Wanders locally in vicinity of breeding range.

SPINUS TRISTIS TRISTIS (Linnaeus)
Eastern American Goldfinch
PLATES 24 AND 25
Contributed by WINSOR MARRETT TYLER

HABITS

The eastern goldfinch belongs to a group of small, short tailed finches which includes the other American goldfinches and the siskins. These birds are closely related to the redpolls (*Acanthis*) and have traits in common; they collect in flocks during most of the year and constantly give their characteristic notes as they fly restlessly from place to place. They give the impression of being high-spirited birds, always happy and full of gaiety.

Bradford Torrey (1885) paints this picture of the goldfinch: "Our American goldfinch is one of the loveliest of birds. With his elegant plumage, his rhythmical, undulatory flight, his beautiful song, and his more beautiful soul, he ought to be one of the best beloved, if not one of the most famous; but he has never yet had half his deserts. He is like the chickadee, and yet different. He is not so extremely confiding, nor should I call him merry. But he is always cheerful, in spite of his so-called plaintive note, from which he gets one of his names, and always amiable. So far as I know, he never utters a harsh sound; even the young ones, asking for food, use only smooth, musical tones. During the pairing season his delight often becomes rapturous. To see him then, hovering and singing—or, better still, to see the devoted pair hovering together, billing and singing—is enough to do even a cynic good." Roger T. Peterson (1935) says: "The responsibilities of life seem to rest lightly on the Goldfinch's sunny shoulders."

Spring.—Spring is not the goldfinch's spring, in the sense that spring is the beginning of a breeding season, because the goldfinch does not build its nest until summer is well advanced when many of its favorite plants have gone to seed.

Francis Beach White (1937) speaks thus of their arrival in Concord, N.H.: "On arrival in the spring, flocks great or small are likely to cluster in the foliage of large trees, and singing goes on by the hour; one of these flocks was estimated at a hundred birds. In June pairs are seen, and the undulations in flight develop till they give the effect of a bouncing ball. On July 7th, a male gave forth a torrent of song while flying on an even course with rapid wing-beats, and then, having perched a moment, left with undulations closely compressed, fifteen feet deep or more.

"* * * In early July, the sexes are still flocking together, though some have apparently long been paired."

Dayton Stoner (1932) describes the goldfinch's occurrence in New York State in spring: "During the entire month of May flocks of eastern goldfinches are to be found almost everywhere about Oneida Lake, singing, and feeding on the buds of apple or the seeds of elm and other trees. * * * The small isolated wooded tracts and the open fields appeal to it and although a considerable local movement is displayed at this season it is without definite direction or objective. Often small flocks can be seen and heard as they pass high above the extensive wooded area north of Cleveland; they may even stop to rest and feed or sing in some of the trees, but they soon move on again.

"* * * Throughout June, also, the goldfinch continues its local wanderings, indulging its sociable tendencies and singing blithely in trees and orchards and on roadside telephone wires. It becomes then one of the most noticeable local species of birds."

The following, from my notes, describes a typical sight in eastern Massachusetts in spring: "A gathering of two or three hundred goldfinches, surely 90 percent males, feeding on the ground in a market garden among chickweed plants in bloom. They often whirled away, dozens at once, to telephone wires and the adjoining woods a field away, later returning to the ground again where they alighted with a quick turn. They sang in chorus from the trees."

Courtship.—John Burroughs (1904) describes an attractive little ceremony which takes place in spring: "When the change [in plumage] is complete, and the males have got their bright uniforms of yellow and black, the courting begins. All the goldfinches of a neighborhood collect together and hold a sort of musical festival. To the number of many dozens they may be seen in some large tree, all singing and calling in the most joyous and vivacious manner. The males sing, and the females chirp and call. Whether there is actual competition on a trial of musical abilities of the males before the females or not, I do not know. The best of feeling seems to pervade the company; there is no sign of quarreling or fighting; 'all goes merry as a marriage bell,' and the matches seem actually to be made during these musical picnics. * * * I have known the goldfinches to keep up this musical and love-making festival through three consecutive days of a cold northeast rainstorm. Bedraggled, but ardent and happy, the birds were not to be dispersed by wind or weather."

PLATE 24

E. Porter

A. D. Du Bois

FEMALE AMERICAN GOLDFINCH AND NEST

Illinois, Aug. 5, 1941

PLATE 2

Medomak, Maine

A. D. Cruicksha

MALE AMERICAN GOLDFINCH FEEDING YOUNG

Playa del Rey, Calif.

D. Bl

WILLOW GOLDFINCH FEEDING MOTH TO YOUNG

Witmer Stone (1937) speaks of a nuptial flight: "Occasionally we see a male Goldfinch flying high in the air more or less in circles, and after covering this imaginary track several times he will relapse into the usual undulating flight and drop back to his perch. This performance is apparently a display, incident to the mating season." Francis H. Allen (MS.) says of the song-flight that "the bird keeps on a level with the wings flapping rapidly and steadily instead of taking the undulating course as in ordinary flight."

Aretas A. Saunders (1938) reports: "On July 27, 1933, I observed what was apparently a courtship flight accompanied by song. The pair of birds was flying about over an open area, not far from a nest discovered later that year. They flew in great circles from 50 to 80 feet from the ground, undulating up and down, and the male singing a long continued song. After circling about several times they flew away, the male changing from song to the ordinary 'perchickery' notes."

I have seen several times a curious modification of this song-flight and find it mentioned twice in my notes: "May 21, 1913. One of four goldfinches, flying about above the trees (good-sized willows), changed from his ordinary flight to a slow, labored flight, the wings moving in leisurely, heavy beats. The performance suggested the flight of a chat when he mounts into the air and dangles his legs. In changing to this labored flight the bird, a male, appeared at once to become twice his former size, for the reason, I suppose, because we associate slow wing-beats with a good-sized bird." And on July 11, 1913: "A male goldfinch flying above trees, singing. Flight is a series of slow flops with his wings, giving the impression of a bird as large as a crow seen in the distance."

Nesting.—The goldfinch breeds so late in the season that full-size leaves afford ample concealment for the nest. Walter P. Nickell (1951) made a study covering 264 nests in Michigan during the period 1933–49. The reader is referred to his lengthy paper. The earliest date on which a nest was found containing eggs was July 6, the latest date for a nest containing young was September 25.

Nesting sites were not over 300 yards from feeding areas and the better the food supply, the greater the density of nests. Greatest density was in swamps. The species is tolerant in respect to territorial boundaries. Food seems more important. No nest was far away from an abundant supply of thistle seed. Territory which lacked thistle but which seemed otherwise appropriate was not used. Nickell lists an overall total of 36 species of trees and shrubs used for nesting. L. H. Walkinshaw (1938) supplies, in addition, an ash, *Fraxinus* sp., and *Sassafras variifolium*.

Nickell found nests ranging in height from 33 feet above the ground, in a red oak, to one foot in a hawthorne. Nests may be located in upright forks with an average of four vertical twigs evenly spaced to form a cradle. At times one side is unsupported. Another type is held between parallel uprights without support underneath. Another type rests in cradles of twigs on a horizontal branch. A fifth type is saddled over and around horizontal branches and fastened to small horizontal twigs or leaves. In two instances nests were wedged between horizontal forks, held in place by the overlapping of the nesting materials and by attachment on two sides, without support underneath. This nest, thus, resembles the semipensile nests of the vireos. Nests are so durable they will last several years, and so tightly woven they will hold water temporarily. The lining is of soft and warm materials, thinning towards the rim, frequently composed of thistle and/or cattail down. Spider silk and caterpillar webs are used to bind the rim of the nest with bark of stronger material such as grape or hawthorne.

Measurements show quite a range in variation. Nests tend to be deeper than wide, but many show equal depth and width. Average measurements for 79 used nests in upright forks were: 2.3 inches inside diameter; 2.9 inches outside: 1.5 inside depth; and 2.8 inches outside.

Margaret Drum (1939) states the feeding area may be more than a mile distant from the nesting site.

Thomas D. Burleigh (1925) found the goldfinch nesting in Georgia among pine trees, one nest "in a large short leaf pine, sixty feet from the ground and six feet out at the outer end of one of the upper limbs."

Several observers have reported goldfinches building in thistles. Clarence H. Bush (1921) says: "On August 8, 1915, while walking in a pasture containing many large thistles, I noticed a Goldfinch fly into one of these thistles, and later found it was building a nest in it. On August 22, there were five eggs in this nest and the bird was sitting. On this day I found three more nests in this same pasture, all in thistles * * *." Mary Emily Bruce (1898) speaks of a nesting in an orchard: "The goldfinches had chosen a tiny pear tree quite close to the house, and the nest was barely four feet from the ground." Walter B. Barrows (1912) reports a very odd site—"a nest with two fresh eggs found in a corn shock."

G. M. Sutton (MS.) accents the close relationship of the nesting site to water; more often than not the nest is over swampy or other wet regions. In Oklahoma he found nests in dogwood, oaks, elm-saplings, dwarf birch, red and sugar maple, quaking aspen, wild cherry, willow, and spiraea. Another 20 nests were built in shrubbery along the edges of marshes.

Andrew J. Berger writes of finding a total of 66 nests near Ann Arbor, Mich., during 1955, all of which were built in *Crataegus* sp within an area of approximately 19 acres. The nests averaged 50.0 inches above the gound, with extremes of 81 and 32 inches. Of these nests, 21 were destroyed (with either eggs or young), and 3 nests were never completed. In addition, one female incubated five eggs for a minimum of 25 days (but less than 30 days) and another female incubated five eggs for a minimum of 25 days (but less than 32 days) before deserting the nest. Forty nests fledged from one young (1 nest) to six young (1 nest). Berger's data indicate a nestling period averaging 13 to 15 days, but he has recorded periods of 16 and 17 days. Berger writes of finding a nest at Ann Arbor, Mich., on the early date of June 11, 1947. On examination "it was discovered that this nest was a double-storied structure and contained three cowbird eggs in the lower story."

Lawrence H. Walkinshaw (1938) speaks of nest building in Michigan, where the bird used the outer parts of dead branches of hawthorn, milkweed, and chickery. "These were stripped off in short pieces by the female, then carried to the nest. This bark fiber together with the soft downy parts of the milkweed and thistle seeds with a few finer grasses constituted the bulk of the nest. The rim was usually circled with a narrow band of strong fibers which helped apparently in holding the nest together when wet and when the young became older. The lining usually consisted of cottony materials entirely and these nests probably withstand the elements better than those of any of our smaller birds." Later (1939) he stated: "It required 4 or 5 days to build a nest, and a period, averaging at six nests, a little over two days followed before the first egg was laid." He says (1938) that the period of rest may last as long as 27 days. G. M. Sutton (MS.) points out that the pair shows so little interest in the nest during this resting period that a casual observer might well consider the nest abandoned.

Alfred O. Gross (1938) tells of the building of a nest he found in Maine, "lodged in a three-pronged fork of one of the slender, upright branches near the top of the birches. The birds were not coming frequently with nesting material. The female was the architect but the male invariably accompanied her, serving as guard and offering moral support and encouragement with his song. Sometimes the male brought nesting material but this was usually presented to his mate who packed it firmly into the growing walls of the structure. The work was not rushed but was done very deliberately. As the nest neared completion, visits were made only during the early morning and again in the hour or two preceding sunset. It was an easy task to record their visits since their arrival was always announced by their loud, cheerful notes, especially those of the male. On some of the visits during the latter stages of construction, no nesting material was brought but the nest was thoroughly inspected—the female, resting in the bowl, carefully shaped the structure and re-arranged bits of vegetable fibers and catkins which made up the bulk of its composition. There was none of the thistle-down which so frequently is a part of the lining of a goldfinch nest."

Gross (1938) writes: "On July 10, six days after the partially built nest was discovered, the structure was completed. It was a beautiful piece of nest architecture—4 inches wide and 2.5 inches deep, with a bowl 2.5 inches wide and 1.25 inches deep. The walls and bottom were so firm and so compact that they seemed tight enough to hold water."

O. W. Knight (1908) mentions: "As the young get older the rim of the nest becomes lined with a fringe of excrement, which is rather exceptional, for most birds carry away the ejecta of their young and drop it where it will not be offensive." Walkinshaw (1939), in accord, states: "The rim of the nest was very filthy during late nesting life but occasionally both parents removed some of the faecal sacs after they had fed the young."

An atmosphere of happiness, characteristic of this cheerful little species, pervades the nest life of the goldfinch. Gross (1938) brings this out:

The female did all the incubating but she was regularly fed by the male. His coming was always announced by a series of clear, warbling notes. The moment the female heard her mate she assumed a characteristic pose which involved throwing her head back with the beak widely opened and rapidly fluttering her wings. This action seemed to initiate the feeding response of the male. * * *

During the first five or six days [after the eggs hatched] the female brooded the young during both day and night. The major part of the food fed to the young was delivered by the male, who also continued to feed the female during his frequent short visits to the nest. No insects were seen in the beaks of the adults at feeding-time, and all of the food delivered was a semi-digested milky pulp of certain seeds. * * *

* * * Several times the female was seen to stand on the rim of the nest opening her beak and twitching her wings precisely as the young [now ten days old] did, in apparent anticipation of receiving food from her mate. Although the male fed her during the time of incubation and early life of the young, he did not respond to her desires at this time.

Walkinshaw (1938) says: "Evidently the reason that the male circles the nesting area so persistently is that he brings food to the incubating female. As he circles overhead, either she remains silent and he continues, or she utters a sharp, often loud, 'tee-tee-tee-tee' at which he immediately drops to the nest to feed her. This procedure has been observed so often from the blind and at different nests that it cannot be accidental."

Margaret Drum (1939) states that males, initially, do not permit other goldfinches to alight in their territories. If the male is absent the female will drive out other females. Once the male has begun to feed the female on the nest, though, the male makes little or no effort to defend his territory. A nesting study by H. Lewis Batts, Jr., (1948) mentions nests in maples, *Acer saccharum* and *Acer rubrum*. While there were four nests, only three pairs of goldfinches were present, and only two nests were occupied at any one time. The male fed the female, but otherwise took no part in nest building, except sometimes to help shape the nest.

Alexander F. Scutch (MS.) gives the following interesting account of the building of the nest by the female goldfinch and of the subsequent life of the pair at the nest:

"On July 31, 1931, I watched a goldfinch building a nest, about nine feet above the ground, on a horizontal limb of a young white pine growing beside a road near Ithaca, New York. The outer shell had apparently been completed, but the lining was still lacking. Between 8:30 and 9:50 a.m. the female brought material eight times; although the male accompained her he did not help to build. First she flew up with long fibers that trailed behind her in the air. While sitting in the nest to work them into the lining, she made a continual sweet chirping, answering the calls of her mate who rested not far off. When this material had been arranged to her satisfaction, she flew away and found a white cocoon-case of a spider. After settling in the nest she stuck it to the outer surface, then took it again in her bill while she rotated to the left, applied it to another spot on the outer surface, took it up anew and rotated farther to the left, placed it on the outside and took it up again—and so on until she had made a complete circuit of the nest. As she moved the cocoon from place to place, some of the silky threads, adhering to the first point of attachment, were drawn out to the second, from the second to the third, and so on; thus the strands of cobweb were drawn over the surface of the nest and helped to bind together the materials of which it was composed. Next the female goldfinch brought a great billful of silky thistle-down and deposited it in the interior of the nest. Sitting in the cup, she proceeded to shape it to her breast. She sank down into the ample hollow until only her tail and the top of her head were visible to me above the rim. From the vibratory movements of her body I inferred that she kneaded the materials with her feet, which of course were hidden from view. In all these operations she generally rotated to the left, or counter-clockwise. Whenever her mate was near, she chirped prettily to him without interrupting her labors.

"At a neighboring nest the male goldfinch, who usually escorted his mate when she brought material for the structure, once carried a billful to it, but hardly took the time to arrange it there.

"Between July 13 and August 3 I found, in the neighborhood of Ithaca, eight occupied nests, all in roadside trees except one that had been built at the outside of a small, isolated clump of pine trees growing in an open field. Six of the eight nests were in young white pines, from eight to eighteen feet above the ground; one was twenty feet up in a white oak; and the highest of all about thirty feet up in a roadside maple. The firm, compact little cups were generally placed well out on horizontal boughs, sometimes straddling the branches; and those in the white pines were situated in the midst of a whorl of branchlets that provided lateral support. One nest that I examined carefully was composed of bits of bark, grass and fibers of various sorts, giving the exterior a dark brown color, while the inside was softly lined with white thistle-down which matched the spotless eggs. Of the nests into which I could look, one contained four eggs, one five, and three held six eggs. At one nest the eggs were laid on consecutive days. By August 3 one goldfinch had just begun to lay, while another had newly hatched nestlings.

"Among goldfinches incubation is performed by the female alone. She sits with a constancy quite unusual in so diminutive a bird, as a rule disregarding trespassing small birds of her own or other kinds, men who move about below her nest and stand or sit without concealment to watch her, and the noisy passage of motorcars if, as often happens, she has built above a busy highway. For food she depends largely upon her mate throughout the period of incubation. She distinguishes him, evidently by voice, from other male goldfinches who fly about the vicinity dropping their little silver coins of sound; and when she hears her partner and is hungry, she calls out from the nest to attract his attention. Then her clear, tinkling, little notes are so sweetly melodious that one not well acquainted with the goldfinch might suppose them to be the bird's song. Once while passing along a road bordered with pine trees, I heard—so I thought—a goldfinch singing, and after considerable scanning of the boughs above me discovered a female sitting in a nest, so well hidden among the pine needles that, had she been silent, I should have passed by without suspecting its presence. Apparently she was hungry and calling her mate to bring food. Thus the pretty hunger call reveals the nest's position to the goldfinches' friends—and I fear that at times it must also betray it to their enemies. On a small scale, it is like the raucous hunger cry of the incubating female White-tipped Brown Jay, which in the Caribbean lowlands of Central America has led me to nests hundreds of yards away.

"Although it has long been known that the male goldfinch feeds his incubating mate, we have not much information on how often he does this, or how constantly the female, with such support, is able to cover the eggs. To learn something about these matters, I watched a nest situated on the bough of an oak tree that reached out above a shady suburban roadway. My first vigil began at sunrise on July 28. At 5:21, three minutes after I saw the sun's earliest rays, the male gold-finch winged close by the oak tree and the female called softly from her nest. After another three minutes he flew into the oak and the sitting bird called more loudly. He approached the nest with nothing visible in his bill but with his throat or crop well stocked with food, stood upon the rim, and regurgitated to her while she fluttered her partially spread wings like a hungry nestling. After delivering the meal he went away, but returned to feed her at 5:45 and again at 6:56. At 7:10, nearly two hours after sunrise, the female, who for the last few minutes had been fidgeting restlessly in the nest, left it for the first time since I began my vigil. She remained out of sight only five minutes, returned and preened her feathers in the nest-tree three minutes more, then settled on the eggs after leaving them uncovered for eight minutes. When, at 7:30, I went for breakfast, she sat raised up and panting, for a little circle of sunshine found its way through the luxuriant foliage of the oak tree and fell upon her nest.

"The following morning I began my vigil earlier, at 4:52, when the light was barely strong enough to reveal the goldfinch sitting in her nest amidst the clustered leafage. She remained quietly covering her eggs until 5:45, when she began to call loudly in a high, warbling voice. She had heard the flight-song of her approaching mate before I did. A moment later he arrived, perched on the nest's rim and fed her by regurgitation. Again at 7:04 she called out before I heard her mate's voice, but was not deceived, for he soon arrived and fed her, passing about thirty mouthfuls in quick succession. At 7:52 I left her on the nest. She had sat continuously for the first three hours after day-break, and during this period had received two generous meals from her mate.

"On August 1 I watched the nest from 3:35 to 7:35 in the afternoon. During this four-hour period the female goldfinch sat continuously except for two short absences from the nest, from 4:24 to 4:34, and again from 7:21 to 7:28—seventeen minutes in all. She returned to her eggs from her second recess just as the sun sank behind the crest of the hill beyond the lake. Her mate came to feed her twice, at 4:48 and at 6:14. At the latter hour I saw clearly for the first time just how the feeding was done—on earlier occasions the female's head had been screened from my view by the rim of the nest. The female goldfinch heard her mate's flight-song while he was still far distant, and called at first loudly, then softly and continuously, until he arrived. He stood on the rim of the nest and held his head above that of his mate, who pointed her bill upward to receive his offering. He took her bill in his, and through my glasses I could glimpse the white, viscid mass that he passed to her. Then he lifted his head slightly in order to regurgitate a second portion. He passed her twenty-one mouthfuls in this manner, then flew off for the night.

"During my nine hours of watching the male goldfinch gave his mate seven substantial meals. She took only three brief recesses from the task of incubation, totalling twenty-five minutes, and kept her eggs covered 95.4 per cent of the time. Of ten other species of finches that I have watched incubate, chiefly in Central America, none has approached the goldfinch in constancy of sitting. The next best, a Variable Seedeater (*Sporophila aurita*) covered her eggs only 81.2 per cent of nine hours, and she was by far the most faithful of four of her kind whose nesting I studied. All the other finches, big and little, incubated between 60 and 75 per cent of the time, during watches that lasted from 6 to 12 hours; a few received occasional morsels from their mates, but none was substantially fed like the goldfinch. Of all the passeriform birds whose mode of incubation I have studied, of whatever family, the only one that matched the goldfinch's record of constancy in sitting was the big White-tipped Brown Jay (*Psilorhinus mexicanus*). Among these birds of the tropical lowlands, the incubating female is fed by her mate and often by one or more unmated helpers in addition."

Eggs.—The goldfinch lays from four to six eggs with sets of five being the most common. They are ovate with a tendency toward rounded ovate, and have very little lustre; they are very pale bluish-white and unspotted. Occasionally, an egg in a set will have a few scattered spots of reddish brown, and rarely an egg will be found well spotted with "vinaceous fawn." Harold M. Holland, of Galesburg, Ill., writes that he has "a set of six eggs, taken locally August 7, 1946, all of which are so thickly and distinctly spotted around their larger ends as to be hardly recognizable, offhand, as goldfinch eggs."

The measurements of 50 eggs average 16.2 by 12.2 millimeters; the eggs showing the four extremes measure *20.0* by 11.5, 18.3 by *13.2*, *14.2* by 11.7, and 15.2 by *11.4* millimeters.

Young.—Henry Mousley (1930a) in a careful study of the nest life of the goldfinch stresses the point that the young birds are fed at long intervals, according to his experience much longer than is the case in wood warblers. He remarks: "* * * during the twenty hours I was at the nest, the young were fed on eighteen occasions, nine by the male, and nine by the female, at intervals of about an hour, or to be exact, once in every 53.3 minutes * * *." Checking his observations the following year, he continues (1930b): "It was about 10:30 a.m. when I arrived at the site, and 3:30 p.m. when I left, and during those five hours the young were fed eleven times, four by the male, and seven by the female, or at the rate of once in every 27.3 minutes, thus proving that a much quicker rate of feeding than about once every hour does at times occur."

Salient points in the life of the young goldfinches, as brought out by Walkinshaw's (1939) study of nests in southern Michigan may be summarized as follows: The body and head at hatching are covered with light grayish natal down. The eyes of some young birds start to open on the second day, but the average date is about 3½ days. Until the age of 6 or 7 days the young made little or no noise in the nest, but afterwards, for several days, they are very noisy when their parents return to feed them. At this stage of their development many more are destroyed than at any other period. They leave the nest between the ages of 11 and 15 days, and by that time they fill the nest to capacity. They often perch on the rim or on the near branches when the day to fly arrives, and some fly as far as 100 feet.

Gross (1938) speaks of the development of the young in a nest observed in Maine. His observations are substantially as follows: "By the tenth day the birds had grown enormously * * *. Feathers on all tracts were at least partially unsheathed, thus offering sufficient protection and insulation to make brooding less necessary. Even at night the female did not cover them, but roosted in the branches near-by. At such times the young huddled down in the bowl of the nest, their bodies producing enough heat to counteract the coolness of the night air." At the age of 12 days the feathers were "unsheathed to such an extent that all the naked parts were concealed. The yellow of the breast-feathers and the tones of olive and fuscous brown gave them an appearance of the completed juvenal plumage save for the tufts of down clinging to the ends of some of the feathers. They had increased so much in size that the little bowl of the nest was scarcely large enough to contain them. * * * The time was fast arriving for the young to leave the nest, and on the next day, when they were thirteen days old, the first young ventured out and climbed up one of the slender branches supporting the nest. He was soon followed by a second, and in the course of the next five hours all were out. By the time the last young had left, the first had attempted short flights from branch to branch. * * * The adults and young were seen in the neighborhood for more than a week, and made regular visits to the feeding-shelves and baths provided for them and other birds." I feel confident that all of the six young survived.

Gross gives the incubation period as 12 days; Walkinshaw (1938) as 12 to 14 days; Burns (1915) as 12 to 14 days.

Andrew J. Berger writes Taber that the oldest birds in a brood are capable of a strong, sustained flight of 50 yards or more when ready to leave the nest, but will flutter to the ground below or near the nest when disturbed prematurely, as by banding. The smallest bird often leaves the nest at a younger age than those hatched first.

Plumages.—Dwight (1900) describes the juvenal plumage of the young male as "above wood-brown, grayer on crown, yellowish on forehead. Below, including sides of head primrose-yellow brightest on chin, washed on sides and flanks and across the throat with deep buff. Wings and tail dull black whitish edged; secondaries, tertiaries, and wing coverts including two wing bands edged with ochraceous buff the outer greater coverts usually partly white. * * *"

He says that the first winter plumage is similar to the juvenal "but a deeper brown above and the yellow below replaced (except on the chin which is a brighter yellow) by pale olive gray, darkest on the throat and washed with wood-brown on the sides. The crissum and middle of the abdomen are white. Dull black, brownish or yellowish edged lesser coverts (the 'shoulders') distinguish young birds from adults which have them bright yellow, the black of the wings and tail is besides less intense, the wing bands are browner and the chin duller yellow."

The first nuptial plumage is acquired by an extensive prenuptial molt, in April and early May, involving all the coutour plumage but not the wings or the tail. "It is interesting to note that the black wings and tail are assumed with the juvenal plumage, the black crown at the prenuptial moult."

Adults have a complete postnuptial molt, beginning about the middle of September, which produces the adult winter plumage, "similar to the first winter but a richer deeper brown above, the crown, throat and sides of breast more distinctly yellow, the edgings of the wings and tail (which are jet black) paler and most important of all the 'shoulders' bright canary-yellow instead of brown. Young and old now become indistinguishable."

Adults also have an extensive prenuptial molt, as in the young bird. Adults in spring can be distinguished from young birds of the first year by the yellow "shoulders."

The molts of the female correspond to those of the male, but her plumage is always duller, her wings and tail are browner, and she never has a black cap.

Food.—The gold finch is primarily an eater of seeds, notably those of the composite family. Among its favorite food plants may be mentioned grey birch, alder, thistle, sunflower, evening primrose, ragweed, and above all, perhaps, the dandelion. It is, however, no uncommon sight to see the birds in spring, when caterpillars are small, picking them from their webs.

William Brewster (1906) says: "The Yellow-birds also subsist largely on the seeds of pitch pines, when these trees are well supplied with ripe cones." O. A. Stevens (1931) reports the bird "feeding upon seeds of the goatsbeard (*Tragopogon pratense*)" in North Dakota. Austin Paul Smith (1915), speaking of the bird in Arkansas, says: "While never seeming to lack a ready food supply, this varied much with the seasons. In the fall, favorite food items were seeds of catmint, burdock, ragweed, etc.; in winter, seeds of sweet gum and sycamore; in spring, the uripe seeds of various plants." Hervey Brackbill (1942), writing of Maryland, gives good evidence that the goldfinches rifle small oak galls growing on the twigs of white oaks to obtain a gall maker "at all stages of development—larva, pupa and adult."

Edward H. Forbush (1913) remarks: "During the spring, when unhampered by family cares, and wandering through fields and orchards, they feed considerably on cankerworms. They sometimes frequent grain fields, where they are said to devour noxious insects, including the Hessian fly. Goldfinches often feed very largely in winter on the eggs of plant lice; this has been observed many times. Mr. Kirkland examined the stomach of one of these birds, and found it contained two thousand, two hundred and ten eggs of the white birch aphis. *Chermaphis laricifoliae* is an aphis that is common on larches. It deposits great numbers of stalked eggs in April and May, which produce the young lice that feed on the trees in summer. Mr. Kirkland saw a flock of over forty goldfinches going systematically over some infested larch trees, beginning at the top of a tree and working gradually down to the lower branches, then repeating the performance on the next tree."

Mrs. Amelia R. Laskey writes to us that the food of the goldfinch includes flower buds and seeds of elms, seeds from the pods of the trumpet vine, and flower buds. Mr. Brackbill in his notes adds berries of Japanese honeysuckle and seeds of wild aster, burdock, chicory, wild lettuce, evening primrose, woodland sunflower, thistle, and tulip tree.

Charles H. Blake (notes) adds buds of the quaking aspen (*Populus tremuloides*) in late March, young leaves of the European mountain ash (*Sorbus aucuparia*) in mid-April, and seeds of the goldenrod (*Solidage rugosa*) in late September.

Mrs. T. E. Winford writes Mr. Bent of watching a number of birds in early March eating the seeds out of rotten apples. H. Lewis Batts, Jr. (1955), mentions seeds of thistle (*Cirsium*), Cinquefoil (*Potentilla*), aster (*Aster*), St. Johnswort (*Hypericum*), and certain grasses as winter food.

Floyd B. Chapman (1948) reports a case of the goldfinch eating fruit, which is not a common habit. He says that the birds came to feed in a very large June berry tree (*Amalanchia laevis*) heavily ladened with fully ripened fruit.

Alexander F. Skutch writes to us:

"All through the third week of April, 1931, large flocks of goldfinches were present in the woods near my parents' house on the outskirts of Baltimore. Here they fed in the elm trees, which at this period were green with their clustered keys, as though with an earlier and transient foliage. There was more music in their confiding call-notes than in many a bird's song. Hanging head downward from the slender elm twigs, the goldfinches plucked the winged fruits; not, so far as I could learn, to eat the small green embryos, but to extract a little white larva, about a millimeter in length, which infested many of the fruits and caused them to take on an abnormal, irregularly swollen aspect. The birds deftly bit the larvae out of the husks, then let the keys flutter to the ground, until large quantities were strewn beneath the trees where they had been feeding."

Economic status.—Forbush (1929) summarizes the economic status: "The Goldfinch is generally regarded as a beneficial bird. Its only injurious habit seems to be the destruction of seeds of cultivated sunflowers, cosmos, lettuce, etc., which is sometimes so serious to the seed grower that he is obliged to take measures to protect his crops."

Behavior.—The goldfinch is an active little bird, always in the best of spirits. It has a definite personality exemplifying light-hearted cheerfulness, restlessness, sociability, and untiring activity. It seeks the company of its own species and, in the winter, that of its relatives, the siskins and redpolls, often moving about with them in large flocks, roving over the fields, feeding together in the birches and alders and among the weeds protruding above the snow. When we come on a lone goldfinch it seems out of its element; it gives a long, sweet call, and appears to look about for companions or to listen for them, and when it sees them or hears their voices in the distance, it goes bounding away to join them. Its flight is deeply undulating; it flies along as if riding the waves of a stormy sea, giving, as it rises to each crest, its little phrase of four happy notes.

Aretas A. Saunders (1929) summarizes the habitat of the bird in the Adirondack Mountains, N.Y.: "The Goldfinch is not a bird of the forest, but prefers more open country with scattered trees. It lives in orchards, among shade trees, along roadsides, and about the edges of forests." Lawrence H. Walkinshaw's (1938) studies were made in Michigan "on an area of approximately thirty-five acres * * * constituting a ditched marsh with its scattered groups of willow, dogwood, buttonbush, other shrubs and small trees, together with a narrow bordering highland also sparingly covered with shrubs, small aspens and occasional larger trees."

William Brewster (1906) speaks of the bird's former occurrence in Cambridge, Mass., and the effect upon it of the introduction of the house sparrow: "Goldfinches used to breed nearly everywhere in and near Cambridge; in shade trees along our city streets; in orchards throughout the farming country; most abundantly of all in the maple woods and willow thickets which once covered so large a portion of the Fresh Pond Swamps. Within the past fifteen or twenty years they have nearly ceased to nest in localities where English Sparrows have become abundant * * *."

Margaret M. Nice (1939), reviewing her own experience and the available literature on the territorial behavior of the goldfinch, concludes that the bird seems to show a "sociable tendency."

Chreswell J. Hunt (1904) speaks on feeding behavior: "I noticed last winter a marked difference in the manner in which the Goldfinch and Tree Sparrow procure the seeds of the evening primrose when feeding upon the stalks sticking above the snow. The Goldfinch flies to the cluster of seed-capsules at the top of the stalk, and clings there while it extracts the seeds with its bill. The Tree Sparrow, on the other hand, alights upon the stalk and shakes it vigorously—making the seed rattle—until it has shaken out a number of the seeds, when it drops down to the snow and picks them up." Alexander Wilson (1832) remarks: "During the latter part of summer they are almost constant visitants in our gardens, in search of seeds, which they dislodge from the husk with great address, while hanging, frequently head downwards, in the manner of the titmouse."

Dr. Charles W. Townsend (1905) reports an interesting note on roosting: "At sunset of a winter's day, late in January, I found one of these birds anxiously flitting about a small pine grove on Heartbreak Hill, alighting at the bases of the trees, and finally popping into a hole about a foot deep in the snow under a stump. Frightened from there, it flew about nervously for a few minutes, but at last returned to the same hole close beside which I was sitting motionless. As it was so nearly dark, I had not been sure of the bird's identity, so I tried to catch it in my hat, but it escaped. It finally cuddled into the protected side of a footprint in the snow, and was there easily captured by my companion. It was evident that the Goldfinch had been searching for a protected hole in which to pass the night—a safe place in that region as the snow showed no mark of prowling animals. I have recorded this, for observations on the sleeping habits of birds are few."

Mr. Skutch says in his notes: "On the evening of July 27, 1931, while walking toward my lodgings, I heard about sunset the *chicoree* of goldfinches in flight, and looking upward saw several males tracing their undulations over the lawns between the houses. They had no particular destination, but circled round and round in an irregular manner and doubled back and forth, always rising and falling as is their wont; only it seemed to me that the hills and valleys they described in the air were steeper and deeper than usual. As they ascended each invisible hillside in their path, they voiced the characteristic flight call; and once one of them burst into full song while on the wing. I watched these pretty maneuvers for about five minutes, when gradually the birds drifted out of sight, perhaps to continue their play in other regions. I call it 'play' because they did not appear to be hawking insects—their flight was too rhythmic for that, yet for a number of minutes it took them nowhere. They seemed merely to rejoice in an exhilarating aerial sport."

G. M. Sutton (MS.) states he has seen a number of times a bird fly deliberately into a net close to a bird already netted and calling. When netted birds gave plaintive cries, other goldfinches flew into the net two by two. On one occasion he had 12 birds to extricate at once.

Charles H. Blake writes that when feeding from gray birch catkin the goldfinch does not as a rule perch on the twig to which the catkin is attached and rarely braces the catkin with a foot.

Walter P. Nickell (1951) comments on the peculiar behavior of abandoning many nests before completion, or at times after completion but before egglaying. Occasionally, nests with eggs, or even with young, are abandoned. He has seen goldfinches dismantling nests of the Baltimore oriole and yellow warbler, and using the materials in its own nest.

Voice.—Aretas A. Saunders in his unpublished manuscript says the song of the goldfinch is a sweet, sprightly, high-pitched one. Most of the time a single song is rather short, but there are occasions in the spring when birds sing long-continued songs, or songs of indefinite length. Often birds will sing together in a chorus. There is, perhaps, greater variation in the detail of song in one individual bird than one finds between the songs of different individuals. The song consists of short notes, groups of such notes on the same pitch, two-note phrases, occasional short trills, and rather rarely slurs. The number of notes per song, omitting the long-continued songs, varies from 7 to 22, averaging between 12 and 13. Songs vary in length from $1\frac{1}{2}$ to $3\frac{3}{5}$ seconds, averaging about 2 seconds. Pitch varies from $F\#_6$ to E_7. The pitch interval varies from one to four tones, averaging two.

Individual birds sing different songs, one after another, up to at least 7. In spite of the great variation on the part of one bird, there is a general likeness between songs of different individuals, and Mr. Saunders doubts that a person could identify an individual bird by the peculiarities of its songs.

In the spring, just after the prenuptial molt when the birds are still in flocks, a dozen or more birds may sing at once. At such times songs tend to be of the long-continued type. This type is often used also during the courtship period when the pair circles around with undulating up and down dips of perhaps 20 to 30 feet. On such occasions the male sings constantly while in flight. After nests are established the male simply sings from a perch, giving one short song after another. Frequently, song is over for the year before the young leave the nest.

The flight call popularly described as *perchickaree* and the sweet, upward slurred *sei silieeee* often are mixed with the song. There are other minor notes. There is the conversational *twit* or *tee-tee-tee*, a reduced flight call, perhaps, heard from feeding flocks. There is a lower toned, roughened *ggee* given in a moment of animosity, which rarely ruffles the tenor of the goldfinch's peaceful nature—"pleasantly quarrelsome" my notes say—suggesting a call of the snow bunting. I once heard a curious low-pitched note, perhaps a modification of the song, which was spoken rather than whistled, repeated quickly several times, and followed by *tee-tee-tee* notes, suggesting the song of the short-billed marsh wren. The note of the young bird, heard often in autumn, sounds like *chipee*, with the accent at the end. It is a pleading, insisting cry.

The song may begin in March before the prenuptial molt is completed, but it most commonly commences in April. Mr. Saunders' earliest record in Connecticut for a 35-year period is Mar. 15, 1936; the latest, May 1, 1938. The average date is between April 6 and 7. His latest record is Aug. 31, 1942; the average for last songs being August 27. In Allegany Park the last date was Aug. 28, 1935, and the average date, August 15. Mr. Saunders also has a number of records of songs during the autumn. He has three November records, the latest being Nov. 20, 1926.

Brand (1938) gives the mean vibration frequency as 4100, with the rather wide range of 7400 and 2750.

Enemies.—In addition to attacks by predators to which small, defenseless birds are subject, several accidents, dangerous or fatal to the life of the goldfinch, have been reported. For example, a goldfinch was killed by an aircraft more than 1000 feet above the ground (V. H. Brown, 1945); a dead goldfinch was found entangled in burdock (B. S. Bowdish, 1906); a bird was immeshed in a spider's web (George H. Mackay, 1929). John Burroughs (1886) tells the following experience: "One day, in my walk, I came upon a goldfinch with the tip of one wing securely fastened to the feathers of its rump by what appeared to be the silk of some caterpillar. The bird, though uninjured, was completely crippled, and could not fly a stroke. Its little body was hot and panting in my hands, as I carefully broke the fetter. Then it darted swiftly away with a happy cry."

Herbert Friedmann (1929) says that the goldfinch is a "fairly common victim" of the cowbird. "At Ithaca [N.Y.], a region where both this species and the Cowbird are common, and where many nest of this bird have been found, there are no cases on record. Dr. A. A. Allen, whose observations on this region extend over a long period, has never known of a Cowbird laying in a Goldfinch's nest, and my observations tend to show that the laying of the Cowbird is on the decline at the time when the Goldfinch starts to nest in numbers. Eaton (1914), however, lists this bird as one of the common victims of the Cowbird in New York, so evidently there is considerable variation locally. * * *

"Occasionally this species covers up the strange egg after the manner of the Yellow Warbler. * * *

"I have found records from Montreal, New England, New York, and Ohio, west to Indiana, Illinois, and North Dakota, and south to Oklahoma."

Walter P. Nickell (1951) mentions finding a nest infested with mites. Arthur A. Allen (1934) states young may drown in the water-holding nest. D. A. Zimmerman (1954) mentions 33 birds found dead on highways.

Winter.—In the parts of the country where it stays the year round the goldfinch is one of our most attractive winter birds. In the countryside about Boston, Mass., for example, we may see them, a hundred together, loosely associated with tree sparrows or more intimately with redpolls, collected in open fields feeding on weeds above the snow. Here they sometimes exhibit a habit common in birds thus gathered together; the whole flock progresses in one direction across the field by the birds in the rear successively flying to the front, over the heads of the others, seeking an advantage over their companions. In spite of this rivalry, however, a spirit of harmony and friendliness seems to pervade all the company. Perhaps the restlessness of the birds and the likelihood of their leaving the vicinity at any moment add to the charm of these gatherings, for at an instant, the whole flock may whirl up and fly away, perhaps out of sight and hearing.

In the winter flocks, goldfinches show so little difference in plumage that it is probable that the sexes are segregated, at least for the most part, at this season.

R. J. Longstreet (1928) reports a remarkable observation. On Dec. 22, 1927, at Daytona Beach, Fla., he saw "a large flock of Goldfinches * * * flying northward back of the sand dunes which line the ocean beach. * * *

"In the 100 minutes of actual counting at a given station, it is estimated that at least 6400 Goldfinches were seen. Inasmuch as the flight extended from at least 7:40 A.M. to 12:20 P.M., or 280 minutes, an average of 50 birds per minute (which seems conservative), gives a total of not less than 14,000 Goldfinches in the movement. How many passed before 7:40 A.M. and after 12:20 P.M., and how many passed too far to the west to be seen, can only be conjectured."

DISTRIBUTION

Range.—Southern Canada to Gulf Coast states.

Breeding range.—The eastern goldfinch breeds from central Nebraska, southern and eastern Minnesota, central Ontario (Lake Nipigon, Fraserdale), southern and eastern Quebec (Rouyn, Gaspé, Anticosti Island), Prince Edward Island, and northern Nova Scotia (Cape North) south to eastern Colorado (Fort Collins, Colorado Springs, Fort Lyon), southern Oklahoma (Sulphur), northeastern Texas (Cooke County), northern Louisiana (Monroe), northern Mississippi (Bolivar County, Oxford), central Alabama (Autaugaville), southwestern and central Georgia (Cuthbert, Macon), and northern South Carolina (Pageland).

Winter range.—Winters from northeastern Colorado (Willard), central Nebraska (Stapleton), southeastern South Dakota (Yankton), northeastern Minnesota (Lake Vermillion), northern Michigan (Ironwood), southern Ontario (London), southwestern Quebec (Lac Bonhomme), central New Brunswick (Fredericton), and central Nova Scotia (Halifax) south to western Texas (Presidio County), central Nuevo León (Mesa del Chipinque), Veracruz (Pánuco), the Gulf coast, and southern Florida (Miami).

Casual records.—Casual in northern Ontario (Moose Factory), Labrador (Cape Mugford), Newfoundland (Barachois Brook, Cuslett), and Bermuda.

Migration.—Early dates of spring arrival are: Virginia—Sweet Briar, March 12. West Virginia—Charleston, March 7. District of Columbia—March 11. Maryland—Laurel, March 20. New Jersey—Morristown, March 19. Connecticut—Danbury, March 14. Massachusetts—Martha's Vineyard, March 15. Vermont—Clarendon and Woodstock, March 28. New Hampshire—New Hampton, April 15 (median of 21 years, May 5). Quebec—Hudson Heights, March 24. New Brunswick—Moss Glen, April 12. Nova Scotia—Wolfville, April 4; Digby, April 9. Newfoundland—St. George Bay, June 10. Illinois—Chicago, April 18 (median of 16 years, May 5). Ohio—Buckeye Lake, median April 12. Iowa—Waterloo, March 21. North Dakota—Bismarck, April 26. Manitoba—Wawanesa, May 8.

Saskatchewan—Prince Albert, April 23. New Mexico—Clayton, March 7; Santa Fe, April 5. Colorado—Colorado Springs, April 17. Wyoming—Casper, April 23. Montana—Libby, April 19 (median of 9 years, May 10). Alberta—Erskine, May 26. Washington—Everson, April 5 (median of 5 years, April 18). British Columbia—Vancouver, April 9.

Late dates of spring departure are: Florida—Tallahassee, May 31. Georgia—Tifton and Demorest, May 7. South Carolina—Charleston, May 28. North Carolina—Raleigh, May 15. Maryland—Laurel, June 11. Louisiana—Baton Rouge, May 18. Arkansas—Stuttgart, May 21. Illinois—Chicago, June 2. Ohio—Buckeye Lake, median May 22. Texas—Tyler, May 23. New Mexico—Clayton, May 29.

Early dates of fall arrival are: Texas—Sinton, October 19. New Mexico—Los Alamos, October 29. North Dakota—Jamestown, September 26. Ohio—Buckeye Lake, median September 15. Kentucky—Bowling Green, September 25. New Jersey—Newark, October 12. Maryland—Laurel, September 23. North Carolina—Weaverville, October 20. South Carolina—Charleston, September 28. Georgia—Fitzgerald, October 15. Alabama—Dauphin Island, October 19. Florida—northwestern Florida, November 7; Tallahassee and Fernandina, November 15.

Late dates of fall departure are: Ohio—Buckeye Lake, median November 8. Kentucky—Danvillle, November 15. New Brunswick—Scotch Lake, November 19. New Hampshire—New Hampton December 30 (median of 21 years, November 30). Massachusetts—Nantucket, November 20. Maryland—Laurel, November 16.

Egg dates.—Georgia: 5 records, June 19 to July 31.

Illinois: 12 records, August 7 to August 29.

Maryland: 40 records, July 26 to September 15; 20 records, August 5 to August 15.

Massachusetts: 36 records, July 26 to August 27; 20 records, August 4 to August 16.

Michigan: 566 records, July 5 to September 17; 300 records, July 25 to August 30.

New Brunswick: 11 records, July 9 to August 8.

New York: 43 records, June 21 to September 2; 22 records, July 26 to August 8.

Ontario: 37 records, June 14 to August 30; 19 records, July 19 to August 7.

SPINUS TRISTIS PALLIDUS Mearns

Pale Goldfinch

HABITS

Dr. Edgar A. Mearns (1890) gave the above name to the goldfinch found breeding in Arizona, and described it as similar to the eastern goldfinch, "but with the black cap larger and extending farther back on the head, the general color decidedly paler, and all of the white markings increased in area. The wing bands, formed by the white tips of the greater and lesser coverts, are considerably broader. The secondaries and tips of primaries are more broadly edged with white."

I cannot find anything in the literature to indicate that the pale goldfinch differs materially in its nesting or other habits from its eastern relative. The sequence of its molts and plumages is the same, bright yellow and black in summer, more sombre colors in winter, but with white wing bars to distinguish it at all seasons. Its food is similar. And it seems to be the same happy bird of sunshine, bounding through the air, rollicking and carefree, with similar cheerful notes at each dip in its erratic flight.

Claude T. Barnes writes to me: "It never seems to know just what its destination is to be; so after making a few bounds in one direction, it appears to find the exertion too great, turns about, slides down the air, circles, zigzags, and at last flutters down to a spot not far distant from its starting point."

The measurements of 15 eggs average 15.5 by 12.0 millimeters; the eggs showing the four extremes measure *16.4* by *12.8*, and *14.7* by *11.7* millimeters.

DISTRIBUTION

Range.—British Columbia and prairie provinces to northern Mexico.

Breeding range.—The pale goldfinch breeds from the southern interior of British Columbia (Okanagan Landing), central Alberta (40 miles north of Belvedere, Athabaska), central Saskatchewan (Emma Lake), southern Manitoba (Lake St. Martin), and extreme western Ontario (Malachi, Wabigoon) south to eastern Oregon (Fort Klamath), central Nevada (Truckee Reservation, Toiyabe Mountains), central Utah (Parley's Park), western Colorado (Durango, Walden), and northwestern Nebraska (Springview).

Winter range.—Winters from southern British Columbia (Okanagan Landing) and central Montana (Missoula, Miles City) south to southern Nevada (Clark County), southern Arizona (Parker, Patagonia), Texas (Fort Davis, Dallas, Huntsville), northern Coahuila (Sabinas), Nuevo León (Galeana), and central Veracruz (Jalapa, Teocelo).

Egg dates.—British Columbia: 20 records, May 24 to August 18; 10 records, June 20 to July 8.

SPINUS TRISTIS JEWETTI van Rossem

Northwestern Goldfinch

HABITS

A. J. van Rossem (1943) bestowed the above name on the goldfinch of the northwest coast region in honor of Stanley G. Jewett. The type is a female in fresh fall plumage and was collected at Ashland, Oreg., in October. He gives it the following subspecific characters: "A small race of *Spinus tristis*, similar in this respect to *salicamans* Grinnell of southern California (wings of 17 males average 69.4 mm., of 9 females 67.2). Both sexes in winter plumage everywhere darker and browner than in *salicamans;* back Saccardo Umber instead of Tawny-Olive; flanks Tawny-Olive to Sayal Brown instead of grayish Tawny Olive; under tail coverts and edging of inner secondaries more strongly suffused with brown. The characters are most evident in newly acquired fall plumage but are observable up to the time of the prenuptial molt.

* * *

"*Salicamans* from southern California differs markedly from other races of *Spinus tristis* in the partial, sometimes nearly complete, suppression of the prenuptial body molt of both males and females. It occurs gradually and in an irregular, patchy manner over a period of several months from about mid-January to late in May and the vast majority of individuals apparently never attain the full summer plumage. Egg laying begins in early April, in the midst of the molting process, and it has been suggested to me that the breeding activity at this time might be in part responsible for the partial suppression. * * * One summer (June) male of *jewetti* has retained the winter plumage on the entire abdominal area; the other nine summer males and all four summer females show a complete prenuptial molt."

Its range seems to be confined to the coastal slope from southern British Columbia to southwestern Oregon. Gabrielson and Jewett (1940) say that it is "a common breeding goldfinch of western Oregon and is equally common during the remainder of the year. It is particularly abundant in the open valleys such as the Rogue, Umpqua, and Willamette valleys. In habits and behavior, it is identical with the goldfinches throughout the United States. Like its eastern Oregon relative, it nests late. Records of numerous fresh or slightly incubated eggs vary from June 15 to July 6."

DISTRIBUTION

Range.—Coastal slope from southern British Columbia to southwestern Oregon.

Breeding range.—The northwestern goldfinch breeds, and is largely resident, west of the Cascade Mountains from southwestern British Columbia (Port Hardy, Chilliwack) south to southwestern Oregon (Rogue River Valley).

Winter range.—Winters north to southwestern British Columbia (Vancouver, Chilliwack).

Casual records.—Casual east of the Cascades in British Columbia (Lillooet).

SPINUS TRISTIS SALICAMANS Grinnell

Willow Goldfinch

PLATE 25

HABITS

Dr. Joseph Grinnell (1897b) named this Pacific Coast race. Its type is a male taken at Pasadena in December. He says that the winter plumage of the male is similar to the winter plumage of the eastern goldfinch, "but browner with much broader wing-markings. In these respects it thus resembles *S. t. pallidus*, but is easily distinguishable by its extreme darkness.* * *

"The female in winter plumage is similar to the male, but the black of the wings and tail is less pure, and the throat is duller colored; bill dusky."

Of the summer plumage he says: "In this plumage the male is scarcely distinguishable from *S. tristis;* the black cap is, if anything, not so extended, and the yellow is not so pure and intense as in the eastern form. The white edgings of the wing-feathers are often entirely worn off, so that the wing is left with barely a trace of white. Bill, in life, darker, almost orange-ochraceous. The wing and tail average shorter, and the bill bulkier.

"The female in breeding plumage is readily separable from the eastern bird by its much darker color. The female *S. tristis* is brightly tinged over the whole breast with yellowish green, while the female *S. t. salicamans* is dull greenish yellow on the throat, becoming still duskier anteriorly. Even juveniles of the Willow Goldfinch just from the nest are deeper and darker colored than those of *S. tristis* proper."

The 1957 A.O.U. Check-List states that it is resident west of Sierra Nevada in California and in northwestern Baja California and that it winters in southern California east to the Mohave and Colorado deserts and south in Baja California. It is casual in northeastern California and Arizona.

The name "willow" seems to have been well chosen for this goldfinch, for its favorite haunts are in the damp areas along streams, ditches, and ponds, where willows grow.

Nesting.—Unlike its eastern relative, the willow goldfinch begins its nest building early in the season. John G. Tyler (1913) says: "Any time from the last week in April until the first of July a pair of Willow Goldfinches may begin the construction of a nest, which later will contain four or five eggs of the palest blue color. These nests are beautiful, compactly woven cups, made of light plant fibers, bark strips, and cotton, and fastened in the forks of a willow or peach tree at a height of from six to fifteen feet from the ground, as a rule."

Dawson (1923) says: "Nesting takes place normally in May or June; but the birds occasionally prolong their efforts into July; and April nests are of record. In their later nesting the Willow Goldfinches show some disposition to colonize. Nests are placed at moderate heights in willow trees, in ceanothus bushes at the lower levels, or even in weeds."

Eggs.—The eggs of the willow goldfinch are indistinguishable from those of the eastern goldfinch. The measurements of 40 eggs average 16.5 by 12.2 millimeters; the eggs showing the four extremes measure *18.3* by 11.4, 15.8 by *15.0*, and *14.5* by *11.1* millimeters.

Young.—Irene G. Wheelock (1912) gives the incubation period as 10 days and says that the young remain in the nest for a similar period, being fed by the regurgitation of their parents. After leaving the nest, they soon learn to forage for themselves, clinging to the top of a thistle or a bunch of goldenrod.

Food.—F. E. L. Beal (1910) studied the contents of 84 stomachs of the willow goldfinch and found the food was 95 percent vegetable and 5 percent animal matter. He says: "They are eminently seed lovers, and rarely eat anything else, except a few insects during the season of reproduction. The only mischief so far imputed to them is the eating of the seeds of useful plants, such as lettuce and other vegetables on seed farms. Investigation has failed, however, to find a case where the damage was considerable.   * * *

"One marked peculiarity of the goldfinches is their bibulous habits. They seem always in need of water, perhaps owing to the habit of eating dry seeds. The writer has seen more goldfinches drinking in one day than he has seen of all other species in his whole life.   * * *

"There are probably few birds that do so little harm as the willow goldfinch. Its animal food, though small in quantity, is composed entirely of harmful insects. It eats no fruit and practically no grain.

Most of its food consists of the seeds of noxious or neutral plants. Its food habits commend the bird, as much as its bright plumage and fine song."

Behavior.—In all of its other habits, in its undulating flight and its happy call notes, it reminds us of the familiar "wild canary" of the eastern states, and we recognize the close relationship. It is a happy, wandering bit of sunshine, pleasing to both eye and ear.

DISTRIBUTION

Breeding range.—The willow goldfinch breeds, and is largely resident, west of the Sierra Nevada in California (Smith River, Edgewood, southeast to Cabezon and Escondido) and in northwestern Baja California (10 miles south of Ensenada).

Winter range.—Winters in southern California east to the Mohave and Colorado deserts (Yermo, Twentynine Palms, Palm Springs) and south in Baja California to lat. 30° 30′ N. (San Ramón, San Quintín Plains).

Casual records.—Casual in northeastern California (Litchfield) and Arizona (Parker).

Egg dates.—California: 112 records, April 10 to July 24; 56 records, May 18 to June 14.

SPINUS PSALTRIA PSALTRIA (Say)

Lesser Goldfinch

Contributed by ALFRED OTTO GROSS

HABITS

Stephen H. Long's expedition to the Rocky Mountains in 1819–20 collected the first known lesser goldfinch on the banks of the Arkansas River between Colorado Springs and Pueblo, Colo., near long. 105° W. Thomas Say (1823) described it and named it *Fringilla psaltria*, and for the next 135 years it was known commonly as the Arkansas goldfinch. This was an unfortunate choice, for after the state of that name was established people tended to associate the bird with the state instead of the lesser-known Colorado river from which the name derived. As the bird has never been recorded in Arkansas, which lies well east of the species' known range, its vernacular name was changed officially to lesser goldfinch in the 5th edition of the A.O.U. Check-List.

In Colorado the lesser goldfinch is a summer resident, arriving usually about mid-June and remaining until September or October. Cooke (1897) reports an early flock seen at Colorado Springs on May 13, 1898. According to Drew (1885) the upper limit of its vertical range in spring is 5,000 feet, in summer 9,500 feet, and in autumn 9,000 feet. It has been found breeding from 5,500 feet to an extreme of 11,500 feet elevation. It nests regularly in the vicinity of Denver (Lincoln, 1920). Hering (1948) found two pairs nesting during a census of a 75-acre tract of yellow pine forest and creek environment. Drew (1881) found the birds in willow bushes along the Rio Animas where he states the birds breed.

In the Panhandle of Oklahoma the lesser goldfinch is a summer resident. Tate (1923) found a nest with three eggs in Cimarron County, Aug. 4, 1921. It is a comparatively common summer resident in the western half of Texas. Stevenson (1942) states that it is resident near Amarillo in the central Texas Panhandle where he observed birds in February, May, August, September, and December. At Kerrville in south-central Texas, Lacey (1911) reports the earliest date of arrival as March 29, the next earliest April 18, and the average arrival date as April 28; it leaves about mid-October. J. E. Stillwell writes me of seeing 35 or more lesser goldfinches on a farm-bordered road about 20 miles southeast of Kerrville on May 16, 1956. They were in handsome nuptial plumage, and a number were singing a song resembling certain phrases of the red-eyed vireo, but he heard nothing like the song of the American goldfinch. In that section of the state many of the nests are in pecan and walnut trees, and complete sets of four eggs have been found the first week in June.

At San Antonio, Bexar County, Tex., Attwater (1892) found them breeding in cedar brakes in the same localities chosen by the golden-cheeked warblers. Van Tyne and Sutton (1937) found the lesser goldfinch common in Brewster County, southwestern Texas, and collected specimens in May. They saw few at Alpine during February, 1935, and on March 20 they saw a flock of five in the Chisos Mountains at an altitude of 5,100 feet. A female taken May 3 and a male on May 12 were still in their prenuptial molt. Specimens taken after May 16 were in full nuptial plumage.

Bailey (1928) presents many records for New Mexico, where the lesser goldfinch is most common at 6,000 to 7,000 feet elevation. Only a few breeding records have been made there below 5,000 feet. Mitchell (1898) found it nesting as high as 10,000 feet in San Miguel county. In none of the warmer, lower parts of New Mexico is the species common, though it breeds in some of the hottest sections of Mexico. Most of the lesser goldfinches desert New Mexico for the winter, but there are a number of winter records.

The range of this subspecies extends westward in eastern Arizona, where Jenks (1936) found it breeding throughout the Upper Sonoran Zone on the north and east slopes of the White and Blue mountains. He collected two typical examples on July 4, 1935, near Springville, one from a group of 20 birds at 2,000 feet elevation, the other from a flock of 5 at 6,250 feet.

Courtship.—The courtship of this race of the lesser goldfinch has not been studied in detail, but presumably it does not differ markedly from that of the western subspecies. Brandt (1940) made an interesting observation in Texas of what he calls the "song circuit." The courting male flies off for a distance of a half mile or more, circles, and then returns to his mate. Throughout the flight he undulates in a characteristic wavelike motion and continuously utters his distinctive exuberant nuptial flight song.

Nesting.—Although these birds are highly gregarious most of the year, they are not so while nesting. Yet occasionally unusually large numbers may nest in a small area. Jensen (1923) reports that 22 pairs nested on the Indian School campus in northern Santa Fe County, N. Mex., during the summer of 1921. He found fresh eggs from June 15 to October 1.

Like most other goldfinches this subspecies is a late nester. Most nests are not built until June, when the reproductive activities of most other birds are well under way. Active nests reported in September and October are probably second nestings. Mrs. J. Murray Speirs writes (in litt.) of a nest she and her husband observed about 18 feet up in an acacia above a stream near the highway at Lyons, Colo., Sept. 8, 1956. The male parent was feeding the young, at least three in number, which seemed almost ready to leave the nest.

A favorite nesting site is in the cottonwood trees which abound along the streams in much of this form's breeding range. It has also been reported nesting in walnut, pecan, yellow pine, fig and other trees as well as in grape vines and in shrubs of various kinds.

The nest is a neat cup of compactly woven plant fibers, fine grass stems, weed bark, and fragments of moss. It is lined with vegetable down such as that of the cottonwood tree or thistle, sometimes with cotton, a few feathers, or other soft materials. One nest measured 3 inches in diameter and 1½ inches in depth. In general the nests are similar in structure to those of the green-backed and American goldfinches.

Eggs.—This species usually lays 4 or 5 eggs, sometimes as few as 3 or as many as 6. The eggs are ovate with some tendency to round-ovate, and have very little lustre, They are very pale bluish-white and unspotted. Occasionally an egg may have a few very small scattered spots of reddish brown.

The measurements of 28 eggs average 15.4 by 12.0 millimeters; the eggs showing the four extremes measure *16.3* by 12.2, 15.0 by *12.5*, *14.5* by 11.6, and 15.0 by *11.0* millimeters.

Food.—Though the food of the lesser goldfinch has not been analyzed in detail, it consists, like that of other goldfinches, primarily of seeds of weeds, grasses, shrubs, and trees of various kinds. It is especially fond of the seeds of the wild sunflower and burr thistle which are abundant in many parts of its range. It has also been reported as feeding on the flowers of cottonwood trees. Several observers state it sometimes feeds on the fruits of the creosote bush and on the long-winged carpels of the cliff rose. At favored feeding spots these gold-finches frequently associate with other birds of similar feeding habits such as siskins.

DISTRIBUTION

Range.—Arizona, Colorado, and Oklahoma to central and southern Mexico.

Breeding range.—The lesser goldfinch breeds, and is largely resident, from central eastern Arizona (Springerville), northern Colorado (Grand Junction, Fort Collins), northwestern Oklahoma (Kenton), and northern and central Texas (Palo Duro Canyon, Kerrville, Austin) south through central, eastern, and southern Mexico to Guerrero (Chilpancingo), Oaxaca (Cerro San Felipe), and central Veracruz (Jalapa).

Winter range.—Winters through much of the breeding range, north at least to western and northern Texas (El Paso, Kerrville, Austin).

Casual record.—Casual in southern Wyoming (Cheyenne).

Egg dates.—Colorado: 1 record, May 10.

Mexico: 1 record, May 30.

SPINUS PSALTRIA HESPEROPHILUS (Oberholser)

Green-backed Goldfinch

PLATE 26

Contributed by JEAN MYRON LINSDALE*

HABITS

The green-backed goldfinch is a common bird in the western states. It breeds from southern Oregon and Utah to southern Lower California, Sonora, and extreme southwestern New Mexico and winters from northern California to Cape San Lucas. It lives on open lands with a sparse tree cover and in brushlands, and occurs through a wide range of climatic conditions. Less plentiful in the humid coastal region, it prefers the dry foothills and the deserts where seeds and

---

*The author's field work on this and the following species at the Hastings Natural History Reservation was facilitated greatly by the generosity of the late Frances Simes Hastings. For further information on both species see Linsdale (1957).

PLATE 26

zusa, Calif., July 1916   R. S. Woods

ona, Calif., May 21, 1916   W. M. Pierce

MALE LESSER GOLDFINCH AND NEST

buds are abundant. The kinds of food it eats require that water be available nearby. Thickets of bushes or trees close to water are occupied consistently through the dry season. Common foraging places are in patches of weeds along roadsides, in pastures, and on hilly slopes.

In August 1931 a severe fire in Napa and Lake counties, Calif., was disastrous to the bird populations in the region. Eight months after the fire H. W. Clark (1935) went over a part of the burned area. A few black oaks and manzanitas had survived, and along a creek the alders and streamside shrubs were unharmed. Wild flowers had sprung up in profusion, and the burned area was a mass of bloom. Green-backed goldfinches were the most abundant birds, supposedly because of the prevalence of seed-bearing plants.

Courtship.—Pair formation is usually accompanied by courtship song, courtship flight, song flight, and a canarylike song. Courtship feeding is important in the maintenance of the bond. These elements resemble the ones observed by Stokes (1950) in his study of the American goldfinch. The species studied on the Hastings Reservation in California contrasts in several ways with the calendar of activity exhibited by the species farther east.

In midmorning of Jan. 29, 1945, on a wooded hill a male perched at the tip of the topmost twig of a 40-foot leafless valley oak. Turning first one way, then the other, he uttered an almost continuous song. This was the first singing green-backed goldfinch observed that season. Earlier in the month there had been snatches of song intermingled with a variety of calls.

In early morning on Feb. 7, 1938, a pair stood within 12 inches of each other on a fence in chamisal. After a flight of 50 feet by the female the male caught up and both birds dived over a ridge in a close, twisting flight. In late March a male led a female in flight and he sang on the wing. At this season goldfinches were frequently scattered in pairs over the reservation. One mid-April afternoon several green-backed goldfinches foraged with Lawrence goldfinches in blue oaks and in fiddleneck patches in an open field. The day was partly cloudy, but the air was warmer than it had been for several weeks. Courtship behavior that day included pursuits—apparently of males by males—displays with feathers raised, tail spread and elevated, and wings waving rapidly, and short flights in which the bird moved slowly but with the wings moving much more rapidly and widely than in ordinary flight. Also there was much singing from perches in the trees.

In May many goldfinches were observed courting along a flowing creek. Attracted there by the water, they were mostly in pairs. Some pursuits were noted, and there were some display flights.

Before noon one male flew about slowly, calling, with wings and tail widely spread and revealing the full extent of the white patches. Another male followed two others along the creek in a display flight.

At the end of May 1942, goldfinches were numerous and active among the blue oaks on a hilltop where they nested each year. The males made many flight displays with fully spread wings. Many females were active that day; apparently they were not yet on nests.

On May 24, observations beginning at 8:30 a.m. were made on a nest in the second day of construction. At times a light breeze swayed the nest limb 3 or 4 inches. The sunshine was bright on the nest and the air was warm. Both birds returned at 8:53, the male 5 feet ahead of the female. The male went to the nest tree 10 feet from the nest; the female went to the nest limb 4 feet from the nest, and then to the nest. There was a mating flight at 8:55. The male was in a valley oak southeast of the nest tree, the female in the nest tree. The male was 8 feet above the female. When the male flew down toward the female, she flew up 2 feet toward him, and he mounted. Both birds fell to bushes 3 feet above the ground, the male seemingly always above. They fell 25 feet in 2 seconds. When the birds struck the bushes they separated and the female flew into the bushes. The male, behind by 2 feet, followed the female around through the bushes under the nest tree. When the female flew to an oak 20 feet from the nest tree, the male flew at her twice from 5 feet away, and she flew off to forage or seek nesting material. When she returned to the nest tree, the male followed 10 feet behind her.

The high flights of the males with wings and tails widely spread reveal the contrasting pattern of white and dark markings conspicuously and attract special attention as the males fly out in circles near the perched females. Near noon on June 7 a male flew in circles 35 feet in diameter, 10 feet up, around a female perched on a barbed wire fence; he spread his tail, fluttered in flight, and uttered a continual series of *dee-dee* notes and snatches of song. The female appeared entirely unmoved by the performance. When she flew off the male followed, singing and calling.

On June 16, the males of five pairs of goldfinches were singing along a creek. One male flew in circles around a female perched on a twig 3 feet from the ground and seemingly oblivious to her mate's display. In midmorning the next day a male in a dense stand of live oaks in a canyon perched in a high tree top and flew out four times over the lower trees, circling once each time, and sang the while much more intensely than the light, whistling notes of the ordinary song. After each flight he paused in the tree tops 60 feet above the ground and sang leisurely. One or two birds uttered occasional notes from adjacent trees during this time; then one flew up from the top of a tree over which the male had flown and a chase ensued for 200 feet around a half circle. The second bird, probably a female, disappeared, and the male, calling softly, perched for 20 seconds at the top of a live oak 75 feet from his original perch and then flew off down the canyon.

A seasonally late example of this type of display occurred in early afternoon on July 14, 1939. A male, perched 3 feet above a female 40 feet up in a valley oak, sang for 2 minutes. He then flew in two wide circles over a ravine in front of his mate, flashing his conspicuous white wing patches, and then perched alongside her.

Nesting.—In central California the normal nesting season extends from the last of March to the last of July, with an exceptionally late nesting (fledged young) on November 18 in Oakland (Mrs. H. K. Trousdale). A nest containing four fresh eggs was found on November 22, 1900, at Parlier, Fresno County, by John M. Miller (1903). Numerous other records for southern California indicate that this bird nests there regularly from September to November.

On the choice of nesting sites Dawson (1923) writes that it is very great, and continues:

Sycamore trees are an early favorite because of the shelter promised by its generous leaves. And in this connection it may be well to note that most birds, whether ground or tree nesters, see to it that their nest is in shadow through the middle of the day. The burning rays of the sun must be avoided, at least by the tender nestlings. It is this fact, and not presumed escape from observation, which is the controlling factor in most nest-building projects. The cypress is also a favorite with the goldfinch, and whether the nests be placed close to the trunk of the tree, or, preferable, well out toward the tip of a branch, is determined again by the shade offered by some overshadowing twig or branch. Live oaks conceal their myriads also. In this case, the bird, securely sheltered by a bristling array of sturdy leaves, prefers the tip of a drooping branch, or at least an outside situation. When the timber gives out, the Green-backs take cheerfully to the major weed-patches, or even invade the open sage, to take potluck with Bell Sparrows and Bush-Tits.

Grinnell, Dixon, and Linsdale (1930) write that in the fourth week of April 1928, several pairs of green-backed goldfinches were nesting among the blue oaks on the hills 6 miles north of Red Bluff, Calif. An unfinished nest in a shrubby tree at the edge of a small clump was 5 feet up on a limb sloping at a 45-degree angle and near the center of the tree. The female kept up a twittering call as she shaped the nest that was made almost entirely of sheep's wool. At Point Lobos in 1934–35 the only nest of green-backed goldfinch found was 8½ feet up, at the end of a bough of a 20-foot Monterey pine. The limb was at the south margin of the woods on the north side of a meadow. The site was thus open to the south and west, but pines standing close on the east provided shade in the morning. On April 26 the female was at the nest, which we thought then to be empty, and the male was near it. The male flew, singing in slow flight, to the top of a dead pine 50 feet from the nest. The female was still brooding on May 11.

Van Rossem (1911) writes that at Mecca, at the north end of Salton Sea, several pairs had nests well underway by Mar. 30, 1911. Thread and cotton from the skinning table went into their makeup.

Bancroft (1930) recorded green-backed goldfinches in central Lower California only from San Ignacio, where the birds were common in the gardens near the reservoir. They began to nest the first week in April, building with plant down and the finest bark. The birds were timid and hid their nests well, by preference in the grapevines, though it was by no means unusual to find them in willow or fig trees.

Nests in California are usually in bushes or trees in fairly dense foliage, from 2 to 30 feet above the ground. They have been reported in the following plants: cottonwood, grapevines, willow, fig, pear, apricot, lemon, live oak, arrowweed, blue oak, walnut, valley oak, box elder, blue gum, and cypress.

On May 11 a female goldfinch flushed from a nest 7 feet up in a 9-foot blue oak halfway up a rocky hillside covered with slender oaks. As the nearest other blue oaks were 10 to 60 feet away, the site was exposed and a cold wind was blowing. The bird stayed within an area 50 feet across, moving from tree to tree and uttering single, loud notes of alarm. The nest's slight, whitish walls were so thin in places the light showed through the dark lining. It contained four eggs.

On July 2, 1948, a female had completed less than one-fourth of a nest in a hanging cluster of leaves about 7 feet up on the west side of a valley oak, and was busily bringing shreds of bark from a willow clump 100 feet away. Ten days later she was incubating. Twice an observer walked within 5 feet of her without flushing her. In the morning on July 17 the nest appeared unattended, but when an observer touched the nest limb, the female leaped out and fluttered to bare ground 12 feet away. She turned, watched for 2 or 3 seconds, and fluttered off, barely clearing the ground and holding her body in flight slanted forward at a 15-degree angle. She seemed to spread her tail as a brake to intensify the effect of the fluttering motion. This bird was the only green-backed goldfinch observed on the reservation that made "injury feigning" displays. At midday on July 23 the nest contained a young bird one or two days old. The female was brooding, and did not leave until a mirror was held over the nest. Then she fluttered off to the tops of some dead grass 14 feet away and fluttered from side to side over a path 3 feet wide for an additional 10 feet. She then flew to a branch 30 feet from the nest and perched, calling a series of slow *kiyah*, *chee-wee*, and *chee* notes. In 3 or 4 minutes she gradually worked back to a perch 15 feet above the nest where she remained calling for an additional 6 or 8 minutes.

When her brooding was again disturbed on July 29, she flew off the nest in a long, fluttering glide and landed 40 feet away, but she returned immediately to a tree near the nest to call in alarm.

The female constructs the nest almost entirely alone. However, the male shows interest in the site and in the early stages of some nests. A pair worked at early stages of nest building in a valley oak on the morning of May 23, when the nest had a thin base 2 inches wide by 3 inches long. On one trip when the pair returned the male went to the nest first, carrying material, but did not remain. The female came to the nest and worked 2½ minutes while the male perched near the center of the tree with the material in his beak until she left; then he brought it to the nest and worked half a minute. Later in the morning he went to the nest for 30 seconds and wove fiber around twigs. Sometimes he flew directly to the nest, sometimes to a branch near it. Once he appeared to climb up to the nest from below, using his bill in parrotlike fashion.

Most of the material came from nearby trees. The female usually flew directly to the nest from a nearby tree, but if she came from farther away she generally lit in the nest tree and then went to the nest. She generally worked from above or inside the nest, less often from the outside. The male sometimes sang nearby while she worked.

In 160 minutes that morning the male made 5 trips to the nest and the female made 33. In the afternoon the female resumed work on the nest at about 3:50 p.m., and spent longer periods at it. The male made only one trip and was not seen near the nest after 3:43. He had evidently ceased working, though his mate made 29 more trips to the nest in the next 3 hours.

On the second day of nest-building, activity was recorded in four periods totalling 9 hours and 20 minutes. In this time the female made 64 trips to the male's 4. The average interval between her trips was 13 minutes in the early morning, 5 minutes in the late morning, 25 minutes in the afternoon, and 6.8 minutes in the late evening. This nest was destroyed by scrub jays soon after it was completed.

A female on another nest was alert to everything that went on about her. Whenever a scrub jay called in the vicinity, her head turned sharply in that direction. She seemed aware of the observer's activity, but she was not unduly excited by it. As she covered the nest, she did so with a rapid, cradlelike, sidewise rocking of her body. Every time she stood up she worked quickly with her bill in the bottom of the nest. When she returned to the nest at midday, she called nine times in the tree before she reached the nest. She moved from perch to perch 10 times in the tree before she reached the nest. When the male came to the nest through the top of the tree, he called continually and fed the female, who appeared to arch her back and flutter her wings as he fed her. After he left she kept up a constant high-pitched, excited chatter, accompanied by a fluttering of the wings.

Eggs.—The usual set of four eggs is pale bluish green and unmarked. Hanna (1924b) weighed 27 eggs of the green-backed goldfinch; these ranged from 0.87 to 1.15 grams and averaged 1.05 grams.

The measurements of 50 eggs average 14.7 by 11.2 millimeters; the eggs showing the four extremes measure *16.3* by *12.2*, and *12.7* by *9.7* millimeters.

Young.—W. Lee Chambers (1915) traced the history of a green-backed goldfinch's nest in southern California in April 1915. The nest was started on April 4 in a lemon tree in which the pair had been present for several days and was lined with feathers and nearly completed by April 11. On the 17th at 6:00 a.m. the nest contained a full set of four eggs and by 6:30 a.m. on April 29 all four eggs had hatched. The incubation period, then, is 12 days, which is what Gross (1938) reported as the incubation period for the American goldfinch.

Law (1929) made the following observations on nesting green-backed and Lawrence's goldfinches at Altadena, Calif.: "In both, with the approach of the breeding season and during incubation, the male feeds the female by regurgitation. The parents of both species feed their young by regurgitation. The young of both species appear to be raised entirely on seed food, mostly seeds 'in the milk.' The nests of each species is * * * kept clean by the parents during the first days after the young emerge from the eggs. By the time the young are half grown, such effort is abandoned, and the rims of the nests become filthy with fecal matter. The feces of the young of both at this stage are without membranous sacs and are, for this reason, less readily eaten or carried off."

Food.—Goldfinches forage in flocks most of the year. They move through the bushes and trees that provide the major part of their food, and they sometimes concentrate on low-growing herbaceous plants. Most of their food is plant material, including buds, leaves, fruits, and seeds. Some animal food is eaten, but the kind and amount are difficult to identify by observation of the living birds. On the Hastings Reservation 55 kinds of plant food have been identified as eaten by the green-backed goldfinch. Prominent among these are chamise, common fiddleneck, vinegarweed, and Napa thistle.

According to Beal (1910) weed seed is the standard food of this goldfinch, representing over 96 percent of the year's diet. In January and March nothing else was eaten. Animal food was found in 50 stomachs collected in June, July, August, and September, more than half of them in August. The great bulk of it was plant lice; one tomach was entirely filled with these insects, and in another 300 were counted.

Peterson (1942) offered salt to birds in a partly wooded pasture on the side of Mount Diablo. The green-backed goldfinches came in flocks and covered the salt-saturated ground, feeding mostly from the earth within a foot of the salt block.

Drinking.—These birds apparently need large amounts of water to help digest the seeds they eat. Availability of water is important in the nesting season, and later when it becomes scarce, its distribution determines where the goldfinches live. In the dry seasons they concentrate about streams and springs.

Mrs. Edwards (1925) has described the behavior of goldfinches at a bird bath. A flock of more than 50 birds crowded over a trap and the water below it, chirping cheerily. While the captives were removed from the trap, the rest of the flock remained at and around the far end of the trap, not 2 feet away. E. D. Clabaugh (1930) reported that in his bird banding, green-backed goldfinches were captured only by using water as bait. He used both the warbler and Potter traps, usually with water dripping into the trap in some manner.

On Sept. 6, 1939, the overflow pipe from a well led to a barrel set on a creek bed under a red willow. The water pouring into it filled the barrel and overflowed so that one edge was wet and the other was dry. After a few minutes many goldfinches in the surrounding willows began to come to the barrel to drink, unlike the juncos which drank from the creek bed. The first one lit on the wet edge, followed in a few seconds by two more, and finally eight were lined up drinking before the first ones started to fly off.

The next morning goldfinches in some coast ceanothus were attracted by an overflow of water. As many as 13 stood and drank in the running water within a radius of 1 foot. When frightened they flew into the ceanothus, then went downhill 10 yards, and reassembled at the water to drink again in a compact group. One afternoon when 20 were drinking, something frightened them, and they all flew off into the nearest trees, except one which remained and continued to drink; this doubtless encouraged the immediate return of the others.

At midmorning on Jan. 10, 1954, at the Hastings Reservation, a flock of juncos and goldfinches visited a water trough where the water was covered with ice. The ice melting at one corner formed a small pool where two goldfinches drank. A male goldfinch stood on the ground beneath one corner, ruffled its feathers, and tried to bathe. An hour later when the surface ice had melted the flock returned to the trough and many of the birds drank.

Bathing.—At noon in early January nine goldfinches, calling continuously, bathed in shallow water in a creek. Each bird stood in water part way up to its flanks, frequently dipped its head and shook its feathers and body vigorously, making drops of water fly in all directions. Some flew momentarily up into nearby willows to shake their feathers and preen. One female stayed in the water and shook herself about every 3 seconds for 26 seconds. The average time each bird remained in the water was close to 15 seconds. One July morning six goldfinches bathed in a pool 9 × 12 × ¾ inches. Standing about 2 inches apart, they dipped their breasts and necks in the water, fluttered their wings to throw water over their backs, and fanned their tails. There was no fighting; when one bird was crowded by another, it swiftly moved out of the way.

Roosting.—At the Grand Canyon, Ariz., Townsend (1925) saw 24 green-backed goldfinches settle for the night in a cottonwood still in leaf close to his cabin. Comby (1944) writes:

A male Green-backed Goldfinch * * * chose as a sleeping perch a tree tobacco plant (*Nicotiana glauca*) in my yard, on San Jose Creek, near Whittier, Calif. He was seen to roost there daily throughout most of January and a part of February, 1944. Each evening he came to the plant early, about an hour and a half before sundown. Here he slept for twenty nights, January 10 to 29, inclusive, but was not to be seen on the 30th or 31st. A light shower or drizzle on the 30th may have been a disturbing factor. He returned to the plant on February 1, to remain through the 16th, although toward the end of this period he came later, just before dark. This was the only individual of the species to perch in the shrub or to be seen in the neighborhood at this time except for two or three occasions when another individual alighted momentarily in a near-by tree tobacco. Although the male goldfinch used the same plant for sleeping, he did not always rest on the same branch or face the same direction; his position varied, it is estimated, from 4½ to 5¾ feet from the ground. Like many other birds he slept with head tucked "under the wing."

The first season's growth of this plant retains its succulent leaves and stems throughout the winter. The yellow-green bird was well camouflaged in the yellowish-green foliage, and careful inspection was necessary to distinguish it; discovery of the roosting place was made as the bird flew into the shrub.

Flocks.—Goldfinches wander widely, sometimes alone, more often in pairs or flocks, in search of food, water, and nesting and roosting sites. Flocking becomes pronounced when the birds assemble to forage, drink, or bathe. They like to assemble with others on the same bush. If frightened, which they often are, they fly off together, but they seldom, if ever, land all together. When alighting they scatter like a thrown handful of sand, some flying straight on, others turning right or left; some land on bushes, some on trees. If a bird finds it has landed without companions, it generally flies to a place where other goldfinches are concentrating.

In October an observer watched a flock of more than 60 goldfinches foraging on an open hilltop. When disturbed, the flock flew up, circled, and generally returned to the same spot. The birds frequently alighted first on the deerweed, which, being taller than the grass and vinegarweed, afforded a better view of the surrounding terrain. Early in the morning in late November about 100 goldfinches foraged in an open field and sunned between times in two blue oaks at the edge of a nearby woodland. In late afternoon in early February between 300 and 400 goldfinches perched in tall valley oaks about a barn. Many sang as they sat in the tops of the bare trees while others foraged in the outer branches of a nearby live oak.

In the Colorado Valley near the Needles in early March, Grinnell (1914b) found large flocks "congregated in the central parts of extensive dense mesquite thickets where, perched from three to four feet above the ground, they were certainly safe from marauders; here they sang volubly in chorus until dusk settled."

Flight.—The green-backed goldfinch flies in the undulating manner typical of all its close relatives. A rapid flurry of wings to gain momentum bears the bird upward, followed by a shallow, swooping glide on closed wings, then another climbing burst of wingbeats and another glide. The white patches under the wings usually show conspicuously in flight, and the birds often sing and call on the wing, the characteristic call notes being uttered in the glides between wingbeats. On long trips the birds tend occasionally to stop and rest briefly in a convenient treetop before continuing on their way.

Voice.—The green-backed goldfinch starts to sing by the first of March or a little earlier. Its song is a pleasing, rapturous, canarylike burst of bird music, frequently uttered on the wing, although this habit is by no means so characteristic of this species as of the house finch. The bird sings actively all spring; during the summer the song gradually wanes, but snatches of it may sometimes be heard in autumn. As Hoffmann (1927) describes it:

In any weedy border of neglected fields small birds with *yellow underparts and white patches in their wings* fly off when disturbed, with a little shivering note like the jarring of a cracked piece of glass. * * * The spring flocks gather in trees near their feeding ground and keep up a concert of twittering song. When a pair are nesting the male utters, either from an upper spray or from the air, a series of sweet twittering notes that suggest the song of a canary. * * * Green-backed goldfinches can always be identified by their calls. These include a plaintive *tee-yee*, both notes on the same pitch, a *tee-ee*, the second note higher, and a single plaintive *tee* and the jarring notes mentioned above. There is more variety in the calls of the Green-backed Goldfinch than in those of the Willow Goldfinch, and a plaintive quality which the latter lacks. Young birds, just before leaving the nest or when following their parents in early summer, utter continually a single sharp *tsi*.

The song of the male goldfinch heard on the Hastings Reservation was a long disorganized series of faintly melodious notes rising and falling many times, but most often rising. Frequently interspersed throughout the long song were sharply rising slurred notes that gave it a quality characteristic of many finch songs. Other notes commonly given by the species are the light metallic clanking sounds uttered frequently both perched and in flight. Another common sound is a clear, plaintive, descending note, slightly less than a second long, usually heard when the bird is in fairly dense foliage, often when alone, and less frequently in the usual groups of 7 to 12.

Field marks.—Grinnell and Storer (1924) distinguish the green-backed goldfinch as follows:

Half the size of Junco. Sexes different from one another both summer and winter. Male: Body plumage dark greenish above, yellow below; whole top of head, and wings and tail, black; in flight a patch of pure white appears on middle of each wing and another shows at base of tail. * * * Female: Dull brown, green-tinged above, and dull yellowish beneath; white patches, showing on wing and tail in flight, small or obscure. Flight course of both sexes undulating. *Voice:* Male has a pleasing canary-like song; both sexes have plaintive-toned call notes. * * *

The Green-backed Goldfinch is slightly smaller than either the Willow or the Lawrence, and differs * * * in having yellow rather than white at the lower base of its tail * * *. The white on the inner webs of the outer tail feathers of the Green-backed Goldfinch extends to the bases of the feathers, but not to the tips, whereas in the * * * Lawrence Goldfinch the white is confined to the middle of the feathers, reaching neither bases nor tips. * * * the marks on the tail are to be seen satisfactorily only when a bird is in flight. * * *

The Green-backed Goldfinch never shows any yellow on the wing, whereas the Lawrence Goldfinch always shows this color in considerable amount. The male Green-backed Goldfinch is quite dark colored above, darker than the males of either of the other two species. * * * The female Green-backed Goldfinch is merely greenish, with the upper surface brown-tinged; and she lacks prominently contrasted markings of any sort.

Enemies.—In their varied relationships with numerous kinds of birds on the Hastings Reservation, green-backed goldfinches apparently recognize the danger in getting too near a Cooper's hawk. In mid-June a male came within three feet of an incubating Cooper's hawk and called repeatedly a series of musical, canarylike chirps until the hawk tried unsuccessfully to catch it. In early August seven goldfinches perched three inches above a juvenal Cooper hawk uttering food cries near the top of a tree. The finches made no attack, but remained above the hawk as if wary of its presence. Later in the month when a Cooper's hawk called, a nesting female goldfinch swung about on her nest, stopped singing abruptly and "froze" for 8 minutes before she again flicked her wings.

One midday in early October 15 goldfinches dived into a willow when a sharp-shinned hawk flew toward the flock. The hawk singled out and pursued one bird, which twisted in flight to escape, turning sharply each time the hawk was within 6 inches, thereby gaining about two feet. The goldfinch finally dropped to safety into a willow clump and the hawk flew off. During the chase neither bird made a sound. Later that month a sparrow hawk dived at a goldfinch perched in the top of an oak; the goldfinch escaped down inside the crown of the oak, leaving the hawk perched in the top. The evening of June 8 a pigmy owl flew by with a green-backed goldfinch, apparently a juvenile, in its talons which it had caught near a water trough that regularly attracted many goldfinches.

A flock of 50 goldfinches chattering in a live oak at the end of January momentarily became quiet as a screaming scrub jay came by. Early in the morning of May 25 a scrub jay flew to a limb 4 inches from the nest of a green-backed goldfinch. Both male and female goldfinches flew about the jay from different directions, not approaching closer than 8 inches, until the jay left. Having discovered the nest the jay returned later in the morning and repeatedly drove its bill into the side of the nest until it was demolished.

Plath (1919), in his studies on nestling birds at Berkeley in the summer of 1913, found 8 of the 13 goldfinch nests examined infested with maggots of *Protocalliphora azurea* (Fallen) (Apaulina). In one nest of young green-backed goldfinches all the nestlings died. Compact nests such as goldfinches build showed a greater infestation than loose-textured nests such as those of the brown towhee.

A. W. Anthony (1923) found Argentine ants (*Iridomyrmex humilis*) in San Diego, Calif., swarming over recently abandoned nests of green-backed goldfinches. In the same area he found a goldfinch less than a week old that he thought had been taken from the nest by the Brewer's blackbird that was vigorously pounding it. In Santa Clara County, W. L. Atkinson (1901) found two green-backed goldfinches that a loggerhead shrike had impaled on a barbed wire fence. Green-backed goldfinches were among the birds destroyed during fumigation of orange trees (A. B. Howell, 1914). Edwards (1919) found newly hatched goldfinches dead under a tree after a wind storm.

Fall.—In early August 1939, the goldfinches on the Reservation were usually paired or in small groups; evidently some families were still united. Perhaps the adults remained paired after nesting while the young congregated in flocks. On September 1 the goldfinches were not numerous in the morning; only two flocks were observed in half an hour and those contained less than 20 birds each. Formerly, from 50 to 100 birds were in evidence. Two days later groups of 5 to 15 went to a tank overflow, but did not remain long, the early rains having removed the need to remain in its vicinity for long periods. In mid-November of one year 15 green-backed goldfinches perched in the tops of oaks at the edge of chamise at the summit of a hill. There was much singing as the clouds broke, but the birds became silent when a drizzle began.

Winter.—On a morning in early December, 30 goldfinches perched in the tops of willows and valley oaks at the edge of a creek. A chorus of almost continuous calls was audible, but the observer had difficulty in seeing all of the birds. During the several minutes he watched them he saw no foraging. Aside from the few individuals occasionally hopping or flitting from one perch to another, they were sunning or preening. On a January morning in 1938 a flock of more than one hundred goldfinches fed on achenes of chamise. The flock moved over the patch, every few minutes flying up to perch in the near-by oaks, and then flying down to another spot in the chaparral. Sometimes eight or more gathered in one small bush, each perched at a cluster of fruits and eating as fast as it could. They seemed completely tolerant of each other and of other species feeding with them. Males and females were present in about equal numbers.

In late afternoon in early February, 200 to 300 goldfinches were in trees beside a barn, many singing their canarylike song. Toward the end of March, 25 or more green-backed goldfinches foraged with a large flock of Lawrence goldfinches, juncos, lark sparrows, and house finches on the abundant crop of seeds produced by annual plants in a deserted vineyard.

DISTRIBUTION

Range.—The green-backed goldfinch is resident from southwestern Washington (Vancouver), western Oregon (Portland, Coos County), northeastern California (Modoc County), northern Nevada (Santa Rosa Mountains), and northern Utah (Tooele, Morgan, and Uintah counties) south through California and central Arizona (Flagstaff, Grand Canyon) to southern Baja California (Sierra de la Laguna) and southern Sonora (Guirocoba).

Casual east to eastern Oregon (Riverside), south central New Mexico (San Antonio), and northwestern Durango.

Egg dates.—Baja California: 16 records, April 23 to August 11; 8 records, May 2 to May 15.

California: 132 records, April 2 to August 3; 66 records, May 12 to June 15.

SPINUS LAWRENCEI (Cassin)

Lawrence's Goldfinch

Contributed by JEAN MYRON LINSDALE*

HABITS

Lawrence's goldfinch is one of the several species of birds restricted largely to the drier, interior parts of California. Fitted to live where

---

*See footnote to preceding species, p. 474.

the seeds it eats and the water it requires may be far from the trees where it nests, this species is the most striking of the goldfinches in California, although not the most plentiful. Noteworthy characteristics include the sharp limitation of its range, the irregularity of its occurrence, its affinity for hot and dry situations, the prominence of seeds of native plants in its food, its dependence on water, the permanence of the flocks, the long period through which the birds remain paired, and the peculiarities in its nesting that appear to be related to these traits.

From Sonoma County along the coast and from Trinity and Shasta counties inland, this bird nests southward into Lower California. In winter some of the birds move southeastward across Arizona as far as New Mexico. In summer, especially northward, the species is not common, and its numbers in one place tend to vary considerably from year to year.

Ralph Hoffmann (1927) writes that "birds are as a rule so regular in their habits that a student can find year after year a pair of birds which may have traveled a thousand miles or more to and from their winter home and yet returned to the same spot to breed. It is interesting, therefore, and puzzling to find a few birds like the Lawrence Goldfinch which are more gypsylike. A valley in southern California may be filled with the black-chinned gray-bodied birds one summer and the next year contain not one. * * * It is a bird of the foothills or mountain valleys, particularly from Los Angeles County southward."

Lawrence's goldfinches occur in summer in Lower California, nesting as far south as Laguna Hanson, on the Sierra Juárez (Huey, 1928). The same observer found the species at La Grulla, San Pedro Mártir. On Feb. 25, 1925, he saw about 100 birds near lat. 30°30', the southernmost locality for the species. The birds are sometimes abundant in winter on the lower Colorado River. Glenn Bradt (MS.) found a nest in Arizona at Cienega Springs, near Parker, about Mar. 15, 1952. The young left the nest on or about April 17.

Van Rossem (1911) found this goldfinch nearly as common as green-backed goldfinches in late March near Mecca at the north end of the Salton Sea, but they were not yet in pairs and specimens showed no signs of sexual activity. Lawrence's goldfinches have been reported on Catalina Island in May and on Santa Cruz Island in April in different years (Howell, 1917).

Observations on the Hastings Reservation in Monterey County, Calif., indicate that the kind and amount of seeds produced each year are important in determining the number of goldfinches present and the length of their stay. They seem to eat the native plants more than the plants introduced to the area. The changes in vegetation, especially the reduction in some of the weedy species with a trend toward stabilization, have tended to attract fewer goldfinches.

In the spring of 1938, annual plants were abundant and produced a heavy crop of small seeds suitable for goldfinches and other finches. Throughout the season the birds fed on them in large numbers. On the same slopes in the spring of 1955 the annual plants were so dwarfed they produced scarcely any seeds, and no goldfinches foraged there.

Courtship.—One morning in mid-February a pair of Lawrence's goldfinches lit in the top of a blue oak. The male sang for 2 minutes as he perched 2 feet away from the female. Next, the female flew down a canyon and the male followed. When he came within a foot of her, she would dive, closely followed by the male, and a moment later the two would shoot upward, the male still following closely. The birds flew out of sight in this manner.

After the middle of March 1938, from 50 to 200 Lawrence's goldfinches were present on the Reservation daily for nearly a month. The large flocks foraged in afternoons on a south-facing slope. At intervals the whole flock stopped feeding and flew off to a fence or to an isolated blue oak where they perched and sang, usually facing into the sun. The birds seemed to be already paired, for the sexes usually perched together in couples.

Courtship display was observed frequently in April, the males perching near the females and extending the head and neck as they sang. In mid-April a pair of goldfinches perched on a valley oak limb 7 feet above the ground. The singing male sat 6 inches from the female with his head outstretched and feathers compressed against the body.

By April 24 the goldfinches were clearly paired; the couples kept close together and followed each other. Singing and posturing among the Lawrence's goldfinches on the afternoon of April 26 became more pronounced than earlier in the season. In a flock watched at this season the 20 birds were obviously paired. Ten or more times males flew at other males in efforts to drive them away from a particular female. This was always a Lawrence's driving away another of the same species, except once when a green-backed male was driven. Usually a move of only 5 or 6 feet was required for the pursued bird to avoid another attack. Both birds would then settle on perches.

At midmorning on May 20 an observer watched a female quivering her wings before a male. The male took no notice, and the female kept flying up to him. On May 22 a male fed an adult female near a nest high in a tree. The quivering wings of the female spread less widely, and they moved less rapidly than the observer had detected in related species.

In the stage before the start of incubation the members of each pair are strongly attached to each other. The male stays with his mate constantly and drives off all interlopers. After incubation starts, the strength of the pair bond wanes. The male becomes less aggressive and his attacks on trespassers are relatively mild. But the female still defends her domain quite fiercely, and drives off all other goldfinches and other species as well.

When a nest-building female leaves the nest on a long trip she utters a flight call that appears to impel the male to follow her. Before short trips she gives no flight call and the male does not follow. The nest-tree is the male's usual song perch, but he may sing from other nearby perches as well. When a strange male settled in a tree 40 feet from the nest-tree, the male owner of the nest chased the intruder away and sang while the female continued to gather material near the nest. After the female started incubating, the male sang from another tree 40 feet away.

Nesting.—According to Dawson (1923) the nests of Lawrence's goldfinch "are exquisite creations, highly varied in construction and sometimes quite picturesque. A dainty cup before me, an inch and a half in diameter and one in depth, is compacted of wool, flower-heads, fairy grasses, horse-hair, and feathers. Another, of coarser construction, boasts several additional ingredients, but dispenses with horse-hair in favor of sheer feathers for lining. A third displays a garland of protruding and highly nutant grassheads, as chic as a Parisian bonnet. The female, naturally, disputes the intruder's claim to such a piece of handiwork; but she does not often have to be lifted from the nest."

Dawson (1923) reports that these birds colonize to some extent in isolated clusters or hedges of the Monterey cypress, and he found as many as 10 nests at once in two adjoining trees. He indicates that there is no flock impulse in the matter, for while some nests were still incompleted, others contained eggs, and still others had young. William Twisselman has told me of a similar colonial nesting of this goldfinch in a short hedge of cypress that formerly lined a road south of Salinas.

Wilson C. Hanna (MS.) found the earliest nest on April 1, in Coachella Valley barely above sea level. His latest nesting date is June 27 in San Bernardino County at over 5,000 feet. His highest altitude for a nest was 6,000 feet in Slover Canyon. He found nests from 3 feet to as high as 40 feet above the ground, with an average of about 15 feet. He usually found Lawrence's goldfinch nesting in solitary pairs, but in 1943 he found a dozen nests in one small juniper on the Mohave Desert, a few in two other junipers a few feet away, and still others in sage (*Artemisia tridentata*) nearby. The site was in a stand of Joshua trees (*Yucca brevifolia*) at least a half mile from the nearest water.

One nest on the Hastings Reservation was 20 feet up in a slender 35-foot blue oak on a steep east-facing slope. Observations were made here on the mornings of May 19 and 20. The nest was supported by small twigs and it was partly exposed. Building was by the female only, but the male was nearly always close by singing while she worked. The two birds seemed markedly aware of each other. The male appeared distressed when the female was not close by, and he nearly always followed her when she left the nest tree, but not when she collected material nearby. Her trips were in a different direction each time. Much of the material was lichen (*Ramalina reticulata*) picked from tree branches.

The second morning the female brought only small pieces of plant material, but she spent much time working around the nest and pressing her body against the sides. In midmorning she brought feathers. Throughout the nest building the male continued to sing while the female worked. He sang in flight when following her, but more persistently when perched near her at the nest. On the first morning the song was spontaneous, not in answer to any other male, and was usually delivered from one of several particular branches in the tree.

During this period each member of the pair often drove off strange goldfinches. The male was quick to chase other males, and the female pursued other females and sometimes strange males. Yet once another pair stayed in the vicinity of the nest for 5 minutes undisturbed, and another time a strange male followed the pair in and perched and sang within 3 feet of the nest while its owners paid no attention. Later the nesting pair followed a strange pair into the tree; the strange female drove off the female owner while the two males perched 9 inches apart without apparent antagonism.

The flocking habit is so strong in Lawrence's goldfinch that a late nest-building pair was regularly followed to the nest by one or more goldfinches, usually of the same species, but sometimes by a green-backed. While the nesting pair usually made some attempt to drive out the strangers, their pursuits tended to be mild and did not extend far. Evidently the impulse to follow other birds in flight and to join other individuals in a flock prevented the establishment of rigid isolation by the nesting pair to the exclusion of all other birds of the same species or even of the same sex.

Eggs.—The number of eggs runs from three to six with four or five most frequently comprising the set. They are ovate in shape with some tendency to rounded ovate, and have very little lustre. They are very pale bluish-white and unmarked, although an occasional egg may be found with a few very small reddish brown spots.

The measurements of 50 eggs average 15.4 by 11.6 millimeters; the eggs showing the four extremes measure *17.3* by 12.0, 16.5 by *12.5*, *14.2* by 11.2, and 14.7 by *10.7* millimeters.

Incubation.—The incubating female goldfinch remains on the nest almost continuously except for short intervals when the male waits for her to leave after a feeding. At one nest in early stages of incubation, the female remained on the nest almost continuously and there was little variety in her activity. On seven days up to June 11, an observer spent 56 hours at this nest. Altogether the female was off the nest only 27 times for a total of 110 minutes or only 3.3 percent of the time. Of the 27 trips off the nest, 10 were for one minute or less, 7 for two minutes, 1 for three minutes, 2 for five minutes, 3 for six minutes, 1 each for seven, nine, thirteen, and thirty-three minutes. She made 16 of these trips before 7:15 a.m., 2 between 9:00 and 10:00 a.m., 3 between 11:00 a.m. and noon, and 6 between 2:00 and 6:00 p.m. In the same period the male made 57 trips to the nest, an average of 1 per hour.

Young.—Feeding of the young in the nest is at fairly uniform hourly intervals. This may be regulated by the time required to gather and prepare the food, and it may also be influenced by the hunger limits of the bird to be fed. Through the 11 days before two young left the nest on July 14, in 109 hours we recorded 139 feedings by a parent bird. The male fed the female 19 times, 6 times on the first day, 7 on the second, 4 on the third, 1 on the fourth, and 1 on the eleventh day. This shows the time required to change from the feeding pattern during incubation when the male delivers all food he brings to the nest to the female and she eats it. The first few days after hatching the tendency is for the female to take the food and deliver it to the young after the male leaves, and he has great difficulty reaching past the begging female to get food to the young. When the female no longer has to brood the young, she accompanies the male on trips for food. Both parents then tend to arrive at the nest together and to take turns in feeding the young. The male nearly always feeds first at the start, but later the female delivers food first almost as often as the male does.

Adults continue to feed the young intermittently for some time after they leave the nest. A post-nesting flock of nearly 50 Lawrence's goldfinches, both adults and young, foraged along the edge of an abandoned field on the Reservation one early afternoon at the end of June. The flock kept in one small area where they fed mostly on the ground, picking up the ripened seeds then available from many annual plants. There was much flying about, and the food calls of the young were the most conspicuous sounds in the vicinity. The young birds, which appeared to outnumber the adults, seemed to feed themselves part of the time, but nearly every adult was closely followed by one or two young birds begging to be fed. Several young ones in chamise bushes pecked at the flowers, and two picked at leaves.

In late July a pair with two young out of the nest fed in a patch of chamise. The parents fed continuously on the newly ripened seeds in the tops of the bushes while their two young perched lower in the bushes between them. They changed perches from time to time and followed the adults chirping loudly and quivering their wings. One young bird fluttered its wings in a wide arc, but the movement involved only the distal parts. The female then fed this bird by regurgitation about eight successive times. When she seemed to gulp more food herself between deliveries, the juveniles made the loudest outcries and fluttered hardest.

Another July morning a female fed a young Lawrence's goldfinch on a road. The young bird followed the old one closely wherever she went. She picked nutlets from fiddleneck and fed them to the youngster. It would lunge at her, utter its tinkling call note several times, open its mouth, and rapidly flap its wings high over its back. At first she backed away, and then fed the young bird several times in succession.

On August 1 a female and a young bird foraging together on seeds were silent except for a few weak *tsip-tsip* notes. The young bird then gave a continuous series of calls with a somewhat nasal quality, and the adult uttered one high-pitched, 2-part note. Although this young one was clearly associated with the adult, it picked its own food from the plants. It was rather clumsy and it lost its balance occasionally, but it was not fed by the parent.

Plumages.—Adult male has anterior portion of head all round, including throat and forepart of crown, black; above brownish gray (the back sometimes tinged with olive green), changing to yellowish olive-green on rump; sides of head and lateral underparts paler brownish gray, becoming white on under tail coverts and abdomen; chest and median portion of breast yellow. Outer webs of wing coverts and remiges partly yellow; inner webs of rectrices (except middle pair) with subterminal white. Adult females are similar to adult males, but without black on head; the colors in general are duller, with the yellow less distinct. The juvenal plumage is similar to that of the adult female, with colors duller, the yellow on the breast less distinct, and upperparts obsoletely streaked.

Food.—Lawrence's goldfinches forage in flocks in patches of low, seed-bearing herbs and shrubs. Though they have been noted eating 20 different plant foods on the Hastings Reservation, they eat fewer kinds of seeds than do the green-backed goldfinches, and they forage over fewer types of plant associations. They concentrate in winter on chamise achenes, and in early summer they are closely restricted to the patches of fiddleneck that furnish most of their food through the nesting period.

For a month after mid-March 1938, large numbers of Lawrence's goldfinches congregated with several other kinds of seed-eating birds, green-backed goldfinches, house finches, juncos, and lark sparrows, to forage in a vineyard on a south-facing gentle slope. Generally the Lawrence goldfinch outnumbered the other species in the flocks. At first the most conspicuous plants they fed on were red-maids. By the end of March other prominent annuals coming into seed were red-stem filaree, annual bluegrass, and common peppergrass. The birds showed a preference for the ripening seeds of peppergrass, and spent much time in the extensive patches of it. By April 15 they were eating seeds of shepherd's purse.

The abundant chamise (*Adenostoma fasciculatum*) provides food for this bird from midsummer until late winter. One July morning a group of goldfinches fed in three bushes in an area 12 feet across. Perched in the highest branches 6 feet up and 8 feet apart, they fed quietly and continuously, keeping the body upright and reaching upward and forward to the clusters of flowers and ripening achenes. They stripped only the basal half of each head, thus taking the drier fruits and leaving the green ones.

One July day 10 or more Lawrence's goldfinches foraged with two or three green-backed goldfinches on a tract that had been burned a year earlier. The Lawrence's goldfinches fed only on the nutlets of the large prickly cryptantha (*Cryptantha muricata*) and were not seen that day on any other kind of plant. The green-backed goldfinches were eating mainly seeds of chia (*Salvia columbariae*) and Indian tobacco (*Nicotiana bigelovii*) and were not seen to eat the cryptantha, an interesting example of how closely related species sometimes contrast sharply in feeding habits, even while foraging together.

The common fiddleneck (*Amsinckia intermedia*) grew abundantly in the deserted hayfields for several years after the Reservation was established. Those were the years when the Lawrence's goldfinch was most abundant. When the patches of fiddleneck became smaller, the number of nesting Lawrence's goldfinches also declined. Continuous observations from early April to late July show the species depends more on this one food than on any other. Almost invariably a feeding goldfinch at that season is in a fiddleneck plant (Linsdale, 1950).

James L. Ortega (1945) saw on June 1 in southern California a female Lawrence's goldfinch fly to a dove's nest, puncture one egg, and eat its contents.

A. E. Culbertson (1946) saw in early August 1944 Lawrence's goldfinches feeding on jumping galls (*Neuroterus saltatorius*) in a heavily infested stand of valley oaks (*Quercus lobata*) near Fresno, Calif. These leaf galls are about one millimeter in diameter and have an extremely thin, dry shell. They seem to jump as the larva within strikes rapidly against the inner wall. A flock of about 30 birds congregated and fed on the galls daily for 3 weeks. They picked up most of the galls from the ground, but when they were disturbed, the birds flew into the trees and picked the galls from the leaves.

Goldfinches show a fondness for salt, especially during the nesting season, and repeatedly visit saltlicks or other ground deposits of it. Peterson (1942) offered salt continuously in a partly wooded pasture on Mount Diablo. Lawrence's goldfinches came in flocks and covered the salt-saturated ground through the nesting season. They picked at crystals occasionally, but fed mostly from the soil within a foot of the block. By June they stopped coming.

Water.—Though Lawrence's goldfinches live in dry habitats, they require water nearly the year round. They drink from the creeks until these cease running, and then they search out overflow water from tanks, wells, and dripping faucets.

In early afternoon on October 22 a flock of more than 20 Lawrence's goldfinches flew into two willows beside a water trough and uttered their thin, plaintive notes for about 12 minutes as they moved about in the dead branches. Finally two fluttered down to the edge of the trough and drank, and others followed immediately. For a few minutes there was great fluttering and flying back and forth between the two willows and the trough. At one time 12 were lined up along the end-board. As two or three left, others immediately took their places and drank. Each bird sipped rapidly, about once each 1½ seconds, tipping its body to dip its beak in the water with its tail up, then throwing its head up and its tail down as it swallowed.

Lawrence's goldfinch is fond of bathing when the opportunity offers, as in the shallow margins of creeks. Flocks going down to water tend to gather around the bolder individuals that land first, as though requiring a nucleus. After splashing about, the birds usually fly up to open perches in the sun or vines or willow branches to sit and preen with feathers fluffed out to dry. Lawrence's goldfinches seem to preen more than other passerine birds studied on the Reservation.

Voice.—Ridgway (1877) reports that this bird "uttered very pleasant and quite peculiar notes." According to A. A. Allen (1932) the songs of this goldfinch are lower in pitch and somewhat rougher than the songs of the other species, and it has among its call notes a harsh *kee-yerr* that is quite different from the notes of the others. J. Grinnell (1912) noted several pairs in early May at Glendora,

Calif., "with their wheezy notes." Grinnell and Storer (1924) characterized the song of the male as weak but varied and distinctive, and the call notes single, low, and with a tinkling quality. They point out that the song and clear, bell-like call notes are so distinctive as to provide, after once learned, the readiest means of identification.

The male's song in spring is high and melodious with many clear notes, but seemingly higher in pitch and weaker in volume than that of the green-backed goldfinch. Its main function appears to be the establishment and maintenance of the pair bond. He sings mainly when he is near the female, and his tones are richest during courtship. He sings more continuously during the nest-building period than some other small birds, though his song seems less strident then. He also sings when attacking other males.

Flocking Lawrence's goldfinches usually keep up a nearly continuous twitter of thin clear-notes, high in pitch, but varied and musical. In the autumn this tinkling twittering is occasionally accented when one or two birds break into a series of high-pitched, rapid, ascending and descending trills, often punctuated by longer clear notes, churrs, and stutterings, some of which have a distinctly finchlike slur.

Field marks.—Lawrence's goldfinch is a small, grayish bird about half the size of a junco. The yellow on the under parts is restricted to the breast; the outer surface of the wing is marked with yellow and white which shows in flight. The flight feathers and tail are chiefly black. The male may be recognized by the black markings encircling the flesh-colored bill which, as he faces the observer, give him a hooded appearance in winter as well as summer plumage. The female is a duller grayish brown, with a bare suggestion of the white markings of the male.

Enemies.—Sharp-shinned and Cooper hawks occur frequently where Lawrence goldfinches live. Even though pursuits are seen often, the goldfinches nearly always escape. Scrub jays threaten them, especially in the nesting season when they are regularly on the lookout for vulnerable nests. One midmorning in July a fence lizard (*Sceloporus occidentalis*) climbed up the nest limb of a pair of Lawrence's goldfinches and up the side of the nest; it paused at the rim, looked into the nest, turned back, and retraced its path back down the limb without touching its contents.

Winter.—Miss Emily Smith (MS.) has observed that Lawrence's goldfinches occasionally winter in the Santa Clara Valley. On Jan. 8, 1948, near Los Gatos, a flock contained about 20 singing birds. The species sometimes remains through the winter on the Hastings Reservation, but the first one observed in the winter of 1950–51 was recorded on January 30.

In some winters Lawrence's goldfinches tend to move south and eastward through Arizona, New Mexico, and Texas. Winter status of the birds in recent years is indicated by evidence summarized from Audubon Field Notes. Gale Monson (1951a) reported a flight of Lawrence's goldfinches southeastward from their summer range, in the fall of 1950. They were common at Tucson, and the species was present on November 30 at Tumacacori National Monument, Ariz. The birds were present at El Paso after November 16, including a flock of 42 at Ascarate Lake on December 2. Monson (1951b) says that in late winter this bird is common in lowland areas, including the Rio Grande Valley from Las Cruces, N. Mex., to Fabens, Tex., the last ones being seen at El Paso on March 20. That was the 3rd year in 20 they had visited the Rio Grande.

In the early winter of 1951 the Lawrence's goldfinches made another eastward flight. About 20 were noted at Tucson on November 4, at Liberty, Ariz., on November 12, and on the Colorado River Indian Reservation on November 9 (Monson, 1952a). In 1953 a flight of this species to central and southern Arizona developed, with records after October 3 at Tucson, Peoria, Wikieup, Hereford, and in Sonora (Monson, 1954a). In 1953–54 more than 50 Lawrence's goldfinches wintered in the El Paso area; nearly 170 were seen at Tucson, January 2, and more than 23 were still present at Tempe by March 17 (Monson, 1954b). That spring these birds were widely reported in southern California.

DISTRIBUTION

Range.—California, southern Nevada, Arizona, and New Mexico, south to northwestern Mexico and extreme western Texas.

Breeding range.—The Lawrence's goldfinch breeds in California west of the Sierra Nevada (Hyampom southeast to Santa Rosa Mountains) and in northern Baja California (Sierra Juárez, Sierra San Pedro Mártir). Casual in summer in southwestern New Mexico (Silver City).

Winter range.—Winters from north-central California (San Francisco, Marysville), southern Nevada, central Arizona (Fort Mohave, near Prescott, Phoenix, Paradise), and southwestern and central southern New Mexico (Fort Bayard, Las Cruces) south to northern Baja California (20 miles south of San Quintín, Cocopah Mountains), northern Sonora (Tecoripa), and western Texas (El Paso).

Egg dates.—California: 74 records, April 1 to July 10; 38 records, May 1 to May 30.

LOXIA CURVIROSTRA CURVIROSTRA Linnaeus

Common Crossbill

Habits

The fact that the common crossbill of the Old World has occurred in Greenland entitles it to a place on our North American Check-List. An inhabitant of the boreal conifer forests of northern Europe, it breeds from the northern British Isles eastward to central western Siberia. It winters irregularly southward to the Mediterranean region, and has strayed to Jan Mayen Land, Iceland, and Greenland (Nappasoq, Kangamuit, Angmagssalik).

Ludlow Griscom (1937) describes it as follows: "Quite different from any New World subspecies; a large Crossbill, wing (male) 98–102 mm.; culmen 18–20 mm.; depth of bill at base 12–14 mm.; consequently as large as the Mexican *stricklandi* with a radically still deeper bill; coloration of both sexes distinctly paler in ground color than the next race, especially noticeable on belly, vent, and under tailcoverts; reds of adult male paler than in any New World race except *benti*, the scarlet tone dulled by a hepatic or pinkish rather than the deeper brick red of our eastern Crossbill; females distinctly yellower, less olive, than our eastern Crossbill, the olive wash below more frequently tinging throat and chin, and more often extensively spotted and tipped with dusky."

European ornithological literature indicates that the nesting habits, sequence of plumages, food, and other habits of the common crossbill of the Old World are very similar to those of the American subspecies. The following from the 1920 edition of Witherby's "Practical Handbook of British Birds" tells the story concisely: "Haunts coniferous woods, frequently nesting in clumps or belts of Scots firs, not as a rule in thickest part, but by preference on outskirts of forest. Nests at varying heights, sometimes not more than 6 ft. from ground. *Nest.*—Characteristic: strong foundation of fir-twigs, with superstructure of grasses, wool, etc., lined grass, rabbit's fur, hair, feathers, etc.; somewhat flattened in shape. *Eggs.*—Usually 4, sometimes 3 only, rarely 5. Ground greenish-white (sometimes faint reddish flush) with few bold spots and streaks of purple-red, sometimes blackish, generally at big end; in some cases markings faint. Average of 25 Norfolk eggs 22.32 × 16.06 mm. *Breeding season.*—Irregular: some laying Jan. and Feb., mostly March and early April; sometimes also June and July."

The Handbook lists its food as: "Normally seeds of cones of Scots fir and other conifers, but also apple-pips, rowan berries, buds, aphides, caterpillars, etc."

DISTRIBUTION

Range.—Europe and western Siberia.

Breeding range.—The common crossbill breeds from Ireland, southern Scotland, northern Scandinavia (from tree limit), northern Russia (Arkhangelsk), and central western Siberia to southwestern Yakutsk, south to northern Spain (the Pyrenees), northern Italy (the Alps), Rumania (the Carpathians), and central Russia (Kaluga, Kazan).

Winter range.—Winters south irregularly to Portugal, southern Spain, Sardinia, Sicily, Malta, the Cyclades, and Palestine.

Casual records.—Accidental in Greenland (Nappasoq, Kangámiut, Angmagssalik), Jan Mayen, Iceland, and Tangiers.

LOXIA CURVIROSTRA PUSILLA Gloger

Newfoundland Crossbill

Contributed by OLIVER L. AUSTIN, JR.

HABITS

In Mr. Bent's files was found the following introductory paragraph to his history of this crossbill, which he was the first to recognize as distinct from other North American populations of the species and to describe accurately:

"While visiting with Dr. Leonard C. Sanford at his camp on Fox Island River in Newfoundland, on June 10, 1912, I noticed two crossbills which he had recently collected there, which were apparently different from any crossbills I had ever seen from eastern North America. At my suggestion he collected 11 more and loaned them to me for study. After comparing these with what specimens I could find in the museums at New York and Washington, I decided to describe and name the Newfoundland bird as a new subspecies. I (1912) named it *Loxia curvirostra percna* and assigned to it the following subspecific characters: 'Similar to *Loxia curvirostra minor* (Brehm) but considerably larger and with a much larger and heavier bill; slightly larger than *Loxia curvirostra bendirei* Ridgway; but somewhat smaller than *Loxia curvirostra stricklandi* Ridgway. In general coloration darker than any of the American subspecies of *Loxia curvirostra;* the reds deeper, richer and more brilliant and the greenish yellow shades richer and brighter than in similar plumages of the other forms. Whereas in the summer plumages of other American forms we find only a few of the most highly colored birds with reds equalling flame scarlet, and most of them show only orange chrome or duller shades of red, with less brilliant greens and yellows; we find in *Loxia curvirostra percna* scarlet, scarlet vermilion, vermilion, poppy red or even geranium red of the most brilliant, glossy shades, with various brilliant shades of greenish yellow.' (Names of colors taken from Ridgway's Nomenclature of Colors, edition of 1886.)"

I suspect that Mr. Bent typed this paragraph 10 years or more before his death and left it to complete later when more information might become available about the subspecies' habits and life history. He certainly wrote it before the A.O.U. Check-List Committee officially recognized Gloger's prior name in 1944, and probably before two revisers of the complicated taxonomy of this often perplexing group (van Rossem 1934, Griscom 1937) pointed out that Gloger's *pusilla*, proposed a century earlier in 1834 for an apparent migrant with no more specific type locality than "eastern United States," was available for and probably applicable to the Newfoundland race.

The 1957 A.O.U. Check-List retains *pusilla* for the red crossbills breeding in Newfoundland and adds that the subspecies "Wanders, chiefly in winter, west and south to western Iowa (Woodbury County), eastern Kansas (Burlington), northern Illinois (Chicago), northern Indiana (Michigan City), southern Ontario (Toronto, Ottowa), northern Virginia (Four-mile Run), and eastern Maryland; casually to Georgia (St. Mary's, Stone Mountain) and Bermuda."

No ornithologist has as yet made an intensive study of the red crossbills in Newfoundland. Peters and Burleigh (1951) characterize its status there as "Resident, fairly common locally in summer but uncommon in winter. Erratic and local in distribution. Common in Codroy Valley in September, indicating a southward migration." They add it "frequently occurs in mixed flocks with the slightly larger White-winged Crossbill in Newfoundland. In spruce forests we often see or hear flocks of crossbills flying overhead when the species cannot be determined." They also make the following observations of interest:

* * * The Red Crossbills often cut the cone from the branch and carry it in their claws to a better perch before breaking it open, while the White-winged Crossbills usually break the cone open while it is still attached to the tree.

Crossbills are quite erratic birds, possibly because they must continually search out supplies of cones for food. They are often very early nesters, sometimes nesting in January or February and at other times not until mid-summer. Perhaps the available food supply influences their breeding cycle. They commonly move southward in the winter but as long as proper food is available some will remain during even the coldest weather.

Crossbills are usually unsuspicious, and when a flock is feeding they may be approached rather closely. A flock feeding on the cones clustered in the top of a spruce * * * climb around the branches like small parrots, using both bills and feet. One may hang by its beak or one foot while reaching for a nearby cone. When frightened one may swing beneath a twig where it is partially concealed by thick foliage. If the flock is thoroughly alarmed it may fly to a considerable distance, but if the tree in which they were feeding contains a considerable supply of food they often return to it.   After they have fed they frequently alight in a tall tree-top, and often sing from such an elevated perch.

Of its nesting the same authors write: "Nests in conifers, building a nest of twigs, rootlets or strips of bark, and lining it with mosses, hair or fur.   The 4 or 5 eggs are pale greenish-blue, spotted with brown and lavender.   They may nest at any time from January to July."   Mr. Harris supplies the following egg data: The measurements of 19 eggs average 21.2 × 15.4 millimeters; the eggs showing the four extremes measure *22.5* × 14.5, 21.0 × *16.7*, *19.5* × 15.2, and 22.1 × *14.1* millimeters."

For field marks Peters and Burleigh (1951) give the following characteristics, which are equally applicable to all races of the species: "Adult males are brick-red; young males are yellow, and females are yellow-gray.   This parrotlike finch is unmistakable if you are close enough to see its crossed bill.   Absence of white on wings separates it from [the white-winged crossbill]."

The same authors say of its voice: "Song is a finch-like warble. Call note is a sharp *kip-kip-kip* or *jip-jip-jip*."

Otherwise its habits and behavior probably do not differ markedly from those of its better-known close relatives elsewhere.

DISTRIBUTION

Breeding range.—The Newfoundland red crossbill breeds in Newfoundland.

Winter range.—Wanders, chiefly in winter, west and south to western Iowa (Woodbury County), eastern Kansas (Burlington), northern Illinois (Chicago), northern Indiana (Michigan City), southern Ontario (Toronto, Ottawa), northern Virginia (Four-mile Run), and eastern Maryland.

Casual records.—Casual in Georgia (St. Marys, Stone Mountain) and Bermuda.

LOXIA CURVIROSTRA MINOR Brehm

Red Crossbill

PLATE 27

HABITS

This is the well known crossbill of eastern North America.   Ludlow Griscom (1937), in his exhaustive study of this species, designates this race (under the name *neogoca*) as "a medium-sized Crossbill with a bill of medium length, but relatively slender, the tip of the upper mandible greatly prolonged beyond the end of the lower; wing 86.5–91; culmen 15.5–17.5; depth of bill 9–10."

PLATE 27

pen, Colo., Mar. 27, 1953   A. W. Gardner

RED CROSSBILL

ncoln County, Maine, August 1949   A. D. Cruickshank

WHITE-WINGED CROSSBILL

He says of its normal breeding range: "Chiefly the Upper Canadian one of North America, east of the treeless areas. Breeding birds examined from Quebec, Nova Scotia, New Brunswick, Ontario, northern New England, northern New York, Michigan, Wisconsin and Minnesota. * * * Breeding most commonly in late winter and early spring, less often in September and October, and still more rarely in May, June and July, such cases involving stray pairs only, never a large population."

Of vagrant breeding, he says: "At irregular intervals invading the lower Canadian zone and breeding in numbers after southward flights. Has bred in numbers at long intervals in the Berkshire Mountains, Mass., the Catskill Mountains, New York, and the mountains of Pennsylvania (where there is as yet no final evidence of a permanently resident population). Still more rarely breeding in the Transition zone (numerous occasions eastern Mass.), twice in southern New York, once in Maryland, Indiana and Ohio. Abundant in the mountains of North Carolina for several years after two great flights, and may have bred there."

Spring.—Although crossbills undoubtedly deserve their reputation for irregular movements, the following note by Wright and Allen (1910) on the regularity of their appearance at Ithaca, N.Y., in June, is of interest:

In all we have about 40 records for the species. Of these, none have been made during the fall migration, but six during the winter, five during the spring, from the middle of March to the first of May, and thirty during the month of June. * * * The first record was made June 16, 1889, by Mr. L. A. Fuertes who with us in recent years has noticed the regularity of their occurrence. In 1900 and 1904 records were also made in June. In 1906 a flock of 10 were seen on the Cornell Campus from June 21 to 24. In 1907 they were first seen on May 28 when twelve were recorded, and they continued common until June 24. In 1908 they were daily noted from June 10 to 17. In 1909 a flock of fifteen appeared June 6 and the species remained until June 14.

In reply to my enquiry, Dr. Allen writes to me in June 1951 that the crossbills have not been reported there in June during recent years. William Brewster (1906) says: "In the neighborhood of Cambridge, where they have been seen during every month of the year, I have repeatedly known them to appear suddenly and rather numerously in May or June * * *." These are good examples of the erratic and unaccountable movements of these nomadic birds, rather than true migrations.

Courtship.—Mrs. Louise de Kiriline Lawrence (1949) writes: "By the middle of January the pairing of the Red Crossbills became an established fact. Birds then began to appear in single pairs rather than in flock, or in small groups of 2 or 3 pairs. * * *

"Courtship-feeding was first observed on February 3 when a male offered his female salted grit. I also noted it on February 22, and this time the male tendered his mate an aspen bud. During early March several pairs of crossbills were apparently establishing territory in a certain place on the south shore of Pimisi Bay near the mouth of the river and here I eventually found 4 nests. The birds were seen flying around in the tops of the trees with much singing, calling and chasing. It was here also, I first witnessed males in flight song. Around the female, usually sitting nibbling cone seeds in the very top of a tree, the male rose on vibrating wings in circle after circle, his brick-red plumage sparkling in the sun, uttering, at first, loud whistled notes which presently ran into an enraptured melody of clarion-like song. The performance usually ended with the female's sudden departure to another tree and the male in hot pursuit after her."

Nesting.—Probably the first authentic nest of the red crossbill to be recorded in North America was found by Eugene P. Bicknell at Riverdale, New York City, late in April 1875, when he discovered a female building a nest that contained three eggs. He (1880) describes it as follows:

The nest was placed in a tapering cedar of rather scanty foliage, about eighteen feet from the ground, and was without any single main support, being built in a mass of small tangled twigs, from which it was with difficulty detached. The situation could scarcely have been more conspicuous, being close to the intersection of several roads (all of them more or less bordered with ornamental evergreens), in plain sight of as many residences, and constantly exposed to the view of passers-by. The materials of its composition were of rather a miscellaneous character, becoming finer and more select from without inwards. An exterior of bristling spruce twigs loosely arranged surrounded a mass of matted shreds of cedar bark, which formed the principal body of the structure, a few strips of the same appearing around the upper border, the whole succeeded on the inside by a sort of felting of finer material, which received the scanty lining of black horsehair, fine rootlets, grass stems, pieces of string, and two or three feathers. This shallow felting of the inner nest can apparently be removed intact from the body of the structure, which, besides the above mentioned material, contained small pieces of moss, leaves, grass, string, cottony substances, and the green foliage of cedar.

The nest measured internally two and one half inches in diameter by over one and a quarter in depth; being in diameter externally about four inches, and rather shallow in appearance.

A few years later, A. H. Helme (1883) reported a nest that he found near Millers Place, Long Island, on Apr. 10, 1883. It was "on a horizontal branch of a pine, about thirty feet from the ground * * *." This nest was composed of fine shreds of chestnut bark and moss, contained a few pieces of caterpillar's silk, and was lined with moss, two or three feathers of a great horned owl, and several of the crossbill itself. Dimensions were 4¼ inches in breadth by 3 inches in depth. The cavity was 2⅛ inches in breadth by 1½ inches in depth.

A nest found near Marblehead, Mass., on Apr. 22, 1917, was brought to William Brewster (1918). It had been placed about 18 feet from the ground on a branch of a pitch pine. In the lining of the nest were "a few Crossbill feathers at least one of which, brick red in color, must have come from an adult male bird. Their presence affords, of course, convincing evidence as to the original ownership of the nest, thereby, indeed, it is 'self-identifying.' "

From the more normal breeding range of the species we have numerous records and plenty of information. The first Nova Scotia nest was recorded by Thomas J. Egan (1889b), a well known and reliable Halifax taxidermist and naturalist. He found the nest on Mar. 30, 1889, in "a pine and spruce wood" near Halifax. "The tree on which the nest was found was a large spruce about seventy-five feet high. The nest was on the end of a branch about thirty feet from the ground. A small branch had been partly broken at some time and had turned back on the main branch. It had continued growing, and had formed a snug, well-sheltered clump. In the little bower formed by the secured branch, the Crossbills had built a neat nest of fine grass and moss."

Harold F. Tufts (1906) published an interesting account of the nesting of this and the white-winged crossbills in Nova Scotia. He says:

"The first nests discovered were those of the American Crossbill (*Loxia curvirostra minor*) Jan. 31, three in number. Of these, two contained young just hatched. The others [sic] held three eggs, advanced in incubation.   * * *

"* * * The sitting female carefully watched my movements as I approached the nest and upon my reaching out to touch her raised the feathers on her crown, opened her bill, and in short made herself look quite ferocious. Finally sliding off the nest, she flitted about within a few feet of me, keeping up an angry chirping, in which she was soon joined by her mate."

Dr. Tufts's brother, Robie W. Tufts, of Wolfville, has sent me data and interesting notes on the nesting of this crossbill in Nova Scotia, in which the following nesting dates are given: Aug. 4, 1896, nest containing three young birds; Feb. 25, 1906, nest with three eggs; Feb. 28, 1906, two nests with four fresh eggs each; and Mar. 31, 1906, nest with three fresh eggs. About the nests he says:

"The nests were all bulky affairs and usually were placed well out on a horizontal branch of a thick, bushy spruce tree. Elevation ranged from about 10 feet to say 40. Other nests were found in hemlocks, but when that tree was used, the nests were invariably placed close to the trunk and concealed by a cluster of thick twigs which often sprout at the point where the branch starts. I recall several nests which we found in dead spruce trees. In such cases the nests were always remarkably well concealed among the beard (*Usnea*) moss which hung from the branches in profusion. Nests were almost invariably discovered by watching the male carry food to the sitting bird. He was accustomed to feed nearby and was conspicuous by his loud and incessant chirping and singing. On one occasion I sat close by the sitting female and waited for him to come to her, so that I might see the manner of his feeding. He soon appeared and, taking no notice of me, was seen to place his bill inside her open mouth. 1 well recall the regurgitory movements of his throat and I could see what looked like thick cream being swallowed by the female. This was, of course, nothing else than the seeds of the conifers.

"The nests were bulky, being composed of twigs and plenty of decayed wood and beard moss (*Usnea*). The lining was sometimes of feathers, but I recall that more often it was made up entirely from the silky fibres which the birds extracted from the seed-pods of the fireweed (*Epilobium angustifolium*) which often was to be found near the nesting colonies."

In Ontario, Mrs. Lawrence (1949) found four nests at Pimisi Bay, which she describes as follows:

* * * Nest A was located in a lone white pine which stood on the crest of a high point overlooking Pimisi Bay. * * * It was saddled on a horizontal branch 8 feet out from the trunk and 6½ feet from the end. The distance from the ground was 23 feet. The nest was made of pine twigs and some spruce twigs on the outside, next dead grasses, green moss and strips of inner bark of white cedar. Inside it was lined with hairs and feathers." This nest was found on April 3, and was abandoned later.

Nest B was discovered on April 6 about 1000 feet north of Nest A. It was built in a red pine about 35 feet from the ground. * * * This three (sic) stood on the periphery of a clump of tall trees on a slope about 30 feet from the lake. This nest was also saddled on a horizontal branch, about 3 feet out from the trunk and 1½ feet from the tip of the branch. * * *

Nest C was discovered on the same date. This nest was located between Nest A and B at a distance of 300 feet from Nest B. It was built deeply seated in the fork of one of the middle branches of a white spruce, very well concealed in a clump of small bushy branchlets. It was at a height of 28 feet from the ground, 4 feet 5 inches from the trunk and 3 feet 9 inches from the tip of the branch. * * *

Nest D was discovered on April 9 when the calling of the birds, presumed to belong to Nest B, was heard continuously during a watch at Nest C. Going to investigate, I found this nest in a white spruce which stood 75 feet south of Nest B. It was placed 4 feet out from the trunk and 3½ feet from the tip of the branch, at height of 32 feet from the ground. This nest was beautifully made with an outer structure of dry spruce twigs, a pattern found in all the nests collected. Next came strips of the inner bark of cedar intermingled with green moss and *Usnea*.

The inner lining was made of a few pine needles, a thick layer of hairs from the white-tailed deer and *Usnea*.

The measurements of these four nests did not vary greatly. The outside diameter varied from 5¼ to 5½ inches; the inner diameter was uniformly about 2 inches; the outside depth varied from 3 to 3½ inches; and the inside depth was from 1⅜₆ to 1¹⁰⁄₁₆ inches.

Dorothy E. Snyder (1951) located a nest at Andrews Point, Cape Ann, Mass., during March 1950. This nest, "about 30 feet up in a pitch pine * * * was saddled on a branch three feet from the tip where the foliage was dense, and only a short distance from the upper windows of a summer cottage." The nest was blown down later and the eggs were broken.

The same observer (1954) found a partially completed nest in northeastern Massachusetts on Mar. 4, 1952, in a large group of exotic Japanese black pines (*Pinus thurbergii*). The latter were fruiting abundantly and provided a convenient food supply. The nest, completed by March 18, was 16 feet 2 inches from the ground—24 inches below the summit of the tree—and saddled in a thick tuft of needles and cones on a branch a half-inch in diameter, only 2½ inches from the trunk. Miss Snyder believes the first egg was laid on this date, but she intentionally kept away from the nest until March 27. On that date it proved necessary to poke the female off the nest. The bird would go to the nearest twig and return as soon as possible to the nest. The three young seen in the nest April 3 were believed to have hatched the previous day. The young were able to hold up their heads and had a gray down covering on April 5, and apparently vacated the nest on April 17. Incubation was performed only by the female. She was fed on the nest by the male while the nestlings were small (up to 4 or 5 days), and then fed the young by regurgitation. Later, both parents fed the young directly. Both parents swallowed the excreta until the last week of occupancy of the nest, after which the outside became whitened. Records at the nearby Coast Guard station indicated an average temperature of 38 degrees F. for the overall period, with extremes of 17 and 51 degrees; during the April period there were 11 days of fog or rain.

Eggs.—The red crossbill usually lays three or four eggs, occasionally five. E. P. Bicknell (1880) describes the eggs very well as follows:

The fresh eggs are in ground color of a decided greenish tint, almost immaculate on the smaller end, but on the opposite side with irregular spots and dottings of lavender-brown of slightly varying shade, interspersed with a few heavy surface-spots of dark purple-brown. There is no approach in the arrangement of these to a circle, but between the apex of the larger end, and the greatest diameter of the egg, is a fine hair-like surface line; in two examples it forms a complete though irregular circle, and encloses the principal spots. In the other egg, which is the largest, this line is not quite complete and the primary blotches are wanting, but the secondary markings are correspondingly larger and more numerous. In another egg there are two perfect figures of 3 formed on the sides by the secondary marks, one of them large and singularly symmetrical. The eggs measure respectively .74×.56, .75×.58, .78×.59.

A. H. Helme (1883) describes the eggs he found slightly differently: "The eggs have a dull white ground with a faint tinge of blue, marked with small spots and lines of brown and black, which tend to form a circle around the larger end. There are also numerous shell markings of a dull lilac color. The eggs measure as follows: .81×.56, .82×.56, 81×55 [sic]."

W. G. F. Harris has supplied the following description: "This species lays from three to five eggs with sets of four most common. The eggs are ovate in shape with a tendency to elongate-ovate, and very little gloss. The ground is very pale bluish-white, or greenish-white, variously marked with spots and blotches of 'cinnamon drab,' 'Natal brown,' 'bone brown,' or 'Mars brown,' with an occasional spot, streak, or even a scrawl of black. Some eggs are very lightly marked, having only a few scattered spots of black or dark brown; others may be quite boldly spotted with dark browns and black, with undertones of drab. There is a general tendency for the markings to concentrate at the large end, but some may be spotted more or less evenly all over. The measurements of 37 eggs average 20.4 by 14.8 millimeters; the eggs showing the four extremes measure *22.4* by 15.5, 21.0 by *16.0*, *18.7* by 14.3, and 20.5 by *14.0* millimeters."

Young.—After going into the nest life and care of the young in detail, Mrs. Lawrence (1949) summarizes it as follows:

* * * Incubation lasts at least 12 days, probably 14 to 18 days. The female alone incubates and her attentive periods are, as a rule, continuous and long. During the day she leaves the nest a few times for short periods. * * *

After the young are hatched the female broods them for long periods without help from the male. As the young grow older the brooding time is gradually shortened. In the case of the nesting described in this paper the female practically ceased brooding on the 5th day. It is probable, however, that in very early nestings the brooding is continued considerably longer.

From the time incubation starts, the male's role becomes exclusively one of provider of food for the family. Thus he practically supports the incubating female by feeding her every 2 to 3 hours. After the young hatch he feeds the young as well as the brooding female. When brooding ceases the male and the female share equally in the task of feeding the young. The parents accompany each other foraging and, as a rule, they feed the young at the same time, the male first and the female waiting until the male has finished.

Apart from the courtship feeding, all feedings of both the female and the young in as well as out of the nest, are done by regurgitation. The feeding of the female both during incubation and while brooding is accompanied by a ritual, consisting of calls and answering food calls on the part of the female which crouches in an attitude of begging while the male feeds her. As soon as the female ceases brooding the ritual is also done away with, and the birds' comings and goings at the ɪest are marked by stealth and silence. Loud calling is resumed after the young ɪeave the nest, now between parents and young, accompanied by begging and ɪursuit on the part of the young.

The young remain in the nest at least 17 days. When the young leave the ɪest their bills are not crossed but during the next following weeks the tips of the ɪnandibles extend and cross as in the adults. The young are fed by the parents ᵗor at least two weeks after leaving the nest. There is no evidence of second ɪnestings, not even after interrupted nesting attempts, at least not in the same ɪerritories.

When nesting was over the birds began to wander and one family group was ɪoined by others. As flocking increased the birds in this area moved out of ɪheir winter and nesting grounds to new, and apparently better, feeding regions.

Ora W. Knight (1908) says: "In Maine I have seen the parent birds with young not long out of the nest in March, April, May, June, July and August in various sections of the State."

Plumages.—In the juvenal streaked plumage the sexes are alike, according to Dwight (1900), who describes this plumage as follows: "Above, streaked with olive-brown, the feathers with whitish edgings, an olive-green on the back and pale buff on the rump. Wings and tail clove-brown the feathers faintly edged with pale buff sometimes greenish tinged. Below, dull grayish white thickly streaked with olive-brown." See Griscom (1937, p. 111).

A partial postjuvenal molt occurs in summer, involving the body plumage but neither the wings nor the tail, producing the first winter plumage. Dwight describes the male in this plumage as follows: "Everywhere a mottled mixture of bright yellows, greens and reds, the former predominating and the reds dull, but individual variation is great. The colors are brightest on the head, rump, throat and side of abdomen. The posterior part of the abdomen and under tail coverts may be red tinged or yellowish or they may fail to moult and remain brown streaked."

The first and following nuptial plumages are produced by wear which results in brightening the plumage, as in the purple finch.

Of the plumages of the female, he says: "In natal down and juvenal plumage indistinguishable from males. The first winter plumage acquired by a partial postjuvenal moult which does not include the wings nor the tail is olive-buff indistinctly mottled or streaked with olive brown; the rump bright olive-yellow. The first nuptial plumage is acquired by wear producing little change. The adult winter plumage varies but little from the first winter, the rump perhaps brighter and the breast tinged with bright olive-yellow. Old birds sometimes show dull red tints on these areas."

Adults and young of both sexes have a complete postnuptial molt in September. At this molt, the young male acquires the "brick-red body plumage with vermilion rump."

Food.—It seems to be the accepted idea that the principal food of the crossbill consists of the seeds of conifers, and various accounts of how the bird uses its specialized bill to extract these seeds from the cones have been published by the earlier writers. C. A. Robbins (1932), with Winsor M. Tyler, made some careful observations at close range of a captive crossbill's method to open the scales and extract the seeds. As their account is too elaborate to be included here, the reader is referred to the above paper for details. Their observations agree in some details with the earlier writers and differ from them in others. Briefly the method "plainly shown us by our bird, involves the use of *two* appliances; *the bill*, which forces and holds apart the scales; and *the tongue*, which lifts the seeds out."

Crossbills eat the seeds from the cones of various pines, firs, spruces, hemlock, and larch. They also eat the seeds of birches, alders, box elders, elms, ragweed, hemp, and probably other weeds. At times they feed on the buds of birches, alders, willows, poplars, elms, and maples, as well as the tender, green buds of spruces.

Perley M. Silloway (1923) says: "The Crossbills eat the seeds from the birch catkins in two different ways. Sometimes they cling to the terminal twigs where the cones are attached and bite out mouthfuls of seeds, often standing with head down in their endeavors to reach the catkins, and detaching seeds with their crossed, forcep-like mandibles, and many seeds fall wasted to the ground. Usually, however, they bite off the cones one at a time, holding them against a branch with their feet, and munch on it in a leisurely manner."

Prof. O. A. Stevens of Fargo, N. Dak., writes me in a letter: "A number of people reported the birds, usually feeding on sunflowers. We had a few sunflowers in the garden. Once I saw a cat jump up and seize one of the birds as it clung to a sunflower head about two feet above the ground."

Crossbills also eat insect food—caterpillars, plant lice, larvae of insects, beetles, ants, etc. Ora W. Knight (1908) observed "several Crossbills engaged in eating larvae of *Vanessa antiopa* and the small green lice which were numerous. I have also seen them picking apart the cottony colonies of lice which are always found in bunches of alders in late summer, and most certainly eating something they took from the cottony bunches.

"Lumbermen have told me of instances where the Crossbills were seen feeding on the material left in salt pork barrels thrown outside of the camps."

P. A. Taverner (1934) writes: "They seem specially fond of the little woolly aphis. It was very interesting to watch a captive specimen open galls on poplar leaves. Seizing the fleshy tissue with the bill tips so that the points crossed within the mass, it gave a little twist of

he head that split the gall wide open and the aphides within were
emoved with the tongue."

The well-known fondness of crossbills and other birds for salt and
alty substances was noted by Mrs. Lawrence (1949) when the roads
vere being sanded with chlorided gravel. She writes: "The Red
Crossbills ate not only the grit but the snow half melted by the salt
oth on the highway and at the saltlick. They put their crossed bills
ideways and lapped it up with their tongues. * * * At the feeding
lace the Crossbills also ate coal ashes on which salt had been thrown.
They showed great liking for soapy dishwater, as previously mentioned,
nd the snow discoloured by the dog's urine.* * *

"Owing to their crossed mandibles, the Crossbills drank by putting
heir bills sideways to the water and then lapping it up with their
ongues * * *."

Behavior.—Crossbills are not particularly shy and can usually be
pproached closely with a little caution. While feeding in the trees
hey move about quietly and deliberately; they are said to resemble
arrots in their movements, probably in part because they may use
heir bills in climbing. While feeding on fallen seeds or cones on the
round, they are apt to be more restless, flying occasionally up into
he trees and then down again to the ground.

Their flight is undulating, suggesting that of a woodpecker or a gold-
inch, though the dips and bounds are not so pronounced and the
light is swifter and often more prolonged, sometimes at a very con-
iderable height.

William Brewster (1938) noticed the following behavior on cold
October mornings in Maine: "Early every morning Crossbills come
n numbers to the brick chimney of a shop here and cluster about its
op, many clinging to the sides but the majority ranged about the top
where they are enveloped in smoke in which they dance up and down
vith quivering wings in evident enjoyment."

Val Nolan, Jr., writes to me of watching a flock near Indianapolis,
Ind., on Dec. 31, 1950, at 2:30 on a sunny afternoon. The flock,
containing two males, had been extremely restive, active, and wild,
not permitting close approach. Finally, by twos and threes, they all
lew to a solitary jack pine about 15 feet high. Investigating after a
ew minutes, he found the flock scattered throughout the tree, resting,
and so tame he came within two feet of a bird while it watched. Some
of the birds had turned their heads and inserted their bills in the
eathers of the back; a few had closed their eyes.

Voice.—Mrs. Lawrence (1949) describes the vocal performances
of the red crossbill as follows:

At the time of the pairing the male apparently comes into song. As far as my
observations show he has two songs, one a perching song and the other a flight

song. During the height of courtship the one song is sometimes protracted into the other and thus a rather prolonged vocal effort is produced that lacks nothing in fervour and melodiousness.

The perching song is loud and rather short. * * * It consists of whistled notes more or less interspersed with warbled phrases. The flight song is rather liquid, a passionate utterance of love by an exalted being. * * *

The Red Crossbill's characteristic location note is a very loud rhythmically whistled note 'plittplitt * * * plittplitt.' It was with this note that the male announced his arrival during incubation, while the female was brooding, and after the young left the nest, and the female answered with the same note. * * * Besides this location call they had a similar but much softer note, 'whuittwhuitt * * * whuittwhuitt', which was of a conversational nature and which the birds used constantly as they travelled together, as they fed, as one waited while the other was feeding. It was this note that the female used when she perched in the top of the nesting tree and called to her young the day they left the nest.

The alarm note was a monosyllabic whistle, very soft, 'lu * * * lu * * * lu', given between rather prolonged intervals. * * *

As mentioned, the female's food call was a continuous 'tchetetetetetetet', which she uttered practically without interruption from the time the male arrived to feed her until he departed again during incubation and brooding. * * *

Francis H. Allen writes to me of a note he heard in Maine in August: "A common phrase of the irregular and disjointed song was *tsi-whir'ree*, *whir'ree*, with a slight pause between the two dissyllabic notes."

Dorothy E. Snyder (1954) describes songs heard before the nest was completed as *pit-pit*, *tor-r-ree*, *tor-r-ree*, and as *whit-whit*, *zzzzt*, *zzzzt*, *zzzzt*, with the last notes low and rasping. The usual song, however, during the first weeks was *z-z-zt* in twos, threes, or fours, all on the same note. On April 16, perhaps two days before the young left the nest, and on the 17th, there was a new song, *whit-wheet and wheet*, *wheet*, *wheet*, changing pitch frequently and using doublets and triplets, with single notes interspersed. The arrival of either bird in the vicinity of the nest was always signaled by *pip-pip*. The female's tones were lower and deeper than, and not as soft as, those of the male.

Mrs. Louise de Kiriline Lawrence sent the following description of the song flight to Taber in January 1957: "February 8, 1954, 9:10 a.m.: A female Red Crossbill came and perched in the top of a tall tree. The next instant a male flew out from a clump of trees in the swooping undulating flight common to crossbills. Suddenly when near the female he reduced his speed until he was almost, but not quite, stationary, beating his wings rapidly and giving forth a continuous, twittering, very sweet song. Slowly, in the apparent ecstasy of this performance, he began circling around the female. Before he had quite completed the full circle around her, he once more and as suddenly resumed his fast and undulating flight. With a fine sweep he reached the top of a tall balsam fir opposite the female and soon after, as she took off, he immediately followed."

Enemies.—Predators, furred or feathered, may occasionally kill the adult birds or rob their nests of eggs or young, but definite reports of such happenings seems to be lacking. Nuttall (1832) saw a northern shrike attack some crossbills. Their fondness for salt may lure them to death on the highways that have been covered with sand and calcium chloride. Gordon M. Meade (1942) reports such a disaster, but the evidence is not clear as to whether the birds were killed by passing vehicles or by the chloride.

The cowbird does not seem to be a serious enemy. Herbert Friedmann (1938) reported only one case of a cowbird laying in a crossbill's nest.

Fall and winter.—Ludlow Griscom's records show (1937) that after the breeding season is over red crossbills wander northward "apparently rarely, into the Hudsonian zone." But southward, "irregularly to Florida (once), Georgia (several times), South Carolina (at least three times in numbers), Tennessee (several times), Alabama and Arkansas (two sight records each, subspecies presumed); western limits, eastern North and South Dakota, eastern Colorado and Kansas. About twice as common in southern New York as Virginia, about four times as frequent in Massachusetts as southern New York. Further west, reaches Missouri more commonly than Kentucky and Virginia, but very much rarer in the Great Plains. Notable flight years in the Atlantic States were 1850, 1870, 1875, 1882, 1884, 1887, 1896, 1900, 1903, 1907, 1919, and 1932."

DISTRIBUTION

Range.—Ontario, Quebec, and Nova Scotia to Missouri and northern Florida.

Breeding range.—The red crossbill breeds, and is largely resident, from northern Minnesota, central Ontario (Lake Manitowick, Canoe Lake, Pakenham), southwestern Quebec (Grand Lac), New Brunswick (Bathurst), and Nova Scotia (Wolfville) south irregularly to northern Wisconsin (Burnett County, Kelley Brook), southern Michigan (Hillsdale), southern Ontario (Toronto), West Virginia (Pocahontas County), eastern Tennessee and western North Carolina (Great Smoky Mountains), Maryland (Laurel), southeastern New York (Bronx, Miller Place), and eastern Massachusetts (Marblehead, Cape Ann).

Winter range.—Same as breeding range except for sporadic wandering northwest to central southern Mackenzie (Fort Simpson, Fort Smith), west to southeastern Saskatchewan (Indian Head) and eastern Colorado (Limon), and south to Missouri (Shannon County), Georgia (Fulton County, Midway), and northern Florida (Sumner).

Migration.—The data apply to the species as a whole. Late dates of spring departure are: Florida—Sumner, February 13. South Carolina—Mount Pleasant, May 26. North Carolina—Highlands, June 17. Virginia—Blacksburg, June 12. West Virginia—Gaudineer Knob, Pocahontas County, June 15. District of Columbia—June 5. Maryland—Salisbury, May 30. Delaware—Lewes, May 19. Pennsylvania—State College, May 19. New York—Cayuga and Oneida Lake basins, June 9 (median of 7 years, May 22); Suffolk County, June 3. Massachusetts—Martha's Vinyard, June 20. New Hampshire—Concord, June 7. Quebec—Rawdon, May 31. New Brunswick—Scotch Lake, June 13. Louisiana—Mandeville, March 27. Arkansas—Clinton, May 5. Tennessee—Nashville, June 20. Missouri—Shannon County, May 1. Illinois—Beach, June 1. Indiana—Burlington, April 23. Ohio—Columbus, June 18. Michigan—Oakland County, May 30. Ontario—London, May 24. Iowa—Sioux City, May 2. Wisconsin—Madison, June 2. Minnesota—Nisswa, May 28. Texas—El Paso, May 10. Kansas—northeastern Kansas, April 15. Nebraska—Holstein, April 25. North Dakota—Devil's Lake, June 23. Manitoba—Trees Bank, June 11. Saskatchewan—Indian Head, June 27. Arizona—Canelo, May 6. Colorado—Fort Garland, June 7.

Early dates of fall arrival are: California—Mount Pinos, October 10. Alberta—Calgary, October 2. Montana—Libby, November 24. North Dakota—northern North Dakota, September 11. South Dakota—Milbank and Brookings, October 6. Nebraska—Bladen, October 29. Kansas—northeastern Kansas, September 25. Texas—El Paso, September 28. Iowa—Davenport, August 30. Ohio—Columbus, October 11. Illinois—Lake Forest, October 29. Arkansas—Texarkana, September 10. Connecticut—New Haven, October 11. New York—Cayuga and Oneida Lake basins, October 1. Pennsylvania—Port Clinton, October 10. Maryland—Ocean City, September 12. Virginia—Bristol, August 10. North Carolina—Raleigh, November 8. Florida—Fernandina, December 4.

Egg dates.—New Brunswick: 1 record, August 6.

Kansas: 1 record, March 24.

New York: 4 records, March 30 to May 1.

Nova Scotia: 6 records, February 25 to April 27.

Ontario: 3 records, April 17 to April 29.

LOXIA CURVIROSTRA BENDIREI Ridgway

Bendire's Crossbill

HABITS

Griscom (1937) describes this crossbill as follows: "Exceedingly close to *neogoea* [=*minor*], some individuals quite indistinguishable; both sexes averaging a little larger, longer winged and with a longer bill; the great majority of adult males bright scarlet, rather than dull brick red; both sexes often with a darker and sootier gray, less brownish mantle in fresh plumage; adult females not otherwise separable in color."

As is true of other crossbills, this subspecies wanders widely in the nonbreeding season; it has been recorded over most of western North America but records in the East are unsatisfactory because of the difficulty of distinguishing *bendirei* from the eastern *minor*.

Nesting.—The breeding habits of this crossbill in British Columbia are well described by J. A. Munro (1919), as observed by him in "a small section of timbered country close to Okanagan Landing, its topography being the familiar Okanagan type of low mountain covered with Douglas fir and yellow pine, including both original forest and second growth.

"* * * A female taken on August 5, and another taken on August 18 [1915], had the worn abdominal patch of breeding birds and a third female in breeding condition, was taken on February 24, 1916."

Munro watched some crossbills on March 1 that were apparently building a nest on a ridge overlooking Okanagan Lake. He continues:

On March 19, while hunting on the same ridge, a nest in process of construction was found, about one hundred yards distant, and I concluded that its owners were the same pair as had been under observation some two weeks earlier. The nest was saddled on a thin branch near the top of a forty foot Douglas fir about fourteen inches from the trunk and was so well concealed as to be all but invisible from below. The female was under observation for half an hour, while she carried material to the nest, moulding the interior with her body after each trip, while her mate remained at the top of a nearby tree chirping excitedly.

Absence from the district prevented my return to the nest until April 9 and it then contained a newly hatched chick, and two eggs on the point of hatching. The ground color of the eggs was pale bluish green lightly flecked with lavender and with a wreath of lavender and ruddy-brown spots around the larger end. No measurements of the eggs were taken and unfortunately I was not successful in preparing them. The nest which is a very handsome one was presented to the Provincial Museum at Victoria. The body of the nest is composed of black tree moss (*Alectoria jubata*), dry grass and weed stalks; the outside, of fine fir twigs, those selected for the rim being decorated with little tufts of vivid green lichen (*Evernia vulpina*). The inside is well felted with black tree moss and contains a few pieces of fine grass and one breast feather of a Red-tailed Hawk. It is 110 mm. in diameter with an outside depth of 60 mm. and an inside depth of 30 mm.

Two other nests were found on March 18. One was in a second growth fir, "on a lower branch ten feet above the ground and ten feet out from the trunk, in plain view from the ground. The female was sitting on one egg * * *." The other nest, containing four young, "was in a tall rugged fir growing on the edge of a rocky bluff. The nest was situated eight feet from the trunk on a stout limb forty feet above the ground and was quite invisible from below."

J. W. Preston (1910) gives an interesting account of the nesting of this crossbill in the vicinity of Spokane, Wash., illustrated with photographs of two nests. He says: "The nest building began about the 10th of July and finish about the 20th."

Earlier he says:

"The nest is built of dead tamarack twigs for a foundation and outer walls, interwoven with much fine grass and a few dry pine needles. The lining is an abundance of long, black moss from tamarack trees, and a few soft feathers, making a good, warm nest, placed in the divergent small branches of a horizontal branch from four to eight feet out from the tree-trunk. One was directly in the center of a heavy bunch of long needles at the very tip of a ninety-foot pine and was so concealed by the denseness of the growth that the nest was not visible. * * * Outside diameter, four by five inches; inside, two and one-half. Outside depth, three; inside, one and one-half."

Dawson and Bowles (1909) describe a nest taken near Tacoma, Wash., on Apr. 25, 1899, that "boasts an inner quilt of felted cow-hair nearly half an inch in thickness." The female had to be lifted off the nest.

Eggs.—J. W. Preston (1910) describes his three sets of eggs as follows:

These eggs are plainly much larger than those of the eastern bird. Set number one contains four splendid eggs, measuring as follows: .85×.60, .86×.61, .87×.62, .88×.62. All are of quite uniform size, all plainly and plentifully markt about the larger end with irregular, kinky strokes and spots, varying from faint purplish to dark chestnut, over a dull greenish white ground somewhat clouded by the weak chocolate flush, which is present in some of these specimens. One egg of this set has the marks somewhat lengthwise giving it a waved or marbled appearance; with no marks darker than cinnamon brown. These extend well over the surface except the point. Three eggs of this set have the subdued purplish at the larger end approaching a wreath.

The eggs of set number two have a clear, bright greenish-white ground color, uniform over the entire surface. They measure: .79×.57, .85×.58, .83×.58. One egg is almost plain at the point, with small specks and spots of faint cinnamon over the larger part of the surface. The other two are almost alike, being sparsely fleckt with cinnamon, with little of this below the center, but heavily speckt with seal brown in an irregular wreath at the larger end. There are also a few kinky lines of the same color. * * *

The eggs of set number three measure as follows: .86.×62, .87×.62, .90×.60, being decidedly elongated. The ground color is a dull greenish, with the markings, mostly at the larger end, consisting of splashes and specks of faint chocolate and cinnamon, forming a washt surface in form of a broad, dull wreath about the large end which is bare at the point, except in one egg in which the blotches extend over the entire surface. Then there is on each of these three eggs a delicate chocolate hair line encircling a small portion of the larger end. Hanging on these lines are a few tear shaped dots of black. In all these sets there is a resemblance to eggs of the Orchard Oriole. In several eggs there is a faint flush of subdued purplish stain.

All of the above measurements are in hundreths of an inch.

Three eggs taken by J. A. Munro (1919) measure 15×20, 15×20 and 14×19 millimeters.

The measurements of 40 eggs average 21.1 by 15.2 millimeters; the eggs showing the four extremes measure *22.8* by 15.3, 20.5 by *16.1*, and *19.0* by *14.0* millimeters.

We seem to have no information on the period of incubation, which is apparently the duty of the female alone. Nor do we know anything about the care and development of the young, except that adults have been seen feeding fully grown young that have left the nest.

McCabe and McCabe (1933) discuss in some detail the possibility of young crossbills nesting the same year they are hatched and conclude that evidence confirms this extraordinary departure at times from usual passerine habits.

Plumages.—The molts and plumages correspond to those of the eastern bird.

Food.—The traditional food of this and other crossbills consists of seeds of coniferous trees, the specialized bill being well fitted for extracting the seeds from the bases of cone scales. They also eat the tender buds and soft green cones of these trees. Miss Ruby Curry writes to me that "While at Tuolome Meadows last summer, we were interested in the activities of the Sierra crossbills, which were hanging like chickadees, working on small fresh cones of the lodge pole pines, cutting them from the ends of the branches, then taking them to larger branches, where they could feed on them more easily."

J. A. Munro (1919) saw a small flock of Bendire's crossbills "feeding on green choke-cherries and tiny salmon-colored lepidopterous larvae that crawled on the under sides of the poplar leaves. To reach these the birds hang head downward in the position they often assume when extracting fir seeds from the cones."

Joe T. Marshall, Jr. (1957) states: "Although there was no evidence of * * * breeding in pine-oak areas, it often fed on seeds of the pines. Examination of eight specimens showed that they cram the esophagus with seeds until it is greatly distended; they also ingest gravel. Apparently they eat their fill in a short time, and this explains their periods of inactivity in shade within clumps of conifers. The stomachs and throats held seeds appropriate to the area of collecting: Engelmann spruce, ponderosa pine, and Chihuahua pine."

Mrs. Amelia S. Allen (1920) observed some of these crossbills feeding on fallen almonds in an orchard; they "picked the almonds from the ground, flew up into the trees and noisily pried open the shells with their bills. After eating the kernels they dropped to the ground again to search for more."

Tracy I. Storer (1921) saw some crossbills feeding on the leaves of a cork elm tree: "They were attacking certain of the leaves which were curled up on one edge, cutting these rolls open and getting something from within." On close examination, "it became evident that a woolly aphis, which had caused the curling of the leaf margin was the item of food being sought by the Crossbills. The attack of this insect causes the blade of the leaf to curl over, forming a cylindrical roll within which the aphis can feed and multiply unmolested by most of their enemies.

"Further watching of the Crossbills showed that the birds had learned the haunt of these particular aphids and also a method for obtaining them. The roll-like cases were cut open lengthwise, but in rather irregular fashion, as well as could be expected of a species with such an unhandy pair of 'scissors'; then the tongue would be inserted and the aphids withdrawn."

P. A. Taverner (1922) explains how the crossbills open leaf galls as follows: "The bird would open its bill and drive both points deeply into the soft mass of the gall until the mandibles were practically closed and crossed. Then, with a slight twist of the head, the gall would be split wide open. The hollow interior was seen to be filled with what appeared to be a sort of woolly aphis, which was rapidly cleaned out with the bird's tongue. The certainty, ease and rapidity with which the operation was performed indicated that the apparently awkwardly crossed bill was a most efficient implement for the work." This operation was closely observed on a captive crossbill that was partially fed on poplar galls.

Grinnell, Dixon, and Linsdale (1930) saw some crossbills apparently feeding on the green cones of hemlocks, but "examination, later, of the contents of the stomach of the bird taken proved that the only food was a smooth, bright-green caterpillar. Thirteen of these caterpillars, uniform in size, 12 to 17 millimeters in length, were found in the one bird."

The fondness of crossbills for salt or salty substances has been noted by several observers. Wherever salty dish water has been spilled, or where salt has been sprinkled on the ground, the birds will alight and lap it up with avidity, turning the head to one side and extending the tongue.

Behavior.—The erratic behavior of crossbills is too well known to be enlarged upon here. They are abundant in a locality one season, rare the next, then entirely absent for a season. They are most unreliable.

Leslie L. Haskin, of Brownsville, Oreg., has sent me the following note: "During the abundant years they are usually hard to observe, as they keep in the tops of the high trees. At times, however, they come down about buildings and camps in a most familiar way. About old camping places on the trail they would gather by hundreds and thousands, apparently attracted by something that they found in the ashes. One of the cabins at the deserted Paywell Mine had become a death trap for the crossbills. The windows of the cabin were still intact. The birds entered through a partially closed door, but seemed unable to find their way out. On a bench below one window, where they had struggled to escape, they lay, literally in heaps, both freshly killed birds and others that were merely dried wings and skeletons."

Voice.—J. W. Preston (1910) writes: "The song is a series of clear, loud, sparrow-like notes, and pretty whistling effects which come riffling down from some pinnacle of a great tall pine tree. An occasional note resembles a quick, clear passage in the song of the rock wren—a rich, clear, single whistle-note. Another resembles a rich portion of the Baltimore Oriole's song. But the common note of the Crossbill is an energetic, strong, metallic 'peet-peet' which is uttered on all occasions, and one seldom sees a Crossbill without also hearing this note. A male bird will gather a flock about him by means of this call. Another effort is like the twittering of the Goldfinch. Most of their movements are accompanied by the 'zeet-zeet-zeet' in a sort of whizzing tone, or 'chink-chink-chink,' 'peet-peet-peet' or 'pit-pit-pit,' metallically. But the real singing is from the tree-tops and it is a happy, cheerful song. At times the male will float about overhead, singing, much as the Horned Lark does."

Fall and winter.—The fall and winter wanderings of Bendire's crossbill are extensive. Crossbills are notoriously nomadic. This race is difficult to distinguish from the eastern bird in the field, and until more eastern specimens have been collected and identified, we do not know what the eastern limits of its wanderings are. It is significant that Thomas D. Burleigh (1941) has reported that a crossbill, collected in North Carolina, has been identified as *bendirei*.

DISTRIBUTION

Range.—Yukon and Saskatchewan south to Baja California, Texas, and Kansas.

Breeding range.—Bendire's crossbill breeds, and is largely resident, from southern Yukon (Kluane Lake, Nisutlin River) and the northern interior British Columbia (Atlin, Telegraph Creek, Nulk Lake) south, east of the Cascade Mountains, to southern Oregon (Fort Klamath, Malheur River), central Idaho (Alturas Lake), northwestern Wyoming (Yellowstone Park), central southern Montana (Shriver), and southwestern Saskatchewan (Cypress Hills); extends southwest to the Trinity Mountains section of California (French Camp, White Rock Ranger Station).

Winter range.—Same as breeding range except for sporadic wandering west to southeastern Alaska (Admiralty Island) and south to Central Baja California (Guadalupe Island, Sierra San Pedro Mártir), southeastern Arizona (Huachuca and Chiricahua mountains), southern New Mexico (Cloudcroft), western Texas (Frijole), and eastern Kansas (Lawrence).

Egg dates.—Alberta: 2 records, March 3 and May 2.

Montana: 1 record, July 27.

LOXIA CURVIROSTRA SITKENSIS Grinnell

Sitka Crossbill

HABITS

When Joseph Grinnell (1909) originally named this small crossbill from the Sitka region of Alaska, he described it as similar "in size to the smaller individuals of *Loxia curvirostra minor* (Brehm) Ridgway, of the Atlantic region of North America, but general coloration different: in adult male about orpiment orange, instead of the deep brownish crimson or coral red as in *minor.*"

L. Griscom (1937) defines the normal breeding range as "The humid coastal strip of the northwestern Pacific coast district from southern Alaska south along the coast of British Columbia, including the Queen Charlotte and Vancouver Islands, to the coastal ranges of Washington and northwestern Oregon."

According to J. A. Munro (1947), in British Columbia *Loxia curvirostra* is "Resident, at some times, in all the forested biotic areas. Violently cyclic in numbers." He states the race *sitkensis* is the one most commonly found in the coast forests while *bendirei* habits the interior parts of the province and is sporadic on the coast.

Griscom (1937) records wandering as far north as Portage Bay, Kodiak Island, Unalaska, and St. Michaels. "*South* irregularly to the northern half of California (numerous years). *East* irregularly through the lower passes into the interior of southern British Columbia and still more rarely crossing the Rocky Mountains. In the winter of 1887–1888 a great irruption eastward took place, paralleling the famous flight of evening grosbeaks in 1890. This Crossbill reached the Atlantic States in numbers from Massachusetts to South Carolina, and in the interior south to Louisiana." His paper gives full details with dates and localities. In the past decade, this subspecies has been reported at a number of localities in the Great Plains and eastern United States.

George Willett (1921) writes, from Craig, Alaska:

During the seven summers and one winter spent by the writer in southeastern Alaska previous to 1920 there was no time when this bird was not in evidence and in most localities it was very common. From observations covering this period it developed that the young were raised in both spring and fall, though whether the same birds nested twice each year was not determined. In late August, 1919, vicinity of Craig, birds were paired and males singing. Fully fledged young were plentiful in late September and early October. Again in late March and early April, 1920, many birds were paired and evidently nesting. A pair of breeding birds was taken April 1 and another pair, also breeding birds, April 2. On April 27 a pair of adults were seen feeding full-grown young on the ground. Since early summer of 1920, though the writer has covered hundreds of miles of territory, not a single crossbill has been met with, and they are apparently absent from the region at present writing. The species is known to be very irregular in its habits, but that it should desert such a large section of territory in which it is normally abundant and should remain absent for such an extended period seems worthy of record.

We seem to have no further information on the nesting habits of this subspecies. Its molts and plumages are apparently similar to those of the other races. Its food is evidently the same, including its extreme fondness for salt. Theed Pearse (1929) describes two interesting feeding habits of the Sitka crossbill, as observed on Vancouver Island. Of some birds feeding in a box elder tree, he writes:

While in the tree it was apparent that some of the birds were collecting food from the leaves, and examination showed that many of the young leaves carried a small grayish black aphis on the under side. With glasses it was possible to watch the bird actually pick off the insect, and this was done in a quite different way than would be done by a bird with a regularly shaped beak. It would be quite impossible for the crossbill to "pick off" a small insect, and they captured them by laying the side of the beak on the leaf and catching the aphis at the intersection of the two mandibles, a sideways motion and invariably successful.

* * * These aphides were not the only food this flock of crossbills were after. Some of the birds in the maples and others in nearby fruit trees were tearing at some plant-like substance held in the feet against the branch. This turned out to be the seedheads of the dandelion (*Taraxacum officinale* Weber); the bird had cut off the head from the growing plant and then carried it to the tree to eat. The heads chosen were those that had just closed after blooming, and the birds tore them open to get at the seeds at the base.

H. B. Tordoff writes Taber: "In all probability, the variations in bill size among North American subspecies of the Red Crossbill reflect differences in dietary preference, but this has yet to be proved for any of the races. The small-billed *sitkensis* should, when studied, prove to be especially informative in this regard."

In all of its other habits, *sitkensis* does not seem to differ materially from other races of the species.

DISTRIBUTION

Range.—Principally the Pacific Northwest.

Breeding range.—The Sitka crossbill breeds along the Pacific coast (including islands) from central southern and southeastern Alaska (Cook Inlet, Sergief Island) south to northwestern California (Big Lagoon).

Winter range.—Same as breeding range except for sporadic wandering east and south to southern Alberta (Jasper Park, Red Deer River), northern Wisconsin (Apostle Islands), northern Michigan (Huron Mountains, Beaver Island), southern Ontario (London, Golden Lake), southwestern Quebec (Grondines, Isle aux Canots), southern California (Riverside), Arizona (Tucson), Colorado (Breckenridge), northeastern Kansas (Lawrence), southeastern Louisiana (Mandeville), South Carolina (Charleston), Virginia (Alexandria), southeastern Pennsylvania (George School), southeastern New York (Hicksville, Hither Plain), and Massachusetts (Chatham).

Casual records.—Casual on Kodiak and St. Michael islands, Alaska.

LOXIA CURVIROSTRA BENTI Griscom

Bent's Crossbill

HABITS

Ludlow Griscom (1937) gave the above name to a crossbill which occupies part of the range formerly assigned to *bendirei*, and which he diagnosed as follows: "A relatively large crossbill, with a long and relatively slender bill; wing (male) 93.0–98; culmen 17.0–19.0; depth of bill at base 10.0–10.5. Coloration of adult male chiefly in fresh fall and winter plumage strikingly rosy red, with paler and whiter belly, less brownish gray; in worn breeding plumage always bright scarlet. Adult female in fresh fall and winter plumage a lighter and brighter yellowish below, the throat whiter and less flecked with gray, more sharply contrasted with the yellowish breast; belly whiter and grayer, less brownish gray; worn breeding birds often inseparable from *bendirei* in coloration." The type, an adult male now in the Museum of Zoology of the University of Michigan, was collected at Grafton, N. Dak., Oct. 8, 1931.

Griscom assigns to it the following range: "Normal breeding area, the pine hills of southeastern Montana, eastern Wyoming (Weston and Crook counties), western North and South Dakota, and the Rocky Mountain region of Colorado. Wandering northward to the

Cypress Hill region of southern Saskatchewan, where abundant in June, 1894 and 1895, and again in 1908. No definite evidence of breeding obtained, and I can find no published evidence of crossbills in this region at any other season or any other year."

I published (1908) the fact that I saw "a flock of 6 crossbills flying over me among the pines in the Cypress Hills," on May 31, 1905.

Allan R. Phillips writes to me that he took a "young bird just out of the nest from a family of three or more in a grove of tall ponderosa pines on the Hualpai Indian Reservation, Coconino County, Arizona, October 7, 1948," and refers it to this subspecies.

Griscom (1937) adds the following to its range: "As a non-breeding vagrant it is of irregular occurrence eastward over the Plains states to Nebraska, Iowa and Kansas (where it has been found locally in abundance on several occasions). Much more rarely westward to Oregon and California (Fort Crook and Mt. Pinos). Status of the crossbill in Utah still unknown, but the few specimens seen are *benti*. Southward to New Mexico and the mountains of southern Arizona (a notable irruption in Nov., 1885).

"Accidental in Michigan (Lane Co., McMillan, Jan. 1, 1932), Tennessee (New Found Gap, Oct. 2, 1932) and Texas (Galveston, Nov. 21, 1924)."

As the range of this subspecies is a part of what was formerly considered to be the range of *bendirei*, much of what has been written about the nesting and other habits of Bendire's crossbill should apply as well to the present race. The habits of both are undoubtedly similar.

Nesting.—Dana P. Snyder and J. Frank Cassel (1951) have published an account of the late summer nesting of this crossbill in Colorado. The reader is referred to their paper for the details of their observations.

In their summary, they write: "A late summer Red Crossbill nest in Colorado was 18 feet from the ground in a 20-foot lodgepole pine. It was started on or about July 26. The first egg was laid on or about July 29. The total clutch consisted of three eggs.

"Incubation did not begin with the laying of the first egg but may have begun with the laying of the second.

"On August 7 (about the ninth day of incubation), the female was on the nest continuously for 15 daylight hours except for six brief periods totalling 26 minutes. While on the nest that day she was fed three times by the male.

"The nest was deserted on or about August 11. The eggs were almost ready to hatch at that time."

Earlier they write:

"The foundation of the nest was of twigs of conifers. The superstructure was of fibrous material stripped from plant stems, a few grass blades, several pieces of herbaceous plant stems, a small tuft of hair, and a fascicle of pine needles (*Pinus flexilis*). The lining was of shredded bark, lichens, and fine hair (no feathers so far as we could see). The nest measured (after collection) 107–123 mm. in over-all diameter, 52 mm. in over-all depth. The cup proper was 60 mm. wide and 27 mm. deep."

A. Lang Baily wrote Mr. Bent that numbers nested on Genesee Mountain, 20 miles west of Denver, commencing Dec. 20, 1951. Nesting was still in progress when he wrote on June 6, 1952. Of 14 nests known to have complete sets of eggs, three nests held four eggs, each; nine nests held three eggs each; and two nests held two eggs each. Egg measurements varied from 22.6 × 16.4 to 21.3 × 16.2 millimeters, averaging 21.95 × 16.26. There was evident color variation.

Later, Baily (Bailey, A. M., Baily, A. Lang, and Niedrach, R. J., 1953) published a full account of this nesting colony, which may be summarized briefly: Nesting began in late December in the yellow pine (*Pinus ponderosa*) stands in the foothills and slowly moved upslope, reaching the Hudsonian zone by midsummer. Territoriality was observed only at the time of nest site selection. Females took the leading role in nest site selection and nest construction. The total time involved in nesting, from start of construction to fledging, was from 43 to 48 days: nest construction, 5 days; completion of nest to laying of first egg, 4 to 5 days; egg laying at one per day, 2 to 4 days; incubation, 14 days; nestling period, 18 to 20 days. Clutches averaged 3, varying from 2 to 4. Only females incubated. Strong evidence of double nesting was found. One nest was used for a second set of eggs after the first set was destroyed. Nesting success averaged one bird fledged for every three eggs laid.

Plumages.—H. B. Tordoff (1952) shows that the first winter plumage of male *benti* is fully as red as adult male winter plumage, *benti* differing in this respect from the eastern North American and Old World subspecies. In first winter plumage, young birds can be distinguished by the color of the edgings of certain flight feathers (red in adults, yellowish in immatures). He also demonstrated that *benti* (and probably other subspecies) has a distinct, although limited, prenuptial molt involving the chin, throat, and to a lesser degree the rest of the head. In northeastern Kansas, where his studies were made, the feathers produced by this prenuptial molt lack red pigment in the males. He suggested that the failure to develop red pigment might be based on hormonal balance of the birds at the time of molt, rather than on the dietary deficiencies usually held responsible for pigment aberrations in captive birds. Age variation in size was demonstrated; this variation is of sufficient magnitude to influence taxonomic studies and is partially masked by the similarity in plumage of first winter males and adult males in *benti*.

Behavior.—H. B. Tordoff (1954) made intensive studies of captive birds. Their resemblance to cones protects them as they roost, far out on the ends of coniferous branches. Before going to sleep birds extend and retract their tongues, three to five times a second, for as many seconds. After a pause, they repeat the process. The tongue may project on either side of the mandibles, and it extends well beyond the tips. Sizable clusters of white frothy bubbles appear at the ends of the bills. These clusters soon break, leaving the mandibles wet and shining. Coincident with the tongue action the birds open and close their bills, but at a slower rate. Also, they close the bill in the "wrong" direction, resulting in a peculiar appearance because the mouth will not close evenly. It is possible that this procedure brings about a wearing down of the nonoccluding edges of the bill by abrasion, with the moisture acting like water on a whetstone. Birds are either right-handed of left-handed in opening cones, according to which way the mandibles are crossed. In feeding, the birds carry pine cones with their bills to a perch, hold the cones with their feet, and insert the tips of the open mandibles. With the long axis of the bird's head approximately at right angles to the long axis of the cone, the tip of the lower mandible presses towards the central axis of the cone and raises a scale against the essentially stationary tip of the upper mandible. The tongue then probes and removes the seeds. There is a peck order of males, another of females, and a dominance of males over females.

Bathing and sun-bathing activities are customarily social. Upon seeing hawks which are barely visible to the human eye the birds become motionless, uttering a single note, *tuck, tuck, tuck*, but resume activities a minute or so after the hawk has passed.

DISTRIBUTION

Range.—Chiefly the Rocky Mountain states.

Breeding range.—Bent's crossbill breeds, and is largely resident, from southeastern Montana (Powder River County), northeastern Wyoming (Weston and Crook counties), and western South Dakota (Harding County, Black Hills) south to eastern Utah (Uinta Mountains, Cedar Breaks; intergrading area between *grinnelli* and *benti*), southeastern Colorado (La Plata County, Fort Garland), and northern New Mexico (Chama).

Winter range.—Same as breeding range, except for sporadic wanderings west to western Oregon (Yaquina Bay, Fort Klamath), Idaho (Moscow), east to eastern North Dakota (Grafton), Minnesota (Minneapolis), and northern Michigan (McMillan), and south to southern California (Mount Pinos, Providence Mountains), southern Nevada (Lake Mead), central and southeastern Arizona (Yavapai County, Huachuca Mountains), western Oklahoma (Kenton), and western and southeastern Texas (Frijole, Galveston).

Casual record.—Casual in southwestern Saskatchewan (Cypress Hills).

Egg dates.—Colorado: 5 records, January 30 to July 27.

LOXIA CURVIROSTRA GRINNELLI Griscom
Grinnell's Crossbill

HABITS

Ludlow Griscom (1937) in naming this race says: "It seems most fitting * * * that the race here described should be named after Dr. Joseph Grinnell, the dean of California ornithologists, and a leader in the study of the crossbills of his State."

His diagnosis follows: "A large crossbill, the adult male scarlet in general coloration throughout the year; wing length and exposed culmen exactly as in *benti;* differing from *benti* in having a much deeper bill, 10.3–11.5, versus 10.0–10.5, and never having the pronounced rosy and paler coloration of that race; easily separable from *bendirei* in much larger size and deeper bill. Also readily separable from *stricklandi,* a still larger bird, with a still deeper bill, and darker coloration, in adult males blood red rather than scarlet."

He gives it the following rather wide range: "*California:* Fairly common resident in the higher Sierra Nevada from Mt. Shasta to Mt. Whitney; also Mt. Pinos, Ventura County, the San Bernardino Mountains, and the San Jacinto Mountains; definitely breeding birds are very rare in collections, as field work in most of this area in late winter and early spring is practically impossible. Occurs sporadically as a vagrant along the Pacific coast from Marin County to San Diego County. *Arizona:* Of fairly common occurrence in the mountains of northern Arizona, all but one of the published breeding records for *stricklandi,* in the State, belonging here. Non-breeding specimens not uncommon in the larger esatern collections and the important western ones. Has definitely bred in the Kaibab National Forest, Grand Canyon, near Williams (Wetmore), in the Mogollon Mountains, and almost certainly on San Francisco Mountain and near Springerville. Field experience proves conclusively that the occurrence of this Crossbill in Arizona is exceedingly erratic and irregular, and that it is absent from any one locality for years at a stretch. Some day its presence or absence in Arizona will be checked with its simultaneous status in the mountains of California, and interesting correlations may be discovered. *Nevada:* In recent years summer specimens have been collected in the Charleston Mountains and the Shell Creek Range. It is a reasonable expectation that some day *grinnelli* will be found breeding in one or more of the higher ranges in western Nevada. *Lower California:* A most irregular vagrant. Recorded from Guadelupe Island in Feb. and March, 1886; as 'common' on Sept. 20, 1896, possibly having bred, to March 22, 1897; common in the San Pedro Martir Mountains in June, 1925, no signs of breeding."

This is another race taken from the range of *bendirei* as we formerly understood it. It is, therefore, fair to assume that much that has been published about Bendire's crossbill should be referred to the present race, if the place where the observation was made seems to indicate it.

DISTRIBUTION

Range.—California, Nevada, Utah, and Arizona.

Breeding range.—The Grinnell's crossbill is resident in interior mountains of California (Mount Shasta, Sierra Nevada, San Jacinto Mountains, San Bernardino Mountains), and in southwestern Nevada (Grapevine Mountains), southwestern Utah, and northwestern and central eastern Arizona (Mount Trumbull, Kaibab Plateau, Flagstaff, White Mountains).

Winter range.—Same as breeding range, wandering sporadically north to central Nevada (Quinn Canyon Mountains), west to the Pacific coast in California (Albion to Escondido), and south to southeastern Arizona (Huachuca Mountains).

Egg date.—California: 1 record, August 19.

LOXIA CURVIROSTRA STRICKLANDI Ridgway
Mexican Crossbill

HABITS

Ludlow Griscom (1937) describes this race as: "The largest of New World crossbills, with deepest and most powerful bill, the depth always 12 mm. or more; in general size averaging appreciably larger than *benti* or *grinnelli;* coloration of adult male deep scarlet to blood red, consequently averaging darker than *grinnelli* with a darker mantle; female averaging darker than *grinnelli*, often but by no means always with a darker, more olive yellow wash below."

Of its range, he says:

Resident in the pine forest belt in the mountains of the tableland of Mexico; all too little known, but apparently of vagrant and erratic habits, with a variable breeding season; apparently much less common or less well known, northward to San Luis Potosi and Chihuahua; unrecorded as yet from Sonora and Oaxaca, and several more central states, but this is probably without significance.

As a vagrant of not infrequent occurrence northward, often in some numbers, to the mountains of southern New Mexico (San Mateo Mts.; San Bernardino Mts., probably bred once); southern Arizona (Santa Rita, Huachuca, Santa Catalina, and Chiricahua Mts., where definitely bred once). Much more rarely or casually north to California (4 records, April to September), Nevada (Snake Mts., Sept. 18, 1934), and Colorado (Aurora, Nov. 2, 1919). Accidental in Kansas (Douglas Co., Jan. 25, 1911) and Wyoming (Weston Co., Newcastle, July 4, 1935).

Found in numbers in the San Pedro Martir Mountains, Lower California, from May–October, 1926, and almost certainly bred; status unknown. In June, 1925, another subspecies was common and did *not* breed, and *stricklandi* was not found.

Reliable accounts of the nesting or other habits of the Mexican crossbill seem to be lacking, but the following note, published by D. R. Dickey and A. J. van Rossem (1923), on the presence and behavior of some of these crossbills on Santa Cruz Island, Calif., is of interest: "The 21 birds taken were submitted to Dr. H. C. Oberholser for determination. He states they are unmistakably *Loxia curvirostra stricklandi* and not *bendirei*. No breeding activity was noticeable in any of the specimens taken, but males were seen courting on April 3. The male birds attracted the attention of the females by squatting, with tail spread, on a limb, and uttering a rather weak, linnet-like twittering. The territory preferred by the birds was a burnt-land pine area on which fire had killed the trees without destroying the cones. The latter had been opened by the heat, thus affording the birds easy access to the seed."

DISTRIBUTION

Range.—Chiefly western and southern Mexico.

Breeding range.—The Mexican crossbill breeds in northern Baja California (Sierra Juárez, Sierra San Pedro Mártir), southeastern Arizona (Chiricahua Mountains), and southern New Mexico (Reserve) south through the tableland of Mexico to Guerrero (Chilpancingo), central western Veracruz (Las Vigas), and Chiapas (San Cristóbal; intergrading between *stricklandi* and *mesamericana*).

Winter range.—Same as breeding range, wandering sporadically north to central California (Pacific Grove), central Nevada (Wheeler Peak, Charleston Mountains), southern Utah (Cedar Mountain, Navajo Mountain), central Colorado (Aurora), eastern Kansas (Lawrence), and central Texas (Fort Worth) and south to Guatemala (Sierra de las Minas).

LOXIA LEUCOPTERA LEUCOPTERA Gmelin

White-winged Crossbill

PLATE 27

Contributed by WENDELL TABER

HABITS

Smoke rises straight in the frosty stillness of an early September morning. Slowly the mist clears to reveal a tiny body of water. Tucked in at the 3,500-foot level in a region where the tree line is around 4,500 feet or less, Speck Pond lies nearly surrounded by the steep, towering, coniferous-clad walls of those wild Maine peaks, Mahoosuc and Old Speck.

From across the lake comes a white-winged crossbill, then another, and yet another. Others appear, seemingly from nowhere. Soon a small inquiring flock has assembled, calling constantly as if to summon yet more birds. As my companion and I stand a foot apart talking, a brilliant male dashes knee-high between us. A bird alights on my friend. Everywhere, birds are busily foraging on the ground, gleaning food too minute for us to see. They explore the rock fireplace or pass beneath those long flattened logs that form the retaining wall and bench at the front of the lean-to. Quickly becoming acclimated, they enter the lean-to itself to pry around in the dried balsam needles of the built-up bottom. I have seen birds, equally at ease in a long, dark, windowless cabin, penetrate into its innermost recesses. Inquisitively, a resplendent male alights on the top of a log resting at an angle against the rock wall of the fireplace. While the bird watches us preparing breakfast, the lower end of the log, not 3 feet distant, burns merrily. Enjoy the birds while we can; next year there will be no enticing crop of cones and the birds will have vanished. Somewhere, coastwise perhaps, they will have located a new food supply.

Courtship.—Joseph Grinnell (1900) observed the courtship of this species in the Kotzebue Sound region of Alaska on Apr. 26, 1899. He says: "Two or three pairs were apparently already mated, for they were detached from the main flock, each by itself. The males were singing very loudly a twitter somewhat resembling that of the American Goldfinch, but coarser. The females were shy, flying covertly from tree to tree and darting through the foliage to avoid the officious advances of the males, who were following them. The latter flew in broad circles above the females, with slowly beating wings, singing continuously, and finally settling on quivering, outstretched wings to a tree-top."

Mrs. Louise de Kiriline Lawrence writes Mr. Bent of a flight display she witnessed at Rutherglen, Ontario, on Dec. 23, 1947. She describes the male as rising almost vertically on rapidly beating wings. The female was not receptive.

Nesting.—Winter may find this bird breeding. A. Leith Adams (1873) discovered a nest with three eggs in New Brunswick in the middle of January 1868. Another nest had been brought to him a few weeks earlier. He describes a nest as composed of black moss, birch bark, and twigs with a lining of wool and moss.

Baird, Brewer, and Ridgway (1874a) describe a nest Adams found in 1868 in Fredericton, New Brunswick. This nest "is deeply saucer-shaped, and composed of a rather thin wall of fibrous pale-green lichens, encased on the outside with spruce twigs, and thinly lined with coarse hairs and fine shreds of inner bark. Its external diameter is a little less than four inches, the rim being almost perfectly circular; the cavity is an inch and a half deep by two and a half broad."

Bertrand E. Smith (1949) mentions two nests found near Calais, Maine, on Feb. 20 and 22, 1948, by Wellington James. The first nest was in a 6-foot spruce and only about 2 feet 8 inches above the ground. Another snowstorm would have covered the nest. All four eggs were broken. The second nest, containing three eggs, was built in a thick spruce about 8 feet high. The cutting down of the first tree may well have accounted for the broken eggs; a falling birch broke two eggs in the second nest. This latter nest is described by Smith as a—

beautifully built structure, the extreme outside diameter of the compact mass is 10 cm., the overall depth 5.5 cm. The nesting bowl is 4.5×4.7 cm. in diameter and 3 cm. in depth. The foundation of the nest consists of delicate grass stems, very slender weed stalks and dead terminal spruce and a few hemlock twigs among which there are tiny bits of Usnea moss and a few small insect cocoons. The nest is lined with intricately woven, long, slender rootlets and tendrils of unknown identity. Some of the tendrils are black in color, very closely resembling horse hair in general appearance, but microscopical examination and tests by burning proved their identity. No hair or feathers were present in any part of the nest.

Robie W. Tufts of Wolfville, Nova Scotia, wrote Mr. Bent of nesting records on Feb. 8, 1906, with three eggs slightly incubated, and on Feb. 26, 1906, with four eggs about one-quarter incubated.

T. J. Egan (1889a) found a nest near Halifax, Nova Scotia, on Mar. 16, 1889. He comments on the absence of feathers or clay in the nest and says: "The female was on the nest and allowed a visitor to come within a few feet before leaving it, when she joined the cock bird, a fine red fellow who was singing on the top of a neighboring tree."

Robie W. Tufts also writes of a nest found on Apr. 1, 1906, containing three eggs about half incubated. On Apr. 26, 1906, he found another nest with four eggs which had not been incubated. On Apr. 2, 1925, at Seal Island in Yarmouth County, Nova Scotia, he observed a female carrying usnea moss and ultimately he located her half-built nest. Visiting the nest again on April 19 he found it contained four eggs which were nearly half incubated. This would seem to imply a rather long period of incubation but I have found no positive information on this point.

Harold F. Tufts (1906) limits nests to spruce, but says, "some were in trees of large growth and seventy feet from the ground, while others were placed low in small bushes." Of the family life he says:

During the period of incubation the sitting females were observed to be fed by the males, in the same manner that the young are fed by their parents—that is by the disgorging of the contents of the crop into the open mouth of the bird to be fed. When bringing his mate food in this manner the male crossbill would announce his coming by loud pipings, and perching upon a near by tree would continue his excited chirpings some minutes and then fly direct to the nest. Often after having thus fed his mate, he would circle in the air about his home on outstretched flapping wings, giving vent to a perfect ecstasy of song.

* * *

The nesting period of these birds seems very extended. Thus on Jan. 31, nests were found with young. The birds have been nesting ever since, and at this date (May 7) flocks of full fledged young can be seen feeding about the woods, while nests with eggs are still to be found.

This protracted period of nesting took place near Wolfville, Nova Scotia.

Joseph Grinnell (1900a) found three nests in a stretch of dwarf spruces on May 28, 1899 in the Kotzebue region of Alaska. He says: "On this date the large flocks had scattered out, and the birds were mostly seen singly or in pairs. Two or three companies of a dozen or so were noted, these probably being non-breeders or yearlings. The first nest was found by spotting a pair of birds and closely watching their movements. * * * Both birds soon left the vicinity and did not return while I remained. The nest was situated close to the trunk, ten feet above the ground, in a mass of foliage so thick as to entirely hide it from view. It contained two eggs, about one-third incubated." The second nest was 12 feet high near the top of a dwarf spruce and was "embedded in a mass of foliage against the stem of the tree, much as in the case of the first nest. It contained two pipped eggs and one newly hatched young. The parents evinced more solicitude in this case, chirping and flying from tree to tree." The third nest was 15 feet up, also hidden in the dense spruce top, and held one fresh egg. The three nests were "just alike in every way. They consist externally of short dry spruce twigs; and internally of a black wool-like lichen, closely felted, and with a scanty admixture of feathers and bits of grasses. The nests are nearly black, and thus present an odd appearance as compared with those of the usual consistency of other birds. The nest measurements are: internal diameter 2.20, depth 1.20; external diameter 4.00, depth 2.50."

James Bond (1938) found the species rare in the Magdalen Islands in June 1934 and 1936, but in June 1935, he says they were "exceedingly abundant everywhere, ranking second in numbers, among forest birds, to the ubiquitous Blackpoll Warbler. * * * A number of young, which had probably hatched in April, were seen being fed by the adult females, while other individuals were obviously nesting or were about to nest. Males were observed singing here and there in the woods and examination of certain of these showed enlarged testes. This was noted not only in the adult male but in the immature as well." A nest which he found on June 8 "was situated near the top of a small spruce about seven feet above the ground. When found, the female was on the nest, covering her four young. On being flushed, she returned immediately to within a few feet of the nest, emitting an incessant, querulous *pit*, while the nest was being examined and photographed. The following morning the female was absent for some time but appeared at the nest about 9 o'clock with a flock of her kind that had been feeding in a stand of taller spruce a quarter of a mile distant. As the flock flew high overhead, she descended and immediately began her monotonous calling, whereupon several others joined her, although for a short time only. One of them, an adult male, was collected but proved not to be the owner of the nest, which I never saw. The males evidently take little or no part in the care of the young. The nest was a rather roughly-built cup composed of dry spruce twigs and was heavily lined with rabbit fur."

Ralph S. Palmer (1949) mentions a nest found by Manly Hardy on which both the male and the female were engaged in adding the lining. The nest was completed on July 19, 1889.

James L. Baillie, Jr., and Paul Harrington (1937) mention a nest found, according to D. A. MacLulich, on Aug. 19, 1926, in a small cedar at Head Lake in Victoria County, Ontario, and another discovered 41 feet up in a spruce tree by Milton B. Trautman on Aug. 20, 1928, at the Michipicoten River in the Northern Algoma district of the province.

J. W. Aldrich and D. C. Nutt (1939) collected an adult male in eastern Newfoundland on Sept. 6, 1938, which, they say, "was in breeding condition, and the plummage was rather worn." It is quite possible, though, that this bird may already have bred.

Analogous is the case of a bird collected by Robie W. Tufts on Sept. 4, 1924, at Tabusintac, New Brunswick. Writing Mr. Bent of this he says, "the testes were normal size of a breeding bird." On the occasion in question he had been watching a colony of about a dozen pairs and says, "I was attracted by their loud singing and boisterous chatterings, all of which suggested nesting birds. * * * I watched the flock for all the time I could spare but was not successful in locating a nest though from time to time a male bird was seen to suddenly leave the feeding flock as though taking food to the mate." He points out that the nest of this species is not distinguishable from that of the red crossbill. Where low spruces grew in open pasture land, "it was a simple matter to locate a nest by watching the noisy male leave the feeding grove. He would alight on a nearby tree and chirp loudly for a moment or two before dropping to the edge of the nest which would invariably be close at hand. A few nests of this species, * * * well out from the trunk" were high up in the trees.

John Macoun (1909) quotes Walter Raine who describes a nest "as made of fine roots and twigs, lined with moss and animals' fur." Henry Nehrling (1896) speaks of a nest near Ascanaba, Mich., which was in "dense evergreen woods, and was placed in the top of a small pine about twenty-five feet from the ground." The inside diameter was 2.75 inches and the depth 1.75 inches.

Frederick C. Schmid writes me of finding a nest July 27, 1945, in southern Yukon territory. The exact location of this far northern record was mile post 843, between Squanga and Little Teslin Lake, on the Alaskan Military Highway. The nest was about the size of that of a robin, rather deep, composed of twigs and a little grass, 10 feet up in a black spruce bog. After flushing an adult off the nest he noted the three young were a sooty black color, eyes not yet opened, gape a brilliant scarlet, bill uncrossed.

Eggs.—Joseph Grinnell (1900a) states the eggs are ovate and gives measurements of .86 by .61 inches and .84 by .60 inches. He says, "The ground-color is an extremely pale tint of blue. One egg has scattering illy-defined spots and blotches of pale chocolate. The other egg has numerous very pale lavender markings, and, mostly at the larger end, a number of spots and four large blotches of dark seal-brown." An egg from another nest was .77×.58, "almost white (before blown, pinkish) with scattering abruptly-defined spots and lines of bay and fawn-color, most numerous at the larger end." O. L. Austin, Jr. (1932) mentions black spots, as does Henry Nehrling (1896), who describes the dots additionally as ashy-lilac. Andrew L. Adams (1873) mentions red streaks on the larger end of bluish-white eggs. E. H. Forbush (1929) states the usual number is 2 to 4 with dimensions of .77 to 86 inches by .56 to .61 inches; ovate;

variable, pale bluish-green to nearly white, with spots or blotches and sometimes lines of various browns and lavenders, chiefly about the large end; figured by Henry Seebohm in a "History of British Birds" (1885, pl. 19).

W. G. F. Harris writes: "Four eggs usually comprises a set of the white-winged crossbill but sometimes only three, or as many as five are laid. They are ovate, sometimes tending toward elongate-ovate, and have very little lustre. The ground is very pale greenish-white, or creamy white, variously spotted and blotched with 'sorghum brown,' 'bay brown,' or 'Vandyke brown,' and occasionally a few scattered spots or scrawls of black. The undermarkings are of pale reddish brown shades, such as 'vinaceous-fawn,' or 'fawn.' On some types the markings are restricted to just the shades of 'fawn.' The spots, generally, are scattered over the entire egg with a slight tendency to become somewhat heavier toward the large end. The measurements of 19 eggs average 20.9 by 15.0 millimeters; the eggs showing the four extremes measure *22.0* by *16.0*, *18.5* by 14.9 and 20.3 by *13.5* millimeters."

Young.—Referring to a nest containing young, James Bond (1938), says: "The young had hatched about three days prior to its discovery. They were covered with down and it was noted that the inside of their mouths was rather bright purplish red in color."

A. Brooker Klugh (1926) watched a pair of adults feeding four young. He says: "The parents fed the young by regurgitation and apparently on comminuted seeds. * * * Three of the young went down beside the laboratory, sat down under the salt-water drip from the experimental jars on the laboratory roof, drank some of the salt water, and then went to sleep. I went down and caught two of them in my hands. They were in the juvenal plumage and their mandibles had not yet started to cross."

F. H. Allen writes Mr. Bent of observing a female feeding young by picking seed from a green spruce cone.

Plumages.—J. Dwight (1900), speaking of the male, says the juvenal plumage is acquired by a complete postnatal molt. The whole plumage is a dull grayish white thickly streaked with clove-brown, the feather edgings grayish, but buffy on the back, rump, and abdomen. The wings and tail are a dull black, the primaries, secondaries, and tertiaries narrowly and the tertiaries and wing coverts broadly edged with buffy white forming two distinct wing bands at tips of greater and median coverts. The bill and feet are brownish black. The birds are decidedly blacker than *Loxia curvirostra minor* in the corresponding plumage.

The first winter plumage is acquired by a partial post-juvenal molt, probably in September, which involves the body plumage, but neither the wings nor the tail. The head, back, rump, throat, and breast are varying shades of chrome yellow with an occasional dash of dull red; the scapulars and upper tail coverts are black. The lores, orbital region, and forehead are a dull black. This plumage wears into the first nuptial plumage which, to the eye, brightens the yellow by loss of the barbules of the feathers. The mouse gray basal portion of the body feathers is somewhat in evidence.

The adult winter plumage is acquired by a complete postnuptial molt. Probably, nearly all young birds assume the full red adult plumage at this molt. The birds become a rosy or hoary brick or geranium red with the wings, tail, and scapularies black. The wing bands and tertiary edgings are white. The abdomen is smoke gray and the under tail coverts dull white, rose tinged, both streaked with clove brown. The colors are much pinker than those of *L. c. minor* in the corresponding dress and the white wing bands are distinctive.

The adult nuptial plumage is acquired by wear, brightening to the eye the rosy tints due in large part to the loss of the barbules from a part of each barb. The general effect is that of a rosy bird mottled with whitish spots.

He says that the female, as in the case of allied species, is probably indistinguishable from the male in the natal down and juvenal plumages. The first winter plumage, acquired by a partial post-juvenal molt which does not involve the wings or tail, is olive bluff, similar to *L. c. minor*, from which it may easily be distinguished by the wing bands. Further, it is more distinctly mottled and streaked with deeper olive brown. The first nuptial plumage is simply the previous plumage modified by wear. The adult winter plumage is, of course, acquired by a complete postnuptial molt and shows a certain amount of yellow scattered through it, somewhat brightened by wear and becoming the adult nuptial plumage. Females never become pink.

Ridgway (1901) mentions specifically the adult male only in connection with the bill, which he describes as horn color, darker terminally, and the "dusky" legs and feet. W. W. Cooke (1885) mentions a male in which the lower mandible turned to the left while in six other specimens the bill turned to the right.

Food.—One might think that this species, with its crossed bill especially adapted to pry open cones, would have a specialized and limited diet. Actually, the bird partakes of a wide and varied diet. Thus, a bird collected on Aug. 9, 1920, in the Pribilof Islands by G. D. Hanna was, according to Preble and McAtee (1923), "apparently feeding on the unripe seeds of wild parsnip. * * * The stomach of this bird was entirely filled with remains of blowflies (*Calliphora* *vomitoria*)." These blowflies were, at the time, predominant among the food items available.

Alfred M. Bailey (1927) quotes Fred Gray of Wrangell, Alaska, as stating that the birds "feed along the beach, among the boulders at low tide, getting a species of snail, or shell fish."

H. S. Swarth (1922), speaking of summering in British Columbia, says that "At Glenora the crossbills were feeding on the seed pods of the cottonwoods, as they were also in some degree at Doch-da-on Creek, but farther down the river, and a littler later in the season, the spruce cones had their undivided attention."

W. H. Moore (1902) includes black alder and birch as sources of food supply.

John F. Ferry (1907) says of birds wintering in northern Illinois that they are "fond of juniper berries and this fall Mr. R. J. Douglass observed them feeding on dried sun-flower seeds, which were still embedded in the withered flower."

T. S. Roberts (1932) lists as food the seeds of crowberry, huckleberry, ragweed, and foxtail grass. He says that they also eat caterpillars and other larvae, and that they will devour greedily earth containing salt. He attributes the presence of the birds at moose-licks to the salt. This also may well be one of the reasons for the quickness with which the species responds to the smoke rising from human camp fires, a potential indication of salt.

W. A. Stearns (1881) mentions decayed garden fruits as food and notes that Mr. Maynard observed birds eating the seeds of beach grass. Baird, Brewer, and Ridgway (1874a) tell of a bird Mr. Maynard shot in Newton, Mass., on June 13, 1869. The bird was found in an apple tree and its crop was full of cankerworms. A pair of caged birds "ate almost every kind of food, but were especially eager for slices of raw apples."

Richard H. Manville (1941) watched birds wintering in the Huron Mountains of northern Michigan. Associated with redpolls, pine siskins, and red crossbills, he says that there were about three of the latter species to one white-winged crossbill and that "At one group of buildings both species were commonly seen in white birches and nearby Norway pines. Often the birds were grouped about the bases of hard maples and hemlocks, pecking at the bark; also they were greatly attracted to spots of dog urine in the snow. During this period the temperature ranged approximately from 10° to 30° F., and the snow depth from 16 to 30 inches on the level."

Arthur H. Norton (1904) watched the species feeding in larch and arborvitae trees. Breaking off the small cones, the birds would seize them and search between the scales for seeds and even insect matter. He says, "Where a flock is feeding the patter of falling cones is audible for a short distance, and they often bear mute testimony to the scene of a recent feast as they lie thick under the trees. A small amount of insect matter was found in some of the stomachs collected in January."

Mrs. Louise de Kiriline Lawrence wrote Mr. Bent an interesting account of her observations of a flock of 52 birds. She says, "They were mostly engaged in feeding on the seeds of the tamaracks which carry a very rich harvest of cones this year. But I also observed that a great many of the spruces had their clusters of cones completely stripped of seeds so that nothing remained but the stems still hanging there. The stripped cones looked like thin silk bobbins without any silk. Some birds were feeding on the highway which has been sanded with chlorided gravel. The birds picked up the apparently salty snow by sideways motions of their crossed bills and separated whatever salty grains and gravel specks they relished from the snow in their bills, so that the snow appeared like froth around their mandibles."

Mrs. Hildegarde C. Allen watched a female on a hard road in winter. She wrote Mr. Bent that the bird "seemed to stay almost completely in one place, and as the sun shone against her pincers, I could see her pink tongue lick out and against the pebble asphalted in. She did not in the least appear to be picking up grit dislodged by her bill, she looked to be licking the black tarred pebble. Since our roads are well salted all winter, then bare this 24th of March, I decided definitely she was licking the salt from its surface!" Gordon M. Meade (1942), however, writes of an instance of the extremely heavy mortality of this and other species observed feeding voraciously on a mixture of sand and calcium chloride surfacing a road in March. Inferentially, this diet may have been responsible for this slaughter since the birds "appeared to be too sick to rise and even though motorists drove slowly they were killed in great numbers."

F. H. Allen wrote Mr. Bent the following: "In feeding on green spruce cones the white-winged crossbill picks off a cone and holds it down with one foot while it rapidly picks out the seeds, letting the scales fall. When a cone is finished it is dropped to the ground. The bird when thus feeding is perched on a small branch or twig. By thus picking the cone off and holding it down the bird can more easily get the seeds out of the unopened cone than if it were left dangling in the air. In dealing with ripe cones, however, the crossbills can, and do, pick out the seeds without detaching the cones." Allen did, on one occasion, see a bird "eating seeds from a green cone without detaching it and without cutting off the scales, probably because the seeds were soft and undeveloped."

Maurice G. Brooks (1943) discusses the occurrence of the species in the red spruce belt on the higher mountain peaks in West Virginia.

He states that he has found the blooming season of the spruces to be by far the best time to find these birds of northern association, that:

This season ordinarily covers the first three weeks in June; June 10 is, generally speaking, near the height of the blossoming period. At this time the young spruces bear, during most years, a light to heavy crop of ovulate strobili containing numerous bract-like carpels which are coated with a waxy or resinous substance that is distinctly sweet to the taste. On many of the carpels this substance forms beads. The coated carpels are eaten avidly by both Red and White-winged Crossbills (*Loxia curvirostra* and *L. leucoptera*) and by Pine Siskins (*Spinus pinus*). These strobili, many of which never ripen into cones, are much more in evidence on young spruces (15 to 25 years old) than on older trees, and they are much more likely to occur annually than are mature cones.

P. B. Hofslund (1955) comments on the wasteful procedure of four birds, including an adult male, feeding on cones of white spruce (*Picea glauca*). Cones were clipped off from the cluster, held on a branch by one foot, a few scales torn off; then the cone was dropped. The procedure was watched for 30 minutes during which 59 cones were clipped and dropped. Few of the 619 cones picked up at the spot had more than four or five scales torn from them.

W. L. Putnam (1955) watched two birds feeding on the seeds of teasel (*Dipsacus sylvestris*).

Behavior.—Though adaptable to a wide range of food, the predilection of this species for cones appears dominant. In the northern coniferous forests, the size of or absence of the cone crop bears a direct relationship to the birds' probable presence. Thus, in late August and early September 1950, they were abundant on Katahdin in Maine, in evidence on every part of the mountain I visited. On September 2 there were four birds flying over the Tableland, a rather level area in comparison to the rest of the mountain which extends for several miles at a minimum altitude of about 4,000 feet. Except for dense growths of stunted conifers that are almost impenetrable to humans on the lower parts of the mountain, the region is above the tree line. Seen often under conditions of unobscured view such as this, the birds impress me as being restless, powerful fliers, capable of rapid sustained flight for distances of several miles or more. On these long flights the birds fly straight and without undulation, calling constantly to each other and at times singing.

Occasionally in a season when cones are scarce, a lone bird or even a small group may be encountered. A lone bird seems self-sufficient, ready to mingle with other fringillids perhaps, but not dependent. On May 31, 1948, I watched at length a stray female at an abandoned open horse shed beside the Carrabassett River in Maine. Several hundred siskins (*Spinus pinus*) were feeding on the ground inside and around the shed or were scattered through the adjoining alders. The crossbill stayed with, yet aloof from, the siskins, moving in a sedate manner in and out of the shed by passing through a crack between two logs in the side wall, disappearing into the alders, and reappearing. The bird associated not at all with a number of purple finches (*Carpodacus purpureus*) scattered in hardwood trees across the road. In 1950 on Katahdin, in a heavily coniferous area where purple finches occur in numbers summer after summer, occasional association of the crossbills with them seemed purely fortuitous. In no instance did I see the two species intermingle closely.

Brewster (1938), as compiled by Griscom, says:

> They seem to have regular beats or routes which they travel every day. Thus the flock noted October 19th regularly passed our camp every morning at about the same hour. They alighted somewhere behind it, and after feeding ten minutes or more took wing again. Like the Red Crossbill they are absolutely silent when feeding. Just before starting to fly one or two birds begin to call, others join in and finally with a general outcry the flock are off. Their flight is undulating, and they fly in a loose scattered flock. * * * They rarely spent more than three or four minutes in one tree usually alighting in a cluster among the cones at the top, then as if struck by a panic whirling off again. Occasionally they would alight in the top of a tall dead pine. I saw one hang head downward and then climb out under a dead branch using its bill like a Parrot.

The tameness of this species has been noted by many observers, including myself. Mr. Bent mentions in his notes attempting to noose birds, but he found they would jump right through the noose. A. Leith Adams (1873) did succeed in catching 30 birds by using a hair noose.

Earle A. Brooks (1920) quotes a correspondent at French Creek, W. Va., on Jan. 22, 1920, a cold day with heavy sleet. He says: "One finely colored male was working busily at a cone on a branch a foot above my head, and I stroked his side with the tip of my umbrella. Instead of flying he edged away, threw his head to one side and scolded me softly for interrupting his feast." The correspondent then proceeded to pick up one of three females which were eating from a cone in the road. He carried the bird home, made sure of the identification, took the bird out onto his porch, and opened his hand. "The bird flew about two feet and alighted on a vine." Another correspondent at Buckhannon, W. Va., wrote on the same day that, "by practising a little Indian stealth, I was able to place my hand over" a full plumaged male.

Baird, Brewer, and Ridgway (1874a) describe the actions of a caged pair, saying: "They were very tame, and were exceedingly interesting little pets. Their movements in the cage were like those of caged parrots in every respect, except that they were far more easy and rapid. They clung to the sides and upper wires of the cage with their feet, hung down from them, and seemed to enjoy the practice of walking with their head downward."

H. Nehrling (1896) writes of several birds being kept in a cage They took food immediately after being captured. They were kep[t] for as long as four years in perfect health, and did not seem to suffe[r] from the summer's heat.

Ridgway (1889) quotes Thomas H. Douglas who described th[e] behavior of red crossbills with the white-winged crossbills. He say[s] that the birds "got along well together when out of doors (would pick seeds out of the same cone), when in captivity (as we had them severa[l] times) the former would not let the latter feed, and killed some b[y] picking them on the head."

James Haynes Hill (1902) says of a captive pair that "during the last week of February 1901, the female wished to go to housekeeping and materials were given them, fine twigs, fine birch bark and a little Usnea moss. But the male bird treated his mate with disdain, quarreling with her and driving her from perch to perch."

T. S. Roberts (1932) says of birds summering in Minnesota: "During midday we found it indulging in prolonged bathing or sitting on low bushes overhanging the water."

John Macoun (1909) writes that the species bred freely on Cape Breton Island in the winter of 1898–99, but left very suddenly in April leaving several broods of young.

John W. Cadbury collected an immature male, now in the Academy of Natural Science in Philadelphia, which came aboard a ship in an exhausted condition about 1158 miles east of Cape May, N.J., and less than 400 miles from Cape Race, Newfoundland.

Charles F. Morrison (1889) quotes the species as occurring in winter in Colorado at 10,000 feet altitude. He (1888) also records a specimen taken at about 9,500 feet.

Voice.—C. W. Townsend (1906) give a lengthy description of the song, saying:

The trills resembled so closely those of the Canary-bird, that several persons who heard it spoke of the bird as the "Wild Canary." Far from being low and feeble, the song was delivered with great vigor and abandon, the birds often flying about in large circles over the woods. Occasionally the song was delivered from the top of an evergreen, but usually its vehemence was so great that the bird was lifted up into the air, where it flew about slowly, pouring out meanwhile a great volume of music. This lasted for minutes at a time, and ceased only when the exhausted bird came to a perch. The song would often be at once taken up by another bird, and occasionally several were singing in the air at a time.

The volume of the sound was constantly swelling and dwindling, at times a low sweet warbling, then a rough rattling, more like a mowing-machine, then a loud all-pervading *sweet, sweet, sweet,* recalling exactly a Canary-bird. Anon the song would die down to a low warbling, and again burst out into a loud sweet trilling *whee, whee, whee.*

When singing from a perch, which was always the tip-top of a spruce or fir, the Crossbill frequently twitched its tail, and erected the feathers of its crown. One fairly good singer appeared to be rather immature, being mostly gray with but a faint tinge of red in the breast. This full nuptial song is certainly very different from the song occasionally heard at other seasons, and would hardly be recognized by one who had heard the latter only.

Olive Thorne Miller (1904) mentions "long bewitching tremolos, varied by rapturous 'sweet! sweet!' and now and then a slurred couplet of thrilling effect, or a long-drawn single note of rich musical quality, or again a rapid succession of sharp staccato notes."

Most of the species with which comparison is made are eastern forms. H. S. Swarth (1922), however, states that the "song-flight especially is suggestive of a similar spring performance of the house finch." Joseph Grinnell (1900a) says: "The bright red adult males seem to have a special note of their own, a sharp metallic 'cheet', to me remarkably like the spring call-note of the Arizona Hooded Oriole in Southern California. This note is often repeated during a flight of the crossbills, and is distinctly recognizable among the medley of ordinary notes." The ordinary call-notes of the species, he says, resemble those of redpolls, but are sharper and more harsh, with several uttered together in rapid succession.

E. M. S. Dale (1924) describes the song as beginning "with a trill on one key, changing to one a little lower in pitch, then to one higher. These three trills were followed by a series of chirps and throaty notes * * *. The song continue with chirps, trills and warbles * * *."

Mrs. Louise de Kiriline Lawrence wrote Mr. Bent of her observations on Jan. 2, 1948, near Rutherglen, Ontario, commenting that during courtship a female was "giving a melodious twitter that almost seemed like a song." She says, further, that an alarm note was a "'tchet, tchet, tchet,' a little rough, a little hoarse or burry, and reminding me somewhat of the hermit thrush's 'chuck-note', or the pine siskin's 'burry' note, though more distinct and loud. There is also another note, which seemed to be given as a warning of something unusual going on. It is a rather long, liquid 'trrrrrrr', to use Thoreau's simile of a 'beady' note, a row of rather large beads strung together. This note I heard the least often and almost always before I myself could spot the bird giving it, who apparently had already spotted me." The song she describes as being similar to that of the red crossbill but "neither as melodious not as varied. It sounded to me something like this: 'trrr-*tweet-tweet-tweet*-trrr-tchet-tchet-*tweet-tweet-tweet*-trrrrr-*tweet-tweet*,' with emphasis on all 'tweets' which often were longdrawn, rising in pitch, and given with great feeling, as it were."

A. Brooker Klugh (1926) states: "The song has considerable carrying-power, as it can be heard at a distance of about seven hundred yards." While this seems a surprisingly long distance, my own observations confirm it under favorable conditions, such as in a natural amphitheatre.

Ridgway (1889), referring to a pair of caged birds kept by Dr. Brewer, says: "They were in full song, and both the male and female were quite good singers. Their songs were irregular and varied, but sweet and musical."

G. M. Sutton, quoted by W. E. C. Todd (1940), encountered birds of this species wintering in Pennsylvania. Sutton says: "While the birds were feeding, there was a constant chattering going on; the notes were either double- or triple-syllabled and very sweet and musical, although not clear. Now and then could be heard a louder, somewhat clearer note, seeming to come from another species of bird; but the chances are that it was another note of one of the crossbills."

L. Griscom (1923), also discussing birds out of their normal breeding habitat, states that wintering birds have as their most common note "a rattle or chatter very like the Redpoll, but much louder, more prolonged, and less hoarse. Another common note is a sweet, whistled *twee*, sometimes given in couplets, which is very like the familiar Goldfinch call, but it lacks the rising inflection at the end. When a flock is quietly feeding, there is also a note which sounds like a Junco singing very badly and hoarsely." I have heard the air full of these sweet whistled *twees*—to me not in the least suggestive of a goldfinch—and looked up to see a flock of 50 to 100 birds fly speedily overhead in a mass formation. All notes seemed to be on the same pitch—a symphonic undertone appearing again throughout the song itself.

Field marks.—The male white-winged crossbill viewed face on might easily be mistaken for a purple finch, which is of similar size and frequently occurs in the same territory summer or winter. The two white wing-bars on the black wing, however, are diagnostic. Only at close range under favorable conditions can the crossed bill be seen. The somewhat similar pine grosbeak is larger, approaching the size of a robin, and lacks the crossed bill. As compared with the red crossbill, the red of the male white-winged crossbill tends to be a sparkling rosy color whereas that of the red crossbill is more nearly a flat brick red. There is much variation in the latter, however, and L. Griscom (1937) points out that the form *benti* is actually rosy also. Absence of the white wing-bars is characteristic in females and immatures as well as in male red crossbills in North America.

Female and immature white-winged crossbills are a blended composition of olive and light brown or gray, but show the dark wing with the two white patches. From this plumage, the amount of red in the case of molting young males progresses until the full adult stage is reached.

Enemies.—This species spends a large portion of its life span in areas little visited by ornithologists or even by persons sufficiently interested to record their observations. Further, the very nature of the terrain hampers the observer. Presumably, the species must fall prey at times to various hawks and owls as do other finches. Its habit of feeding on the ground must occasionally subject the bird to attacks from rodents and other animals. L. Griscom (1937) stresses the effect of competition between this species and the red crossbill. Although the white-winged crossbill is the more northern, the breeding ranges of the two species overlap in a broad belt across the continent, equivalent to about half the breeding range of either species. Griscom emphasizes the point that wherever one species is present in numbers, the other is absent, or at most represented by a vagrant flock or two.

Winter.—Joseph Grinnell (1900a) mentions finding the species in tracts of dwarf spruces bearing great clusters of cones along the bases of the mountains in the Kotzebue Sound region of Alaska. He says: "During the winter they were usually noted in flocks of a dozen to fifty or more, flying from place to place. They then readily attracted attention by their chorus of notes." When feeding, "they were invariably quiet."

While on excursions in the winter away from the forested regions of the north, the species occurs, as H. Nehrling (1896) says, "in large flocks and in company with the common Crossbills, Pine Grosbeaks, Red-polls, Evening Grosbeaks, and Waxwings * * *. Like its ally it is a very gregarious bird, being never seen alone, but always in flocks." He also points out that the species may not be found again in the same locality for the next 5 or 10 years.

My own experience has been at variance with this in that, while I have a number of times encountered small flocks composed of both species of crossbills in the Maine forests in summer, intermingling of the species in winter in more open country has been at a minimum. Also, I have at times occasionally recorded a lone individual in Massachusetts. In such instances, however, possibly the bird was merely separated momentarily from a flock overlooked in densely timbered areas.

W. E. C. Todd (1940) attributes incursions to lack of cones in the far north inasmuch as the bird is, he says, a "truly boreal species, fitted to withstand the severe cold of the northern latitudes * * *." In western Pennsylvania the species frequents Norway spruces but seems to favor hemlocks particularly. The flocks are usually small but may at times amount to 300 birds. They scatter out and recombine in divers permutations. The snow beneath the trees in which the birds feed is always well littered with cones and scales. In March the birds hop around on bare places on the ground. Todd quotes notes of G. M. Sutton for Jan. 20 and 27, 1923, stating that the birds "also drank from the stream. When feeding unmolested, they were nearly silent, but they broke out into chirping before flying away. * * * They swung about erratically through the air, apparently without any particular object or destination in view. * * * Masses of them would leave one feeding ground for another and progress in a constant stream along the steep, hemlock-covered slope. They were not particularly wild, nor were they (as literature had led me to believe) especially tame."

Aretas A. Saunders (1921) mentions a male and three females taken at Miles City, Mont., on Nov. 16, 1919, which "were in a draw among wild rose bushes and spanish bayonet, three-quarters of a mile from the nearest trees and twelve miles from the nearest pines."

T. S. Roberts (1932) records an observation of three birds "out on the prairie in high weeds" in the last week of October 1908. He also refers to birds seen feeding in weeds by the roadside on Nov. 7, 1919.

Perhaps the most extraordinary instance of the wanderings of this species is a bird picked up dead at Demarcation Point, Alaska, in January 1937, recorded by Laurence M. Huey (1938). The bird was taken to Charles D. Brower of Barrow, Alaska, who verbally confirmed the identification to Huey, who comments on "the peculiar phenomenon of the bird's wandering such a great distance from the coniferous forest belt, and ending its journey of life on the tundra so far within the Arctic Circle in the dead of winter!"

DISTRIBUTION

Range.—Alaska, Mackenzie, Labrador, Scandinavia, Russia, and central Siberia south to northern United States, England, Italy, and southern Siberia. (An isolated subspecies is resident in Hispaniola.)

Breeding range.—Breeds, and is largely resident, from north-central Alaska (Kobuk River, Fort Yukon), central Yukon (Bern Creek, McMillan River), central Mackenzie (Fort Wrigley, Fort Rae, Thelon River), central Manitoba (Grand Rapids), northern Ontario (Fort Severn, Fort Albany, Moose Factory), northern Quebec (Paul Bay, central Ungava), central Labrador (Okak, Hopedale), and Newfoundland south to south central Alaska (Palmer, McCarthy), northern and interior British Columbia (Flood Glacier, Indianpoint Lake, Monashee Pass), central Alberta (Stony Plain), northern Minnesota (Lake and Cook counties), northern Wisconsin (Kelley Brook), northern Michigan (Escanaba), southern Ontario (Michipicoten River, Head Lake), southern Quebec (Mount Orford), southern New Brunswick (Grand Manan), and Nova Scotia (Barrington, Halifax); reported breeding sporadically south to Washington (Mount Rainier), northeastern Oregon (Wallowa Mountains), Montana (Fortine, Glacier Park, near Red Lodge), northeastern New York (eastern Lewis County, Long Lake), northern Vermont (Lunenburg), New Hampshire (White Mountains), and southern Maine (Mount Desert Island).

Winter range.—Same as breeding range, wandering sporadically south to central Oregon (Big Cultus Lake), southern Idaho (Minidoka), Colorado (Bakers Park; Denver), southeastern New Mexico (Clayton), Kansas (Hays, Halstead, Lawrence), Oklahoma (Bartlesville), Missouri (Shannon County), Illinois (Warsaw), Indiana (Bloomington), Kentucky (Louisville), Tennessee (Memphis), and North Carolina (Lenoir, Raleigh); west and north to western and northern Alaska (St. Paul Island, Malchatna River, Afognak Island, Demarcation Point), northwestern Mackenzie (Fort Anderson), northern Manitoba (Churchill), and Franklin (Repulse Bay, Baffin Island, Lake Harbour).

Casual records.—Accidental in Bermuda, Greenland (Frederikshaab, Julianehaab), Scotland, and England.

Migration.—Late dates of spring departure are: North Carolina—Cullowhee, May 9. Virginia—Fort Hunt, May 2. District of Columbia—May 20. Maryland—Laurel, April 27. Pennsylvania—State College, May 19. New York—Cayuga and Oneida Lake basins, May 30 (median of 7 years, April 22); Scarborough, May 29; New York City, May 10. Connecticut—Portland, May 12. Massachusetts—Concord, May 30. Vermont—Montpelier, May 4. New Hampshire—New Hampton, May 8 (median of 21 years, March 20). Quebec—Senneville, May 7. Missouri—Shannon and Carter Counties, April 18. Indiana—Michigan City, June 26; Bloomington—June 24; Camden, March 16. Ohio—Toledo, May 8. Michigan—Escanaba, May 1. Iowa—Ames, February 15. Kansas—Wichita, March 21. Nebraska—Holstein, Bladen, April 20. South Dakota—Brookings, March 6. North Dakota—Fargo, June 1. Manitoba—Lake St. Martin, May 1. Colorado—Silver Lake, May 17. Washington—Tacoma, May 19.

Early dates of fall arrival are: Washington—Echo Lake, Pierce County, September 22. Alberta—Edmonton, October 28. Montana—Big Sandy, September 12. Wyoming—Laramie Park, August 25. New Mexico—Clayton, November 3. Manitoba—Oak Lake, August 10. North Dakota—October 23. South Dakota—Faulkton, October 1. Nebraska—Omaha, November 10. Kansas—Hays City, September 15. Minnesota—Hallock, October 25. Wisconsin—Shiocton, November 3. Iowa—Davenport, November 3. Michigan—McMillan, October 31. Ohio—Toledo, November 2. Illinois—Chicago, September 9. Missouri—St. Louis, November 16. Ken-

tucky—Louisville, November 27. Quebec—Morin Heights, Septem
ber 28. Vermont—Stratton, October 7. Massachusetts—Concord
October 27. Rhode Island—Johnston, November 20. Connecticut–
Saybrook, November 6. New York—Babylon, October 6. Pennsyl
vania—Hawk Mountain, Hamburg, October 17; Media, October 22
Delaware—Hoops Dam, November 16. Maryland—Laurel, Novem
ber 13. District of Columbia—October 23. North Carolina—Piney
Creek, December 13.

Egg dates.—Nova Scotia: 5 records, February 8 to April 26.

ARREMONOPS RUFIVIRGATA RUFIVIRGATA Lawrence

Olive Sparrow

PLATE 28

Contributed by OLIVER L. AUSTIN, JR.

HABITS

First described by George Newbold Lawrence in 1851 from a specimen taken along the Rio Grande near Brownsville, Tex., this species
was known commonly for the next century as the Texas sparrow
In 1957 the A.O.U. Check-List adopted olive sparrow as a more fitting
vernacular name. The species occurs within Check-List limits only
in extreme southern Texas, in Kinney, Atascosa, and Nueces counties.
From there its range extends southward along both coasts of Mexico
to Yucatan and Chiapas, and an isolated population lives along the
the Pacific coast of Costa Rica. Some eight subspecies are recognized.

A modest little greenish finch, the olive sparrow is nonmigratory,
and the various populations are resident throughout the species'
range. It inhabits scrubby chaparral, weedy thickets, and the undergrowth near forest edges from sea level to altitudes of 6,000 feet
locally in Mexico (Blake, 1953). Though somewhat quiet and retiring, it is not particularly shy, and is even inclined to be a bit inquisitive at times. While not an uncommon bird, its habits and behavior
have not been studied intensively, and little has been written about
its life history.

While in Texas in 1923 Mr. Bent (MS.) wrote: "While resting in a
shady resaca near Brownsville, I noticed a small, plainly colored bird
hopping about among the fallen leaves on the floor of a thicket, where
it was decidedly inconspicuous. As I could see no distinctive markings in its plain, olive-green plumage in the dim light of its shady
retreat, I concluded that it must be a Texas sparrow. I was not
greatly impressed with its beauty at this first glimpse, but when I

PLATE 28

wnsville, Texas · A. D. Cruickshank

OLIVE SPARROW

lumne County, Calif., June 14, 1938 · J. S. Rowley

NEST OF GREEN-TAILED TOWHEE

PLATE 29

heard its pretty little song later on, I found it both pleasing and distinctive."

George M. Sutton (1951) thus describes his first encounter with the species in Nuevo León, Mexico:

But what were these mousey, olive-backed finches which moved like shadows from bush to bush; which so reminded us of undersized Green-tailed Towhees; and which had that species' amusing habit of kicking up the dead leaves while searching for food? If we walked toward them, even though slowly and noise-lessly, they kept well ahead of us. But if we sat down and remained quite still, they resumed their feeding, chased each other playfully, and gave their faint chirps of alarm and beady squeals of contentment almost under our noses. Their eyes were light brown. Frequently as many as three or four of them fed close by, scratching diligently a moment or two, then racing across an open stretch to the shelter of the next thicket. They were birds we had never seen before —Olive Sparrows * * *. The neat brown and gray striping of the head, gray of the breast, and touch of yellow at the bend of the wing made the Olive Sparrow a very attractive bird, we thought, and its manners were winsome. We judged it to be a common nesting species in the vicinity of Monterrey though we heard no songs and witnessed neither courtship nor pairing.

Nesting.—S. N. Rhoads (1892) "found the Texas Sparrow thoroughly at home in the Corpus Christi and San Patricio chaparral, and secured their nests and fully fledged young." Dr. James C. Merrill (1879) says: "I have found the nests with eggs at intervals from May 9 to September 7. These are placed in low bushes, rarely more than three feet from the ground; the nests are rather large, composed of twigs and straws, and lined with finer straws and hairs; they are practically domed, the nests being placed rather obliquely, and the part above the entrance being somewhat built out."

George B. Sennett (1878) claims "* * * they raise at least two broods within our limits, one in May and June, the other in August and September," and adds (1879):

The domed nests are situated in the heart of bushes, generally from two to five feet above the ground. They were found in all sorts of open thickets. One I detected close by the roadside, in a clump of bushes, under a small tree; another on a dry knoll, which was covered with cacti, thorny bushes of various kinds, and scattering trees of mesquite and ebony, and in close proximity to nests of the Long-billed Thrasher and the Yellow-billed Cuckoo. Most frequently, however, nests were found in those depressions near woods, where water stands during the wet season, which, when dry, abound with grass hummocks and bunches of rank weeds covered with wild-tomato vines. The nests are nearly round in shape, large for the size of the bird, and constructed of dried weed-stems, pieces of bark. grasses, and leaves—sometimes with a little hair for lining of the bottom, but more frequently without.

Herbert Friedmann (1925) found five nests near Brownsville, "all in prickly pear cacti." Dean Amadon and Don R. Eckleberry (1955) found a nest about 3 feet above the ground in the center of a large mass of candelabra cactus.

Eggs.—The olive sparrow usually lays four or five eggs, sometimes only three. They are white, unspotted, and quite glossy; in shape they vary from rounded ovate to ovate. The measurements of 45 eggs average 21.8 by 16.2 millimeters; the eggs showing the four extremes measure *24.2* by *17.3, 19.9* by 16.0, and 21.7 by *15.0.*

Plumages.—F. M. Chapman (1914) writes:

Few birds show less change of plumage than does this bush-haunting sparrow. The male resembles the female; there is practically no difference between the winter and the summer dress, and after the post-juvenal molt the bird of the year cannot be distinguished from its parents.

The juvenal, or nestling plumage, however, is strongly streaked with fuscous both above and below. At the post-juvenal molt apparently only the wing-quills and tail feathers are retained, and the bird passes into its first winter plumage, which, as just remarked, resembles that of the adult.

There appears to be no spring molt, and summer birds differ from winter ones only in being more worn.

Witmer Stone (*in* Rhoads, 1892, footnote) thus describes the fully fledged young: "The young have the feathers of the head and inter-scapulum centered with black and bordered with ochraceous. Beneath, the breast and flanks are tinged with olivaceous and are marked with dark longitudinal markings; belly yellowish-white."

Food.—G. B. Sennett (1879) says the olive sparrow "feeds upon larvae and seeds, especially the seeds of the wild-tomato." Sutton (1951) describes "two in plain enough sight under a fallen branch, kicking away like little towhees; another off in the shrubbery, invisible but scratching noisily; and two more in a vine, a short way above the ground, busily preening their wings."

Voice.—R. T. Peterson (1941) says: "Song, a series of dry notes all on one pitch, starting off deliberately and trailing off into a Chippy-like rattle. 'Also an insect-like buzz as the birds chase each other through the thickets' (Irby Davis)." George M. Sutton (1951) writes: "For the first time we heard the full song of the Olive Sparrow— a simple, deliberate series of unmusical chips, somewhat suggestive of the song of a Swamp Sparrow (*Melospiza georgiana*)."

Field marks.—E. R. Blake (1953) characterizes the olive sparrow as "an olive-backed sparrow with a prominent *brown eye-streak*, and two *dull brown crown-stripes*. A strip of bright yellow on the edge of the wing helps verify the identification." Mr. Bent (MS.) writes that the species "may be recognized by its plain, grayish, olive-green upper parts, brighter on the wings and tail, and dull whitish under parts. There is no conspicuous field mark that is visible at a distance. The brown stripes on the head, the white eye-ring and the yellow edge of the wing are noticeable only at short range." Peterson (1941) adds that the bird is about the size of a house sparrow, and that its olive-green back gives it some resemblance to the larger green-tailed towhee which sometimes occurs in the same range in winter.

Enemies.—Mr. Bent (MS.) writes the olive sparrow "is sometimes imposed upon by the red-eyed cowbird; there are two eggs of this parasite, said to have been taken from a nest of this sparrow, in the American Museum of Natural History."

Dean Amadon and Don R. Eckleberry (1955) relate: "On April 15, about 30 miles south of Brownsville, Texas, in Tamaulipas, we were attracted by a protesting pair of Olive Sparrows. A coachwhip snake, *Coluber (Masticophis) flagellum*, was found with its head in the sparrows' nest, which was about three feet above the ground in the center of a large mass of candelabra cactus. The young (or eggs) had been eaten. This was shortly after noon on a not, sunny day."

DISTRIBUTION

Range.—The olive sparrow is resident from southern Texas (Val Verde, Atascosa, and Nueces counties) south to eastern Coahuila (Sabinas) and central Tamaulipas (Victoria).

Egg dates.—Texas: 50 records, March 16 to September 1; 26 records, May 11 to May 31.

CHLORURA CHLORURA (Audubon)

Green-tailed Towhee

PLATES 28 AND 29

Contributed by ROBERT A. NORRIS

HABITS

In describing the green-tailed towhee as *Fringilla chlorura*, Audubon (1839) manifestly regarded it as a finch. Since that time the bird has been placed in one genus after another, no less than eight generic names being listed in Ridgway's (1901) synonymy of the species. "It seems absurd to call this bird a Towhee at all," wrote W. L. Dawson (1923), whose further, uncritical comment was, "To appearance it is, rather, an overgrown Warbler, or a cross, say, between a Yellow-breasted Chat and a Chipping Sparrow." While Dawson may have penned these remarks in a spirit of levity, he appears to have noticed in this species' song an unmistakable resemblance to that of the bona fide towhees.

Reasons for considering the green-tailed towhee a species of *Pipilo*, as set forth by C. G. Sibley (1955) and supported by K. C. Parkes (1957), seem to me strong and convincing, and I would prefer to include it in this genus rather than in *Chlorura*, where the 1957

A.O.U. Check-List puts it. Briefly, the arguments offered by Sibley are that the rufous cap, white throat, yellow carpal edge, olive-green upper parts, and other color characters of this towhee are also found in the collared towhee (*Pipilo ocai*) of Mexico, and that the relatively long, pointed wing of the greentail is simply correlated with its migratory habit. As described earlier (see especially Sibley, 1950), extensive hybridization occurs between the collared towhee and the rufous-sided towhee (*P. erythrophthalmus*), leaving little doubt as to their being properly considered congeneric. Consequently, "it remains only to demonstrate the close relationship between *P. ocai* and the Green-tailed Towhee in order to show the latter also to be a *Pipilo*" (Sibley, 1955). As well as in adult color pattern, in habitat preferences, songs and call-notes, and color of eggs, as indicated by Sibley (1955), and in juvenal color pattern, as noted by Parkes (1957), there is an essential similarity between these two species. Sibley adds that "if one is to disagree with this proposal he must justify the inclusion of the brown towhees [*P. fuscus, rutilus,* and *aberti*] in *Pipilo* because they are without doubt less closely related to the type species, *Pipilo erythrophthalmus,* than is the Green-tailed Towhee." These reasons for placing the greentail in *Pipilo* are weighty and should be convincing to many. Even so, a measure of caution is still in order. I feel that additional characteristics, such as skeletal and other anatomical features and types of behavior, need to be investigated before students can best piece together, on the basis of all the potentially available, neontological evidence, the phyletic relationships in the towhee group. Only then can the best possible natural classification be achieved.

The green-tailed towhee breeds in montane and high plateau regions in the western United States, from Oregon and Montana to southern California and western Texas. It winters from more southerly parts of California, Arizona, and Texas south into Mexico. A short, sprightly introduction to it in its native haunts is provided by Ralph Hoffmann (1927):

"A cat-like call, *pee-you-wee* is often heard in summer from the low bushes on open mountain-sides or high sage-brush plains east of the Sierras or Cascades. Presently a bird with *reddish brown cap* mounts to the top of some bush and utters a lively song. The singer has a *white throat,* which shows like a bit of cotton when the notes are poured forth. The Green-tailed Towhee is an active bird, slipping in and out of the sage or deer-brush, inquisitive about intruders and not shy."

Among 39 records of specific altitudes at which breeding individuals or populations have been recorded, some of the lowest points were 2,500 feet (Nevada County, Calif.), 3,450 feet (Siskiyou County,

Calif.), and 4,350 feet (Fremont National Forest, Colo.) above sea level; the highest point was 10,500 feet (San Francisco Mountains, Ariz.). A median or average elevation based on this series of records is about 7,300 feet. Southerly populations tend to breed at higher elevations than more northerly ones do. Although present in much of the transition zone, this brush inhabitant is perhaps most character-istic of the Canadian zone, as was graphically illustrated for the Yosemite region by J. Grinnell and T. I. Storer (1924). The range also extends well up into the Hudsonian zone in areas such as the San Francisco Mountains, where R. Jenks (1934) found that "these birds inhabit the mountain willow and wild gooseberry thickets on the borders of alpine meadows, from altitudes of 8,300 up to 10,500 feet."

Especially prominent among shrubs that characterize its breeding-season habitats are sagebrush (*Artemisia*), deerbush and snowbush (*Ceanothus*), wild rose and spiraea (*Rosa* and *Spiraea*), manzanita (*Arctostaphylos*), waxberry (*Symphoricarpos*), and chokecherry (*Prunus virginianus*). Other plants, either less widespread or less important for the greentail, are mountain mahogany (*Cercocarpus*), gooseberry (*Ribes*), antelope brush (*Purshia*), ninebark (*Physocarpus*), serviceberry (*Amelanchier*), and ocean-spray (*Holodiscus*). Fre-quently open stands of piñon and juniper are interspersed in the chaparrallike vegetation or ponderosa pine forms a partial canopy above it. This species' habitat and niche, as found in California, are suc-cinctly described by J. Grinnell and A. H. Miller (1944):

"* * * Forest is avoided; only scattered trees within the brushland are tolerated, but they may be used as song posts. The brush cover is typically low (2 to 4 feet) and spreading, affording runways between plants and underneath the foliage. Within forested areas, the places occupied are comparatively dry and well insolated; in the Great Basin region the lower, warmer flats are avoided even though grown to sagebrush. The sphere of activity is low, foraging taking place on the ground in the leaf litter and in the tangle of branches.* * *"

Spring.—W. W. Cooke (1914) says: "From its winter home in northern Mexico and along the border of the United States, the Green-tailed Towhee moves slowly northward, occupying more than two months—late February to early May—in passing across the less than a thousand miles from the northern limit of the winter home to the northern boundary of the breeding range."

Many of the migrants trickle into southern parts of California, Arizona, and New Mexico in the first week in April. Representative arrival dates for Silver City, N. Mex., and Carson City, Nev., are April 12 and 25, respectively, while an average early date (based on data from 7 years) for Laramie, Wyo., is May 11. In California, say J. Grinnell and A. H. Miller (1944), the "spring movement occurs in April, lasting well through May in the desert mountains." A. A. Saunders (1911) reports that in Gallatin County, Mont., the species appears "in the latter part of May".

The transients often move through the mountains; less often, perhaps, they pass through relatively low country. In 1902, in the Huachuca Mountains of southern Arizona, H. S. Swarth (1904) reported spring-migrant greentails "frequenting the lower canyons up to an altitude of about 6000 feet." But the next year these birds were unusually late in arriving (May 6) and "all that were seen were in washes issuing from the canyons, specimens being taken a mile or more from the mountains." It would seem that this change of pattern might have been due to a retarded spring in 1903. In Utah these birds are said to migrate "chiefly through the mountains, seldom descending to streamside thickets in low altitudes (A. M. Woodbury, C. Cottam, and J. W. Sugden, 1949); in the same state, however, W. H. Behle (1944) has referred to the species as a "transient in the lowlands."

Mr. Bent (MS.) writes: "We saw a part of [spring] migration in southern Arizona on April 4, 1922; a valley near Bisbee was filled with migrating birds, mainly western chipping sparrows, white-crowned sparrows, and green-tailed towhees, all moving steadily northward." Evidently it accomplishes much of its northward movement in daylight hours.

This towhee could, I believe, be classed as semihardy. On May 24, 1941, Robert T. Moore and Wendell Taber (MS.) watched a single bird at 8,000 feet on Mount San Jacinto, in southern California, under well-nigh wintry conditions and report: "The location was a natural flat clearing in the dense yellow pine forest. Snow, hard-packed, was between three and four feet deep, but ground was appearing at the edges of a rushing brook which varied in width from five to perhaps twenty-five yards. The willows were not yet in full leaf. The towhee seemed perfectly at home and was apparently gleaning food under the willows rather than along the ground bared by the stream. A flight of but a few hundred yards would have taken the bird to the precipitous drop to the snow-free slopes."

An interesting sidelight on the vernal ecology of this bird is offered by K. W. Kenyon (1947) in the following passage:

The Green-tailed Towhee * * * is typically found on wooded mountain sides and among the mesquites in the lowlands of the Cape district of Lower California in winter. However, it appeared entirely out of place on a small sandy and windswept islet in Scammon's Lagoon. One Green-tailed Towhee lived a precarious existence on such an island near the camp of several Mexican fishermen. It picked up the bits of food and drank the water the fishermen offered it, becoming quite tame. The towhee was first observed in the area on

April 20, 1946, and it was still there when I left on May 7. It sought shelter from the almost constant wind under the many carapaces of the green turtle (*Chelonia mydas*) which lay scattered about near the fishermen's camp. Although the salt marsh near-by supported a population of Savannah Sparrows (*Passerculus sandwichensis*), the towhee made no attempt to search for food in that area. Conversely the Marsh Sparrows infrequently entered the vicinity of the camp.

Evidence of this species' propensity to return to its nesting ground or birthplace is presented in notes from northern Arizona by Allan R. Phillips (MS.), who states that "our latest captures of definitely breeding birds in 1935 were on September 17–21 (birds recaptured in May–July 1936); but a bird banded Sept. 29, 1935 got into a trap not in operation on May 19, 1936 and evidently froze overnight, probably being also a breeding bird here. All October birds captured here failed to return, being probably migrants."

Territory.—No information is available on the territory size of the greentail and its interspecific relations. One of the chief co-occupants of its scrub habitat in California mountains is the fox sparrow (J. Grinnell and H. S. Swarth, 1913; W. M. Pierce, 1921; H. W. Clark, 1932). A. K. Fisher (1893), in reporting on the Death Valley Expedition, states that in "May and June Mr. Nelson found [this species] common among the sage brush on the Panamint and Grapevine mountains, where it was associated with Brewer's sparrow." Other fringillid species observed sharing its breeding habitat— and which might well compete with the green-tailed towhee—are the rufous-sided towhee and the lazuli bunting (V. M. Tanner and C. L. Hayward, 1934). That the fox sparrow in particular may be something of a competitor is indicated by the following observation (H. W. Clark, 1932): "An interesting case of conflict between birds occupying nearly the same ecologic niche was observed at Black Butte. Here I found a number of individuals of the Green-tailed Towhee * * * singing from the same places used by the Fox Sparrows. One morning there was quite a spirited battle between a Fox Sparrow and a towhee over the possession of a small red fir. After several sallies at the towhee, the sparrow finally allowed him to remain in the same tree, and the two sat close together in the upper twigs and sang alternately for some minutes."

Nesting.—The green-tailed towhee nests on or near the ground. Some 27 records indicate that heights of nests range from ground level to 28 inches, the average height being 16 inches. Of these nests, 11 were placed in or at the base of sagebrush, 7 were in waxberry, and 4 were in snowbush. There are two records of nests associated with scrubby oaks, including *Quercus gambelii*, and one instance each of association with chokecherry, juniper, and gooseberry. Although nests are often well concealed in brushy growth, this is not always true. Thus, J. Grinnell (1908), in writing on this towhee in the San Bernardino

Mountains, mentions a nest that "was built in a slight hollow in the ground at the base of a small and scraggly specimen of sage * * * in an open space on the cañon bottom fully twenty feet from any more pretentious bush, such as we had expected to find this bird selecting as a shelter for its home." Apparently the species nests in cactus at times (F. M. Bailey, 1902). L. Hering (1948), among others, points out that the greentail may show a preference for stream environments wherever these are available.

Although nest-building activity seems not to have been recorded, there have been a number of partial descriptions of finished nests. These are generally rather large, thick-walled, and fairly deeply cupped; in one, as reported by J. Grinnell and T. I. Storer (1924), "the cavity measured 67 millimeters across by 40 millimeters deep." The major part of the structure usually includes twigs and stems, grasses, and bark (including that of sagebrush); the lining comprises fine plant stems, rootlets, and in most instances strands of horsehair from mane or tail. Sometimes other kinds of hair, as that of the porcupine (I. N. Gabrielson and S. G. Jewett, 1940), may be used.

Sets of eggs are to be found over a period of approximately two months, from May 20 to July 21. The median date, based on 26 sets, is June 17. These records pertain to findings in six states, from Oregon and California to New Mexico. Some observers (R. B. Rockwell and A. Wetmore, 1914; A. J. van Rossem, 1936) have suspected that the green-tailed towhee normally has two broods, but a larger compilation of nesting data or a careful study of color-banded birds would seem necessary to establish this as fact. There is circumstantial evidence of a replacement nesting or second nesting attempt (Allan R. Phillips, MS.).

One wonders what sort of role in the species' breeding program might have been played by the hermaphrodite example which J. A Jeffries (1883) has described in this manner: "A short time ago I received the body of a Green-tailed Towhee * * *. The bird was shot by Mr. Brewster, at Colorado Springs, on May 16, 1882. In plumage it resembled females of the species, but on dissection to determine the sex, both an ovary and a testicle were found; the one on the left the other on the right side.

"* * * the two generative mounds took on the two sexes and * * * the accessory structures followed the master organs. So the Wolffian duct remained on one side and the Mullerian on the other."

Eggs.—According to notes provided by A. R. Phillips, the eggs, as observed at one nest, are laid one a day in the early morning. The first was known to have appeared before 10:45 on May 27, 1936, the second before 8:35 on the 28th, and the third before 8:45 on the 29th. The eggs were cold throughout this period, but a bird sometimes was seen near the nest. By 9:20 a.m., May 30, incubation was under way; it began, presumably, with the laying of the fourth and last egg, which was not actually seen until the 31st, when Phillips deliberately flushed the incubating bird from the nest.

The greentail lays from two to five eggs. For 28 sets recorded in the literature, the average size was 3.65 eggs, the distribution being as follows: 3 sets of two, 7 sets of three, 15 sets of four, and 3 sets of five. Egg weights of this species as recorded by W. C. Hanna (1924b) average 2.91 grams (55 eggs), with extremes of 2.16 and 4.02 grams.

W. G. F. Harris describes the eggs as follows:

"Four eggs comprises the usual set of this species although sometimes as few as three or as many as five are laid. They are ovate to rounded ovate, and moderately glossy. The eggs are white, profusely speckled, and finely spotted with such shades of reddish brown as "snuff brown," "Rood's brown," "russet," or "avellaneous" with undertones of "light mouse gray" and "pale mouse gray." The majority of eggs are heavily speckled over the entire surface, and often these markings are confluent at the large end forming a solid cap. Some of the gray undertones and the brown spots are so close and intermingled that they run together; others have the spots of the two colors sharply defined and separated; on still others the gray undertones may be entirely lacking. The measurements of 50 eggs average 21.8 by 16.4 millimeters; the eggs showing the four extremes measure *25.2×18.3*, *18.3*×15.2, and *19.6×14.5* millimeters."

Young.—We find no observations on the normal sequence of hatching. However, the following remarks of R. W. Hendee (1929) on hatchability under suboptimal conditions are worthy of note: "On June 12 two nests were found * * *. The eggs from these sets were carried to our base camp and three days later when I unwrapped them to blow them I found to my chagrin that one set was just hatching, the young birds being still alive." The word "chagrin," incidentally, reveals something of the observer's viewpoint, which evidently was more that of the traditional oologist than that of the avian biologist. In occasional nests the hatchability of eggs may be low. In reporting on several nests found in the San Bernardino Mountains, G. Willett (1921) says that "all contained young except one found on June 15, which held three addled eggs."

Hatching takes place from early June through July; fledglings leave the nest from mid-June until August. Almost no information is available on parental care or development of nestlings. Although brooding has been recorded (Phillips, MS.), neither this nor feeding of young, including the role of the sexes, appears to have been studied. J. Grinnell (1908) mentions a nest holding four half-grown young whose parents "showed mild solicitude, by uttering their kitten-like mew, varied with the sharp 'peep,' from a neighboring bush." After leaving the nest the juveniles are fed by their parents for an indefinite period. Immatures were reported by J. E. Law (1926) to be surprisingly tame at a feeding station in the San Bernardino Mountains. Remarking on one bird that visited a feeding box inside his cabin, Law says "breakfast at dawn was the program, and it seemed not to matter to the bird if my fingers were in the box, nor if its tail brushed my fingers."

Plumages.—According to F. M. Chapman's (1914) description, "the adult male and female are alike in color, and there is essentially no difference between their summer and winter plumages. The young male, also, after the first post-juvenal molt, resembles its parents; but the young female * * * in corresponding (first winter) plumage has the chestnut crown-cap largely concealed by the grayish tips of the feathers, and the back is grayer than in the adult." Apparently some individuals among first-year males are also rather dully colored, for H. S. Swarth (1904) mentions that a "male bird, presumably of the previous year, taken on May 8, 1903, has hardly a trace of the rufous crown, and is generally of a duller color and with the markings less sharply defined than in the fully adult bird."

K. C. Parkes (1957) remarks that the juvenal plumage, which is streaked with dusky blackish both dorsally and ventrally, "conforms precisely to the *Pipilo* pattern: uniformly streaked above, with no indication of the contrast in color between back and crown of the adult; unstreaked on the throat (which is white in the adult); streaked on the remainder of the underparts, with the markings heaviest across the chest, where the adult has a gray band with a poorly-defined posterior edge." F. M. Chapman (1914) says: "At the post-juvenal molt, only the wing-quills, primary coverts and tail-feathers of this plumage are retained, when the young male * * * acquires a plumage resembling that of the adults, while in the young female the crown-cap is absent."

Among juveniles collected by J. Grinnell and H. S. Swarth (1913) in the San Jacinto area of southern California, from July 1 to August 4, "some [were] in full juvenal plumage, and others variously advanced in the post-juvenal molt. An immature female secured August 2 * * * has already acquired complete first winter plumage."

F. M. Chapman (1914), reports that "the prenuptial or spring molt appears to be confined to the throat and anterior parts of the head. Probably the immature female acquires fresh chestnut feathers in the crown, and with the wearing away of the grayish tips of the winter plumage her crown-cap becomes like that of the adult. Aside from this, the summer plumage differs from winter plumage only through the effects of wear and fading, the upper parts being grayer, the flanks paler."

Food.—Among the relatively little information published on the species' food habits, J. Grinnell (1908) noted greentails in abundance at the north base of Sugarloaf in the San Bernardino mountains where "they were feeding on service-berries [*Amelanchier alnifolia*] in company with many other birds." According to F. M. Bailey (1928), the species takes weed seeds and insects, including the alfalfa weevil and other injurious beetles and bugs. In the Bull Run mountains of Nevada, Ira La Rivers (1941) found this towhee, among other species, feeding on small, third-instar Mormon crickets (*Anabrus simplex*).

The green-tailed towhee often visits feeding stations, where it accepts chick-feed, cracked corn, bread crumbs, and birdseed. C. H. Merriam (1890) noted that this bird's "habit of searching for food on the ground led to the death of several individuals which got into our traps set for Mice and other small mammals." Similar experiences were recorded by L. M. Huey (1936a) and also by J. Grinnell and T. I. Storer (1924), who specified that the source of the birds' undoing was the rolled oats placed on the traps as bait.

Behavior.—In the words of I. N. Gabrielson and S. G. Jewett (1940), "the trim, alert Green-tailed Towhee is a somewhat shy bird, although its ringing song and catlike call notes are familiar sounds of the sage country." F. M. Bailey (1939) writes of "its usual appealing air of timidity" and of its running "over the ground with round crest up and tail in motion ready for flight, its deprecatory calls * * * also bespeaking its gentle timid nature." Activity in dense growth has aptly been called "skulking" (A. Wetmore, 1920), which seems applicable to movements both on and above the ground.

As to foraging characteristics, Grinnell and Storer (1924) say that "the combination of conical bill, long tail, short wings, and stout legs and feet, proclaim the Green-tailed Towhee to be adapted for foraging beneath brush patches." The bird's food-searching motions usually involve "a little jump forward and a little kick back" (F. M. Bailey, 1939), or scratching not unlike that of other kinds of towhees. That this habit is well ingrained is illustrated by J. E. Law (1926), who, while observing rather confiding young greentails at a feeding box near Bluff Lake, San Bernardino mountains, set down the following notes: "It seemed strange * * * how the scratch habit could not be overcome. Every few pecks, standing in this box half filled with bread crumbs, it just had to give a scratch or two, which sent the crumbs flying in every direction." R. Hoffmann (1927) was apparently in error when he stated that this bird "does not scratch with both feet after the manner of the larger Towhees."

One of the more peculiar, if not species-specific attributes of the green-tailed towhee is the "rodent-run," as it has been termed by A. H. Miller (1951a). In Colorado, a greentail running across an open space was taken for a chipmunk and shot by mistake (R. B. Rockwell and A. Wetmore, 1914). Not dissimilar running has been observed in birds associated with nests; thus F. M. Bailey (1902) says: "One that Mr. Bailey found on its nest on Donner Peak, California, ran silently for five or six rods through the brush, and then stopped, to tempt him away from its brood." In Utah, A. H. Miller (1934) reported a nest from which a bird flushed "in the characteristic 'green-tail' manner, that is, by dropping to the ground and running with tail elevated, thus resembling a chipmunk running through the brush." In focusing attention on the "rodent-run," A. H. Miller (1951a), after pointing out that the species commonly places its nests a foot or two above the ground in sagebrush and other low bushes (between which are open alleyways), provides the following discussion:

The resemblance of the flushing towhee to a chipmunk [of which several related species were common in the sagebrush country] has the following specific aspects: the size of the bird is similar to that of a chipmunk; the tail of similar length and breadth, is held elevated in both; the motion is fast and even, that is, distinct saltations are absent, whereas they are present in the usual hopping gait of the towhee; the run is in a straight line except as altered by major obstructions; the take-off from the bush by dropping nearly straight down without use of wings is mammal-like. Although the back of the towhee is not striped as in chipmunks, it is to be noted that the longitudinal stripes of rapidly running chipmunks are not conspicuous anyway. The dull green and brown of the running towhee actually presents a dusky streak that is similar to that presented by the prevailingly brown-backed chipmunk.

The effectiveness of the towhee-chipmunk resemblance is attested by the dozen or more instances in which I have been deceived by it, not realizing until after the towhee had run into cover fifteen yards or more away that it was a bird and was now giving an alarm note. A retracing of my steps then disclosed a nest. Of course I do not know how many more times I have been completely deceived. Surely coyotes, which are common predators in the region, must frequently be led to pursue the apparent chipmunk racing through a clearing rather than to relate the movement to the easily attacked towhee nest from which the bird has dropped. Whether or not pursued, the bird would at least momentarily be confused with a chipmunk, and the significance of the bird-and-nest situation escape the predator.

Williamson * * * has postulated the origin of the rodent-run in shore birds, or at least that in the Purple Sandpiper, from a substitute or displacement activity which, first by chance, has had special value in protection, and under selective forces has become perfected and regularly utilized at appropriate times. In the Green-tailed Towhee, origin from substitute activity is not evident to me. The rodent-run here would seem to be a direct modification of a general tendency to run or hop rapidly on the ground when closely pursued. But it should be stressed that for distraction purposes the modifications and refinements of the escape movement entailed in the nest-departure run to varying degree all bear resemblance to the mammalian copy.

Whether bona fide injury-feigning occurs in this species with any regularity is a moot point. Probably it does not. R. W. Hendee's (1929) observation is nevertheless suggestive: "On June 9, I flushed a towhee from a bush near the spring. Flying a few feet to one side it gave the customary imitation of a crippled bird, which led me to believe that there was a nest in the vicinity. However, after careful examination I failed to find a nest, and, though I returned to the locality a number of times, I never located a nest or saw a bird in the vicinity again."

The intelligence of the greentail and its response to kind treatment is shown by J. E. Law's (1926) account of his experiences with it, to which the reader is referred. One particularly memorable item Law recorded is that whereas a bird would freely enter his cabin for a "handout" in a feeding box, it would never allow a person to come between it and the door—the only escape passage. One had only to move toward the door to elicit the towhee's "escape" reaction, which was rapid and effective. Such a "blocking experiment" was not a serious deterrent, however, in that one or more of the towhees, apparently throughout their sojourn in the area, remained confiding—and hungry—visitors in and about the cabin.

Voice.—F. M. Bailey (1902) writes: "His mewing call-note, a soft *mew, mew-ah-eep*, seems his most chewink-like character and proclaims his presence, as does his song when the ear has caught the difference between it and *Passerella*. Though phrased somewhat like the song of the *maculatus* [rufous-sided towhee] group, it is wholly different in quality and rendering, being more of the bright finch type with the *Chondestes*-like burr heard in so many finch songs, and its two emphasized notes standing out in a medley of short notes." Otto Widmann (1904) also likens the species' vocal effects to those of the lark sparrow, remarking, in fact, that the towhee's song is strongly reminiscent of that of the sparrow.

W. L. Dawson (1923) describes the song as follows: "Of song the bird possesses a surprising repertory. There is something dashing and wren-like about his more familiar ditties, and also something faintly reminiscent of the Vesper Sparrow (*Pooecetes gramineus*). *Meay, tsit sit sit sit* reminds me of orthodox *Pipilo*, and *Ah fewgee weeee pilly willy willy* will carry one right back to *Pipilo erythrophthalmus*—or will, that is, when one gets over the surprise of the opening notes, which in the case of two birds heard at Goose Lake were strikingly like those of the Eastern Phoebe (*Sayornis phoebe*)."

Further record and interpretation of the bird's vocal efforts are found in J. Grinnell and T. I. Storer's (1924) study of animals in the Yosemite:

During the courting season the male Green-tailed Towhee sings at frequent intervals, although on the whole somewhat less often than the male fox sparrow. For singing the bird mounts to the topmost twig of his selected thicket and there says in rapid wheezy sequence, *sŭp-sĕ-tew'-sĭ-sĕ*, or *eet-ter-te-te-te-si-si-si-seur* (according to the transcriptions of two different observers). Individual syllables may be added or dropped, but the general plan of the song remains about the same. The song is buzzy, distinctly like that of the Western Lark Sparrow, and not so much like the impressively clear lay of the fox sparrow. Between songs the cat-call is given at irregular intervals, and it is frequently uttered when the bird is disturbed or excited. Thus when the two nests mentioned above were being examined, the owners remained in the vicinity, at a distance of 30 or 40 feet, hopping about on the ground, exhibiting some concern, and voicing a kitten-like *mew-wée*.

Claude T. Barnes, who observed the greentail in a scenic setting in the Wasatch mountains, Utah, contributes the following notes: "About every thirty seconds he would raise his chestnut-capped head towards the sky with a little twist of his neck, and, his throat fairly billowing with the effort, utter a song that after many attempts I felt best represented by these letters: 'klū', klŏw', klee, klee, klee, klee, klee,' the first two syllables being strongly accented, the five ending 'klees' being of ordinary finchlike character." Further description of the song is provided by R. Hoffmann (1927), who says; "The song varies greatly in different individuals and even the same bird frequently changes his song after a few repetitions."

Earlier writers referred to call-notes in much the same way as did Grinnell and Storer (1924). H. D. Minot (1880) mentions "a petulant *week*, and a characteristic *pe-u-ee* in a Towhee's voice (three syllables)," while J. C. Merrill (1888) says that "besides its pleasant song and the alarm note, there is another, rarely heard and apparently only when the bird's curiosity is excited without alarming it; this is a loud and distinct *mew-wée*, which is very characteristic." One of the commoner calls, apparently the *week* or alarm note, C. G. Sibley (1955) describes as "a mewing note, which may be written, 'zree' or 'zew.'" If these reports are considered in the light of Grinnell and Storer's (1924) account, it would seem that the two types of utterance referred to by Merrill in reality intergrade; if this is so, the various call-notes expressing alarm, solicitousness, or mild curiosity, might relate more to modifications in volume and intonation than to differences in quality or syllabification.

R. B. Rockwell and A. Wetmore (1914) could not distinguish the calls of immature greentails near Golden, Colo., from those of young of the local rufous-sided towhees.

A. K. Fisher (1893) reported several instances of night singing.

Field marks.—This towhee, which is a little larger than the house sparrow, is easily recognized by its reddish brown cap, its white throat bordered by black stripes, its olive green upper parts—brightest on the wings and tail—and its gray breast and whitish belly. Immatures are brownish on the back, lack the rufous crown, and are streaked with dusky.

Enemies.—This towhee is sometimes victimized by the brown-headed cowbird (*Molothrus ater*), one of the more recent instances having been noted by N. K. Carpenter in Mono County, Calif. (H. Friedmann, 1934).

While no evidence of predation has come to my attention, probably adults as well as eggs and young of this low-nesting bird occasionally fall prey to mammalian predators, as is suggested by A. H. Miller (1951a) in his discussion of the "rodent-run."

Other hazards besetting the greentail, in common with other birds, include weather inclemencies such as severe hailstorms, which may destroy sets of eggs (L. Huey, 1936a), and "modern La Brea tar pits," in which the birds may become entrapped (A. E. Borèll, 1936).

One specimen examined by C. M. Herman, Jankiewicz and Saarni (1942) was infected with the coccidian parasite, *Isospora*, which was also found in brown and rufous-sided towhees and several other species of birds.

Fall.—Prior to fall migration proper, there is an up-mountain scattering of birds after the breeding season, and immatures are prevalent among these wanderers (Grinnell and Storer, 1924). This well-known phenomenon, as observed in Utah, has been treated by C. L. Hayward (1945) as follows: "This post-nesting up-drift of bird populations is less marked in the Uinta Mountains * * * than it is in the Wasatch, but it is nevertheless evident. The green-tailed towhee, western vesper sparrow, Macgillivray's warbler, western wood pewee, yellow warbler, and Brewer's sparrow are the more common species to follow this procedure in both the Wasatch and Uintas."

There is also evidence of downslope scattering of individuals in late summer (J. Grinnell, 1908).

In many areas migration is well under way in September. Late fall records for localities in Oregon (Jackson County and Rogue River Valley), Nevada (Carson City and the Charleston Mountains), and Wyoming (Laramie) have been in the last week in September; others for the Yosemite Valley, Utah (Pine Valley), Arizona (San Francisco Mountains), Colorado (Golden), and New Mexico (Silver City), have fallen within the first week in October. In Kern and Inyo counties, Calif., this towhee has been recorded as late as October 24 and 25 (see J. Grinnell and A. H. Miller, 1944, who furnish representative data on migrants in the state). As a transient, the green-tail may be uncommon (Grand Canyon region; R. K. Grater, 1937) or it may be abundant (Yosemite Valley; Grinnell and Storer, 1924).

In early October, in Yosemite Valley, the species has been found "frequenting the same thickets as the Golden-crowned Sparrows [*Zonotrichia atricapilla*] which had then just arrived from the north," (Grinnell and Storer, 1924), while R. Hoffmann (1927) states that "in migration it associates with Gambel Sparrows [*Zonotrichia leucophrys gambelii*] in the bushes in the deserts of southeastern California * * *." In fall it has also been noted in Stillwater County, Mont., in association with rufous-sided towhees (C. M. Welch, 1936). There is but little tendency, however, toward actual gregariousness. Statements by Grinnell and Storer (1924) and L. Huey (1942) indicate that the green-tail is basically nonsocial after the breeding season.

Winter.—Some of the wintering populations may be fairly dense. In giving the species' status in the Organ Pipe Cactus National Monument area of Arizona, Huey (1942) states that it is "perhaps the most generally distributed winter visitor. While never in concentrated numbers, it was found singly in almost every place where vegetation was dense enough to given it shelter." From middle or late September until mid-May it is common to abundant in parts of Sonora and Sinaloa (A. H. Miller *in* Miller, Friedmann, Griscom, and Moore, 1957), to mention but two sections of Mexico in which it sojourns in the nonbreeding season.

Among the rare individuals that have been found wintering in the eastern United States, two showed an attraction to white-throated sparrows (*Zonotrichia albicollis*). First, G. C. Embody (1908) writes of a vagrant greentail collected in Virginia that was "in company with White-throated Sparrows, in a thicket along the edge of an open field * * *." Second, S. A. Eliot (1948) tells of a bird, evidently a first-year male, which appeared as an accidental visitor at a North-hampton, Mass., feeding station: "From January 22 on, its favorite companion was a White-throated Sparrow * * *, and as it matured its behavior towards this female White-throat became more and more devoted. In April it came but little to the feed but could be found nearby, always with the White-throat. On April 15, Mrs. Risley had her last look at it, closely following the White-throat and apparently courting it. We supposed that the White-throat went north that evening with the Green-tail in pursuit, but on April 26 a group from Pittsfield found it moping by itself in the forsythia! What happened next, nobody knows."

The apparent special "affinity" between the green-tailed towhee and the *Zonotrichia* sparrows certainly merits further study. As this towhee does appear to be a true *Pipilo*, one is tempted to speculate whether the genera *Pipilo* and *Zonotrichia* are more closely related than the 1957 A.O.U. Check-List indicates.

DISTRIBUTION

Range.—Washington and Montana to central Mexico.

Breeding range.—The green-tailed towhee breeds from southwestern and central Oregon (Onion Mountain, Wheeler County), southeastern Washington (Blue Mountains), southern Idaho, southwestern Montana (18 miles northwest of Dillon), and northwestern, central, and southeastern Wyoming (Yellowstone Park, Wheatland) south through the interior mountains to southern California (San Jacinto Mountains), southern Nevada (Charleston Mountains), central Arizona (San Francisco Mountains, White Mountains), and southern New Mexico (Black Mountains, Sacramento Mountains).

Winter range.—Winters from southern California (Los Angeles, casually), southern Arizona (Fort Mohave, Gila River Valley), and western and southern Texas (Sierra Blanca, Brownsville) south to southern Baja California (San José del Cabo), Jalisco, Guanajuato (Guanajuato), Morelos (Cuernavaca), Nuevo León (Galeana), and Hidalgo (Metztitlán); occasionally north to central California (Marysville); in migration to western Kansas and western Oklahoma (Cimarron County).

Casual records.—Casual north to Saskatchewan (Dollard, Tregarva), Wisconsin (Prescott), and Quebec (Portneuf County), and east to Massachusetts (6 localities), New Jersey (Englewood, Newton, Whitesville), Delaware (Wilmington), Virginia (Bowers Hill), South Carolina (Mount Pleasant), Georgia (Rome), Tennessee (Elizabethton), and Louisiana (Cameron Parish).

Migration.—Early dates of spring arrival are: New Mexico—Los Alamos, April 27 (median of 7 years, May 6). Wyoming—Laramie, April 30 (average of 7 years, May 11). Idaho—Paris, April 26. Montana—Bozeman, May 17. California—Twin Oak, April 23; Cabezon, May 13. Nevada—Carson City, April 25. Oregon—Powder River Mountains, April 10.

Late dates of spring departure are: Georgia—Rome, April 27. Wisconsin—Prescott, May 10. Texas—Frijole, May 1; Fort Davis, April 10. Oklahoma—Guymon, May 16. Arizona—Tucson, May 16.

Early dates of fall arrival are: Arizona—Fort Whipple, September 15. Texas—Sinton, September 26. New Mexico—Los Alamos, October 4.

Late dates of fall departure are: Oregon—Rogue River Valley, September 23. Nevada—Humboldt Valley, September 16. California—Pinecrest, September 15. Montana—Bozeman, October 3. Wyoming—Laramie, December 15 (average of 5 years, September 26). Colorado—Beulah, October 23.

Egg dates.—California: 115 records, May 28 to July 29; 60 records, June 1 to June 20.

Colorado: 10 records, May 19 to June 30.

New Mexico: May 20 to July 10 (number of records not stated).

Oregon: 17 records, May 25 to July 16.

PIPILO ERYTHROPHTHALMUS (Linnaeus)

Rufous-sided Towhee: Eastern U.S. Subspecies*

PLATES 30 AND 31

Contributed by JOSHUA C. DICKINSON, JR.

HABITS

Mark Catesby (1731) in his description of the "towhee-bird," commented "* * * It is a solitary Bird; and one seldom sees them but in Pairs. They breed and abide all the Year in *Carolina* in the shadiest Woods." Vieillot, in redescribing Catesby's "towhee-bird" as "*Le Touit Noir*" in 1819, added the following to the already growing store of information (translated from the French):

This species is numerous in the center of the United States where it remains through the summer and from where it migrates in Autumn to spend Winter in the South of the States. The Towhees, because of their short wings, cannot fly at much altitude or stay in the air for a long time; so they travel only by fluttering from hedge to hedge, from bush to bush, and they are never seen at the top of tall trees. They hunt on the ground for the different seeds they feed on, pushing the leaves and weeds that hide those seeds aside with their bill and feet; they seemed to me to be quite fond of small acorns [*petits glands*], eating usually only those that are fallen; they live in pairs through summer, gathering in families during September and large flocks toward the end of October, which is the time of their migration voyage which they accomplish in company with *sparrows* and *blue* and *red fallow-finches*. Those birds like to stay in summer in the thickness of thickets and at the edge of woods. Then we can see the male on the top of a medium height tree where he sings for hours at a time; his song is made of only a single short and often repeated musical phrase, but it seemed to me sonorous and pleasant enough to make me regret that the bird would stop as soon as there were young ones. The female makes her nest on the ground, in the weeds or under a thick bush, gives it a thick and specious shape; she makes it out of leaves, vines, and bark strips outside and lines it inside with fine weed stems. Her laying consists of five eggs of a pale flesh color with freckles more abundant at the larger end.

Since these early writings, many details of the life history of this ever popular bird have come to light. Presumably, both Catesby

---

*The following subspecies are discussed in this section: *Pipilo erythrophthalmus erythrophthalmus* (Linnaeus), *P. e. rileyi* Koelz, *P. e. alleni* Coues, *P. e. canaster* Howell.

PLATE 30

eechobee, Fla.   A. D. Cruickshank

MALE WHITE-EYED TOWHEE

itylene, Ala., Apr. 17, 1940   F. S. Barkalow, Jr.

NEST OF ALABAMA TOWHEE

Oyster Bay, Long Island, N.Y.   A .D. Cruicksha

MALE RED-EYED TOWHEE

Ashland, Oreg., June 1922   J. E. Patterso

NEST OF OREGON TOWHEE

and Vieillot were referring to the bird that breeds in the northeastern United States, although Catesby was more likely to have been familiar with the form occurring in Georgia and the Carolinas. Studies of geographic variation in morphology, migratory behavior, and breeding habits have today documented the propriety of recognizing four sub-species of eastern towhees (Dickinson, 1952). C. G. Sibley's (1950) study of the allied western forms has confirmed their close relation-ship to the nominate eastern stock.

The four eastern races the 1957 A.O.U. Check-List recognizes are characterized as follows (Dickinson, 1952):

P. e. erythrophthalmus (Linnaeus). A large, small-billed, vividly colored, red-eyed form, showing a large amount of white on the rectrices. It breeds in the Transition and Upper Austral Zones east of the Great Plains from southern Saskatchewan, Manitoba, Ontario, and Maine southward through middle North Dakota, Iowa, Kansas, and northern Arkansas, and eastward through middle Tennessee, northern Georgia, and western South Carolina to the Atlantic coast in southern Virginia.

P. e. rileyi Koelz. A medium sized, large-billed race with variable eye color, and showing less white on the rectrices than its northern relatives. It breeds from western Florida and southeastern Alabama northeastward through southeastern Georgia and South Carolina to central coastal North Carolina.

P. e. alleni Coues. A small, medium-billed, pale-eyed race, showing very little white in the rectrices. It breeds in Florida from Franklin, Columbia, and Duval counties south to southern Dade County.

P. e. canaster Howell. A large, large-billed, pale race, with variable eye color, showing a medium amount of white on the rectrices. It breeds from eastern Louisiana and western Mississippi northward to southern Tennessee, eastward across northern Alabama and central Georgia and South Carolina to south-central North Carolina, and southward to the Gulf coast from extreme western Florida westward to central Louisiana.

Authors vary widely in their choice of terms describing the preferred habitat of the rufous-sided towhee. Some areas noted are hedgerows, thickets, brushy hillsides, and "slashings" (E. H. Eaton, 1914); wood-lands and swamps (E. E. Murphy, 1937); dry uplands near edges of woods or high tracts covered with a low brushwood (Baird, Brewer, and Ridgway, 1874b); brushy pastures (C. J. Maynard, 1896); and "thick-ets of willows, cottonwoods, and young sycamores, where wild sun-flowers, horse-weeds and poke grow rampant, the whole woven together by the interlacing of wild cucumber vines" (A. W. Butler, 1898). Forbush (1929) says "He is a ground bird—an inhabitant of bushy land. No other sparrow in New England seems to be so wedded to life in thicket and tangle. * * * He spends most of his life in thicket, 'scrub' or sprout land, and so the bushy lands of Marthas Vineyard and Cape Cod are favorite resorts. He is not a dooryard bird except in winter, when necessity now and then drives one to a feeding station, but even then he spends most of his time in the shrubbery, coming out only to secure food. He may be found along bushy fences and roadsides, and often finds food or sand in country roads." B. H. Warren (1890) states that they occasionally "visit potato vines and other plants on which the destructive Colorado potato-beetle feeds."

F. M. Chapman (1932), writing of the "southern race" of the towhee, comments that it "does not associate with the northern bird, which is abundant in the south in the winter. The latter selects haunts of much the same nature as those in which it passes the summer, while the southern bird lives in heavy growths of scrub palmetto."

My own experiences in the Gainesville region (where Chapman spent much of his time) and elsewhere over the entire range of *P. e. alleni* do not confirm Chapman's observations. Racially mixed flocks do occur in winter, and frequently. *P. e. alleni* is quite commonly found in habitats other than that of scrub palmetto. Sandpine (*Pinus clausa*) scrub in both the coastal dune and "Big Scrub" areas of Florida have this white-eyed towhee as a very conspicuous element along with the Florida Jay *Aphelocoma c. coerulescens*. When I spent a summer on Cape Cod, Mass., I was impressed by the obvious gross similarity of the species preferred habitats there and in Florida. The habitat of birds from near the type locality of *P. e. canaster* (Mobile, Ala.) and *P. e. rileyi* (Brunswick, Ga.) do not differ radically from those in which the towhee is abundant in peninsular Florida. In my experience, the species frequents early seral stages in both xeric and mesic successions, and whenever ruderal conditions approximate these natural situations one can usually expect to find towhees in abundance.

Courtship.—Few comments have been made on the species' courtship behavior. J. J. Murray (MS.) writes of his observations on Elliott's Knob, Augusta County, and Lexington, Va. "Late in the afternoon I heard a towhee call and then saw him fly to the top of a bush. He then spread his tail into a fan with the white spots showing distinctly, raised his wings, and fluffed out his feathers until in the fog he looked twice his natural size. Almost at once a female appeared in a nearby bush. At another time, in my yard at Lexington, on October 22d, I saw a male, all alone, go through what was similar to a courtship display. Restlessly flying from branch to branch and from bush to bush, with fluttering wings and tail, he paused at times to sing a 'whisper song.' It was not the usual song, but a broken warble, low and husky and full of squeaks."

W. E. C. Todd (1940) writes of this activity in Pennsylvania: "When the females appear, the wooing begins with a lively chase through the thickets. The white-marked wings and tails flash impressively as they are rapidly spread and folded in the courtship display."

Frederic W. Davis writes me from Amherst, Mass., that "The males arrive first in late April, followed by the females a few days later. Adult and first-year males arrive together and seem about equally represented throughout the breeding season. For the first few days after their arrival the males are often found in small groups of four to eight birds.

"Females being pursued in full flight by two courting males are a common sight up through mid-May. The male whisper song is as prominent a part of courtship as the male-female chase. Another common courtship phenomenon is the male carrying nesting material such as dead leaves to the vicinity of the female, who then manipulates it. This behavior is particularly noticeable during pairing before the first nesting, less so before the second. In precopulatory display the female holds her back horizontal, raises her bill and tail, and utters a rapid high-pitched *tetetetete*."

Nesting.—F. W. Davis continues in his letter: "Site search and nest-building are carried on entirely by the female, who gathers all nesting materials within 60 feet of the site she chooses. Although building one nest covered a 5-day span, the female devoted only a few hours each day to placing the materials. The day after she finished the nest she visited it but once and remained only about 2½ minutes. She came once the following day with a long piece of sedge and remained almost a half hour, but did nothing to the nest. She deposited the first egg the morning of the third day after nest completion.

"Incubation may start with the second egg of the clutch, or be delayed until the last egg is laid. Incubation takes 12 to 13 days. Two nests per season seem to be normal; the same mates are retained and the second nests are within the original territories. The laying of the first egg of the second clutch in four cases observed ranged from 8 to 21 days after the fledging of the first brood. A banded pair whose first brood was destroyed 7 days after hatching laid the first egg in a second and new nest 9 days later."

J. S. Y. Hoyt (1948) describes a nest found June 6, 1942, in a heavily wooded area near Ithaca, N.Y. It was built not more than three feet from the ground between two stems of a white pine and contained three young birds about 5 days old and one unhatched egg.

A. A. Saunders (1923) reports a nest found in New York on July 6 in a "silky dogwood" and another on July 13, also in a bush that contained four eggs. M. B. Trautman (1940) writes of finding nine nests. Of the nine, one contained six eggs, three contained four eggs or young, three contained five eggs or young, one contained four young and one cowbird young, and one contained six young and one cowbird egg. He continues:

> The nest was made of grasses, rootlets, twiglets, bits of leaves, string, or shreds of bark; a few nests were lined with cattle hair. Four nests were built upon the ground beneath brush tangles, 2 were built in piles of dead brush over which a dense leafy tangle had grown, and the remaining 3 were 1 to 5 feet above the ground in vine tangles or upon small branches of bushes. The earliest nest with eggs was recorded April 30 (1929, 4 eggs), and the latest July 12 (1931, 5 eggs); the earliest nest with young was found May 11 (1929, 4 one-third grown young in same nest as of April 30), and the latest July 17 (1932, 4 young); the first fledging out of the nest was seen May 20 (1931), and the last August 4 (1930, at least 2 young being fed by parents).

Dayton Stoner (1932), writing of his experiences in New York, states that all nests he observed were located on the ground, but that on occasion a low bush served as a support or hiding place. He adds that the nests are made of "Dead leaves, grass and strips of bark * * * with a lining of fine grass." He records both 4 and 5 eggs per nest. In Ohio, G. M. Allen (1909) discovered nests in the "higher, more open woods, as well as in the brushy tangles." Merriam (1877), quoting the notes of the Stadtmüller brothers, describes a nest found under a cedar tree as being "composed externally of cedar bark, lined with grass and horse hair."

B. H. Warran, writing in 1890, adds "a grass tuft" to the type of site that may be chosen. W. B. Barrows (1912) comments that in Michigan the towhee almost invariably nests on the ground. He adds that "Possibly one nest in fifty is built in a bush or tangle of vines a foot or two above the ground." Also reported in Barrows are records by Wolcott of a single nest at Grand Rapids 8 feet above the ground in a tree and another at Ann Arbor placed on top of a stump. Barrows also states that two broods are reared almost always, one in June and another in July. Minnesota records from T. S. Roberts (1932) include a single nest found by Dr. Patton in a matted grape vine 11 feet 4 inches from the ground. L. H. Porter (1908), in writing of the nesting habits of birds at Stamford, Conn., following the cold spring of 1907, suggests that his finding of towhee nests in trees might have been the result of the unusual weather, but the many records of this habit under average conditions contradict this suggestion.

Russell E. Mumford kindly furnished this following condensation of his (1953) observation of what appears to be the highest towhee nest on record:

"On June 26, 1952, I was walking along an old road through a strip of second growth woodland near Freetown, Jackson County, Ind. I observed a bulky nest about 18 feet above the road placed in a bushy tangle where the tops of two small saplings of shagbark hickory (*Carya ovata*) and the vine of a wild grape (*Vitis* sp.) were interlaced. By shaking the trees lightly, I failed to flush off any bird, but a vigorous shaking caused a female Red-eyed Towhee to burst from the nest noisily scolding me. I could not examine the nest at this time, but on the following day took a pole with a mirror attached and noted that there were eggs in the nest. The adult towhee was not present at this visit. The distance from the base of the nest to the ground was measured and found to be 17 feet, 5 inches. About an hour later, I passed the tree again, shook the nest, and the adult female was again flushed off. As before, she was very excited and scolded me soundly as long as I remained in the vicinity of the nest.

"On July 4, the eggs were found beside the nest on the ground, both having been knocked from the tree in some way. The predominate trees at the nest site were saplings of shagbark hickory and white oak (*Quercus alba*). The nearest clearing was about 75 yards from the nest site and the tree canopy was completely closed over the nest."

In peninsular Florida, where *P. e. alleni* is the resident subspecies, A. H. Howell (1932) writes that the nest is commonly placed in small bushes, 1 to 4 feet above the ground. Nests are occasionally found on the ground under palmetto leaves or brush piles. Howell adds that three eggs comprise the usual complement and that two or three broods are raised. Early nests are found in April, second broods in June, and third broods in August. H. H. Bailey (1925) describes a Florida nest as made of dry leaves, leaf stems, pine needles, and grasses, lined with fine grasses.

As expected, birds in the northern parts of the breeding range begin nesting activities somewhat later. However, it is interesting to note that by early May there are records from such points as Virginia, Pennsylvania, Massachusetts, and Indiana (F. M. Chapman, 1932).

F. W. Davis writes me from Amherst that "The nesting season in our section of Massachusetts, based on estimated first egg dates, extended from May 15 through July 5, 1960, from May 18 through July 8, 1961, and from May 22 through July 14, 1962." He continues: "I believe the male assists neither in incubating nor brooding. During incubation the female tends to join the male to forage, and he often accompanies her back to the vicinity of the nest, but I have never seen a male take part in any activities at the nest before the young hatched, except for occasional anticipatory food-bringing. The female develops a very prominent brood patch, the male no sign of one, nor has a male ever been observed on a nest. The female deprived of her mate can successfully fledge a brood, but no males have succeeded unless the young were old enough to need no brooding when the female was lost.

"Both parents are active in feeding the young and in nest sanitation. They eat the egg shells as soon as the young are out of them, and for the first few days they eat the fecal sacs; later they carry more and more of these away. Both parents also were seen to eat nest parasites. At first the adults feed the young by placing their bills into the gullet and pumping vigorously, seeming to vibrate their bodies as they do so. As the young grow this method diminishes and finally ceases. When the male brings food the female usually leaves, but in the early stages while she is still brooding the nestlings, she often just hops on the nest rim and watches while the male feeds them. Occasionally he gives her the food, or she takes some from him, and both feed the young together."

F. L. Burns (1915) gives the incubation period for the nominate race as "12 to 13 days." O. L. Austin, Jr., informs me that at a nest in his garden in Gainesville, Fla., the period from the laying of the last egg to the hatching of the last egg was 13 days.

Eggs.—The rufous-sided towhee lays from two to six eggs, most often three or four. They are usually short-ovate or ovate and slightly glossy. The ground color is grayish or creamy white and occasionally greenish white. They are more or less evenly speckled or spotted with "russet," "chestnut brown," "Carob brown," "pecan brown," or "Mars brown," with underlying spots of "light neutral gray," "or pale purplish gray." On some eggs the undermarkings are quite numerous and on others practically nonexistent. The brown spots are quite sharply defined in most instances, often so profuse that they almost obscure the ground, but occasionally the markings are clouded. The spottings generally tend to become heavier toward the large end where frequently they form a solid cap. The measurements of 50 eggs of *P. e. erythrophthalmus* average 23.1 by 17.0 millimeters; the eggs showing the four extremes measure *25.7* by 18.3, 24.4 by *19.3*, *20.3* by 17.3, and 21.3 by *16.8* millimeters.

Plumages.—As described by A. A. Saunders (1956), the skin of the newly hatched young bird is flesh colored, the mouth is edged with pale yellow, and the lining of the mouth is pink. The down is medium gray and occurs on the capital, dorsal, humeral, femoral, and secondary tracts.

J. Dwight (1900) describes the natal down of this species as "Pale clove-brown." G. M. Sutton (1935) appears to be in agreement with Dwight. David K. Wetherbee has written me that "drab-gray" is a better description. Both Dwight and Wetherbee used specimens of *P. e. erythrophthalmus* for their observations. My own observations of *P. e. alleni* conform with those of Wetherbee. Dwight's (1900) detailed description goes on to state that the juvenal plumage of the male is—

acquired by a complete postnatal moult. Above, including sides of head, cinnamon-brown (often darker) somewhat obscurely striped, broadly on the back, more narrowly on the crown, with deep olive-brown. Wings dull black, the primaries with edgings and a patch at their bases white, the tertiaries with broad edgings of buff and walnut-brown, the innermost white edged, the wing coverts with buff or pale cinnamon edgings. Tail deeper black than the wings, the three outer rectrices with subterminal areas of white. Below, dull white, strongly washed with buff or pale yellow, cinnamon tinged on breast, flanks and crissum, and streaked on the throat and sides with dull black. Bill and feet pinkish buff, the former becoming slaty black, the latter dusky sepia-brown. Iris, sepia-brown becoming deep red during the winter.

Dwight (1900) further states that the first male winter plumage is—

acquired by a partial postjuvenal moult, beginning the middle of August, which involves the body plumage, the wing coverts, the tertiaries and the tail but not the primaries, their coverts, and the secondaries. Young and old become almost indistinguishable except by the browner primary coverts of the young birds. Whole head, throat, breast, back, rump, wing coverts and tertiaries jet black; abdomen pure white, the sides and flanks rich chestnut, the crissum cinnamon. The upper tail coverts are usually edged with cinnamon and the back sometimes has obscure Vandyke-brown edgings. The tertiary endings are pale buff with walnut, those of the inner tertiary nearly white.

G. M. Sutton (1935) comments that Dwight of course refers to New York birds and that in other areas the onset of the post-juvenal molt is much earlier than August. Sutton presents records of the beginning of the molt in mid-July in specimens from Michigan and Georgia.

Dwight's (1900) description of the molts continues:

First nuptial plumage acquired by wear which is marked by the end of the breeding season producing a ragged plumage, but the black areas do not fade perceptibly and the chestnut flanks fade but very little. The brown primary coverts are the distinguishing feature of young birds.

Adult winter plumage acquired by a complete postnuptial moult beginning early in August. Differs from first winter dress chiefly in the blacker wings, especially the primary coverts and deeper wing edgings. Old and young now become indistinguishable.

Adult nuptial plumage acquired by wear and differing from first nuptial by black instead of brown primary coverts. A few feathers may be assumed by moult on the chin and elsewhere, but they are insignificant in numbers.

In the female juvenal plumage olive-brown wings and tail replace the black ones of the male. The first winter plumage, acquired by a molt of similar extent to that of the male, differs in having the head, back, throat, and breast brown instead of black. The earliest record of the first molt I have seen is a female I took near Brunswick, Ga., June 24, 1949, that shows a few buff flank feathers. Adult and young females cannot be distinguished in this plumage. The first nuptial is acquired by wear and the adult winter by a complete postnuptial molt. Subsequent plumages do not differ, females never assuming the black areas of the male.

F. W. Davis writes me: "Certainly August is far too late for the onset of the postnuptial molt in Massachusetts. A breeding female banded June 4, 1961, with a well-developed brood patch, was retaken July 4, 1961, and had then molted all her upper tail coverts except the central pair; an adult male taken the same day had shed all his upper tail coverts."

My own observations indicate that the sequence and method of acquisition (molt or wear) of plumage is the same for the four eastern subspecies. The variations in color with locale have been discussed at some length in an earlier study (Dickinson, 1952). These changes are generally characterized by a marked paling of the flank colors and a lessening of the amount of white at the bend of the wing and at the tips of the outer rectrices in southern latitudes.

Food.—The towhee is principally a ground feeder, and this is reflected in its diet. W. L. McAtee (1926) comments on the food habits of this species as follows:

The food of the Chewink consists of a great variety of items, the bird taking apparently almost everything unearthed in its rummaging of the forest floor. About three-tenths of the food is animal matter and seven-tenths vegetable. Of the latter portion seeds, mast, and wild fruits are the important items. The mast consists chiefly of acorns; the favorite seeds are those of ragweed, foxtail grass, smartweed, and dock; and the fruits that are most frequently taken are those of strawberry, huckleberry, blueberry, bayberry, and blackberry. The towhee has very rarely been observed to feed on any agricultural product.

Beetles are eaten more frequently than any other insects and among them weevils are especially favored. Moths and caterpillars, bugs, and ants are other insect food items of importance. Besides insects numerous spiders and snails, smaller numbers of daddy-long-legs, millipeds, and sowbugs, and a very few small salamanders, lizards, and snakes are consumed. The insects eaten include various agricultural pests such as the potato beetle, plum curculio, strawberry crown girdler, flea beetles, cutworms, striped and spotted cucumber beetles, and the cornfield ant. Pests of trees which are known to be on the bill-of-fare of the chewink embrace nut weevils, bark beetles, adults of round-headed and flat-headed wood borers, leaf beetles including the locust leaf miner, and the variable leaf beetle (*Typophorus canellus*) which injures mountain ash and butternut among other trees, leaf chafers, junebugs, the goldsmith beetle, the yellow case-bearer (*Chlamys plicata*) which feeds on the leaves of numerous deciduous trees, click beetles, scale insects, cicadas, tree hoppers, carpenter ants, sawflies, and tent caterpillars and a great variety of other caterpillars. The chewink is an exemplary woodland citizen and should receive our best protection.

In addition to this rather complete account, many unusual food items have been recorded. G. H. Breiding (1946) quotes A. L. Nelson (*in* litt.) as informing him of a single record of a towhee eating the drupes of moonseed (*Menispermum canadense*) in Maryland, which Breiding notes is claimed to be poisonous to humans. Holly berries were eaten by a towhee observed by G. A. Petrides (1942). E. H. Forbush (1929) states that Arthur T. Wayne says that when spring arrives in South Carolina, these birds go to the tallest trees and feed upon the buds. E. G. Holt (1918) noted towhees feeding on mulberries in a small orchard in Alabama. F. H. King (1883) examined 17 specimens and found that "five had eaten small seeds; one, wheat; one, oats; one, raspberries; one, seven moths; three, nine beetles; one, ants; one, a wasp; one, an ichneumon; two, three grasshoppers; two, two cockroaches; one, a walkingstick (*Spectrum femoratum*), and four of its eggs; and one, a larva." T. S. Roberts (1932) quotes Dr. G. H. Leudtke's notes on the behavior of a towhee that remained at a feeding station at Fairmont, Mich., beyond the usual time for fall departure. This bird ate suet, oats, and flax during the period October 25–November 1. H. C. Oberholser (1938) adds the boll weevil to the varied insect items included in the diet of this exceedingly beneficial species.

It should be noted that no writer since L. J. P. Vieillot (1819) has reported "acorns" as being an item of diet for the towhee.

Frederic W. Davis (in litt.) adds the following notes from his observations in Amherst, Mass.:

"When feeding on the ground the towhee usually progresses by 'kick' foraging, scattering the ground debris with its feet to expose potential food as it goes. When insect larvae and other food are plentiful on top of the substrate, the birds resort to 'visual' or 'peck' foraging without scratching the debris aside. Occasionally towhees will attempt short 'flycatching' sallies on the wing, either from the ground or from a perch. In the few instances of this I have seen, the intended prey was always a conspicuous and slow-moving insect, and the bird's sallies were too awkwardly executed to be successful.

"In late May or early June the birds are often seen in highbush blueberry, *Vaccinium corymbosum*, eating the blossoms. Arboreal foraging predominates during the first week or two of June, and throughout the month the towhees frequent a variety of deciduous trees to glean larvae from the foliage. Fruits of the aromatic winter green, blueberries, and huckleberries are consumed not only by the adults, but are fed in quantity to the nestlings. One nestling about six days old was fed a wintergreen berry so large the young bird could not swallow it, and succeeded in spewing it out only after 45 minutes of trying.   In addition to smooth larvae, the nestlings are also given hairy caterpillars such as those of the gypsy moth, which the adults first soften well by chewing.   Adults also consume large numbers of ant pupae, which they seem to prefer to the adult ants when they uncover and ant nest."

Behavior.—F. M. Chapman (1932) says: "There is a vigorousness about the towhee's notes and actions which suggests both a bustling, energetic disposition and a good constitution."   He continues, "The dead leaves fly before his attack * * *.   It is only when singing that the Towhee is fully at rest.   Then a change comes over him; he is in love, and, mounting a low branch, he repeatedly utters his *sweet bird s-i-n-n-g* with convincing earnestness."   Such comments are typical expressions of almost all who have observed this attractive bird. T. E. Musselman (1923), in writing of trapping experiences with towhees in Georgia, adds some interesting notes to the recorded behavior patterns.   A male bird "upon being seized * * * commenced singing and kept up his song until I released him."   This unusual reaction occurred on each of 30 captures of this individual.   Injury feigning has been recorded for the species by S. A. Grimes (1936) who states that he observed it "rarely."   Baird, Brewer, and Ridgway (1874b) note that "They are much attracted to their young, and when approached evince great anxiety, the female thrusting herself forward to divert attention by her outcries and her simulated lameness." E. H. Forbush (1929) adds the following comments concerning the behavior of nesting pairs:

While the female is incubating, the male waits upon her and occasionally relieves her on the nest.   As the nest is exceedingly well concealed, and the female dull colored, she can sit until almost trodden upon before she leaves the nest; when finally driven from it she is likely to act as if disabled, thus attempting to lure the intruder away.   The young usually remain in the nest ten or twelve days, if not disturbed, until their wings grow strong, but if disturbed they may leave it before they are able to fly.   When the young have learned to fly, the family keeps together for a time, but seldom, even in migration, is anything like a close flock formed, for Towhees are not normally gregarious.   During and after the molt in August all are rather quiet, and shy.   When severe frosts come most of them disappear in the night on their southward migration.

From his studies of the species in Massachusetts, F. W. Davis writes me:

"The towhee, when conspicuous, is very much so.   It calls, sings, and forages with little or no attempt at concealment, and even flies short distances noisily in what I term the 'flut flight,' its wings making a thuttering sound audible at some distance.   But when it wants to, the bird can be most inconspicuous, remaining quietly out of sight in the underbrush or flying silently away well ahead of the intruder. The towhee's sense of hearing is apparently very keen, for birds I have been watching have often taken alarm at another person's approach long before I became aware of it.

"The species has a phenomenal ability to keep itself hidden from view. I have so often been unable to find or flush towhees I have watched fly into certain covers that I presumed they must have flown away unnoticed. In August, 1960, I saw a male bird fly into a dense but isolated patch of hardhack and sweetfern not more than 20 feet across. After trying my best to flush him for 30 minutes, I gave up in disgust and left. I had retreated only a short distance however, when a well-modulated *twee* from the copse announced he was still there.

"Then in June, 1962, another adult male flew into a dense cover of cinnamon fern and lit near me on the ground. He evidently saw me at once, for he froze motionless in a hunched-over crouch. He stayed still when I moved so long as I did not shorten the distance between us. Every time I tried to approach him, however, he scurried without a sound, still in his crouch, a few feet to one side or the other, always at right angles to my approach. Thus his tactics in evading me were displacement rather than flight.

"Reaction to disturbance at the nest varies considerably. Usually the brooding female remains on the nest until the intruder is within a few feet, sometimes until the vegetation over the nest is parted, and in a few cases until she is actually touched. She generally leaves the nest in a crouch and scuttles off silently for some distance under cover before she rises and returns to scold the intruder. During incubation she may desert the area temporarily, or she and her mate may *twee* apprehensively from the nearby cover. When the young are about five days old both the male and female become bolder, and will often dash to within 3 or 4 feet of the intruder, *twee*ing excitedly with wings and tail spread and crown raised, before retiring to continue scolding from the trees at a safer distance. The male often sings and scolds alternately. Several times in reaction to disturbances near but not at the nest, the parents led 7-day or older young away from it.

"While his mate was incubating in June, 1960, a male towhee discovered his reflection in the windows of a nearby house. From crack of dawn until dark he attacked his image with time out only to feed. He would flutter against a pane for a few seconds, take a few tentative but firm pecks at it, retreat, give a few *drink-your-tea* calls, and then return to drive off the interloper. Apparently his reflection in the glass was clear a few feet away, but disappeared closer by. When a mirror was substituted he remained at it for two hours at a stretch, feinting at his reflection, pecking at it, rising and striking the glass with beak and feet simultaneously. Then he would pause, sing a few times, and renew the attack. He continued this behavior even after the eggs hatched. On his way to feed the young with a beakful of larvae he usually tarried long enough to make a few sallies. Ultimately he fought with—and smeared—every window in the house.

"Towhees in captivity consume quantities of water and are avid bathers. Wild birds in suburban areas are frequent visitors to bird baths. In most of our study areas free surface water is scarce, even after heavy rains, because the heavy layer of humus absorbs it. After a very heavy dew the morning of June 17, 1961, I watched a male towhee fly into one cluster of red maple leaves after another and flutter among them. After becoming thoroughly drenched, he flew to a gray birch where he fluffed vigorously and then preened his plumage as it dried."

Voice.—The towhee is a vigorous songster. R. T. Moore (1913) uses him as the epitome when he comments that the song of the fox sparrow is "quite as strenuous as that of his cousin, the Chewink." While many of its various vernacular names are of course phonetic interpretations of its call, the towhee has a considerable repertoire and it is interesting to note the many observations and interpretations various authors have recorded.

C. J. Maynard (1896) comments that "when disturbed, it constantly reiterates its name of 'towhee' given very decidedly with the accent on the last syllable. This note is oftentimes interpreted as being chewink * * *." E. H. Forbush (1929) provides these descriptive terms: *"towhee', chewink', joree', wink rrrink; chuck, chuck; 'whit-a whit-a-whit'* (H. D. Minot); song, *'drink-your-tea'; dick' you, fiddle fiddle fiddle,* or better yet *'chuck-burr, pill-a-will-a-will-a'* (E. T. Seton), most of the force expended on the *chuck*, the *burr* on a lower key, and the rest uttered rapidly; also a 'quavering warble difficult of description' (E. A. Samuels); an unusual song *jung* (low) *dee-dee-dee-dee-dee* (high) *ees-ees* (higher) *yŭ-yŭ-yŭ-yŭ-yŭ* (low) (F. H. Allen)."

H. A. Allard (1928) adds his observations of "strange winter singing" of a group of towhees which passed the winter near Chapel Hill, N.C.—

a strange, squeaky song * * * interspersed with its familiar *tur-ee—tur-ee.* [I heard] a peculiar bird expression delivered for some seconds in a sweet conversational way, somewhat hushed in quality. * * * an almost indescribable song-babble or warble, the notes uttered in succession, with warbler-like variations. * * * interspersing his expressions with the familiar well known *tur-ee—tur-ee—tur-ee,* now uttered in an excited manner. [On March 2, 1904] * * * It was a happy courtship scene, in which brilliantly attired males were trying to win the approval of the female. Again I heard its new, mysteriously soft, affectionate expressions, almost a subdued whispering chant, warbler-like. * * * It is evidently his true love-song or murmur, remotely reminding one of the Bobolink's sweetness at times, and delivered while in company with the females, and doubtless during the active courtship period * * *.

T. S. Roberts (1932), after considering other authors' attempts to describe the song of this species, states his preference thus: "* * * chipper-chee-e-e-e-e, the first two syllables sharp and clear, the latter part a trill of a slightly lower pitch." A. W. Butler (1897) adds the interesting note that the "female does not sound the final k in chewink, which is distinctly given by the male." To Roberts the song sounds something like " 'look-out, ter-r-r.' The first syllable has a rising inflection; the second is slurred." E. H. Eaton (1914) finds a distinction between the call notes "chewink" and "tow-hee" and comments that the former is often followed directly by the latter. C. R. Mason wrote to Mr. Bent in 1945 of his observation of what he assumed to be a single individual that frequented his place three successive summers. "Instead of the 'Drink Your Tea' song its notes are 'Drink, Drink, Drink, Tsit, Tsit.' The last two notes are inaudible fifty feet from the bird, but the 'Drink' notes are quite loud and ringing." From an unpublished manuscript provided by A. A. Saunders, the following information has been extracted. "The song * * * is short and, in its commonest form, fairly simple. This form consists of two notes, usually on different pitches, followed by a short trill, or a series of rapid notes all on the same pitch. A still simpler form consists of one note and a trill. There are many other variations. The songs vary in length from one to two and three-fifths seconds, and in pitch from A_5 to D_7. The pitch interval varies from none at all to seven and a half tones, the average being three and two-fifths tones.

"The quality of Towhee songs is exceedingly variable. Some are quite musical, others decidedly rattle-like or buzzy. Some are partly musical and partly rattle. The musical part may be the first notes or the trill. One bird that lived on the grounds of the Allegany school for three summers was outstanding in its extremely fine first notes, musical and bell-like.

"In 36 years of records in southern Connecticut, the first spring song of the Towhee averages April 19, the earliest being Apr. 2, 1938, and the latest May 2, 1924. The occasional birds that winter here may start singing in March. I have three dates of March singing, the earliest being Mar. 16, 1944, but I have not used them in working out the average first date for spring arrivals.

"Song ceases in August. In Allegany Park the last song heard averages August 5, the latest Aug. 13, 1937. In Connecticut the last song averages August 12, the latest Aug. 19, 1949. Revival of song in fall is rare; I have three October dates; Oct. 12, 1935, Oct. 8, 1939, and Oct. 3, 1946."

Val Nolan (MS.) reports his interesting observations on the song of a female Towhee: "At 0430 on Apr. 23, 1957, a cloudy morning with the temperature at 65°, I heard a loud and unfamiliar song, faintly reminiscent of the utterance of the male towhee. A female Towhee was perched 14 feet high in the top of a flowering dogwood in an old field; in 5 minutes she sang 15 times, then flew down and fell silent.

"Her song was made up of five and sometimes six notes, a long 'dee' followed by a series of rapid 'da' sounds on the same key. The quality was labored and unmusical, flat and somewhat squeaky.

"I heard her no more, although I passed the spot daily and in June spent two full days watching warbler nests nearby. A male towhee held territory there, but he was not in evidence within 15 minutes of the time when the female sang. A towhee nest with eggs was being incubated there in May.

"This is reminiscent in certain particulars of the singing of the female song sparrow mentioned by Mrs. Nice (1943), whose song 'is confined to the period in early spring before nest building begins * * *; it is always given from an elevation—a large weed, a bush or even a tree, in contrast to the female's usual behavior of staying close to the ground; it is short, simple, and entirely unmusical.' And, like the female song sparrow's performance, the female towhee's apparently elicited no response from other birds of the same species."

Field marks.—The rufous-sided towhee is about the size of the catbird but much more robust. The male is black above and below from bill to breast, has chestnut sides, white belly, and conspicuous white patches on the tail. The tail is used vigorously, flicking, opening and closing almost constantly. The female has the black replaced by brown. Young birds of both sexes are markedly streaked on the breast and the flank colors are poorly developed. E. H. Forbush (1929) points out that a bird scratching noisily in dense brush is usually a towhee or a brown thrasher.

Enemies.—Records of the towhee as a host for both internal and external parasites include the following: H. J. Van Cleave (1942), an acanthocephalan, *Plagiorhynchus formosus* Van Cleave; O. W. Olsen (1939), a spiruroid nematode, *Dispharynx pipilonis* Olsen; H. E. Ewing (1929), the North American chigger, *Trombicula irritans*; C. M. Herman (1938), *Haemaphysalis leporis-palustris*. The species has been recorded as a food item of the Cooper's hawk (F. N. and Frances Hammerstrom, 1951).

Herbert Friedmann (1929) states that the towhee is a very common victim of the cowbird, and continues:

At Ithaca, this species is uncommon and so extremely local that I have not had any experience with it as a molothrine host. This bird is called one of the commonest victims in New York by Eaton; in Connecticut by Sage; in Ohio by Jones; in Indiana by Evermann; in Iowa by Anderson, etc. The Towhee is one of the larger of the common victims of the Cowbird, and with none of its dupes is the latter more uniformly successful. Larger numbers of parasitic eggs have been reported from single nests of this species than from any other bird, and there is not one case on record of a Towhee covering up, or in any way trying to get rid of the strange eggs. The highest record is a nest containing eight eggs of the Cowbird together with five of the Towhee, a set taken in northern Iowa, and now in the collection of Mr. R. M. Barnes. Sanborn and Geolitz (Wilson Bull. XXVII no. 4, Dec. 1915, p. 444), record a nest of this species, May 14, 1914, Lake County, Illinois, with one egg of its own and eight of the Cowbird. A similar set, one and eight of the parasite, is recorded in the Oologist XXXI, no. 6, June 15, 1914, p. 119. There are also instances of five, four and three eggs of the Cowbird in single nests.

About a hundred and eighty definite records have come to my notice, ranging from New York, Connecticut, and Pennsylvania, south to West Virginia, and west to Ohio, Indiana, Illinois, Michigan, and Iowa.

Friedmann (1938) also adds the Nevada cowbird to the list of parasites of the species.

F. W. Davis writes me: "Cowbirds were common on all our study areas before, during, and after the towhee nesting period, but their incidence of parasitism seems comparatively low. Of 81 towhee nests found during the course of the study, only 4, or slightly less than 5 per cent, were victimized, each to the extent of 1 egg per nest. Our data are not adequate to show any effect of cowbird parasitism on the towhee's nesting success."

Banding records.—Longevity records based on bandings indicate that 4–6 years is not an uncommonly long life span for this species. M. T. Cooke (1950) notes an individual that was banded Mar. 21, 1937, and retrapped Dec. 16, 1944, and Mar. 3, 1946. This bird was at least 10 years old when released the last time. An outstanding record of movement is that of Marie V. Beals (1939) of a female banded Oct. 5, 1937, at Elmhurst, N. Y., and killed Apr. 29, 1938, at Crystal River, Fla.

DISTRIBUTION

Red-eyed Towhee (*P. e. erythrophthalmus*)

Range.—Southern Manitoba, Great Lakes area, and northern New England south to southern Texas and the Gulf states.

Breeding range.—The red-eyed towhee breeds from southern Manitoba (Treesbank, Winnipeg), northern Minnesota (Duluth), northern Wisconsin, northern Michigan (Isle Royale, McMillan), southern Ontario (Sault Ste. Marie, North Bay, Ottawa), northern New York, northern Vermont (Burlington, St. Johnsbury), central New Hampshire (Ossipee), and southwestern Maine (Norway, Christmas Cove) south to central northern and northeastern Oklahoma (Nash, Tulsa), northern Arkansas (Winslow, Ravenden), southern Tennessee (Raleigh), northeastern Georgia (Rabun County), northwestern South Carolina (Anderson and Cherokee counties), central North Carolina (Sampson County), and Virginia (except Princess Anne County).

Winter range.—Winters from Nebraska (Lincoln), Iowa (Sioux City, Polk County), Wisconsin (Portage County), southern Michigan (Washtenaw County), southern Ontario (Essex County), Pennsylvania (Beaver, Harrisburg), southeastern New York (New York City), and Massachusetts (Pleasant Valley, Belmont) south to western Oklahoma (Woodward County), central southern and southeastern Texas (San Antonio, Brownsville, Galveston), the Gulf Coast, and south central Florida (Basinger).

Casual records.—Casual north to northern Ontario (Fort Severn, James Bay), Quebec (Buckingham, Quebec City), New Brunswick (Irishtown, Fredericton), and Nova Scotia (Northport) and west to Colorado (Boulder).

Migration.—The data apply to the species as a whole. Early dates of spring arrival are: West Virginia—Bluefield, March 1. District of Columbia—March 30. Maryland—Baltimore County, March 8; Laurel, March 14 (median, March 25). Pennsylvania—Cambridge Springs, March 4. New Jersey—Cape May, March 8. New York—Prospect Park, March 23; Cayuga and Oneida Lake basins, March 30 (median of 21 years, April 16). Connecticut—Fairfield, April 2. Rhode Island—Charlestown, April 7. Massachusetts—Belmont, April 13. Vermont—Burlington, April 20. New Hampshire—New Hampton, April 17 (median of 21 years, May 2). Maine—Auburn, May 3. Quebec—Mt. Royal, April 21. New Brunswick—Irishtown, May 8. Missouri—St. Louis, March 1. Illinois—Chicago, March 12 (average of 16 years, March 29). Indiana—Wayne County, March 6. Ohio—Buckeye Lake, February 21 (median, March 8); Oberlin, March 6 (median of 19 years, March 17). Michigan—Battle Creek, March 13 (average of 44 years, April 2). Ontario—Ottawa, April 29. Iowa—Sioux City, April 11. Minnesota—Houston County, April 10 (average of 15 years for southern Minnesota, April 16). Kansas—northeastern Kansas, April 2. Nebraska—Falls City, March 14; Omaha, March 27; Red Cloud, April 5 (average of 21 years, April 24). South Dakota—Yankton, March 28. North Dakota—Cass County, May 4. Manitoba—Margaret, April 22; Treesbank, April 30 (average of 21 years, May 14). Saskatchewan—McLean, April 15. Idaho—Moscow, March 7. Montana—Libby, March 12 (median of 9 years, March 24). Oregon—Malheur National Wildlife Refuge, March 16.

Late dates of spring departure are: Florida—Leon County, April 29. Georgia—Athens, April 10. Maryland—Laurel, May 13.

Louisiana—Baton Rouge, April 17. Mississippi—Gulfport, May 15. Arkansas—Hot Springs, April 18. Ohio—Buckeye Lake, median May 12.

Early dates of fall arrival are: Kansas—northeastern Kansas, September 10. Texas—Sinton, November 3. Mississippi—Saucier, October 28. Arkansas—Delight, October 8. Louisiana—Reef Light, October 23. Nova Scotia—Digby County, September 27. Maryland—Ocean City, September 20. Cecil County and Tilghman Island, September 23. South Carolina—Charleston, September 28. Georgia—Hinesville, October 10. Florida—Leon County, October 8.

Late dates of fall departure are: Saskatchewan—Muscow, September 30. Manitoba—Treesbank, October 6 (average of 12 years, September 18). North Dakota—Cass County, September 14. Nebraska—Scottsbluff, October 23. Minnesota—Minneapolis, November 15 (average of 10 years for southern Minnesota, October 14). Iowa—Sioux City, October 18. Ohio—Columbus, November 28 (median for central Ohio, October 29). Indiana—Wayne County, November 8. Illinois—Chicago, November 6 (average of 16 years, October 24). Nova Scotia—Northport, October 27. New Brunswick—Salisbury, October 24. Quebec—St. Helen's Island, November 4. Maine—Gardiner, November 21. New Hampshire—New Hampton, October 23 (median of 21 years, October 2). Vermont—Putney, October 20. Massachusetts—Belmont, November 12. Connecticut—Portland, November 11. New York—Cayuga and Oneida Lake basins, December 5 (median of 16 years, November 3). New Jersey—Island Beach, October 31. Pennsylvania—Beaver, November 16. Maryland—Baltimore County, November 24; Laurel, November 5 (median, October 30). District of Columbia—November 12. Virginia—Naruna, November 22.

Egg dates.—Connecticut: 52 records, May 17 to June 25; 26 records, May 20 to June 7.

Illinois: 38 records, May 1 to August 11; 20 records, May 14 to June 3.

Maryland: 75 records, April 22 to August 28; 38 records, May 22 to June 14.

Massachusetts: 65 records, May 13 to July 9; 35 records, May 21 to June 10.

Michigan: 27 records, April 28 to July 22; 15 records, May 16 to May 31.

New York: May 8 to June 25 (number of records not stated).

Rhode Island: 21 records, May 15 to June 26; 14 records, May 27 to June 9.

Tennessee: 2 records, May 8 and May 26.

Riley's Towhee (*P. e. rileyi*)

Range.—Low country of South Atlantic states from southeastern Virginia to northern Florida.

Breeding range.—Riley's towhee breeds, and is largely resident, from southeastern Alabama (Houston County), central Georgia (Crisp, Jones, and McDuffie counties), coastal South Carolina (Dorchester and Horry counties), coastal North Carolina (Carteret County), and extreme southeastern Virginia (Pungo, apparently not typical) south to central northern Florida (Walton, Wakulla, and Madison counties) and southeastern Georgia (Camden County).

Winter range.—Winters from near the northern limit of the breeding range south to western Florida (Escambia County) and mid-peninsular Florida (Charlotte and Brevard counties).

Egg dates.—Georgia: 52 records, April 19 to July 7; 26 records, May 19 to June 19.

South Carolina: 18 records, April 5 to July 16; 10 records, May 3 to May 24.

White-eyed Towhee (*P. e. alleni*)

Range.—The white-eyed towhee is resident in Florida from Franklin, Columbia, and Duval counties south to southern Dade County.

Casual record.—Casual in Florida Keys (Key West).

Egg dates.—Florida: 8 records, April 15 to June 20.

Alabama Towhee (*P. e. canaster*)

Range.—Tennessee and western North Carolina to Louisiana and northwestern Florida.

Breeding range.—The Alabama towhee breeds, and is largely resident, from northeastern Louisiana (West Carroll Parish), northwestern Mississippi (Rosedale, intermediate toward *P. e. erythrophthalmus*), extreme southwestern Tennessee (Germantown, Wayne County), northern Alabama (Cobert, Limestone, and Calhoun counties), northern Georgia (Chattooga and Jackson counties), central South Carolina (northeast to York and Sumter counties), and western North Carolina (Murphy, Rocky Bald) south to central southern Louisiana (Iberia Parish), east along the Gulf coast to northwestern Florida (Okaloosa County), and to central eastern Alabama (Russell County) and north central Georgia (Putnam and Taliaferro counties).

Winter range.—Winters in breeding range, and south to north central northern Florida (Wakulla and Leon counties), southeastern Georgia (Toombs County), and coastal South Carolina (north to Georgetown County).

Egg dates.—Alabama: 85 records, April 6 to July 24.

Georgia: 2 records, May 19 and June 11.

PIPILO ERYTHROPHTHALMUS ARCTICUS (Swainson)

Arctic Towhee

Contributed by OLIVER L. AUSTIN, JR.

HABITS

This and the following 11 subspecies, plus some 8 more races resident extralimitally in Mexico and Guatemala, form a complex commonly called the spotted-backed towhees. All show varying amounts of white streaks or spots on the scapulars and wing coverts, which occur very rarely in the four eastern races treated in the preceding account. In addition, females of these western races have the black of the male replaced by dark gray instead of the reddish brown of eastern females. Until recently they were regarded as specifically distinct from the eastern forms and grouped together in the species *Pipilo maculatus*. In suggesting the conspecificity of the *maculatus* and *erythrophthalmus* groups, Charles G. Sibley (1950) notes that "many specimens of otherwise typical *P. e. erythrophthalmus* have varying amounts of white spotting on the same feathers which are normally spotted in the races inhabiting Mexico and the western United States" and adds:

1. In all plumage characters other than the dorsal spotting, the two are identical except for normal geographic variation.

2. Eggs and nests are no more different than is to be expected between subspecies.

3. Ecological requirements vary more within the spotted races than between the spotted and the eastern ones.

In a later paper, Sibley (1959) suggests:

The geographical distribution of the dorsal color pattern suggests that it has adaptive significance in some way correlated with climate. The races which are spotted dorsally (*maculatus* group) tend to live in areas which are more arid than those occupied by the unspotted *erythropthalmus* group. The vegetation occupied by the spotted races is usually a "chaparral" formation of woody shrubs without an arboreal cover. The unspotted races tend to occupy the understory shrubbery of eastern deciduous woodlands, a formation of more humid climates. Common observation indicates that the amount of sunlight reaching the ground and producing a sun-dappled pattern will be greater in a chaparral habitat than in a woodland habitat where the canopy will intercept more of the light. Hence we suggest that the dorsal spotting is a cryptic pattern induced by selection through predation and correlated indirectly with climate through the effects described.

In appearance *arcticus* is closest to *P. e. montanus*, from which it differs chiefly in having heavier white dorsal spotting and a more olivaceous back. In his original description of the form Swainson (1831) states he observed it "only on the plains of the Saskatchewan," where it frequented shady and moist clumps of wood, being generally seen on the ground. He says "It feeds on grubs, and is a solitary and retired, but not a distrustful bird." P. A. Taverner (1926) remarks:

"Like the Eastern Towhee, the Spotted is a bird of the brush and almost identical with it in general habits. To those familiar with the former, the latter presents nothing strikingly new. The notes are similar enough to be recognized as a Towhee's, but with a sufficiently different tone and accent to attract attention. On the whole, the Spotted Towhee's voice is hoarser, and its song less clearly musical than that of its eastern relative."

E. S. Cameron (1908) states that in Custer and Dawson Counties, Mont., the average date of the towhee's arrival is the second week in May, and its departure for winter at the end of September. He mentions sage brush as the common nesting site; on June 20, 1898, he found a nest containing five eggs of the towhee and two of a cowbird. A. A. Saunders (1921) adds that in Montana this race breeds in June in the Transition Zone in thickets of willow, wild rose, and other shrubs. J. C. Merrill (1881) found it abundant in Montana wherever a stream with bordering underbrush afforded the needed shelter. He writes: "There is a great diversity in the time of laying, or rather in the contents of nests found on about the same dates from the middle of May until late in July, which I attribute more to the great number of nests that must be destroyed by snakes, birds, and small mammals, and to the attempts of the parents to raise another brood, than to any other cause." He found nests on the ground usually under a bush, often a cherry bush. He describes them as strongly built, with an internal diameter of about 2¼ inches; the rim is flush with the ground, the birds scratching a hollow large enough to contain it; externally it is made of dead leaves and broad strips of bark, then a wall of finer strips of bark and blades of dry grass, and finally a lining usually of yellow straws.

Wilbur C. Knight (1902) mentions two nests at Newcastle in extreme northeastern Wyoming which were built on the sloping sides of a canon about six feet from the bottom beside small rocks. The nests were made of pine needles and lined with fine grass.

Eggs.—The Arctic Towhee lays from two to five eggs with three or four being the most common. They are short ovate or ovate, only slightly glossy, and practically indistinguishable from those of the eastern races. The ground is grayish or creamy white, sometimes very pale greenish white, and generously speckled all over with "russet," "Mars brown," "chestnut brown," or "Carob brown," with undermarkings of "light purplish gray" or "light neutral gray." The markings on most eggs tend to become concentrated toward the larger end, where they are often so thick as to obscure the ground. Although some eggs are blotched, in most instances the markings are numerous, well-defined, small spots or speckles.

The measurements of 50 eggs average 24.1 by 18.0 millimeters; the eggs showing the four extremes measure *27.0* by 17.9, 24.9 by *19.3*, *21.1* by 17.3, and 23.4 by *17.0* millimeters.

DISTRIBUTION

Range.—Great plains from southern portion of the prairie provinces south to central northern Mexico.

Breeding range.—The Arctic towhee breeds from central Alberta (Fort Saskatchewan), central Saskatchewan (Carlton), and central northern North Dakota (Turtle Mountains) south, east of the Rocky Mountains, to southeastern Wyoming (Laramie), northeastern Colorado (Wray), and central northern Nebraska (Long Pine).

Winter range.—Winters from Colorado (Boulder) and Kansas (St. John, Lawrence) south to southwestern New Mexico (Deming), central Chihuahua (Chihuahua), central Nuevo León (Monterrey), and southern Texas (Laredo, 15 miles west of Bastrop).

Casual records.—Casual west to Utah (Provo) and Arizona (Camp Verde) and east to Minnesota (Madison), Iowa (Woodbury and Plymouth counties), Illinois (North Evanston), New York (Bronx Park, Jones Beach), New Jersey (Metuchen), and North Carolina (Fayetteville). Sight records (presumably this race) southeast to Tennessee, Mississippi, Louisiana, and Arkansas.

Egg dates.—Alberta: 5 records, June 10 to June 22.

Montana: 2 records, June 14 and June 19.

PIPILO ERYTHROPHTHALMUS MONTANUS Swarth
Spurred Towhee
Contributed by TRAVIS G. HAWS and C. LYNN HAYWARD

HABITS

The spurred towhee is a common and characteristic bird in central Utah, particularly along the western bases of the Wasatch Mountains. Its most favored habitat seems to be large clumps of Gambel's oaks, *Quercus gambelii*, that grow in scattered patches on the hot, dry slopes. Here the birds may be seen the year round, although in winter they may drift downward into the valleys or more protected canyons where they can scratch for food among the ground debris.

Broadly speaking, Utah marks the center of the east–west breeding range of this race, which the 1957 Check-List defines as extending from central eastern Califronia, southern and central eastern Nevada, northern Utah, and northern Colorado south to southeastern California, southern Arizona, northeastern Sonora, northwestern Chihuahua, and central New Mexico. In southern Arizona and adjacent Mexico,

Joe T. Marshall, Jr. (1956) notes that while the towhee spans several vegetation zones, it is partial to bush growth, particularly chaparral and brush within woods or forests at altitudes above the deserts.

More recently Marshall writes us from Arizona that this race "is a common breeding bird in the mountains here wherever any brush or bushes grow under the trees or beside creeks, but only in the zones well above the desert. It breeds in patches of manzanita among the oaks, in manzanita or ceanothus under the pines or among the pinons, and in snowberry bushes and under aspens in the high forests. It is most abundant where true chaparral grows, as on the Pinal Mountains near Globe in central Arizona. In the Rincon and other southern mountains it is plentiful only where heavy brush growth has replaced the forests after fires or logging operations."

In the common with other *Pipilos*, the spurred towhees are inseparable from dense cover throughout their range. They are rarely seen in the open except as they may be flushed from one bush and fly for the closest thicket, usually close to the ground. In spring and summer the casual observer will most likely see the male as he sings from the top of a favored clump of oakbrush or similar shrub. When too closely approached, the male invariably darts downward into the thickest cover available. The female is less often seen, for she usually stays on or near the ground where she rustles among the dried fallen leaves in the dense underbrush, or goes quietly about the tasks of nest-building, incubating, and brooding. Rarely is either sex seen in long, sustained flight.

Spring.—About the first of April the winter flocks of towhees break up and the birds pair and establish their nesting territories. By mid-April the males sing vigorously. At this time the leaves have not yet appeared on the oakbrush or other deciduous shrubs, and the males are often conspicuous as they sing from vantage points on the tops of shrubs where they can overlook their domains. By the first of May when most of the nesting activity is well under way, leaves have usually appeared on the shrubs and the birds have ample protective cover.

Courtship.—J. T. Marshall, Jr. (1957) comments that the territories the towhees battle over in spring seem rather small. He has sent us in a letter the following excerpts from his field notes describing a territorial conflict he witnessed in an abandoned orchard within the pine forest on El Tigre Mountain in Sonora on Apr. 7, 1953: "Two males battling over a female. All three birds squalling loudly. Real fight in clump of locust, banging wings, flying at each other, tumbling down, calling. Then out to middle of flat. Ticking call and mew call both used. Female joins them and both males begin to sing. Intruder male moves off to north and owner follows him, both still singing from high up in the trees. Female squalling from middle of orchard. Intruder male sings farther off to north for quite a while. Original male returns and seen later scratching in oak leaves around house. No more singing."

Nesting.—In Utah nesting begins in April. The female builds her nest in such great secrecy that we have never been able to witness the entire process. We have seen females carrying nesting material, and observed one just starting to build a nest under a small sagebrush Apr. 21, 1938. All the nests we have found were on the ground under low bushes, usually sagebrush, and not in the dense, taller thickets of scrub oak from which the males do most of their singing. The nest is placed in a depression with the rim level with the ground surface. It has an outer coarse shell of dried oak leaves and bark and is lined with finer grasses. The cup ranges in diameter from 7 to 9 centimeters and in depth from 5 to 6 centimeters.

A summary of nesting dates for the vicinity of Provo, Utah, is as follows: May 5, nest and four fresh eggs found under a sagebrush; May 6, nest and four fresh eggs under a sagebrush; May 29, nest with four eggs well advanced in incubation under a sagebrush, these hatched June 2. For this same general area R. G. Bee and J. Hutchings (1942) give nesting dates of May 20, May 25, June 1, June 10, and June 26.

Eggs usually number four, but we have seen as many as five and as few as three apparently forming a full clutch. Their color, using Ridgway's Color Standards, is near pale olive gray but lighter, and finely speckled or spotted with army brown and sometimes blotched with light mouse gray. Most of the eggs are heavily pigmented at the large end.

The measurements of 40 eggs average 23.6 by 17.8 millimeters; the eggs showing the four extremes measure *25.9* by *18.5*, *20.8* by 18.3, and 23.9 by *16.8* millimeters.

Incubation is apparently carried out entirely by the female. She sits very closely during that period and may be approached within a few feet or even a few inches before she will flush. She leaves the nest by slinking rapidly over the ground to the nearest cover, and her movements are so swift she may easily be mistaken for a small mammal. She returns to the nest the same way, never by direct flight to the site. Insofar as we have been able to observe, the male does not approach the nest during the incubation period. We have not been able to determine the length of the incubation periods in *P. e. montanus* accurately, but our meagre information suggests that it agrees with that of the eastern subspecies, *P. e. erythrophthalmus*, recorded by F. L. Burns (1915) as 12 to 13 days.

Young.—On June 2, 1956, we were able to observe the hatching of the young and their development through the first week. At 8:00 a.m. on June 2, two eggs had hatched and the third was pipped. When the nest was revisited about six hours later, the young of the third egg was dead half out of the shell and the fourth egg was pipped. By 7:30 p.m. the fourth egg had hatched successfully. The empty shells are removed apparently soon after hatching, though we were unable to observe the process.

The young at hatching were naked except for a few down feathers along the spinal and capital pterylae. The day after hatching the feather papillae had darkened and enlarged noticeably. By the third day the sheaths were emerging, especially on the wings, and by the sixth day they had begun to open. In common with most passerines, the growth of the young towhees is very rapid. The weight of these nestlings increased about fourfold during the six days of observation.

Brooding is seemingly entirely by the female. At first her periods off the nest are brief, but they become more sustained by the fourth or fifth day. Feeding the young is apparently largely the responsibility of the male. On June 6 a male was observed to feed the young six times during a 160 minute period. Each time he approached the nest he gave the *pshew* call, softly and muffled by the food in his beak. The female left the nest immediately and he fed the young. After feeding them he usually returned to his perch to sing for awhile before setting out to scratch for food and feed the young again.

Voice.—In addition to the spring song of the male, which shows considerable variation from individual to individual, the spurred towhee has two distinct calls which vary but little and are used by both sexes. The first of these we designate as the *tseep* note. The female gives it as she approaches the nest containing young, and it is the first sound the young make. It is not very loud, and can be heard only at distances of a few feet. It is heard most commonly during the winter as the birds move about through the shrubbery and underbrush.

The *pshew* call is uttered commly by both sexes at all seasons. This is a scolding call, and usually indicates disturbance of some sort, but it may also be heard when the birds are feeding and apparently unexcited. At the close of a period of vigorous singing, the male will often fly down into his shrubby habitat and call *pshew* steadily for a considerable period. Frequently, and especially during the mating season, the *pshew* call is answered by several nearby males.

The spring or mating song, given by the male only, consists of one to five introductory notes followed by a trill usually higher than the introductory tones, sometimes at the same pitch, more rarely at a lower one. Singing starts in Utah late in February or early in March, and continues until after the young leave the nest, but is most intense in April and May. Song is most pronounced on clear, warm days. Males start to sing at the first indication of daylight and continue singing intermittently throughout the day until dark, with two apparent periods of intensity, one just before, and the other just after sunrise.

The longest sustained period of singing by a single bird, heard soon after sunup on Apr. 14, 1955, lasted 42 minutes. In this time the bird sang 260 consecutive songs involving 6 variations. The males continue to sing while the females are brooding, while the young are in the nest, and between their own periods of feeding the young.

J. T. Marshall, Jr., writes us from Arizona: "There are differences in the songs in different areas, and each male has several different songs. When a male uses a particular song, those near him often respond with the same song. The most frequent pattern consists of two sharp notes followed by a trill, such as *clip-clip-cheeee*. One bird in northern Sonora changed to a song exceedingly like a brown towhee's for several minutes, and then changed back to his own again. A common variation you hear in Sonora is the trill preceded by a whistle like the call of the evening grosbeak, which is very confusing."

Summer.—Our observations in Utah indicate that after the young leave the nest the family stays together near the nesting site all summer. Young of the year in full juvenal plumage are seen regularly in July. As the singing of the males diminishes after the nesting season, the birds become relatively inconspicuous as they forage quietly in the dense cover of their preferred habitat.

In the southern part of its range this towhee is apparently double-brooded. J. T. Marshall, Jr., writes us from Arizona that "in mid-July in the Pinal Mountains independent juveniles were everywhere in the brush within the aspens and firs. The males were singing all day, and were often seen chasing the juveniles as if to get them out of their territories." He sends us the following notes from northern Mexico: "Northern Sonora mountains, July 8: female carrying nesting material and another feeding young just out of the nest; July 16: juveniles fully grown; July 28: a pair hovering in alarm around juveniles just out. Both adults and juveniles had the same call note, a piercing *chip* so ventriloquial you could not locate the birds by the sound. Chihuahua, August 22: independent juveniles in complete juvenal plumage; August 25: juvenile male half molted into the rich adult plumage."

Food.—Herbert H. Frost (1947) studied the food habits of the spurred towhees along the Wasatch foothills east of Provo, Utah. He found that their principal food in winter was vegetable, with the fruits of the hackberry (*Celtis*) most commonly identified. In summer, animal matter increases in the diet markedly. Remains of coleoptera and orthoptera were found in many stomachs. It must be recognized, however, that examination of stomach contents alone may not give a true picture of the bird's food habits, as the hard fruits of the hackberry add the chitinous exoskeletons of the insects are more likely to remain identifiable than any softer material ingested.

The towhee obtains most of its food by scratching in the leaves and other ground litter beneath the shrubbery in which the birds live. A. M. Woodbury (1933) describes its method of feeding as follows:

The Spurred Towhee (*Pipilo maculatus montanus*) is a perching bird that has entered the field of scratching to earn a living. In Zion Canyon in Utah it is an inhabitant of the dense thickets of oak, sarvis-berry, squawbush and streamside deciduous trees. It is primarily a ground-dwelling bird, nesting among the thickets and hunting its food chiefly among the trash and leaves, but does not hesitate to ascend the trees and brush at other times.

* * * If the visible food supply on the surface is not sufficient for its needs, the towhee takes to turning over the leaves and scratching among the trash with its feet. This is a complex operation that it is fitted admirably to perform. * * *

Scratching birds like chickens stand on one leg and scratch with the other, but not so with the towhee. Being a small bird, it would have a difficult time turning over a leaf with one foot while standing on it with the other. Such difficulties are solved by using both feet in scratching. In order to use both feet, the body must be balanced in the air during the scratching operation.

This is accomplished by jumping into the air and drawing the feet backward while the upward momentum lasts. Drawing the feet backward and raking trash or leaves at the same time tends to overbalance the body forward. The bird uses several methods to hold its balance, either singly or in combination. Nearly always, the scratching motion of the feet is accompanied by an upward and forward jerk of the tail. Sometimes the wings flutter forward, and always after the scratching stroke the feet are brought forward quickly to catch the body and keep it from falling. Sometimes a backward movement of the body is made in jumping and the feet rake the trash while the momentum lasts. This is accompanied by a downward movement of the tail. All of these movements are carried on automatically and seemingly with the greatest of ease.

Sometimes, when the jump is made, the feet are thrust forward and trash in front of the bird is caught and pulled backward. Other times material underneath is moved, while occasionally material just behind the feet will be kicked out of the way by vigorous backward strokes.

Sometimes the trash is kept flying by quick successive strokes, but if insects, spiders, or other interesting food items are exposed to the eye of the bird, it suddenly stops and picks up such items one by one. And thus it taps a food supply not available to its competitors in Zion Cañon. On one occasion, I saw a Woodhouse Jay make a dart at a towhee. The smaller bird merely flitted away a few feet and stopped. The jay did not pursue any farther. At another time a gray rock squirrel came nosing around very close to the towhee, evidently paying no attention to the bird. The bird, however, flitted quietly out of the way a few feet and went on scratching.

Winter.—In Utah the spurred towhees begin to gather into small flocks in September. However, the flocks are loosely organized, and many of the birds remain more or less solitary. Flocking seems to result from a tendency to gather in favored localities rather than true gregariousness, and the closeness of the flock depends largely on the size and density of the cover. By about September 21 the post-juvenal molt seems to have been completed, and from then on adults and juveniles cannot be distinguished readily from one another in the field.

Their winter distribution and activities here seem to be governed to a large degree by the amount and duration of snowfall. Usually the lower west- and south-facing slopes of the Wasatch Mountains are free of snow except for short intervals. However, when the ground is covered for longer periods in midwinter and food becomes difficult to find, the birds tend to drift downward to streamside thickets and other suitable cover along ditchbanks and elsewhere in the lower valleys. Ordinarily no marked wholesale exodus occurs from the summer habitats to the valleys, and some birds may be seen regularly in the foothill brushlands throughout the year.

From Arizona, J. T. Marshall, Jr., writes us: "We find a few towhees here in winter high in the mountains, and we also have it as an uncommon winter visitor in the lowlands around Tucson, where it is confined to mesquite woods. On a mountain near Hermosillo, Sonora, where we have never found the bird in summer, we have taken specimens in winter up in the oak zone. The most abundant winter population I have seen was in manzanita scattered among oaks at the east base of the Rincon Mountains, where I recorded about 25 in about ½ mile on January 21, 1951."

DISTRIBUTION

Range.—Eastern California, Utah, and Colorado south to northwestern Mexico.

Breeding range.—The spurred towhee breeds from central eastern California (Benton), southern and central eastern Nevada (Grapevine Mountians, Lehman Creek), northern Utah (Stansbury Island, Unita Mountains), and northwestern and central northern Colorado (Boulder) south to southeastern California (Providence Mountains), central western and central southern Arizona (Harquahala Mountains, Baboquivari Mountains), northeastern Sonora (San Jose and San Luis mountains), northwestern Chihuahau (Sierra Madre, south to lat. 29° N.), and central southern and northeastern New Mexico (Mesilla Park, Sierra Grande).

Winter range.—Winters from southern Utah (Beaverdam Mountains), central Colorado (Golden), and western Texas (Palo Duro Canyon) south to northern Sonora (Sierra Carrizal, Nacozari) central Chihuahua (Chihuahua), and central Texas (Del Rio, Kendall County); casually farther southeast in Texas (Victoria, Eagle Lake).

Casual records.—Casual in Nebraska (North Platte) and Kansas (Morton County).

Egg dates.—California: 7 records, April 24 to June 7.

PIPILO ERYTHROPHTHALMUS GAIGEI Van Tyne and Sutter

Texas Towhee

Contributed by KEITH L. DIXON

HABITS

The rufous-sided towhee of western Texas was separated under the name *Pipilo maculatus gaigei* by Van Tyne and Sutton in 1937 during their avifaunal studies in Brewster County, Tex. The type locality of this subspecies, which they named in honor of Frederick M. Gaige, is "southeast of Boot Spring, 6800 feet" in the Chisos Mountains.

In voice and behavior, the rufous-sided towhees occupying the mountain ranges of east-central and southeastern New Mexico, western Texas, and northern Coahuila appear to differ in no important respects from other populations of the species. For the most part, these birds have been reported from forested areas above 6,000 feet, but they are limited either to wooded areas with a brushy understory or to rather dense shrub communities. A feature common to the places I have seen them is the presence of clumps of shrubby canopy from one to several feet above the ground and leaf litter on the surface of the ground. In the Chisos Mountains of Texas, such cover is provided by a variety of shrubs, including *Rhus trilobata*, *Salvia regla*, and *Cercocarpus eximius*, as well as the oaks, *Quercus grisea* and *Q. emoryi*. On a slope west of the Laguna in the Chisos Mountains in late July 1955, this towhee was found with black-chinned sparrows (*Spizella atrogularis*) and Bewick's wrens (*Thryomanes bewickii*) in a shrub growth which included squaw bush (*Rhus trilobata*), silk tassel bush (*Garrya lindheimeri*), scrub oak (*Quercus intricata*), and *Viguiera stenoloba*.

The distribution range of this form, according to Van Tyne and Sutton (1937), extends northward to the vicinity of Cabra Springs in east-central New Mexico. In that area, some 30 miles north of Santa Rosa, Vernon and Florence M. Bailey found this towhee in the oak brush understory of yellow pine timber at 7,400 feet elevation in June 1903 (F. M. Bailey, 1910). The form is known from the Capitan and Guadalupe mountains of New Mexico and also from the latter range in Texas, from the Davis (A. P. Smith, 1917) and Chisos mountains of Texas, and the Sierra del Carmen of Coahiula (A. H. Miller, 1955a). Van Tyne and Sutton's report (1937) of specimens of *gaigei* taken in late May on Mount Ord and the Glass

Mountains, which lie in northern Brewster County between the Chisos and Davis mountains, suggests its breeding there also. However the rufous-sided towhee is absent from the low mountain ranges between the Davis and Guadalupe mountains, as the woodland of juniper and pinyon there appears too open for it (William B. Davis, pers. comm.).

Spring.—A. H. Miller (1955a) reported only sporadic singing of males in the higher parts of the Sierra del Carmen in the period Apr. 4–Apr. 18, 1953, and he noted a preponderance of males present at this time. These males, although not in full breeding condition, appeared to be spaced on territories.

Nesting.—Although W. W. Cooke (F. M. Bailey, 1928) stated that this species "nests commonly in June" in New Mexico, the breeding season appears to be a long one. Van Tyne and Sutton (1937) reported that "specimens taken on April 27, 1935, in the Chisos Mountains were obviously breeding," and my observation of a male gathering food at 5,700 feet elevation on the north side of that range on May 28, 1957, indicates early nesting. Further, I found that singing was not conspicuous in Boot Canyon in the Chisos Mountains (6,500 to 7,000 feet) from July 11–26, 1955, suggesting that the peak of breeding had passed. However, in the Guadalupe Mountains of New Mexico, Vernon Bailey found a nest with eggs on August 12 (F. M. Bailey, 1928) and A. P. Smith (1917) took "young, barely able to fly" at 6,500 feet elevation in the Davis Mountains on Sept. 10, 1916.

Although Van Tyne and Sutton (1937) spoke of this towhee as being of "common" occurrence in the Chisos Mountains, I recorded it as "infrequent" in the upper Chisos as a whole in the latter half of July, due in part to its restricted habitat distribution. Miller (1955) likewise found rufous-sided towhees "sparsely distributed" in the neighboring Sierra del Carmen.

Winter.—The 1957 A.O.U. Check-List uses the expression "resident, in part at least" in referring to the montane distribution of *P. e. gaigei.* Some evidence for altitudinal migration of this form in the Guadalupe Mountains was provided by T. D. Burleigh and G. H. Lowery, Jr. (1940). In December and January they found *P. e. montanus* the only wintering towhee (two specimens), and neither of these was taken or recorded above 6,000 feet elevation, whereas *gaigei* ranged upward to 8,750 feet in June. W. B. Davis took a specimen in pinyon-juniper woodland at 4,400 feet elevation in the Delaware Mountains (south of the Guadalupes) on Mar. 8, 1942, and Van Tyne and Sutton (1937) reported a few individuals wintering in live oak groves at 5,000 feet elevation in the vicinity of Alpine. In the area surrounding the Chisos Mountains, however, there appears to be little habitat suitable for wintering rufous-sided towhee, and I know of no records of their occurrence in winter below 5,200 feet. Although dense brush may be found, in the desert lowlands, there usually is no accumulation of leaf litter.

DISTRIBUTION

Range.—The Texas towhee breeds, and is resident at least in part, in mountains of central eastern and southeastern New Mexico (Cabra Springs, Guadalupe Mountains), western Texas (Guadalupe, Davis, and Chisos Mountains), and northern Coahuila (Sierra del Carmen).

PIPILO ERYTHROPHTHALMUS CURTATUS Grinnell

Nevada Towhee

Contributed by WENDELL TABER

HABITS

Joseph Grinnell (1911c) described this race as being most nearly like *P. e. montanus*, from which it differs mainly in being shorter winged and darker colored. (For a lengthy discussion of these races, see Swarth, 1913.)

Grinnell and A. H. Miller (1944) describe its habitat as similar to that of the race *montanus*, in brushy cover including willow thickets, artemisia, and rabbit brush. In winter in the Colorado River Valley, it occurs in thickets of arrowweed and in atriplex bushes. J. M. Linsdale (1951) states that in eastern and southern Nevada this race is resident in the mountains and higher valleys, but that an appreciable movement takes place in winter to lower valleys and more southern parts of the state.

It is doubtful that the habits and behavior of this race vary greatly if at all from those of other races described in greater detail.

The measurements of 20 eggs average 24.0 by 17.9 millimeters; the eggs showing the four extremes measure *26.0* by 17.5, 23.9 by *18.9*, *22.9* by 17.5, and 24.9 by *17.3* millimeters.

DISTRIBUTION

Range.—Southern British Columbia and Idaho to northwestern Mexico.

Breeding range.—The Nevada towhee breeds from central southern British Columbia (Lillooet, Okanagan Landing, Robson) and northern Idaho (5 miles west of Cocolalla) south, east of the Cascades, to northeastern California (south to Mono Lake), western and central Nevada (Tybo), and southeastern Idaho (Craters of the Moon).

Winter range.—Winters in part in the breeding range and also south to southeastern California (Potholes), northwestern Sonora (Sonoyta), and southeastern Arizona (Huachuca and Chiricahua mountains).

Egg dates.—British Columbia: 30 records, Apr. 21 to July 8; 15 records, May 5 to June 2.

PIPILO ERYTHROPHTHALMUS OREGONUS Bell

Oregon Towhee

PLATE 31

Contributed by OLIVER L. AUSTIN, JR.

HABITS

The Oregon towhee is the darkest and least spotted of the western complex of spotted-backed *Pipilos*. Ira N. Gabrielson and Stanley G. Jewett (1940) consider it "one of the most common permanent resident birds in western Oregon, where every rose thicket and evergreen blackberry patch has its pair of Oregon Towhees. They are present throughout the year so commonly that it is unusual to walk along the bottom lands at any season without seeing a handsome black and white and reddish fellow flirting his tail nervously as he glides to a landing around a clump of bushes or hops about in the thickets."

In Washington State, Stanley G. Jewett, Walter P. Taylor, William T. Shaw, and John W. Aldrich (1953) say it "spends most of its time in the shelter of the shrubbery of its humid environment. It is found in the brush of abandoned clearings, along roadsides, in burns, coastal gulches, and in swamps. Log heaps in timbered areas often shelter it; and on Mt. Rainier towhees presumed to be of this subspecies were observed in the azalea, mountain-ash, and huckleberry brush."

The same authors continue:

Brown found a nest and 4 eggs in Kings County, June 29, 1909, and a nest and 3 eggs in Seattle on July 13, 1908. Dates for full sets of fresh eggs are as follows: early, May 4, mean, May 17, late, June 20 * * * . Bowels reports a pair feeding young in the nest at Gravelly Lake, Pierce County, August 21, 1933 * * * .

Burleigh * * * says nests found by him were invariably sunk flush with the ground, at times at the base of an old stub or small sapling, and were quite well concealed by Oregon grape and clusters of ferns. Of 9 nests examined 7 held 3 eggs, two 4 eggs. Rathbun flushed a female from a nest on the ground in an open spot among scattered tall firs, and alongside a path running through a dense growth of salal. This nest was unusual in that it contained 5 eggs. On another occasion Rathbun found a nest containing 2 eggs only, both heavily incubated. Immature birds are commonly observed into September.

A little patience enables the observer to watch the towhee as it forages among the leaves in the shelter of the brush. It hops industriously over the ground, its whole attention, apparently, given to the work in hand. * * * On catching sight of the observer the bird may retreat to the inner fastnesses, its spotted tail becoming conspicuous as it flies. It sometimes becomes quite familiar, and is a characteristic bird visitor to food tables provided in fall and winter. The trill of the male Oregon spotted towhee is much like that of the Nevada, though Dawson * * * says "the damps of ten thousand winters have reduced his song to a pitiful wheeze." The call note is a mewing *jo-ree*.

In the fall the species becomes scattered. Individuals are often found associated in flocks with other species such as song sparrows and juncos. Since the Oregon spotted towhee is observably scarcer in winter than at other seasons it seems a fair assumption that some of the birds migrate, but the fact that a large proportion of individuals stay very close to the same area throughout the year is attested by the record of 12 Seattle banded towhees which were trapped and recovered in both winter and breeding season at the same station. * * *

Gordon W. Gullion wrote Mr. Bent of his experiences with this race in the Willamette Valley of Oregon, where the birds inhabit "most of the brush piles and blackberry tangles throughout the valley. They always seem to occur in pairs, and very seldom is a single bird encountered holding a territory. In fact it rather seems that they pair for life. In the fall of 1946 I banded a pair of towhees at my home. As they were the only banded towhees in the vicinity, it was quite easy to keep tab on their activities. Whenever one was seen, the other would be found close by. They were seen almost daily from the time of banding until late December 1947. Then the female vanished. The male remained around about another two weeks, then he too disappeared. Within a few days another and unbanded pair came in and took possession of the territory. Now they are also banded, and they maintain the same sort of constant companionship the first pair exhibited."

Gabrielson and Jewett (1940) state that in Oregon "The eggs are usually laid in May. Our nesting dates extend from May 3 to June 25, although young of the year are always on the wing before the latter date."

The measurements of 17 eggs average 23.3 by 18.3 millimeters; the eggs showing the four extremes measure *25.5* by 19.5, 24.5 by *20.0*, *22.5* by 19.1, and 24.5 by *17.0* millimeters.

DISTRIBUTION

Range.—Pacific Coast from British Columbia to California.

Breeding range.—The Oregon towhee breeds, and is largely resident, from southwestern British Columbia (Comox, Chilliwack) south through western Washington to southwestern Oregon (Roseburg).

Winter range.—Winters south to northwestern California (Trinidad, Willow Creek); casually south to central (Colusa) and southern California (San Clemente Island).

Egg dates.—California: 1 record, June 9.
Oregon: 4 records, May 10 to May 14.
Washington: 5 records, April 13 to July 26.

PIPILO ERYTHROPHTHALMUS FALCINELLUS Swarth

Sacramento Towhee

PLATE 32

Contributed by OLIVER L. AUSTIN, JR.

HABITS

Harry S. Swarth (1913) described this race as "Most nearly similar to *Pipilo maculatus megalonyx* Baird, from which it differs in weaker foot, with noticeably short, weak, hind claw, in somewhat greater extent of white markings, and olivaceous or grayish rump."

Joseph Grinnell and Alden H. Miller (1944) point out that within its range "there is some altitudinal movement up mountain slopes after nesting and descent from higher parts of breeding range in winter, but no migration is known that carries birds outside the limits of breeding range." They describe its habitat as "Chaparral, river bottom thickets, and brush patches in open forests. Among the widespread plant formations of such types available in the range of this race, the Spotted Towhees are to be found especially where there is a good accumulation of leaf litter and humus. For this reason partly dead or dying brush, ravine and river bottoms, and bases of cliffs or of steep slopes are favored situations. If the ground forage beat is thus supplied, sufficient screening plant cover is usually present and nest sites on the ground or in well supported vine tangles are also available. Some common plant associates are ceanothus bushes of several species, poison oak, willows, blackberry, cascara, and manzanitas."

William B. Davis (1933) gives May 1 as his earliest nesting date in Butte County, Calif. Near Fyffe in the central Sierra Nevadas on June 8, 1897, Chester Barlow (1901) "found a nest containing three unfeathered young and one egg on a hillside under a bush. By far the prettiest nest found was on June 11 of the same year. The situation was a small clearing in the forest grown up to cedar saplings about two feet high. Beneath one of these reposed the nest and its three eggs, the lining of light grasses setting them off to good advantage. As in the valley this towhee does not nest on the ground entirely, for Mr. Taylor found a nest on June 12, 1897 containing two eggs, placed six feet up in a bush beside a ditch. It was composed of pine and spruce bark and lined with light yellowish grass."

From the small portion of this subspecies' range that penetrates into south-central Oregon, Gabrielson and Jewett (1940) state "Patterson (MS.) furnished dates of numerous nests at Ashland between May 2 and June 14 * * *."

The measurements of 20 eggs average 24.2 by 17.9 millimeters; the eggs showing the four extremes measure *25.4* by 17.8, 23.9 by *18.8*, *23.1* by 17.8, and 23.5 by *17.1* millimeters.

DISTRIBUTION

Range.—The Sacramento towhee is resident from the interior of southwestern Oregon (Grants Pass, Medford) south through the northern interior coast ranges, the western and southeastern slopes of the Sierra Nevadas, and the Great Valley of California (Hoopa and Mount Shasta to Vacaville, and Kings and Tulare counties; Laws, Olancha).

Egg dates.—California: 4 records, May 1 to June 12.

PIPILO ERYTHROPHTHALMUS FALCIFER McGregor

San Francisco Towhee

Contributed by OLIVER L. AUSTIN, JR.

HABITS

Harry S. Swarth (1913) characterizes this subspecies as "Coloration dark; white markings more restricted than in *megalonyx* but much more extensive than in *oregonus*. Hind claw smaller and weaker than in *megalonyx*." Within its narrow range along the northwest California coast, Grinnell and Miller (1944) consider it a "Permanent resident. Common generally, although sparse in extreme northwestern part of range." They describe its habitat as:

"Chaparral and forest undergrowth as in other races of Spotted Towhees * * *. Apparently avoids the dense brushlands of the fog-swept coastal slopes of Humboldt and Del Norte counties, although *P. m. oregonus* finds suitable wintering grounds there in some of the less compact tracts of plant growth. Elsewhere *falcifer* occupies heavy chaparral on shaded canyon slopes, as also streamside tangles, low second growths of forest trees and the understory of oak and madrone woodlands. Blackberry vines, willow thickets, baccharis and poison oak brush, and ceanothus and manzanita bushes commonly constitute the essential plant cover."

Milton S. Ray (1906) notes this race "nests in low bushes, scrub oaks or willows, or among overhanging blackberry vines. I have never found a nest placed on the ground, except once." Emerson A. Stoner

PLATE 32

shland, Oreg., May 25, 1924   J. E. Patterson
NEST OF SACRAMENTO TOWHEE

epulveda Canyon, Calif., May 25, 1950   R. Quigley, Jr.
NEST OF SAN DIEGO TOWHEE

(1931) reports a case of its multiple nesting and reuse of an old nest in Palo Alto, Calif., as follows:

"The first nest was constructed early in May among some geranium bushes growing against a private garage. After the young had been successfully reared and had left the first nest, a second nest was built closer to the house in a hedge of cherry oak some thirty feet from the first one. The young left this second nest about July 10. Within a week after the departure of the young from the second nest, the parents returned to the first nest and successfully raised a third brood therein, the young of the third brood leaving the nest on August 9."

The measurements of 25 eggs average 23.6 by 17.8 millimeters; the eggs showing the four extremes measure *25.9* by 18.3, 25.4 by *18.5*, *22.7* by 18.1, and 23.6 by *16.2* millimeters.

Alden H. Miller (1942) presents the following observations on the bathing habits of this subspecies:

In the long dry summers of coastal central California, chaparral-dwelling species may find water locally scarce except as it collects on foliage from the nightly fogs that blow in from the ocean. Use of this supply for drinking is probably widespread, but its availability for bathing had not been appreciated by me.

The morning of July 29, 1942, was cool and foggy in Berkeley, and on the hillside at my home * * * the trees and bushes were dripping with water. An adult Spotted Towhee * * * came to the feeding tray at 7:15 and ate some of the cracked grain offered there. It was a dejected looking individual, with bare patches of skin showing around the head, for it was in the middle of its annual molt; indeed it left a spotted tail feather behind on the tray. It flew but a short distance, stopping on top of a tangle of baccharis bushes and poison oak. At once it began scuttling about under and over the wet foliage, rubbing against it and shaking down drops from overhead. The wings were half spread and were fluttered in the fashion customary in bathing; also the bird bent the legs, crouching down rather than standing normally erect. It moved about within a radius of about two feet, always in the crowns of the bushes, three to four feet above the ground. After approximately a minute of this the towhee moved on, but it was detected at a distance, perched, fluttering its wings and preening. The bath was not by my standards especially effective, as the bird was only slightly wet, but it had apparently satisfied an instinct at least. All this time there had been a pan of water on the feeding tray, but it was small and fairly deep and evidently was not so stimulating of the bathing reaction as the natural supply of water.

DISTRIBUTION

Range.—The San Francisco towhee is resident along the coasts of northwestern and central western California (Smith River south through Santa Cruz and San Benito counties).

Egg dates.—California: 2 records, May 7 and May 13.

PIPILO ERYTHROPHTHALMUS MEGALONYX (Baird)

San Diego Towhee

PLATES 32 AND 33

Contributed by JAMES E. CROUCH

HABITS

The rufous-sided towhee of southwestern California was described by Baird in 1858 under the name *Pipilo megalonyx*. The type locality is Fort Tejon, Kern County, Calif. The distinguishing characteristics of *P. e. megalonyx*, according to Swarth (1913), are "Coloration very dark, and white markings restricted. Adult male (and sometimes the immature male as well) with the entire back uniformly deep black (except for the usual white markings), the rump being deep black instead of more or less grayish or olivaceous. Hind claw longer than in any other California race of *Pipilo maculatus.*"

The behavior of *P. e. megalonyx* differs in no important way from that of other populations of the rufous-sided towhee. The bird seldom forages in the open or on bare ground. It shows a strong preference for situations which give a good overhead cover, some lateral cover, and a ground surface well supplied with humus and litter. This provides protection and desirable foraging. These conditions are provided by the coast live oaks (*Quercus agrifolia*), said by Davis (1957) to be "optimal undertree foraging sites for Spotted Towhees." Other oaks (*Q. douglassi* and *Q. lobata*) are commonly used, as are willow (*Salix* sp.) and other streamside species of plants. Rufous-sided towhees are found in chaparral, but mostly where there are clumps of larger shrubs. The chamise (*Adenostoma fasciculatum*) and California sagebrush (*Artemisia californica*) provide good cover, but little litter. Where there are large isolated shrubs of Toyon (*Photinia arbutifolia*), blue elderberry (*Sambucus coerulea*), or lemonade berry (*Rhus integrifolia*), the towhees are likely to be found. Other plants forming good cover and forage areas are coffeeberry (*Rhamnus californica*), redberry (*Rhamnus crocea* var. *ilicifolia*), poison oak (*Rhus diversiloba*), California blackberry (*Rubus ursinus*), California wild rose (*Rosa californica*), and coast ceanothus (*Ceanothus ramulosus*).

In the forested mountain areas such as at Palomar and the Laguna Mountains of San Diego County the rufous-sided towhees are seen mostly in the clumps of brush at the forest edge or isolated brushy areas out in the meadows. Where the forests give way at the abrupt eastern sides of the mountains these towhees are commonly seen in the heavy brush of the upper slopes. Here they are found in the company of black-chinned sparrows (*Spizella atrogularis*).

This towhee is reported occasionally from high altitudes. Grinnell (1908), writing of the San Bernardino Mountains, states: "It was found on the south side of the ranges as high as 7,000 feet. A few were seen as far up the Santa Ana as the mouth of Fish Creek, 6,500 feet." Again Grinnell and Swarth (1913) writing about the birds and mammals of the San Jacinto area of Southern California report towhees at 8,000 feet on Toro Peak on July 1 and at 9,000 feet at Round Valley on July 10. They state that these birds, full-grown juvenals, were "probably far above normal breeding range."

Cardiff (1956) collected an adult male *megalonyx* below sea level on Oct. 8, 1949, from a growth of arrow-weeds and salt brush along the New River northwest of Westmoreland, Imperial County, Calif. This specimen was identified by Alden H. Miller. Gilman (1903) reports these towhees about a half mile from Palm Springs, Calif.

Eggs.—The measurements of 32 eggs average 23.4 by 17.9 millimeters; the eggs showing the four extremes measure *25.1* by *18.9*, *23.5* by 17.5 and 23.8 by *16.8* millimeters.

Food.—The rufous-sided towhee gets most of its food by scratching in the litter under shrubs and trees. Sometimes it feeds up in trees or shrubs. Seeds, seed capsules, and bracts of miner's lettuce (*Montia perfoliata*) are eaten by these birds between April and June, according to Davis (1957). Also, he says that they eat various fruits such as elderberries between July and September, coffeeberries between August 22 and December 24, and that acorns constitute an important part of their diet in the winter. I have seen them occasionally "hawking" for insects and they quite often pick up insects as they forage for seeds.

Voice.—In his lengthy study of the song and breeding of the rufous-sided towhee made at the Hastings Reservation in northern Monterey County, Calif., John Davis (1958) states: "Singing usually starts between mid-January and the first week of February, and it comes to an end in early August. In September and October, there is a slight but regular appearance of singing, involving only a few males.

"Singing is widespread by mid-March, but in early April there is a noticeable decrease in the amount of song. By the last week in April, at the time that nesting gets under way, singing is again at a high level. Nesting males sing a higher percentage of the time during incubation than after the young have been hatched. Unmated males are the most persistent singers of all."

For description and analyses of the various types of song in this race, the manner of its delivery, and its correlation with season, time of day, and the reproductive cycle, the reader is referred to this soundly detailed report.

DISTRIBUTION

Range.—The San Diego towhee is resident in southwestern Califor-- nia (Monterey and west slope of Walkers Pass south to Santa Cruz Island, Little San Bernardino Mountains, and San Diego County) and northwestern Baja California (south to about lat 32° N.).

Casual record.—Casual on San Miguel Island, Calif., and in south-eastern California (Westmorland).

Egg dates.—California: 5 records, April 19 to May 22.

PIPILO ERYTHROPHTHALMUS CLEMENTAE Grinnell

San Clemente Towhee

Contributed by RICHARD FOURNESS JOHNSTON

HABITS

This subspecies was described by Grinnell (1897a). Ridgway (1901) states it is "Similar to *P. megalonyx* but bill and feet larger (at least relatively) and coloration grayer; adult male with the black of a duller or grayer cast, and the adult female with coloration much lighter * * *." Miller (1951b), however, states that he is not able to demonstrate the difference in bill length between *clementae* and *megalonyx*.

This bird is a permanent resident on Santa Rosa, Santa Catalina, and San Clemente Islands off the coast of southern California. It inhabits, according to Grinnell and Miller (1944), "Fairly tall chaparral, especially along watercourses. Wild cherry thickets are favored both because of associated ground conditions and the protection and fruit supply they afford. Towhees also have been noted in cactus patches and in scrub oak and toyon." It is remarkable that this race is found, among the northern channel islands, only on Santa Rosa Island, and not on Santa Cruz (Miller, 1951b); these islands are closer to one another than are either to Santa Catalina and San Clemente.

Eggs.—The four eggs in the Harvard Museum of Comparative Zoology measure 25.7 by 18.5, 25.3 by 17.9, 25.0 by 17.8, and 25.0 by 18.2 millimeters.

DISTRIBUTION

Range.—The San Clemente towhee is resident on Santa Rosa, Santa Catalina, and San Clemente islands off southwestern California.

Egg date.—California: 1 record, May 9.

PIPILO ERYTHROPHTHALMUS UMBRATICOLA Grinnell and Swarth
Cape Colnett Towhee
Contributed by RICHARD FOURNESS JOHNSTON

HABITS

This race of towhee is restricted to northern Baja California and is characterized in the original description (Grinnell and Swarth, 1926) as follows: "Differs from *P. m. megalonyx*, to which it is nearest both geographically and in appearance, in smaller bill and darker coloration. Color differences are most apparent in females, these being decidedly slaty dorsally in *umbraticola* as compared with the browner tinge seen in female *megalonyx*. * * * The bill and feet * * * are on the average decidedly blacker than in any other of the western subspecies of *Pipilo maculatus*." Morphologic intergradation between the two races is extensive near the northern boundary of the range outlined below for *umbraticola*.

Grinnell (1928b) says the distribution of this resident race extends "locally, north of latitude 30°, from San Ramón, at the mouth of the Santo Domingo River, north, centrally, to very near the United States boundary, and east in the San Pedro Mártir section from the seacoast at Colnett to mouth of El Cajón Cañon at east base of the San Pedro Mártirs; reaches an altitude of 7500 feet toward the tops of those mountains." The preferred habitat is found within chaparral associations. Deep, shaded ravines are especially favored. In ecology and general behavior *umbraticola* probably differs little from *megalonyx*.

DISTRIBUTION

Range.—The Cape Colnett towhee is resident in northwestern Baja California between latitudes 32° and 30° N. (Sierra Juarez and Sierra San Pedro Mártir west to the coast).

PIPILO ERYTHROPHTHALMUS CONSOBRINUS Ridgway
Guadalupe Towhee
Contributed by RICHARD FOURNESS JOHNSTON

HABITS

Ridgway (1901) remarks skins of this towhee to be "Similar to *P. m. oregonus* in restriction of the white markings on the wings, tail, scapulars, etc., but wing and tail much shorter, and hind claw much larger; adult male with the black much duller, dark sooty rather than black."

The bird, now extinct, formerly was resident on Guadalupe Island, off the coast of Baja California. It apparently inhabited the under-story of the cypress (*Cupressus*) grove, large individuals of which are still to be found on the high part of the island. Howell and Cade (1954) note with reference to this bird, "We found no trace, of course, of any of the endemics considered extinct. Indeed, the complete absence today of shrubs or understory of any kind in the forests of the island make it difficult to believe that the towhee, *Pipilo erythrophthalmus consobrinus* * * * once existed there, and this utter lack of suitable habitat should convince even the most hopeful skeptic that [this form is] totally extinct.

"* * * The goats continue to be the greatest threat to the biota of the island through their destruction of vegetation." The towhee was last seen alive in June, 1897 (Thoburn, 1899).

DISTRIBUTION

Range.—Extinct. It was formerly resident on Guadalupe Island off northwestern Baja California.

PIPILO ERYTHROPHTHALMUS MAGNIROSTRIS Brewster

Large-billed Towhee

Contributed by RICHARD FOURNESS JOHNSTON

HABITS

Ridgway (1901) says this large-billed, pale spotted towhee is "similar to *P. m. megalonyx* but wing and tail decidedly shorter, bill larger, hind claw averaging larger, white on outermost tail-feathers decidedly more extensive, and color of sides and flanks much paler (buff-tawny instead of cinnamon-rufous)."

P. e. magnirostris is one of the most highly geographically isolated forms of the species; this is to a certain extent evident in its gross morphological characteristics. The range is restricted in southern Baja California. Grinnell (1928b) states that the bird is a "Common resident of mountainous portions of the Cape district. Appertains to brushy tracts chiefly within the Upper Sonoran life-zone. A few come down to sea level in winter (C. C. Lamb, MS.). * * * Northern-most known station of occurrence, Triunfo * * * southernmost, Miraflores * * *."

DISTRIBUTION

Range.—The large-billed towhee is resident in the mountains of southern Baja California (Triunfo, Sierra de la Laguna).

Casual record.—Casual at lower levels at Miraflores.

A CATALOGUE OF SELECTED DOVER BOOKS
IN ALL FIELDS OF INTEREST

A CATALOGUE OF SELECTED DOVER BOOKS
IN ALL FIELDS OF INTEREST

AMERICA'S OLD MASTERS, James T. Flexner. Four men emerged unexpectedly from provincial 18th century America to leadership in European art: Benjamin West, J. S. Copley, C. R. Peale, Gilbert Stuart. Brilliant coverage of lives and contributions. Revised, 1967 edition. 69 plates. 365pp. of text.

21806-6 Paperbound $3.00

FIRST FLOWERS OF OUR WILDERNESS: AMERICAN PAINTING, THE COLONIAL PERIOD, James T. Flexner. Painters, and regional painting traditions from earliest Colonial times up to the emergence of Copley, West and Peale Sr., Foster, Gustavus Hesselius, Feke, John Smibert and many anonymous painters in the primitive manner. Engaging presentation, with 162 illustrations. xxii + 368pp.

22180-6 Paperbound $3.50

THE LIGHT OF DISTANT SKIES: AMERICAN PAINTING, 1760-1835, James T. Flexner. The great generation of early American painters goes to Europe to learn and to teach: West, Copley, Gilbert Stuart and others. Allston, Trumbull, Morse; also contemporary American painters—primitives, derivatives, academics—who remained in America. 102 illustrations. xiii + 306pp. 22179-2 Paperbound $3.50

A HISTORY OF THE RISE AND PROGRESS OF THE ARTS OF DESIGN IN THE UNITED STATES, William Dunlap. Much the richest mine of information on early American painters, sculptors, architects, engravers, miniaturists, etc. The only source of information for scores of artists, the major primary source for many others. Unabridged reprint of rare original 1834 edition, with new introduction by James T. Flexner, and 394 new illustrations. Edited by Rita Weiss. 6⅝ x 9⅝.

21695-0, 21696-9, 21697-7 Three volumes, Paperbound $13.50

EPOCHS OF CHINESE AND JAPANESE ART, Ernest F. Fenollosa. From primitive Chinese art to the 20th century, thorough history, explanation of every important art period and form, including Japanese woodcuts; main stress on China and Japan, but Tibet, Korea also included. Still unexcelled for its detailed, rich coverage of cultural background, aesthetic elements, diffusion studies, particularly of the historical period. 2nd, 1913 edition. 242 illustrations. lii + 439pp. of text.

20364-6, 20365-4 Two volumes, Paperbound $6.00

THE GENTLE ART OF MAKING ENEMIES, James A. M. Whistler. Greatest wit of his day deflates Oscar Wilde, Ruskin, Swinburne; strikes back at inane critics, exhibitions, art journalism; aesthetics of impressionist revolution in most striking form. Highly readable classic by great painter. Reproduction of edition designed by Whistler. Introduction by Alfred Werner. xxxvi + 334pp.

21875-9 Paperbound $3.00

VISUAL ILLUSIONS: THEIR CAUSES, CHARACTERISTICS, AND APPLICATIONS, Matthew Luckiesh. Thorough description and discussion of optical illusion, geometric and perspective, particularly; size and shape distortions, illusions of color, of motion; natural illusions; use of illusion in art and magic, industry, etc. Most useful today with op art, also for classical art. Scores of effects illustrated. Introduction by William H. Ittleson. 100 illustrations. xxi + 252pp.
21530-X Paperbound $2.00

A HANDBOOK OF ANATOMY FOR ART STUDENTS, Arthur Thomson. Thorough, virtually exhaustive coverage of skeletal structure, musculature, etc. Full text, supplemented by anatomical diagrams and drawings and by photographs of undraped figures. Unique in its comparison of male and female forms, pointing out differences of contour, texture, form. 211 figures, 40 drawings, 86 photographs. xx + 459pp. 5⅜ x 8⅜.
21163-0 Paperbound $3.50

150 MASTERPIECES OF DRAWING, Selected by Anthony Toney. Full page reproductions of drawings from the early 16th to the end of the 18th century, all beautifully reproduced: Rembrandt, Michelangelo, Dürer, Fragonard, Urs, Graf, Wouwerman, many others. First-rate browsing book, model book for artists. xviii + 150pp. 8⅜ x 11¼.
21032-4 Paperbound $2.50

THE LATER WORK OF AUBREY BEARDSLEY, Aubrey Beardsley. Exotic, erotic, ironic masterpieces in full maturity: Comedy Ballet, Venus and Tannhauser, Pierrot, Lysistrata, Rape of the Lock, Savoy material, Ali Baba, Volpone, etc. This material revolutionized the art world, and is still powerful, fresh, brilliant. With *The Early Work*, all Beardsley's finest work. 174 plates, 2 in color. xiv + 176pp. 8⅛ x 11.
21817-1 Paperbound $3.00

DRAWINGS OF REMBRANDT, Rembrandt van Rijn. Complete reproduction of fabulously rare edition by Lippmann and Hofstede de Groot, completely reedited, updated, improved by Prof. Seymour Slive, Fogg Museum. Portraits, Biblical sketches, landscapes, Oriental types, nudes, episodes from classical mythology—All Rembrandt's fertile genius. Also selection of drawings by his pupils and followers. "Stunning volumes," *Saturday Review*. 550 illustrations. lxxviii + 552pp. 9⅛ x 12¼.
21485-0, 21486-9 Two volumes, Paperbound $10.00

THE DISASTERS OF WAR, Francisco Goya. One of the masterpieces of Western civilization—83 etchings that record Goya's shattering, bitter reaction to the Napoleonic war that swept through Spain after the insurrection of 1808 and to war in general. Reprint of the first edition, with three additional plates from Boston's Museum of Fine Arts. All plates facsimile size. Introduction by Philip Hofer, Fogg Museum. v + 97pp. 9⅜ x 8¼.
21872-4 Paperbound $2.00

GRAPHIC WORKS OF ODILON REDON. Largest collection of Redon's graphic works ever assembled: 172 lithographs, 28 etchings and engravings, 9 drawings. These include some of his most famous works. All the plates from *Odilon Redon: oeuvre graphique complet*, plus additional plates. New introduction and caption translations by Alfred Werner. 209 illustrations. xxvii + 209pp. 9⅛ x 12¼.
21966-8 Paperbound $4.00

DESIGN BY ACCIDENT; A BOOK OF "ACCIDENTAL EFFECTS" FOR ARTISTS AND DESIGNERS, James F. O'Brien. Create your own unique, striking, imaginative effects by "controlled accident" interaction of materials: paints and lacquers, oil and water based paints, splatter, crackling materials, shatter, similar items. Everything you do will be different; first book on this limitless art, so useful to both fine artist and commercial artist. Full instructions. 192 plates showing "accidents," 8 in color. viii + 215pp. 8⅜ x 11¼. 21942-9 Paperbound $3.50

THE BOOK OF SIGNS, Rudolf Koch. Famed German type designer draws 493 beautiful symbols: religious, mystical, alchemical, imperial, property marks, runes, etc. Remarkable fusion of traditional and modern. Good for suggestions of timelessness, smartness, modernity. Text. vi + 104pp. 6⅛ x 9¼.
20162-7 Paperbound $1.25

HISTORY OF INDIAN AND INDONESIAN ART, Ananda K. Coomaraswamy. An unabridged republication of one of the finest books by a great scholar in Eastern art. Rich in descriptive material, history, social backgrounds; Sunga reliefs, Rajput paintings, Gupta temples, Burmese frescoes, textiles, jewelry, sculpture, etc. 400 photos. viii + 423pp. 6⅜ x 9¾. 21436-2 Paperbound $5.00

PRIMITIVE ART, Franz Boas. America's foremost anthropologist surveys textiles, ceramics, woodcarving, basketry, metalwork, etc.; patterns, technology, creation of symbols, style origins. All areas of world, but very full on Northwest Coast Indians. More than 350 illustrations of baskets, boxes, totem poles, weapons, etc. 378 pp.
20025-6 Paperbound $3.00

THE GENTLEMAN AND CABINET MAKER'S DIRECTOR, Thomas Chippendale. Full reprint (third edition, 1762) of most influential furniture book of all time, by master cabinetmaker. 200 plates, illustrating chairs, sofas, mirrors, tables, cabinets, plus 24 photographs of surviving pieces. Biographical introduction by N. Bienenstock. vi + 249pp. 9⅞ x 12¾. 21601-2 Paperbound $4.00

AMERICAN ANTIQUE FURNITURE, Edgar G. Miller, Jr. The basic coverage of all American furniture before 1840. Individual chapters cover type of furniture—clocks, tables, sideboards, etc.—chronologically, with inexhaustible wealth of data. More than 2100 photographs, all identified, commented on. Essential to all early American collectors. Introduction by H. E. Keyes. vi + 1106pp. 7⅞ x 10¾.
21599-7, 21600-4 Two volumes, Paperbound $11.00

PENNSYLVANIA DUTCH AMERICAN FOLK ART, Henry J. Kauffman. 279 photos, 28 drawings of tulipware, Fraktur script, painted tinware, toys, flowered furniture, quilts, samplers, hex signs, house interiors, etc. Full descriptive text. Excellent for tourist, rewarding for designer, collector. Map. 146pp. 7⅞ x 10¾.
21205-X Paperbound $2.50

EARLY NEW ENGLAND GRAVESTONE RUBBINGS, Edmund V. Gillon, Jr. 43 photographs, 226 carefully reproduced rubbings show heavily symbolic, sometimes macabre early gravestones, up to early 19th century. Remarkable early American primitive art, occasionally strikingly beautiful; always powerful. Text. xxvi + 207pp. 8⅜ x 11¼. 21380-3 Paperbound $3.50

ALPHABETS AND ORNAMENTS, Ernst Lehner. Well-known pictorial source for decorative alphabets, script examples, cartouches, frames, decorative title pages, calligraphic initials, borders, similar material. 14th to 19th century, mostly European. Useful in almost any graphic arts designing, varied styles. 750 illustrations. 256pp. 7 x 10.   21905-4 Paperbound $4.00

PAINTING: A CREATIVE APPROACH, Norman Colquhoun. For the beginner simple guide provides an instructive approach to painting: major stumbling blocks for beginner; overcoming them, technical points; paints and pigments; oil painting; watercolor and other media and color. New section on "plastic" paints. Glossary. Formerly *Paint Your Own Pictures*. 221pp.   22000-1 Paperbound $1.75

THE ENJOYMENT AND USE OF COLOR, Walter Sargent. Explanation of the relations between colors themselves and between colors in nature and art, including hundreds of little-known facts about color values, intensities, effects of high and low illumination, complementary colors. Many practical hints for painters, references to great masters. 7 color plates, 29 illustrations. x + 274pp.
20944-X Paperbound $2.75

THE NOTEBOOKS OF LEONARDO DA VINCI, compiled and edited by Jean Paul Richter. 1566 extracts from original manuscripts reveal the full range of Leonardo's versatile genius: all his writings on painting, sculpture, architecture, anatomy, astronomy, geography, topography, physiology, mining, music, etc., in both Italian and English, with 186 plates of manuscript pages and more than 500 additional drawings. Includes studies for the Last Supper, the lost Sforza monument, and other works. Total of xlvii + 866pp. $7\frac{7}{8}$ x $10\frac{3}{4}$.
22572-0, 22573-9 Two volumes, Paperbound $10.00

MONTGOMERY WARD CATALOGUE OF 1895. Tea gowns, yards of flannel and pillow-case lace, stereoscopes, books of gospel hymns, the New Improved Singer Sewing Machine, side saddles, milk skimmers, straight-edged razors, high-button shoes, spittoons, and on and on . . . listing some 25,000 items, practically all illustrated. Essential to the shoppers of the 1890's, it is our truest record of the spirit of the period. Unaltered reprint of Issue No. 57, Spring and Summer 1895. Introduction by Boris Emmet. Innumerable illustrations. xiii + 624pp. $8\frac{1}{2}$ x $11\frac{5}{8}$.
22377-9 Paperbound $6.95

THE CRYSTAL PALACE EXHIBITION ILLUSTRATED CATALOGUE (LONDON, 1851). One of the wonders of the modern world—the Crystal Palace Exhibition in which all the nations of the civilized world exhibited their achievements in the arts and sciences—presented in an equally important illustrated catalogue. More than 1700 items pictured with accompanying text—ceramics, textiles, cast-iron work, carpets, pianos, sleds, razors, wall-papers, billiard tables, beehives, silverware and hundreds of other artifacts—represent the focal point of Victorian culture in the Western World. Probably the largest collection of Victorian decorative art ever assembled—indispensable for antiquarians and designers. Unabridged republication of the Art-Journal Catalogue of the Great Exhibition of 1851, with all terminal essays. New introduction by John Gloag, F.S.A. xxxiv + 426pp. 9 x 12.
22503-8 Paperbound $5.00

A HISTORY OF COSTUME, Carl Köhler. Definitive history, based on surviving pieces of clothing primarily, and paintings, statues, etc. secondarily. Highly readable text, supplemented by 594 illustrations of costumes of the ancient Mediterranean peoples, Greece and Rome, the Teutonic prehistoric period; costumes of the Middle Ages, Renaissance, Baroque, 18th and 19th centuries. Clear, measured patterns are provided for many clothing articles. Approach is practical throughout. Enlarged by Emma von Sichart. 464pp. 21030-8 Paperbound $3.50.

ORIENTAL RUGS, ANTIQUE AND MODERN, Walter A. Hawley. A complete and authoritative treatise on the Oriental rug—where they are made, by whom and how, designs and symbols, characteristics in detail of the six major groups, how to distinguish them and how to buy them. Detailed technical data is provided on periods, weaves, warps, wefts, textures, sides, ends and knots, although no technical background is required for an understanding. 11 color plates, 80 halftones, 4 maps. vi + 320pp. 6⅛ x 9⅛. 22366-3 Paperbound $5.00

TEN BOOKS ON ARCHITECTURE, Vitruvius. By any standards the most important book on architecture ever written. Early Roman discussion of aesthetics of building, construction methods, orders, sites, and every other aspect of architecture has inspired, instructed architecture for about 2,000 years. Stands behind Palladio, Michelangelo, Bramante, Wren, countless others. Definitive Morris H. Morgan translation. 68 illustrations. xii + 331pp. 20645-9 Paperbound $3.00

THE FOUR BOOKS OF ARCHITECTURE, Andrea Palladio. Translated into every major Western European language in the two centuries following its publication in 1570, this has been one of the most influential books in the history of architecture. Complete reprint of the 1738 Isaac Ware edition. New introduction by Adolf Placzek, Columbia Univ. 216 plates. xxii + 110pp. of text. 9½ x 12¾. 21308-0 Clothbound $10.00

STICKS AND STONES: A STUDY OF AMERICAN ARCHITECTURE AND CIVILIZATION, Lewis Mumford. One of the great classics of American cultural history. American architecture from the medieval-inspired earliest forms to the early 20th century; evolution of structure and style, and reciprocal influences on environment. 21 photographic illustrations. 238pp. 20202-X Paperbound $2.00

THE AMERICAN BUILDER'S COMPANION, Asher Benjamin. The most widely used early 19th century architectural style and source book, for colonial up into Greek Revival periods. Extensive development of geometry of carpentering, construction of sashes, frames, doors, stairs; plans and elevations of domestic and other buildings. Hundreds of thousands of houses were built according to this book, now invaluable to historians, architects, restorers, etc. 1827 edition. 59 plates. 114pp. 7⅞ x 10¾. 22236-5 Paperbound $3.50

DUTCH HOUSES IN THE HUDSON VALLEY BEFORE 1776, Helen Wilkinson Reynolds. The standard survey of the Dutch colonial house and outbuildings, with constructional features, decoration, and local history associated with individual homesteads. Introduction by Franklin D. Roosevelt. Map. 150 illustrations. 469pp. 6⅝ x 9¼. 21469-9 Paperbound

THE ARCHITECTURE OF COUNTRY HOUSES, Andrew J. Downing. Together with Vaux's *Villas and Cottages* this is the basic book for Hudson River Gothic architecture of the middle Victorian period. Full, sound discussions of general aspects of housing, architecture, style, decoration, furnishing, together with scores of detailed house plans, illustrations of specific buildings, accompanied by full text. Perhaps the most influential single American architectural book. 1850 edition. Introduction by J. Stewart Johnson. 321 figures, 34 architectural designs. xvi + 560pp.
22003-6 Paperbound $4.00

LOST EXAMPLES OF COLONIAL ARCHITECTURE, John Mead Howells. Full-page photographs of buildings that have disappeared or been so altered as to be denatured, including many designed by major early American architects. 245 plates. xvii + 248pp. 7⅞ x 10¾. 21143-6 Paperbound $3.50

DOMESTIC ARCHITECTURE OF THE AMERICAN COLONIES AND OF THE EARLY REPUBLIC, Fiske Kimball. Foremost architect and restorer of Williamsburg and Monticello covers nearly 200 homes between 1620-1825. Architectural details, construction, style features, special fixtures, floor plans, etc. Generally considered finest work in its area. 219 illustrations of houses, doorways, windows, capital mantels. xx + 314pp. 7⅞ x 10¾. 21743-4 Paperbound $4.00

EARLY AMERICAN ROOMS: 1650-1858, edited by Russell Hawes Kettell. Tour of 12 rooms, each representative of a different era in American history and each furnished, decorated, designed and occupied in the style of the era. 72 plans and elevations, 8-page color section, etc., show fabrics, wall papers, arrangements, etc. Full descriptive text. xvii + 200pp. of text. 8⅜ x 11¼.
21633-0 Paperbound $5.00

THE FITZWILLIAM VIRGINAL BOOK, edited by J. Fuller Maitland and W. B. Squire. Full modern printing of famous early 17th-century ms. volume of 300 works by Morley, Byrd, Bull, Gibbons, etc. For piano or other modern keyboard instrument; easy to read format. xxxvi + 938pp. 8⅜ x 11.
21068-5, 21069-3 Two volumes, Paperbound $10.00

KEYBOARD MUSIC, Johann Sebastian Bach. Bach Gesellschaft edition. A rich selection of Bach's masterpieces for the harpsichord: the six English Suites, six French Suites, the six Partitas (Clavierübung part I), the Goldberg Variations (Clavierübung part IV), the fifteen Two-Part Inventions and the fifteen Three-Part Sinfonias. Clearly reproduced on large sheets with ample margins; eminently playable. vi + 312pp. 8⅛ x 11. 22360-4 Paperbound $5.00

THE MUSIC OF BACH: AN INTRODUCTION, Charles Sanford Terry. A fine, nontechnical introduction to Bach's music, both instrumental and vocal. Covers organ music, chamber music, passion music, other types. Analyzes themes, developments, innovations. x + 114pp. 21075-8 Paperbound $1.50

BEETHOVEN AND HIS NINE SYMPHONIES, Sir George Grove. Noted British musicologist provides best history, analysis, commentary on symphonies. Very thorough, rigorously accurate; necessary to both advanced student and amateur music lover. 436 musical passages. vii + 407 pp. 20334-4 Paperbound $2.75

JOHANN SEBASTIAN BACH, Philipp Spitta. One of the great classics of musicology, this definitive analysis of Bach's music (and life) has never been surpassed. Lucid, nontechnical analyses of hundreds of pieces (30 pages devoted to St. Matthew Passion, 26 to B Minor Mass). Also includes major analysis of 18th-century music. 450 musical examples. 40-page musical supplement. Total of xx + 1799pp.
(EUK) 22278-0, 22279-9 Two volumes, Clothbound $17.50

MOZART AND HIS PIANO CONCERTOS, Cuthbert Girdlestone. The only full-length study of an important area of Mozart's creativity. Provides detailed analyses of all 23 concertos, traces inspirational sources. 417 musical examples. Second edition. 509pp.
21271-8 Paperbound $3.50

THE PERFECT WAGNERITE: A COMMENTARY ON THE NIBLUNG'S RING, George Bernard Shaw. Brilliant and still relevant criticism in remarkable essays on Wagner's Ring cycle, Shaw's ideas on political and social ideology behind the plots, role of Leitmotifs, vocal requisites, etc. Prefaces. xxi + 136pp.
(USO) 21707-8 Paperbound $1.50

DON GIOVANNI, W. A. Mozart. Complete libretto, modern English translation; biographies of composer and librettist; accounts of early performances and critical reaction. Lavishly illustrated. All the material you need to understand and appreciate this great work. Dover Opera Guide and Libretto Series; translated and introduced by Ellen Bleiler. 92 illustrations. 209pp.
21134-7 Paperbound $2.00

BASIC ELECTRICITY, U. S. Bureau of Naval Personel. Originally a training course, best non-technical coverage of basic theory of electricity and its applications. Fundamental concepts, batteries, circuits, conductors and wiring techniques, AC and DC, inductance and capacitance, generators, motors, transformers, magnetic amplifiers, synchros, servomechanisms, etc. Also covers blue-prints, electrical diagrams, etc. Many questions, with answers. 349 illustrations. x + 448pp. 6½ x 9¼.
20973-3 Paperbound $3.50

REPRODUCTION OF SOUND, Edgar Villchur. Thorough coverage for laymen of high fidelity systems, reproducing systems in general, needles, amplifiers, preamps, loudspeakers, feedback, explaining physical background. "A rare talent for making technicalities vividly comprehensible," R. Darrell, *High Fidelity*. 69 figures. iv + 92pp.
21515-6 Paperbound $1.25

HEAR ME TALKIN' TO YA: THE STORY OF JAZZ AS TOLD BY THE MEN WHO MADE IT, Nat Shapiro and Nat Hentoff. Louis Armstrong, Fats Waller, Jo Jones, Clarence Williams, Billy Holiday, Duke Ellington, Jelly Roll Morton and dozens of other jazz greats tell how it was in Chicago's South Side, New Orleans, depression Harlem and the modern West Coast as jazz was born and grew. xvi + 429pp.
21726-4 Paperbound $3.00

FABLES OF AESOP, translated by Sir Roger L'Estrange. A reproduction of the very rare 1931 Paris edition; a selection of the most interesting fables, together with 50 imaginative drawings by Alexander Calder. v + 128pp. 6½x9¼.
21780-9 Paperbound $1.50

AGAINST THE GRAIN (A REBOURS), Joris K. Huysmans. Filled with weird images, evidences of a bizarre imagination, exotic experiments with hallucinatory drugs, rich tastes and smells and the diversions of its sybarite hero Duc Jean des Esseintes, this classic novel pushed 19th-century literary decadence to its limits. Full unabridged edition. Do not confuse this with abridged editions generally sold. Introduction by Havelock Ellis. xlix + 206pp. 22190-3 Paperbound $2.00

VARIORUM SHAKESPEARE: HAMLET. Edited by Horace H. Furness; a landmark of American scholarship. Exhaustive footnotes and appendices treat all doubtful words and phrases, as well as suggested critical emendations throughout the play's history. First volume contains editor's own text, collated with all Quartos and Folios. Second volume contains full first Quarto, translations of Shakespeare's sources (Belleforest, and Saxo Grammaticus), Der Bestrafte Brudermord, and many essays on critical and historical points of interest by major authorities of past and present. Includes details of staging and costuming over the years. By far the best edition available for serious students of Shakespeare. Total of xx + 905pp.
21004-9, 21005-7, 2 volumes, Paperbound $7.00

A LIFE OF WILLIAM SHAKESPEARE, Sir Sidney Lee. This is the standard life of Shakespeare, summarizing everything known about Shakespeare and his plays. Incredibly rich in material, broad in coverage, clear and judicious, it has served thousands as the best introduction to Shakespeare. 1931 edition. 9 plates. xxix + 792pp. (USO) 21967-4 Paperbound $3.75

MASTERS OF THE DRAMA, John Gassner. Most comprehensive history of the drama in print, covering every tradition from Greeks to modern Europe and America, including India, Far East, etc. Covers more than 800 dramatists, 2000 plays, with biographical material, plot summaries, theatre history, criticism, etc. "Best of its kind in English," New Republic. 77 illustrations. xxii + 890pp.
20100-7 Clothbound $8.50

THE EVOLUTION OF THE ENGLISH LANGUAGE, George McKnight. The growth of English, from the 14th century to the present. Unusual, non-technical account presents basic information in very interesting form: sound shifts, change in grammar and syntax, vocabulary growth, similar topics. Abundantly illustrated with quotations. Formerly Modern English in the Making. xii + 590pp.
21932-1 Paperbound $3.50

AN ETYMOLOGICAL DICTIONARY OF MODERN ENGLISH, Ernest Weekley. Fullest, richest work of its sort, by foremost British lexicographer. Detailed word histories, including many colloquial and archaic words; extensive quotations. Do not confuse this with the Concise Etymological Dictionary, which is much abridged. Total of xxvii + 830pp. 6½ x 9¼.
21873-2, 21874-0 Two volumes, Paperbound $7.90

FLATLAND: A ROMANCE OF MANY DIMENSIONS, E. A. Abbott. Classic of science-fiction explores ramifications of life in a two-dimensional world, and what happens when a three-dimensional being intrudes. Amusing reading, but also useful as introduction to thought about hyperspace. Introduction by Banesh Hoffmann. 16 illustrations. xx + 103pp. 20001-9 Paperbound $1.00

POEMS OF ANNE BRADSTREET, edited with an introduction by Robert Hutchinson. A new selection of poems by America's first poet and perhaps the first significant woman poet in the English language. 48 poems display her development in works of considerable variety—love poems, domestic poems, religious meditations, formal elegies, "quaternions," etc. Notes, bibliography. viii + 222pp.

22160-1 Paperbound $2.50

THREE GOTHIC NOVELS: THE CASTLE OF OTRANTO BY HORACE WALPOLE; VATHEK BY WILLIAM BECKFORD; THE VAMPYRE BY JOHN POLIDORI, WITH FRAGMENT OF A NOVEL BY LORD BYRON, edited by E. F. Bleiler. The first Gothic novel, by Walpole; the finest Oriental tale in English, by Beckford; powerful Romantic supernatural story in versions by Polidori and Byron. All extremely important in history of literature; all still exciting, packed with supernatural thrills, ghosts, haunted castles, magic, etc. xl + 291pp.

21232-7 Paperbound·$2.50

THE BEST TALES OF HOFFMANN, E. T. A. Hoffmann. 10 of Hoffmann's most important stories, in modern re-editings of standard translations: Nutcracker and the King of Mice, Signor Formica, Automata, The Sandman, Rath Krespel, The Golden Flowerpot, Master Martin the Cooper, The Mines of Falun, The King's Betrothed, A New Year's Eve Adventure. 7 illustrations by Hoffmann. Edited by E. F. Bleiler. xxxix + 419pp. 21793-0 Paperbound $3.00

GHOST AND HORROR STORIES OF AMBROSE BIERCE, Ambrose Bierce. 23 strikingly modern stories of the horrors latent in the human mind: The Eyes of the Panther, The Damned Thing, An Occurrence at Owl Creek Bridge, An Inhabitant of Carcosa, etc., plus the dream-essay, Visions of the Night. Edited by E. F. Bleiler. xxii + 199pp.

20767-6 Paperbound $1.50

BEST GHOST STORIES OF J. S. LEFANU, J. Sheridan LeFanu. Finest stories by Victorian master often considered greatest supernatural writer of all. Carmilla, Green Tea, The Haunted Baronet, The Familiar, and 12 others. Most never before available in the U. S. A. Edited by E. F. Bleiler. 8 illustrations from Victorian publications. xvii + 467pp. 20415-4 Paperbound $3.00

MATHEMATICAL FOUNDATIONS OF INFORMATION THEORY, A. I. Khinchin. Comprehensive introduction to work of Shannon, McMillan, Feinstein and Khinchin, placing these investigations on a rigorous mathematical basis. Covers entropy concept in probability theory, uniqueness theorem, Shannon's inequality, ergodic sources, the E property, martingale concept, noise, Feinstein's fundamental lemma, Shanon's first and second theorems. Translated by R. A. Silverman and M. D. Friedman. iii + 120pp.

60434-9 Paperbound $1.75

SEVEN SCIENCE FICTION NOVELS, H. G. Wells. The standard collection of the great novels. Complete, unabridged. First Men in the Moon, Island of Dr. Moreau, War of the Worlds, Food of the Gods, Invisible Man, Time Machine, In the Days of the Comet. Not only science fiction fans, but every educated person owes it to himself to read these novels. 1015pp. (USO) 20264-X Clothbound $6.00

LAST AND FIRST MEN AND STAR MAKER, TWO SCIENCE FICTION NOVELS, Olaf Stapledon. Greatest future histories in science fiction. In the first, human intelligence is the "hero," through strange paths of evolution, interplanetary invasions, incredible technologies, near extinctions and reemergences. Star Maker describes the quest of a band of star rovers for intelligence itself, through time and space: weird inhuman civilizations, crustacean minds, symbiotic worlds, etc. Complete, unabridged. v + 438pp.   (USO) 21962-3 Paperbound $2.50

THREE PROPHETIC NOVELS, H. G. WELLS. Stages of a consistently planned future for mankind. *When the Sleeper Wakes,* and *A Story of the Days to Come,* anticipate *Brave New World* and *1984,* in the 21st Century; *The Time Machine,* only complete version in print, shows farther future and the end of mankind. All show Wells's greatest gifts as storyteller and novelist. Edited by E. F. Bleiler. x + 335pp.   (USO) 20605-X Paperbound $2.50

THE DEVIL'S DICTIONARY, Ambrose Bierce. America's own Oscar Wilde—Ambrose Bierce—offers his barbed iconoclastic wisdom in over 1,000 definitions hailed by H. L. Mencken as "some of the most gorgeous witticisms in the English language." 145pp.   20487-1 Paperbound $1.25

MAX AND MORITZ, Wilhelm Busch. Great children's classic, father of comic strip, of two bad boys, Max and Moritz. Also Ker and Plunk (Plisch und Plumm), Cat and Mouse, Deceitful Henry, Ice-Peter, The Boy and the Pipe, and five other pieces. Original German, with English translation. Edited by H. Arthur Klein; translations by various hands and H. Arthur Klein. vi + 216pp.
20181-3 Paperbound $2.00

PIGS IS PIGS AND OTHER FAVORITES, Ellis Parker Butler. The title story is one of the best humor short stories, as Mike Flannery obfuscates biology and English. Also included, That Pup of Murchison's, The Great American Pie Company, and Perkins of Portland. 14 illustrations. v + 109pp.   21532-6 Paperbound $1.25

THE PETERKIN PAPERS, Lucretia P. Hale. It takes genius to be as stupidly mad as the Peterkins, as they decide to become wise, celebrate the "Fourth," keep a cow, and otherwise strain the resources of the Lady from Philadelphia. Basic book of American humor. 153 illustrations. 219pp.   20794-3 Paperbound $1.50

PERRAULT'S FAIRY TALES, translated by A. E. Johnson and S. R. Littlewood, with 34 full-page illustrations by Gustave Doré. All the original Perrault stories—Cinderella, Sleeping Beauty, Bluebeard, Little Red Riding Hood, Puss in Boots, Tom Thumb, etc.—with their witty verse morals and the magnificent illustrations of Doré. One of the five or six great books of European fairy tales. viii + 117pp. 8⅛ x 11.   22311-6 Paperbound $2.00

OLD HUNGARIAN FAIRY TALES, Baroness Orczy. Favorites translated and adapted by author of the *Scarlet Pimpernel.* Eight fairy tales include "The Suitors of Princess Fire-Fly," "The Twin Hunchbacks," "Mr. Cuttlefish's Love Story," and "The Enchanted Cat." This little volume of magic and adventure will captivate children as it has for generations. 90 drawings by Montagu Barstow. 96pp.
22293-4 Paperbound $1.95

THE RED FAIRY BOOK, Andrew Lang. Lang's color fairy books have long been children's favorites. This volume includes Rapunzel, Jack and the Bean-stalk and 35 other stories, familiar and unfamiliar. 4 plates, 93 illustrations x + 367pp.

21673-X Paperbound $2.50

THE BLUE FAIRY BOOK, Andrew Lang. Lang's tales come from all countries and all times. Here are 37 tales from Grimm, the Arabian Nights, Greek Mythology, and other fascinating sources. 8 plates, 130 illustrations. xi + 390pp.

21437-0 Paperbound $2.50

HOUSEHOLD STORIES BY THE BROTHERS GRIMM. Classic English-language edition of the well-known tales — Rumpelstiltskin, Snow White, Hansel and Gretel, The Twelve Brothers, Faithful John, Rapunzel, Tom Thumb (52 stories in all). Translated into simple, straightforward English by Lucy Crane. Ornamented with headpieces, vignettes, elaborate decorative initials and a dozen full-page illustrations by Walter Crane. x + 269pp.

21080-4 Paperbound $2.00

THE MERRY ADVENTURES OF ROBIN HOOD, Howard Pyle. The finest modern versions of the traditional ballads and tales about the great English outlaw. Howard Pyle's complete prose version, with every word, every illustration of the first edition. Do not confuse this facsimile of the original (1883) with modern editions that change text or illustrations. 23 plates plus many page decorations. xxii + 296pp.

22043-5 Paperbound $2.50

THE STORY OF KING ARTHUR AND HIS KNIGHTS, Howard Pyle. The finest children's version of the life of King Arthur; brilliantly retold by Pyle, with 48 of his most imaginative illustrations. xviii + 313pp. 6⅛ x 9¼.

21445-1 Paperbound $2.50

THE WONDERFUL WIZARD OF OZ, L. Frank Baum. America's finest children's book in facsimile of first edition with all Denslow illustrations in full color. The edition a child should have. Introduction by Martin Gardner. 23 color plates, scores of drawings. iv + 267pp.

20691-2 Paperbound $2.50

THE MARVELOUS LAND OF OZ, L. Frank Baum. The second Oz book, every bit as imaginative as the Wizard. The hero is a boy named Tip, but the Scarecrow and the Tin Woodman are back, as is the Oz magic. 16 color plates, 120 drawings by John R. Neill. 287pp.

20692-0 Paperbound $2.50

THE MAGICAL MONARCH OF MO, L. Frank Baum. Remarkable adventures in a land even stranger than Oz. The best of Baum's books not in the Oz series. 15 color plates and dozens of drawings by Frank Verbeck. xviii + 237pp.

21892-9 Paperbound $2.25

THE BAD CHILD'S BOOK OF BEASTS, MORE BEASTS FOR WORSE CHILDREN, A MORAL ALPHABET, Hilaire Belloc. Three complete humor classics in one volume. Be kind to the frog, and do not call him names . . . and 28 other whimsical animals. Familiar favorites and some not so well known. Illustrated by Basil Blackwell. 156pp.

(USO) 20749-8 Paperbound $1.50

EAST O' THE SUN AND WEST O' THE MOON, George W. Dasent. Considered the best of all translations of these Norwegian folk tales, this collection has been enjoyed by generations of children (and folklorists too). Includes True and Untrue, Why the Sea is Salt, East O' the Sun and West O' the Moon, Why the Bear is Stumpy-Tailed, Boots and the Troll, The Cock and the Hen, Rich Peter the Pedlar, and 52 more. The only edition with all 59 tales. 77 illustrations by Erik Werenskiold and Theodor Kittelsen. xv + 418pp. 22521-6 Paperbound $3.50

GOOPS AND HOW TO BE THEM, Gelett Burgess. Classic of tongue-in-cheek humor, masquerading as etiquette book. 87 verses, twice as many cartoons, show mischievous Goops as they demonstrate to children virtues of table manners, neatness, courtesy, etc. Favorite for generations. viii + 88pp. $6\frac{1}{2}$ x $9\frac{1}{4}$. 22233-0 Paperbound $1.25

ALICE'S ADVENTURES UNDER GROUND, Lewis Carroll. The first version, quite different from the final *Alice in Wonderland*, printed out by Carroll himself with his own illustrations. Complete facsimile of the "million dollar" manuscript Carroll gave to Alice Liddell in 1864. Introduction by Martin Gardner. viii + 96pp. Title and dedication pages in color. 21482-6 Paperbound $1.25

THE BROWNIES, THEIR BOOK, Palmer Cox. Small as mice, cunning as foxes, exuberant and full of mischief, the Brownies go to the zoo, toy shop, seashore, circus, etc., in 24 verse adventures and 266 illustrations. Long a favorite, since their first appearance in St. Nicholas Magazine. xi + 144pp. $6\frac{5}{8}$ x $9\frac{1}{4}$. 21265-3 Paperbound $1.75

SONGS OF CHILDHOOD, Walter De La Mare. Published (under the pseudonym Walter Ramal) when De La Mare was only 29, this charming collection has long been a favorite children's book. A facsimile of the first edition in paper, the 47 poems capture the simplicity of the nursery rhyme and the ballad, including such lyrics as I Met Eve, Tartary, The Silver Penny. vii + 106pp. (USO) 21972-0 Paperbound $1.25

THE COMPLETE NONSENSE OF EDWARD LEAR, Edward Lear. The finest 19th-century humorist-cartoonist in full: all nonsense limericks, zany alphabets, Owl and Pussycat, songs, nonsense botany, and more than 500 illustrations by Lear himself. Edited by Holbrook Jackson. xxix + 287pp. (USO) 20167-8 Paperbound $2.00

BILLY WHISKERS: THE AUTOBIOGRAPHY OF A GOAT, Frances Trego Montgomery. A favorite of children since the early 20th century, here are the escapades of that rambunctious, irresistible and mischievous goat—Billy Whiskers. Much in the spirit of *Peck's Bad Boy*, this is a book that children never tire of reading or hearing. All the original familiar illustrations by W. H. Fry are included: 6 color plates, 18 black and white drawings. 159pp. 22345-0 Paperbound $2.00

MOTHER GOOSE MELODIES. Faithful republication of the fabulously rare Munroe and Francis "copyright 1833" Boston edition—the most important Mother Goose collection, usually referred to as the "original." Familiar rhymes plus many rare ones, with wonderful old woodcut illustrations. Edited by E. F. Bleiler. 128pp. $4\frac{1}{2}$ x $6\frac{3}{8}$. 22577-1 Paperbound $1.00

Two Little Savages; Being the Adventures of Two Boys Who Lived as Indians and What They Learned, Ernest Thompson Seton. Great classic of nature and boyhood provides a vast range of woodlore in most palatable form, a genuinely entertaining story. Two farm boys build a teepee in woods and live in it for a month, working out Indian solutions to living problems, star lore, birds and animals, plants, etc. 293 illustrations. vii + 286pp.

20985-7 Paperbound $2.50

Peter Piper's Practical Principles of Plain & Perfect Pronunciation. Alliterative jingles and tongue-twisters of surprising charm, that made their first appearance in America about 1830. Republished in full with the spirited woodcut illustrations from this earliest American edition. 32pp. 4½ x 6⅜.

22560-7 Paperbound $1.00

Science Experiments and Amusements for Children, Charles Vivian. 73 easy experiments, requiring only materials found at home or easily available, such as candles, coins, steel wool, etc.; illustrate basic phenomena like vacuum, simple chemical reaction, etc. All safe. Modern, well-planned. Formerly *Science Games for Children*. 102 photos, numerous drawings. 96pp. 6⅛ x 9¼.

21856-2 Paperbound $1.25

An Introduction to Chess Moves and Tactics Simply Explained, Leonard Barden. Informal intermediate introduction, quite strong in explaining reasons for moves. Covers basic material, tactics, important openings, traps, positional play in middle game, end game. Attempts to isolate patterns and recurrent configurations. Formerly *Chess*. 58 figures. 102pp.   (USO) 21210-6 Paperbound $1.25

Lasker's Manual of Chess, Dr. Emanuel Lasker. Lasker was not only one of the five great World Champions, he was also one of the ablest expositors, theorists, and analysts. In many ways, his Manual, permeated with his philosophy of battle, filled with keen insights, is one of the greatest works ever written on chess. Filled with analyzed games by the great players. A single-volume library that will profit almost any chess player, beginner or master. 308 diagrams. xli x 349pp.

20640-8 Paperbound $2.75

The Master Book of Mathematical Recreations, Fred Schuh. In opinion of many the finest work ever prepared on mathematical puzzles, stunts, recreations; exhaustively thorough explanations of mathematics involved, analysis of effects, citation of puzzles and games. Mathematics involved is elementary. Translated by F. Göbel. 194 figures. xxiv + 430pp.   22134-2 Paperbound $3.50

Mathematics, Magic and Mystery, Martin Gardner. Puzzle editor for Scientific American explains mathematics behind various mystifying tricks: card tricks, stage "mind reading," coin and match tricks, counting out games, geometric dissections, etc. Probability sets, theory of numbers clearly explained. Also provides more than 400 tricks, guaranteed to work, that you can do. 135 illustrations. xii + 176pp.

20335-2 Paperbound $1.75

MATHEMATICAL PUZZLES FOR BEGINNERS AND ENTHUSIASTS, Geoffrey Mott-Smith. 189 puzzles from easy to difficult—involving arithmetic, logic, algebra, properties of digits, probability, etc.—for enjoyment and mental stimulus. Explanation of mathematical principles behind the puzzles. 135 illustrations. viii + 248pp.
20198-8 Paperbound $1.75

PAPER FOLDING FOR BEGINNERS, William D. Murray and Francis J. Rigney. Easiest book on the market, clearest instructions on making interesting, beautiful origami. Sail boats, cups, roosters, frogs that move legs, bonbon boxes, standing birds, etc. 40 projects; more than 275 diagrams and photographs. 94pp.
20713-7 Paperbound $1.00

TRICKS AND GAMES ON THE POOL TABLE, Fred Herrmann. 79 tricks and games— some solitaires, some for two or more players, some competitive games—to entertain you between formal games. Mystifying shots and throws, unusual caroms, tricks involving such props as cork, coins, a hat, etc. Formerly *Fun on the Pool Table*. 77 figures. 95pp.
21814-7 Paperbound $1.00

HAND SHADOWS TO BE THROWN UPON THE WALL: A SERIES OF NOVEL AND AMUSING FIGURES FORMED BY THE HAND, Henry Bursill. Delightful picturebook from great-grandfather's day shows how to make 18 different hand shadows: a bird that flies, duck that quacks, dog that wags his tail, camel, goose, deer, boy, turtle, etc. Only book of its sort. vi + 33pp. 6½ x 9¼. 21779-5 Paperbound $1.00

WHITTLING AND WOODCARVING, E. J. Tangerman. 18th printing of best book on market. "If you can cut a potato you can carve" toys and puzzles, chains, chessmen, caricatures, masks, frames, woodcut blocks, surface patterns, much more. Information on tools, woods, techniques. Also goes into serious wood sculpture from Middle Ages to present, East and West. 464 photos, figures. x + 293pp.
20965-2 Paperbound $2.00

HISTORY OF PHILOSOPHY, Julián Marias. Possibly the clearest, most easily followed, best planned, most useful one-volume history of philosophy on the market; neither skimpy nor overfull. Full details on system of every major philosopher and dozens of less important thinkers from pre-Socratics up to Existentialism and later. Strong on many European figures usually omitted. Has gone through dozens of editions in Europe. 1966 edition, translated by Stanley Appelbaum and Clarence Strowbridge. xviii + 505pp.
21739-6 Paperbound $3.50

YOGA: A SCIENTIFIC EVALUATION, Kovoor T. Behanan. Scientific but non-technical study of physiological results of yoga exercises; done under auspices of Yale U. Relations to Indian thought, to psychoanalysis, etc. 16 photos. xxiii + 270pp.
20505-3 Paperbound $2.50

Prices subject to change without notice.
Available at your book dealer or write for free catalogue to Dept. GI, Dover Publications, Inc., 180 Varick St., N. Y., N. Y. 10014. Dover publishes more than 150 books each year on science, elementary and advanced mathematics, biology, music, art, literary history, social sciences and other areas.